SECOND EDITION

VOLUME A

Worlds Together, WORLDS APART

GLOBAL SATELLITE MOSAIC

The beauty and complexity of Earth's landscape—above and below the oceans—is revealed with the Global Satellite Mosaic. The mosaic was produced for the National Geographic Society by NASA's Jet Propulsion Laboratory using more than 500 satellite images from the National Oceanic and Atmospheric Administration. The cloud-free images show Earth in its natural colors as it would be seen from space. One can easily identify the world's major glaciers, deserts, mountain ranges, and rain forests. For example, follow the green ribbon of lush vegetation across the Pole into the stark, dry Sahara. The mountain ranges seem to rise off the map thanks to digital elevation databases from the Department of Defense. The deepest areas of the ocean realm are colored dark blue in contrast to the light blue areas highlighting continental shelves, submarine ridges, and underwater mountains.

BIOSPHERE

Thousands of satellite images were combined to show a picture of biological productivity in the oceans, red, yellow, and green indicate waters rich in phytoplankton. On land, dark green areas show high-potential plant productivity; the lighter areas suffer from productivity limitations due to aridity and temperature.

THE W

SATEL

OCEAN

EUROPE

ASIA

SIBERIA

URAL MOUNTAINS

Franz Josef Land

North Land

BARENTS SEA

Lake Baikal

Kamchatka Peninsula

Aral Sea

Black Sea

Caspian Sea

HIMALAYA

Plateau of Tibet

ARABIAN PENINSULA

ARABIAN SEA

INDIA

BAY OF BENGAL

SAHARA

AFRICA

Congo Basin

Lake Victoria

Lake Tanganyika

Lake Malawi

Madagascar

Kalahari Desert

Cape of Good Hope

SOUTHWEST INDIAN RIDGE

NINETYEAST RIDGE

INDIAN OCEAN

SOUTHEAST INDIAN RIDGE

KERGUELEN PLATEAU

INDONESIA

NORTH PACIFIC OCEAN

TROPIC OF CANCER

PHILIPPINE SEA

SOUTH CHINA SEA

Philippine Islands

MICRONESIA

MELANESIA

EQUATOR

New Guinea

AUSTRALIA

TROPIC OF CAPRICORN

CORAL SEA

New Caledonia

Fiji Islands

SOUTH PACIFIC OCEAN

TASMAN SEA

North Island

NEW ZEALAND

South Island

Tasmania

0°

20°

20°

40°

SOUTH POLAR REGION

Drake Passage

Weddell Sea

Antarctic Peninsula

Alexander I.

Queen Maud Land

ANTARCTICA

WEST ANTARCTICA

EAST ANTARCTICA

South Pole

Marie Byrd Land

Ross Ice Shelf

Ross Sea

Wilkes Land

ANTARCTIC CIRCLE

South Magnetic Pole

30°

60°

90°

120°

150°

180°

Wilkes Land

THE NEED FOR SATELLITES

The Global Satellite Mosaic along with the biosphere image (lower left) and the temperature image (lower right) provides an integrated view of our world. Even very high elevations of the Himalaya and Tibet show up as a cold area (blue). Temperature imaged as a plant-poor area (tan; biosphere image). Temperature, plant life, and landscape are interrelated. The need to understand the forces shaping environmental change has led to a space race among various countries. In 1997 alone some 85 rockets launched more than 140 satellites—mostly from China, Europe, Japan, Russia, and the United States. Some satellites provide vital communication links propelling economic development; other satellites supply data on patterns and trends associated with agricultural productivity, pollution monitoring, weather forecasting, and many other environmental concerns.

WINKEL TRIPEL PROJECTION, CENTRAL MERIDIAN 0°
SCALE 1:38,931,000
1 CENTIMETER = 389 KILOMETERS; 1 INCH = 614 MILES AT THE EQUATOR

20° 40° 60° 80° 100° 120° 140° 160° 180°

TICA

ORLD
MAP

SURFACE TEMPERATURE

Reddish colors vividly show average high temperatures on the two largest continents, Africa and Asia, from the Sahara to Central Asia. Latitude, mountains, and oceans influence land temperatures.

WORLD · POLITICAL

NATIONAL BOUNDARIES

While man's impact is quite evident, and even striking, on many remotely sensed scenes, sometimes, as in the case with most political boundaries, it is invisible. State, provincial, and national boundaries can follow natural features, such as mountain ridges, rivers, or coastlines. Artificial constructs that possess no physical reality—for example, lines of latitude and longitude—can also determine political borders. The world political map (right) represents man's imaginary lines as they slice and divide Earth.

The National Geographic Society recognizes 192 independent states in the world as represented here. Of those nations, 185 are members of the United Nations.

Winkel Tripel Projection

ROBERT TIGNOR

JEREMY ADELMAN

PETER BROWN

BENJAMIN ELMAN

XINRU LIU

HOLLY PITTMAN

BRENT SHAW

SECOND EDITION
VOLUME A
BEGINNINGS TO 1200

Worlds Together, WORLDS APART

A HISTORY OF THE WORLD FROM THE MONGOL EMPIRE TO THE PRESENT

W · W · NORTON & COMPANY
NEW YORK · LONDON

W. W. Norton & Company has been independent since its founding in 1923, when William Warder Norton and Mary D. Herter Norton first published lectures delivered at the People's Institute, the adult education division of New York City's Cooper Union. The Nortons soon expanded their program beyond the Institute, publishing books by celebrated academics from America and abroad. By mid-century, the two major pillars of Norton's publishing program—trade books and college texts— were firmly established. In the 1950s, the Norton family transferred control of the company to its employees, and today—with a staff of four hundred and a comparable number of trade, college, and professional titles published each year— W. W. Norton & Company stands as the largest and oldest publishing house owned wholly by its employees.

Editor: Jon Durbin
Developmental Editors: Sandy Lifland, Alice Falk
Copy Editors: Alice Falk, Ellen Lohman
Project Editor: Rebecca Homiski
Photo Researchers: Stephanie Romeo, Jennie Bright, Julie Tesser
Production Manager: Roy Tedoff
Managing Editor, College: Marian Johnson
Emedia Editor: Steve Hoge
Book Designer: Rubina Yeh
Ancillary Editors: Matthew Arnold, Alexis Hilts
Layout Artist: Brad Walrod
Editorial Assistants: Rob Haber, Alexis Hilts
Cartographer: Carto-Graphics

About the Cover Image: The "flying horse" was unearthed along the Silk Road in western China. "Horses of Heaven" came from Ferghana in the Eurasian steppe lands and were highly prized within the Han Dynasty for their swiftness and superb balance.

ISBN: 978-0-393-93208-9

W. W. Norton & Company, Inc., 500 Fifth Avenue, New York, NY 10110
wwnorton.com

W. W. Norton & Company Ltd., Castle House, 75/76 Wells Street, London W1T 3QT

1 2 3 4 5 6 7 8 9

Contents in Brief

Contents

CHAPTER 1 BECOMING HUMAN 3

Global Connections & Disconnections Features

Primary Source Documents

Maps

Preface

THE MAKING OF *Worlds Together, Worlds Apart*

Most books have a back story, though authors often hesitate to trot out the truly revealing details. In this case, however, some details should be disclosed because they illuminate the shape and substance of the narrative. The story begins nearly twenty years ago, when the Princeton University history department established its first course in world history. Called "The World and the West," the course surveyed the major developments in the history of the modern world from 1500 to the present. Although the importance of the course for students of an increasingly globalized era was immediately recognized, the course placed immense demands on teachers and students. The greatest challenge was how to treat the many regions of the world and the many centuries in an integrated way and in a single semester. The instructors searched in vain for a textbook that would provide both coverage and integrated analysis. Some of the books available at the time were written by a single author; these tended to have a clear narrative framework but to suffer from the limitations that a single individual, no matter how well read, necessarily encountered when dealing with the immensity of world history. Others were written by a team of regional experts and had authoritative treatments of regions but lacked integration and balance.

With the full support of Princeton University, a small group of modern historians in the Princeton history department decided to try our hand at world history, agreeing to meet on a regular basis to plan a text that addressed the weaknesses in the other books. Each of us had a regional specialization as well as an interest in how our regions fitted into larger cross-regional relationships. For an entire year we met to discuss the ways in which we would craft a modern world history and the global themes we wanted to stress. After intensive and sometimes contentious discussions, we decided on an overarching framework, the chapter divisions, and the global themes and regional variations. During these meetings, we also settled on the all-important idea of building each chapter around a turning point or central story in world history, such as the spread of the Black Death or the rise of the nation-state, that would enable us to integrate all the regions of the world into most chapters. Then we began to write. We wrote a lot—and a lot of what we wrote ended up in recycling bins. We all wrote sections in each of the chapters, shared them with one another, and then gave one of our group the assignment of integrating each chapter. All this meant that every one of us wrote something for each of the chapters. Different individuals coordinated the chapters, after which the drafts circulated to everyone once again for additional thoughts and revisions. The general editor then wrote the final draft to ensure that a strong, single voice would emerge and that the level of presentation would be consistent throughout. *Worlds Together, Worlds Apart: A History of the Modern World* (WTWA), the final product, was truly a collaborative work. No section, no matter how seemingly specialized, was the product of just one author.

We were pleased to discover, very soon after publication, that teachers and students liked WTWA. The original text (now Volume Two) was adopted widely in its first year of publication and has gone on to be used at over 200 colleges and universities worldwide and has sold over 40,000 copies. Then, instructors began to ask, Why not apply the WTWA model to the early period of world history? In 2003 we set out to do just that, with Robert Tignor and Jeremy Adelman from the modern volume joining forces with a distinguished group of historians of the earlier periods. In crafting the stories and chapters that would cover the earlier periods of world history, we have used the same highly collaborative writing model that proved so successful with the original volume, and we have built the chapters covering the earlier periods around turning points and central stories in world history, such as the formation of the Silk Road and the rise of universal religions, just as we did the chapters in the original volume. While we were hard at work writing the chapters covering the earlier periods, the authors of the modern chapters set about revising them so that all the chapters would fit seamlessly together. Ten years after we began our work, we are very pleased to offer *Worlds Together, Worlds Apart: A History of the World from the Beginnings of Humankind to the Present.*

Over the ten-year period of work on this book, world history has gained even more prominence in college classrooms and historical studies. Courses in the history of the world now abound, often replacing the standard surveys of European history and western civilization overviews. Graduate history students receive training in world history, and journals routinely publish studies in this field. A new generation of textbooks is needed to help students and instructors make sense of this vast, complex, and rapidly evolving field. WTWA hopes to be the first to plot this new course and to inspire its readers to continue their studies in this increasingly critical field.

OUR GUIDING PRINCIPLES

Five principles inform this book, guiding its framework and the organization of its individual chapters. The first is that **world history is global history**. There are many fine histories of the individual regions of the world, which we have endeavored to make good use of. But unlike the authors of many other so-called world histories, we have chosen not to deal with the great regions and cultures of the world as separate units, reserving individual chapters to East Asia, South Asia, Southwest Asia, Europe, Africa, and the Americas. Our goal is to place each of these regions in its largest geographical context. It would be misleading to say that the context is the world, because none of these regions, even the most highly developed commercially, enjoyed commercial or cultural contact with peoples all over the globe before Columbus's voyage to the Americas and the sixteenth century. But the peoples living in the Afro-Eurasian landmass, probably the single most important building block for our study, were deeply influenced by one another, as were the more scattered peoples living in the Americas and in Africa below the Sahara. Products, ideas, and persons traveled widely across the large land units of Eurasia, Africa, and the Americas. Indeed, Afro-Eurasia was not divided or thought of as divided into separate landmasses until recent times. It is in this sense that our world history is global.

The second principle informing this work is **the importance of chronology in framing world history**. Rather than telling the story of world history by analyzing separate geographical areas, we have elected to frame the chapters around significant historical turning points or periods that transcended regional and cultural boundaries—moments or periods of meaningful changes in the way that human beings organized their lives. Some of these changes were dramatic and affected many people. Environments changed; the earth became drier and warmer; humans learned to domesticate plants and animals; technological innovations in warfare, political organization, and commercial activities occurred; and the appeal of new religious and cultural beliefs spread far and wide. These changes swept across large landmasses, paying scant heed to preexisting cultural and geographical unity. They affected peoples living in widely dispersed societies. In other cases, changes occurred in only one locality while other places retained their traditions or took alternative routes. Chronology helps us understand the ways in which the world has, and has not, shared a common history. Chapter headings give a clue to the turning points or periods that paid no heed to geography and culture. At the outset of human existence, after *Homo sapiens* populated the world and became truly human (Chapter 1), men and women established the first cities and hierarchical polities and societies in the riverine basins of the Near East and northwest India (4000–2000 BCE; Chapter 2). Several millennia later, nomadic invaders provided a stimulus to re-create powerful territorial polities, employing horse-drawn chariots to undermine the old polities and to fashion new ones (2000–1200 BCE; Chapter 3). During the next millennium, powerful Asian monarchs established the first large-scale kingdoms that even aspired to world domination (1200 BCE–250 CE; Chapters 4 through 6). In more modern times, the spread of the bubonic plague across the Afro-Eurasian landmass brought great loss of life and undermined existing polities, preparing the groundwork for a new set of political organizations that proved to be long-lived (Chapter 11). The discovery of large silver mines in Spanish America in the sixteenth century provided a precious metal that brought the economies of the world into closer contact (Chapter 12). In the nineteenth century, ideas of freedom swept across the world, propelled by the American and French revolutions, only to be superseded by European imperial ambitions (Chapters 16 through 18). Two world wars linked the entire international community on battlefields and in great loss of life (Chapters 19 and 20).

The third principle is **historical and geographical balance**. Ours is not a history focused on the rise of the West. We seek to pay attention to the global histories of all peoples and not to privilege those developments that led directly into European history as if the rest of the history of the world was but a prelude to the rise of western civilization. We deal with peoples living outside Europe on their own terms and try to see world history from their perspective. Even more significantly, while we describe societies that obviously influenced Europe's historical development, we do so in a context very different from that which western historians have stressed. Rather than simply viewing these cultures in terms of their role in western development, we seek to understand them in their own terms and to illuminate the ways they influenced other parts of the world. From our perspective, it is historically inaccurate to annex Mesopotamia and Egypt to western civilization, because these territories lay well outside Europe and had a large influence on Africa, South Asia, and East Asia as well as on Europe. Indeed, our presentation of Europe in the period leading up to and including the founding of the Roman Empire is different from many of the standard treatments. The Europeans we describe are rather rough, wild-living, warring peoples living on the fringes of the settled parts of the world and looked down on by more politically stable communities. They hardly seem to be made of the stuff that will catapult Europeans to world leadership a millennium later—indeed, they were very different people from those who, as the result of myriad intervening and contingent events, founded the nineteenth- and twentieth-century empires whose ruins are still all around us.

Our fourth principle is **an emphasis on connections and what we call disconnections across societal and cultural boundaries**. World history is not the history of separate regions of the world at different periods of time. It is the history of the connections among peoples living often at great distances from one another, and it is also the history of the resistances of peoples living within and outside societies to connections that threatened to put them in subordinate positions or to rob them of their independence.

A stress on connections inevitably foregrounds those elements within societies that promoted long-distance ties. Merchants are important, as are military men and political potentates seeking to expand their polities. So are scholars and religious leaders, particularly those who believed that they had universalistic messages with which to convert others to their visions. Perhaps most important of all in premodern world history, certainly the most understudied, are the nomadic pastoral peoples, who were often the agents for the transmission of products, peoples, and ideas across long and harsh distances. They exploded onto the scene of settled societies at critical junctures, erasing old cultural and geographical barriers and producing new unities, as the Arabs did in the seventh century CE and the Mongols in the thirteenth century. *Worlds Together, Worlds Apart* is not intended to convey the message that the history of the world is a story of increasing integration. What for one ruling group brought benefits in the form of increased workforces, material prosperity, and political stability often meant enslavement, political subordination, and loss of territory for other groups. The historian's task, then, is not only to represent the different experiences of increased connectedness, describing worlds that came together, but also to be attentive to the opposite trends, describing peoples and communities that remained apart.

The fifth and final principle is that **world history is a narrative of big themes and high-level comparisons**. *Worlds Together, Worlds Apart* is not a book of record. Indeed, in a work that covers the whole of the historical record of humankind from the beginnings of history to the present, the notion that no event or individual worthy of attention would be excluded is the height of folly. We have sought to offer clear themes and interpretations in order to synthesize the vast body of data that often overwhelms histories of the world. Our aspiration is to identify the main historical forces that have moved history, to highlight those monumental innovations that have changed the way humans lived, and to describe the creation and evolution of those bedrock institutions, many of which, of course, endure. In this regard, self-conscious cross-cultural comparisons of developments, institutions, and even founding figures receive attention to make students aware that some common institutions, such as slavery, did not have the same features in every society. Or, in the opposite fashion, the seemingly diverse terms that were used, say, to describe learned and religious men in different parts of the world—monks in Europe, ulama in Islam, Brahmans in India, and scholar-gentries in China—often meant much the same thing in very different settings. We have constructed *Worlds Together, Worlds Apart* around big ideas, stories, and themes rather than filling the book with names and dates that encourage students only to memorize rather than understand world history concepts.

❧ OUR MAJOR THEMES

The primary organizing framework of *Worlds Together, Worlds Apart*—one that runs through the chapters and connects the different parts of the volume—is the theme of **interconnection and divergence**. While describing movements that facilitated global connectedness, this book also shows how different regions developed their own ways of handling or resisting connections and change. Throughout history, different regions and different population groups often stood apart from the rest of the world until touched by traders or explorers or missionaries or soldiers. Some of these regions welcomed global connections. Others sought to change the nature of their connections with the outside world, and yet others resisted efforts to bring them into the larger world. All, however, were somehow affected by their experience of connection. Yet, the history of the world is not simply one of increasing globalization, in which all societies eventually join a common path to the present. Rather, it is a history of the ways in which, as people became linked, their experience of these global connections diverged.

Besides the central theme of interconnection and divergence, other themes also stand out in WTWA. First, the book discusses **how the recurring efforts of people to cross religious, political, and cultural borders brought the world together**. Merchants and educated men and women traded goods and ideas. Whole communities, in addition to select groups, moved to safer or more promising environments. **The transregional crossings of ideas, goods, and peoples produced transformations and conflicts**—a second important theme. Finally, the movement of ideas, peoples, products, and germs over long distances upset the balance of power across the world and within individual societies. Such movements changed the relationship of different population groups with other peoples and areas of the world and led over time to dramatic shifts in the ascendancy of regions. **Changes in power arrangements within and between regions explain which parts of the world and regional groups benefited from integration and which resisted it.** These three themes (exchange and migration, conflict and resistance, and alterations in the balance of power) weave themselves through every chapter of this work.

In *Worlds Together, Worlds Apart,* we tell the stories of people caught in these currents of exchange, conflict, and changing power relations. We describe those historical actors, such as Roman legionnaires, early Christian and Muslim proselytizers, Indian Ocean merchants in the sixteenth century, and late-nineteenth-century European imperialists, who sought a more closely integrated world economy and polity. But we also describe those individuals who led movements in defense of cherished historical and cultural heritages. Jewish prophets under Roman rule, the Indian prophet Tenskwatawa in North America, and the religious cleric al-Wahhab on the Arabian Peninsula all urged their people to return to traditional identities. Others, such as Shiite clerics under Umayyad rule in the seventh and eighth centuries CE, Indian rebels in 1857, and advocates of a third way after World War II, sought a less unified world and used their historical and cultural traditions to favor new arrangements of world power.

From the beginnings of humanity to the present, in examining the forces that brought peoples and cultures together and those that kept them apart, this book explores not only the changing power relations between societies but also those within societies. Chief among these have been the divisions between rulers and subjects, between commoners and nobles, and between men and women. The **gender divide** has been one of the most important factors in shaping the evolution of societies, and this theme receives attention in Volume One and fresh accenting in the revised chapters of Volume Two.

Women and men lived in small-scale, relatively egalitarian societies until about 8,000 years ago, when hierarchical, urbanized, and centralized societies sprang up in three of the major river basins of Afro-Eurasia. One of the primary divides across all societies was the difference between men and women. If there was a world apart, from the time of the early agrarian breakthrough, it was within the family itself, as divisions of labor sharpened between men and women. Not all societies stratified themselves along gender lines in the same way. Indeed, many left open the possibility of women exercising influence and authority. But what underlay so many of the world's first civilizations was the way in which societies defined some traits as virtuous (such as the ability to fight) or created new social roles for rulers but restricted them mainly to men (such as scribes or priests). In this fashion, the social order took on gendered features from the very start. This was a long-term legacy that evolved over the ensuing centuries of human history.

By the same token, over the sweep of the millennia people acquired more and more skills and aptitudes for changing the environment to suit their needs and wants. They went from adapting to nature to controlling it, though this was hardly a linear process. There was plenty of backsliding. As with gender, not all societies related to their environments in the same way. To a very large extent, the differences in habitat were influential. In arid steppe lands, nomads followed their food around, while in large river basins, urban zones and complex, stratified societies emerged because water helped with transportation and settled agriculture. Similarly, societies coped with nature's vagaries in different ways. Some learned from experience, such as when China developed vast hydraulics to control flooding. Others could not cope with shocks, such as when the bubonic plague ravaged Afro-Eurasian populations in the fourteenth century and, most devastatingly, Old World diseases were introduced to the New World after 1492. A recurring theme, however, is **the way in which adaptation to environmental constraints was the source of large-scale unintended consequences that often brought societies face to face with similar plights**. In this sense, environmental history was a force that divided and united world societies.

OVERVIEW OF VOLUME ONE

Volume One of *Worlds Together, Worlds Apart* deals with the period from the beginnings of human history through the Mongol invasions of the thirteenth century and the spread of the Black Death across Afro-Eurasia. It is divided into eleven chapters, each of which marks a distinct historical period. Hence, each chapter has an overarching theme or small set of themes that hold otherwise highly diverse material together.

Chapter 1, "Becoming Human," presents biological and cultural perspectives on the way that early hominoids became truly human. World history books now have a nearly mandatory opening chapter on prehistory. We believe that this chapter is important in establishing the global context of world history. We believe too that our chapter is unique in its focus on how humans became humans, so we discuss how early humans became bipedal and how they developed complex cognitive processes such as language and artistic abilities. Recent research indicates that *Homo sapiens* originated in Africa, probably no more than 200,000 years ago. These early men and women walked out of the African landmass sometime between 120,000 and 50,000 years ago, gradually populating all regions of the world. What is significant in this story is that the different population groups around the world, the so-called races of humankind, have only recently broken off from one another. Also in this chapter, we describe the domestication of plants and animals and the founding of the first village settlements around the globe.

In **Chapter 2, "Rivers, Cities, and First States, 4000–2000 BCE,"** we focus on five of the great river basins where extraordinary breakthroughs in human activity occurred. On the flood plains of the Tigris and Euphrates in Mesopotamia, the Nile in Egypt, the Indus valley in modern-day northern India and Pakistan, and the Yellow and Yangzi rivers in China, men and women mastered annual floods and became expert in seeding and cultivating foodstuffs. In these areas, populations became dense. Riverine cultures had much in common. They had highly developed hierarchical political, social, and cultural systems, priestly and bureaucratic classes, and organized religious and cultural systems. But they also differed greatly, and these differences were passed from generation to generation. Compare ancient Egypt, which had a dearth of large cities, with Mesopotamia, which was the heartland of urban development. Consider as well the Chinese ruling elites, who early on displayed a talent for organizing large swaths of territories with heavy population densities and gradually imposing on them a unified culture. The development of these major complex societies certainly is a turning point in world history.

In **Chapter 3, "Nomads, Territorial States, and Microsocieties, 2000–1200 BCE,"** extensive climatic and technological changes serve as major turning points. Drought, en-

vironmental degradation, and political instability brought the first riverine societies to a crashing end around 2000 BCE. When aridity forced tribal and nomadic peoples living on the fringes of the settled populations to move closer to settled areas, they brought with them an insurmountable military advantage. They had become adept at yoking horses to war chariots, and hence they were in a position to subjugate or intermarry with the peoples in the settled polities in the river basins. Around 2000 BCE these peoples established new territorial kingdoms in Mesopotamia, Egypt, the Indus valley, and China, which gave way a millennium later (1000 BCE) to even larger, militarily and politically more powerful states. In the Americas, the Mediterranean, sub-Saharan Africa, and the Pacific worlds, microsocieties arose as an alternative form of polity in which peoples lived in much smaller-scale societies that showcased their own unique and compelling features.

Chapter 4, "First Empires and Common Cultures in Afro-Eurasia, 1200–350 BCE," describes the different ways in which larger-scale societies grew and became unified. In the case of the world's first empires, the neo-Assyrian and Persian, political power was the main unifying element. Both states established different models that future empires would emulate. The Assyrians used brutal force to intimidate and subjugate different groups within their societies and neighboring states. The Persians followed a pattern that relied less on coercion and more on tributary relationships, while reveling in cultural diversity. The Zhou state in China offered yet a third way of political unity, basing its rule on the doctrine of the mandate of heaven, which legitimated its rulers' succession as long as they were able to maintain stability and order. Vedic society in South Asia offers a dramatically different model in which religion and culture are the main unifying forces. Religion moves to the forefront of the narrative in other ways in this chapter. The birth of monotheism occurred in the Zoroastrian and Hebrew faiths and the beginnings of Buddhism—all three religions endure today.

During the last millennium before the common era, the worlds surrounding these centralized, riverine polities emerged as major players on the historical stage just as these first empires were declining. As **Chapter 5, "Worlds Turned Inside Out, 1000–350 BCE,"** demonstrates, these worlds took advantage of the small-scale and more intimate relationships to create highly individualistic cultures, even in some cases to experiment with a democratic polity. They also developed new strategies for understanding the natural world and humankind. The Greek city-states were the most dynamic of these new cultures, and they spread their Hellenistic culture far and wide. In China, Confucians and Daoists debated how best to create a well-ruled and stable society during the Warring States period. Similar debates occurred in South Asia, where early Buddhists and Brahmin priests in Vedic society strove to provide a more spiritually compelling belief system for their followers. In Greece, Plato, Socrates, and the Sophists discussed nature and humanity. In Africa, the Bantu peoples spread across sub-Saharan Africa, and the Sudanic peoples of Meroe created a society that blended Egyptian and sub-Saharan influences. These were all dynamic hybrid societies building on existing knowledge. Equally dramatic transformations occurred in the Americas, where the Olmec and Chavín peoples were creating hierarchical societies of the like never before seen in their part of the world.

Chapter 6, "Shrinking the Afro-Eurasian World, 350 BCE–250 CE," describes three major forces that simultaneously integrated large segments of the Afro-Eurasian landmass culturally and economically. First, Alexander and his armies changed the political and cultural landscape of North Africa and Southwest and South Asia. Culturally, Alexander spread Hellenism through North Africa and Southwest and central Asia, making it the first cultural system to achieve a transregional scope. Hellenism's appeal to peoples with varying historical and cultural backgrounds was irresistible. Alexander and his men followed existing pathways across Southwest Asia on their way to South Asia, but it was in the post-Alexander world that these commercial roads were stabilized and intensified. For the first time, a trading network, known as the Silk Road, stretching from Palmyra in the West to Central Asia in the East, came into being. Buddhism was the first religion to seize on the Silk Road's more formal existence as its followers moved quickly with the support of the Mauryan Empire to spread their ideas into central Asia. Finally, we witness the growth of a "silk road of the seas" as new technologies and bigger ships allowed for a dramatic expansion in maritime trade from South Asia all the way to Egypt and East Africa.

Chapter 7, "Han Dynasty China and Imperial Rome, 300 BCE–300 CE," describes Han China and the Roman Empire. The world's first empires appeared in Chapter 4, and developments introduced in previous chapters paved the way for the massive Roman and Han empires, which provided two political, economic, and cultural systems that dominated much of the Afro-Eurasian landmass from 200 BCE to 200 CE. Both the Han Dynasty and the Roman Empire ruled effectively in their own way, providing an instructive comparative case study. Both left their imprint on Afro-Eurasia, and rulers for centuries afterward tried to revive these glorious polities and use them as models of greatness. This chapter also discusses the effect of state sponsorship on religion, as Christianity came into existence in the context of the late Roman Empire and Buddhism was introduced to China during the decline of the Han.

Chapter 8, "The Rise of Universal Religions, 300–600 CE," describes how out of the crumbling Roman Empire new polities and a new religion emerged. The Byzantine Empire, claiming to be the successor state to the Roman Empire, embraced Christianity as its state religion. The Tang rulers patronized Buddhism to such a degree that Confucian statesmen feared it had become the state religion. Both Buddhism and Christianity enjoyed spectacular success in the politically fragmented post-Han era in China and in the feudal world of western Europe. These dynamic religions represent a decisive turning point in world history. Christianity enjoyed its eventual successes through state sponsorship via the Roman and Byzantine empires and by providing spiritual comfort and hope during the chaotic years of Rome's decline. Buddhism grew through imperial sponsorship and significant changes to its fundamental beliefs, when adherents to the faith deified Buddha and created notions of an afterlife. In Africa we see a wide range of significant developments and a myriad of cultural practices, yet we also witness the ongoing development of large common cultures. The Bantu peoples spread throughout the southern half of the landmass, spoke closely related languages, and developed similar political institutions based on the prestige of individuals of high achievement. In the Americas the Olmecs established their own form of the city-state, while the Mayans owed their success to a decentralized common culture built around a strong religious belief system and a series of spiritual centers.

In **Chapter 9, "New Empires and Common Cultures, 600–1000 CE,"** we look at how from a relatively remote corner of the Arabian Peninsula arose another world religion, Islam, which enjoyed unanticipated political, military, cultural, and economic successes. The rise of Islam, clearly another turning point in world history, provides a contrast to the way in which universalizing religions and political empires interacted. Islam and empire arose in a fashion quite different from Christianity and the Roman Empire. Christianity took over an already existing empire—the Roman—after suffering persecution at its hands for several centuries. In contrast, Islam created an empire almost at the moment of its emergence. Toward the end of his life, the Prophet Muhammad was already establishing the rudiments of an empire as he contemplated taking control of the whole Arabian Peninsula and extending his influence to Syria and Iraq. By the time the Abbasid Empire came into being in the middle of the eighth century, Islamic armies, political leaders, and clerics exercised power over much of the Afro-Eurasian landmass from southern Spain, across North Africa, all the way to Central Asia. Islam worked its way into West and East Africa, as Muslim clerics and traders crossed the Sahara and the Indian Ocean. They reached far into the interior of the sub-Saharan region. The Tang Empire in China, however, served as a counterweight to Islam's power both politically and intellectually. Confucianism enjoyed a spectacular recovery in this period. With the Tang rulers, Confucianism slowed the spread of Buddhism and further reinforced China's development along different, more secular pathways. Japan and Korea also enter world history at this time, as tributary states to Tang China and as hybrid cultures that mixed Chinese customs and practices with their own. The Vikings highlight the role that nomadic peoples played in developing trade in Afro-Eurasia. The Christian world split in this period between the western Latin church and the eastern Byzantine church. Both branches of Christianity played a role in unifying societies, especially in western Europe, which lacked strong political rule.

Chapter 10, "Becoming 'The World,' 1000–1300 CE," looks at the increase of prosperity and population across most of Afro-Eurasia and into West and East Africa. Just as importantly, the world in this period divided into regional zones that are recognizable today. And trade grew rapidly. A look at the major trading cities of this time demonstrates how commerce transformed cultures. Sub-Saharan Africa also underwent intense regional integration via the spread of the Mande-speaking peoples and the Mali Empire. The Americas witness their first empire in the form of the Chimu peoples in the Andes. This chapter ends with the Mongol conquests of the twelfth and thirteenth centuries, which brought massive destruction. The Mongol Empire, however, once in place, promoted long-distance commerce, scholarly exchange, and travel on an unprecedented scale. The Mongols brought Eurasia and North Africa and many parts of sub-Saharan Africa into a new connectedness. The Mongol story also underscores the important role that nomads played throughout the history of the early world.

Finally, **Chapter 11, "Crises and Recovery in Afro-Eurasia, 1300s–1500s,"** brings into relief the turning point of the Black Death, which turned this period into one where many traditional institutions and polities gave way and peoples were compelled to rebuild their cultures. The polities that came into being at this time and the intense religious experimentation that took place effected a sharp break with the past. The bubonic plague wiped out as much as two-thirds of the population in many of the densely settled locations of Afro-Eurasia. Societies were brought to their knees by the Mongols' depredations as well as by biological pathogens. In the face of one of humanity's grimmest periods, peoples and societies demonstrated tremendous resilience as they looked for new ways to rebuild their communities, some turning inward and others seeking inspiration, conquests, and riches elsewhere. Volume One concludes on the eve of the "Columbian Exchange," the moment when "old" worlds discovered "new" ones and a vast series of global interconnections and divergences commenced.

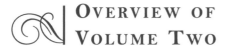

OVERVIEW OF VOLUME TWO

The organizational structure for Volume Two reaffirms the commitment to write a decentered, global history of the world. Christopher Columbus is not the starting point, as he is in so many modern world histories. Rather, we begin in the eleventh and twelfth centuries with two major developments in world history. The first, set forth in **Chapter 10, "Becoming 'The World,' 1000–1300 CE,"** describes a world that was divided

for the first time into regions that are recognizable today. This world experienced rapid population growth, as is shown by a simple look at the major trading cities from Asia in the East to the Mediterranean in the West. Yet nomadic peoples remain a force as revealed in the Mongol invasions of Afro-Eurasia. **Chapter 11, "Crises and Recovery in Afro-Eurasia, 1300s–1500s,"** describes how the Mongol warriors, through their conquests and the integration of the Afro-Eurasian world, spread the bubonic plague, which brought death and depopulation to much of Afro-Eurasia. Both these stories set the stage for the modern world and are clear-cut turning points in world history. The primary agents of world connection described in this chapter were dynasts, soldiers, clerics, merchants, and adventurers who rebuilt the societies that disease and political collapse had destroyed. They joined the two hemispheres, as we describe in **Chapter 12, "Contact, Commerce, and Colonization, 1450s–1600,"** bringing the peoples and products of the Western Hemisphere into contact and conflict with Eurasia and Africa. It is the collision between the Eastern and Western Hemispheres that sets in motion modern world history and marks a distinct divide or turning point between the premodern and the modern. Here, too, disease and increasing trade linkages were vital. Unprepared for the advanced military technology and the disease pool of European and African peoples, the Amerindian population experienced a population decline even more devastating than that caused by the Black Death.

Europeans sailed across the Atlantic Ocean to find a more direct, less encumbered route to Asia and came upon lands, peoples, and products that they had not expected. One item, however, that they had sought in every part of the world and that they found in abundance in the Americas was precious metal. In **Chapter 13, "Worlds Entangled, 1600–1750,"** we discuss how New World silver from Mexico and Peru became the major currency of global commerce, oiling the long-distance trading networks that had been revived after the Black Death. The effect of New World silver on the world economy was so great that it, even more than the Iberian explorations of the New World, brought the hemispheres together and marks the true genesis of modern world history. We also discuss the importance of sugar, which linked the economies and polities of western Europe, Africa, and the Americas in a triangular trade centered on the Atlantic Ocean. Sugar, silver, spices, and other products sparked and expanded commercial exchanges and led to cultural flourishing around the world.

Chapter 14, "Cultures of Splendor and Power, 1500–1780," discusses the Ottoman scientists, Safavid and Mughal artists, and Chinese literati, as well as European thinkers, whose notable achievements were rooted in their own cultures but tempered by awareness of the intellectual activities of others. In this chapter, we look closely at how culture is created as a historical process and describe how the massive growth in wealth during this period, growing out of global trade, led to one of the great periods of cultural flourishing in world history.

Around 1800, transformations reverberated outward from the Atlantic world and altered economic and political relationships in the rest of the world. In **Chapter 15, "Reordering the World, 1750–1850,"** we discuss how political revolutions in the Americas and Europe, new ideas about how to trade and organize labor, and a powerful rhetoric of freedom and universal rights underlay the beginning of "a great divide" between peoples of European descent and those who were not. These forces of laissez-faire capitalism, industrialization, the nation-state, and republicanism not only attracted diverse groups around the world; they also threatened groups that put forth alternative visions. Ideas of freedom, as manifested in trading relations, labor, and political activities, clashed with a traditional world based on inherited rights and statuses and further challenged the way men and women had lived in earlier times. These political, intellectual, and economic reorderings changed the way people around the world saw themselves and thus represent something quite novel in world history. But these new ways of envisioning the world did not go unchallenged, as **Chapter 16, "Alternative Visions of the Nineteenth Century,"** makes clear. Here, intense resistance to evolving modernity reflected the diversity of peoples and their hopes for the future. This chapter looks at Wahabbism in Islam, the strongman movement in Africa, Indian resistance in America and Mexico, socialism and communism in Europe, the Taiping Rebellion in China, and the Indian Mutiny in South Asia. Prophets and leaders had visions that often drew on earlier traditions and that led these individuals to resist rapid change.

Chapter 17, "Nations and Empires, 1850–1914," discusses the political, economic, military, and ideological power that thrust Europe and North America to the fore of global events and led to an era of nationalism and modern imperialism, new forces in world history. Yet this period of seeming European supremacy was to prove short-lived. **Chapter 18, "An Unsettled World, 1890–1914,"** demonstrates that even before World War I shattered Europe's moral certitude, many groups at home (feminists, Marxists, and unfulfilled nationalists) and abroad (anticolonial nationalists) had raised a chorus of complaints about European and North American dominance. As in Chapter 14, we look at the processes by which specific cultural movements arise and reflect the concerns of individual societies. Yet here, too, syncretistic movements emerged in many cultures and reflected the sway of global imperialism, which by then had become a dominant force.

Chapter 19, "Of Masses and Visions of the Modern, 1910–1939," briefly covers World War I and then discusses how, from the end of World War I until World War II, different visions of being modern competed around the world. It is the development of modernism and its effects on multiple cultures that integrate the diverse developments discussed in this chapter. In the decades between the world wars, proponents of liberal democracy struggled to defend their views and often to impose their will on authoritarian rulers and anticolonial nationalists.

Chapter 20, "The Three-World Order, 1940–1975," presents World War II and describes how new adversaries arose after the war. A three-world order came into being— the First World, led by the United States and extolling capitalism, the nation-state, and democratic government; the Second World, led by the Soviet Union and favoring authoritarian polities and economies; and the Third World, made up of former colonies seeking an independent status for themselves in world affairs. The rise of this three-world order dominates the second half of the twentieth century and constitutes another major theme of world history.

In **Chapter 21, "Globalization, 1970–2000,"** we explain that, at the end of the cold war, the modern world, while clearly more unified than before, still had profound cultural differences and political divisions. At the beginning of the twenty-first century, capital, commodities, peoples, and ideas move rapidly over long distances. But cultural tensions and political impasses continue to exist. It is the rise of this form of globalism that represents a vital new element as humankind heads into a new century and millennium. We close with an **Epilogue,** which tracks developments since the turn of the millennium. These last few years have brought profound changes to the world order, yet we hope readers of *Worlds Together, Worlds Apart* will see more clearly how this most recent history is, in fact, entwined with trends of much longer duration that are the chief focus of this book.

The history of the world is not a single, sweeping narrative. On the contrary, the last 5,000 years have produced multiple histories, moving along many paths and trajectories. Sometimes these histories merge, intertwining themselves in substantial ways. Sometimes they disentangle themselves and simply stand apart. Much of the time, however, they are simultaneously together and apart. In place of a single narrative, the usual one being the rise of the West, this book maps the many forks in the road that confronted the world's societies at different times and the surprising turns and unintended consequences that marked the choices that peoples and societies made, including the unanticipated and dramatic rise of the West in the nineteenth century. Formulated in this way, world history is the unfolding of many possible histories, and readers of this book should come away with a reinforced sense of the unpredictability of the past, the instability of the present, and the uncertainty of the future.

Let us begin our story!

PEDAGOGICAL PROGRAM

Worlds Together, Worlds Apart is designed for maximum readability. The crisp, clear narrative, built around stories, themes, and concepts, is accompanied by a highly useful pedagogical program designed to help students study while engaging them in the subject matter. Highlights of this innovative program are described below.

STELLAR MAP PROGRAM WITH ENHANCED CAPTIONS

The book's more than 120 beautiful maps are designed to reinforce the main stories and concepts in each chapter. Every chapter opens with a two-page map of the world designed to highlight the main story line of the chapter. Within the chapter appear four to five more maps that focus on the regions covered. Enhanced captions encourage more interaction with the map program. Each caption provides contextual information and then asks three types of questions:

- *Factual.* Understanding basic geography
- *Analytical.* Understanding patterns and trends on the map
- *Interpretive.* Thinking beyond the map

FOCUS-QUESTION SYSTEM

The focus-question system helps the reader remain alert to key concepts and questions on every page of the text. Focus questions guide students' reading in three ways: (1) a focus-question box at the beginning of the chapter previews the chapter's contents, (2) relevant questions reappear at the start of the section where they are discussed, and (3) running heads on right-hand pages keep these questions in view throughout the chapter.

PRIMARY SOURCE DOCUMENTS

The authors have selected three to five primary source documents for each chapter. Unlike the primary sources found in other books, which are designed to cover only the greatest hits, our selections reinforce the book's main themes and provide colorful material to augment the chapter's main story line. Perhaps most importantly, many of them challenge students to see world history through the eyes of others and from different perspectives. Each excerpt is accompanied by at least two study questions. Additional primary sources are available on the Digital History Reader, which is part of the Norton StudySpace website.

GLOBAL CONNECTIONS & DISCONNECTIONS FEATURES

Each chapter contains one thematic feature built around key individuals or phenomena that exemplify the main emphasis of the text. Among the many topics included are how historians use technology to date bones and objects from early history, the use of ritual funeral objects in the contexts of religion and trade, the role of libraries in early world history, the travels of Marco Polo and Ibn Battuta, coffee drinking and coffeehouses in different parts of the world, cartography and maps as expressions of different worldviews, the growth of universities around the world, and Che Guevera

as a radical visionary who tried to export revolution throughout the Third World.

NEW CHAPTER CHRONOLOGIES

With the Second Edition come new chronologies that are organized regionally rather than temporally. Each chapter ends with a chronology. The chronologies allow students to track unifying concepts and to see influences across cultures and societies within a given time period.

STUDY QUESTIONS

Following each chapter's conclusion is a series of study questions to help ensure that students have grasped the major concepts and ideas.

FURTHER READINGS

Each chapter includes an ample list of suggested further readings, annotated so that students can see what each book or article covers.

ACKNOWLEDGMENTS

Worlds Together, Worlds Apart would never have happened without the full support of Princeton University. In a highly unusual move, and one for which we are truly grateful, the university helped underwrite this project with financial support from its 250th Anniversary Fund for undergraduate teaching and by allowing release time for the authors from campus commitments.

The history department's support of the effort over many years has been exceptional. Two chairs—Daniel Rodgers and Philip Nord—made funds and departmental support available, including the department's incomparable administrative talents. We would be remiss if we did not single out the department manager, Judith Hanson, who provided us with assistance whenever we needed it. We also thank Eileen Kane, who provided help in tracking down references and illustrations and in integrating changes into the manuscript. We also would like to thank Pamela Long, who made all of the complicated arrangements for ensuring that we were able to discuss matters in a leisurely and attractive setting. Sometimes that meant arranging for long-distance conference calls. She went even further and proofread the entire manuscript, finding many errors that we had all overlooked.

We drew shamelessly on the expertise of the departmental faculty, and although it might be wise simply to include a roster of the Princeton history department, that would do an injustice to those of whom we took most advantage. So here they are: Robert Darnton, Sheldon Garon, Anthony Grafton, Molly Greene, David Howell, Harold James, William Jordan, Emmanuel Kreike, Michael Mahoney, Arno Mayer, Kenneth Mills, John Murrin, Susan Naquin, Willard Peterson, Theodore Rabb, Stanley Stein, and Richard Turits. When necessary, we went outside the history department, getting help from L. Carl Brown, Michael Cook, Norman Itzkowitz, Martin Kern, Thomas Leisten, and Heath Lowry. Two departmental colleagues—Natalie Z. Davis and Elizabeth Lunbeck—were part of the original team but had to withdraw because of other commitments. Their contributions were vital, and we want to express our thanks to them. David Gordon, now at the University of Maryland, used portions of the text while teaching an undergraduate course at the University of Durban in South Africa and shared comments with us. Shamil Jeppie, like David Gordon a graduate of the Princeton history department, now teaching at the University of Cape Town in South Africa, read and commented on various chapters.

Beyond Princeton, we have also benefited from exceptionally gifted and giving colleagues who have assisted this book in many ways. Colleagues at Louisiana State University, the University of Florida, the University of North Carolina, the University of Pennsylvania, and the University of California at Los Angeles, where Suzanne Marchand, Michael Tsin, Holly Pittman, and Stephen Aron, respectively, are now teaching, pitched in whenever we turned to them. Especially helpful have been the contributions of James Gelvin, Naomi Lamoreaux, Gary Nash, and Joyce Appleby at UCLA; Michael Bernstein at the University of California at San Diego; and Maribel Dietz, John Henderson, Christine Kooi, David Lindenfeld, Reza Pirbhai, and Victor Stater at Lousiana State University. It goes without saying that none of these individuals bears any responsibility for factual or interpretive errors that the text may contain. Xinru Liu would like to thank her Indian mentor, Romila Thapar, who changed the way we think about Indian history.

The quality and range of reviews on this project were truly exceptional. The final version of the manuscript was greatly influenced by the thoughts and ideas of numerous instructors. We wish to particularly thank our consulting reviewers, who read multiple versions of the manuscript from start to finish.

First Edition Consultants
Hugh Clark, Ursinus College
Jonathan Lee, San Antonio College
Pamela McVay, Ursuline College
Tom Sanders, United States Naval Academy

Second Edition Consultants
Jonathan Lee, San Antonio College
Pamela McVay, Ursuline College
Steve Rapp, Georgia State University
Cliff Rosenberg, City University of New York

We are also indebted to the many other reviewers from whom we benefited greatly.

First Edition Reviewers
Lauren Benton, New Jersey Institute of Technology
Ida Blom, University of Bergen, Norway
Ricardo Duchesne, University of New Brunswick
Major Bradley T. Gericke, United States Military Academy
John Gillis, Rutgers University
David Kenley, Marshall University
John Kicza, Washington State University
Matthew Levinger, Lewis and Clark College
James Long, Colorado State University
Adam McKeown, Columbia University
Mark McLeod, University of Delaware
John Mears, Southern Methodist University
Michael Murdock, Brigham Young University
David Newberry, University of North Carolina, Chapel Hill
Tom Pearcy, Slippery Rock State University
Oliver B. Pollak, University of Nebraska, Omaha
Ken Pomeranz, University of California, Irvine
Major David L. Ruffley, United States Air Force Academy
William Schell, Murray State University
Major Deborah Schmitt, United States Air Force Academy
Sarah Shields, University of North Carolina, Chapel Hill
Mary Watrous-Schlesinger, Washington State University

Second Edition Reviewers
William Atwell, Hobart and William Smith Colleges
Susan Besse, City University of New York
Tithi Bhattacharya, Purdue University
Mauricio Borrerero, St. John's University
Charlie Briggs, Georgia Southern University
Antoinne Burton, University of Illinois, Urbana-Champaign
Jim Cameron, St. Francis Xavier University
Kathleen Comerford, Georgia Southern University
Duane Corpis, Georgia State University
Denise Davidson, Georgia State University
Ross Doughty, Ursinus College
Alison Fletcher, Kent State University
Phillip Gavitt, Saint Louis University
Brent Geary, Ohio University
Henda Gilli-Elewy, California State Polytechnic University, Pomona
Fritz Gumbach, John Jay College
William Hagen, University of California, Davis
Laura Hilton, Muskingum College
Jeff Johnson, Villanova University
David Kammerling Smith, Eastern Illinois University
Jonathan Lee, San Antonio College
Dorothea Martin, Appalachian State University
Don McGuire, State University of New York, Buffalo
Pamela McVay, Ursuline College
Joel Migdal, University of Washington
Anthony Parent, Wake Forest University
Sandra Peacock, Georgia Southern University
David Pietz, Washington State University

Jared Poley, Georgia State University
John Quist, Shippensburg State University
Steve Rapp, Georgia State University
Paul Rodell, Georgia Southern University
Ariel Salzman, Queen's University
Bill Schell, Murray State University
Claire Schen, State University of New York, Buffalo
Jonathan Skaff, Shippensburg State University
David Smith, California State Polytechnic University, Pomona
Neva Specht, Appalachian State University
Ramya Sreeniva, State University of New York, Buffalo
Charles Stewart, University of Illinois, Urbana-Champaign
Rachel Stocking, Southern Illinois University, Carbondale
Heather Streets, Washington State University
Tim Teeter, Georgia Southern University
Charlie Wheeler, University of California, Irvine
Owen White, University of Delaware
James Wilson, Wake Forest University

We do want to pay special thanks to our most ardent supporter of the *Worlds Together, Worlds Apart* enterprise. Jon Lee, San Antonio College, has played many important roles on this project. He has served as a super reviewer on both editions, reading the draft manuscripts multiple times. He also created many of the original support materials that accompanied the First Edition. With the Second Edition, he was the primary force behind the map and pedagogy program for Volume One. He also has taken on the responsibilities for creating the digital history reader that accompanies the text. We are ever grateful to him for his ongoing support and contributions. We also want to thank Nancy Khalek (Ph.D. Princeton University), who has just taken her first tenure-track job, at Franklin and Marshall College. Nancy was our jack-of-all-trades who helped in any way she could. She attended all the monthly meetings during the development of the early volume. She provided critiques of the manuscript, helped with primary research, worked on the photo program and the Global Connections and Disconnections features, and contributed content to the student website. She was invaluable.

Our association with the publisher of this volume, W. W. Norton & Company, has been everything we could have asked for. Jon Durbin took us under the wing of the Norton firm. He attended all of our monthly meetings spanning the better part of four years across the creation of both volumes. How he put up with some of our interminable discussions will always be a mystery, but his enthusiasm for the endeavor never flagged, even when we seemed to grow weary. Sandy Lifland was the ever-watchful and ever-careful development editor for each volume. She let us know when we were making sense and when we needed to explain ourselves more fully. We also want to thank newcomers to the project Alice Falk and Rebecca Homiski. Alice Falk was our talented and insightful co-developmental editor and copyeditor on Volume One. Between the efforts of Sandy and Alice, we couldn't have asked for more from our manuscript editors. Rebecca Homiski did a fabulous job as our project editor, coordinating the responses of up to twelve authors on both volumes combined and locking down all the details on the project. We also want to thank Ellen Lohman for copyediting the Volume Two manuscript ably and with just the right touch under a very tight schedule and Sarah England for providing comments on our Volume Two revisions in a timely and thoughtful fashion. Stephanie Romeo, Jennifer Bright, and Julie Tesser shared duties in finding wonderful photos for both volumes. Rubina Yeh created a beautiful design. Roy Tedoff guided the manuscripts through the production process under a very tight schedule. On the media front, we want to thank Steve Hoge for creating the Norton Study-Space website, which includes the impressive Norton Digital History Reader. On the print ancillary front, we'd like to thank Matt Arnold for finding an excellent group of authors to create the instructor's manual, test bank, and study guide. We also want to thank Alexis Hilts, the most recent newcomer to the project, for helping to pull together many loose ends during the copyediting and production stages.

Finally, we must recognize that while this project often kept us apart from family members, their support held our personal worlds together.

About the Authors

ROBERT TIGNOR (Ph.D. Yale University) is Professor Emeritus and the Rosengarten Professor of Modern and Contemporary History at Princeton University and the three-time chair of the history department. With Gyan Prakash, he introduced Princeton's first course in world history nearly twenty years ago. Professor Tignor has taught graduate and undergraduate courses in African history and world history and written extensively on the history of twentieth-century Egypt, Nigeria, and Kenya. Besides his many research trips to Africa, Professor Tignor has taught at the University of Ibadan in Nigeria and the University of Nairobi in Kenya.

JEREMY ADELMAN (D.Phil. Oxford University) is currently the chair of the history department at Princeton University and the Walter S. Carpenter III Professor of Spanish Civilization and Culture. He has written and edited five books, including *Republic of Capital: Buenos Aires and the Legal Transformation of the Atlantic World,* which won the best book prize in Atlantic history from the American Historical Association. Professor Adelman is the recent recipient of a Guggenheim Memorial Foundation Fellowship and the Frederick Burkhardt Award from the American Council of Learned Societies.

STEPHEN ARON (Ph.D. University of California, Berkeley) is professor of history at the University of California, Los Angeles, and executive director of the Institute for the Study of the American West, Autry National Center. A specialist in frontier and Western American history, Aron is the author of *How the West Was Lost: The Transformation of Kentucky from Daniel Boone to Henry Clay* and *American Confluence: The Missouri Frontier from Borderland to Border State.* He has also published articles in a variety of books and journals, including the *American Historical Review,* the *Pacific Historical Review,* and the *Western Historical Quarterly.*

PETER BROWN (Ph.D. Oxford University) is the Rollins Professor of History at Princeton University. He previously taught at London University and the University of California, Berkeley. He has written on the rise of Christianity and the end of the Roman Empire. His works include *Augustine of Hippo, The World of Late Antiquity, The Cult of the Saints, Body and Society, The Rise of Western Christendom,* and *Poverty and Leadership in the Later Roman Empire.* He is presently working on issues of wealth and poverty in the late Roman and early medieval Christian worlds.

BENJAMIN ELMAN (Ph.D. University of Pennsylvania) is professor of East Asian studies and history at Princeton University. He is currently serving as the director of the Princeton Program in East Asian Studies. He taught at the University of California, Los Angeles, for over fifteen years. His teaching and research fields include Chinese intellectual and cultural history, 1000–1900; the history of science in China, 1600–1930; the history of education in late imperial China; and Sino-Japanese cultural history, 1600–1850. He is the author of five books: *From Philosophy to Philology: Intellectual and Social Aspects of Change in Late Imperial China; Classicism, Politics, and Kinship: The Ch'ang-chou School of New Text Confucianism in Late Imperial China; A Cultural History of Civil Examinations in Late Imperial China; On Their Own Terms: Science in China, 1550–1900;* and *A Cultural History of Modern Science in China.* He is the creator of Classical Historiography for Chinese History at www.princeton.edu/~classbib/, a bibliography and teaching website published since 1996.

STEPHEN KOTKIN (Ph.D. University of California, Berkeley) is professor of history and teaches European and Asian history at Princeton University, where he also serves as director of Russian studies. He is the author of *Armageddon Averted: The Soviet Collapse, 1970–2000* and *Magnetic Mountain: Stalinism as a Civilization* and is a coeditor of *Mongolia in the Twentieth Century: Landlocked Cosmopolitan.* He is currently finishing a book entitled *Lost in Siberia: Dreamworlds of Eurasia,* which is a study of the Ob River valley over the last seven centuries. Professor Kotkin has twice been a visiting professor in Japan.

XINRU LIU (Ph.D. University of Pennsylvania) is assistant professor of early Indian history and world history at the College of New Jersey. She is associated with the Institute of World History and the Chinese Academy of Social Sciences. She is the author of *Ancient India and Ancient China, Trade and Religious Exchanges, AD 1–600; Silk and Religion, an Exploration of Material Life and the Thought of People, AD 600–1200; Connections across Eurasia, Transportation, Communication, and Cultural Exchange on the Silk Roads,* co-authored with Lynda Norene Shaffer; and *A Social History of Ancient India* (in Chinese). Professor Liu promotes South Asian studies and world history studies in both the United States and the People's Republic of China.

SUZANNE MARCHAND (Ph.D. University of Chicago) is associate professor of European and intellectual history at Louisiana State University, Baton Rouge. Professor Marchand also spent a number of years teaching at Princeton University. She is the author of *Down from Olympus: Archaeology and Philhellenism in Germany, 1750–1970* and is currently writing a book on German "orientalism."

HOLLY PITTMAN (Ph.D. Columbia University) is professor of art history at the University of Pennsylvania, where she teaches art and archaeology of Mesopotamia and the Iranian Plateau. She also serves as curator in the Near East Section of the University of Pennsylvania Museum of Archaeology and Anthropology. Previously she served as a curator in the Ancient Near Eastern Art Department of the Metropolitan Museum of Art. She has written extensively on the art and culture of the Bronze Age in the Middle East and has participated in excavations in Cyprus, Turkey, Syria,

Iraq, and Iran, where she currently works. Her research investigates works of art as media through which patterns of thought, cultural development, and historical interactions of ancient cultures of the Near East are reconstructed.

GYAN PRAKASH (Ph.D. University of Pennsylvania) is professor of modern Indian history at Princeton University and a member of the Subaltern Studies Editorial Collective. He is the author of *Bonded Histories: Genealogies of Labor Servitude in Colonial India* and *Another Reason: Science and the Imagination of Modern India.* Professor Prakash edited *After Colonialism: Imperial Histories and Postcolonial Displacements* and has written a number of articles on colonialism and history writing. He is currently working on a history of the city of Bombay. With Robert Tignor, he introduced the modern world history course at Princeton University.

BRENT SHAW (Ph.D. Cambridge University) is the Andrew Fleming West Professor of Classics at Princeton University, where he is director of the Program in the Ancient World. He was previously at the University of Pennsylvania, where he chaired the Graduate Group in Ancient History. His principal areas of specialization as a Roman historian are Roman family history and demography, sectarian violence and conflict in Late Antiquity, and the regional history of Africa as part of the Roman Empire. He has published *Spartacus and the Slaves Wars*; edited the papers of Sir Moses Finley, *Economy and Society in Ancient Greece*; and published in a variety of books and journals, including the *Journal of Roman Studies,* the *American Historical Review,* the *Journal of Early Christian Studies,* and *Past & Present.*

MICHAEL TSIN (Ph.D. Princeton) is associate professor of history and international studies at the University of North Carolina at Chapel Hill. He previously taught at the University of Illinois at Chicago, Princeton University, Columbia University, and the University of Florida. Professor Tsin's primary interests include the histories of modern China and colonialism. He is the author of *Nation, Governance, and Modernity in China: Canton, 1900–1927.* His current research explores the politics of cultural translation with regard to the refashioning of social and institutional practices in China since the mid-nineteenth century.

NORTH

AMERICA

ATLANTIC
OCEAN

SAHARA

PACIFIC
OCEAN

SOUTH

AMERICA

0   1000   2000 Miles

0   1000   2000 Kilometers

THE GEOGRAPHY OF THE ANCIENT AND MODERN WORLDS

Today, we believe the world to be divided into continents, and most of us think that it was always so. Geographers usually identify six inhabited continents: Africa, North America, South America, Europe, Asia, and Australia. Inside these continents they locate a vast number of subcontinental units, such as East Asia, South Asia, Southeast Asia, the Middle East, North Africa, and sub-Saharan Africa. Yet this geographical understanding would have been completely alien to premodern men and women, who did not think that they inhabited continents bounded by large bodies of water. Lacking a firm command of the seas,

they saw themselves living on contiguous landmasses, and they thought these territorial bodies were the main geographical units of their lives. Hence, in this volume we have chosen to use a set of geographical terms, the main one being *Afro-Eurasia*, that more accurately reflect the world that the premoderns believed that they inhabited.

The most interconnected and populous landmass of premodern times was Afro-Eurasia. The term *Eurasia* is widely used in general histories, but we think it is in its own ways inadequate. The preferred term from our perspective must be *Afro-Eurasia*, for the intercon-

ARCTIC OCEAN

A F R O — E U R A S I A

EUROPE

INNER EURASIA

Danube R.

BLACK SEA

CASPIAN SEA

ARAL SEA

AEGEAN SEA

CENTRAL ASIA

TAKLAMAKAN DESERT

MEDITERRANEAN SEA

TAURUS MTS.

IRANIAN PLATEAU

Tigris R.

Yellow R.

YELLOW SEA

DESERT

Euphrates R.

SOUTHWEST ASIA

Indus R.

HIMALAYA MTS.

Yangzi R.

EAST ASIA

RED SEA

ARABIAN SEA

SOUTH ASIA

Pearl R.

PACIFIC OCEAN

Lake Chad

Nile R.

SOUTHEAST ASIA

SOUTH CHINA SEA

Congo R.

Lake Victoria

SUB-SAHARAN AFRICA

INDIAN OCEAN

AUSTRALIA

nected landmass of premodern and indeed much of modern times in-
cluded large parts of Europe and Asia and significant regions in Africa.
The major African territories that were regularly joined to Europe and
Asia were Egypt, North Africa, and even parts of sub-Saharan Africa.

Only gradually and fitfully did the divisions of the world that we
take for granted today take shape. The peoples inhabiting the northwestern part of the Afro-Eurasian landmass did not see themselves as
European Christians, and hence as a distinctive cultural entity, until
the Middle Ages drew to a close in the twelfth and thirteenth centuries. Islam did not arise and extend its influence throughout the
middle zone of the Afro-Eurasian landmass until the eighth and ninth

centuries. And, finally, the peoples living in what we today term the
Indian subcontinent did not feel a strong sense of their own cultural
and political unity until the Delhi Sultanate of the thirteenth and
fourteenth centuries and the Mughal Empire, which emerged at the
beginning of the sixteenth century, brought political unity to that vast
region. As a result, we use the terms *South Asia, Vedic society,* and
India in place of *Indian subcontinent* for the premodern part of our
narrative, and we use *Southwest Asia* and *North Africa* to refer to what
today is designated as the *Middle East*. In fact, it is only in the period
from 1000 to 1300 that some of the major cultural areas that are familiar to us today truly crystallized.

SECOND EDITION

VOLUME A

Worlds Together, WORLDS APART

Chapter

1

BECOMING HUMAN

*I*n a remote and desolate corner of the Ethiopian highlands, a University of California team of evolutionary biologists came upon a remarkable cache of fossil remains. The task of identifying and reassembling these finds took six years of painstaking work, but the researchers eventually reconstructed one of the most revealing sets of human fossils ever found: a nearly complete skeleton of an adult male and the partial remains of another adult and a juvenile. The bones were lodged in volcanic rock. By dating this rock through analysis of its chemical structure, the team was able to determine that the bones were about 160,000 years old. Although the skeletal remains were not identical to those of modern men and women—who are technically *Homo sapiens sapiens*, a specific biological subspecies that emerged approximately 200,000 years ago and is the only surviving subspecies of *Homo sapiens*—they were close enough to form part of the family of modern humans. In short, the bones represented the oldest record of *Homo sapiens*. The fossil finds confirmed what earlier blood analyses and DNA studies had already suggested: *Homo sapiens*, or modern humans, first emerged in a small region of Africa about 200,000 years ago and migrated out of Africa only about 100,000 years ago. As Tim White, the team leader, proclaimed, "We are all Africans."

Not everyone agrees with the "Out of Africa" thesis, a label that emphasizes the contention that modern human beings are all recent descendants of people from Africa. The doubters have continued to believe that the "races" of the world evolved separately in the different regions of the world for up to one million years after their original but distant exodus out of Africa. They contend that as these early descendants of modern men and women evolved, they took on distinctive physical appearances and diverse personality traits in widely dispersed geographical settings, with the result that they appear today as different "races." In their view, the story of humanity was about deep and fundamental differences. But what is now becoming clear is the opposite: all humans share a common heritage, and humanity's differences are not genetic or crudely physical, but mainly cultural. We are also much newer than was once imagined.

Recent and mounting evidence suggests that humans have a common African heritage and that they spread to the rest of the world a relatively short time ago. This is an important insight: as a consequence of the relatively brief period of time spent living separately from one another, all of the world's "races" have a great deal in common. The characteristics that make us human are in fact quite recent in origin. Most of the common traits of human beings—an ability to make tools, to engage in family life, to use language, and to refine cognitive abilities—evolved over many millennia and crystallized on the eve of the exodus from Africa. Only in the last 100,000 years did modern humans gradually make their way out of Africa and populate the world. Only with the advent of settled agriculture did significant cultural divergences become apparent, as seen in material remains (for example, tools, cooking devices, and storage containers) uncovered by archaeologists. The big differences in humankind's cultures are less than about 15,000 or 20,000 years old.

This chapter lays out the origins of humanity from its common source. It will show how many different earlier hominids (humanlike beings who walked erect) preceded modern humans, and that humans came from only one—very recent—stock of migrants out of Africa. Then, fanning out across the world, our ancestors devised new ways to adapt to environmental constraints and opportunities. They created languages, families, and clan systems, often innovating to defend themselves against predators. One of the biggest breakthroughs was the domestication of animals and plants—the creation of agrarian settlements. With this development, humans could dispense with following food and begin producing it in their own backyards.

PRECURSORS TO MODERN HUMANS

> → *What traits differentiated early hominids from other animal species?*

To understand the origins of modern humans, we must confront what is common to all humans and what divides them from each other. We must also come to terms with time. Though the hominids that finally evolved into modern humans (*Homo sapiens*) lived millions of years ago, we have only recently developed the tools to analyze these precursors to modern humans. What is now known about the origins of human existence and the evolution into modern humans over the millennia would have astonished individuals all around the globe a century ago. Only 350 years ago, learned English clerics claimed on the basis of biblical calculations and early Christian tradition about the earth's origin that the first day of creation was Sunday, October 23, 4004 BCE. One scholar even refined the figures to specify that creation happened at 9:00

Focus Questions BECOMING HUMAN

- → *What traits differentiated early hominids from other animal species?*
- → *How did* Homo sapiens *become the only hominid species?*
- → *How did art and language increase* Homo sapiens' *chances of survival?*
- → *What factors contributed to the domestication of plants and animals?*
- → *What factors contributed to autonomous innovation in agriculture versus early borrowing?*
- → *How did agricultural revolutions foster new communal hierarchies and interaction?*

 WWNORTON.COM/STUDYSPACE

→ *What traits differentiated early hominids from other animal species?*

Human Evolution

Australopithecus anamensis	4.2 million years ago
Australopithecus afarensis (Lucy)	3.4 million years ago
Australopithecus africanus	3.0 million years ago
Homo habilis (Dear Boy)	2.5 million years ago
Homo erectus (Java and Peking Man)	1.8 million years ago
Neanderthals	120,000 years ago
Homo sapiens	200,000 years ago
Homo sapiens sapiens (modern humans)	35,000 years ago

A.M. on the morning of that day. Now we see things differently. The origin of the universe dates back some 15 billion years; and the hominid separation from African pongids, or members of the ape family, began some 6 or 7 million years ago. These discoveries have proved as mind-boggling to Hindus and Muslims as to Christians and Jews, all of whom believe, in their different ways, in a creationist account of humanity's origins.

Modern discoveries about humanity's origins have also challenged other major cultural traditions. The Chinese from East Asia, who did not appear to have an indigenous creation story, and Buddhists believed in an apparently endlessly repeated reappearance of human and animal souls over time. But no cultural tradition ever developed the idea that creatures evolved into new kinds of life, that humans were related to apes, and that all of humanity originated in a remote corner of Africa. Take as an example the creation story of the Yoruba peoples of West Africa, representative of many African creation accounts. The Yorubas believed that in the beginning God descended from the heavens in human form, becoming the godlike king of the Yorubas, Oduduwa, who established the Yoruba kingdom and laid down the tenets by which his subjects were to conduct their lives. Or as another example consider the creation story of the Buddhists, who believed in a cosmos of thousands, even millions of worlds, each of which consisted of a central mountain encircled by four continents, its seas surrounded by a girdle or wall of iron. Or consider the time frame for creation as described in the Brahmanical Vedas and the Upanishads, which date to the seventh or sixth century BCE and are still fundamental to Hindu faith today; they count the age of the world in millions, not billions, of years. Moreover, note that Chinese Han dynasty (202 BCE to 220 CE) astronomers believed that at the beginning of the world, perhaps some 23 million years ago, the planets had been conjoined and were likely to merge again at the end of time. Even the million-year time frames and multiple planetary systems that ancient Asian thinkers endorsed did not prepare them for the idea that humans are related to apes. In all of the traditional cosmologies, humans came into existence fully formed, at a single moment, as did the other beings that populated the world.

EVOLUTIONARY FINDINGS AND RESEARCH METHODS

In their study of the origins and descent of species, evolutionary biologists and archaeologists have recently transformed humanity's understanding of its own history, a shift comparable to the realization some five centuries ago that the earth rotates around the sun. And so we see that understanding the long sweep of human history, calculated in millions of years, requires a radically new sense of time. Moreover, the findings have important, if often unsettling, implications concerning who we are as human beings. A mere century ago, who would have accepted the fact that the universe came into being 15 billion years ago, that the earth appeared about 4.5 billion years ago, and that the earliest life forms began to exist 3.8 billion years ago? The great cultural traditions would not have even considered the idea that human beings are part of a long evolutionary chain, stretching from microscopic bacteria to cells and algae and finally to African apes who appeared about 23 million years ago. And they would not have countenanced the findings, which are even more at variance with their origin stories, that Africa's great ape population had broken off into three different groups: one becoming present-day gorillas; the second becoming chimpanzees; and the third group, the one that we call

Selection of Stone Tools from Essex, Southeastern England. The tools shown include a pounder, macelike hammers, a knife, and axes (one of flint). They are typical of the range of implements being made by agriculturalists in the period between 2700 and 1800 BCE, when agricultural settlements were beginning to develop in the region. Tools made of bone, wood, and other perishable materials were also part of the tool-kit used by these same peoples.

A HINDU CREATION MYTH

This hymn of Rig-Veda describes the creation of the universe by the gods' sacrifice of a creature—
Purusha, which means "Man." From the body of Purusha come four different kinds of people: the
Brahman, the Rajanya, the Vaishyas, and the Shudra. They are ritually the four forefathers of the
four castes of India.

Thousand-headed Purusha, thousand-eyed, thousand-footed—he, having pervaded the earth on all sides, extends ten fingers beyond it.

Purusha alone is all this—whatever has been and whatever is going to be. Further, he is the lord of immortality and also of what grows on account of food.

Such is his greatness; greater, indeed than this is Purusha. All creatures constitute but one-quarter of him, his three-quarters are the immortal in the heaven.

With his three-quarters did Purusha rise up; one-quarter of him again remains here. With it did he variously spread out on all sides over what eats and what eats not.

From him was Viraj born, from Viraj the evolved Purusha. He, being born, projected himself behind the earth as also before it.

When the gods performed the sacrifice with Purusha as the oblation, then the spring was its clarified butter, the summer the sacrificial fuel, and the autumn the oblation.

The sacrificial victim, namely, Purusha born at the very beginning, they sprinkled with sacred water upon the sacrificial grass. With him as oblation, the gods performed the sacrifice, and also the Sādhyas [a class of semidivine beings] and the rishis [ancient seers].

From that wholly offered sacrificial oblation were born the verses [rc] and the sacred chants; from it were born the meters [chandas]; the sacrificial formula was born from it.

From it horses were born and also those animals who have double rows [i.e., upper and lower] of teeth; cows were born from it, from it were born goats and sheep.

When they divided Purusha, in how many different portions did they arrange him? What became of his mouth, what of his two arms? What were his two thighs and his two feet called?

His mouth became the brāhman; his two arms were made into the rājanya; his two thighs the vaishyas; from his two feet the shūdra was born.

The moon was born from the mind, from the eye the sun was born; from the mouth Indra and Agni, from the breath [prāna] the wind [vāyu] was born.

From the navel was the atmosphere created, from the head the heaven issued forth; from two feet was born the earth and the quarters (the cardinal directions) from the ear. Thus did they fashion the worlds.

Seven were the enclosing sticks in this sacrifice, thrice seven were the fire-sticks made when the gods, performing the sacrifice, bound down Purusha, the sacrificial victim.

With this sacrificial oblation did the gods offer the sacrifice. These were the first norms [dharma] of sacrifice. These greatnesses reached to the sky wherein live the ancient Sādhyas and gods.

→ *What makes the Brahman the highest, and Shudra the*
lowest, caste in the hierarchy? What is the origin of the
varnas?

SOURCE: *Sources of Indian Tradition*, vol. 1, *From the Beginning to 1800*, edited and revised by Ainslie T. Embree, 2nd ed. (New York: Columbia University Press, 1988), pp. 18–19.

hominids, becoming modern-day humans only after following a long and complicated evolutionary process.

At what stage did humanity's earliest ancestors, the first hominids, initially appear? What traits distinguished hominids from other animals? In fact, no single variable separated these early humanlike beings from other creatures; instead, a combination of traits began to set off hominids from other animals as they evolved over several million years. These include lifting the torso and walking on two legs—a trait called *bipedalism*—thereby freeing hands and arms to carry objects and hurl weapons; controlling and then making fire; fashioning and using tools; developing an enlarged brain and therefore the capacity for language; and acquiring a consciousness of one's "self." Taken together, these traits began to differentiate hominids from other animal species and in the long (long!) run provided humans with the capacity to become the dominant species on the globe. Moreover, all of these traits were fully in place 50,000 years ago. Yet this was just a beginning in human development. It was only about 12,000 years ago that modern humans were ready to make another spectacular advance: domesticating plants and animals and living sedentary lives in village communities.

EARLY HOMINIDS AND ADAPTATION

What was it like to be a hominid, an ancestor of modern humans, in the millions of years before the emergence of modern humans? The first clue came from an important discovery made in 1924 at Taung, not far northwest of where the city of Johannesburg, South Africa, is now located. There, a scientist named Raymond Dart happened upon a skull and the bones of various body parts that appeared to be partly human and partly ape. Believing the creature to be "an extinct race of apes intermediate between living anthropoids (apes) and man," Dart labeled the creature the "Southern Ape of Africa," or *Australopithecus africanus*. This *Australopithecus africanus* had a brain capacity of approximately one pint, or a little less than one-third of the brain size of a modern man and about the same size as modern-day African apes. Yet these beings were different from other animals, for—however shakily or wobbly—they walked on two legs. (See Map 1-1.) In the vicinity of Dart's hominid fossils were scattered the bones of animals. Dart mistakenly concluded that our early ancestors were violent and bloodthirsty creatures who carried their prey to slaughtering grounds. In fact, early hominids were only about five feet tall and weighed at most 110 pounds. They were no match for the big, muscular, and swift animal predators: they were the hunted, not the hunters. That they survived at all in such a hostile environment is a bit of a miracle. But they did, and over the first million years of their existence in Africa, the australopithecines managed to develop into more than six distinct species. Yet it must be strongly emphasized that these australopithecines were not humans, but rather had the genetic and biological material out of which modern humans would later emerge.

Australopithecines not only were found in southern Africa but were discovered in the north as well. In 1974, an archaeological team working at a site in present-day Hadar, Ethiopia, unearthed a relatively intact skeleton of a young adult female australopithecine in the valley of the Awash River. The researchers gave the skeleton a nickname, "Lucy," based on the popular Beatles' song "Lucy in the Sky with Diamonds."

Lucy was remarkable. She stood a little over three feet tall, she walked upright, her skull contained a brain within the ape size range, and her jaw and teeth were humanlike. Her arms were long, hanging halfway from her hips to her knees, suggesting that she might not have been bipedal at all times and still often resorted to arms for locomotion, in the fashion of a modern baboon. Above all, Lucy's skeleton was relatively complete and was very, very old. In fact, it was a solid half million years older than any other complete hominid skeleton found up to that time. Lucy showed us that human precursors were walking around as early as 3 million years ago. Her skeleton provided some big answers. But it also raised some big questions: Was Lucy a precursor to modern-day humans? If so, what kind of a precursor? What species did she represent? Or was she a modern human?

To survive, hominids had to adapt and evolve as their environments altered. During the first millions of years of human existence, these adaptations and changes were slow. They entailed far more physical adaptations to the environment than cultural transformations. Hominids, like the rest of the plant and animal world, had to keep pace with rapidly

Fossil Bones of Lucy. Archaeologist Donald Johanson discovered the fossilized bones of this young female in the Afar region of Ethiopia. They are believed to date from approximately 3.2 million years ago and provide evidence of some of the first hominids to appear in Africa. This find was of great importance because the bones were so fully and completely preserved.

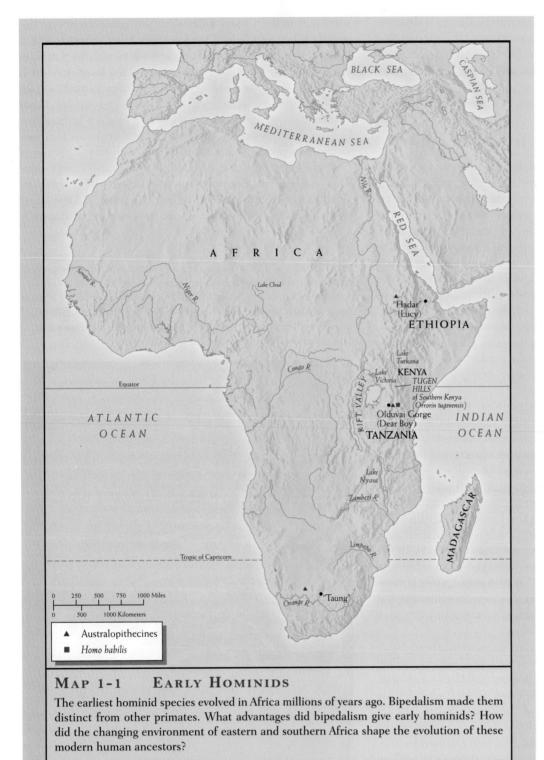

MEDITERRANEAN SEA

BLACK SEA

CASPIAN SEA

RED SEA

Nile R.

A F R I C A

Senegal R.

Niger R.

Lake Chad

"Hadar"
(Lucy)

ETHIOPIA

Congo R.

Lake
Turkana

Lake
Victoria

KENYA

TUGEN
HILLS
of Southern Kenya
(Orrorin tugenensis)

Olduvai Gorge
(Dear Boy)

TANZANIA

RIFT VALLEY

INDIAN
OCEAN

Equator

ATLANTIC
OCEAN

Lake
Nyasa

Zambezi R.

MADAGASCAR

Limpopo R.

Tropic of Capricorn

Orange R.

"Taung"

| 0 | 250 | 500 | 750 | 1000 Miles |
| 0 | 500 | 1000 Kilometers |

▲ Australopithecines
■ *Homo habilis*

MAP 1-1   EARLY HOMINIDS

The earliest hominid species evolved in Africa millions of years ago. Bipedalism made them distinct from other primates. What advantages did bipedalism give early hominids? How did the changing environment of eastern and southern Africa shape the evolution of these modern human ancestors?

ern Africa had environments that changed radically from lush and heavily forested and watered locales to arid, waterless, desertlike wastelands, and then back again. Survival required constant adaptation, and some of the hominid groups happened to be better at it than others.

In adapting, early hominids began to distinguish themselves from other mammals that were physically similar to themselves. It was not their hunting prowess that made them stand out; plenty of other species chased their prey with skill and dexterity. The single trait that gave early hominids a real advantage for survival was bipedalism: they became "two-footed" creatures who stood upright. At some point, the first hominids were not just able to stand up on two feet, they were able to remain upright and move about, leaving their arms and hands free to perform other useful tasks, like carrying food over longer distances. Once they ventured into open savannas (grassy plains with a few scattered trees), about 1.7 million years ago, hominids had a tremendous advantage. They were the only primates to move consistently on two legs. They could move continuously and could travel great distances, and they were therefore able to migrate out of hostile environments and into newer and more hospitable environments as needed.

The physical design of the

changing physical environments, for if they did not, they would die out. Many of the early hominid groups did just that. No straight-line genealogical tree exists from the first hominids to modern men and women. The places in which early hominid remains have been found in southern and east-

body of the earliest hominids represents a fundamental overhaul of the basic body design of tree-living apes. That hominids ever came down out of the trees was also a bit of a miracle. The process took a very long time, and was erratic and unpredictable; but once it took hold, it went beyond the

HOW WE KNOW WHAT WE KNOW

What we know of our recent and shared origins has been the result of some remarkable scientific breakthroughs. The past four or five decades have been critical for charting humankind's earliest history. Only recently have scholars been able to date fossil remains and to use biological and linguistic research to understand the past relationship of the peoples of the world to each other. The first major advance in the study of prehistory (before there were written historical records) occurred immediately after World War II. It involved the use of radiocarbon dating for determining the age of objects of great antiquity. All living things contain the radiocarbon isotope C^{14}, which plants acquire directly from the atmosphere and animals acquire indirectly when they consume plants or other animals. When these living things die, the C^{14} isotope begins to decay into a stable nonradioactive element, C^{12}. Because the rate of decay is regular and measurable, it is possible to ascertain the date of fossils that leave organic remains for ages of up to 40,000 years.

A second major dating technique, known as the *potassium-argon method*, is based on the changing chemical structure of objects over time. Scientists can calculate the age of nonliving objects by measuring the ratio of potassium to argon in them, since over time potassium decays into argon. This method makes possible the dating of objects up to a million years old, and it enables scientists to date the sediments in which fossils are found—as a gauge of the age of the fossils themselves.

DNA (deoxyribonucleic acid) analysis is a third innovation that provides a crucial tool for unraveling the beginnings of modern humans. DNA analysis makes it possible for researchers to pinpoint human descent from an original African population to populations that lived approximately 100,000 years ago. DNA, which determines biological inheritances, is found in two different places within the cells of all living organisms, including the human body. DNA occurs in the nucleus of every cell, where it is known as *nuclear DNA*. It is also found outside the nucleus of cells, where it serves as their microscopic power packs and is known as *mitochondrial DNA*. Examining mitochondrial DNA enables researchers to measure the genetic variation among living objects, including human beings. By studying the mitochondrial DNA of a broad sample of humans, researchers have concluded that there is remarkable genetic homogeneity among the world's peoples today. Gorilla populations now living in the same African valley display more genetic variation than the most widely dispersed human populations. The genetic similarity of modern humans suggests that the human population from whom all modern men and women descended, *Homo sapiens*, originated in Africa about 200,000 years ago. These humans then moved out of Africa about 100,000 years ago, dispersing eastward into the area of Southwest Asia and then through the rest of Afro-Eurasia. One branch moved across to Australia about 50,000 years ago. Another group moved westward into the area of Europe about 40,000 years ago. When the scientific journal *Nature* published these findings in 1987, it inspired a groundswell of public interest and astonishment—and a scientific debate that remains hotly contested today.

point of return. The hominids became permanent land-dwelling rather than tree-dwelling creatures.

Explaining why and how hominids began to walk on two legs is critical to understanding long-term human origins. The first hominids enjoyed, along with the other primates, the advantages of being long-limbed, tree-loving animals, with good vision and dexterous digits. But why did these primates, in contrast to their closest relatives, gorillas and chimpanzees, leave the shelter of trees and venture out into the open grasslands, where they were vulnerable to attack? The answer is not at all self-evident. Explaining how and why some apes took these first steps also sheds light on why humanity's origins lie in Africa. Fifteen million years ago there were apes all over the world—so why did a small number of them evolve new traits in Africa?

What eastern and southern Africa offered was a climate conducive to the development of a diversified milieu of plant and animal species. At a critical moment, the environment in this region changed dramatically. The world had entered its fourth great Ice Age approximately 40 million years ago, during which the earth's temperatures diminished and its continental ice sheets, polar ice sheets, and mountain glaciers increased. This Ice Age was to last until 10,000 years ago. Like all Ice Ages, it was characterized by warming and cooling phases that usually lasted between 40,000 and 100,000 years. Between 10 and 15 million years ago, the climate in

Africa went through one such cooling and drying cycle. To the east of Africa's Rift Valley, stretching from South Africa north to the Ethiopian highlands, the cooling and drying forced forests to contract and savannas to spread. It was in this region, where the environment changed dramatically, that apes came down from trees, stood up, and learned to walk, run, and to live in savanna lands—thus becoming the precursors to humans, and more and more distinctive as a new species of animal.

Using two feet for locomotion did more than augment the means of survival for creatures whose environments were changing, sometimes quite fundamentally. It increased their options for subsistence and led to the acquisition of a variety of cognitive skills, such as thought, memory, problem-solving, and ultimately language, to obtain food and avoid predators. Cognition itself became the basis for further developments. Thus, as hands were freed from the drudgery of pulling bodies around, they could be used for carrying around other things, and eventually for making the first tools. A free hand could be used for holding a spear or the ever-useful digging stick.

In addition to being bipedal, hominids had another feature that helped them to survive and create and use tools—opposable thumbs. This trait, shared with other primates such as apes and monkeys, gave hominids great physical dexterity, enhancing their ability to explore and to alter materials that they found around them. Manual dexterity and standing upright also enabled them to carry their own young family members if they needed

With larger brains, hominids could do more things and become what we call more "human."

to relocate, or to throw missiles with deadly accuracy to protect themselves or to obtain food. They used their increased powers of observation and memory to gather wild berries and grains and to scavenge the meat and marrow of animals who had died of natural causes or who had been killed by large predators. These are activities at which all primates are good, but at which hominids came to excel.

These early hominids were highly social. They lived in small bands of about twenty-five individuals, trying to survive in hostile environments by hunting small game and by gathering wild plants and their produce. They were not yet a match for large predators, however, and had to find safe havens in which to hide. They were also looking for specialized habitats or ecological niches where a diverse supply of wild grains and fruits and abundant wildlife ensured a secure, even comfortable existence. In such highly diversified environmental niches, small hunting bands of twenty-five could swell through alliances with other bands to as many as 500 individuals. The hominids soon learned to communicate mainly through gestures, but they also may have developed a simple early form of language that facilitated the establishment of distinct cultural codes such as common rules and customs.

The early hominids lived in this manner for as many as 3 million years, changing their way of life very little, except for moving around the African landmass in their never-ending search for more favorable environments. Even so, their survival is somewhat surprising. There were relatively few of them, and they struggled in often hostile environments, surrounded by a huge diversity of very large mammals, some of which were threatening carnivores. As the environment changed over the millennia, these early hominids gradually altered in appearance, with small modifications in their bodies reflecting the effects of their adaptation to the changing environment. Fossils from 3 million years ago reveal that their brains became larger, almost doubling in size; their foreheads became more elongated; their jaws became less massive; and they took on a much more modern look. Similarly, adaptation to changes in the environment also created new skills and aptitudes, which in turn expanded cognitive capacities—the ability to store and to analyze information. With larger brains, hominids could do more things and become what we call more "human." A larger brain gave hominids the capacity to form mental maps of their worlds—to learn, to remember what they learned, and to convey these lessons to their neighbors and offspring. In this fashion, larger groups of hominids created communities with shared understandings of their immediate environments, which enhanced the advantages of those with larger brains as they underwent natural selection—the process whereby offspring inherit traits that improve the probability of survival and reproduction.

We know that hominids are much older than we thought, but it also turns out that there was much more diversity than we thought in this early hominid world. A series of startling finds in Ethiopia and Kenya have recently transformed the understanding of these early stages of hominid development. In the Tugen Hills of southern Kenya, bone remains dating to at least 6 million years ago have been discovered of a chimpanzee-sized hominid, named *Orrorin tugenensis*, who walked upright on two feet, indicating that bipedalism must be millions of years older than previously thought. Moreover, the teeth of these hominids seem to indicate that they were closer to modern humans than to australopithecines. But in their arms and hands, which display the characteristics needed for tree climbing, the *Orrorin* hominids seemed more apelike than the australopithecines. So *Orrorin* hominids were still at least half tied to an environment in the trees. Also, recent discoveries of the bones of five individuals in the Afar depression in Ethiopia (in an area just south of where Lucy was found) have revealed the existence of bipedal ho-

→ *What traits differentiated early hominids from other animal species?*

Searching for Hominid Fossils. Olorgasalie in Kenya has proved to be one of the most important archaeological sites for uncovering evidence of early hominid development. Rick Potts, a leader in the field, is shown here on-site. Among his discoveries were hand axes and indications that hominids in this area had learned to use fire.

minids of a yet different kind that dates to at least 5 million years ago. And still another recent discovery, this time in northern Kenya, has revealed another species of early hominids. The fact that quite different kinds of early hominids were living side by side in the same environment in eastern Africa between 3 and 4 million years ago shows that there was much greater diversity and development among early hominid populations than has been previously imagined. The environment in eastern Africa was generating a fair number of different hominid populations, a few of which would provide our genetic base, but most of which would not survive in the long run. In fact, the survival of any of these hominid lines was no certain thing. The bones of *Orrorin* hominids discovered in Kenya had been chewed and broken by the shearing teeth of a large carnivore. A huge leopardlike cat had torn them to pieces.

THE FIRST HUMANS:
HOMO HABILIS

The fossil record reveals that nearly 1 million years after Lucy, the first examples of human beings, to whom we give the name *homo* or "true human," appeared. They, too, were bipedal, possessing a smooth walk based on true upright posture. They had an even more important advantage over other hominids: they had large brains. They were also the first beings to create and use tools systematically, consistently, and on a large scale in order to exploit the resources in their en-

vironment (and, presumably, to defend themselves) more efficiently. These important traits were identified by Mary and Louis Leakey, who made astonishing fossil discoveries in the 1950s at Olduvai Gorge (part of the Great Rift Valley) in present-day northeastern Tanzania. Theirs are regarded as the most significant discoveries of early humans in Africa—especially one find of a totally intact skull that potassium-argon dating methods indicated was 1.8 million years old.

The Olduvai Gorge is a thirty-mile-long canyon through which a winding stream has exposed many layers of volcanic rock containing abundant fossil remains. Louis S. B. Leakey, the son of Anglican missionary parents who had been living in the central highlands of Kenya since the turn of the twentieth century, was a paleontologist (a scientist studying fossil remains from past geological periods) educated at the University of Cambridge. In 1931, Leakey launched a small research project in Olduvai, along with his wife, Mary Nicol Leakey, who was a trained archaeologist. Together, they defied their Cambridge mentors, who had rejected the notion of humanity's African origins. After decades of frustrating work and financial troubles, Mary Leakey could hardly believe her good fortune when she stumbled upon an almost totally intact skull. The Leakeys nicknamed it "Dear Boy."

Other objects discovered with Dear Boy demonstrated that by this time, early humans had begun to fashion tools and to use them for butchering animals and also, possibly, for hunting and killing smaller animals. The tools were flaked stones with sharpened edges that enabled these early humans to cut apart animal flesh and to scoop out the marrow from

Louis Leakey (1903–1972). The Leakeys (Louis and his wife, Mary) were dedicated archaeologists whose work in East Africa established the area as one of the starting points of human development.

mental changes with which it was confronted than other hominids had been. Only with the hindsight of millions of years can we understand the decisive advantage of having larger brains over having larger teeth. This story was not a predictable triumph. There were many more failures than successes in the gradual changes that led *Homo erectus* to be the one species of hominids that would survive until the arrival of *Homo sapiens*.

One of the traits that contributed to the survival of the *Homo erectus* species was the early development of extended periods of caring for their young, which further distinguished them from other primates. Having a brain more than twice the size of the australopithecines gave these hominids real advantages over the rest of the animal world. But an enlarged brain brought one significant problem in its wake: the pelvises of *Homo erectus* females were only big enough to allow an infant with a cranial capacity that was about a third an adult's size to pass through at birth. As a result, infants required a

animal bones. To mimic substitutes for the slicing teeth that lions, leopards, and other carnivores used in stripping meat from a carcass, the Oldowans had devised these tools—deliberately crafting them by careful chipping. Mary Leakey found that Dear Boy and his companions had carried usable rocks over long distances to places where they made their implements and had learned to employ special hammer stones, tools to make tools; sometimes they even carried their favorite toolmaking devices around with them. Unlike other tool-using animals (for example, the chimpanzees), early human men and women were now intentionally fashioning implements, not simply finding them when they were needed. Even more important, they were passing on knowledge of these new tools to their offspring, and in the process they were gradually improving the tools. Because these beings were making tools and because the Leakeys believed that making and using them represented a new stage in the evolution of human beings, they gave these creatures a new name, *Homo habilis*, or "Skillful Man." This toolmaking ability truly made them the forerunners, though very distant, of modern men and women.

EARLY HUMANS ON THE MOVE: MIGRATIONS OF *HOMO ERECTUS*

All the different species of hominids flourished together in Africa between 1 and 2.5 million years ago. By 1 million years ago, however, almost all had gradually died out. The one surviving species, which emerged about 1.5 million years ago, had a large brain and walked truly upright; it therefore was named "Standing Man," or *Homo erectus*. But the success of *Homo erectus* was hardly a foregone conclusion, even though this species was better adapted to the challenging environ-

Tracking Footprints. Mary Leakey was among the most successful archaeologists studying hominids in Africa. Her finds, including the one in this photograph from Laetoli, Tanzania, highlight the activities of early men and women in Africa. The footprints, believed to be those of an *Australopithecus afarensis*, date from 3.7 to 3 million years ago.

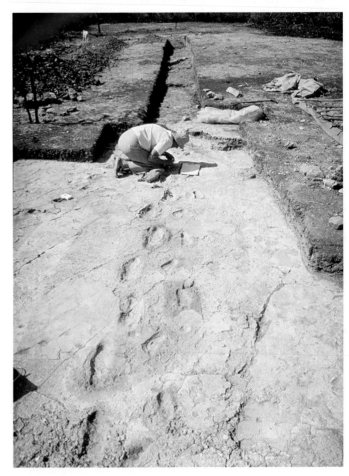

→ *What traits differentiated early hominids from other animal species?*

Olduvai Gorge, Tanzania. Olduvai Gorge is arguably the most famous archaeological site containing hominid finds. Mary and Louis Leakey, convinced that early human beings originated in Africa, discovered the fossil remains of *Homo habilis* ("Skillful Man") in this area between 1960 and 1963. They argued that these findings represent a direct link to *Homo erectus.*

long period during which they would be protected by adults as they matured and their brain size tripled.

This big difference from other species also affected family dynamics. A long process of maturing rendered children dependent on their parents for protection against the dangers of the world, but it also provided the adult members of hunting and gathering bands with the opportunity to train their offspring in those activities. In addition, maturation and brain growth required years of energy transfers from mothers to their infants, via long lactation cycles and the preparation of food for dependent children after weaning. This investment was such a critical part of survival that mothers devised means to disperse the risks of accidents (or attacks) and to share the burden of helping their children's brains grow. Sometimes mothers even had to fend off assaults by predatory fathers and other males. In effect, mothers relied on other women (their own mothers, sisters, and friends) and girls (often their own daughters) to help in the nurturing and protecting, a process known as "allomothering" (literally, "other mothering").

There were two main features of *Homo erectus* that distinguished them from their competitors. Since they were fully bipedal, they were able to move with a smooth rapid gait, which meant they were able to move over large distances quickly. They were the world's first long-distance travelers, forming the first truly mobile human communities. In addition, they began to make rudimentary attempts to control their environment. Not only did these early human ancestors become proficient at making stone tools for hunting and food preparation, they also began to control fire, another significant marker in the development of human culture. It is very hard to tell from the fossil evidence when humans learned to use fire.

The most reliable evidence of fire mastery comes from cave sites, less than 250,000 years old, where it seems that people cooked. By less conservative estimates, fire had become more than an accidental luxury as early as 500,000 years ago. Fire provided heat, protection, a gathering point for small communities, and a way to cook food. It was also symbolically powerful: here was a source of energy that humans could extinguish and revive at will. The uses of fire had enormous long-term effects on human evolution. Because they were able to boil, steam, and fry wild plants, early humans could expand their diets; fire rendered palatable otherwise indigestible foods—especially raw muscle fiber, which human stomachs are ill equipped to handle—and expanded the potential food base, making it possible to exploit food sources that could not be used without fire. Mastery of fire also made it possible for early humans to survive in the colder regions of the world. Without fire, Africans might not have ventured out of their continent.

As scientists gained a clearer sense of when and where the early hominids lived, they also had to figure out how—and, just as important, which—hominids fanned out across the world. What their research indicated was that hominids migrated out of Africa about 1.5 million years ago and gradually spread throughout much of the world. Members of the *Homo erectus* species proved to be the first globe-trotters. Yet despite their tremendous success in moving rapidly to populate most of the globe (except the Americas), these hominids were still not modern humans. They were only the ancestors, or precursors, of modern humans.

The populating of the world by hominids proceeded in waves. Around 1 or 2 million years ago, *Homo erectus* individuals migrated first into the lands of Southwest Asia; then, according to some scholars, they traveled along the Indian Ocean shoreline, moving into South Asia and Southeast Asia and later northward into what is now China. Their movement out of Africa was a response in part to the huge environmental changes that were transforming the world. The Northern Hemisphere was shaken by thirty major cold phases during this period marked by the advance of glaciers (huge sheets of ice) over vast expanses of the northern parts of Eurasia and the Americas. The glaciers had been formed by widespread intense cold that froze much of the water in the world's oceans, lowering them some 325 feet below their present-day levels. So it was possible for the migrants to travel across land bridges into Southeast Asia and from East Asia to Japan, as well as from New Guinea to Australia. The last part of the Afro-Eurasian landmass to be occupied consisted of areas in Europe, at the time one of the most forbidding regions in the world because of its extensive ice cover. The geological record

Zhoukoudian Cave. Located in a cluster of limestone hills twenty-six miles west of Beijing, China, Zhoukoudian is the largest and most important early Stone Age site in China. In addition to the bones of Peking Man, a *Homo erectus* found there, archaeologists discovered two piles of ash residues on a big limestone block, which was used to preserve a fire after kindling. Peking Man's average cranial capacity was approximately 80 percent that of modern man.

indicates that mantles of ice completely blanketed present-day Scotland, Ireland, Wales, Scandinavia, and the whole of northern Europe, including the areas where today's cities of Berlin, Warsaw, Moscow, and Kiev are located. Here, too, however, a lowered ocean level enabled early human predecessors to cross by foot from areas in what we now know as Europe into what is now England.

It is truly astonishing how far these *Homo erectus* hominids traveled. The discoveries of the bone remains of "Java Man" and "Peking Man" (as archaeologists named specific *Homo erectus* hominids, from where their remains were discovered) confirmed early settlements of *Homo erectus* hominids in Southeast and Eastern Asia. The remains of Java Man, found in 1891 on the banks of the Solo River in central Java, were later verified as an early *Homo erectus* that had dispersed into Asia perhaps as early as 2 million years ago. This would mean that the first *Homo erectus* walked out of Africa almost a million years earlier than had been originally believed. In 1969, at Sangiran (also on the island of Java), archaeologists uncovered remains with a fuller cranium, which was very thick, indicating that the individual's brain was about half the size of a modern human's. The most complete discovery from Southeast Asia, it dates from about 800,000 years ago. Accordingly, scientists realized that African hominids were moving north and eastward into Asia at least a million years ago, and more likely 2 million years ago, and had reached Java, which was then connected by land to the rest of the Afro-Eurasian landmass.

Similar finds made in China in the early twentieth century give us a clearer picture of the daily lives of these pioneering hominids, who retained many of the lifeways of their African ancestors. Peking Man was a cave dweller, toolmaker, and hunter and gatherer (surviving by hunting animals and gathering wild fruit such as berries and wild plants), who settled in the warmer climate in northern China perhaps 400,000 years ago. Peking Man's brain was larger than that of his Javan cousins, and there is evidence that he controlled fire and cooked meat, in addition to hunting big animals. He made tools with vein quartz, quartz crystals, flint, and sandstone. The *Homo erectus* hominids proved to be even more adept at making tools than were their predecessors. Their major innovation, dated as far back as 1.7 million years ago, was the double-faced axe, a stone instrument that was whittled down on both sides to make a sharp edge capable of being used as a hand axe, a cleaver, a pick, and probably as a weapon to be hurled against foes or animals. Even so, and in spite of their enlarged brains, these early predecessors still had a long way to go before becoming modern humans.

Rather than seeing human evolution as a single, gradual development, increasingly scientists see our origins as shaped by progressions and retrogressions, as hominids adapted or failed to adapt and went extinct. As the climate changed, especially with the cyclical fluctuations of warming and cooling that were typical of the ice ages, weather conditions altered the course of what is called *speciation* (species formation). Several species could exist simultaneously, but some would be more suited to changing environmental conditions—and thus more likely to survive—than others. Although those in the *Homo habilis* and *Homo erectus* species were some of the world's first humanlike inhabitants, they are unlikely to have been direct ancestors of modern man and woman. The early settlers of Afro-Eurasia from the *Homo erectus* group went extinct, unable to compete against more highly evolved hominids. They were followed by later waves of hominids who walked out of the African landmass just as their predecessors had done. Certainly, by 500,000 years ago, caves in areas of Afro-Eurasia were full of residents who made fire, flaked stones into implements, and formed settlements. Yet we are not their descendants. In effect, the existence of *Homo erectus* hominids may have been a necessary precondition for the evolution into modern humans, or *Homo sapiens*. But it was not, in itself, sufficient.

THE FIRST MODERN HUMANS

> → *How did* Homo sapiens *become the only hominid species?*

Homo sapiens moved out of Africa and became the sole "human" species on the earth sometime between 120,000 and 50,000 years ago. If we can think of the 5 million years of hominid life as a single hour of our time, then the history of *Homo sapiens* has occurred in slightly less than two minutes. The history that we study has happened in an incredibly short interval within the hominid time frame.

The early hominids did not and could not form large communities, as they had limited communication skills. Although hominids could utter simple commands and communicate with hand signals, complex linguistic expression eluded them. This achievement was one of the last in the evolutionary process of becoming truly human. Developing language apparently did not occur until sometime between 100,000 and 50,000 years ago. Many scholars view it as the most critical ingredient in distinguishing human beings from other animals. It is this skill that ultimately made *Homo sapiens* "sapiens," which is to say "wise" or "intelligent": humans who could create culture. Creating language enabled humans to become modern humans.

HOMO SAPIENS AND THEIR MIGRATION

About 200,000 years ago, large-scale ecological shifts in climate and environment in Africa put huge pressures on all types of mammals, including hominids. In these new extremely warm and dry environments, the smaller, quicker, and more adaptable mammals survived. All forms of mammalian life, including early humans, began to become smaller. It was no longer large size and brute strength but rather the ability to respond quickly, to have great agility in responding to challenges, and to be able to move with great speed that counted.

Caught up in these environmental transformations, early humans were no different from other mammals. It is therefore no surprise that a bigger-brained, more dexterous, and more agile species of humans appeared in the highlands of eastern Africa. Referred to technically as *Homo sapiens*, these humans differed notably from their precursors. The eclipse of *Homo erectus* by *Homo sapiens* was hardly inevitable. After all, the *Homo erectus* species of humans was

Skulls of Ancestors of *Homo sapiens*. Shown here are seven skulls of ancestors of modern-day men and women, arranged to highlight brain growth over time. The skulls represent (left to right): *Adapis*, a lemur-like animal that lived 50 million years ago; *Proconsul*, a primate that lived about 23 million years ago; *Australopithecus africanus*; *Homo habilis*; *Homo erectus*; *Homo sapiens* from the Qafzeh site in Israel, about 90,000 years old; and Cro-Magnon from France, about 22,000 years old.

The Physical Evolution of Hominids. These three figures show the femur bones of Lucy, *Orronin tugenensis* (one of the earliest of the hominids, who may have existed as much as 6 million years ago), and *Homo sapiens*. *Homo sapiens* has a larger femur bone and was bigger than Lucy—a representative of the hominid species *Australopithecus afarensis*—but has the same bone structure.

already scattered around Africa and Eurasia; in contrast, even as late as 100,000 years ago there were no more than 10,000 *Homo sapiens* adults, and they were still confined to a small part of the African landmass. But when *Homo sapiens* moved out of Africa and the two species did find each other in the same places across the globe, *Homo sapiens* individuals were better suited to survive, certainly in part because of their greater cognitive and language skills compared to members of the *Homo erectus* species.

The *Homo sapiens* newcomers followed the trails blazed earlier by other migrants from Africa. (See Map 1-2.) In many places, they moved into the same ecological areas as their genetic cousins, migrating from Africa by way of the Levant (the area encompassing modern-day Lebanon, Israel, and Syria), moving across the area of Southwest Asia, and from there migrating into central Asia—but not at this time into the area of Europe. They flourished and reproduced. By 30,000 years ago, the population of *Homo sapiens* had grown to about 300,000. Between 50,000 and 12,000 years ago, these modern humans were moving with extraordinary rapidity into areas that were tens of thousands of miles from the Rift Valley and the Ethiopian highlands of Africa—for example, into what is now China, where they were thriving and even creating distinct regional cultures, with differences between those who lived in the north and those who lived in the south. Shandingdong

Man, for example, was a *Homo sapiens* whose fossil remains and relics can be dated to about 18,000 years ago. His physical characteristics were closer to those of modern humans, and he had a similar brain size. His stone tools, which included choppers and scrapers used to prepare food, were similar to the tools of the *Homo erectus* Peking Man. His bone needles, however, were the first stitching tools of their kind found in China, and they indicated that garments were being made. Some of the needles measured a little over an inch in length and had small holes drilled in them. Shandingdong Man also buried his dead. A tomb of grave goods includes ornaments suggesting that these individuals already had developed aesthetic tastes and religious beliefs. The social unit of the Upper Cave Man appeared to be some sort of clan descended from a common ancestor and thus linked by genealogy.

Homo sapiens were also moving into the furthest northeastern fringe of East Asia. In the more frigid climate, they learned to follow the herds of big Siberian grazing animals. Mastodon bones and dung, for instance, made decent fuel and good building material. They pursued their prey ever eastward as the herds looked for pastures in the steppes (treeless grasslands) and marshes. These groups migrated east across the ice to Japan, also following animal herds. A mammoth fossil has been uncovered in the colder north of Japan, for example, and an elephant fossil in the warmer south. Elephants in particular roamed the warmer parts of East Asia that stretched thousands of miles across inner Eurasia from 300,000 years ago until 15,000 years ago. The hunters and gatherers who moved into Japan hunted animals and gathered wild plants for their sustenance. Meat was dried, smoked, or broiled using fire, practices that the migrants refined once the seas separated the islands from Asia and limited the supplies of game and plants.

Several thousand years later, about 18,000 years ago, *Homo sapiens* went further than their predecessors had gone, edging into the weedy landmass that linked Siberia and North America (which had not been populated by hominids). This prehistoric thousand-mile-long land bridge, called "Beringia," must have seemed to the people who crossed over it simply an extension of familiar steppeland terrain. For thousands of years, modern humans poured eastward and south into the uninhabited terrain of North America. The oldest currently known location of human settlement in the Americas is Broken Mammoth, a 14,000-year-old site in central Alaska. A second, and last, migration seems to have taken place about 8,000 years ago and was by boat, since by then the land bridge had disappeared under the waters of the sea.

Once in the Americas, these mobile and expansionist migrants began to fill up the landmasses. They were the first discoverers of America, and they found ample prey in the herds of wooly mammoths, caribou, giant sloths (weighing nearly three tons), and 200-pound beavers. But the explorers could also themselves be prey—for they encountered saber-toothed tigers, long-legged eagles, and giant bears that moved faster than horses. The melting of the glaciers about 8,000 years ago and

→ *How did* Homo sapiens *become the only hominid species?*

Migrations of *Homo sapiens*	
Homo erectus leave Africa	c. 1.5 million years ago
Homo sapiens leave Africa	c. 100,000 mya
Homo sapiens migrate into Asia	c. 60,000 mya
migrate into Europe	c. 50-40,000 mya
migrate into Australia	c. 40,000 mya
migrate into the Americas	c. 16–11,000 mya

the resulting disappearance of the land bridge eventually cut off the first Americans from their Afro-Eurasian origins. Thereafter, the Americas became a world apart.

CRO-MAGNON *HOMO SAPIENS* REPLACE NEANDERTHALS

Homo sapiens spread out and occupied habitats previously inhabited by earlier hominid migrants. Over the millennia between 100,000 and 30,000 years ago, they eventually migrated over the whole globe and gradually eclipsed their earlier precursors. By that date, as DNA reveals, all genetic cousins to the *Homo sapiens* were extinct, leaving only modern humans' ancestors to populate the world. Neanderthals, members of an early wave of hominids from Africa, had settled in the western area of Afro-Eurasia, ranging from present-day Uzbekistan and Iraq to Spain, perhaps 150,000 years ago. They were there well before *Homo sapiens*. Therein lies a tale, for Western scholars have had a long fascination with these hominids.

Many believed that Neanderthals were the precursors to modern-day Europeans. We now know that this is not true. The first knowledge of Neanderthals came with the discovery in 1856 of a skull in the Neander Valley of present-day Germany—hence their name (*thal* or *tal* is the German word for "valley"). Some authorities wondered if the skull represented the so-called missing link between apes and humans. Not only did Neanderthals have big brains, probably slightly larger than those of modern humans, but they also used tools, buried their dead, hunted, and lived in caves. Yet their brains were not as complex in their structure as those of modern humans, and so their cognitive abilities were far more limited than those of *Homo sapiens*, especially in their perception and creation of symbols.

These characteristics prompted some to conclude that the Neanderthals were the ancestors of modern humans, with important implications for how "racial" differences were explained. Carleton Coon, a leading American anthropologist in the 1940s and 1950s, was an admirer of Neanderthal culture. He also firmly believed that the races of the world were not of recent origin (thus rejecting the "Out of Africa" thesis); he instead maintained that they had been evolving separately

from each other for at least a million years (the multiregional thesis). Disputing the prevailing reputation of Neanderthal man at the time "as a squat, slouching, low-browed, stupid, and vicious brute, wooing his women by clubbing them over the head and eating his deceased parents" (Coon, *The Story of Man*, 39), he advanced the radical claim that if a Neanderthal were dressed up in modern garb, wearing a fedora, a shirt, and a tie, he could enter a New York City subway and pass as a modern man. Coon and others were uncomfortable with the idea that modern humans had emerged from common origins in Africa a mere 100,000 years ago and shared the same genetic foundations. They used fossil remains of Neanderthal Man, Java Man, and Peking Man to attempt to prove that modern men and women, *Homo sapiens*, had evolved separately from *Homo erectus* in markedly different geographical settings. Coon and others erroneously believed that these different groups had taken on deep-seated, nearly unbridgeable racial differences based on lengthy genetic distances from the first humans.

Neanderthals turned out not to be the ancestors of modern humans at all. They eventually gave way to a group of *Homo sapiens* known as the Cro-Magnon peoples (named after the 1868 fossil discoveries in Cro-Magnon in France). Although Neanderthal and Cro-Magnon communities overlapped in Europe for thousands of years, the Neanderthals were not nearly as well equipped to survive as the Cro-Magnon *Homo sapiens*. The Neanderthals' short arms and legs and bulky torso probably made them stronger than modern men and women but extremely awkward and clumsy. Assuming that Neanderthals had proficiency in language (an assumption that cannot be made easily), the location of their voice box put them at a great disadvantage in comparison with modern humans. They would have found it impossible

Skulls of a Neanderthal Man (left) and Cro-Magnon (right).
These two skulls show that Neanderthals had a large brain capacity and a larger head than modern man. However, Neanderthals lost out to *Homo sapiens* in the struggle to survive as they spread across the globe.

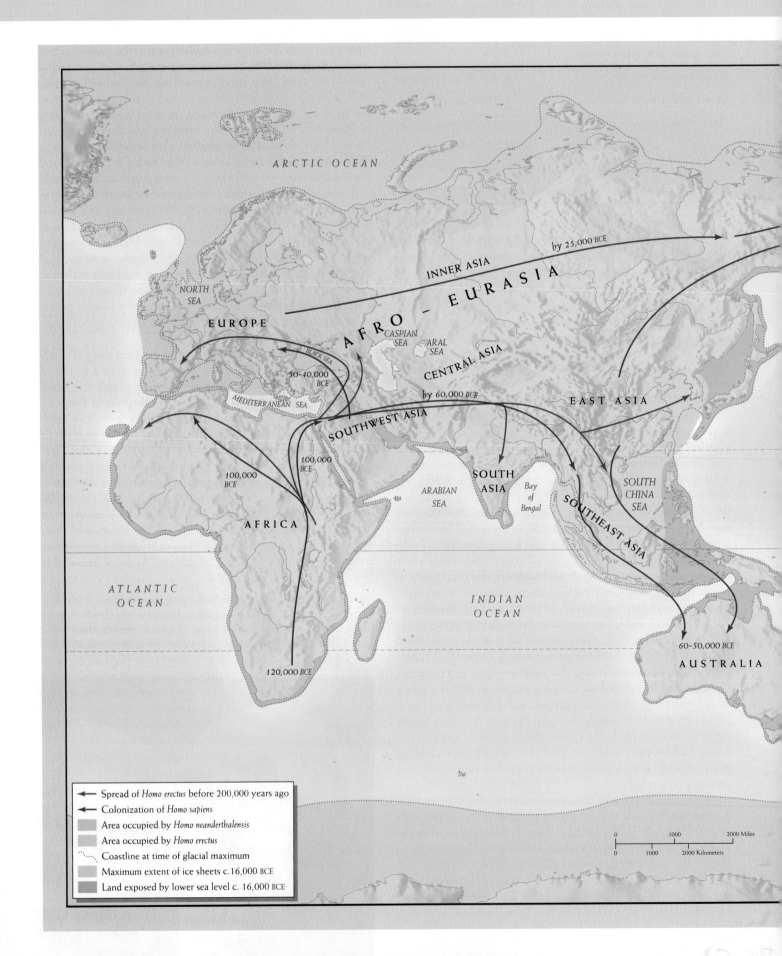

ARCTIC OCEAN

by 25,000 BCE

INNER ASIA

AFRO – EURASIA

NORTH
SEA

EUROPE

BLACK SEA

50-40,000
BCE

CASPIAN
SEA

ARAL
SEA

CENTRAL ASIA

EAST ASIA

MEDITERRANEAN SEA

by 60,000 BCE

SOUTHWEST ASIA

100,000
BCE

SOUTH
ASIA

*Bay
of
Bengal*

SOUTH
CHINA
SEA

100,000
BCE

ARABIAN
SEA

SOUTHEAST ASIA

AFRICA

ATLANTIC
OCEAN

INDIAN
OCEAN

60-50,000 BCE

AUSTRALIA

120,000 BCE

→ Spread of *Homo erectus* before 200,000 years ago
→ Colonization of *Homo sapiens*
    Area occupied by *Homo neanderthalensis*
    Area occupied by *Homo erectus*
 ⋯⋯ Coastline at time of glacial maximum
    Maximum extent of ice sheets c. 16,000 BCE
    Land exposed by lower sea level c. 16,000 BCE

0   1000   2000 Miles
0   1000   2000 Kilometers

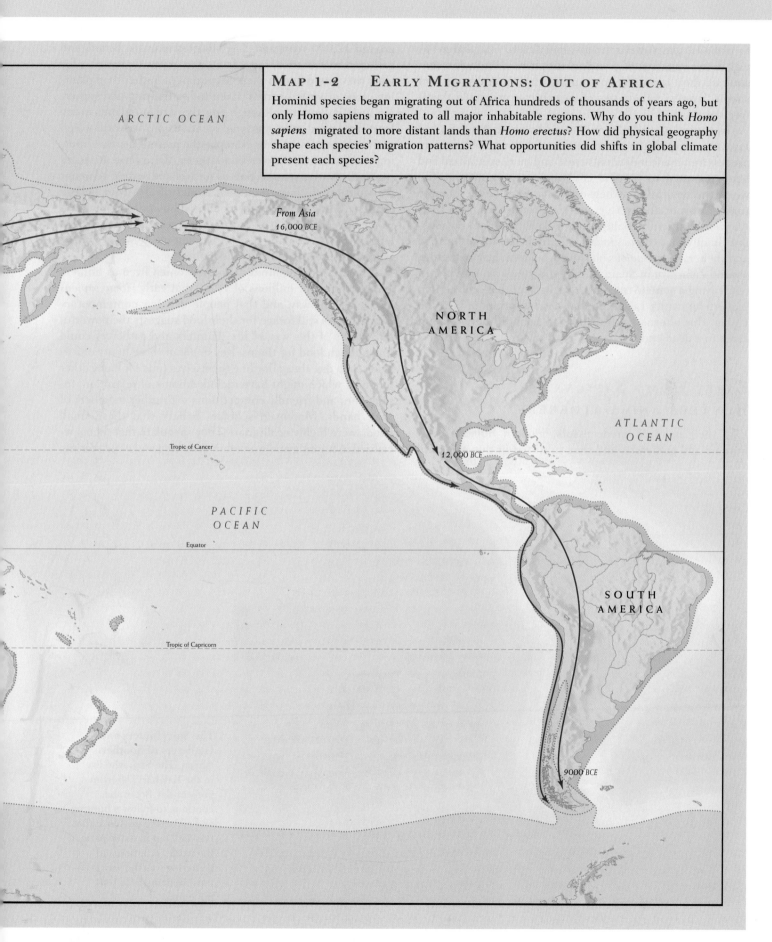

MAP 1-2   EARLY MIGRATIONS: OUT OF AFRICA

Hominid species began migrating out of Africa hundreds of thousands of years ago, but only Homo sapiens migrated to all major inhabitable regions. Why do you think *Homo sapiens* migrated to more distant lands than *Homo erectus*? How did physical geography shape each species' migration patterns? What opportunities did shifts in global climate present each species?

ARCTIC OCEAN

From Asia
16,000 BCE

NORTH AMERICA

ATLANTIC OCEAN

Tropic of Cancer

12,000 BCE

PACIFIC OCEAN

Equator

SOUTH AMERICA

Tropic of Capricorn

9000 BCE

to make certain vowel sounds—specifically, *i, u,* and *a*—as well as two consonants, *k* and *g*. This physical limitation constrained their repertoire to grunting, calling, and some very simple "words." Whole sets of speech patterns could therefore not evolve.

Neanderthals and other advanced hominids in China and Java represented the culmination of a long evolutionary process that made individuals more and more specialized and better adapted to specific environmental conditions. So, when the environment began to change, and the climate turned warmer and wetter, these earlier descendants from Africa had difficulty coping. They lacked the range and adaptive fluidity that *Homo sapiens* had. In the scramble for food and shelter, *Homo sapiens* had an edge. From their last refuge around Zafarraya in Spain, the Neanderthals vanished without leaving a genetic trace in the gene pool that evolved into modern humanity. Like the *Homo erectus* species in Java and China, this alternative trajectory of hominid development came to a dead end.

EARLY *HOMO SAPIENS* AS HUNTERS AND GATHERERS

Like their hominid predecessors, modern humans were hunters and gatherers, and they subsisted in this way until around 12,000 years ago. They hunted animals, fished, and gathered wild berries, nuts, fruit, and grains by foraging for what they could find in their environment, rather than planting crops or vines or trees. Even today, hunting and gathering societies endure, although now they are found only in the least fertile and most marginal locations of the world, often at the edge of deserts. For example, the present-day San hunting and gathering peoples of southern Africa have attracted researchers who see the San as an isolated, exotic remnant still continuing their traditional modes of life. They believe that the San can reveal to modern scholars how men and women lived hundreds of thousands of years ago. Yet even as late as 1500 CE, as much as 15 percent of the world's population still lived by hunting and gathering.

The fact that hominid men and women lived as hunters and gatherers for millions of years, that early *Homo sapiens* also lived this way, and that people in a few contemporary communities still forage for their food suggests the powerful attractions of this way of life. Hunters and gatherers could find enough food for themselves in about three hours of foraging each day, thus affording themselves time for many other pursuits, which might have included hours of relaxation, interaction, and friendly competitions with other members of their bands. Moreover, scholars believe that these small bands were highly egalitarian. They speculate that men specialized in hunting and women in gathering and child rearing,

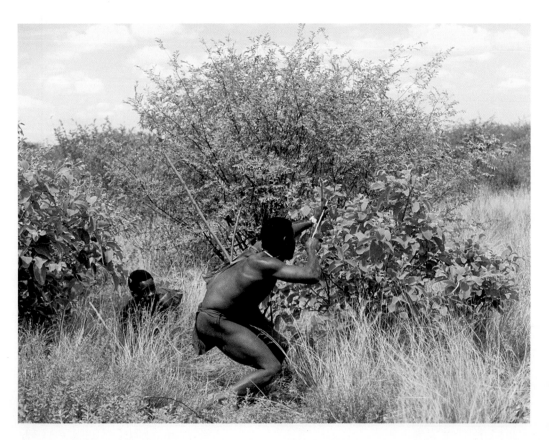

The San Hunters and Gatherers of Southern Africa. The San, who live in the Kalahari Desert in present-day Botswana, continue to follow a hunting and gathering existence that has died out in many parts of the world. Hunting and gathering was the way that most humans lived for millennia.

PROBLEMS IN THE STUDY OF HUNTERS AND GATHERERS

One of the main challenges in studying prehistory and the origins of humanity is that the evidence available to us is incomplete. Archaeologists and anthropologists are forced to theorize and speculate on the basis of what they can lay their hands on. In the case of archaeologists, these are fossil records. In the case of anthropologists, their subjects are tribal peoples—such as the San of southern Africa— whose lifeways today are thought to be similar to those of their ancestors, tens of thousands of years ago.

To date, the hunting way of life has been the most successful and persistent adaptation man has ever achieved. Nor does this evaluation exclude the present precarious existence under the threat of nuclear annihilation and the population explosion. It is still an open question whether man will be able to survive the exceedingly complex and unstable ecological conditions he has created for himself. If he fails in this task, interplanetary archeologists of the future will classify our planet as one in which a very long and stable period of small-scale hunting and gathering was followed by an apparently instantaneous efflorescence of technology and society leading rapidly to extinction. "Stratigraphically" the origin of agriculture and thermonuclear destruction will appear as essentially simultaneous.

On the other hand, if we succeed in establishing a sane and workable world order, the long evolution of man as a hunter in the past and the (hopefully) much longer era of technical civilization in the future will bracket an incredibly brief transitional phase of human history—a phase which included the rise of agriculture, animal domestication, tribes, states, cities, empires, nations, and the industrial revolution. These transitional stages are what cultural and social anthropologists have chosen as their particular sphere of study. We devote almost all of our professional attention to organizational forms that have emerged within the last 10,000 years and that are rapidly disappearing in the face of modernization.

It is appropriate that anthropologists take stock of the much older way of life of the hunters. This is not simply a study of biological evolution, since zoologists have come to regard behavior as central to the adaptation and evolution of all species. The emergence of economic, social, and ideological forms are as much a part of human evolution as are the developments in human anatomy and physiology . . .

. . . Ever since the origin of agriculture, Neolithic peoples have been steadily expanding at the expense of the hunters. Today the latter are often found in unattractive environments, in lands which are of no use to their neighbors and which pose difficult and dramatic problems of survival. The more favorable habitats have long ago been appropriated by peoples with stronger, more aggressive social systems.

. . . Taking hunters as they are found, anthropologists have naturally been led to the conclusion that their life (and by implication the life of our ancestors) was a constant struggle for survival.

At the dawn of agriculture 12,000 years ago, hunters covered most of the habitable globe, and appeared to be generally most successful in those areas which later supported the densest populations of agricultural peoples. By 1500 CE the area left to hunters had shrunk drastically and their distribution fell largely at the peripheries of the continents and in the inaccessible interiors. However, even at this late date, hunting peoples occupied all of Australia, most of western and northern North America, and large portions of South America and Africa. This situation rapidly changed with the era of colonial expansion, and by 1900, when serious ethnographic research got under way, much of this way of life had been destroyed. As a result, our notion of unacculturated hunter-gatherer life has been largely drawn from peoples no longer living in the optimum portion of their traditional range.

To mention a few examples, the Netsilik Eskimos, the Arunta, and the Kung Bushmen are now classic cases in ethnography. However, the majority of the precontact Eskimos, Australian aborigines, and Bushmen lived in much better environments. Two-thirds of the Eskimos, according to Laughlin, lived *south* of the Arctic circle, and the populations in the Australian and Kalahari deserts were but a fraction of the populations living in the well-watered regions of southeast Australia and the Cape Province of Africa. Thus, within a given region the "classic cases" may, in fact, be precisely the opposite: namely, the most isolated peoples who managed to avoid contact until the arrival of the ethnographers. In order to understand hunters better it may be more profitable to consider the few hunters in rich environments, since it is likely that these peoples will be more representative of the ecological conditions under which man evolved than are the dramatic and unusual cases that illustrate extreme environmental pressure. Such a perspective may better help us to understand the extraordinary persistence and success of the human adaptation.

→ *Why is it important to study hunting and gathering communities? Why did these societies give way to other ways of life?*

SOURCE: *Man the Hunter*, edited by Richard B. Lee, Irven DeVore, and Jill Nash (Chicago: Aldine Publishing, 1968), pp. 3, 5.

but that men and women alike contributed equally to the bands' welfare. If anything, they believe that women made a larger contribution and enjoyed a higher status because the main items in the diet were cereals and fruits, whose harvesting and preparation were thought to be the responsibility of women.

ART AND LANGUAGE

> → *How did art and language increase* Homo sapiens' *chances of survival?*

Despite the remorselessly nature-bound quality of everyday life for early humans, the first *Homo sapiens* made a noteworthy evolutionary breakthrough. They developed cultural forms that reflected their consciousness of themselves and

Painting of a Bison from the Cave at Altamira, Northern Spain. When descriptions of the Altamira paintings were first published in 1880, they shocked scholars who did not believe that the earliest modern humans in this region of Europe would be capable of such artistic expression. Dating much later than similar cave paintings recently discovered at Chauvet (compare the bison on the opposite page) and rather different from them, the Altamira paintings show that distinctive regional traditions of cave art developed in different parts of Europe.

their quests to survive and to forge indispensable relationships with their environments.

ART

Few of the cultural achievements of early communities of *Homo sapiens* have captured the attention of modern-day observers more completely than their artistic endeavors. These accomplished drawings by early humans were created in areas in Europe, probably in part as a response to the harsher environment there and also in part because of intense competition with the Neanderthals. The ability to draw allowed *Homo sapiens* to understand their environment, to bond tightly among their kingroups, and to establish important mythologies. In times of stress, these behaviors certainly gave these individuals an adaptive advantage to survive in extremely challenging circumstances. The drawings and reliefs (raised wall carvings) that men and women made on the walls of caves are so vivid and realistic that modern scholars at first did not want to attribute them to artists living thousands of years ago. Take, for example, a brilliant set of images of bison, horses, wolves, boars, and deer that was discovered in a cave in northern Spain in the 1870s. The images fairly bristle with life and energy; the color and figure formations have an uncanny quality of realism.

"Look, Daddy, oxen!" That is what Maria, the daughter of Marcelino Sanz de Sauruola, cried to her father as she looked at the ceiling of a deep cave on his property at Altamira in Spain that he was exploring one summer afternoon. As he looked up, Sauruola could not believe what he saw. Arranged across the ceiling of the huge chamber were more than two dozen life-size figures of bison, horses, and wild bulls, all painted in vivid colors of red, black, yellow, and brown. He did not think that anyone would believe that these fabulous images were made tens of thousands of years ago, but he knew in his heart that they were. That was in 1879. Only in 1906 did the world finally accept that the paintings in Altamira, and those in other caves that were later discovered, were in fact the work of early humans. Even today, with more than 50,000 works of art of early humans found in Europe, these paintings compel wonder and awe at the innate artistic abilities unique to humans.

The images on cave walls were painted over a period of 25,000 years, and they changed very little in that time. The subjects are most often large game, animals that would not have been often hunted but would have been considered powerful symbols. These animals were rendered with a striking economy of line. Frequently they were placed so that the natural contours of the cave wall defined a bulging belly or the socket of an eye. Many were drawn more than once, suggesting that they were made on several occasions or by several artists. There are remarkably few images of humans, but those that exist are often male and are usually shown dancing. There are also many handprints that were made by blowing paint

Primary Source

THE ART OF CHAUVET CAVE

A spectacular discovery made at Chauvet Cave in southwestern France in 1994 upset all previously held ideas about the place and development of prehistoric art. Dating to about 35,000 years ago—much older than the 20,000-year-old paintings from Lascaux in southeastern France, discovered in 1940, or the 17,000-year-old paintings from Altamira in northwestern Spain—they are the oldest prehistoric cave paintings known in Europe. The hundreds of representations found at Chauvet Cave are more detailed and more brilliant than the ones at Altamira and Lascaux. There are detailed drawings of mammoths, musk oxen, horses, lions, bears, and even rhinoceroses, as well as human palm prints (together with footprints on the floor of the cave) and striking "Venus" female figures that feature exaggerated depictions of female genitalia—these last obviously connected to a preoccupation with human fertility. These amazing engravings and paintings shocked scholars—they come only a few thousand years after the first appearance of modern humans in Europe.

Almost as soon as their first appearance in western Europe, modern humans seemed to have rapidly developed a sense, ability, and desire to portray other living beings in their environment. This brilliant drawing shows the detail in a depiction of horses' heads.

This image uses a doubling effect—drawing additional hindquarters and legs for the animal—to give the bison the appearance of motion and speed. This ability to portray dynamic movement was once thought to be a skill that humans developed only much later.

> ⤳ *Are these drawings evidence of an early impulse to artistic creation? If so, what does that tell us about modern humans during this period? What does their decision to portray certain animals but not others tell us?*

SOURCE: French Ministry of Culture and Communication, Regional Direction for Cultural Affairs—Rhône-Alpes Region—Regional Department of Archaeology.

around a hand placed on the stone wall, or by dipping hands in paint and then pressing them to the wall. Finally, there are abstract symbols such as circles, wavy lines, and checker-boards; these are most likely to appear at places of transition in the caves.

Lacking any writings to indicate what the images meant to ancient humans, we can only speculate about their meaning. At first, decoration seemed to be their purpose—art for art's sake. But that explanation has long been discarded. Why would these peoples have decorated caves deep in the earth that were not their homes and that had no natural light that would allow the images to be seen? Perhaps, as some scholars have proposed, the paintings were ways in which humans defined themselves as separate from other parts of nature. Other more interesting interpretations have also been put forward. Most recently, the cave drawings have been described as the work of powerful shamans, individuals believed to hold special powers to understand and control the tremendous forces of the cosmos. The subjects and the style of the paintings in the caves of Europe are very similar to images engraved or painted on rocks by some hunter and gatherer societies living today, especially the San and the !Kung peoples of southern Africa. In those societies, paintings are used to mark important places of ritual. Often they are made during trances by shamans who intercede with the spirit world on behalf of their community.

Paintings were not the only form of artistic expression for early humans. Small sculptures of animals that were shaped out of bone and stone tools are dated as being even older than the paintings. Most famous are the three-dimensional figurines of enormously fat and pregnant females. Statuettes like the so-called Venus of Willendorf, found in Austria, demonstrate that successful reproduction was a very important theme, requiring special attention. Some of the most exquisite of the sculptures are of animals carved in postures that fit the shape of bone spear-throwers. The ancient artist captured the essence of the animal either in movement or at rest.

While the paintings found in the caves of Europe are the most spectacular examples of prehistoric art, there were other types as well. Sculpture and drawing are the oldest forms of visual expression, which was a fundamental part of the life of early humans; yet very few examples exist that were produced by hominid lines, with the possible exception of the Neanderthals. Only members of *Homo sapiens* exploited and developed this cognitive capacity for symbolic expression by permanently leaving their mark on the landscape.

Did ancient art have an important social function? What can be said is that early ornamental and decorative expressions covering Afro-Eurasian cave rock faces marked the dawn of human culture and of a consciousness of men and women's place in the world. Symbolic activity of this sort helped early humans to make sense of themselves, nature, and the relationships between humanity and nature.

Because dance, music, and other performance activities do not survive the ages, while paintings and drawings do, historians must use the surviving artifacts to probe the psyche of early men and women. Art historians have come to believe that the drawings contained underlying social messages, conveying mood and meaning to those who stood around the fire pit gazing at the walls of the cave, deeply inspired by the magic of the animal depictions as they prepared to hunt creatures whose meat and bones would bring them life-sustaining strength. Yet many of the most frequently employed images were of animals that were rarely hunted or eaten, and this observation has prompted some

Willendorf Venus. This squat limestone statuette—only about six inches in height—was discovered in 1908 near the village of Willendorf, Austria, and dates back about 25,000 years. As one of the earliest representations of a female figure found in Europe, it is one of the most famous icons of prehistoric art. The emphasis on the woman's breasts and reproductive organs—to the exclusion, for example, of her facial features—and the presence of a red ochre dye on her genitalia suggest the maker's concern with the woman's fertility and procreative functions.

Paleolithic Bone Carving. This decorated piece of bone from Germany probably dates to about the same time as the Altamira cave paintings in Spain. Both pieces depict a common subject matter—the capture of wild animals—but this carving is notable for its material and degree of preservation. Prehistoric representations once existed on a wide range of materials like bone and wood, but most of these pieces are now lost.

scholars to suggest that certain animals were simply interesting to observe because they projected maleness (horses) or femaleness (bison).

LANGUAGE

In the final analysis, few things set humans off from the rest of the animal world more starkly than their use of language, whose genesis and evolution are wrapped in heated controversies. (See Map 1-3.) What is generally agreed is that the cognitive abilities involved in language development marked an evolutionary milestone. It is important to make the distinction between vocal-utterance speech, possessed by many precursor hominids (such as the Neanderthals), and natural language (words arranged in particular sequences to convey meaning), which is unique to modern humans. Its development necessitated a large brain and complex cognitive organization to create words that would verbally convey symbolic meanings. Verbal communication thus required an ability to think abstractly and to communicate abstractions. The invention of language was a huge breakthrough, because words could be taught to neighbors and offspring and could be used to integrate communities for human survival. Language expanded the lessons that could be learned and shared with others. It enhanced the ability to communicate and to accumulate bodies of knowledge that could be transmitted across both space and time.

Biological research has demonstrated that humans can make and process many more primary and distinctive sounds,

Art, language, learning, and teaching were developed by early humans to increase their chances of survival.

called *phonemes*, than can other animals. Whereas a human being can utter fifty phonemes, an ape can form only twelve. What is more, humans can mentally process sounds far more quickly than can other primates. With fifty phonemes, it is possible to create more than 100,000 words; and by arranging those words in different sequences and developing syntax in language, individuals can express an almost infinite number of subtle and complex meanings. Recent research suggests that the breakthrough in the use of complex languages occurred about 50,000 years ago and that the nearest approximation to humanity's proto-language (earliest language) existing today belongs to two small click-speaking African peoples, the !Kung of southern Africa and the Hadza of Tanzania. These peoples make a clicking sound by dropping the tongue down from the roof of the mouth and exhaling—a sound similar to that made by vervet monkeys warning one another of impending danger. As humans moved out of Africa and dispersed around the globe, they expanded their original language into nineteen separate and basic language families, from which all of the world's languages then evolved.

Art, language, learning, and teaching were developed by early humans to increase their chances of survival. All of these behaviors accelerated the rate of change and augmented humans' ability to adapt to environmental changes. What is more, their combination gave humans the ability to fundamentally change their relationship to their environment. Though still dependent on the natural world, increasingly humans turned to the challenge of manipulating it to their advantage, a process we first see in the flaking of stones to make tools.

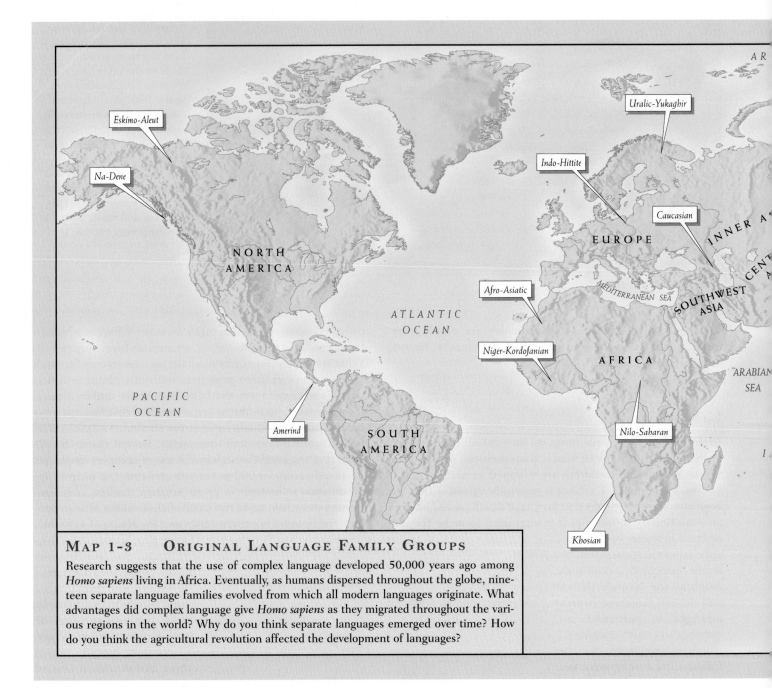

MAP 1-3 ORIGINAL LANGUAGE FAMILY GROUPS

Research suggests that the use of complex language developed 50,000 years ago among *Homo sapiens* living in Africa. Eventually, as humans dispersed throughout the globe, nineteen separate language families evolved from which all modern languages originate. What advantages did complex language give *Homo sapiens* as they migrated throughout the various regions in the world? Why do you think separate languages emerged over time? How do you think the agricultural revolution affected the development of languages?

THE BEGINNINGS OF FOOD PRODUCTION

> → *What factors contributed to the domestication of plants and animals?*

About 12,000 years ago, at a time when the earth's population may have been around a million people, one of the world's most fundamental changes occurred. It involved an extended and huge shift in the way that humans controlled and produced food for themselves—what some have called a revolution in agriculture and ecology. (See Map 1-4.) In this era of major change, humans established a firmer control over nature, especially over plants and animals, resulting in changes in human modes of life. In at least five (and perhaps as many as nine) separate locations and over a period of 5,000 years, men and women engaged in experiments that led to basic changes in food production. This transformation consisted of the cultivation of wild grasses and cereals and the domestication (human control) of wild animals. For the

→ *What factors contributed to the domestication of plants and animals?*

cause, it was certainly a precipitating element. The population could not have continued to increase if it had had to subsist through hunting and gathering. It is just possible, though difficult to verify, that some regions of the world had reached the saturation point for a hunting and gathering way of existence (exhausting the food supply that could be gathered to feed the larger population with no cultivation of crops or domestication of animals). Without doubt, the agricultural revolution led to a vast population expansion, since men and women could now produce many more calories per unit of land than they had in the past. To be sure, learning to control environments and domesticate resources did not liberate humans from the risks of drought, floods, storms, or other natural "disasters." Indeed, without food storage systems, a sharp drought could wipe out or uproot entire communities.

EARLY DOMESTICATION OF PLANTS AND ANIMALS

Why and how did the domestication of plants and animals come about? To begin with, the changeover from a mobile way of life dependent on hunting and gathering to agriculture, which requires people to stay in one place, unfolded gradually. It was an evolutionary process that depended not on physical changes in nature but on accumulated knowledge of plants and animals. Climatic change, beginning with the ending of the last ice age (10,000 years ago) and culminating in the onset of drought, was a catalyst, causing hunters and gatherers living in a specific part of Southwest Asia—the southern Levant (roughly the area covered in modern times by Israel, Palestine, and Jordan) and its environs—to disperse to neighboring regions. Around 9000 BCE, when the rains returned and temperatures rose, abundant rainfall in the summer and mild winters created optimal conditions in Southwest Asia for settled life. These conditions lasted about 3,000 years, during which time humans experimented with new ways of organizing themselves and thought about the meaning of what it was to be human. The foundations were laid for modern societies as we know them now.

Hunters and gatherers, now able to meet all of their subsistence needs in one diverse ecological niche, could afford to settle in a single location. They did so throughout Southwest Asia, in considerably greater numbers than had ever come together before, learning to exploit mountainous areas covered with forest vegetation and home to wild sheep, wild goats, and aurochs (long-horned wild oxen). Here, in especially attractive locations such as the valleys of the Taurus Mountains in Upper Mesopotamia (present-day Iraq) and the Anatolian plateau (in modern-day Turkey), permanent settlements were established.

The formation of settled communities enabled humans to take advantage of favorable regions and to take risks, thus spurring agricultural innovation. In areas that were full of abundant wild game and edible plants, people began to

first time, nature was essentially, deliberately, and consciously refashioned by human intelligence to meet human needs. The five locations acknowledged to be independent centers of this agricultural revolution were Southwest Asia, East Asia, Southeast Asia, Mesoamerica, and northeastern America. Four other regions may also have been independent regions for this revolution, although the evidence strongly suggests some borrowing. These were East Africa, inland West Africa, southeastern Europe, and South America.

A large number of factors triggered the move to settled agriculture. While population pressure was not a direct

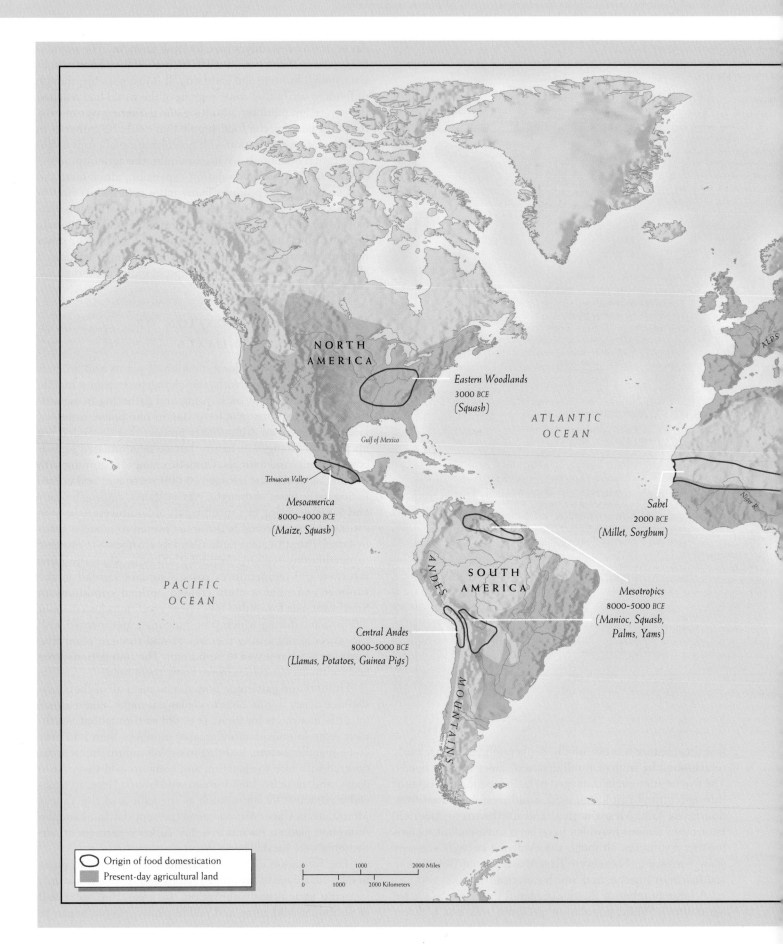

NORTH
AMERICA

Eastern Woodlands
3000 BCE
(Squash)

ATLANTIC
OCEAN

Gulf of Mexico

Tehuacan Valley

Mesoamerica
8000–4000 BCE
(Maize, Squash)

Sahel
2000 BCE
(Millet, Sorghum)

Niger R.

PACIFIC
OCEAN

ANDES

SOUTH
AMERICA

Mesotropics
8000–5000 BCE
(Manioc, Squash,
Palms, Yams)

Central Andes
8000–5000 BCE
(Llamas, Potatoes, Guinea Pigs)

MOUNTAINS

ALPS

Origin of food domestication
Present-day agricultural land

| 0 | 1000 | 2000 Miles |
| 0 | 1000 | 2000 Kilometers |

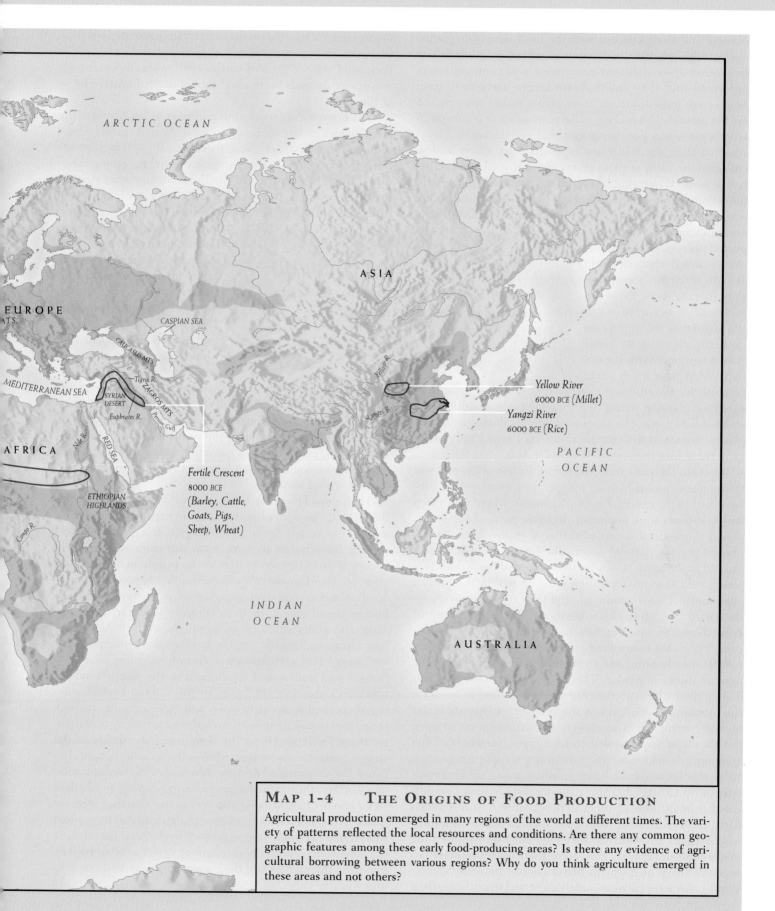

ARCTIC OCEAN

ASIA

EUROPE

CASPIAN SEA

CAUCASUS MTS

Tigris R.

MEDITERRANEAN SEA

ZAGROS MTS

SYRIAN
DESERT

Euphrates R.

Persian Gulf

AFRICA

Nile R.

RED SEA

ETHIOPIAN
HIGHLANDS

Congo R.

Fertile Crescent
8000 BCE
(Barley, Cattle,
Goats, Pigs,
Sheep, Wheat)

Yellow R.

Yangzi R.

Yellow River
6000 BCE (Millet)

Yangzi River
6000 BCE (Rice)

PACIFIC
OCEAN

INDIAN
OCEAN

AUSTRALIA

MAP 1-4   THE ORIGINS OF FOOD PRODUCTION

Agricultural production emerged in many regions of the world at different times. The variety of patterns reflected the local resources and conditions. Are there any common geographic features among these early food-producing areas? Is there any evidence of agricultural borrowing between various regions? Why do you think agriculture emerged in these areas and not others?

observe and to experiment with the most adaptable plants. For ages, people gathered grains by relying on seeds falling freely from their stalks. At some point, observant collectors perceived that they could obtain larger harvests if grain seeds were pulled directly from plants rather than picked off the ground. The process of domestication of plants probably began when people noticed that certain edible plants retained their nutritious grains longer than others and so collected the seeds of these grains and scattered them across fertile soils. When ripe, these plants produced bigger and more concentrated crops. It took a great deal of time for the overall pattern of these steps to be completed, but by the end, a community that supported this kind of innovation realized that it could sustain a larger population than its neighbors. Plant domestication occurred when the structure of the plant naturally retained its seeds even when ripe. With the domesticated plant, seeds could be easily harvested. Most were used for food but some were saved for planting in the next growing cycle, resulting in a steady food supply. The process of gradual domestication of plants happened first in the southern Levant and spread from there into the rest of Southwest Asia.

The domestication of animals ultimately led to one of the great divides in Afro-Eurasian history: the pastoralists versus the agriculturalists.

At about the same time, the domestication of animals was taking place, probably as an independent development concentrated in the central Zagros Mountains, where wild sheep and wild goats were abundant. In other parts of the world, animal domestication preceded that of plants. It, too, was a gradual process that did not require force or domination. A favored explanation is that hunters returned home with very young wild sheep, which then grew up within the human community. They reproduced, and their offspring never returned to the wild. The animals accepted their state of dependence because the humans fed them. Gradually it became clear that controlling animal reproduction was more reliable than hunting, and so domesticated herds became the primary source of protein. This shift probably happened first and quite quickly with the wild sheep that lived in herds on the mountain slopes. When the number of animals under human control and living close to the settlement outstripped the supply of food needed to feed them, members of the community could move them to grassy steppes for grazing. Later this lifeway, called pastoralism, became an important alternative to settled farming. Pastoralists herded domesticated animals, moving them to new pastures on a seasonal basis. Goats, the other main domesticated animal of Southwest Asia, are smarter than sheep but more difficult to bring under control. Probably goats were gradually introduced into herds of sheep as a way to better control herd movement. While goats were far more widely dispersed than sheep, their natural habitat was mountain slopes, not grassy steppes. Furthermore, they were far more independent and less docile in their wild state. Pigs and cattle, even more important domesticated animals, were also brought under human control at this time.

The domestication of animals ultimately led to one of the great divides in Afro-Eurasian history: the pastoralists versus the agriculturalists, or those from the steppe lands versus those from the arable zones (regions suited for crop cultivation). The northern areas of the Eurasian landmass stretching from what is today the Ukraine across Siberia and Mongolia to the Pacific Ocean became the preserve of pastoral peoples, for this region has not been able to support the extensive agriculture necessary for large settled populations until recent times. From here would come the Turkic-speaking peoples of the eighth century CE, who would migrate into the Islamic empire, and the Mongol peoples of the thirteenth century, who would erupt out of the eastern steppe lands and establish the far-flung Mongol empire. As these examples demonstrate, from time to time the pastoral, often nomadic peoples living in northern Afro-Eurasia descended through the natural gateways that linked northern and southern Afro-Eurasia to impose their authority over settled societies.

Historians know much less about these pastoral peoples than about the agriculturalists. Their numbers were small, and they have left fewer archaeological traces or historical records for scholars to work with. But their role in world history is as important as that of the people in settled societies. In Afro-Eurasia, they domesticated horses and developed weapons and techniques that at certain points in history would enable them to conquer sedentary societies. They also transmitted ideas, products, and people across long distances, maintaining the linkages that connected east and west. The archaeological record indicates that full-fledged pastoralism had crystallized in the steppe lands of northern Eurasia by 3000 BCE. By this time, the peoples living there had learned to yoke and ride animals, to milk them, and to use their hair for clothing, as well as to slaughter them for food. Of all the domesticated animals in the steppe lands, the horse was to prove the most important. Because horses provided decisive advantages in transportation and warfare, they gained more value in people's minds than other equally hardworking and serviceable domesticated animals. Thus, horses soon became the measure of household wealth and prestige. Steppe peoples made good use of their horsemanship repeatedly throughout Afro-Eurasian history, imposing themselves and their ways on the settled communities to the south.

SOUTHWEST ASIA: THE REVOLUTION BEGINS

The world's first agricultural revolution occurred in Southwest Asia in an area bounded by the Mediterranean Sea in the west and the Zagros Mountains in the east. Known today as the Fertile Crescent because of the rich soils and regular rainfall that once were characteristic of the region, the area played a leading role in the domestication of wild grasses and the taming of the animals most important to humans. Of the five large mammals that have been vital to humankind for meat, milk, skins (including hair), haulage, and transportation (goats, sheep, pigs, cattle, camels, and horses), only horses were not first domesticated in Southwest Asia, though they soon spread into the area and assumed great importance.

Given the presence of so many of the wild ancestors of humankind's most valuable plants and animals, it is scarcely surprising that Southwest Asia led the agricultural revolution

and was the region in which many of the world's first major city-states appeared (see Chapter 2). An event that prepared the way was a significant warming trend that began about 13,000 years ago and resulted in a profusion of plants and animals, large numbers of which began to live closer to humans.

Around 9000 BCE, in the southern corridor of the Jordan River valley, humans began to domesticate the wild ancestors of barley and wheat. (See Map 1-5.) Many different kinds of wild grasses were already growing abundantly in this region, and barley and wheat proved the easiest to adapt to settled agriculture and the easiest to transport to new locales. Although this changeover from the mere gathering of wild cereals to regular cultivation took many centuries and was marked by failures as well as successes, by the end of the ninth millennium BCE cultivators were selecting and storing seeds and then sowing these seeds in prepared seedbeds. Moreover, as already noted, in the valleys of the Zagros Mountains on the eastern side of the Fertile Crescent, the same kind of experimentation was taking place with animals at around the same time.

One place conspicuous by its lack of involvement in the early spread of these new ways of producing food is the valley of the Tigris and Euphrates rivers, a region that became central to the story of humanity a few thousand years later. There, in what is often called "the cradle of the world's earliest urban civilization," humans lived in very small communities. They found the region's hot, dry summers and harsh, cold winters inhospitable. Annual floods were terrifying and could be highly destructive; all animals, including humans, had to retreat to safer, higher ground. In low flood years, plant life perished for want of water. In high flood years, the destruction of the physical environment from the raging waters was even more devastating. As a consequence, before 5500 BCE, the Tigris-Euphrates floodplain, like many other of the great floodplains of the Eurasian and North African landmass, showed little evidence of human habitation.

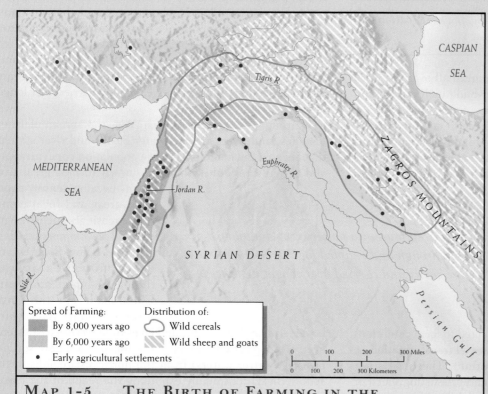

Spread of Farming:
- By 8,000 years ago
- By 6,000 years ago
- Early agricultural settlements

Distribution of:
- Wild cereals
- Wild sheep and goats

0   100   200   300 Miles
0   100   200   300 Kilometers

MAP 1-5 THE BIRTH OF FARMING IN THE FERTILE CRESCENT

Agriculture production first appeared in the Fertile Crescent, starting roughly at 9000 BCE. Though the process was slow, farmers and herders domesticated a variety of plants and animals over time, a process that led to the rise of large-scale, permanent settlements. What does the map reveal about the environment and natural resources in the Fertile Crescent? What relationship existed between cereal cultivators and herders of goats and sheep? Why was agriculture absent in the region of the southern Tigris and Euphrates rivers during this period?

But as the populations in the surrounding regions began to rise and competition for land and grazing lands became more intense, some enterprising communities slowly moved into the river valley. They developed primitive methods of seasonal irrigation, drawing water from feeder streams into shallow canals that the community maintained. The land was very fertile, as long as it was properly watered, and it produced extraordinarily successful harvests. As a consequence, the communities in the river valley gradually grew until some groups had created small villages and had introduced simple irrigation techniques in the region (see Chapter 2).

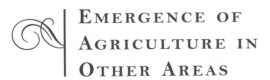

EMERGENCE OF AGRICULTURE IN OTHER AREAS

> → *What factors contributed to autonomous innovation in agriculture versus early borrowing?*

Similar agricultural revolutions occurred all over the world in these four or five millennia. They had much in common. The same factors of climatic change, increased knowledge about plants and animals, and the need to develop more efficient ways to feed, house, and promote the survival of larger numbers led peoples in Eurasia, Africa, and the Americas to see the advantages of cultivating plants and domesticating wildlife. In at least five of these locations, and perhaps another four areas, these agricultural revolutions were internally generated, with no influence from the outside. In some locations, notably western Europe, the new ideas and techniques were largely borrowed, and then adapted to local conditions. But wherever this agricultural and social transformation occurred, local variations were important. These variations stemmed from climate, geography, and preexisting social organizations, but they especially reflected the different plants and animals that were suitable to the particular locations. By examining early agriculture in Southeast Asia and the southern part of China in East Asia, where water and rice were critical; in western Europe, where the new cultivators borrowed much from Southwest Asia; in the Americas, which had the disadvantage of few animals that could be domesticated; and finally in Africa, where a fishing culture had many of the same features of the agricultural revolution that was taking place elsewhere, we can observe the broad array of patterns with which humans experimented as they settled down as farmers and herders.

RICE AND WATER IN EAST ASIA

When the glaciers began to melt around 13,000 BCE, and the ocean levels began to rise, environmental changes affected living and subsistence patterns for coastal dwellers in East Asia. Here, too, although under different circumstances, a revolution in food production occurred. (See Map 1-6.) As the temperature warmed, the sea level rose, creating the Japanese islands. Hunters there tracked a diminishing supply of large animals, like giant deer, but all such big game eventually became extinct. Men and women had to find other ways to support themselves, and before long they settled down and became cultivators of the soil. In this postglacial period, divergent human cultures flourished in both northern and southern Japan. In the south, hunters created relatively primitive pebble and flake tools. Those in the northernmost island of Hokkaido prepared sharper blades about a third of an inch wide. Earthenware pottery production also seems to have begun in this period in the south. Converting mud into pottery—a hard, lightweight substance that could be transported—was a major breakthrough and enabled food to be stored more easily and carried over longer distances.

Throughout the rest of East Asia, the spread of lakes, marshes, and rivers created water basins and river systems that became the habitats for large population concentrations and agricultural cultivation. Two newly formed great river basins became densely populated areas and focal points for increasingly intensive agricultural development. These were the Yellow River, which flowed from west to east through the more arid North China plain, and the Yangzi River in central China, which

Converting mud into pottery was a major breakthrough and enabled food to be stored more easily and carried over longer distances.

traversed a land of streams and lakes from west to east. Moreover, winds carried alluvial loess topsoil (a loamy soil deposited by river waters) from the northwest regions of the Yellow River, continually extending the reach of the North China coastline as the soil entered the sea. The same loess topsoil was deposited on the North China plain by fierce winter winds sweeping across the Mongolian steppe. In addition to good soil, the region had ample fresh water. Heavy rains brought by strong monsoon winds that blew in from the oceans in the spring and summer watered the crops. Much later on, farmers developed intricate irrigation systems for rice crops (see Chapter 4).

Rice in the south and millet in the north were for East Asia what barley and wheat were for western Asia—staples

→ *What factors contributed to autonomous innovation in agriculture versus early borrowing?*

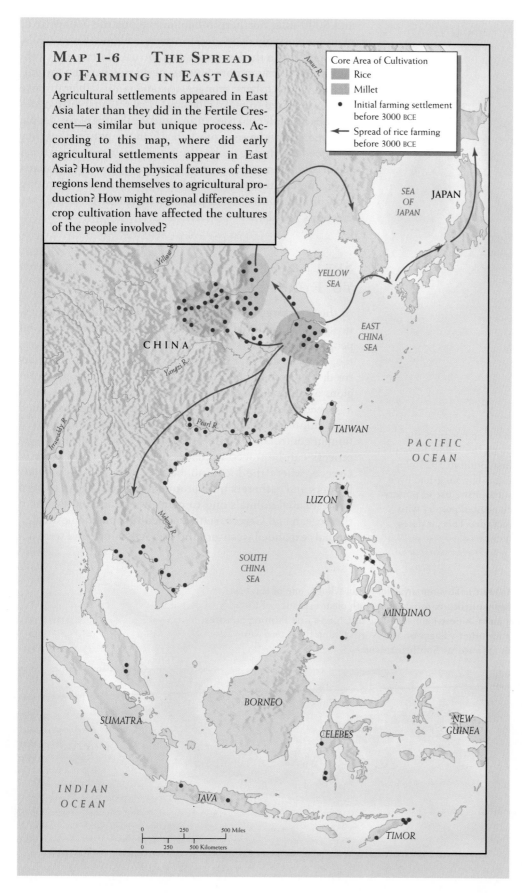

MAP 1-6   THE SPREAD OF FARMING IN EAST ASIA

Agricultural settlements appeared in East Asia later than they did in the Fertile Crescent—a similar but unique process. According to this map, where did early agricultural settlements appear in East Asia? How did the physical features of these regions lend themselves to agricultural production? How might regional differences in crop cultivation have affected the cultures of the people involved?

Core Area of Cultivation
- ▨ Rice
- ▨ Millet
- • Initial farming settlement before 3000 BCE
- ← Spread of rice farming before 3000 BCE

adapted to local environments that humans could domesticate. Archaeologists have found evidence of rice cultivation in the Yangzi River valley in 6500 BCE, and millet cultivation in the Yellow River valley in 5500 BCE. Rice and millet cultivation supported a much larger sedentary population. Innovations in grain production came early and spread fairly widely, thanks in part to internal migration and wider contacts. When farmers migrated east and south, they carried with them domesticated millet and rice. In the south, they also came into contact with southern strains of faster-ripening rice originally from Southeast Asia, which they adopted. There is also evidence of early plow cultivation and a wide dissemination of stone shards. Ox plows and water buffalo plowshares were the technical prerequisites for large-scale millet planting in the drier north and the rice-cultivated areas of the wetter south.

Rice was the principal staple, but millet and wheat (which spread to China around 1500 BCE from Southwest Asia) were also fundamental to the food-producing revolution in East Asia. There is some evidence that early maize was grown in China as well, although it soon dropped out of the mix. Each crop depended on ecological suitability and the human knowledge of how to manipulate plants.

The economic breakthrough in China occurred around the early eighth millennium BCE. As elsewhere, the move to settled agriculture was crucial. But also important were advances in pottery making, which enabled the harvesters to store products, and the use of polished stone axes for clearing fields. Each region struck its own adapted combination of crops and animals. Between 8000 and 5000 BCE, northern inhabitants along the Yellow River plain increasingly depended for their livelihoods on cereals, such as millet in the loess soils, and the use of hemp for clothing. In the warmer, more humid south, rice became the staple, along with tubers, oranges, tea, and ramie (a plant whose fibers were used to make clothing). The regional differences in crops also affected the culture and aesthetics of the people involved, as can be seen most clearly in the pottery that they produced for storing crops. Recent discoveries at many East Asian sites demonstrate that food was produced in many places before the more complex royal states arose limiting food production to fewer places but on a larger scale (see Chapters 3 and 4).

SPREAD OF AGRICULTURE TO EUROPE

At the far western fringe of Afro-Eurasia, in Europe, domestication was achieved by the diffusion of existing ideas and peoples from centers where it had already developed. Here, too, as in East Asia, once the new ideas and techniques arrived, they spread rapidly. By 6000–5000 BCE, people in regions of Europe close to the societies of Southwest Asia, such as Greece and the Balkans, were already being transformed from hunters and gatherers into agriculturists who exerted human control over plants and animals. (See Map 1-7.) The process can be traced in places like the Franchthi Cave in Greece, where the local inhabitants, who had been solely hunters and gatherers until around 6000 BCE, began to herd domesticated animals and to plant wheat and barley. From the Aegean and Greece, settled agriculture and domesticated animals expanded westward throughout Europe and were ac-

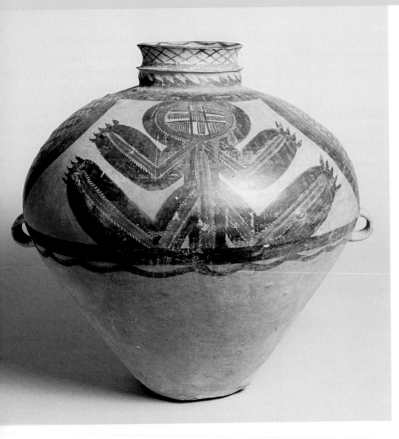

Large Two-handled Yangshao Pot. This pot comes from the village of Yangshao in Henan Province, along the Yellow River in Northwest China, where remains were first found in 1921 of a people who lived more than 6,000 years ago. The Yangshao lived in small, rammed-earth fortresses and, without the use of pottery wheels, created fine white, red, and black painted pottery with human faces and animal and geometric designs. This jar dates back to the third or second millennium BCE.

Pottery in Banpo Village (c. 4800–4200 BCE). This remarkable, intact village, one of the best-known ditch-enclosed settlements of Yangshao culture, provides us with clear evidence of a sophisticated agriculture based on millet and Chinese cabbage. One of China's first farming cultures, the people of Banpo interacted directly with other villages on the North China Plain and were indirectly in contact with peoples from as far away as Southeast Asia.

MAP 1-7　THE SPREAD OF AGRICULTURE IN EUROPE

The spread of agricultural production into Europe after 7000 BCE represents an example of geographic diffusion. Europeans borrowed agricultural techniques and technology from other groups and adapted those to their own situations. Through what two pathways did agriculture spread through Europe? Where did the ideas and techniques originate? How did the spread of agriculture throughout the region alter the physical and social landscape?

companied by the development of communities in which people resided in concentrated groups.

The emergence of agriculture and village life occurred in Europe along two separate paths. The first and most rapid trajectory took place along the northern rim of the Mediterranean Sea. In this area, domestication of crops and animals would have moved westward, following the prevailing sea currents of the Mediterranean, from what is now Turkey through the islands of the Aegean Sea to mainland Greece, and from there to southern and central Italy and Sicily. Whether domestication was accomplished through migration of individuals or through the spread of ideas, connections by sea quickened the pace of the transition. Once the basic elements of domestication had been introduced into the Mediterranean from Southwest Asia, the speed and ease of seaborne communications aided what were astonishingly rapid changes. Almost overnight, hunting and gathering gave way to domesticated agriculture and herding.

The second trajectory took an overland route from Anatolia, across northern Greece into the Balkans, then northwestward along the Danube River into the Hungarian plain, and from there further north and west into the Rhine River valley, in modern-day Germany. Here change was likely the result of the transmission of ideas rather than of population migrations, for community after community adapted to domesticated plants and animals and the new mode of life. This route of agricultural development was slower than that along the Mediterranean for two reasons. First, domesticated crops, or individuals who knew about them, had to travel by land, as there were few large rivers like the Danube. Second, new groups of domesticated plants and animals had to be found that could be grown or herded in the colder and more heavily forested lands of central Europe. Crops had to be planted in the spring and harvested in the autumn, rather than the other way around. Cattle rather than sheep became the dominant herd animals in this northern area.

In Europe, the main cereal crops were wheat and barley, and the main animals herded were sheep, goats, and cattle (all of which were first domesticated in Southwest Asia). Additional plants, such as olives and grape-producing vines, were later domesticated. These changes, however fundamental and important they were, did not bring dramatic material progress. The normal settlement in Europe at this time consisted of a few dozen mud huts. These settlements, although small in numbers, were often made up of typical large "long houses" built of timber and mud, designed to store produce and shelter animals during the long winters. Some settlements were larger, with perhaps sixty to seventy huts—in some rare cases, up to a hundred. Hunting, gathering, and fishing still supplemented in important ways the new settled agriculture and the herding of the newly domesticated animals. The innovators dynamically blended the new ways with the old. About 6000 BCE, hunter-gatherers in southern France, for example, adopted the idea of herding domesticated sheep, but they decided not to plant domesticated crops—*that* would have conflicted too much with their preference for a more mobile life of hunting, which was a traditional part of their economy.

By about 5000–4000 BCE, areas around rivers and in the large plains and flatlands, even where forest cover had yet to be

Franchthi Cave. This cave in southern Greece was used as a living space from about 20,000 years ago until about 3000 BCE. It is one of the most important prehistoric sites for tracing the transmission of ideas and goods from Southwest Asia and the Mediterranean into Europe. Some of the tools found here were constructed of obsidian originating from the island of Melos (well over eighty miles to the east), indicating seaborne contacts at a very early date. There is also evidence that domesticated cereal grains were used here as early as 8,000 years ago, signaling a major change from the inhabitants' previous hunter-gatherer lifestyle.

"Long House." The people who opened up the whole of central Europe to agriculture typically lived in communities of six to twelve "long houses." Although large in size (varying between 60 and 120 feet in length), long houses were built on simple principles: a framework of wooden beams and posts with walls made of mud and woven branches beneath a thatched roof. These dwellings probably sheltered large extended family or kinship units that cooperated to provide the hard work needed to carve out pioneer farming settlements along river valleys. This cutaway reconstruction of a longhouse shows the placement of wall timbers and internal support posts.

fully stripped away, had embraced the new food-producing economy. Elsewhere, notably in the rugged mountain lands that still account for much of Europe's modern-day landscape, hunting and foraging remained the dominant way that humans related to nature. But the transition to settled farming and herding brought with it an enormous rise in population. As agricultural communities produced more and more people, such communities came to be the dominant social organization.

AGRICULTURE IN THE AMERICAS

When people crossed Beringia and trekked southward through the Americas, they set off a major ecological transformation. But they also adapted to habitats that humans had not previously encountered. The flora and fauna of the Americas were different enough to induce the early settlers to devise ways of living that distinguished them from their ancestors in Afro-Eurasia. Then, when the glaciers began to melt around 12,500 BCE, and the land bridge between East Asia and America eventually was covered by water, the Americas and their peoples truly became a whole world apart.

Early humans in America made use of basic chipped blades and pointed spears, pursuing their prey among the herds of large mammals that included mastodons, large woolly mammoths, and bison. In doing so, they extended the hunting traditions they had learned in Afro-Eurasia, establishing campsites and moving with their herds. These hunters were known as "Clovis people" because the typical arrowhead point that they used was first found by archaeologists at a site near Clovis, New Mexico. They were so mobile that the remains of the weaponry are scattered in archaeological sites all over North America.

For many years, scientists thought that the Clovis communities had wiped out the large Ice Age mammals that they found in America. But recent research suggests that it is more likely that climatic change destroyed the indigenous plants and trees, and thus the feeding grounds of large prehistoric mammals, and that what was once abundant forage became scarce. The vast spruce forests that had fed the great mastodons, for instance, shrank into isolated pockets, leaving increasingly isolated and undernourished mastodons vulnerable to human and animal predators, until they vanished. The tall grassland prairies gave way to areas with short grass; and where there had been short grass, cacti took over. As in Afro-Eurasia, the advent of a long warming cycle compelled those who entered the Americas to adapt to different ecological niches and to create new subsistence strategies. Thus, in the woodland area of the present-day northeastern United States, hunters learned to trap smaller wild animals for food and furs. To supplement the protein gained from meat and fish, these people also dug for roots and gathered berries. What is important is that most communities adapted to the settled agricultural economy, but they did not fully abandon basic survival strategies of hunting and gathering.

Food-producing changes in the Americas were different from those in Afro-Eurasia because this area did not witness the same relatively sudden cluster of innovations that revolutionized agriculture in Southwest Asia and elsewhere. Tools ground from stone, rather than chipped implements, appeared in the Tehuacán Valley by 6700 BCE, and evidence of plant domestication there can be dated as far back as 5000 BCE. But villages, pottery making, and sustained population growth came later. For many of the early American inhabitants, the life of hunting, trapping, and fishing went on much as it had for millennia. The remains of ancient shell fishing can be found throughout the coastal Americas, from California to Brazil. Along the Pacific coast, for instance, communities formed around fishing cultures, many relying on dugout canoes and spears to obtain food.

On the coast of what is now Peru, people primarily found their food by fishing and gathering shellfish from the Pacific, and archaeological remains include the remnants of fishnets, bags, baskets and textile implements, gourds for carrying water, and stone knives, choppers, scrapers, bone awls, and thorn needles. Oddly enough, however, there is no evidence of watercraft used in this area. Hundreds if not thousands of villages dotted the seashores and riverbanks of the Americas. Some had made breakthroughs in the management of fire that enabled them to manufacture pottery; others devised irrigation and water sluices in floodplains. And some even began to send their fish catches inland in return for agricultural produce.

The earliest evidence of plant experimentation in Mesoamerica dates from around 7000 BCE, and it went on for a long time. Maize, squash, and beans were first found in what is now central Mexico and became staples of Mesoamerican diets. Small seeds of maize were foraged, peeled from ears that were no longer than a few inches long, and planted by early settlers. Maize offered some real advantages to its consumers. It was easily stored, relatively imperishable, nutritious, and easy to cultivate alongside other plants, though it was mostly complementary to plants like beans, which replenished the soils with nitrogen that maize plants sucked up. Nonetheless, it took fully 5,000 years, until about 2000 BCE, for farmers to domesticate maize completely—that is, to settle in one place, live there year-round, plant maize, and stay beyond a single growing and harvesting cycle. Over the years, farmers had to mix and breed different strains of maize for it to evolve from the thin spikes of seeds to cobs rich with kernels, with a single plant able to yield big, thick ears to feed a growing permanent population. Thus the agricultural

changes afoot in Mesoamerica were slow and late in maturing. The same gradual process of change was even more marked in South America, where early settlers relied even more heavily on hunting and gathering.

Across the Americas, the settled, agrarian communities, when they finally did appear, relied on a variety of crops. They found that legumes (beans), grains (maize), and tubers (potatoes) all complemented each other in keeping the soil fertile and offering a balanced diet. Yet as peoples in the Americas formed permanent communities, they did not turn to domesticated animals as an alternative source of protein. Unlike in Afro-Eurasia, where people used domesticated animals for meat or milk, in the Americas animals were not generally domesticated as a source of food (aside from some Andean camelids such as the llama and the vicuña, and the turkey in Mesoamerica). In only a few pockets of the Andean highlands in South America is there evidence of the domestication of tiny guinea pigs, which were, at best, tasty but unfilling meals.

Head of Mayan Corn God. Corn, or maize, was a revered crop in Mesoamerica, where people ritually prayed to their deities for good harvests. Notice the crown made not of precious metals and stones but of corn husks as an example of the cultural emphasis on maize.

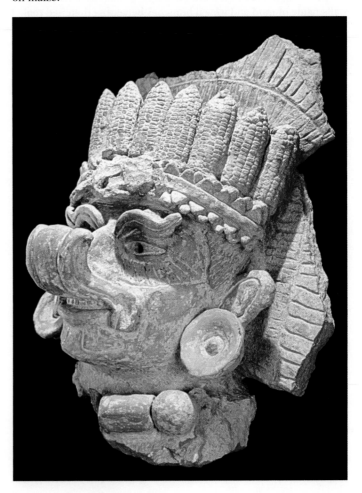

Primary Source

A MESOAMERICA CREATION MYTH

The discovery and cultivation of maize was so central to the livelihood of Mesoamericans that the crop was seen by many as the fount of humanity. This excerpt from the Mayan classic text Popol Vuh *describes the making of the first humans from ears of corn.*

Here, then, is the beginning of when it was decided to make man, and when what must enter into the flesh of man was sought.

And the Forefathers, the Creators and Makers, who were called Tepeu and Gucumatz said: "The time of dawn has come, let the work be finished, and let those who are to nourish and sustain us appear, the noble sons, the civilized vassals: let man appear, humanity, on the face of the earth." Thus they spoke.

They assembled, came together and held council in the darkness and in the night; then they sought and discussed, and here they reflected and thought. In this way their decisions came clearly to light and they found and discovered what must enter into the flesh of man.

It was just before the sun, the moon, and the stars appeared over the Creators and Makers.

From Paxil, from Cayalá, as they were called, came the yellow ears of corn and the white ears of corn.

These are the names of the animals which brought the food: *yac* (the mountain cat), *utiú* (the coyote), *quel* (a small parrot), and *hob* (the crow). These four animals gave tidings of the yellow ears of corn and the white ears of corn, they told them that they should go to Paxil and they showed them the road to Paxil.

And thus they found the food, and this was what went into the flesh of created man, the made man; this was his blood; of this the blood of man was made. So the corn entered [into the formation of man] by the work of the Forefathers.

And in this way they were filled with joy, because they had found a beautiful land, full of pleasures, abundant in ears of yellow corn and ears of white corn, and abundant also in *pataxte* and cacao, and in innumerable *zapotes, anonas, jocotes, nantzes, marasanos,* and honey. There was an abundance of delicious food in those villages called Paxil and Cayalá. There were foods of every kind, small and large foods, small plants and large plants.

The animals showed them the road. And then grinding the yellow corn and the white corn, Xmucané made nine drinks, and from this food came the strength and the flesh, and with it they created the muscles and the strength of man. This the Forefathers did, Tepeu and Gucumatz, as they were called.

After that they began to talk about the creation and the making of our first mother and father; of yellow corn and of white corn they made their flesh; of corn meal dough they made the arms and the legs of man. Only dough of corn meal went into the flesh of our first fathers, the four men, who were created.

→ *How does this text represent the relationship between (maize) food and (human) flesh? What were the variety of ways that maize served creation?*

SOURCE: *Popol Vuh: The Sacred Book of Ancient Quiché Maya*, English version by Delia Goetz and Sylvanus G. Morley from the Spanish translation by Adrián Recinos (Norman: University of Oklahoma Press, 1950), pp. 165–67.

Nor did people in the Americas tame animals capable of protecting villages (as dogs did in Afro-Eurasia), or carrying heavy loads over long distances (as camels did in Afro-Eurasia). Only llamas could be made to haul heavy loads—but their patience and cooperation were notoriously limited. Llamas can be considered at best only semidomesticates, mainly useful for clothing. Nonetheless, the domestication of plants and animals in the Americas, as well as the concentration of population into villages and clans, does suggest a great deal of diversification and refinement of technique. But the centers

Llamas. The peoples of the Americas were unable to domesticate beasts of burden such as camels, horses, or oxen. Their closest option was the finicky llama, which had neither the strength nor the stamina of its counterparts in Afro-Eurasia. Llamas were more prized as a source of wool than as pack animals.

of this kind of activity were many, scattered, and more isolated from each other than those in Afro-Eurasia, and thus were much more narrowly adapted to local ecozones, without much exchange and learning between them. This fragmentation in human migration and communication was a major distinguishing force in the gradual pace of change in the Americas and contributed to their taking a path of development separate from Afro-Eurasia's.

AFRICA: THE RACE WITH THE SAHARA

Some societies, like those in Southwest Asia and East Asia, were autonomous innovators, while others, like those in Europe, were early borrowers. What about Africa, where the story began? The evidence for settled agriculture in different African regions is still uncertain and far from uniform. But most scholars believe that the Sahel area—a territory running across Africa just south of the Sahara Desert—was most likely the location where hunters and gatherers became settled farmers and herders without any outside help. In this area, what now appears to be a move to settled agriculture, including the domestication of larger herd animals, took place two millennia before it did along the Mediterranean in North Africa. In fact, the Sahel agricultural revolution was so early that it cannot be seen as an example of a diffusion of techniques from Southwest Asia via the Nile River valley. From this innovative heartland, Africans carried their agricultural breakthroughs elsewhere across the landmass. (See Map 1-8.)

The Sahel was colder and moister 10,000 years ago than it is today. The region was lush with grassland vegetation and

teeming with animals. Before long, the inhabitants had made sorghum their principal food crop. Yet as the world became warmer and more arid and the Sahara Desert expanded, men and women living in this region had to disperse and take their agricultural and herding skills into other parts of Africa. Some went south to the tropical rain forests of West Africa, while others trekked eastward into the Ethiopian highlands. In their new environments, farmers searched for new crops that could be domesticated. The rain forests of West Africa yielded root crops, particularly the yam and cocoyam, both of which became the principal life-sustaining foodstuffs for these populations. The enset plant, which is similar to the banana, played the same role in the Ethiopian highlands.

In sub-Saharan Africa, the area extending far southward below the Sahara Desert, where population grew it did not concentrate into major urban hubs. But in the wetter and more temperate locations in the vast Sahel region, particularly in the upland massifs and their foothills, villages and towns came into being. Residents constructed stone dwellings and underground wells and granary storage areas. In one such population center, fourteen circular houses were built facing each other so as to form a main thoroughfare, or a street. Recent archaeological investigations have unearthed remarkable rock engravings and paintings, one often composed on top of another, filling up vast expanses of the cave dwellings' walls. Many images portray in fascinating detail the changeover from hunting and gathering to pastoralism that was in full swing 5,000 to 6,000 years ago. Caves abounded with pictures of cattle, which were a mainstay of these early men and women. The cave illustrations also depict day-to-day activities, for the artists drew men and women undertaking household chores, living in conical huts, crushing grain on stone, and riding bareback on their oxen, with women always sitting behind the men. Yet, around 4,000 years ago, the warming and drying of the earth's climate drove the Sahelian inhabitants out of the region in search of a place where they could preserve their way of life.

If the definition of settled agriculture includes the systematic collection of aquatic life from lakes and streams, then it is quite possible that the move to settled agriculture, with an accompanying creation of settled village life, occurred all across the southern Sahara region approximately 11,000 years ago, even before its emergence in Southwest Asia. This, at least, is the view of Christopher Ehret, an ethnolinguistic historian of Africa. The region where Ehret believes that this agricultural revolution occurred was around the shores of Lake Chad, in the central zone of West Africa, which is today at the edge of the Sahara Desert. Then, the lake covered an area ten times its current size. Harvesting the lake's fish enabled the peoples living in this area to expand their populations, establish substantial villages, and create a distinctive way of life that included elaborate rites of passage from childhood to adult status, burial ceremonies, and an elaborate set of highly sophisticated religious beliefs. Unfortunately for Africa's first settled aquatic cultivators, the world grew hotter

MAP 1-8 THE SPREAD OF FARMING IN AFRICA

African societies living south of the Sahara Desert developed their own version of agricultural production after 6000 BCE. Locate the Sahel region on this map. How did the expansion of the Sahara Desert affect the diffusion of agriculture in the Sahel? Compare the diffusion of agriculture in the Sahel versus that in Europe (Map 1-7). What similarities and differences are evident?

- Sahara Desert c. 6000 BCE
- Sahara Desert today
- Lakes in the Sahara c. 6000 BCE
- Early farming site
- Early herding site
- Movement of peoples to western tropical rainforests
- Movement of peoples to Ethiopian highlands

Original Areas of Crop Domestication
- Sorghum
- Yam
- Teff, ensete, and other Ethiopian crops

North African Cave Painting. This cave painting comes from Tassili n'Ajjer, highlands in the Sahara Desert, and dates from the second millennium BCE. In this illustration, early men and women covered the walls with pictures of daily life: children tending calves tethered to a rope. The white ovals to the left represent huts.

and more arid. Small lakes dried up, and so did rivers and streams. The largest lakes did survive, but they lacked the fish stocks that had fed expanding human populations. Apart from the extraordinary visual record that they left, Africa's first settled agrarian and fishing communities disappeared virtually without a trace, only to be discovered 11,000 years later at the hands of ingenious archaeologists.

REVOLUTIONS IN SOCIAL ORGANIZATION

→ *How did agricultural revolutions foster new communal hierarchies and interaction?*

With the domestication of plants and animals came settlement in agricultural villages. These villages were near fields for accessible sowing and cultivating, and pastures for herding livestock. Villagers worked together to clear fields, plant crops, and celebrate rituals in which they sang and danced and sacrificed to nature and the spirit world for fertility, rain, and successful harvests. They also produced stone tools to work the fields and clay and stone pots or woven baskets to collect and store the crops. As populations rose, and lands yielded surplus food, some villagers stopped working the fields to become specialized craftworkers, devoting their time to producing pottery, baskets, textiles, or

tools, which they could trade to farmers and pastoralists for food. Craft specialization and the buildup of surpluses contributed to early stratification, as some people accumulated more land and wealth while others led the rituals and sacrifices.

EARLY SETTLEMENT IN VILLAGES

The earliest dwelling places of the first settled communities were quite simple structures—little more than circular pits with stones piled on top of each other to form walls, above which was stretched a cover that rested on poles. Social structures were equally simple; they were clanlike and based on kinship networks. With time, however, population growth enabled clans to expand their size. As the use of natural resources intensified, specialized tasks evolved and divisions of labor came into being. Some members of the community procured and prepared food; others built terraces and defended the settlement. Later, walls were built and clamped together with wooden fittings. And as construction techniques changed, the shape of the houses altered from the traditional circular plan to a rectangular one. The rectangular shape is not found in nature, and it is thus a truly human mark on the landscape. Certainly this new shape reflected new mental attitudes and social behaviors. In rectangular houses, walls did more than support and protect: they also divided and separated. Because it was easier to build interior walls leaning against flat surfaces, privacy improved and family members were physically parted. Human relations would never be the same as they had been in the highly egalitarian arrangements of the mobile hunters and gatherers.

Although the food-producing changes were gradual and widely dispersed, a few communities stand out as pioneers in the long transition from hunting and gathering to agrarian and pastoral life. Around Wadi en-Natuf, located about ten miles from present-day Jerusalem, a group of people known historically as Natufians began to dig sunken pit shelters and to chip stone tools around 12,500 BCE. Over the course of the next two millennia or so, these bands stayed in one place, improving their toolmaking techniques, building circular shelters, and developing a variety of ways to preserve and prepare food. They dwelled in solidly built structures, buried their dead, and harvested grains. Although they did not plant seeds and did not give up hunting, their growing knowledge of wild plants paved the way for later breakthroughs.

It was only a matter of time before the full transition to settled agriculture and full-scale pastoralism took place. As noted above, the agricultural revolution spread in all directions. In the highlands of eastern Anatolia, the area that encompasses modern-day Turkey, large settlements were arranged around monumental public buildings with impressive stone carvings that attest to the complexity of social organization. In central Anatolia, at the site of Çatal Höyük, a dense honeycomb of settlements was filled with rooms that were covered with wall paintings and sculptures of wild bulls, hunters, and pregnant women. The use of art and imagery to provide identity and to master the powerful forces of the cosmos is a human characteristic continued unbroken from the time of the early cave artists. The difference now was that men and women made their own structures, where they gathered to worship the forces of nature and the spirit world, interacting with each other according to rituals that defined their place in society.

After 5500 BCE, people began to move into the river valley in Mesopotamia (in present-day Iraq) along the Tigris and Euphrates rivers, and small villages began to appear. They began to work together to build simple irrigation systems to water their fields. Perhaps because of the increased demands for community work to maintain the irrigation systems, the communities in southern Mesopotamia became stratified, with some people having more power than others. We can see from the burial sites and the large number of public buildings uncovered by archaeologists that for the first time, communities had people who were born into a higher status rather than acquiring high status through the merits of their work. A class of people who had access to more luxury goods, and who lived in bigger and better houses, now became part of the social organization.

The agricultural revolution created farmers and herders where once there had been only hunters and gatherers. Agriculture required settled communities and because it provided surplus food, populations could easily increase. As populations grew, they eventually began to concentrate in ever larger centers, where they formed the first towns. Settled agricultural societies could finally produce enough sustenance to feed large numbers of people who did not themselves have to produce food and could move from the countryside to urban settings. The next chapter will explore early urbanization in more detail. What is important for us to emphasize here is that changes dependent on agriculture enabled larger numbers of people to live together in/denser concentrations. Rapid population expansion also followed in the wake of agriculture and herding. By 1000 BCE, the world's population had reached 50 million, and the household, with its dominant male, had replaced the small, relatively egalitarian band as the primary social unit.

MEN, WOMEN, AND THE GROWTH OF DRUDGERY

Over the 4- to 5-million-year-long history of humans and their hominid ancestors, one of the fundamental divisions manifest in the fossil remains of early hominids and humans is that between males and females. The existence of this division naturally raises questions about what relationships between the two sexes were like in prehistoric times. Certainly, for millions of years, basic differences in biology affected differences in the roles played by men and women. The fact that females gave birth to offspring and that males did not was the driving force that determined female and male actions and behaviors and attitudes toward each other, at least up to the appearance of *Homo erectus*. Thus, it is a mistake to think of male-female interactions as "gender" (social and cultural) relations when, in reality, they are biologically based sexual

Çatal Höyük. Discovered in 1958 by the British archaeologist James Mellaart, this site is notable for providing information on the global transition from hunting and gathering to urban dwelling. Çatal Höyük is located in modern Turkey and dates from the eighth millennium BCE.

MOTHERING AND MILKING

One of the dividing lines among all animals, humans included, involves child rearing and the division of labor between mothers and fathers. In this text, the renowned primatologist Sarah Blaffer Hrdy argues that breast-feeding among mammals was a major factor shaping women's fortunes.

"Is sex destiny?" When this question is posed, it's a safe bet that the underlying agenda has to do with what women *should* be doing. Should they be home caring for their children or off pursuing other interests? A comparative look at other creatures that (like humans) breed cooperatively and share responsibilities for rearing young with other group members reveals that sex *per se* is not the issue. Lactation is.

Caretakers of both sexes, wet-nurses, even "daycare"— none of these are uniquely human, nor particularly new. They are standard features of many cooperatively breeding species. As we saw, cooperative breeding is exquisitely well developed in insects such as honeybees and wasps. Shared provisioning is also common among birds such as acorn woodpeckers, bee-eaters, dunnocks, and scrub jays. Although cooperative breeding is uncommon among mammals generally, it is richly developed in species such as wolves, wild dogs, dwarf mongooses, elephants, tamarins, marmosets, and humans. In all these animals, individuals other than the mother ("allomothers") help her provision or otherwise care for her young. Typically, allomothers will include the mother's mate (often but not necessarily the genetic progenitor). Individuals other than either parent ("alloparents") also help. These helpers are most often recruited from kin who are not yet ready to reproduce themselves, or from subordinates who do not currently—or may never have—better options. In the human case, the most important alloparents are often older, post-reproductive relatives who have already reproduced.

Among mammals, the trend toward having young who require costly long-term care began modestly enough. It probably began with an egg-laying brooding reptile that started to secrete something milklike. Such egg-layers gradually developed glands especially equipped for milk production. Only among mammals did one sex come to specialize in manufacturing custom-made baby formula, to provide something critical for infant survival that the other sex could not. This peculiarity has had many ramifications, especially as infants became dependent for longer periods in the primate line.

The ante was upped substantially when primate mothers, instead of bearing litters, began focusing care on one baby at a time. These singletons were born mature enough to cling to their mother's fur, to be carried by her right from birth and for months thereafter. Whether or not this intimate and prolonged association is the mother's destiny, *sex* is not the issue. Lactation is.

What Is Lactation About?

Other forms of caretaking—fathers brooding eggs, bringing food, protecting babies—are not nearly so sex-specific. Even gestation is a function that in rare cases (for example, the sea horse) a male takes on. But not lactation. Why—with the sole exception of one rare fruit bat—does lactation appear to be exclusively female? How did these curious secretions get started?

At first glance, a mother sea horse might seem to have a sweet deal. She sallies up to her mate, injects her eggs into his belly pouch, and then, carefree, propels herself off to feed and make more eggs. Meanwhile, back at the male's pouch, the sea-mare's last batch is fertilized, toted, and kept safe in the ballooning brood chamber of the now extremely pregnant male. At birth, as many as 1,500 fully formed but still minuscule and defenseless sea-foals are sprayed out into the open ocean. The sea around them teems with predators and competitors, many bigger than they are. Forced to fend for themselves immediately after birth, almost all starve.

Viviparity means keeping infants safe inside some sealed chamber within the parent's body till they can be born alive, as opposed to protected in an egg fill hatching. But by itself, viviparity offers tiny, still helpless creatures only the slimmest toehold on posterity. Why not linger in the womb longer, and grow bigger before venturing into the world?

→ *How does human child rearing affect mothers differently from fathers? Why is the difference more marked among humans than other species?*

SOURCE: From Sarah Blaffer Hrdy, *Mother Nature: Maternal Instincts and How They Shape the Human Species* (New York: Ballantine Books, 2000), pp. 121–23.

relations. One can speak of the emergence of "gendered" relations and roles only with the appearance of modern humans (*Homo sapiens*) and perhaps Neanderthals. Only when humans began to think imaginatively and in complex symbolic ways and when they gave voice to these perceptions in a spoken language, perhaps no sooner than 150,000 years ago, did such true gender categories as *man* and *woman* crystallize. As these cultural aspects of human life took shape, the distinction between "men" and "women," rather than between "males" and "females," began to be made, and culture joined biology in governing human interactions.

Gender roles became more pronounced and fixed in the stages leading up to and during the food-producing revolution. As human communities became larger, more stratified, and more powerful following the transition to an agriculturally based way of life, the rough gender egalitarianism of hunting and gathering societies eroded. An enhanced human power over the environment did not confer equal power on all. In one view, women were the net losers of the agricultural revolution. Women's knowledge of wild plants had contributed decisively to early settled agriculture, but women did not necessarily benefit from the transition to which their expertise contributed. Indeed, a well-known student of primate behavior, Sarah Hrdy, has called the settled agricultural transformation a "Great Leap Sideways," because advances for some people meant losses for others.

Advances in agrarian tools, notably the plow, made heavy work much more onerous for some people than for others, especially undermining the status women had held as farmers. Men, who had been more involved in hunting and gathering, took charge of yoking animals to plows, leaving to women the backbreaking and repetitive tasks of planting, weeding, harvesting, and grinding the grain into flour. Thus, although agricultural innovations augmented productivity, they also increased the drudgery of work, especially for women. The unequal effects on men and women are visible, for instance, in fossils found in Abu Hureyra, Syria, where the bones found by archaeologists displayed the evidence of a harsh working life. Damage to the vertebrae, osteoarthritis in the toes, and curved and arched femurs suggest that the work of bending over and kneeling in the fields especially took its toll on female agriculturalists. These maladies do not usually appear among the bone remains of hunters and gatherers.

The stratification of men and women during this era also affected power relations within households and communities. The senior male figure became the dominant figure in these households—and even beyond, in the new political and cultural hierarchies, where societies favored males over females in leadership positions. The agricultural revolution marked a greater division among men, and particularly between men and women. Where the agricultural transformation was most widespread, and where population densities especially began to grow in Afro-Eurasia, the social and political differences created inequalities within society, especially along gender lines, and patriarchy, or the "rule of senior males" within households, began to spread around the globe.

 # CONCLUSION

Over thousands of generations, African hominids evolved from other primates into *Homo erectus* hominids, who then wandered very far from their native habitats to fill other landmasses. They did so in successive waves, each responding to worldwide alternations of glaciation and melting. These predecessors of humans had some common features with modern humans. They stood erect, made stone tools, lived in extended families, and, to a certain extent, communicated with each other (by means other than language). An ability to adapt to environmental change was what increasingly separated humans from other animal species. *Homo sapiens*, who had larger brains than other hominids and are what we know as "modern humans," also emerged in Africa and trickled out of the world's largest landmass about 100,000 years ago. Since *Homo sapiens* had greater adaptive skills, when a cooling cycle returned they were better prepared to face the elements, and eventually they eclipsed their genetic cousins. One critical variable was their ability to use language, to engage in abstract, representational thought, and to convey the lessons of experience to their descendants and neighbors. Thus it was that modern humans stored and shared knowledge, thereby enhancing their adaptive abilities.

While modern men and women share a recent African heritage, people adapted over hundreds of generations to the specific environments that they encountered as they began to fill the earth's corners. Some settled near lakes and took to fishing, while others hunted large mammals in northern steppes. But everywhere, the dependence on nature yielded broadly similar social and cultural structures. It took another warming cycle for people from Africa to the Americas slowly to put down their hunting weapons and begin to domesticate animals and plants.

The changeover to settled agriculture was not uniform across the world. There were some basic commonalities: reliance on wood, stone, and natural fibers to make tools, shelter, and materials for cultural expressions, as well as increasing social hierarchies, especially a status differential between men and women. But with time, the social geography of the world's regions began to vary as communities became more settled. The process of divergence between the world's parts gathered speed as humans learned to modify nature to fit their needs. The varieties of animals that could be domesticated, as well as differences in climatic conditions and topography, all shaped the early ways in which people drifted apart in spite of their recent common origins.

Still, there was one important commonality: the scale and complexity of settlements and communities across the world had a limit. The vast majority of people in the age before the agricultural revolution continued a life of foraging for food supplies. Villages grew—but they did not become cities. Moreover, although fishing and farming enabled settled communities to spring up, pastoral communities that followed moving herds of animals or migrating schools of fish also spread. These peoples moved across mountains or deserts to find fresh pastures for their animals or seek waters where fish were spawning. Around the world, the remains of rudimentary pottery, stone tools, and rustic adobe and stone villages give us pictures of worlds that were almost exclusively rural, largely horizontal in social structure, and still very much dependent on the natural flow of fresh water and fertility of soils. As we will see in the next chapter, another round of technical advances would be necessary before humans in some areas could further change their relationship to nature and in so doing create the foundations for the world's first highly complex societies.

STUDY QUESTIONS

WWNORTON.COM/STUDYSPACE

1. Explain how evolutionary biologists and archaeologists in recent decades have transformed our understanding of human origins. What tools and discoveries led them to their conclusions?
2. Describe the evolutionary process through which *Homo sapiens* emerged. Was it a linear progression?
3. Analyze the advantages that art and language gave *Homo sapiens* over other species. How did art and language contribute to the domestication of plants and animals and the spread of agriculture?
4. List the nine regions where agricultural production first emerged. What common factors existed in all of these places that allowed for the domestication of plants and animals?
5. Explain the conditions that allowed agriculture to emerge first in Southwest Asia.
6. Analyze the advantages and disadvantages of agricultural production versus nomadic foraging. How were agricultural or pastoral communities different from those of hunters and gatherers?

FURTHER READINGS

Arsuaga, Juan Luis, *The Neanderthal's Necklace: In Search of the First Thinkers*, translated by Anthony Klatt (2002). A stimulating overview of prehistory that focuses on the Neanderthals and compares them with *Homo sapiens*.

Barker, Graeme, *Agricultural Revolution in Prehistory: Why Did Foragers Become Farmers* (2006). The most recent, truly global, and up-to-date study of this momentous event in world history.

Bellwood, Peter, *First Farmers: The Origins of Agricultural Societies* (2005). A state-of-the-art global history of the origins of agriculture including recent archaeological, linguistic, and microbiological data.

Bogucki, Peter, *The Origins of Human Society* (1999). An authoritative overview of prehistory.

Cauvin, Jacques, *The Birth of the Gods and the Origins of Agriculture*, translated by Trevor Watkins from the original French published in 1994 (2000). An important work on the agricultural revolution of Southwest Asia and the evolution of symbolic thinking at this time.

Cavalli-Sforza, Luigi Luca, *Genes, Peoples, and Languages*, translated by Mark Selestad from the original French published in 1996 (2000). An expert's introduction to the use of gene re-

Chronology

	15 mya*	10 mya	5 mya	1 mya

▌ *Global climate cooling; apes move down from trees and become bipedal, 10–15 mya*

Orrorin tugenensis *appears, 6 mya* ▌

Australopithecus africanus *hominid species appears, 3 mya* ▌

Homo habilus *appears, 2.5 mya* ▌

Homo erectus *appears, 1–2.5 mya* ▌

Beginnings of Ice Age across the Northern Hemisphere ▌

Homo erectus *migration across Afro-Eurasia*

*millions of years ago

search for revealing new information about the evolution of human beings in the distant past.

Childe, V. Gordon, *What Happened in History* (1964). A classic work by one of the pioneers in studying the early history and evolution of human beings. Though superseded in many respects, it is still an important place to start one's reading and a work of great power and emotion.

Clark, J. Desmond, and Steven A. Brandt (eds.), *From Hunters to Farmers: The Causes and Consequences of Food Production in Africa* (1984). Excellent essays on the agricultural revolution.

Coon, Carleton Stevens, *The Story of Man; from the First Human to Primitive Culture and Beyond*, 2nd ed. (1962). An important early work on the evolution of humans, emphasizing the distinctiveness of "races" around the world.

Cunliffe, Barry (ed.), *The Oxford Illustrated Prehistory of Europe* (1994). The definitive work on early European history.

Ehrenberg, Margaret, *Women in Prehistory* (1989). What was the role of women in hunting and gathering societies, and how greatly were women affected by the agricultural revolution? The author offers a number of stimulating generalizations.

Ehret, Christopher, *The Civilizations of Africa: A History to 1800* (2002). Although this is a general history of Africa, the author, a linguist and an expert on early African history, offers new information and new overviews of African peoples in very ancient times.

Fagan, Brian, *People of the Earth: An Introduction to World Prehistory* (1989). An authoritative overview of early history, widely used in classrooms.

Fage, J. D., and Roland Oliver (eds.), *The Cambridge History of Africa*, 8 vols. (1975–1984). A pioneering work of synthesis by two of the first and foremost scholars of the history of the African continent. Volume 1 deals with African prehistory.

Frison, George C., *Survival by Hunting: Prehistoric Human Predators and Animal Prey* (2004). An archaeologist applies his knowledge of animal habitats, behavior, and hunting strategies to an examination of prehistoric hunting practices in the North American Great Plains and Rocky Mountains.

Gebauer, Anne Birgitte, and T. Douglas Price (eds.), *Transition to Agriculture in Prehistory* (1992). Excellent essays on the agricultural revolution, especially those written by the two editors.

Johnson, Donald, Lenora Johnson, and Blake Edgar, *Ancestors: In Search of Human Origins* (1999). A good overview of human evolution, with insightful essays on *Homo erectus* and *Homo sapiens*.

Jones, Steve, Robert Martin, and David Pilbeam (eds.), *The Cambridge Encyclopedia of Human Evolution* (1992). A superb guide to a wide range of subjects, crammed with up-to-date information on the most controversial and obscure topics of human evolution and early history.

Ki-Zerbo, J. (ed.), *Methodology and African Prehistory*, vol. 1 of the UNESCO General History of Africa (1981). A general history of Africa, written for the most part by scholars of African descent.

Klein, Richard G., and Blake Edgar, *The Dawn of Human Culture* (2002). A fine and reliable guide to the tangled history of human evolution.

Leakey, Richard, *The Origin of Humankind* (1994). A readable and exciting account of human evolution, written by the son of the pioneering archaeologists Louis and Mary Leakey, a scholar of equal stature to his parents.

Lewin, Roger, *The Origin of Modern Humans* (1993). Yet another good overview of human evolution, with useful chapters on early art and the use of symbols.

Loewe, Michael, and Edward Shaughnessy (eds.), *The Cambridge History of Ancient China: From the Origins of Civilization to 221 B.C.* (1999). A good review of the archaeology of ancient China.

Mellaart, James, *Çatal Höyük: A Neolithic Town in Anatolia* (1967). A detailed description of one of the first towns associated with the agricultural revolution in Southwest Asia.

Mithen, Steven, *The Prehistory of the Mind: The Cognitive Origins of Art and Science* (1996). A stimulating discussion of the impact

200,000 ya**	150,000 ya	100,000 ya	50,000 ya	1 CE

Climate and environmental shift in Africa
Neanderthal evident in Europe, 200,000 ya

Homo sapiens emerges in Africa and migrates ∎
to other regions, 120,000–50,000 ya

Cave art develops in Europe, 30,000 ya ∎
Human migration from Afro-Eurasia to Americas begins, 18,000 ya ∎
Ice age, 16,000–10,000 BCE ∎
Beginnings of agricultural revolution in Southwest Asia, 9000 BCE ∎
Millet cultivation in Yellow River valley develops, 6500 BCE ∎
Rice cultivation in Yangzi River valley develops, 5500 BCE ∎
Domestication of plants and animals begins, 6700–2000 BCE ∎
Agricultural settlements using Southwest Asian domesticants emerges, 6000–5000 BCE ∎
Pastoralism begins in Inner Asia, 3000 BCE ∎
Maize cultivation emerges in central Mexico, 2000 BCE ∎

*years ago

of biological and cultural evolution on the cognitive structure of the human mind.

Olson, Steve, *Mapping Human History: Genes, Race, and Our Common Origins* (2003). Using the findings of genetics and attacking the racial thinking of an earlier generation of archaeologists, the author writes powerfully about the unity of all human beings.

Price, T. Douglas (ed.), *Europe's First Farmers* (2000). A discussion of the agricultural revolution in Europe.

Price, T. Douglas, and Anne Birgitte Gebauer (eds.), *Last Hunters-First Farmers: New Perspectives on the Prehistoric Transition to Agriculture* (1996). An exciting collection of essays by some of the leading scholars in the field studying the transition from hunting and gathering to settled agriculture.

Scarre, Chris (ed.), *The Human Past: World Prehistory and the Development of Human Societies* (2005). An encyclopedia and an overview rolled up into one mammoth volume, written by leading figures in the field of early human history.

Shaw, Thurstan, Paul Sinclair, Bassey Andah, and Alex Okpoko (eds.), *The Archaeology of Africa: Food, Metals, and Towns* (1993). Up-to-date research on the earliest history of human beings in Africa.

Smith, Bruce D., *The Emergence of Agriculture* (1995). How early humans domesticated wild animals and plants.

Stringer, Christopher, and Robin McKie, *African Exodus: The Origins of Modern Humanity* (1996). Detailed data on why Africa was the source of human origins and why *Homo sapiens* is a recent wanderer out of the African continent.

Tattersall, Ian, *The Fossil Trail: How We Know What We Think We Know about Human Evolution* (1995). A passionately written book about early archaeological discoveries and the centrality of Africa in human evolution.

Van Oosterzee, Penny, *Dragon Bones: The Story of Peking Man* (2000). Describes how the late-nineteenth-century unearthing of sites in China containing fossils of animals used for medicinal purposes led to the discovery of the fossils of the Peking Man.

Weiss, Mark L., and Alan E. Mann, *Human Biology and Behavior: An Anthropological Perspective* (1996). The authors stress the contribution that biological research has made and continues to make to unravel the mystery of human evolution.

Chapter 2

RIVERS, CITIES, AND FIRST STATES, 4000–2000 BCE

One of the oldest cities and first centers of society in the world was the ancient city of Uruk, known in the Bible as Erech and in modern Arabic as Warka. Located in the southernmost part of the Mesopotamian alluvium in Southwest Asia on one of the many winding branches of the Euphrates River, it had at least 10,000 inhabitants and many large public structures and temples by the late fourth millennium BCE. A temple probably dedicated to the god An, the Sumerian god of the sky, had been built before 3000 BCE. Known today as the White Temple because of its bright lime-plastered surface, it was constructed on a high platform that towered more than thirty feet above the level of the plain, with niched mud-brick walls forming stepped indentations up and down the surface. In another sacred precinct of the city dedicated to the Sumerian goddess Inanna (also called Ishtar in the semitic Akkadian language), huge administrative buildings and temples stood in courtyards defined by tall columns. The surfaces of these buildings were covered with colored stone cones arranged in elaborate geometric patterns. These buildings must have been visible from far away, making Uruk the "shining city" of the epic devoted to its later king, Gilgamesh.

The city of Uruk had once been a mere town, but over the years it grew into an immense commercial and administrative center—a location where jobs, adventure, and new ideas were to be found. A huge wall with seven massive gates surrounded the metropolis. Down the middle ran a canal whose waters had been diverted from the Euphrates River. On one side were gardens, pottery kilns, and enormous textile workshops where hundreds of men and women made beautiful clothes, fit for the goddess Inanna and her royal consorts; on the other side was the temple quarter, where the priests and their households lived, where scribes kept their records, and where the LU-GAL, or the big man, met the elders when they held their important discussions about the future of the city.

As Uruk grew, it became home to laborers, craftworkers, farmers, and scribes, as well as ruling elites. By the middle of the fourth millennium BCE, all kinds of specialists lived and worked in Uruk. Many of the industries, previously small and localized, now became centralized to address the burgeoning demand for their services and the increasing sophistication of construction and manufacturing. Potters made significant technical breakthroughs using a fast wheel that enabled them to mass-produce vessels in many different shapes. Metalsmiths, stone bowl makers, and brickmakers all worked under the centralized city administration. They, along with other workers, were paid in rations allocated from central storehouses—probably doled out in crude, standardized beveled-rim bowls that archaeologists have found by the millions at Uruk and other sites occupied during this period.

> *Uruk was the first city of its kind in world history; its appearance marked a new phase in human development.*

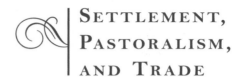

SETTLEMENT, PASTORALISM, AND TRADE

> → *What diverse strategies did people across the globe develop to live in their environments?*

Uruk was the first city of its kind in world history; its appearance marked a new phase in human development. In earlier times, humans had settled in small communities that were equal in size and distributed over the landscape at a level of density ensuring that water and land were easily accessible to all. Gradually some communities grew to a larger size, becoming focal points of trade and settlements that attracted specialists. Eventually a few of these centers became cities—centers with large populations, containing institutions of economic, religious, and political power. At these centers, most of the inhabitants would no longer be involved in producing their own food. Rather, they would be engaged in other professions or tasks necessary for the larger community. Workers would be fed with rations, and the elite would receive their support through taxes levied on those over whom they held authority.

Over many millennia, people had slowly developed strategies to make the best of their environments. But around 3500 BCE, a series of remarkable cultural changes, demographic leaps, and technological innovations gave rise to a major revolution in social organization that was relatively swift (compared to the pace of earlier developments) and that

Focus Questions RIVERS, CITIES, AND FIRST STATES

- → *What diverse strategies did people across the globe develop to live in their environments?*
- → *What role did cities play in Mesopotamian society?*
- → *Why do we know less about Harappan culture than about others in Afro-Eurasia?*
- → *How did the Nile River shape the development of early Egyptian society?*
- → *What hallmarks of urban life emerged in China during this period?*
- → *How did the growth of urban societies in river basins affect people living in the Aegean region, Anatolia, and Europe?*

 WWNORTON.COM/STUDYSPACE

Aerial View of Ur. The ancient city of Ur is now an archaeological mound, known as a Tell or Tal in Arabic. Ur was a medium-sized city in the third millennium BCE located on one of the important canals connected to the mouth of the Persian Gulf. It was there that the first true ziggurat, or temple tower, was built by Ur-Nammu, the founder of the Third Dynasty of Ur, which controlled all of Mesopotamia, Khuzistan, and the central Zagros Mountains at the end of the third millennium BCE.

fundamentally changed human life. In combination, these changes enabled complex, hierarchical societies to form, and they were reinforced in turn by the emergence of cities and the institutions that define them. The physical, social, and cultural achievements of city life would begin to have a profound impact on the human experience.

Village conglomerations arose as people gathered together to live near a reliable water source that would enable them to grow the crops so vital to feeding larger populations. Although the first groupings appeared in regions with abundant rainfall, the larger foundations of the new cities were established in drier zones, where rich alluvial soils were irrigated with river water. Equally important, a warming cycle caused temperatures around the world to rise and growing seasons to expand. These changes in the natural environment provoked a revolutionary response, fundamentally altering the very fabric of the human experience.

At the beginning, cities were scarce and could be found only in very select places. To begin with, cities required the conducive environments of stable river systems. As their waters cut through mountains, steppe lands (vast treeless grasslands), and deserts, the rivers deposited rich soils around the deltas before finally reaching the sea. The combination of fertile soils, access to water for irrigation, and the widespread availability of domesticated plants and animals made these particular places attractive for human habitation. Abundant water and arable soil made the city possible.

With the dense settlement of large numbers of people in the new cities also came labor specialization, and craftworkers began to concentrate solely on making textiles, pottery, and other goods. Soon these goods were used not only in the cities themselves but also in trade with outlying areas. Such trade would expand over longer distances, bringing in raw materials such as metal, timber, and precious stones that could be used to construct and decorate city walls, temples, and palaces, as well as to fashion tools and weapons.

EARLY CITIES ALONG RIVER BASINS

At first, these material and social advances occurred in a remarkably short period of time in three locations: the basin of the Tigris and Euphrates rivers in modern Iraq, at the heart of Southwest Asia; the Indus River basin in modern Pakistan, in the northwest corner of South Asia; and the northern parts of the Nile River, which flows north from the heart of Africa through modern-day Egypt before it enters the Mediterranean Sea. (See Map 2-1.) In these three regions, from roughly 4000 to 2000 BCE, humans altered how they farmed and fed themselves—turning to intensive irrigation agriculture; where they lived—with more people moving to cities inhabited by rulers, administrators, priests, and specialized craftworkers; and how they organized communities—now controlled by divinely inspired monarchs and elaborate bureaucracies. They also transformed what and how they worshipped—praying to a multitude of anthropomorphic gods who communicated with believers through kings and priests living in palace complexes and temples that were the centers of the early cities. These far more complex modes of living required new means of record keeping that finally led to the invention of writing systems. The same development took place at the same time but on a smaller scale along the inland river valleys of the Iranian plateau and in central

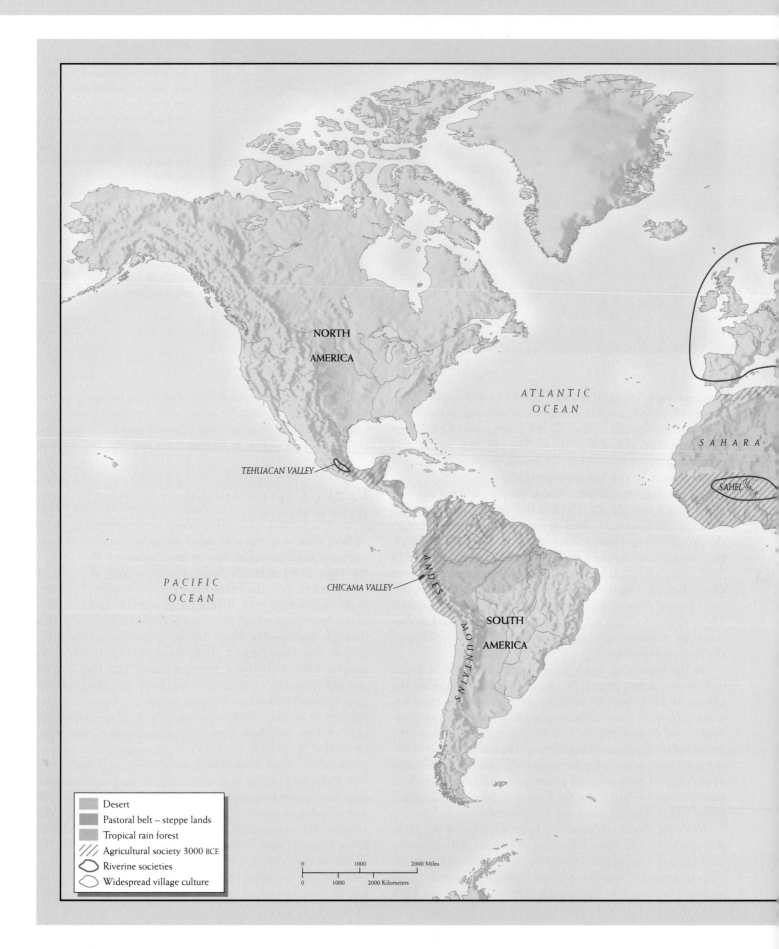

NORTH
AMERICA

ATLANTIC
OCEAN

SAHARA

SAHEL

TEHUACAN VALLEY

PACIFIC
OCEAN

CHICAMA VALLEY

A
N
D
E
S

M
O
U
N
T
A
I
N
S

SOUTH
AMERICA

Desert

Pastoral belt – steppe lands

Tropical rain forest

Agricultural society 3000 BCE

Riverine societies

Widespread village culture

0   1000   2000 Miles

0   1000   2000 Kilometers

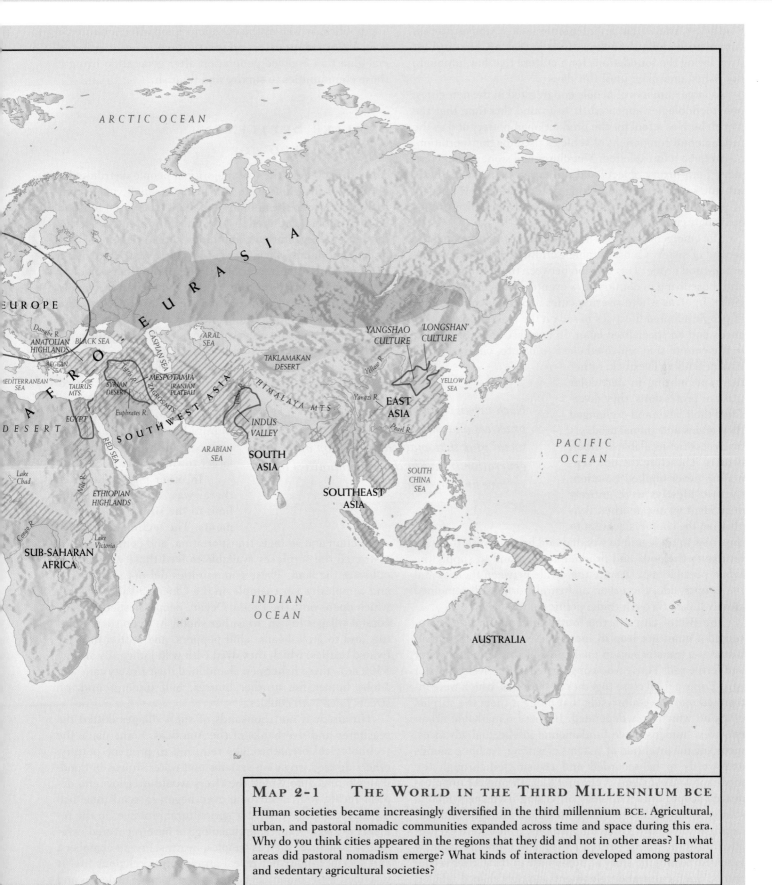

ARCTIC OCEAN

A F R O E U R A S I A

EUROPE

Danube R.
ANATOLIAN BLACK SEA
HIGHLANDS
*AEGEAN
SEA*
MEDITERRANEAN
SEA
TAURUS
MTS.
EGYPT
DESERT
RED SEA

CASPIAN SEA
Tigris R.
SYRIAN
DESERT
ZAGROS MTS.
MESOPOTAMIA
IRANIAN
PLATEAU
Euphrates R.

ARAL
SEA

TAKLAMAKAN
DESERT

Yellow R.

YANGSHAO
CULTURE

'LONGSHAN'
CULTURE

YELLOW
SEA

HIMALAYA MTS

Yangzi R.

EAST
ASIA

Pearl R.

S O U T H W E S T A S I A

INDUS
VALLEY

ARABIAN
SEA

SOUTH
ASIA

SOUTHEAST
ASIA

SOUTH
CHINA
SEA

PACIFIC
OCEAN

*Lake
Chad*
Nile R.
ETHIOPIAN
HIGHLANDS
Congo R.
*Lake
Victoria*

SUB-SAHARAN
AFRICA

INDIAN
OCEAN

AUSTRALIA

MAP 2-1   THE WORLD IN THE THIRD MILLENNIUM BCE

Human societies became increasingly diversified in the third millennium BCE. Agricultural, urban, and pastoral nomadic communities expanded across time and space during this era. Why do you think cities appeared in the regions that they did and not in other areas? In what areas did pastoral nomadism emerge? What kinds of interaction developed among pastoral and sedentary agricultural societies?

Southwest Asia. About a millennium later, a similar process commenced along the Yellow River in North China in East Asia, laying the foundations for a culture that has, uniquely, flourished unbroken until this day.

As large numbers of people congregated in the new cities, new technologies appeared. It is around this time that the wheel, both as a tool for the production of pottery and as the fundamental component of vehicles used for transportation, began to be fully exploited. Metallurgy and stoneworking provided both luxury objects and utilitarian tools. With these, urbanites also developed writing systems and a new imagery of power and control, which they used to organize the increasingly complex society.

The emergence of cities as population centers created the second of history's most durable worldwide distinctions—the urban-rural divide. This division between those living in cities and those living in countrysides eventually encompassed the globe. In areas where riverine cities appeared, communities of people adopted lifestyles based on the mass production of goods and on specialized labor. In contrast, those still living in the countryside remained close to nature, cultivating the land or tending livestock; rather than specializing in particular tasks or professions, they diversified their labor and exchanged their grains and animal products for necessities available in urban centers. Therefore the new separation never implied isolation; the two lifeways were entirely dependent on one another. People from the countryside went to the cities to trade and to worship and brought with them offerings to the gods and produce to feed and to supply the urban populations. Despite the divide between the city and the countryside, the urban and rural worlds still remained closely linked through trade, politics, and religion.

The rise of cities in the fourth millennium BCE represented a quantum leap in increased complexity in human history—a transformation made possible by abundant water and fertile soil. Those who congregated in the river valleys of Afro-Eurasia lived close together in the cities, which were integrated into the countryside that brought them the surplus crops on which they depended. In these remarkable urban enclaves, humans made fundamental intellectual advances, including the invention of systems of writing, enabling sounds and words to be recorded and transmitted through the medium of visual signs. A cultural breakthrough of unprecedented scope, the technology of writing used the symbolic storage of words and meanings to extend human communication and memory. Oral compositions, which were eventually transformed into written annals and literature, quickly followed, telling the story of human life in these river settlements. Such cultural developments strongly shaped religion

Each urban culture developed its own practices and institutions, providing the social glue that enabled generation after generation living in these communities to survive and flourish.

and politics, as well as the economy. Each urban culture developed its own practices and institutions, providing the social glue that enabled generation after generation living in these communities to survive and flourish.

SMALLER SETTLEMENTS AROUND 3500 BCE

Around 3500 BCE, the vast majority of people distributed in all parts of the globe were still living in small village communities close to the animals and plants they used for food. As they hunted, gathered, fished, and cultivated plants, they formed small egalitarian communities organized on the basis of clan and family allegiances. Tools were restricted mainly to wood and stone materials, though containers made of gourds were used to transport water and food over long distances. In a few special locations, early artisans regularly formed and then fired malleable clay to make vessels and dishes for storing and preparing food. More rarely still, craftworkers pounded native copper into small items of personal adornment. In such places where the population increased, divisions between artisans and manual laborers emerged, community life became more hierarchical, and villages grew into larger towns.

In other places, however, there was an environmental limit to the size of these settlements. The techniques of food production and storage, transportation, and communication restricted the surpluses available to feed those who did not cultivate the land. These communities did not grow in size and complexity. For example, in the Chicama Valley of Peru, which opens onto the Pacific Ocean, people nestled in small coastal villages to fish, to gather shellfish, to do some hunting, and to grow beans, chili peppers, and cotton to make twined textiles, which they dyed with wild indigo. By around 3500 BCE, these fishermen abandoned their rickety cane and adobe homes for sturdier houses, half underground, on streets lined with cobbles.

Hundreds if not thousands of such villages dotted the seashores and riverbanks of the Americas. Some made the technological breakthroughs required to produce pottery; others devised irrigation systems and water sluices in floodplains (areas onto which the rivers would overflow and deposit fertile soil). And some even began to send their fish catches inland in return for agricultural produce. In the remains of these villages, archaeologists have recovered ceremonial structures such as temples, hearths, fire-pit chambers, and special tombs that reveal an elaborate religious life. It was filled with communal devotion and homage to deities and with rituals to celebrate the momentous events of birth and death, as well as to perpetuate the memory of ancestors.

In the Americas, the largest population center at the time was located in the valley of Tehuacán near current-day Mexico City. The domestication of corn in this region created a subsistence base that enabled people to migrate from caves to cluster in a mosaic of pit-house villages that supported a growing population. But by 3500 BCE, the valley held nothing resembling a large city, though it teemed with inhabitants.

The same can be said of sub-Saharan Africa, where the population grew but did not concentrate into major urban communities. About 12,000 years ago, when there was more rainfall and temperatures increased, small encampments of African hunting, gathering, and fishing communities congregated around the large lakes and big rivers that flowed through what is now the largest desert in the world. Elephants, rhinoceroses, gazelles, antelopes, lions, and panthers roamed, both posing a threat to humans and providing them a source of food. Over millennia, in the wetter and more temperate locations of this vast region—particularly in the upland massifs and their foothills—permanent villages slowly came into being. As the Sahara gradually became drier, people moved to the edges of the desert, to areas along the Niger River and the Sudan. They settled along Lake Chad in what is today eastern Nigeria and southern Cameroon, where they grew yams, oil palms (a palm tree whose fruit and seeds produce oil), and plantains (a fruit similar to bananas). In the Sudan, settlers grew grains such as millet and sorghum, which later spread to areas along the Niger River as well. Residents constructed stone dwellings and dug underground wells and food storage areas. As an increasing population strained resources, groups of migrants moved south toward the Congo River and east toward Lake Victoria; there they established new farms and villages. Although population centers were often hundreds and even thousands of miles apart, they maintained trading and cultural contacts. We know of their connection because villagers from present-day Mali in the west to Kenya in the southeast used much the same style of pottery, characterized by bowls with rounded bottoms and similar wavy-line decorations.

PASTORAL NOMADIC COMMUNITIES

While many peoples continued to live in settled agricultural villages, where they fished and farmed and raised a few animals, some instead turned to pastoralism—herding and breeding sheep and goats as their primary means of subsistence. As their herds expanded, they found it necessary to move to the periphery of the settled areas to find sufficient pastures. Around 3500 BCE, western Afro-Eurasia witnessed the growth and spread of pastoral nomadic communities that herded domesticated animals whose grazing requirements were sizable. Rather than living permanently in settled com-

munities, these pastoral nomads moved their herds from highland to lowland pastures in an annual cycle. Their communities were small, and their settlements were impermanent, without substantial public buildings or infrastructure, but the herders' patterns of moving seasonally between specific pasturelands were stable. Across the vast expanse of Eurasia's great mountains (Taurus, Zagros, Himalaya, Tianshan, and Kunlun) and its desert barriers (Sahara, Gobi, and Taklamakan), and from its steppe lands ranging across inner and central Eurasia to the Pacific Ocean, these pastoral peoples lived alongside settled agrarian people when they were on their lowland pastures. The herders traded meat and animal products for the grains and pottery and tools produced in the settled agrarian communities.

As in western Afro-Eurasia, in the arid environments of Inner Mongolia and central Asia people initially engaged in a combination of herding animals and crop cultivation. But the environment on the Eurasian steppes was not conducive to large-scale farming, and they began to turn primarily to animal breeding and herding; they continued to engage in fishing and hunting and farming small plots of land in their winter pastures as secondary pursuits. Their economy centered on domesticated cattle and the sheep and horses that they raised. As their herds increased, they had to move often to new, ungrazed pastures. By the second millennium BCE, full-scale nomadic communities dominated these steppe lands. The horse-riding nomads moved their large animal herds across immense tracts of land within zones defined by rivers, mountains, and other natural features of the geography. In the arid zones of central Eurasia, the nomadic economies made horses—which enabled riders to move easily over large areas—a crucial component of survival.

THE RISE OF TRADE

Whether seeking to ensure their physical existence or providing luxury items conveying status or magical powers, humans from the time of their earliest groupings have exchanged things with one another. When they settled in one place, their need to exchange goods with those in other communities became even greater, as no one place had everything that people need. At the same time, settlements make it possible for humans to accumulate material wealth. By the advent of the earliest farming villages around 7000 BCE, trade patterns across Eurasia were well established. Most often this trade was in exotic materials such as obsidian, a black volcanic glass used to make superb chipped stone tools. Its proximity to one of the richest and best sources of this volcanic glass in all of Southwest Asia helps explain why the village at Çatal Höyük in central Anatolia (present-day Turkey) grew to such an extraordinary size (see Chapter 1). The obsidian was passed from one village to another in a process called "trickle trade" or "down the line trade."

More important to the people of the cities of southern Mesopotamia was long-distance trade. Because they lacked many basic raw materials that developed settlements require, they needed to find sources of wood, stones, and metal to augment their locally available building materials—mud and reeds. Indeed, these communities established outposts close to the sources of these materials so that they could coordinate and monitor the resources' import. In exchange, they offered manufactured goods, especially luxury textiles. This long-distance trade began around 5000 BCE, carried out by boats along the shores of the Persian Gulf. By 3000 BCE, there was extensive interaction between southern Mesopotamia and the highlands of Anatolia, the forests of the Levant (present-day Lebanon, Syria, Israel, and the Palestinian territories, bordering the eastern Mediterranean), and the rich mountains and vast plateau of Iran. (See Map 2-2.)

Throughout the millennia, trade and exchange between peoples increased. By the mid-third millennium BCE, trading communities were established in the oases (fertile areas with water in the midst of arid regions) dotting the deserts of western Syria, the plateau of Iran, northern Afghanistan, and Turkmenistan. Trading stations, or entrepôts, at the borders between several communities made possible exchanges among many partners. Caravans of pack animals—first donkeys and onagers (an Asian wild ass) and later camels—were used to take goods across long distances over land. These caravans

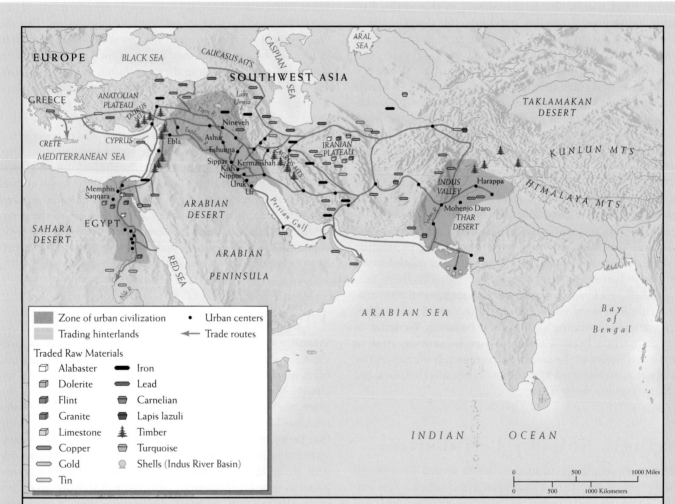

MAP 2-2 TRADE AND EXCHANGE IN SOUTHWEST ASIA AND THE EASTERN MEDITERRANEAN—THIRD MILLENNIUM BCE

Extensive commercial networks linked the urban cores of Southwest Asia in the third millennium BCE. According to the map, why was Mesopotamia the crossroads of Afro-Eurasia? Why do you think there were more extensive trade connections between Mesopotamians and people to their northwest and east than with Egypt to the west? How did trade shape societies living beyond urban cores in Mesopotamia, Egypt, and the Indus Valley?

would cross deserts, stopping at oasis communities where water and supplies could be exchanged for their wares. They traveled over routes that passed through deserts, steppes, and forests, carrying goods and ideas across Afro-Eurasia.

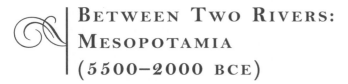

BETWEEN TWO RIVERS: MESOPOTAMIA (5500–2000 BCE)

> → *What role did cities play in Mesopotamian society?*

The common social geography of the world in 3500 BCE saw people living close to the land in small clans and settlements, some mobile, some stationary, but a breakthrough occurred in one place: the Mesopotamian river basin in Southwest Asia, where the world's first complex society came into existence. There the city and the river changed how people lived.

TAPPING THE WATERS

Mesopotamia, whose name is a Greek word meaning "[country] between two rivers," is not at first glance a hospitable place. From their headwaters in the mountains to the north and east, the Tigris and Euphrates rivers are wild and unpredictable, flooding in periods of heavy rainfall and snow, and dry during the parched months of summer. Thus, water was both scourge and blessing for the pioneers who moved to the Tigris and Euphrates river basin. It could wipe out years of hard work; but, properly handled, water could also transform the landscape into verdant fields. In retrospect, the simple irrigation systems created by the earliest Mesopotamians were nothing short of revolutionary. A large landmass that includes all of modern-day Iraq and parts of Syria and southeastern Turkey, Mesopotamia embraces a richly varied topography and a wide variety of cultures—all unified by interlocking drainage basins. Both rivers provided water for irrigation, and although hardly navigable, both served as important routes for transportation and communication by pack animal and by foot.

The first advances occurred in the foothill zones of the Zagros Mountains along the banks of the smaller rivers that feed into the Tigris. Here, men and women discovered that simple irrigation techniques enabled them to achieve higher agricultural yields and greater surpluses on these lands than were possible on rain-fed areas to the north. Gradually they ventured out of the foothills onto the southern alluvial plain of the Tigris and Euphrates River basin. There floods were larger, and the water harder to harness, but the land held greater promise of abundant harvests.

Early Mesopotamian Waterworks. From the sixth millennium BCE, irrigation was necessary for successful farming in southern Mesopotamia. By the first millennium BCE, sophisticated feats of engineering allowed the Assyrians to redirect water through constructed aqueducts, like the one illustrated here on a relief from the palace of the Assyrian king Sennacherib at Nineveh.

Converting the floodplain of the Euphrates River into a breadbasket required mastery over the unpredictable rivers. Both the Euphrates and (to an even greater degree) the Tigris, unless controlled by waterworks, were rivers profoundly unfavorable to cultivators. The annual floods and low-water seasons came at exactly the wrong times in the farming sequence. Floods occurred at the height of the growing season, when crops were most vulnerable. Irrigation waters, conversely, were needed when the floodwaters had receded and the river was at low ebb. In order to prevent the river from overflowing during the flood stage, farmers put up and maintained levees (barriers to the waters) along the river's banks, and dug ditches and canals to drain away floodwaters. To ensure a plentiful supply of water in the later growing stages, they needed highly developed water-lifting devices. In pioneering water storage, Mesopotamians were the world's first hydraulic engineers.

The great technological breakthrough in Mesopotamian societies was in irrigation, not necessarily in agrarian methods. The soils were fine and rich, constantly replenished by silt carried by the floodwaters, so soil tillage was light work. Farmers sowed a combination of wheat, millet, sesame, and especially barley (which doubled as the basis for beer, a staple of their diet), with yields possibly as high as those afforded by current-day wheat fields in Canada.

CROSSROADS OF SOUTHWEST ASIA

Though its soil was rich and water was abundant, southern Mesopotamia had few other natural resources apart from the abundant mud and marsh reeds in the immediate vicinity of the river basin that provided primitive building materials. In order to get wood, stone, metal, and all of the other raw materials on which complex settled societies relied to construct cities and the temples and palaces within them, Mesopotamians had to interact with the inhabitants of surrounding regions. They imported the cedars of Lebanon, the copper and stones of Oman, more copper from what is now Turkey and Iran, and the precious blue gemstone called lapis lazuli from faraway Afghanistan in return for textiles, oils, and other commodities. Maintaining trading contacts with their neighbors was relatively easy, given Mesopotamia's open boundaries on all sides. In this crucial respect, Mesopotamia contrasted with Egypt, whose long and narrow land was cut off by impassable deserts to the east and west, and by the Nile River rapids to the south.

Mesopotamia's natural advantages—its rich agricultural land and water combined with easy access to neighboring regions—were propitious for the growth of cities. But this very openness made the river valleys vulnerable to invaders from the deserts and the mountains. Mesopotamia thus became a crossroads for the peoples of Southwest Asia, the meeting grounds for several distinct cultural and linguistic groups of people. Among the dominant groups were Sumerians, who were concentrated in the south; Hurrians, who lived in the north; and the Semitic-speaking Akkadians, who concentrated in western and central Mesopotamia. In general, people engaged in pastoralism outside the core agricultural regions, and they provided the settled communities with animal products in exchange for agricultural produce.

FIRST CITIES

Archaeological surveys suggest that sometime during the first half of the fourth millennium BCE, a large-scale demographic transformation occurred. The population in the region had expanded as a result of its agricultural bounty, and swelling ranks of Mesopotamians migrated from the villages scattered across the countryside to particular centers that eventually became cities. The earliest of these cities, Eridu, Nippur, and Uruk, dominated their environs by 3500 BCE. Rather than appearing suddenly, the first cities in the southern part of the Mesopotamian floodplain grew gradually over about 1,000 years. Buildings of mud brick were erected in successive layers of accumulated urban development. Consider Eridu, which had first been settled as a village around 6000 BCE. Home to the Sumerian water god, Ea, Eridu was a sacred site where temples full of fish bones were built one on top of the other for more than 4,000 years. During the course of more than twenty reconstructions, the temples became increasingly elaborate, built on an ever-higher base. Eventually, the temple was raised on a platform like a mountain, looming over the featureless landscape and visible for miles in all directions. Not only had the temple grown up but the village had expanded horizontally, becoming a city, with its god overseeing its growth.

There were some thirty-five cities with major divine sanctuaries widely scattered across the southern plain of Mesopotamia. Sumerian ideology glorified a way of life and a territory composed of politically equal city-states, each with its own principal guardian deity and sanctuary, supported by its inhabitants. Local communities in these urban hubs expressed their homage to individual city gods and took great pride in the temple, the god's home.

Early Mesopotamian cities served as meeting places for peoples and their deities. In fact, it was the city's status as a devotional and economic center that elevated it over the countryside. Whether enormous, like Uruk or Nippur, or modest, like Ur or Abu Salabikh, all cities performed these complex roles as spiritual, economic, and cultural homes for Mesopotamian subjects.

Layout of Eridu. Over several millennia, temples of increasing size and complexity were built atop each other at Eridu in southern Iraq. The culmination came with the elaborate structure of level VII.

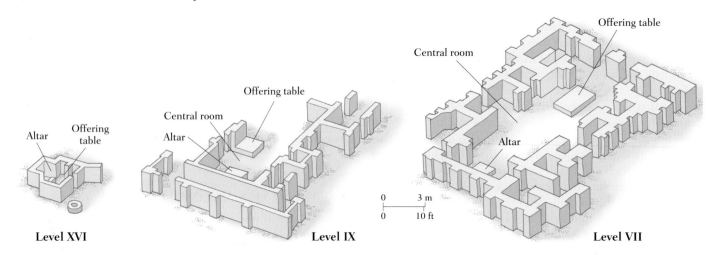

Level XVI   Level IX   Level VII

Ziggurat. The first ziggurat of Mesopotamia, dedicated to the moon god Nanna, was built by the founder of the Neo-Sumerian dynasty, Ur-Nammu (2112–2095 BCE). Although temples had been raised on platforms since early times, the distinctive stepped form of the ziggurat was initially borrowed from the Iranian plateau. It became the most important sacred structure in Mesopotamia.

Simply making a city was therefore not enough: it had to be made great. Urban design reflected the role of the city as a wondrous place to pay homage to the gods and their human intermediary, the king. The early cities contained enormous spaces within their walls. Initially, houses were large and separated by great plantations of date palms. Within the city limits were also located extensive sheepfolds (which became a frequent metaphor for the city). As populations grew, the fabric of the cities of Mesopotamia became denser. Even houses belonging to the well-to-do became considerably smaller. And often urbanites established new suburbs, either settling beyond the city perimeter or simply breaking through the old walls and spilling into the countryside.

The original layout of Mesopotamian cities conformed to a common pattern. Through their middle invariably ran a canal, around which neighborhoods housing specific occupational groups emerged. The temple marked the city center, while the palace and other official buildings often arose on the periphery. In separate quarters for craft production, families passed down their trades from generation to generation.

The emergence of politically autonomous and essentially equal cities was a recurring theme in lower Mesopotamia, where Sumerians and Semites lived side by side. The city-states were bound together through a common culture, intense trade, and a shared environment. Urban life and irrigated agriculture demonstrate how much ancient peoples depended on the nearby rivers to produce their distinctive cultures.

GODS AND TEMPLES

The worldview of the Sumerians and, later, the Akkadians revolved around a pantheon of gods who were believed to inhabit the lands of Sumer and Akkad, shaping political institutions and controlling everything, including the weather, fertility, harvests, and the underworld. As depicted in the *Epic of Gilgamesh,* a later composition based on a cycle of several oral tales about Gilgamesh (a historical but much mythologized king of Uruk), the gods could give, but they could also take away—with searing droughts and unmerciful floods and with natural and violent death. Gods, and the natural forces they controlled, had to be revered and feared. Faithful subjects imagined their gods as immortal, all-powerful, anthropomorphic beings whose habits were capricious, contentious, and gloriously work-free. Each of the major gods of the Sumerian pantheon had its home in a particular floodplain city, which it was believed to have created; therefore each gave his or her city its particular character, distinct institutions, and individual patterns of relationships with its urban neighbors.

Temples, and especially the main temple, were thought of as the home of the gods and the symbol of urban identity.

Cylinder Seal of Adad Carved from Green Stone. Many people in Mesopotamia involved with administration and public life had one or more cylinder seals. Cylinder seals were carved with imagery and inscriptions and were impressed into clay tablets and other documents while they were still malleable in order to guarantee the authenticity of a transaction. The cylinder seal shown here carries the inscription of the scribe Adda. The imagery includes representations of important gods of the Akkadian pantheon. The sun god Shamash rises from between the mountains in the center. Ishtar as a warrior goddess stands to the left. To the right is Ea, the god of wisdom, who is associated with flowing water and fish. Behind him is the servant Usmu, whose double face allows him to see everything. At the far left is a god of hunting.

Temples represented the ability of the gods to hoard wealth at sites where mortals exchanged goods and services. They were the single most important marker distinguishing the urban from the rural world, and rulers lavished resources on their construction and adornment to demonstrate the power of their cities. Because the temple was the symbolic focus of the entire city-state, it was important for rulers and other important members of the community to contribute to its upkeep. Communal efforts would often be channeled to temple projects. Many royal inscriptions commemorate the construction and later renovation of a temple as one of the ruler's major duties.

Inside the temple was an altar, on which the cult image was placed. Frequently benches lined the walls, with statues of humans standing in perpetual worship of the deity's images. By the end of the third millennium BCE, the elevated platform base of the temple was transformed into a stepped platform called a *ziggurat*. On top of the temple tower itself stood the main temple. Surrounding the ziggurat was a conglomeration of buildings that composed the temple precinct, which housed priests, officials, laborers, and a copious retinue of servants—all bustling about to serve the city's god.

While the temple was the god's home, it was also the god's estate. As such, temples functioned like large households engaged in all sorts of productive and commercial activities.

Their dependents cultivated cereals, fruits, and vegetables, all of which required extensive irrigation. The temples owned vast flocks of sheep, goats, cows, and donkeys. Those located close to the river employed workers to collect reeds, to fish, and to hunt. Enormous labor forces were required to maintain this high level of production. Other temples operated huge workshops (embryonic factories), where textiles and leather goods were manufactured. Temple workshops employed legions of craftworkers, metalworkers, masons, and stoneworkers. Since southern Mesopotamia lacked many raw materials, temples as well as the palaces sponsored long-distance trade, often commissioning independent merchants and traders to organize commercial expeditions to distant lands. The model of the household extended beyond the temple to all aspects of the Sumerian and Akkadian economy. The royal court was organized around the king's household; and in the private sector, large landowning extended families functioned as a household economic unit.

THE PALACE AND ROYAL POWER

The palace, both as an institution and as a set of buildings, appeared around 2500 BCE, about a millennium later than the Mesopotamian temple. But the palace quickly joined the temple as a defining landmark of city life. As life became more complex and cities grew in size, palaces began to supplement temples in upholding order and diffusing a sense of shared membership in city affairs. Over time, the palace became a source of power rivaling the temple. Palace and temple life often blurred, with rulers doubling as secular governors and sacred figures. Indeed, rulers embodied gods in such rituals as the Sacred Marriage, in which the king, as high priest, took on the role of the god Dumuzi, a Sumerian god of fertility and agrarian productivity, as in the temple he engaged in sexual relations with the high priestess, who embodied the goddess Inanna. Although located at the edge of cities in previously uninhabited locations, palaces quickly became the visible expression of permanent secular, military, and administrative authority, as distinct from the spiritual and economic power of the temples. Their builders expanded their city's influence—and thereby also disrupted the balance of power within and among Mesopotamian cities.

Rulers tied their status to their gods through elaborate burial arrangements of the kind well known from Egypt and China. The Royal Cemetery at Ur offers spectacular archaeological evidence of how Sumerian rulers dealt with death. Of the more than 2,000 graves that archaeologists uncovered in the 1930s, 16 were the burial sites of highborn persons. The royal burials were distinguished from others by being housed in a structure of mud brick. Further, they held not only the primary remains but also the bodies of other humans who had been sacrificed. In one case, more than eighty men and women accompanied the deceased to the afterlife. Many of the graves containing human sacrifices also demonstrate the elaborateness of the burial festival rituals. From the huge vats for cooked food, the bones of animals, the drinking vessels, and the musical instruments recovered from the grave sites, we can reconstruct the lifestyle of those who were required to join their masters in the graves. Honoring the dead by including their followers and possessions in their tombs reinforced the social hierarchies—including the vertical ties between humans and gods—that were the cornerstone of these early states.

SOCIAL HIERARCHY AND FAMILIES

Social hierarchies were an important part of the fabric of Sumerian city-states. The origins of the first states and hierarchies topped by powerful elites that supported them and profited from them can be traced to the very breakthrough

The Royal Tombs of Ur. The Royal Tombs of Ur, excavated in the 1930s, contained thousands of objects in gold, silver, lapis lazuli, and shell that were buried along with elites of the First Dynasty of Ur. One tomb belonged to the king, Mes-KALAM-dug. Next to his head was a gold helmet with the bun and braid that was headdress of the ruler. In another grave, along with the skeletons of more than sixty members of a royal household, were musical instruments, including this large harp with a golden bull's head. Such instruments would have been played at the ritual meal associated with these fabulously rich burials. Pu-Abi, identified as a queen by the cylinder near her body, was buried in a separate chamber. She was interred in full regalia, including the elaborate headdress shown here.

that made the region so special: irrigation. Whereas plows and sickles—the basic implements of farming—were tools employed by individuals for their own benefit, dikes, canals, banks, and hydraulic lifts required collective effort, investment, and organization. No single individual or family could sustain the challenge. Early irrigation societies therefore created communal ways of building infrastructure and maintaining it, collecting taxes and drafting labor to expand and preserve waterworks. These efforts laid the foundations of the first Afro-Eurasian states.

City-states at first were run by assemblies of elders and young men who made collective decisions for the community. From the outset, specially empowered elites were intermittently appointed to tackle emergencies; with time, these elite power holders became permanent features of the political landscape. The social hierarchy set off the rulers from the ruled. Ruling groups secured their privileged access to economic and political resources by erecting systems of bureaucracies, priesthoods, and laws. Priests and bureaucrats served their rulers well, championing rules and norms that legitimized the political leadership.

Occupations within the cities were highly specialized. A list of professions was formalized and transmitted across the land so that everyone could know where he or she fit within the newly emerging social order. The king and priest in Sumer were at the top of the list. Following them were bureaucrats (scribes and accountants of the household economy), supervisors, and specialized craftworkers. These included cooks, jewelers, gardeners, potters, metalsmiths, and traders. The biggest group, which was at the bottom of the hierarchy, consisted of the male and female workers who were not slaves but who were dependent on their households. Frequently several households would operate as a closed economic unit, producing most of the necessities within a closed system. Property was held collectively by the family or extended household. All members were party to land transfers or sale. Movement between these economic classes was not impossible but, as in many traditional societies, it was unusual. There were also independent merchants who assumed the risk of long-distance trading ventures, hoping for a generous return on their investment.

Sumerian society was organized around the family and the household, and the Sumerian family was also hierarchical: the senior male dominated as the patriarch of the family. Most Sumerian households were made up of a single extended family, all living under the same roof. The family consisted of the husband and wife bound by a contract; she would provide children, preferably male, while he provided support and protection. Monogamy was the norm, unless a son was not produced, and in such cases it was common to take a second wife or to bring a slave girl into the house to bear male children who would be considered the married couple's offspring. Sons would inherit the family's property in equal shares, while daughters were supported through gifts that were meant to provide the dowry necessary for a successful marriage. Adoption was also a common way for a family to gain a male heir. Most women lived inside the contract of marriage, but a special class of women joined the temple staff as priestesses. By the second millennium BCE, these priestesses were allowed broad economic autonomy that included ownership of estates and productive enterprises. Yet even in the case of the female temple personnel, their fathers and brothers remained ultimately responsible for their well-being.

FIRST WRITING AND EARLY TEXTS

The first recorded words of history were set down in the cities of Mesopotamia, and they promoted the power of the temples and kings in the expanding city-states. The people who controlled the production and distribution of goods used writing to enhance communication among large numbers of individuals and to keep track of the products of their realm. Oral communication and human memory had adequately served the needs of small-scale hunting and gathering and village farming communities, but they imposed limits on a society's scale and complexity. As people developed more specialized skills and roles, they had to communicate with other specialists and convey messages over longer distances. Writing facilitated transactions and information sharing across wider spans of distance and time.

We now take reading and writing for granted, but they emerged independently in only a few locations. Mesoamerica was one such area, and China, too, saw the autonomous development of literacy. What is certain is that at approximately the same time, Mesopotamians and Egyptians became the world's first record keepers and readers. The precursors to writing appeared in Mesopotamian societies when farming peoples and officials who had been employing clay tokens and images carved on stones to seal off storage areas began to use them to convey messages. Originally intended simply to identify those responsible for the vessels and storerooms where valuable commodities were held, these images, when combined with numbers also drawn on clay tablets, began to record the distribution of goods and services.

In a flash of human genius, someone, probably in Uruk, understood that the marks, usually pictures of objects, could also represent words and then distinct sounds. A representation that transfers meaning from the name of a thing to the sound of that name is called a *rebus*. For example, a picture of a bee can be used to represent the sound "b." Such pictures opened the door to writing: a technology of symbols that uses marks to record specific discrete sounds. Before long, scribes connected symbols with sounds, and sounds with meanings. As people combined rebus symbols with other ways to store meaning in visual marks, they became able to record and transmit messages over long distances by using

Primary Source

THE ORIGINS OF WRITING ACCORDING TO THE SUMERIANS

One Sumerian myth records the invention of writing by the Lord of Kullaba, Enmerkar, who sought to transmit complex messages across the vast distances to the Land of Aratta, where his rival for the love of the goddess Inanna lived. Messengers would memorize their responses and deliver them orally after an arduous journey across the mountains. Enmerkar felt he could not trust the memory of his messenger to deliver one particularly complicated response, and so he invented writing in the form of cuneiform script.

His speech was substantial, and its contents extensive. The messenger, whose mouth was heavy, was not able to repeat it. Because the messenger, whose mouth was tired, was not able to repeat it, the lord of Kulaba patted some clay and wrote the message as if on a tablet. Formerly, the writing of messages on clay was not established. Now, under that sun and on that day, it was indeed so. The lord of Kulaba inscribed the message like a tablet. It was just like that. The messenger was like a bird, flapping its wings; he raged forth like a wolf following a kid. He traversed five mountains, six mountains, seven mountains. He lifted his eyes as he approached Aratta. He stepped joyfully into the courtyard of Aratta, he made known the authority of his king. Openly he spoke out the words in his heart. The messenger transmitted the message to the lord of Aratta:

"Your father, my master, has sent me to you; the lord of Unug, the lord of Kulaba, has sent me to you." "What is it to me what your master has spoken? What is it to me what he has said?"

"This is what my master has spoken, this is what he has said. My king is like a huge *meš* tree, ... son of Enlil; this tree has grown high, uniting heaven and earth; its crown reaches heaven, its trunk is set upon the earth. He who is made to shine forth in lordship and kingship, Enmerkar, the son of Utu, has given me a clay tablet. O lord of Aratta, after you have examined the clay tablet, after you have learned the content of the message, say whatever you will say to me, and I shall announce that message in the shrine E-ana as glad tidings to the scion of him with the glistening beard, whom his stalwart cow gave birth to in the mountains of the shining *me,* who was reared on the soil of Aratta, who was given suck at the udder of the good cow, who is suited for office in Kulaba, the mountain of great *me,* to Enmerkar, the son of Utu; I shall repeat it in his *gipar,* fruitful as a flourishing *meš* tree, to my king, the lord of Kulaba."

After he had spoken thus to him, the lord of Aratta received his kiln-fired tablet from the messenger. The lord of Aratta looked at the tablet. The transmitted message was just nails, and his brow expressed anger. The lord of Aratta looked at his kiln-fired tablet. At that moment, the lord worthy of the crown of lordship, the son of Enlil, the god I_kur, thundering in heaven and earth, caused a raging storm, a great lion, in .... He was making the mountains quake ......, he was convulsing the mountain range ......; the awesome radiance ...... of his breast; he caused the mountain range to raise its voice in joy. (lines 500–551)

➔ *What aspects of Sumerian history are preserved and transmitted in the mythic story of the struggle between Enmerkar and the Lord of Aratta? "Enmerkar and the Lord of Aratta" is a text that was written down about 500 years later than the events that it describes. What other kinds of evidence do historians use to reconstruct the history of the early Sumerian period?*

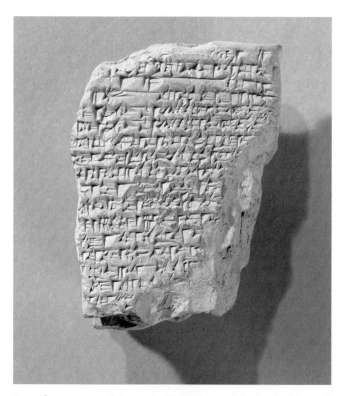

Cuneiform version of the myth "Enmerkar and the Lord of Aratta."

Source: J. A. Black, G. Cunningham, E. Fluckiger-Hawker, E. Robson, and G. Zólyomi, *The Electronic Text Corpus of Sumerian Literature* (Oxford, 1998–2006), www-etcsl.orient.ox.ac.uk/. Italics signify Akkadian glosses.

Early Uruk Writing. The earliest tablets found at the site of Uruk were first impressed with cylinder seals and subsequently with wedge-shaped signs. Appearing around 3200 BCE, these earliest tablets are no more than aids to memory, recording, for example, quantities of goods transferred to workers. It is not until six hundred years later that the cuneiform script is developed enough to record complete sentences that would be read by everyone in the same way.

abstract symbols or signs to denote concepts; such signs later came to represent syllables, which could be joined into words.

From the beginning, scribes occupied a special place in Mesopotamian societies. By impressing these signs into wet clay with the cut end of a reed, the scribes engaged in a form of wedge-shaped writing that we call *cuneiform*; it could be used to fill clay tablets with information. What looked like gibberish to someone who was illiterate was actually intelligible to anyone who could decipher it—even those in faraway locations or in future generations. This Sumerian innovation powerfully enhanced the ability of urban elites to produce and trade goods, to control property, and to transmit ideas of society through literature, historical records, and sacred texts. Once again, the human experience had changed fundamentally, this time because human communication and memory were extended by being stored in the symbols of natural spoken language.

By taking these gradual steps, Mesopotamians opened the door into the world of literacy. The cuneiform script was exceedingly complicated, using a large set of signs that only a very small proportion of the population was trained to decipher. Therefore literacy, though a fundamental part of the

civilizing process in cities, was a skill mastered by only a tiny but influential scribal elite.

Much of what we know about Mesopotamia rests on our ability to decipher cuneiform script. Writing that employed the rebus first appeared sometime around 3200 BCE, but not until about 700 years later could the script record spoken utterances completely. By around 2400 BCE, texts began to describe the political makeup of southern Mesopotamia, giving details of its history as well as its economy. At that time, the land of Sumer in the southern floodplain consisted of at least a dozen city-states. Northern cities also borrowed the cuneiform script to record economic transactions and political events, but in their own Semitic tongue. Cuneiform's adaptability to different languages is one of the main reasons its use spread so widely. As city life and literacy expanded, they gave rise to more than documents; they also spawned the first written narratives, the stories of a "people" and their origins.

One famous set of texts written down around 2100 BCE, "The Temple Hymns," describes the thirty-five major divine sanctuaries on the southern plain. The magnificent Sumerian King List is among the texts that recount the making of political dynasties and depict great periodic floods. Written down around 2000 BCE, it organizes the reigns of kings by dynasty, one city at a time. The Sumerian King List also refers to the Great Flood, which is just one of many traditional Mesopotamian stories that were transmitted orally from one generation to another before being recorded (this story was borrowed and incorporated into the book of Genesis as part of the traditional creation story of the Bible). The Great Flood, a crucial event in Sumerian memory and identity, explained Uruk's demise as the gods' doing. Flooding was the most riveting of natural forces in the lives of a riverine folk, and it helped shape the material and symbolic foundations of Mesopotamian societies—societies whose breakthroughs were a consequence of tapping the waters of massive rivers.

SPREADING CITIES AND FIRST TERRITORIAL STATES

Although no single state dominated the history of fourth and third millennium BCE Mesopotamia, a few stand out. Easily the most powerful, influential, and fully studied were the Sumerian city-states of the Early Dynastic Age (2850–2334 BCE) and their successor, the Akkadian territorial state (2334–2193 BCE), which was founded by the warrior king Sargon of Akkad (r. 2334–2279 BCE).

While the city-states of southern Mesopotamia flourished and competed, giving rise to the land of Sumer, the rich agricultural zones to the north inhabited by the Hurrians also became urbanized. (See Map 2-3.) Northern urbanization, beginning around 2600 BCE, was rapid and soon yielded cities comparable in size to those in the south, including ancient

→ *What role did cities play in Mesopotamian society?*

Nagar and Urkesh. In western Syria, ancient Ebla (modern Tell Mardikh) was the center of another Semitic-speaking city-state. Though their inhabitants were culturally related to the Sumerians and Akkadians of the alluvium, the northern cities had economic, political, and social organizations that were distinct and independent.

It was their very success that eventually destabilized the balanced world of the early Sumerian city-states. Southern Mesopotamia contained many cities with burgeoning populations that were vying for access to agrarian lands, to increasingly scarce water, and to lucrative trade routes. As the region's bounty became known to pastoralists far and wide, they journeyed in greater numbers to Mesopotamian cities, fueling urbanization and competition. Thus, as cities grew up, they also became important crossroads.

The world's first great conqueror emerged from one of these cities. By the end of his long reign, he had successfully united the independent Mesopotamian

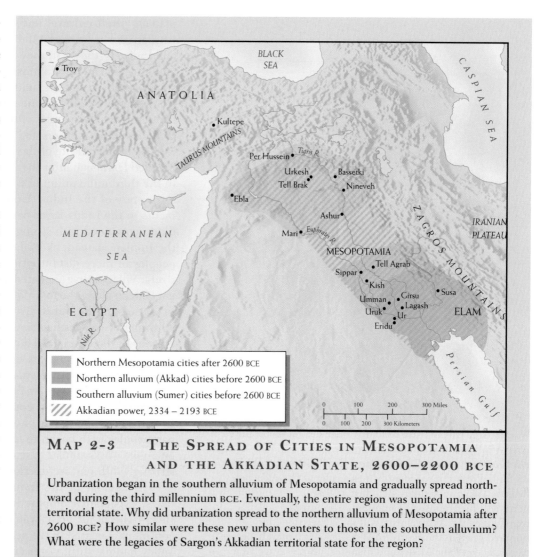

MAP 2-3   THE SPREAD OF CITIES IN MESOPOTAMIA AND THE AKKADIAN STATE, 2600–2200 BCE

Urbanization began in the southern alluvium of Mesopotamia and gradually spread northward during the third millennium BCE. Eventually, the entire region was united under one territorial state. Why did urbanization spread to the northern alluvium of Mesopotamia after 2600 BCE? How similar were these new urban centers to those in the southern alluvium? What were the legacies of Sargon's Akkadian territorial state for the region?

Map legend:
- Northern Mesopotamia cities after 2600 BCE
- Northern alluvium (Akkad) cities before 2600 BCE
- Southern alluvium (Sumer) cities before 2600 BCE
- Akkadian power, 2334 – 2193 BCE

cities south of modern Baghdad by force. The legendary Sargon the Great, king of Akkad, a city-state close to modern Baghdad, brought the era of increasingly competitive independent city-states to an end. Remembered for two millennia as a conqueror, Sargon was a ruler whose remarkable achievement was not simply to dominate the southern lands but to unify their cities, forging a single political, economic, and cultural alliance in a land called Agade or Akkad. Although the unity forged by Sargon lasted only three generations, he established the first multiethnic collection of urban centers—the territorial state—capable of combining the northern and southern parts of the alluvium, thus laying the foundations for the integration of the territorial states that we describe in Chapter 3.

The most obvious legacy of the dynasty established by Sargon was sponsorship of monumental architecture, artworks, and literary works. These cultural achievements

stood for centuries and were copied by many generations of builders, architects, artists, and scribes. And by encouraging contact with distant neighbors, many of whom incorporated various aspects of Mesopotamian culture into their own distinct traditions, the Akkadian kings also increased the geographic reach of Mesopotamian influence. Although his historical reputation has endured, Sargon's "empire" was short-lived. Foreign tribesmen who came out of the Zagros Mountains to the east of the Tigris River infiltrated the heartland of Akkad, conquering the capital city around 2190 BCE. As legend has it, these "barbarians" wreaked havoc on "civilization," but we will see that this interpretation was promoted by the conquered and may not have reflected the reality of the conquest (see Chapter 3). Nonetheless, this cycle of urban magnificence, punctuated by nomadic destruction, would become the stuff of epic history writing—and it continues to captivate readers to the

Naram Sin. This life-size head of a ruler cast of almost pure copper was found at Nineveh in northern Iraq in the destruction levels of the Assyrian Empire. The style and imagery of this sculptural masterpiece identify it as a ruler of Old Akkadian dynasty. While sometimes identified as Sargon, it is most likely a portrait of his grandson, Naram Sin, who consolidated and transformed the Akkadian state. It must have stood for over fifteen hundred years in the courtyard of a temple at Nineveh, before it was defaced by the Medes and Elamites, whose savage attack on Nineveh cause the Assyrian Empire to fall.

present, even while creating a myth of urban civility and rural backwardness.

INDUS VALLEY: A PARALLEL CULTURE

> → *Why do we know less about Harappan culture than about others in Afro-Eurasia?*

Mesopotamian developments had spillover effects across much of Eurasia. As an outward-looking people, Mesopotamians depended on trade for many of their most basic needs. Mesopotamian commercial trails reached across the Iranian

plateau (Jiroft culture) and beyond what is now called the Khyber Pass as far as the Indus River in present-day Pakistan and India. To the west, they reached the Mediterranean Sea and entered the floodplains of the Nile. Riverine settings, such as the Nile and the Indus rivers, produced parallel flourishing states. While in some ways influenced by Mesopotamian examples, the peoples of the Nile and Indus created their own distinctive cultures and societies.

The urban culture of the Indus and the surrounding area is called Harappan after the urban site of Harappa that arose in the third millennium BCE on the banks of the Ravi River, a tributary of the Indus. Unlike in Mesopotamia, developments in the Indus River basin reflected an indigenous tradition combined with strong influences from the peoples of the Iranian plateau, as well as indirect influences from the peoples of more distant cities on the Tigris and Euphrates rivers. Villages first appeared around 5000 BCE on the Iranian plateau along the foothills of the Baluchistan Mountains, to the west of the Indus. By the early third millennium BCE, a frontier of villages had spread from these mountains in an eastwardly direction until it reached the fertile alluvial banks of the Indus River and its numerous tributaries. (See Map 2-4.) The riverine settlements soon yielded agrarian surpluses that supported greater wealth, more trade with neighbors, and more surpluses that could be devoted to public works. In due course, urbanites of the Indus region and the Harappan peoples both began to fortify their cities and to embark on public works similar in scale to those in Mesopotamia, but strikingly different in function.

The ecology of the Indus Valley boasted many advantages, especially compared to the area near the Ganges River—the other great waterway of the South Asian subcontinent. Located in the semi-tropical latitudes, the Indus Valley had plentiful water coming from the Himalayas that ensured flourishing vegetation without suffering the torrential monsoon downpours that caused heavy flooding every year on the Ganges plain. The expansion of agriculture in this basin, like those in Mesopotamia, Egypt, and China, depended on the river's annual floods. Here the river provided the land with predictable amounts of water, drawn from the melting snow on the Himalayas and beyond, that replenished the soil and averted droughts. From June to September, the rivers inundated the plain. Once the waters receded, farmers planted wheat and barley on fertile soft alluvium. They harvested the crops the next spring as temperatures rose. And as they took advantage of the fertility created by the river, the villagers on the banks of the Indus also improved their tools of cultivation. Researchers have found evidence of furrows, probably made by plowing, that they have dated to around 2600 BCE. Farmers were soon able to achieve harvests like those of Mesopotamia—yielding a surplus that freed many of the inhabitants from having to produce food and thus allowed them to specialize in other activities.

In time, rural wealth produced urban splendor. More abundant harvests, now stored in large granaries, brought migrants into the area and supported ever-growing populations. By 2500 BCE, cities began to take the place of villages throughout the Indus River valley, and within a few generations towering granaries became prominent features of the urban skyline. Harappa and Mohenjo Daro, the two largest cities, each covered an area about 250 acres (a little less than half a square mile) and probably housed 35,000 residents. As in Mesopotamia, such population densities were unprecedented departures from the common dispersal of peoples into self-sufficient agrarian hamlets, villages, or nomadic communities.

The floodplain over which Harappan cities sprawled was vast, totaling an area of 500,000 square miles—two or three times the area covered by the Mesopotamian cultural zone.

At the height of their development, the Harappan peoples reached the edge of the Indus ecological system and came into contact with the cultures of the northern part of Afghanistan, as well as with the inhabitants of the infertile desert frontier, the nomadic hunter-gatherers to the east, and western traders.

HARAPPAN CITY LIFE

We know less about Harappan culture than about the other cultures of Afro-Eurasia of a comparable age. Many of its remains are buried today under a water table raised through years of heavy flooding and accumulated silt deposits. To complicate matters further, scholars have thus far been unable to identify the spoken language of the Indus peoples, who devised a script of about 400 symbols. Indeed, it is unclear if the script even represents a spoken language: it may instead be a nonlinguistic symbol system. Most of what remains of the Indus script is carried on some thousand or more stamp seals and small plaques, excavated from the region; these may represent the names and titles of individuals rather than complete sentences. Moreover, because the Harappans did not produce King Lists, as did the Mesopotamians and the Egyptians—and may not even have had kings— scholars are unable to chart a political history by tracing the rise and fall of dynasties and kingdoms.

What we know about Harappa is therefore not based on literary accounts. It is pieced together from archaeological reconstructions, and it is inevitably and disappointingly sketchy. The sketchiness reminds us that "history" is not what happened but only what we know about what happened. Unable to read documents from the Harappan period

MAP 2-4 THE INDUS RIVER VALLEY IN THE THIRD MILLENNIUM BCE

Historians know less about the urban society of the Indus Valley in the third millennium BCE than they do about its contemporaries in Mesopotamia and Egypt. Still, archaeological evidence affords insight into this urban complex. Where were cities concentrated in the Indus Valley? How did the environment of the region shape urban development? What functions do you think outposts such as Lothal played in Harappan society?

THE MYSTERY OF HARAPPAN WRITING

Harappa culture in the Indus Valley is one urban culture of the third millennium BCE whose writing system has not yet been deciphered. The Indus script appeared on seals and tablets, and in Dholavira, a recently discovered site, even on a board for public display. Though no one can read the script, and no one is sure which language it represents, certain of its characteristics provide scholars with fuel for speculation.

As for verbal communication through writing, it needs to be understood that no one has as yet succeeded in deciphering the Harappan script and that this will remain an unlikely eventuality unless a bilingual inscription—in Harappan and a known form of writing—is found, that incorporates the names of people or places. The Harappan script is logographic: there are 375 to 400 signs, which rules out an alphabet (where one sign stands for one vowel or consonant) because alphabets usually have no more than thirty-six signs. Often Harappan bangles or metal tools are inscribed with just one sign. Harappan writing goes from right to left, as can be made out from close examination of overlapping signs scratched on pots. Short strokes indicate numbers, and numerals precede other signs, which could mean that in the Harappan language adjectives preceded the nouns they qualified. Certain signs, computer concordances reveal, tend to occur frequently at the end of inscriptions, which points to a language using a set of phonetic suffixes.

The Harappan language was probably agglutinative, or a language which added suffixes to an unchanging root. This feature is characteristic of the Dravidian language family rather than the Indo-Aryan languages. This, and the fact that the earliest Indo-Aryan text, the *Rigveda*, shows Dravidian influence (indicating that the early Indo-Aryans in the northwest had some contact with Dravidian speakers), make it likely that the language of the Harappans was a Dravidian one. (Note, also, that Brahui, spoken in the hills of southern Baluchistan today, is a Dravidian language.)

The inscriptions on the seals being brief, on average five to six signs long, they probably gave little more than the owner's name and designation. Perhaps it was the pictorial (often solo animal) emblem, rendered with great skill, that indicated the lineage, ancestry or social origins of the owner. There is no geographic pattern to the occurrence of the various seal animals (unicorn, bull, rhinoceros, antelope, tiger or elephant), so the animal could not possibly have signified the place of origin of the seal owner. Perhaps it was this pictorial image that lent authority to any spoken message that accompanied a seal or an object stamped with one. It may be noted that so far it

is Harappa and Mohenjo-daro—and mound E rather than the 'citadel mound' AB at Harappa—that have yielded the evidence for the most intensive writing activity. These were probably centres of administration.

Harappan writing occurs on pots, seals, bullae, terracotta (stoneware) and shell bangles, copper tablets and tools, and ivory rods. Large numbers of scored goblets with pointed bases that occur at Harappa and Mohenjo-daro are important as they are one of the very few pottery forms that can occasionally carry seal impressions (as distinct from scratched signs)—their use remains a mystery. We get the impression that writing was for humdrum purposes. A striking exception to this is the occurrence of a huge "public" inscription that seems to have been set up on a street at Dholavira in Kutch, with letters about thirty-seven centimetres high cut out of stones and, R. S. Bisht suggests, fastened on a wooden board.

The most important point, however, is the enormous intellectual advance that the emergence of writing signifies. When we speak we utter sounds in one or other language using a series of sound sequences that carry specific meanings in that language. What writing does is to encode in visual form, that is, through a set of distinct symbols or signs, those sounds and sound sequences—thereby conveying meaning or information. Further, writing makes possible the storage of information or the maintenance of records for future reference. It makes communication at a distance possible. It requires of the writer knowledge of the signs and some amount of manual dexterity, and of the reader, knowledge of how the visual signs are vocalized and of course familiarity with the relevant language. Writing has been termed the most momentous invention human beings have ever made.

→ *Even though we cannot read Harappan script, why is the knowledge that the Harappans wrote in script important? Judging from the information above about Harappan writing, what language do you think the script most likely represents?*

SOURCE: Shereen Ratnagar, *Understanding Harappa Civilization in the Greater Indus Valley* (New Delhi: Tulika, 2002), pp. 60–61.

Mohenjo Daro. Mohenjo Daro, the "mound of dead," is a large urban site of the Harappan culture. The view of the city demonstrates a neat layout of houses and civic facilities such as sewer draining.

and forced to rely on fragmentary archaeological evidence, scholars have been unable to draw the rich portraits of the Harappan way of life that they have supplied for the Mesopotamians and the Egyptians.

Still, what we know is impressive. The layout of Harappan cities and towns followed the same general pattern. A fortified citadel housed public facilities, alongside which was located a larger residential area. Both the citadels and the residential areas of Harappan cities were well planned. The main street cut through the city and had covered drainage on both sides. Because the house gates and doors opened onto back alleys, the main street, flanked by blank walls of houses, probably looked rather dull. Citadels were most likely centers of political and ritual activities. At the center of the citadel of Mohenjo Daro was the famous great bath, a brick structure that was 39.3 feet by 23 feet and 9.8 feet deep. Flights of steps led to the bottom of the bath, while other stairs went up to a level of rooms surrounding it. The bath was well sealed with mortar and bitumen, and its water was supplied by a large well nearby. The water then drained through a channel leading from one corner of the bath to lower land to the west of the small mound where the bath was located. The location, size, and quality of the structures all suggest that the bath served ritual purposes.

The Harappans used brick extensively. Houses for notables, the city walls, and underground water drainage systems were all built of bricks manufactured in large ovens, where they were baked into tough, durable, but costly construction materials, made and laid so skillfully that basic structures remain intact to this day. A well-built house had private bath-rooms, showers, and toilets that drained into durable municipal sewers—also made of bricks. Less durable, and less costly, sun-baked bricks, a ubiquitous building material throughout the southern stretches of Eurasia even today, were employed in constructing houses in small towns and villages.

TRADE

The Harappans engaged in trade along the Indus River and through the mountain passes to the Iranian plateau, as well as along the coast of the Arabian Sea as far as the Persian Gulf and Mesopotamia. They traded such resources as copper, flint, shells, and ivory, as well as pottery, flint blades, and jewelry created by their craftworkers, for gold, silver, gemstones, and textiles from afar. Some of the Harappan trading towns were located in remote but strategically important places. Lothal, a well-fortified town at the head of the Gulf of Khambhat (Cambay), was distant from the center of the Harappan society. Yet it was a vital port, providing access to the sea and to valuable raw materials. Its many workshops processed precious stones, both those available locally and those brought in by traders—especially carnelian, a red stone. The demand for these gemstones was high on the Iranian plateau and even higher in Mesopotamia, and Harappans knew that controlling their extraction and trade was essential to maintaining economic power. Carnelian was found nearby, but lapis lazuli had to be imported from what is now northern Afghanistan, and the Harappans built fortifications and settlements near its sources. Extending their

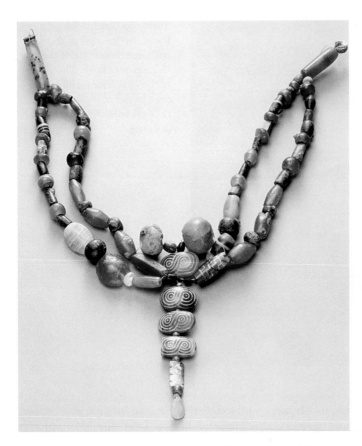

Harappan Gemstone Necklace. Beadmakers perforated lapis lazuli and other semi-precious stones using a bow drill to make tiny holes for suspension.

frontier to control resources did not stop at gemstones. Metals such as copper and silver also had strategic importance in the Afro-Eurasian commercial systems, and Harappans set up settlements near their copper mines.

Through a complex and vibrant trading system, the Harappans maintained access to mineral and agrarian resources. To facilitate trade across the Indus riverine area, rulers relied not just on Harappan script but on a system of weights and measures that they devised and standardized. Harappan seals, used to stamp commodities with the names of their owners or the nature of the goods, have been found in archaeological sites as far away as the Persian Gulf, Mesopotamia, and the Iranian plateau (see "Global Connections & Disconnections").

The high degree of uniformity in Harappan sites suggests a centralized and structured state. Unlike the Mesopotamians, however, the Harappans seem to have built neither palaces nor grand royal tombs, nor even impressive monumental structures of any kind. Unlike the Egyptians and Mesopotamians, the Harappan elites expressed their elaborate urban culture in ways that did not loudly proclaim their high standing in the world. The Harappans were as reticent as the Egyptians and Mesopotamians were boastful. This

quality has puzzled scholars, but it clearly underscores the profound differences in ancient societies: they did not all value the same things. The advent of writing, urban culture, long-distance trade, and large cities did not necessarily produce the same social hierarchies and the same ethos. What the people of the Indus River show us is how much even the urbanized parts of the world were diverging from each other, even as they borrowed from and imitated their neighbors.

THE GIFT OF THE NILE: EGYPT (5000–2000 BCE)

> → *How did the Nile River shape the development of early Egyptian society?*

The earliest inhabitants along the banks of the Nile River, where another of the great founding riverine cultures of the third millennium BCE arose, were a mixed people. Some had migrated from the eastern and western deserts in Sinai and

Harappan Seal Stamps. The stamp seals of the Indus Valley culture are distinctive. Cut from the soft stone steatite and fired to a white color to make them hard, they have a rounded boss pierced for suspension on the back. The images carved on their surface are usually animals: elephants, tigers, bulls. Occasionally human figures, perhaps deities, perhaps rulers, are depicted seated on a platform, or dancing, or surrounded by animals. Many of the stamp seals have inscriptions across the top edge. The script of the Harappan people has not been deciphered, nor has its underlying language been identified.

Libya as these areas became nearly barren. Still others came from the Mediterranean, but equally important were the peoples who trekked northward from Nubia and central Africa. Ancient Egypt was a melting pot, where early immigrants to the river basin blended cultural practices and technologies from southwestern Asia, northern Africa, the Mediterranean basin, and central Africa.

Egypt had much in common with Mesopotamia and the Indus Valley. Like them, it had densely populated areas whose inhabitants depended on irrigation for their economic well-being, employed monumental architecture, endowed their rulers with immense authority, and created a social order of great complexity. Tapping the Nile water gave rise to agrarian wealth, commercial and devotional centers, early states, and new techniques of communication.

Yet the ancient Egyptian culture was profoundly distinct from its contemporaries in Mesopotamia and the Indus Valley. To understand its unique qualities, we must begin with Egypt's geography. The country and its inhabitants were, and continue to be, dominated by the environment and the natural boundaries of deserts and river rapids and the sea. What is today the Arab Republic of Egypt, roughly the core area of the ancient Egyptians, consists of 386,560 square miles, of which only 7.5 million acres (11,720 square miles) are cultivable. And of this total, no fewer than 6 million acres are located in the Nile delta, that vast agriculturally rich alluvial land that lies between the two main branches of the Nile River as it flows north of Cairo into the Mediterranean Sea.

THE NILE RIVER AND ITS FLOODWATERS

Because knowing Egypt requires appreciating the pulses of the Nile, we must turn first to this extraordinary body of water, the world's longest river, which stretches 4,238 miles from its sources in the highlands of central Africa to its ultimate destination in the Mediterranean Sea. In this way and many others Egypt was, and remains to this day, deeply attached to sub-Saharan Africa. Not only did its life-giving irrigation waters and its rich silt come from African highlands, but much of its population originally migrated into the valley of the Nile from the south.

The Upper Nile is a sluggish river that cuts deeply through a merciless desert. Rising out of central Africa and Ethiopia, the two main branches of the Nile—the White and Blue Niles—join together at the present-day capital city of the Sudan, Khartoum, and then scour out a single riverbed 1,500 miles long to the river's outlet on the Mediterranean. The floods were annual, which gave the basin a regular injection of moisture and alluvial richness. But when the waters spilled over the banks, they did not fertilize or irrigate fields as broad as those in Mesopotamia or Harappa. Floodwaters created something more closely resembling green belts flank-

ing the thick brown waterway. The result was a society whose highly coherent culture stretched out along the navigable axis of the river and its carefully preserved banks. Further away from the banks of the river, on both sides, lay a desert, rich in raw materials but largely uninhabitable. Egypt had no vast fertile hinterland like the sprawling plains of Mesopotamia and the Indus Valley. In a sense, Egypt was the most "riverine" of the riverine cultures.

The predictability of the Nile as the source of life and abundance fundamentally shaped the character of ancient Egypt. In contrast to the wild and uncertain Euphrates and Tigris rivers, whose floods often brought great destruction, the Nile was gentle and bountiful, leading Egyptians to view the world as beneficent. The White Nile, rising in the heart of Africa and traversing the great lakes of central Africa, including Lake Nyanza, yielded Egypt a steady stream of water, varying little from one season to the next or one year to the next. The same was not true of the Blue Nile, which rose in the highlands of Ethiopia and was fed by the monsoon rains of East Africa and by melting snows. The Blue Nile provided Egypt's floodwaters, while the White Nile ensured that these would be predictable and relatively easy to regulate.

Once the Egyptians began to occupy the Nile River valley, they devised a simple but highly effective system for turning the Nile floodwaters to their advantage and rendering the area one of the most fertile spots in the world. During the summer months, as the Nile swelled, local villagers, unsupervised by any central administration, built earthen walls

Nile Agriculture. The Nile is fed by the Blue Nile, which has its source in the Ethiopian highlands, and the White Nile in southern Sudan. It rises and falls according to a regular pattern that was the basis for the ancient Egyptian agricultural cycle. Flooding the valley in August and September, the Nile recedes, depositing a rich layer of silt in which the crops were planted in the fall and harvested in April and May.

that carved the floodplain into basins. As the flood spilled over the banks the waters were trapped in the basins, where they deposited the rich silt of the Ethiopian highlands. The waters stood in the flood basins long enough to provide silt for the growing season; then the earthen dams were breached, allowing the water to drain into adjacent basins and eventually back into the river. Annual flooding meant that each year the land received a new layer of rich topsoil.

The light fertile soils made planting simple. Peasants cast seeds into the ooze and then had their livestock trample them to the proper depth. The never-failing sun, which the Egyptians worshipped, ensured that the fields would yield an abundant harvest as long as they were properly weeded. In the early spring, when the Nile waters were at their lowest and no crops were being grown, the sun dried out the soil, allowing it to shed the harmful salts that ultimately destroyed the fertility of southern Mesopotamia.

The contrasts with Mesopotamia are clear: large-scale hydraulic engineering was not required to domesticate the Nile. Because villagers and households could create and maintain the basic waterworks, the Egyptian state played no essential role in controlling the Nile flood. This is not to say that Egyptians had no need of public infrastructure provided by the state. Accordingly, the state built vast storehouses to hold grain for the next growing season.

EGYPT'S UNIQUE RIVERINE CULTURE

The peculiarities of the Nile region had effects that distinguished it from Mesopotamia and the Indus Valley. Some 2,500 years ago, the Greek historian and geographer Herodotus famously observed that Egypt was the gift of the Nile. He also noted that the Nile basin—from its first cataract (a rough river rapid), south of Aswan, to the sea—was one of the world's most self-contained geographical entities. Bounded on the north by the Mediterranean Sea, on the east and west by harsh deserts, and on the south by cataracts, Egypt was destined from its earliest days to achieve a sense of common destiny. It was a region far less open to outsiders than were Mesopotamia and the Indus River basin.

Reinforcing a sense of separation from the outside was the region's bounty: nearly all of the natural resources that the ancient Egyptians needed were available locally. In the desolate landscapes of the western and eastern deserts were abundant sources of copper, silver, lead, and other metals, as well as colorful stones like turquoise. Gold, exotic woods, plants, animals, and extra manpower were available to the south in Nubia and were transported along the Nile River in vessels with sails and oars. This was a far cry from the resource-poor alluvium of Mesopotamia, which from the fourth millennium BCE onward required copper, timber, and stones to be imported from the surrounding plateaus and mountain regions.

Yet, like the other pioneering societies, Egypt created a common culture by balancing regional tensions and reconciling regional rivalries. Ancient Egyptian history can be told as a struggle of sharply competing dualistic forces: the north or Lower Egypt versus the south or Upper Egypt; the sand, the so-called red part of the earth, versus the rich soil, described as black; life versus death; heaven versus earth; and order versus disorder. For Egypt's ruling groups—most notably the kings, known as pharaohs, at the apex of the political system—the primary task was to bring stability or order, referred to as *ma'at*, out of these antagonistic impulses. The Egyptians believed that keeping chaos, personified by the desert and its marauders, at bay through vigilant attention to *ma'at* was what allowed all that was good and right to occur.

THE RISE OF THE STATE AND DYNASTIES

Once the Nile was harnessed to agriculture, Egypt quickly developed from a scarcely inhabited area to a complex society. Whereas the pace of development in Mesopotamia and Harappa was gradual and cumulative, Egypt grew seemingly overnight; it changed from being only a few small village communities into a powerhouse, projecting its splendor along the full length of the river valley.

The king's primary responsibility was to ensure that the fundamental forces of nature, in particular the regular flooding of the Nile, continued without interruption. In addition, the king had to protect his people from the invaders of the eastern desert, as well as from the Nubians who pressed against Egypt's southern borders. These groups threatened Egypt with intolerable social chaos. As guarantors of the social and political order, the early kings depicted themselves as shepherds. In wall carvings, artists portrayed them carrying the crook and the flail, indicating their responsibility for the welfare of their flocks (the people) and of the land. Moreover, under the king, an elaborate bureaucracy organized labor and produced public works, sustaining both his vast holdings and general order throughout the realm.

The narrative of ancient Egyptian history has been organized around its dynasties—a structure that gives Egyptian history a sense of deep continuity. According to a third-century BCE Egyptian cleric named Manetho, Egypt was ruled by no fewer than thirty-one dynasties, stretching out over nearly three millennia from 3100 BCE down to its conquest by Alexander the Great in 332 BCE. Since the nineteenth century, however, scholars have found it easier to group the dynasties and recast the story of ancient Egypt around three great periods of dynastic achievement: the Old Kingdom (dynasty III or IV to dynasty VI, from 2649 to 2152 BCE); the Middle Kingdom (dynasties XI to XIII, from 2040 to 1640 BCE), and the New Kingdom (dynasties XVIII to XXI, from 1550 to 1070 BCE). At the end of each of these eras, cultural flourishing was interrupted by a breakdown in central authority, known respectively as the First, Second, and Third Intermediate Periods. But no other region of the world has charted its history across a continuum of such extraordinary length and durability.

RITUALS, PYRAMIDS, AND TRUE ORDER

The Third Dynasty (2649–2575 BCE) launched the long foundational period of ancient Egyptian culture known as the Old Kingdom, the golden age of ancient Egypt. (See Map 2-5.) By the time it began, the basic institutions of the Egyptian state were in place, and the ideology and ritual life that gave legitimacy to dynastic rulers were fully integrated into the region's culture.

The king as god presented himself to the population by means of impressive architectural spaces. The priestly class performed rituals that reinforced his supreme status within the natural order of the universe. The most important royal ceremony, especially in the Old Kingdom, was the Sed festival, which renewed the vitality of the king after he had ruled for thirty years (sometimes fewer). Although it focused on the vitality of the king, its origins lay in ritually ensuring the perpetual presence of water.

King Djoser (r. 2630–2611 BCE), the second king of the Third Dynasty, celebrated the Sed festival in his tomb complex at Saqqara. This magnificent monumental complex, the world's oldest stone edifice (rather than the mud brick of the temples and palaces of Mesopotamia), was

MAP 2-5   OLD KINGDOM EGYPT, 2686–2181 BCE

Old Kingdom Egyptian society was strongly influenced by its unique geographical location. How does this map offer insight into early Egyptians' view of their place in the world? Compare this map with Map 2-2. Why do you think Old Kingdom Egyptians had less contact with other societies than did their counterparts in Mesopotamia?

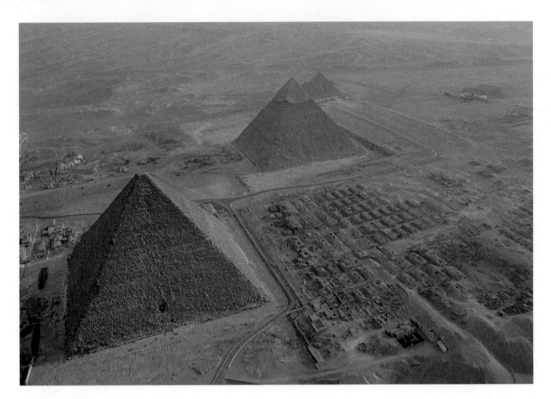

The Pyramids of Giza. The Pyramid Fields of Giza lie on the western side of the Nile just south of the modern city of Cairo. The Old Kingdom Pharaohs built their eternal resting places there, surrounded by the smaller pyramids and mastaba tombs of their relatives and courtiers. The largest pyramid of Khufu is to the north. Khephren's is linked to the Nile by a causeway flanked by the famous Sphinx. The smallest is that of Menkaure, the penultimate king of the glorious Fourth Dynasty.

built during his reign. It began as a huge flat structure—a *mastaba,* which means "bench" in Arabic—identical to earlier royal tombs. Remarkably, we know the name of the architect of Djoser's funerary complex: Imhotep, who was himself deified and became a mythic hero of Egyptian lore. Imhotep was not satisfied with the modest shape of earlier burial chambers. Through the course of six separate renovations, he transformed the *mastaba* into a step pyramid that in its final form rose some 200 feet above the plain, dominating the landscape as did the later Mesopotamian ziggurats. This mountainlike structure stood at the center of an enormous walled precinct that had five individual courts in which the king performed various rituals that emphasized the divinity of kingship and the unity of Upper and Lower Egypt. Because most of the structures were facades, the whole complex resembled a stage on which state rituals were performed. The symbolism of the unity of Upper and Lower Egypt was pervasive, embodied in the entwined lotus and papyrus—symbols of each region. The step pyramid complex incorporated the artistic and architectural forms that would characterize Egyptian culture for millennia.

The Egyptian pharaoh—the king as god—used the royal tomb to embody the state's ideology and the fundamental ideas of the Egyptian cosmos. The ritual of death, leading to everlasting life, became part of the cultural myth. So, too, did a common ideology that stressed the underlying unity of the distinct regions of the long river valley. The pharaoh also used symbols (for example, the dual crown representing Upper and Lower Egypt), throne names, and many descriptive titles for himself and his advisers to represent his power and that of his

administrators, the priests, and the landed elite. The Egyptian cosmic order was from the beginning one of inequality and stark hierarchy. Established at the time of creation, the universe was the king's responsibility to maintain for eternity. The insistence, in Egypt and elsewhere, that the king was a god, or was like a god, has often been misunderstood as exalting the power of the king. In fact, the belief that the king was a god compelled the ruler to behave like one. And therefore, like a god, he had to be serene, orderly, merciful, and perfect. An expression of divine peace (not the angry snarl of mere human power) had always to be on his lips.

Pyramid building evolved rapidly from the step version of Djoser to the grand pyramids put up in the Fourth Dynasty (2575–2465 BCE). The Fourth Dynasty kings erected their magnificent structures at Giza, just outside modern-day Cairo and not far from the early royal cemetery site of Saqqara. The pyramid of Khufu is the largest stone structure in the world, and it was built to almost perfectly exact measurements.

Khephren's pyramid, though smaller, is even more alluring because of the protective presence of the famous recumbent sphinx. These royal tombs were surrounded on all sides by the tombs of the high officials, almost all of whom were members of the royal family. The amount of labor involved in constructing these monuments was enormous and provides another measure of the degree of centralization and the large surpluses that existed in Egyptian society at this time. The manpower was drawn from the peasants and workers who were obliged to work for the state at certain times of the year. Their numbers were augmented by slaves brought from Nubia, as well as by captured peoples from the Mediterranean.

RELIGION OF ANCIENT EGYPT

Religion stood at the center of this ancient world. All aspects of the culture of the ancient Egyptians were suffused with spiritual expression. Egyptians understood the world in which they lived to be inhabited by three groups: gods, kings, and the rest of humanity. Official records, especially pictorial but also written texts, exclusively bore representations of gods and kings. Yet rarely were kings confused with gods—at least during their lifetimes. Mortality was the bar between rulers and deities; after death, kings joined the gods whom they had represented while alive.

As in Mesopotamia, every region in Egypt had its resident god. The fate of each deity was mirrored in the history of its region. Some gods, such as Amun, who was believed to reside and be physically present in Thebes, transcended regional status because of the importance of their hometown. Over the centuries, the Egyptian gods evolved, combining often contradictory aspects into single deities who were represented by symbols: animals and human figures that often had animal as well as divine attributes. They included Horus, the hawk god; Osiris, the god of regeneration and the underworld; Hathor, the goddess of childbirth and love; Ra, the sun god; and Amun, a creator who was considered the hidden god.

Official religious practices took place in the main temples, the heart of ceremonial and festive practices. The king and his agents cared for the gods in their temples, giving them respect, adoration, and thanks. In return, the gods, who were embodied in sculptured images, maintained order and gave sustenance to the king and through him all humanity. In this contractual relationship between the gods and humans, gods were invariably passive and serene while the kings were active, a difference that reflected the inherent inequality in their relationship. The practice of religious rituals and communication with the gods formed the cult, whose goal was to preserve cosmic order—and achieving that goal required constant exertion on the part of human worshippers.

The task of upholding the cult, regulating yearly rituals according to a cosmic calendar, and mediating between gods, kings, and the rest of society fell to one specialist class: the priesthood. In the Egyptian order of things, the priesthood was more important than a cadre of tax collectors. Creating a priesthood required elaborate rules for selecting and training the priests to project the organized power of spiritual authority. And as was true of all Egyptian society, that organization was highly stratified. That the priests alone could enter the inner sanctum of the temple drove home their exceptional and exalted status. The god, embodied in the cult statue, left the temple only on the occasion of great festivals. Even then the divine image remained hidden in a portable shrine, out of sight of the general populace. This arrangement ensured that priests monopolized the channels of communication between spiritual powers and their subjects—and thereby made certain that Egyptians understood and embraced their subservience to the priesthood.

While the priesthood helped integrate Egyptians into one unified realm and focused the attention of all subjects on the central role of temple life, the priests coexisted with less visible local protectors of the divine order. Unofficial, popular religion was equally important in the cosmic system. Ordinary people in ancient Egypt matched their elite rulers in faithfulness to the gods. But their distance from temple life required that they fulfill their religious needs and duties in different ways. Common Egyptian people frequented the many scattered local shrines, just as those of higher status visited the temples. There they prayed, made requests, and left offerings to the gods.

Magic held a special importance for commoners, who attributed extraordinary powers to amulets—for example, expecting them to ward off illness and ensure safe childbirth. Marked with the images and symbols of deities, amulets were especially useful because they were easily moved, able to accompany—and therefore watch over—humble believers wherever they went. To deal with the most profound questions of life, commoners looked to omens and divination—a practice that was also used both in Mesopotamia and in ancient China to help predict and control future events.

Like Egyptian elites, commoners attributed supernatural powers to animals. Chosen animals were entitled to special treatment in life and were looked after in death. Special cemeteries and mourning rituals were reserved for Apis bulls, sacred to the god Ptah; ibises, dogs, jackals, cats, baboons, lizards, fish, snakes, crocodiles, and other beasts associated with deities enjoyed similar privileges.

A "Chosen" Animal. In the popular religion of ancient Egypt, gods were thought to be manifest through certain animals, which were mummified when they died. Bulls were sacred to several gods. The Apis bull at Memphis was considered the earthly manifestation of Ptah, the creator god through whom he gave oracles. Pious individuals would dedicate a calf to the gods as a token of their devotion. This is a typical example of such a mummy.

Egyptian Gods. Osiris (*top left*) is the dying god who rules over the netherworld. Most frequently he is depicted as a mummy wearing a white crown with plumes and holding the scepter and flagellum across his chest. The god Horus (*top right and bottom*), who was also rendered as Ra-Horakhty, is the falcon-headed Egyptian sky god. Horus is the earliest state god of Egypt and is always closely associated with the king. Horus is a member of the ennead of Heliopolis and is the son of Osiris and Isis.

WRITING AND SCRIBES

Egypt, like Mesopotamia, was a scribal culture. A common statement that circulated among Egyptians was that peasants toiled so that scribes could live in comfort; literacy sharpened the divisions between rural and urban worlds. By the middle of the third millennium BCE, literacy was already firmly established among tiny circles of experts in the cultures of Egypt and Mesopotamia. Because it was limited to relatively few individuals, its possession heightened scribes' social status. Although in both cultures writing emerged in response to economic needs, its utility for commemorative and religious purposes was grasped immediately: as soon as literacy took hold, Mesopotamians and Egyptians were drafting historical records and literary compositions.

Both the early Mesopotamian and Egyptian scripts were complex. Indeed, one feature shared by all writing systems is that over time they became simpler and more efficient at representing the full range of spoken utterances. Only when the first alphabet appeared (to record Aramaic in the middle of the second millennium BCE) did the potential for wider literacy surface. To judge from remaining records, it seems that more Egyptians than Mesopotamians were literate. Most high-ranking Egyptians were also trained as scribes who were employed by the king's court, the army, or the priesthood. Occasionally, kings and members of the royal family also learned to write.

Two basic forms of Egyptian writing were used in conjunction throughout antiquity. *Hieroglyphs,* a term derived from a Greek word meaning "sacred carving," were employed exclusively in temple, royal, or divine contexts. From the early appearance of writing in the tombs of the First Dynasty, records were also kept in a cursive script that was written with ink on papyrus, on pieces of pottery, or on other absorbent media. This was called *demotic writing* and was the most common and practical form of writing in Egypt. Used for administrative record keeping, demotic writing was also employed in private or pseudo-private forms, like letters, and for works of literature, including narrative fiction, manuals of instruction and philosophy, cult and religious hymns, love poems, medical and mathematical texts, collections of rituals, and mortuary books.

Becoming literate required being taught by scribes, and often the skills clustered in extended families. Usually students started their training when they were young; after its completion, they entered the bureaucracy. They began by repeatedly copying standard texts in demotic cursive or hieroglyphs. After mastering these texts, students moved on to

Egyptian Hieroglyphics and "Cursive Script." The Egyptians wrote in two distinctive types of scripts. The more formal is hieroglyphics, which is based on pictorial images that carry values of either ideas (idiograms) or sounds (phonemes). All royal and funerary inscriptions, such as this funerary relief from the Old Kingdom, are rendered in hieroglyphic script. Daily documents, accountings, literary texts, and the like were most often written in a cursive script called demotic, which was written with ink on papyrus. The form of the cursive signs is based on the hieroglyphics but is more abstract and can be formed more quickly.

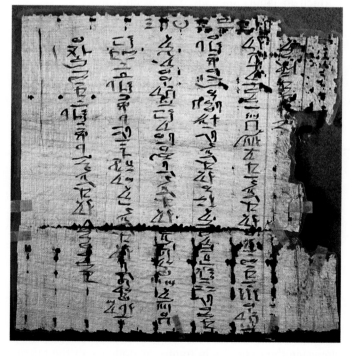

Primary Source

THE ADMONITIONS OF IPUWER

In order to maintain his power during a period of increasing drought, Pepy II (r. 2246–2152 BCE) gave away many advantages and tax exemptions to provincial nobles. At the end of his long reign, no strong successors emerged who were capable of maintaining centralized power. The collapse of the central state was traumatic, and Egyptian society was for a time reduced to chaos. This social condition was poignantly captured in a number of texts written by prophets and wise men. One of the most moving was by Ipuwer.

Behold, the fire has gone up on high, and its burning goes forth against the enemies of the land.

Behold, things have been done which have not happened for a long time past; the king has been deposed by the rabble.

Behold, he who was buried as a falcon [is devoid] of biers, and what the pyramid concealed has become empty.

Behold, it has befallen that the land has been deprived of the kingship by a few lawless men.

Behold, men have fallen into rebellion against the Uraeus, the [...] of Re, even she who makes the Two Lands content.

Behold, the secret of the land whose limits were unknown is divulged, and the Residence is thrown down in a moment.

Behold, Egypt is fallen to pouring of water, and he who poured water on the ground has carried off the strong man in misery.

Behold, the Serpent is taken from its hole, and the secrets of the Kings of Upper and Lower Egypt are divulged.

Behold, the Residence is afraid because of want, and [men go about] unopposed to stir up strife.

Behold, the land has knotted itself up with confederacies, and the coward takes the brave man's property.

Behold, the Serpent [...] the dead: he who could not make a sarcophagus for himself is now the possessor of a tomb.

Behold, the possessors of tombs are ejected on to the high ground, while he who could not make a coffin for himself is now [the possessor] of a treasury.

Behold, this has happened [to] men; he who could not build a room for himself is now a possessor of walls.

Behold, the magistrates of the land are driven out throughout the land: [...] are driven out from the palaces.

Behold, noble ladies are now on rafts, and magnates are in the labor establishment, while he who could not sleep even on walls is now the possessor of a bed.

Behold, the possessor of wealth now spends the night thirsty, while he who once begged his dregs for himself is now the possessor of overflowing bowls.

Behold, the possessors of robes are now in rags, while he who could not weave for himself is now a possessor of fine linen.

Behold, he who could not build a boat for himself is now the possessor of a fleet; their erstwhile owner looks at them, but they are not his.

Behold, he who had no shade is now the possessor of shade, while the erstwhile possessors of shade are now in the full blast of the storm.

Behold, he who was ignorant of the lyre is now the possessor of a harp, while he who never sang for himself now vaunts the Songstress-goddess.

Behold, those who possessed vessel-stands of copper [...] not one of the jars thereof has been adorned.

→ *What were the causes of the collapse of Egypt's Old Kingdom? How can we use such a document as "The Admonitions of Ipuwer" to understand what conditions were like in Egypt at the end of the third millennium BCE?*

SOURCE: Translated by John A. Wilson in *Ancient Near Eastern Texts Relating to the Old Testament*, edited by J. B. Pritchard (Princeton: Princeton University Press, 1950), pp. 442–43.

literary works. The upper classes prized the ability to read and write almost above all else, regarding it as proof of high intellectual achievement. When they died, those who had attained literacy often had their student textbooks placed alongside their corpses in tombs, as evidence of the talents they had displayed during their lifetimes. The literati produced texts mainly in temples, where these works were also preserved. Writing hieroglyphs and transmitting texts continued without break in ancient Egypt for almost 3,000 years, coming to an end only in the third century BCE.

THE PROSPERITY OF EGYPT

Under pharaonic rule, Egypt prospered. Its population grew at a steady, and in some periods spectacular, rate, swelling from 350,000 in 4000 BCE to 870,000 in 3000 BCE, 1 million in 2500 BCE, 2 million in 1800 BCE, 2.9 million in 1250 BCE, and nearly 5 million by 1500 BCE.

The success of the state depended on administering resources skillfully, and especially on managing agricultural production and labor. Everyone, from members of the most powerful elite groups to the workers in the field, was part of the system. In principle, no one possessed private property; in practice, Egyptians treated land and tools as their own—but submitted to the intrusions of the state. Indeed, a strong state exerted its control, especially over matters of taxation, prices, and the distribution of goods, with unchallenged powers. Such strength was rooted in a large bureaucracy that maintained records, watched over society, and of course regulated and stored the Nile's floodwaters. While land had to be tilled by farmers, the precious source of prosperity was African water, the gift of the gods and the exclusive right and responsibility of the rulers. Mirroring the predictability of the Nile's flow, the bureaucracy and the culture at large became highly resistant to change, counting on tried and true practices and resisting fundamental transformation.

During this period of Egypt's growing social and occupational complexity, when large urban conglomerates were appearing elsewhere, the continued absence of cities on the scale of those in Mesopotamia was extraordinary. In striking contrast to Mesopotamia, ancient Egypt was a land of extensive settlements that had many metropolitan centers. Hence, the divide between rural and urban settings was not as stark in the Nile River basin as it was in Mesopotamia. There were, to be sure, administrative headquarters, where the ruling family and the bureaucrats who supported it resided—Memphis during the Old Kingdom, and Thebes later on—but Egypt neither had nor needed massive cities. It was not nearly so vital a crossroads of trade and population movements as the Tigris-Euphrates region. Its peoples lived tightly compacted into the Nile River basin, and they could easily reach one another by boat. Because the Nile and the surrounding countryside provided most of the goods that men and women needed for a comfortable existence, those dwelling in ancient Egypt could live in communities—constructed just beyond the floodplain, safe from the Nile overflows—that were largely self-contained.

THE LATER DYNASTIES AND THEIR DEMISE

As the Old Kingdom matured and expanded without a powerful uniting or dominating city like those found in Mesopotamia or Harappa, the Egyptian state became more dispersed. The patterns of monumental architecture tell us that Fifth Dynasty policies were less centralized than those of the Fourth Dynasty. The state's expansion, driven by economic growth, led to local variation and adaptation. That private tombs were more highly decorated with images and inscriptions than before testifies to an enhanced freedom of expression. As this era came to an end, high officials were beginning to use magical spells and imagery that originally had been the sole preserve of kings. By the beginning of the Middle Kingdom, such officials began in special cases to have the same access as kings to immortality through burial rituals.

Fifth Dynasty Egypt no longer looked inward. By the Sixth Dynasty, texts, reliefs on tombs, and archaeological evidence suggest that Egypt had extended its power militarily in Palestine to the east, in Libya in the west, and in Nubia in the south. Trade also increased, and the southern Egyptian oases of El Kharga and El Dakhla bustled with traders driving caravans of donkeys loaded with goods.

Expansion and decentralization eventually exposed the weaknesses of dynastic genealogies. The shakeup resulted not from external invasion or of bickering between rival city-states but from feuding between factions of the political elite. In addition, an extended drought that began in northern Africa sometime around 2250 BCE put impossible strains on Egypt's extensive irrigation system, which could no longer water the lands that kept the population of about a million inhabitants fed. Imagery of great suffering filled the texts and depictions on the walls of the royal tombs. The long reign of Pepy II (2246–2152 BCE), at the end of the Sixth Dynasty, proved to be the swan song of the Old Kingdom. Upon his death, royal power collapsed completely. For the next hundred years, many rivals jostled for the throne; some fell within a year. Local magnates assumed hereditary control of the government in the provinces and treated the lands previously controlled by the royal family as their own personal property. Descriptions of life were filled with internecine feuding, as local leaders plunged into bloody regional struggles to keep the irrigation works functioning for their own communities. This so-called First Intermediate Period lasted roughly from 2150 to 2040 BCE.

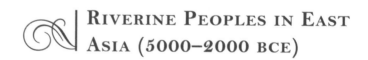

RIVERINE PEOPLES IN EAST ASIA (5000–2000 BCE)

> → *What hallmarks of urban life emerged in China during this period?*

Like the inhabitants of Mesopotamia and Egypt, East Asian peoples tended to cluster in river basins. Their settlements along the banks of the Yellow River in the north and the Yangzi River in the south became the foundation of the future Chinese state, unlike the Jomon in Japan, who were tied to a hunting-gathering subsistence economy. Already by 5000 BCE, both millet in the north and rice in the south were being

MAP 2-6   RIVERINE PEOPLES IN EAST ASIA, 5000–2000 BCE

Complex agricultural societies emerged in East Asia during the third millennium BCE. Using the map above, identify the regional cultures that flourished in East Asia during this time. How were they different from and similar to the cultures in other contemporary riverine societies? How did regional cultures in East Asia influence each other?

widely cultivated. Yet in the following three millennia, during an era when Mesopotamia, Egypt, and the Indus Valley were creating populous, socially complex, and city-based cultures, the Chinese moved more slowly. China's great riverine cultures did not arise until the second millennium BCE. (See Map 2-6.) Like the waterways in the other regions, the Yellow and Yangzi rivers also had annual floods and extensive floodplains that proved eminently suitable for high agricultural yields and capable of supporting dense populations. But in China the evolution of hydraulic works, big cities, priestly and bureaucratic classes, and a new writing system took longer.

Living conditions and the environment played a strong role in ancient Chinese society just as it did in the riverine culture of Southwest Asia. In the riverine basins of China, food was abundant and communities were spread out, encouraging localized agrarian cultures. Complex cities would come later. The early Chinese peoples simply did not feel the same kinds of pressure compared to the societies bordering the deserts in Southwest Asia. Other factors contributing to their different course of development included the paucity of easily domesticated animals and plants, as well as geography. Geography worked to isolate China, for the Himalayan Mountains and the Taklamakan and Gobi deserts prevented large-scale population movements between East Asia and Central Asia and hindered the rapid diffusion of intellectual and cultural breakthroughs occurring elsewhere in Afro-Eurasia.

FROM YANGSHAO TO LONGSHAN CULTURE

China's classical histories place the society's beginnings at the foundation of the Xia dynasty, dating from 2200 BCE. Archaeological studies of riverine environments in East Asia tell a story that challenges the traditional account. Whether or not the Xia actually existed as a historical dynasty, it is clear that our study of the Yellow River basin and Yangzi delta should begin earlier, in the two millennia from 4000 to 2000 BCE.

Although somewhat isolated in comparison to Southwest Asia, China was never completely sealed off from outside influences. Unlike the Americas, East Asia was not separated from the rest of Afro-Eurasia by great oceans. Indeed, some travelers arrived via the ocean, though not on a large scale until the invention of truly seaworthy vessels. More importantly, the Mongolian steppe provided an opening to China through which such important technologies as the chariot were introduced by nomads sometime in the second millennium BCE. Nomads were drawn to the agricultural settlements in China as they were in Mesopotamia, and they brought with them innovations and bronze and other goods from afar. Through trade and migration, nomadic cultures and technologies filtered from the steppes to communities settled on the rivers.

The combination of agrarian settlements and increasing contact with neighbors gave rise to greater cultural complexity. The telltale signs include breakthroughs in communication. Although the Chinese did not create a graphic writing system until the middle of the second millennium BCE, preliterate signs and marks found at Jiahu, on the south banks of the Yellow River, have been dated as early as the seventh millennium BCE—long before similar systems appeared in Mesopotamia and Egypt.

Markings on red pottery, which archaeologists found in ancient sites near the village of Yangshao along the Yellow River in northwestern China, likewise represent a pioneering system of signs and symbols from as early as 5000 BCE. Some

Yangshao Bowl with Dancing Figures, c. 5000–1700 BCE. The Yangshao, also referred to as the "painted pottery" culture, produced gray or red pottery painted with black geometric designs and occasionally with pictures of fish or human faces and figures. Because the potter's wheel was unknown at the time, the vessels were probably fashioned with strips of clay.

of the signs may be precursors of script. Archaeologists have also discovered analogous signs on early pottery in southern China. A complex society that required writing, such as that of the Sumerians, did not emerge until much later. Nevertheless, shamans—many of them women—in the emerging villages of the fourth and third millennium BCE may have used signs in performing rituals, music, and healing, as well as in divination to interpret omens and predict the future.

China's early riverine societies produced stone and pottery storage vessels of the sort that we associate with permanent, increasingly urban settlements. Near the village of Longshan in Shandong province on the eastern end of the North China plain, for example, archaeologists in 1931–1932 discovered highly polished black pottery and a complete town enclosure of compacted earth. Such finds contrast sharply with the simpler artifacts of the Yangshao sites in the northwest. Furthermore, Longshan residents burned deer scapulas to communicate with the dead: the cracks that formed were interpreted by diviners. This ritual was likely the precursor of the inscribed oracle bones introduced in the Shang dynasty (1600–1045 BCE), which like the deer bones were consulted by those who wished to get the advice of their dead ancestors when making important decisions.

We do not know where the Longshan people originally came from, but they likely migrated in several waves from the peripheries of East Asia to the eastern China seashore, and they helped form the many villages then dotting China. Their achievements, compared to those of the earlier Yangshao peoples, suggest marked development between 5000 and 2000 BCE. Several regional cultures in northern and southern China, which arose independently, began to produce similar

Primary Source

ARCHAEOLOGICAL EVIDENCE FOR LONGSHAN CULTURE

Over the course of a millennium, multiple cultures with strong similarities emerged in north and northwest China. Some scholars have argued that a single Longshan culture grew out of these various close-knit groups. Even if its cohesiveness did not rise to the level of forming a fully integrated interaction sphere, the changes that Longshan represented were nonetheless remarkable.

Let us take a quick look at the kind of innovations that sprouted everywhere and that, because of the similarities of style, must be interrelated:

1. Archaeologically acceptable evidence of copper objects, mostly trinkets and small tools of no agricultural value, has been unearthed in Shantung, western Honan, southern Shansi, and Ch'i-chia from archaeological horizons comparable in age. The finds do not suffice to point to a major metal industry as yet, but in light of what happened later on one must regard the Lung-shan metallurgy as worthy of note. The bronze vessel fragment from Wang-ch'eng-kang is of special significance.

2. Industrially much more important is the extremely widespread use of potter's wheels for the manufacture of ceramics. There was tremendous variation in the pottery wares of the various Lung-shan Cultures, but the overwhelming change from red to gray and the general decline of painted decoration must have been the result of a conscious choice on the part of the potters, who, armed with improved kilns and the wheel, must have represented a specialized profession in the Lung-shan society.

3. The stamped-earth construction technology and the construction of town walls using that technology are separate issues, but the town walls in Shantung, east Honan, north Honan, and west Honan indicate both the transmission of a technology and the rise of the necessity for defensive public works.

4. Related to the rise of defensive ramparts is the archaeological evidence of institutionalized violence. This takes two forms—evidence of raids or wars, such as the Chien-kou-ts'un finds of skulls and bodies in the water well; and burials of possible ritual victims relating to the construction of chiefly or royal monuments.

5. There are several manifestations of rituals, especially ones closely tied to persons of high political status. The first is the role of some animals and birds in ritual art, such as those found or identified recently in Liang-ch'eng, Shantung; the Liang-chu sites, in Kiangsu and Chekiang; and T'ao-ssu, Shansi.

6. The *ts'ung* tube, especially if associated with animals and birds, is a very distinctive ritual object manifesting a unique cosmology. Its discovery in Liang-chu on the coast and T'ao-ssu in the interior cannot be accidental; it indicates without question an interregional transmission of cosmology or even a spherewide substratum featuring that cosmology. If we include jade rings (*pi*) in this cosmological bag, the Ch'i-chia Culture also becomes involved.

7. The virtually universal occurrence of scapulimancy among the Lung-shan Cultures is another manifestation of the spherewide communication or substratum of cosmology.

8. The archaeological evidence for violence and for ritual on an institutional basis almost inevitably means a society featuring sharp political and economic divisions, and that is exactly what we find in the mortuary remains of many of the Lung-shan Cultures. We have already seen archaeological indications of social ranking in the mortuary remains of the Neolithic sites of the fifth and fourth centuries B.C. (see chapters 3–4). These trends accelerated and further intensified in the Lung-shan cemeteries. Furthermore, as the Ch'eng-tzu (Shantung) and T'ao-ssu (Shansi) cemeteries show, the economic and political polarization appears to have taken place within the framework of the unilinear clans and lineages.

All of the above happenings are plainly indicated by archaeological evidence, but they do not point to a single Lung-shan Culture. Instead, they indicate a series of interrelated changes in culture and society that took place within each of the regional cultures in the Chinese interaction sphere. From the point of view of each of the regional sequences, both the external interaction network and internal changes during a period of two thousand years were essential for its readiness, toward the end of the third millennium B.C., to step over the next threshold into the state society, urbanism, and civilization.

→ *What were the key ingredients of Longshan culture? What does the evidence of violence reveal about Longshan society?*

SOURCE: Kwang-chih Chang, *The Archaeology of Ancient China*, 4th ed. (New Haven: Yale University Press, 1986), pp. 287–88. Note: Chang uses Wade-Giles romanization.

pottery and tools and to plant the same crops, probably reflecting their contact with one another. They did not yet produce city-states, but agriculture began to flourish and small settlements covered the increasingly populated Yellow River valley in the northwest and the coastal areas.

Some of the hallmarks of the beginnings of urban life are evident. Members of the Longshan cultural complex buried their dead in cemeteries outside their villages. Several thousand graves have been uncovered in southern Shanxi province; the largest ones contain ritual pottery vessels, musical instruments made of wood, copper bells, and painted murals. Specialized shamans performed rituals employing axes of jade. Jade quarrying in particular indicated the group's highly developed technical power, as skilled craftworkers translated stone tablets into powerful expressions of ritual and military authority. The recent discovery in the middle part of the Yellow River's flow across the North China Plain of a Longshan household whose members were all scalped after being killed demonstrates the power and danger of organized violence. Attackers filled the water wells with five layers of human skeletons, some decapitated. The defensive walls that surrounded newly established villages were clearly needed.

Longshan Beaker, c. 2500 BCE. Longshan has been called the "black pottery" culture, and its exquisite black pottery was not painted but rather decorated with rings, either raised or grooved. Longshan culture was more advanced than the Yangshao culture, and its distinctive pottery was likely formed on a potter's wheel.

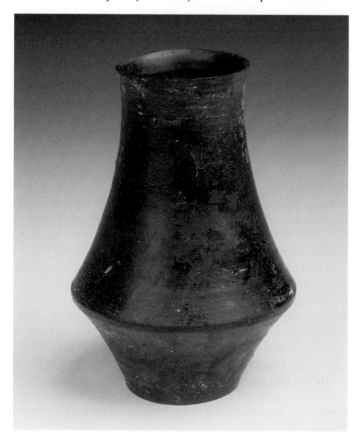

As communities became more centralized, contact between regions also increased. Interregional links between northern and southern China took shape in the middle of the third millennium BCE, when peoples originally from Longshan villages began to migrate along the East Asian coast to Taiwan and the Pearl River delta in the far south. Similarities in the artifacts found along the coast and at Longshan sites in northern China, such as the form and decoration of pottery and jade items, also point to a shared cultural and trading sphere. Many of the early peoples in the south, whom we also call Austronesians (a diverse group of people stretching roughly from Madagascar to Easter Island whose languages were similar), then moved by boat into the Pacific from East Asian coastal islands (see Chapter 3).

Finally, archaeologists have found evidence of small-scale, short-lived, and scattered political organizations. Although they did not aggregate into anything resembling the trans-local alliances that created dynastic systems in Egypt, Mesopotamia, and the Indus Valley, they did not consist simply of chieftains ruling impoverished hamlets. These were wealthy—if localized—polities, which constituted what scholars have called the era of Ten Thousand States (*Wan'guo*). One of them, the Liangzhu, has drawn particular interest because of its remarkable jade objects.

LIFE IN LIANGZHU

The Liangzhu people, like their Longshan relatives to the north, were sophisticated agriculturalists, growing rice and fruits along the banks of the Qiantang River where it flows into Hangzhou Bay. Among their implements were flat and perforated spades, as well as rectangular and curved sicklelike knives with holes. They raised domesticated water buffalo, pigs, dogs, and sheep. Archaeologists have discovered the remains of net sinkers, wooden floats, and wooden paddles, which demonstrate that the Liangzhu were familiar with watercraft and fishing. Also surviving in wood are pieces of boats, the foundations of houses, tools, and utensils. Their stone and bone artifacts were highly developed as well. Liangzhu artisans produced a black pottery from soft paste thrown on a wheel. And like the people of the Longshan culture, they devoted much labor to creating ritual objects from several varieties of jade; they mined it in the silt-formed Great Lake (Taihu) area of the Yangzi delta, close to the Liangzhu tombs.

In the late third millennium BCE, a long drought hit China as it did Egypt, Mesopotamia, and India. The Chinese recovered during the early centuries of the second millennium BCE, creating elaborate agrarian systems along the Yellow and Yangzi rivers that in many respects were similar to the irrigation systems established earlier along the Euphrates, Indus, and Nile. Extensive trading networks and a highly stratified social hierarchy based on age and gender then emerged; like the other river basin complexes of Asia and North Africa, China became a centralized polity. Here, too, a powerful

Liangzhu Jade Axe Blade, c. 3400–2250 BCE. The Liangzhu represented the last new Stone Age culture in the Yangzi River Delta. Their culture was highly stratified, and jade, silk, ivory, and lacquer artifacts were found exclusively in elite burial sites.

monarchy eventually devised the political and military means to unite the independent communities of riverine peoples. But what developed in China was a social and political system that ideologically emphasized an idealized past and tradition represented by sage-kings. In this and numerous other ways, China diverged from the rest of Afro-Eurasia.

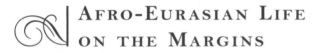

AFRO-EURASIAN LIFE ON THE MARGINS

> → *How did the growth of urban societies in river basins affect people living in the Aegean region, Anatolia, and Europe?*

Those who lived in river basins and who looked to cities and their hierarchies as a model of dependable order, protected by bureaucracies and strong militaries, were inclined to see outsiders—particularly those who lived in the countryside, and especially those who were nomads—as "barbarians" and primitives. The imagery and narratives produced by city peoples in which they sought to distinguish themselves from rural and nomadic folk by depicting people from the periphery as backward and less civilized should not be accepted at face value. The city folk were less concerned with accurate portraits of the nomads than with enhancing their own self-image. Certainly, those who lived on the margins would not have recognized themselves as savages who were bereft of culture, faith, and organized life. They had frequent contact with the urbanites in river basins and became adept users of the technologies that radiated from cities. (See Map 2-7.) Despite being less urbanized, settled, and stratified than city dwellers, they fashioned institutions and belief systems that were as durable as those that flourished in the metropolitan centers.

AEGEAN WORLDS

One distinctive characteristic of people who lived outside the river basins was their warrior-based ethos. The top tiers of the social ladder, to which priests and scribes rose in cities, were held by chiefs and military men in less-stratified societies. This feature could be observed with particular clarity north of the Mediterranean Sea—especially in Europe and Anatolia, where weaponry rather than writing, palisades rather than palaces, and conquest rather than commerce dominated everyday life. Here, too, the inhabitants moved beyond stone implements and hunting and gathering, but they remained more egalitarian than riverine folk and politically did not evolve much above the level of small-scale societies led by a chief.

Contact with Egypt and Mesopotamia affected the worlds around the Aegean, but it did not lead to their basic transformation. Mountains and large bodies of water kept apart communities that lacked the unifying effects of a great river. Geography stood in the way of urban conglomerations arising on the mountainous islands, on the Anatolian plateau, and in Europe. People from Anatolia, Greece, and the Levant took to boats and populated the Aegean islands in the sixth millennium BCE. Their small villages endured almost unchanged for 2,000 years, not becoming more complex until the early third millennium BCE.

On mainland Greece and on the Cycladic islands in the middle of the Aegean Sea, large fortified settlements became the habitations of local rulers who controlled a small area of agriculturally productive countryside. Metallurgy developed both in Crete and in the Cyclades. There is evidence of a more formal administration and organizations in some communities by 2500 BCE, but the norm for the region was scattered settlements separated by natural obstacles. Consider rocky and mountainous Crete, the largest island in the Aegean. Occupied by sea-

MAP 2-7   **SETTLEMENTS ON THE MARGINS: THE EASTERN MEDITERRANEAN AND EUROPE, 5000–2000 BCE**

Urban societies in Southwest Asia profoundly influenced peripheral societies in the third millennium BCE. How did the spread of flint and copper tools and weapons transform Aegean and European societies during this time? What other influences did societies in Southwest Asia have on these settlements? How does this map demonstrate the growth of distinct cultures in these regions?

faring peoples, the island had hamlets and settlements sprinkled through its rugged interior. By the early third millennium BCE, it had made intermittent contact with distant neighbors—Egypt to the south and the coastal towns of the Levant to the east. Through these contacts, Cretans brushed up against new ideas, technologies, and materials as new waves of people arrived on their shores to trade or to stay. People came in ships with goods from the coast of Anatolia and from Egypt and the Levantine

coast. They brought with them such items as stone vessels and other luxury objects, which they traded for the abundant copper that could be found on the islands.

Lacking a rich agrarian base, communities remained small villages; most had no more than 100 inhabitants, and only a few grew over time. By the middle of the third millennium BCE, a more complex society was emerging on the eastern part of the island. During the second millennium BCE, Knossos, located in the middle of a rich agricultural plain,

RITUAL OBJECTS IN THE IRANIAN PLATEAU, CHINA, AND EGYPT

An important aspect of religious practice is the interaction between the worldly and the divine, between the living and the dead, between heaven and earth. Thousands of years ago ritual objects, such as amulets, statues, or carved objects representing the gods, were tangible representations of the connection between the earthly and the sacred. Other objects carried images of important myths and other stories that helped bind people together. Such objects could be used in specific ceremonies marking major events, such as a birth or a death. They may also have acted as more permanent signs of the divine, in shrines or temples. In both cases, ritual objects represented the sacred in everyday life.

From earliest times humans have deposited symbolic objects with the dead to ease the journey to the world beyond and to provide the sustenance and tools that the deceased would need in the afterlife. Both illicit and scientific excavations in the region of Jiroft in south-central Iran have revealed thousands of symbolic objects as well as utilitarian vessels that were put in graves. Most frequently interred with the body was a jar or cylindrical vessel made of soft green stone (locally available steatite or chlorite), whose sides were carved with elaborate designs that undoubtedly carried symbolic meaning. Furniture inlays and rectangular slabs with handles were also carved from the green stone and were decorated with similar designs.

While many of the designs featured repeating patterns of a grid or depicted curls or scorpions, some carried representations of gods in human form, who wore bull horns on their head as a sign of their divinity. A common motif portrayed a bird of prey grasping a snake in its talons; a leopard confronts the snake. Both the body of the bird and the snake are covered with holes that would originally have been filled with multihued stones, making the overall pattern very colorful and lively. The struggle between forces of nature is represented by the confrontation of the snake and the leopard. Neither wins; rather, they are always seen in a perfectly balanced equilibrium.

Vessels from Jiroft have been found in the Persian Gulf and in Mesopotamia. Some historians have argued that they were objects of trade no different from semiprecious lapis lazuli and carnelian. In fact, the centrality of these very distinctive objects to the funerary cult in their homeland makes it much more likely that they were carried to distant lands by traders and craftsmen who found work and lucrative markets for their commodities in the large cities of the great river valleys. These items were carried as personal effects; there is no evidence that the objects were ever exchanged in trade.

The Liangzhu people of ancient China carefully crafted ritual objects from several varieties of jade that they mined in the silt-formed Great Lake (Taihu) area of the Yangzi delta. Many of these jade pieces were decorated with animal masks or bird designs. Especially important in these rituals were circular jade objects called *bi* discs (found in tomb sites) and *cong* tubes. The *cong* jades, used in divination practices, were round in their hollow interior but squared on the outside. The rounded portion of the tube represented heaven and the square portion the earth; the jade tubes thus signified interaction between heaven and earth, the dead and the living. Both heaven and earth were penetrated by a central axis running through the jade's shaft, which symbolized the sacred mountains dividing the land of the living from the place of the dead.

Jade was the most important precious substance in East Asia. It was associated with the qualities of being

would become the primary palace-town in an extended network of palaces. The evidence from burial sites suggests that some households belonged to an elite class, for they were buried in their gold jewelry and took other exotic objects to their graves. Aegean elites did not spurn the niceties of civilized life. At the same time, they never forgot that their power rested as much on their ability to extract a living from a rugged landscape as on self-defense and on trade and interaction with others.

ANATOLIA

The emergence of regional cultures that were focused on the control of vital trade routes and mining outposts is especially clear on the highland plateau of Anatolia, which had been populated almost from the time that humans walked out of Africa. The pace of change was slow, as people clung to their village ways and stone tools. True cities did not develop in Anatolia until the third millennium BCE; even then, they were not the sprawling, densely packed centers of humanity typi-

Egyptian Funeral Amulet. This winged scarab is a symbol of rebirth and would have been placed in the wrapping of the mummy along with other amulets to assure the successful passage of the deceased into the afterlife. The Egyptians understood the dung-beetle who pushes a ball of dung as Khepri, the divine protector of the daily solar cycle.

good, pure, lucky, and virtuous, and it was carved into such items as ceremonial knives, blade handles, religious objects, and elaborate jewelry. Because jade is an especially hard stone, its intricate carving required much time and great skill. Smaller objects, such as blades and amulets, could serve a ceremonial purpose in ancient China. Jade objects used in a funerary function might be placed in the mouths and on the eyes of the deceased, or jade ornaments, jewelry, and ritual objects might be buried with them. Men and women had different ornaments, including necklaces and headdresses, swords and seals.

In ancient Egypt, precious stones and metals shaped into jewelry and ritual objects also played an important role, especially in burying the dead. Indeed, much of what we know about Egyptian amulets rests on discoveries made in tombs. Archaeologists often find amulets and funerary jewelry placed in specific positions on the bodies of mummies. The system for preparing a body for mummification was so specialized that it mandated a special type of funerary jewelry distinct from what ordinary people wore during their lives. Funerary amulets were thought to protect a mummy from potential suffering in the afterlife. The Egyptian *Book of the Dead* contains drawings and small paintings, along with spells, explaining how certain jewelry amulets should be used.

In addition, amulets of stone or precious metal—also described in the *Book of the Dead*—could be entombed with a mummified body. Nearly every mummy archaeologists have discovered has been found with one such amulet, made variously of stone, glass, or wood, in the shape of a pillar with cross bars at its top, perhaps mimicking the form of a tree (see Carol Andrews, *Egyptian Mummies*). Other types of amulets were made to resemble parts of the body, particularly an arm or a foot, indicating that the person had suffered in that body part or that a limb was missing, and the amulet could serve as its substitute. In either case, embalmers appear to have desired to make the deceased person as whole as possible for his or her passage into the afterlife. And Egyptian amulets of this sort often complemented the features of the person with whom they were placed.

Whether they were used to express religious or social status in this world or fend off evil spirits in the next, ritual objects played a major role in the practice of religion in China and Egypt. Amulets and ritual jewelry were the ultimate way of personalizing the divine, as they represented a connection to heaven that could belong to an individual. In this way, the creation and use of ritual objects stressed the interconnectedness of worldly and spiritual life.

cal of the Mesopotamian plain. Instead, small communities that were organized around fortified citadels housing competing local rulers were the usual settlement type. The most impressive of these fortified centers were Horoz Tepe and Alaça Hüyük, which we know primarily from more than a dozen very rich graves, apparently of royalty, full of gold jewelry, ceremonial standards, and elaborate weapons.

Another important third millennium BCE site in Anatolia was Troy to the far west. Troy is legendary as the place of the famous war launched by the Greeks (the Achaeans) and recounted by Homer in the *Iliad*. Troy, the modern mound of Hissarlik, was founded around 3000 BCE on the coast of the Mediterranean in a fertile and productive plain. First investigated by the German archaeologist Heinrich Schliemann in the 1870s, Troy level I was identified as a third-millennium BCE fortified settlement with monumental stone gateways and stone-paved ramps. Troy level II was extremely rich and had five large buildings called *megarons*, the forerunners of the classic Greek temple. Here, Schliemann found gold and silver objects, vessels, jewelry, and other artifacts. Many of these are similar to the ones found in the graves at Alaça Hüyük in the east. Moreover, since they closely parallel finds in the graves at Mochlos on Crete and at sites on the Greek mainland, they indicate that Troy was active in the trade system that linked the Aegean and Southwest Asian worlds during the third millennium BCE. Precious objects such as these may have been obtained through trade, but Troy still had to be defended against predatory neighbors and pirates who attacked from the sea—a necessity that helps explain its impressive fortifications.

THE WESTERN FRONTIER: EUROPE

At the far western reaches of the Eurasian landmass was a region that contained both more temperate and more frigid climates with much smaller population densities Its peoples—forerunners of present-day Europeans—began to make things out of metal, moved into permanent settlements, and started to create complex societies. Here, too, hierarchies replaced older egalitarian ways. Yet, as in the Aegean worlds, density and complexity here also had their limits.

More strongly than in the Mediterranean or Anatolia, it was in Europe—partly because of the persistent fragmentation of the region's peoples, partly because of the type of agrarian development they pursued—that warfare dominated social development. The introduction of the plow and the clearing of woodlands expanded agriculture. Agrarian development was driven by households and communities wielding axes both for defense and to cut down trees, not city-states or dynasties organizing irrigation and settlement. Compared to the riverine societies, even those of East Asia, Europe was a wild frontier, where day-to-day confrontations and violent conflicts over resources were common.

The effects of the gradual frontier expansion of agricultural communities were cumulative and eventually reached a critical turning point. The huge growth of flint mining to an industrial level, such as the thousand shafts sunk at Krzemionki in Poland or the large flint-mining complex of Grimes Graves in England, indicate a large-scale social and economic transformation. Most important, mining output slashed the cost and increased the availability of the raw materials needed to make tools that could more efficiently clear forested lands and till them into arable fields. Agricultural communities proliferated throughout the continent; some grew into villages capable of dominating their regions.

By 4000 BCE, the more developed agrarian peoples had coalesced into large communities. They supplied labor for the construction of large fixed monuments that are visible today. In western Europe, the building of large ceremonial centers shared the same model: enormous shaped stones, sometimes weighing several tons each, were set together in common patterns—in alleyways, troughs, or circles—that we call *megalithic* (literally, "great stone") constructions. These large-scale projects were certainly evidence of some kind of

Stonehenge. This spectacular site, located in the Salisbury Plain in Wiltshire in southwestern England, is one of several such megalithic structures found in the region. Constructed by many generations of builders, the arrangement of the large stone uprights enabled people to determine precise times in the year through the position of the sun. Events such as the spring and autumn equinoxes were connected with agricultural and religious activities.

Primary Source

THE MALE WARRIOR BURIALS OF VARNA AND NETT DOWN

In the burials arranged for elite individuals across the whole region from the Black Sea to the Atlantic, we witness the kinds of precious objects and weapons associated with a competitive warrior culture. At Varna, on the Black Sea coast of Bulgaria, the lifestyle of the "big men" associated with a farming village dated to around 4000 BCE was suddenly revealed in 1972 when a farmer driving a tractor uncovered graves from an ancient cemetery. The burials at Varna seem to represent a relatively powerful and well-connected settlement of the period, since most other contemporary sites do not display such high levels of wealth. In the grave of a man who died at about age forty-five, large pots used for drinking and storage were found. Much more striking were the 990 separate gold objects: most were decorative devices sewn onto his clothing, but they also included bracelets on both arms, a necklace, and small axe with a gold handle. The weapons buried with him—daggers, axes, and spearheads, and points—were still made of flint.

A second individual burial—from the far western parts of Europe, at Nett Down in Wiltshire, England, and at the end of our period, around 2500 BCE—reveals a less highly developed culture. In this case, a young male warrior was buried in a small tomb cut into the chalk ground and covered with a small circular mound of earth. He was buried with the two most significant representative objects connected with his life: a bronze dagger and, lower down, by his hands, a large bell beaker. No gold or precious metal ornaments were found with the man, who was clearly part of a more basic and poorer society than Varna's. As one scholar has remarked, "the grave neatly encapsulates the ideal male image of drinking and fighting."

→ *What does the fact that most individualized burial sites contain male bodies tell us about gender relations in these societies? When we compare these sites to those in Egypt and China, what can we learn about the importance of burying the dead across these societies? What can we perceive more generally about the differences between these societies?*

cooperative planning and work. In the British Isles, where such developments tended to come later than those on the continent, the famous megalithic complexes at Avebury and Stonehenge probably reached their highest stages of development in the centuries just before 2000 BCE.

European societies intensified communication, exchange, and mobility among the various communities. This increased interaction was an important source of wealth, but it also sparked organized warfare, especially as peoples vied for frontier lands and sought to conquer sites that contained valuable resources. Integration of local communities, ironically, led to greater friction and produced regional social stratification. The first material sign of an emerging warrior culture was the appearance of drinking cups. The violent men who now provided the protection that these communities needed were buried ceremonially with their drinking cups and weapons. These warrior burials have been found in a huge swath of European lands, from areas in present-day France and Switzerland in the west to areas in present-day central Russia in the east. The agricultural communities now were producing surplus wealth that could be stored, boosting populations to levels at which land and resources had to be fought over, conquered, and defended from encroaching neighbors.

A rough and aggressive culture based on violent confrontations between adult males organized in larger "tribal" groups was taking shape. War cultures became deeply entrenched in all western European societies, marked by a universal presence of a new drinking instrument, the "bell beaker"—so named by archaeologists because it was shaped like an inverted bell. These cups were transported across Europe from their place of origin among armed groups on the lower Rhine River, where they were widely used to swig beer and mead that was distilled from a mixture of grains, honey, herbs, and nuts. As beer drinking spread across Europe, many local variations on beer mugs appeared, again illustrating the constant interplay between external communication and local forces.

As new tools and weapons spread across Europe, the region adopted similar cultural practices. But a split between its eastern and western flanks also began to emerge. In the millennium following 2500 BCE, western Europe witnessed a more elaborate working out of its combative ethos in which warriors battled for territory and resources. The twin pillars of agriculture and metalworking, initially in copper, became the normal supports of daily life almost everywhere.

Warfare had the ironic effect of accentuating the borrowing among the competing people of the region as each tried to best, or at least to check, all rivals. The violent warrior culture of central Europe exerted tremendous pressure to produce more effective weaponry. Warrior elites borrowed from Anatolia the technique of combining copper with tin to produce harder-edged weapons made of an alloy that we call *bronze*. The war economy also provoked universal demand for these better weapons; smiths therefore began to produce them in bulk—as evidenced by the great hoards of copper and bronze tools and weapons from the period found in several archaeological sites in central Europe. Traders used the networks of water communication offered by the rivers of central and northern Europe to exchange their prized metal products, creating one of the first widespread commercial networks that covered the continent.

Constant warfare propelled Europe to become a hugely innovative frontier society. The violent struggles between communities and emerging kinship groups fueled a massive demand for weapons, alcohol, and horses. The culture of violence and conflict that now was driving a basic agricultural economy served to integrate European kinship-based oral societies in a realm of their own, and to separate them from rather than to integrate them with the Mediterranean—a seemingly ordered world of palaces, scribes, and well-disciplined commoners.

Chronology

	5000 BCE		4000 BCE	
SOUTHWEST ASIA AND NORTH AFRICA			*Earliest Sumerian cities in southern Mesopotamia appear, 3500 BCE* ▌	
SOUTH ASIA				
EAST ASIA	▌ *Yangshao culture thrives in northwest China along Yellow River, 5000 BCE* ▌ *Longshan culture emerges in northeast Yellow River valley between 5000 and 2000 BCE* ▌ *Jomon culture in Japan, 5000–2500 BCE*			
THE EASTERN MEDITERRANEAN AND EUROPE		*Megalithic stone constructions begin in western Europe, 4000 BCE* ▌		
THE AMERICAS			*Chicama Valley along Pacific Ocean coast in modern-day Peru thrives, 3500 BCE* ▌ *Tehuacán Valley in modern-day Mexico thrives, 3500 BCE* ▌	
SUB-SAHARAN AFRICA		*Dense village life by Lake Chad and Niger River, Congo River, and Lake Victoria, 3500 BCE* ▌		
INNER AND CENTRAL EURASIA		*Growth and spread of nomadic pastoralism begins, 3500 BCE* ▌		

CONCLUSION

Over the course of the fourth and third millennia BCE, the social geography of the world changed in remarkable ways. In a few key locations, where giant rivers irrigated fertile lands, complex human cultures began to emerge. These areas were the world's most densely populated regions, and they experienced all of the advantages and difficulties of big populations: occupational specialization; social hierarchy, with haves and have-nots; rising material standards of living; highly developed systems of art and science and centralized production and distribution of food, clothing, and other goods for expanding populations. Ceremonial sites and trading entrepôts became cities that were, in turn, the emerging cores of centralized religious and political systems. Cities became the homes for the scribes, priests, and rulers who labored to keep complex societies together. As they did so, urbanites—both men and women—sharpened the distinction between country folk and city dwellers. In effect, urbanization exemplified the many ways in which societies were becoming more complex and stratified, creating social and cultural distinctions within each of these worlds. Social distinctions affected the distinct roles of men and women, as urban families began to take different forms from the kinship groups in the countryside.

But while the riverine cultures shared basic features, the evolution of each followed a distinctive path. Where there was a single river—the Nile or the Indus—the agrarian hinterlands that fed the cities lay along the banks of the mighty waterway. In these areas, cities tended to be smaller, and the Egyptian and Harappan worlds probably enjoyed more political stability and less rivalry. In contrast, cities in the immense floodplain between the Tigris and Euphrates needed large hinterlands to sustain themselves as they became the home for larger populations. Because of their growing power and prestige and their need for resources, Mesopotamian cities vied for preeminence, and their competition often became violent. As we will see in Chapter 3, a similar pattern emerged after 1500 BCE in China, where the Yellow and Yangzi rivers provided the environmental foundations for the rapid expansion of Chinese settlements into cities.

Cities stood at one end of the spectrum of social complexity. At the other end, in most areas of the world, people still lived in relatively simple, horizontal societies, supporting themselves by hunting, gathering, and basic agriculture, as in the settlements of the Americas and Africa. In between, of course, were worlds such as Anatolia, as well as Europe and large parts of China, where towns emerged and agriculture advanced—but not with the leaps and bounds made by the great riverine cultures. Beyond these frontiers, farmers and nomads survived as they had for many centuries.

In spite of these global differences, changes in climate affected everyone and could slow or even reverse development. How—and indeed whether—cultures adapted depended on local circumstances. As the next chapter will show, the human agents of change often came from the fringes of larger settlements and urban areas.

3000 BCE	**2000** BCE	**1000** BCE

First Dynasty emerges in Egypt, 3100 BCE

  ▌ *First writing appears, 3200 BCE*

    ▌ *Early Dynastic Age, 2850–2334 BCE*

      ▌ *Old Kingdom Egypt, 2649–2152 BCE*

Sargon's Akkadian territorial state, 2334–2193 BCE ▌   ▌ *Middle Kingdom Egypt, 2040–1640 BCE*

      ▌ *Cities began to appear in Indus Valley, 2500 BCE*

▌ *Troy founded in Western Anatolia, 3000 BCE*

Fortified villages in Aegean, 2500 BCE ▌   ▌ *Stonehenge constructed in modern-day England just before 2000 BCE*

▌ *Nomadic pastoral communities dominate Central Asian steppe lands by the second millennium BCE*

STUDY QUESTIONS

WWNORTON.COM/STUDYSPACE

1. Explain how the rise of cities in the fourth millennium BCE represented a quantum leap forward in complexity in human history. How did urban dwellers shape political, economic, and cultural developments in their region?
2. Describe how cities in Mesopotamia, the Indus Valley, and Egypt differed from small village communities across the globe. Why did cities emerge in a relatively few places between 5000 and 2000 BCE?
3. Define *pastoralism*. Where in Afro-Eurasia did this form of social organization develop and thrive?
4. Identify major common characteristics that urbanites in Mesopotamia, the Indus Valley, and Egypt shared. What features distinguished each from the others?
5. Compare and contrast the ways in which early writing emerged in the urban societies between 5000 and 2000 BCE. How did each use this new technology? How common was literacy?
6. Compare and contrast early state structures in Egypt and Mesopotamia. Why was Egypt more politically unified than Mesopotamia?
7. Analyze the influence of long-distance trade on the political and economic development of urban societies in Egypt, Mesopotamia, and the Indus Valley. How was each society influenced by contacts with other people?
8. Explain East Asia's relative physical isolation from other Afro-Eurasian societies during this time period. To what extent did this isolation shape social development in this region between 5000 and 2000 BCE?
9. Identify major common characteristics shared by European, Anatolian, and Aegean settlements between 5000 and 2000 BCE. How did settlements in these regions on the margins differ from urban settlements in river basins?

FURTHER READINGS

Adams, Robert McCormick, *The Evolution of Urban Society* (1966). A classic study of the social, political, and economic processes that led to the development of the first urban civilizations.

Algaze, Guillermo, *The Uruk World System: The Dynamics of Expansion of Early Mesopotamian Civilization* (1993). A compelling argument for the colonization of the Tigris and Euphrates valley by the proto-Sumerians at the end of the fourth millennium BCE.

Andrews, Carol, *Egyptian Mummies* (1998). An illustrated summary of Egyptian mummification and burial practices.

Assmann, Jan, *The Mind of Egypt: History and Meaning in the Time of the Pharaohs* (2002). A superb analysis of the cultural and philosophical foundations of Pharaonic culture.

Bagley, Robert, *Ancient Sichuan: Treasures from a Lost Civilization* (2001). Describes the remarkable findings in Southwest China, particularly at Sanxingdui, which have challenged earlier accounts of the Shang dynasty's central role in the rise of early Chinese civilization.

Bar-Yosef, Ofar, and Anatoly Khazanov (eds.), *Pastoralism in the Levant: Archaeological Materials in Anthropological Perspectives* (1992). Classic study of the role of nomads in the development of societies in the Levant during the Neolithic period.

Bruhns, Karen Olsen, *Ancient South America* (1994). The best basic text on pre-Columbian South American cultures.

Butzer, Karl W., *Early Hydraulic Civilization in Egypt: A Study of Cultural Ecology* (1976). The best work on how the Egyptians dealt with the Nile floods and the influence that these arrangements had on the overall organization of society.

Habu, Junko, *Ancient Jomon of Japan* (2004). Study of prehistoric Jomon hunter-gatherers on the Japanese archipelago that incorporates several different aspects of anthropological studies, including hunter-gatherer archaeology, settlement archaeology, and pottery analysis.

Jacobsen, Thorkild, *The Treasures of Darkness: A History of Mesopotamian Religion* (1976). Best introduction to the religious and philosophical thought of ancient Mesopotamia.

Kemp, Barry J., *Ancient Egypt: Anatomy of a Civilization* (1989). A synthetic overview of the culture of the Pharaohs.

Kramer, Samuel Noah, *The Sumerians: Their History, Culture and Character* (1963). Classic study of the Sumerians and their culture by a pioneer in Sumerian studies.

Kuhrt, Amelie, *The Ancient Near East c. 3000–330 BCE* (1995). Comprehensive and authoritative history through the Achaemenid period of the societies of the Ancient Near East, including Mesopotamia, Egypt, Anatolia, and Western Iran.

Lamberg-Karlovsky, Carl C., *Beyond the Tigris and Euphrates Bronze Age Civilizations* (1996). A thought-provoking essay on the social, economic, and political development of the wider Near East during the fourth and third millennia BCE.

Pollock, Susan, *Ancient Mesopotamia: The Eden That Never Was* (1999). An analysis of the social and economic development of Mesopotamia from the beginnings of settlement until the reign of Hammurapi.

Possehl, Gregory L., *Indus Age: The Beginnings* (1999). The second of four volumes analyzing the history of the Indus Valley civilization.

Postgate, J. N., *Early Mesopotamia: Society and Economy at the Dawn of History* (1992). A study of the economic and political development of the Sumerian civilization.

Preziosi, Donald, and L. A. Hitchcock, *Aegean Art and Architecture* (1999). One of the best general guides to the figurative and decorative art produced both by the Minoans and Mycenaeans and by related early societies in the region of the Aegean.

Ratnagar, Shereen, *Trading Encounters: From the Euphrates to the Indus in the Bronze Age*, 2nd ed. (2004). A comprehensive presentation of the evidence for the relationship between the Indus Valley and its western neighbors.

———, *Understanding Harappa: Civilization in the Greater Indus Valley* (2001). Harappan site archaeological data of the last century organized into a historical narrative comprehensible to the general audience.

Rice, Michael, *Egypt's Legacy: The Archetypes of Western Civilization, 3000–300 BC* (1997). The author argues for the decisive influence of Egyptian culture on the whole of the Mediterranean and its later historical development.

Roaf, Michael, *Cultural Atlas of Mesopotamia and the Ancient Near East* (1990). A comprehensive compendium of the historical and cultural development of the Mesopotamian civilization from the Neolithic background through the Persian Empire.

Shaw, Ian (ed.), *The Oxford History of Ancient Egypt* (2000). The most up-to-date and comprehensive account of the history of Egypt down to the Greek invasion.

Thorp, Robert, *The Chinese Neolithic: Trajectories to Early States* (2005). Uses the latest archaeological evidence to describe the development of early Bronze Age cultures in North and Northwestern China from about 2000 BCE.

Van de Mieroop, Marc, *A History of the Ancient Near East, ca. 3000–323 BC* (2004). A political history of Mesopotamia and its neighbors from the late fourth millennium rise of first cities through the first centuries CE.

Warren, Peter, *The Aegean Civilizations: From Ancient Crete to Mycenae,* 2nd ed. (1989). An excellent textual and pictorial guide to all the basic aspects of the Minoan and Mycenaean societies.

殷代车马坑 Chariot Pit of the Shang Dynasty
(No. AGM5146)

编号:(AGM5146)

坑内葬1车、2
马、1人、2000
年发现于孝民屯
东地。

One chariot, 2
horses and one per-
son were buried in
this pit, which were
discovered and un-
earthed in the east-
ern land of Xiaomi-
ntun Village in 2000.

3

NOMADS, TERRITORIAL STATES, AND MICROSOCIETIES, 2000–1200 BCE

The big states of the river basins collapsed—and collapsed brutally—around 2000 BCE when a subsistence crisis gripped much of Afro-Eurasia. For all their achievements and complexity, urbanites existed on a precarious edge. Also severely threatened when the world entered a dry phase were people living in decentralized communities who relied on rainfall rather than on irrigation to supply water for their crops. In the homelands of the large urban cultures of the Nile, Indus, and Mesopotamian floodplains, disaster struck. The crisis was above all environmental. Many centuries of farming had degraded the soils, trees had been stripped from the land for firewood, and rains and floods had washed away layers of topsoil. And as if humanity's ability to unwittingly destroy natural resources was not enough, climatic cycles made things worse. The world entered a warming and drying cycle that converted into deserts lands that had already become less fertile. Irrigation could no longer sustain regular crops when the land became parched.

Urban worlds suffered most. In the great cities of Afro-Eurasia, food shortages led to hunger, and hunger soon gave way to famine. The decline lasted some generations, but by the end of this period of severe drought, the inhabitants of some cities, unable to procure food from their hinterlands, staggered about the streets until they collapsed. Transhumant herders—that is, those who moved their herds back and forth seasonally between microenvironments—from the desert and mountain areas and horse-riding pastoral nomads from the Inner Eurasian steppes, who moved over much longer distances, also felt the pinch. And as they searched for sustenance they more frequently raided permanent settlements. Political vacuums opened up: governing structures in Egypt, Mesopotamia, and the Indus Valley collapsed. Everywhere, in urban centers, political crises in state-level societies disrupted their two millennia of impressively rapid development. In a sense, Afro-Eurasian societies were the first to experience the inescapability of global warming: the emergence of great pioneering cities may have created unprecedented differences between elites and commoners, and between urbanites and rural folk, but everyone felt the effects of this disaster.

Such a radical loss of life-sustaining water did not destroy everything that pioneering city people had created. Writing, ideologies of kingship, architecture, skill at metalworking, and forms of transportation such as sailing vessels and wheeled vehicles were durable cultural creations not easily forgotten. When nomadic and transhumant peoples from the peripheries entered into the fabric of these weakened settled societies, they brought with them their beliefs and customs, but they were also strongly influenced by the settled people, adapting indigenous beliefs and accommodating their own cultural practices to fit with those of the people they had joined. Just as earlier cultural achievements had set the stage for a preliminary round of intense growth in social complexity, so the cultural innovations of Mesopotamia, Egypt, the

Indus River valley, and the North China plain set the stage for another cycle of human cultural development: polities would expand beyond their previous urban frontiers to encompass more cohesive territorial states. But like their riverine predecessors, the regimes that arose in the second millennium BCE created new kinds of tensions between peoples even as they augmented humanity's achievements. Much further away, among the islanders of the Pacific and the Aegean, and in the cut-off world of the Americas, regimes did not bump against each other with the same intensity—and therefore their political systems evolved differently. In those locales, the norm was small-scale micro-states.

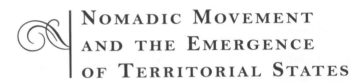

NOMADIC MOVEMENT AND THE EMERGENCE OF TERRITORIAL STATES

> → *How did nomadic groups recast the cultural landscape and geography of Afro-Eurasia during the second millennium BCE?*

Drought and food shortages led to political turbulence and the collapse of the power of kings and ruling elites throughout central and western Afro-Eurasia. Walled cities could not defend their hinterlands. Trade routes lay open to predators, and pillaging became a lucrative enterprise. Clans of pastoral nomads from the Inner Eurasian steppes (north of the Caucasus Mountains and west of the Black, Caspian, and Aral seas) moved across vast distances on horseback and increas-

Focus Questions NOMADS AND TERRITORIAL STATES

→ *How did nomadic groups recast the cultural landscape and geography of Afro-Eurasia during the second millennium BCE?*

→ *What was the impact of the interactions triggered by the drought on the organization of societies?*

→ *How did Vedic migrations influence South Asia?*

→ *What methods did the Shang state employ to maintain its rule?*

→ *How did Austronesian migrations affect the South Pacific?*

→ *How did long-distance trade influence the Aegean world?*

→ *Why did politics remain small-scale in Europe?*

→ *How did the ecology of the Central Andes influence early state systems?*

WWNORTON.COM/STUDYSPACE

NOMADIC MOVEMENT AND THE EMERGENCE OF TERRITORIAL STATES | **99**

→ *How did nomadic groups recast the cultural landscape and geography of Afro-Eurasia during the second millennium* BCE?

ingly threatened the settled people of the mighty cities. In much the same way, transhumant herders from the borderlands of the Iranian plateau and the Arabian Desert advanced on the more densely populated areas near cities searching for food and resources for themselves and for their animals. Similar migratory patterns would also occur in the Indus River valley and the Yellow River valley, causing fundamental changes within the societies there as well. (See Map 3-1.)

The change in environmental conditions now forced humans throughout Afro-Eurasia to adapt or perish. When the pastoral nomads and transhumant herders proved able to adjust more quickly to the new dry conditions of the second millennium BCE, they provided the historic catalyst for the rise of new but still localized territorial states from pharaonic Egypt and Mesopotamia to Vedic South Asia and Shang China. Using chariots, the horse-mounted pastoral nomads introduced technologies that led to new forms of warfare whose spread transformed the ancient Afro-Eurasian world. Moreover, the state building of the new rulers produced changes in society and government that enabled humans not only to survive the climate change but even to thrive in it.

NOMADIC AND TRANSHUMANT MIGRATIONS

As noted in Chapter 2, pastoral nomads rode their horses across the steppe lands of inner Eurasia herding a wide array of livestock. They were perpetually in motion as they covered tremendous areas. Transhumant migrants tended to live closer to city-states and riverine societies; they moved from lowland to highland areas with their livestock, depending on the season of the year.

The changes in climate and landscape affected both migratory groups. The same droughts that ravaged city-states and riverine societies at the end of the third millennium BCE devastated the homelands of nomads and transhumant herders. Both types of peoples were therefore driven to search for secure water sources and pastures for their livestock. Many of them migrated onto the highland plateaus that border the Inner Eurasian steppe lands. From there, some continued into the more densely populated river valleys and soon were jostling with the farming communities over space and resources. They also came from the western and southern deserts in Southwest Asia. For example, the Amorites, pastoral nomads speaking a Semitic language, moved into southern Mesopotamia from the western Syrian Desert. Indo-European-speaking steppe peoples migrated into Anatolia (in present-day Turkey) and eastern Europe, probably entering the plateau from both sides of the Black Sea, especially through the Caucasus Mountains.

The newly arrived pastoral nomadic and transhumant populations settled in the agrarian heartlands of Mesopotamia and the Indus River valley for their tribesmen. After the first wave of newcomers, more immigrants gradually arrived by foot or in wagons pulled by draft animals. Sometimes they came looking for temporary work; sometimes they came to resettle permanently. Nomadic peoples of inner and Central Asia began to fan out across much of Eurasia, including China, Europe and South Asia, bringing with them horses and new technology that could be used for making war. They also brought with them their religious practices and languages, as well as new pressures to feed, house, and clothe an ever-growing population. Taken together, all this human motion caused major changes in the cultural landscape and geography in western Eurasia.

Not all nomadic activity took place on the land. Numerous Greek peoples took to the sea in search of new opportunities, establishing complexes across a wide range of islands in the Aegean Sea. Around the same time, Austronesians set out from the shores of East Asia, hopping from island to island in mammoth sea canoes. They would ultimately populate many of the large habitable islands throughout the Pacific Basin.

The hard-riding pastoral nomads linked disparate cities and towns of South Asia and China for the first time into regional networks connected by tribal clan relations and trade. Using weapons, the horsemen controlled trade and maintained peace in their enclaves. But they could not control how the more literate elites they conquered would write about them. Those who lost their power described the nomadic warriors as "barbaric" and inhuman, painting them as cruel and heartless enemies of "civilization." And in the annals of world history, the label *barbarian* has generally stuck to these nomads. Yet what we know of them today suggests that they were anything but barbaric.

When nomads and transhumant herders conquered settled peoples, they carried with them inventions and ideas that urban and agricultural elites adapted to revitalize and rebuild their societies. Chariots, and especially the horses that pulled them, brought by the pastoral nomadic warriors from the steppes became the favored mode of transportation for an aristocratic warrior class from the cities and for other men of power in agriculture-based societies like China. Kings learned to make alliances with chariot-driving warriors. They also came to use chariots as the centerpiece of their own armies. Control of chariot forces was the foundation of the new balance of power across Afro-Eurasia during the second millennium BCE.

HORSES AND CHARIOTS On the vast steppe lands north of the Caucasus Mountains, as early as the late fourth millennium BCE, the settled people had successfully domesticated the horse. Elsewhere, as on the northern steppes of what is now Russia, horses served as a food source. It was only during the late third millennium BCE that fashioned cheek pieces and mouth bits were used. Horses are faster than any other draft animals, but harnessing horses for

Spread of wheeled vehicles
Spread of war chariots
Dispersal of nomads
Pastoral nomads c. 2000 – 1500 BCE
Southwest Asian Society
Zone of urban civilization

MAP 3-1 NOMADIC MIGRATIONS IN AFRO-EURASIA, 2000–1000 BCE

How did the domestication of horses transform nomadic societies in Afro-Eurasia? How did nomadic pastoral migrations affect settled, agriculture-based societies? To what extent did pastoral peoples bring various worlds together in the second millennium BCE?

S I A

Lake Baikal

ALTAI MOUNTAINS

GOBI DESERT

N SHAN MTS.

LAMAKAN ESERT

Yellow R.

EAST ASIA

SEA OF JAPAN

JAPAN

YA MOUNTAINS

SIA Ganges R.

Yangzi R.

SOUTHEAST ASIA

Bay of Bengal

SOUTH CHINA SEA

PACIFIC

OCEAN

pulling is a complicated matter. Unlike cattle, onagers, or donkeys, which stretch their necks ahead when walking, a horse raises its head. The drivers needed headgear to control horses' speed and direction. In the tombs of nomads scattered around the steppe, archaeologists have found various parts of horse harnesses made from wood, bone, bronze, and iron. These reveal the evolution of headgear from simple mouth bits to full bridles with headpiece, mouthpiece, and rein.

Sometime around 2000 BCE, pastoral nomads on the far northern edge of the broad Mesopotamian plains fashioned a vehicle with one axle and two wheels, and harnessed the newly invented chariot to horses. Early versions had been attached to lumbering oxen or to onagers or donkeys. But harnessing horses was much more complicated than making bullocks draw plows and wagons. Horses were the fastest animals domesticated by human beings and remained the speediest means of transportation until the invention of the steam engine, but they were rarely used as draft animals, for they could not haul sizable loads at high speeds.

Pastoral nomads borrowed transportation techniques developed among agrarian peoples to make chariots light enough for horses to pull at high speeds. Spoked wheels demanded special wood and the carpentry skills to bend it into a circle; wheel covers, axles, and bearings were produced by settled people. The moving parts of the chariot were made of durable metal, first bronze and later—around 1000 BCE—iron. Initially iron was a decorative and experimental metal and bronze was the metal of all tools and weapons. Iron's hardness and flexibility, however, eventually made it more desirable than

copper or bronze (it was also more plentiful) for reinforcing moving parts and protecting wheels. Similarly, solid wood wheels that easily shattered gave way to spokes and hooped bronze and later iron rims. The horse chariots, properly speaking, were the result of a creative combination of the innovations of both nomadic people and agrarian people in western Afro-Eurasia. These innovations—combining new engineering skills, metallurgy, and animal domestication—and their ultimate diffusion revolutionized how humans made war and therefore changed history.

The horse chariot slashed the time it took to travel between capitals and altered the machinery of war. Slow-moving infantry gave way in the second millennium BCE to battalions of chariots. Each vehicle carried a driver and an archer, and charged into the melee of battle with deadly precision and speed. The mobility, accuracy, and shooting power of warriors in horse-drawn chariots tilted the political balance so dramatically that after the nomads perfected chariot warfare by 1600 BCE, they were able to challenge the political systems of Mesopotamia and Egypt and soon were affecting war making in regions as far removed as present-day Greece, India, China, and Sweden. Only with the advent of cheaper armor after 1000 BCE could foot soldiers—in China, armed with crossbows—recover their military importance. For much of the second millennium BCE, charioteer elites prevailed over huge swaths of Afro-Eurasia.

City dwellers in the river basins must have found their first sight of horse-drawn chariots terrifying, but they knew that war making had changed forever and scrambled to adapt. The Shang kings of China and the pharaohs in Egypt probably learned about and copied chariots from nomads or neighbors who already had them, and they came to be valued almost as highly as the throne itself. The young pharaoh Tutankhamun (c. 1350) was portrayed as a chariot archer; when he died, his chariot and other accoutrements of a warrior were laid in his tomb. A century later, horse chariots were displayed in the tombs of the Shang kings in the Yellow River valley, the heartland of agricultural China.

Horse Figurines. Around 1500 BCE, a group of people who spoke an Indo-European language, the Vedic Sanskrit, entered South Asia. These people were nomads with horse chariots, a novelty in South Asia. Because they cremated their dead and roamed around, few traces of them have survived. These horse figurines from the northwest region of South Asia, in modern Pakistan, are probably among the few material remains of the migrants.

PASTORAL NOMADS, HERDERS, AND TRADE Transhumant herders, whose lowland pastures were often on the periphery of cities in riverine societies, traded their surplus meat and animal products for items produced by artisans in the cities. When the production of goods in the cities fell because of environmental or political pressures, the herders might instead raid the cities in order to gain access to what they needed. Drought affecting their usual pasturelands might also force them to move their herds closer to the riverine cities in order to find grass and water.

Horse-riding nomads from the steppes ranged more widely. Some of these nomads engaged in long-distance trade, traveling quickly over great expanses and bearing goods and ideas back and forth across Afro-Eurasia. Traveling by horse or camel in relatively small bands over unsettled areas, they

War Chariots. *Bottom left:* A large vase typical of Mycenaean art on the mainland areas of Greece. The regular banding and presentation of scenes reflect a society that is more formally ordered and rigidly hierarchical than that on Minoan Crete. Note the presence of the horse-drawn chariot. Possessing this more elaborate means of transport and warfare characterized the warrior elites of Mycenaean society and linked them to developments over wide expanses of Afro-Eurasia at the time. *Upper left:* This wooden chest covered with stucco and painted on all sides with images of the Egyptian pharoah in his war chariot was found in the fabulously wealthy tomb of Tutankhamun in the Valley of the Kings in Egypt. The war chariot was introduced into Egypt by the Hyksos. By the reign of Tutankhamun in the New Kingdom, depictions of pharaoh single-handedly smiting the enemy from a war chariot drawn by two powerful horses were common. *Upper right:* The Shang fought with neighboring pastoral nomads from the central Asian steppes. To do this, they imported horses from central Asia and copied the chariots of nomads they had encountered. This gave Shang warriors devastating range and speed for further conquest.

could carry such prestige goods as precious stones or textiles, or metals such as copper, tin, or silver. In small bands, they also might raid trading caravans organized by merchants, or they might offer protection to such caravans for a fee. Early nomads did not write down their achievements, as did the kings of sedentary societies. Yet archaeologists have uncovered some of what the nomads accomplished as traders, for they have found jade from Central Asia's Khotan Desert in tombs at Anyang, one of the Shang capitals, and amber pieces in Greece that likely originated in Nordic lands.

THE EMERGENCE OF TERRITORIAL STATES

From the riverine cities in Mesopotamia, overwhelmed by the arrival of displaced nomadic peoples, emerged a new political form—the territorial state—that broke out of the urban confines of its predecessors. (See Map 3-2.) Power reaching from cities into distant hinterlands was the chief political innovation of this epoch. Great centralized kingdoms, organized around charismatic rulers heading large households, achieved

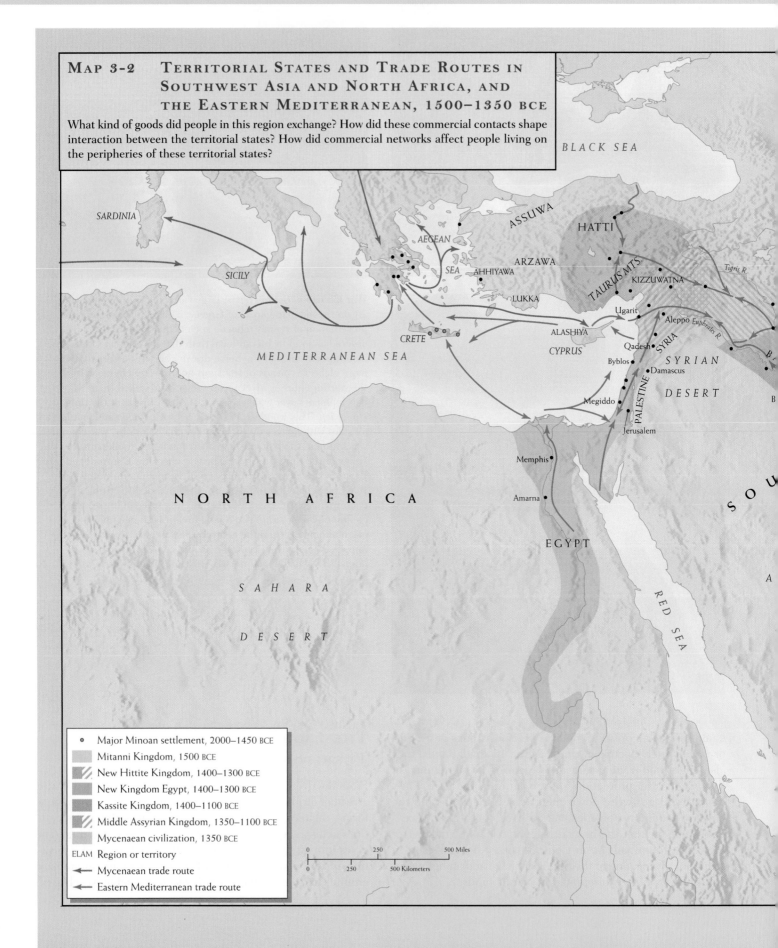

MAP 3-2   TERRITORIAL STATES AND TRADE ROUTES IN SOUTHWEST ASIA AND NORTH AFRICA, AND THE EASTERN MEDITERRANEAN, 1500–1350 BCE

What kind of goods did people in this region exchange? How did these commercial contacts shape interaction between the territorial states? How did commercial networks affect people living on the peripheries of these territorial states?

Map legend:
- Major Minoan settlement, 2000–1450 BCE
- Mitanni Kingdom, 1500 BCE
- New Hittite Kingdom, 1400–1300 BCE
- New Kingdom Egypt, 1400–1300 BCE
- Kassite Kingdom, 1400–1100 BCE
- Middle Assyrian Kingdom, 1350–1100 BCE
- Mycenaean civilization, 1350 BCE
- ELAM   Region or territory
- Mycenaean trade route
- Eastern Mediterranean trade route

0   250   500 Miles
0   250   500 Kilometers

NOMADIC MOVEMENT AND THE EMERGENCE OF TERRITORIAL STATES | 105

→ *How did nomadic groups recast the cultural landscape and geography of Afro-Eurasia during the second millennium* BCE?

political stability for a while by passing the torch of political command from one generation to the next. People now identified themselves as more than simply residents of cities—they felt allegiance to their territories, their rulers, and their widely dispersed linguistic and ethnic communities. These territories for the first time had identifiable borders, and those living within them began the long process of creating a shared identity.

Territorial states differed from the city-states that preceded them. The earlier city-states of the riverine societies, organized around the temple and palace, were each autonomous polities and were separated by buffer zones that were increasingly contested. The new territorial states in Egypt and Mesopotamia based their authority on divine monarchs, large and widely dispersed bureaucracies, elaborate and widely administered legal codes, large territorial expanses, definable borders, and plans for continuous expansion. Although power still emanated from central cities, the rulers had changed: the once-marginalized peoples of the Syrian Desert (the Amorites) and of the northern steppe lands and Anatolia (the Hittites) now held considerable power. Their drive to conquer and expand overcame and replaced the earlier models of competition and coexistence. Territorial states also emerged for the first time in Greece and China; there the newcomers from the outside who took power more completely adopted local ways.

Each of these societies was different, but they all shared the drive to integrate dominions within a landscape that had definable boundaries. In the second millennium BCE, when rulers created large-scale territorial states for the first time, they were literally remapping their known world and dividing it into specific areas and zones to be "governed" by an authority recognized—sometimes loved, sometimes feared—by the people. Such states brought two major changes to the lives of their inhabitants. First, people now identified themselves as part of an entity with territorial limits; those living beyond them belonged to "other" territorial states, were seen as unlike them in significant respects, and had to be dealt with (mainly through new forms of diplomacy and advanced warfare). Second, people welcomed the return of "government," which first restored and then upheld order. Achieving that order was made possible not only by the formal laws or codes developed by these territorial states, laws that all subjects were expected to obey, but also by the subjects' adherence to a shared set of norms and values. During the second millennium BCE, people came to view a good king as one who could command the respect of neighboring states and bring security to his subjects. Their feelings of safety, however, were often the result of a long and bloody process as territorial states expanded their borders to their geographical or demographic limits. It was one of the great paradoxes of the era that upheavals and surges of great violence could yield unprecedented political innovation and security.

The long-term political consequences of ecological and demographic upheavals played out during this period. The

Afro-Eurasia-wide droughts had forced peoples to move in search of new lands. Nomads from the north moved southward in pursuit of arable land, while settled peoples from the southern coastal areas went north as salt from overirrigation and the seas encroached on the land and poisoned water supplies. The resulting shift of the population axis across much of central and southwestern Asia ultimately contributed to the creation of the new territorial states. As city-states fell, undone by these climatic and demographic changes, new political structures emerged in their place.

Other regions of the world were undergoing similar developments but more slowly; they would not feel the full effects of the changes attending the formation of their states for a few more centuries. In one way, East Asia and especially the Americas were fundamentally different from the lands that stretched from North Africa to South Asia: because these regions were not as densely packed as the emerging territorial states, they experienced less rivalry and consequently less struggle over borders and populations. High density of states brought greater pressure on borders, which state builders were then forced to defend. Within those borders, ruling classes sought to integrate their dominions and thereby increase loyalty to the capital and its laws. Ever larger territorial states began the long-term process of giving the world a political map, divided into specific areas tied to different sovereign authorities.

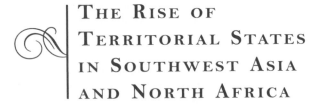

THE RISE OF TERRITORIAL STATES IN SOUTHWEST ASIA AND NORTH AFRICA

> → *What was the impact of the interactions triggered by the drought on the organization of societies?*

Environmental pressures and conquering pastoral nomads and transhumant herders transformed the city-states of Southwest Asia and North Africa. As the newcomers became assimilated, they competed for positions of leadership and resources among themselves and with the rulers they encountered. From 2000 to 1600 BCE, small kingdoms, organized according to territorial and ethnic identity, dominated the landscape from the Aegean Sea through Mesopotamia and Iran. In 1600 BCE, a renewed wave of pastoral nomadic conquests and migrations brought the fledgling territorial kingdoms—never very stable—to their knees. After a century of turmoil, the balance of power shifted irrevocably, and a new order of territorial states based in urban capitals but

commanding large hinterlands with definable boundaries and common cultures took form.

The five great territorial states of Southwest Asia and North Africa during this period consisted of the Egyptians, who extended their power to the eastern Mediterranean and Palestine; the Hittites in Anatolia; the Mitanni (later replaced by the Middle Assyrians), who controlled Syria and northern Mesopotamia; the Kassites in southern Mesopotamia; and the Middle Elamites, who controlled the southwestern Iranian plateau. These large states were so well balanced and competed with each other so intensely that over time, they were compelled to learn the techniques of coexistence. They produced highly developed forms of statecraft and international diplomacy that served this area well for several centuries. Not so fortunate were the smaller kingdoms, such as the Syro-Palestinian vassal realms, squeezed between the major powers. They were relegated to the status of buffer zones between the regions that the large territorial powers dominated.

EGYPT

The first and probably best known of the five great territorial kingdoms of Southwest Asia was Egypt. There the pharaohs of the Middle Kingdom and later the pharaohs of the New Kingdom unified the river valley and expanded both south and north into adjacent lands. The long era of prosperity associated with the Old Kingdom of the third millennium BCE had ended abruptly when the Afro-Eurasia-wide drought brought catastrophe to the area. For several decades, the Nile did not overflow its banks, and Egyptian harvests withered. The pharaohs lost legitimacy and fell prey to internecine feuding among pretenders to the title. Regional powers took the place of a unifying, centralized state. Egypt, which had been one of the most stable corners of Afro-Eurasia, would endure more than a century of tumult before a new order emerged.

MIDDLE KINGDOM EGYPT (2040–1640 BCE) Around 2050 BCE, after a century of drought, the floodwaters of the Nile returned to normal. Crops grew again. But who would restore order and reunite the kingdom? From about 2061 to 1991 BCE, two rulers at Thebes—far south of the Old Kingdom's seat of power in Memphis—named Mentuhotep consolidated power in Upper Egypt and began building activity in much of the country. By taming rivals and co-opting pretenders, they ushered in a new phase of stability that later historians have called the Middle Kingdom. For 350 years, the new pharaonic line built on earlier foundations to develop institutions far beyond their original forms.

GODS AND KINGS Just as rulers of this new phase came from the margins, so too did its gods. The Twelfth Dynasty

(1991–1783 BCE), with its long, unbroken line of succession, dominated the epoch of the Middle Kingdom, in part because it brought a new sacred order to replace the chaos that had visited drought and despair on the Egyptian people. Amenemhet I (1991–1962 BCE) elevated a formerly insignificant god, Amun, to prominence. The king capitalized on the god's name, which means "hidden" in ancient Egyptian, to convey a sense of his invisible omnipresence throughout the realm.

Because Amun's attributes were largely hidden, he could with relative ease be embraced by believers in a different theological system. Amun's cosmic power was attractive to those in areas that had recently experienced impoverished independence. As the pharaoh elevated the cult of Amun, he also brought the parts of his kingdom into a more unified, if not always fully integrated, whole, thereby further empowering Amun—as well as his worldly sponsor, the pharaoh. Thus, during the Twelfth Dynasty, Amun eclipsed all of the other gods of Thebes. Grafted onto the sun god Re, Amun emerged as "Amun-Re": a supreme deity, the king of the gods. His champion among the Egyptian kings also became the ruler of the rulers. The power of the gods and kings was intertwined, increasing the sway of both. But the cult of Amun was more than simply a tool of political culture: it also had a strong spiritual impact on the pharaoh and on Egyptian society.

Amun. This sculpture of the head of the god Amun was carved from quartzite during the Eighteenth Dynasty, around 1335 BCE. At Thebes in Upper Egypt, a huge temple complex was dedicated to the combined god Amun-Re. The powerful kings of the Middle and New Kingdoms each added a courtyard or a pylon, making this one of the largest religious structures in the ancient world.

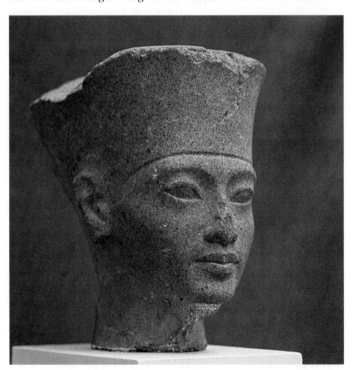

ROYAL SPLENDOR AND ROYAL CARE Middle Kingdom rulers tapped into the bounty of their kingdom, the loyalty of their subjects, and the work of untold slaves and commoners to build what would become the largest and longest-lasting public works project ever undertaken. For 2,000 years, Egyptians and slaves captured in war or raids set about erecting monumental gates, enormous courtyards, and other structures in a massive temple complex at Thebes dedicated to Amun-Re to exhibit the power of the pharaohs and the gods.

Gradually the Middle Kingdom pharaohs reasserted royal power over the regions that had broken off from the old regime, deploying ideology and administrative innovation as well as religion. Unlike the perfect and removed rulers of the Old Kingdom, the Middle Kingdom rulers nurtured a cult of the pharaoh as the good shepherd whose prime responsibility was to fulfill the needs of his human flock. By instituting charities, offering homage to gods at the palace to ensure cyclical floodwaters, and performing ritualized ceremonies to honor their own generosity, the pharaohs portrayed themselves as the stewards of their people.

MERCHANTS AND TRADE NETWORKS Prosperity gave rise to an urban class of merchants and professionals who used their wealth and specialized skills to carve out places in the cities for their own leisure and pastimes. What was new was that they did not depend directly on the kings for such benefits. Indeed, in a sign of their upward mobility and autonomy, some members of the middle class constructed tombs that they filled with representations of the material goods they would use in the afterlife as well as the occupations that would engage them for eternity—a privilege that during the Old Kingdom had been reserved exclusively for the royal family and a few powerful nobles.

Centralized and reforming kingdoms also drove the expansion of more actively extended and more wealth-producing trade networks. The Egyptian floodplains had long since been deforested. Wood had to be imported by ship, in massive quantities; especially prized were cedars from Byblos (a city in the land that would soon be known as Phoenicia, corresponding roughly to present-day Lebanon), used to make furniture for the living and coffins for the dead. Superb examples are preserved from the tombs of nobles and pharaohs. Commercial networks extended south through the Red Sea as far as present-day Ethiopia to bring back precious metals, ivory, livestock, slaves, and exotic animals such as panthers and monkeys to the pharaoh's palace. Expeditions were also undertaken to the Sinai Peninsula in search of copper and turquoise. Egyptians looked south for gold, which was highly desired for personal and architectural ornamentation. To acquire it, they crossed into Nubia, where they ran into some stiff resistance; eventually they colonized the area to broaden their trade routes and secure needed resources. A series of forts extended as far south as the second cataract of the Nile River. (See Map 2-5.)

HYKSOS INVADERS AND NEW FOUNDATIONS   Pharaonic peace brought prosperity, but it did not ensure that the pharaohs' rule would continue uninterrupted. Egypt found itself open to migration and foreign invasion, coming once again from the margins. First, the very success of the new commercial networks lured pastoral nomads from the frontiers who were in search of work. Later, a new people from Southwest Asia attacked Egypt, initially destabilizing the kingdom but ultimately putting it on stronger foundations.

Beginning in 1780 BCE, large numbers of Amorites, who were Semitic-speaking transhumants, reached the banks of the Nile after being forced out of the Syrian Desert by drought. Over the course of the next century, they were absorbed into Egyptian society as agricultural workers, especially in the region of the delta in Lower Egypt, and gradually their numbers and power increased. Sometime around 1640 BCE, a western Semitic-speaking people, whom the Egyptians called the Hyksos (literally, "Rulers of Foreign Lands"), overthrew the unstable Thirteenth Dynasty. The Hyksos had mastered the art of horse chariots, and with those chariots and their superior bronze axes and composite bows (made of wood, horn, and sinew) they were able to defeat the pharaoh's foot soldiers. Yet the victors did not destroy the conquered land; if anything, they were assimilated into it. By adopting Egyptian ways, they also reinforced them. The Hyksos settled down and ruled as the Fifteenth Dynasty, taking control of the northern part of the country and transforming the Egyptian military force.

> *No longer cut off as a world apart, Egypt became a major player in the politics of Southwest Asia.*

After a century of political conflict, an Egyptian who controlled the southern part of the country, Ahmosis (r. 1550–1525 BCE), successfully used the Hyksos weaponry—horse chariots—against the invaders themselves and became pharaoh. The Egyptian rulers had learned an important lesson from the invasion: they had to pay closer attention to their frontiers, for they could no longer rely on deserts as natural buffers. Ahmosis built up large, mobile armies and drove the "foreigners" back into the Levant. Diplomats followed in the army's path, and the pharaoh initiated a strategy of interference in the affairs of the Levantine states. Such policies laid the groundwork for developing statecraft and an international diplomatic system that future Egyptian kings used to dominate the eastern Mediterranean world.

The migrants and invaders from the west introduced new ideas and techniques that the Egyptians quickly adopted to consolidate their power. The new techniques included bronze working, which the Egyptians had not perfected, preferring to import already alloyed bronze or to work with a copper arsenic alloy that was dangerous and more difficult to work. The migrants also introduced an improved potter's wheel and a vertical loom. South Asian animals such as humped zebu cattle, as well as vegetable and fruit crops, appeared on the banks of the Nile for the first time.

Probably the most significant innovations pertained to war: the horse and chariot, the composite bow, the scimitar, and other weapons associated with fighters from western Eurasia. These weapons rapidly transformed the Egyptian army from a standing infantry to a high-speed, mobile, and deadly fighting force. As Egyptian armies drove the military frontier as far south as the fourth cataract of the Nile River, the kingdom now stretched from the Mediterranean shores to Ethiopia. West Eurasian military technology enabled the pharaohs to pacify the frontiers and to maintain command over distant provinces. No longer cut off as a world apart, Egypt became a major player in the politics of Southwest Asia.

NEW KINGDOM EGYPT   By the beginning of the New Kingdom (1550–1070 BCE), Egypt was projecting its interests outward: it defined itself as a superior, cosmopolitan society that drew its strength from an efficient bureaucracy run by competent and socially mobile individuals. For 100 years, Egypt expanded its control south into Nubia, a source of gold, exotic raw materials, and manpower. This expansion is most strongly identified with the reign of Egypt's most powerful woman ruler, Hatshepsut. Hatshepsut served as regent for her young son Thutmosis III, who came to the throne in 1479 BCE. When he was seven years old, she proclaimed herself "king," ruling as co-regent until she died. During her reign, there was little military activity, but trade contacts both into the Levant and Mediterranean and south into Nubia flourished.

Thutmosis III (r. 1479–1425 BCE) launched an even more expansionary phase that lasted for 200 years. The direction of Egypt's expansion was northeastward into the Levant, where Egyptians collided with the ambitions of the Mitanni and the Hittite kingdoms. At the Battle of Megiddo (1469 BCE), the first recorded chariot battle in history, Thutmosis III defeated vassals of the Mitanni and established an Egyptian presence in Palestine. Egypt was now poised to engage in commercial, political, and cultural exchanges with the rest of the region (see "The Community of Major Powers" later in this chapter).

ANATOLIA AND THE RISE OF THE HITTITES

Anatolia was an overland crossroads that linked the Black and Mediterranean seas. Like so many other semi-arid plateaus of Afro-Eurasia—high tablelands, easy to crisscross and hospitable to large-scale herding societies and clans—

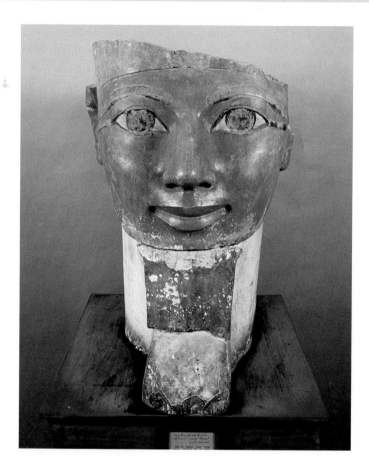

Hatshepsut. The only powerful queen of Egyptian pharonic history was Hatshepsut, seen here in a portrait head created during her reign. Because a woman on the throne of Egypt would offend the basic principles of order (*ma'at*), Hatshepsut usually portrayed herself as a man, especially late in her reign. This was reinforced by the use of male determinatives in the hieroglyphic renditions of her name.

during the third millennium BCE Anatolia had become home to a number of powerful independent polities run by indigenous elites, combining pastoral lifeways, agriculture, and urban commercial centers. Before 2000 BCE, peoples speaking Indo-European languages began to infiltrate onto the plateau, probably coming from the steppe lands north and west of the Black Sea. The newcomers lived in fortified settlements and often engaged in regional warfare, and their numbers grew. Splintered into competing clans, the peoples of Anatolia fought for regional supremacy. They borrowed extensively from the cultural developments of the Southwest Asian urban cultures, especially those of Mesopotamia.

THE OLD AND NEW HITTITE KINGDOMS (1800–1200 BCE) In the early second millennium BCE, the chariot aristocracies, which were the most powerful of the competing groups in the Anatolian area, thrived on the commercial activity between east and west. Chief among them

were the Hittites, who would form one of the five great territorial states of this period. Their chariots carried lancers and archers across vast expanses to plunder recalcitrant neighbors and enforce tax and tribute collection from those they subdued. These chariot aristocracies were finally unified during the seventeenth century BCE under the reign of Hattusilis I.

During Hattusilis's reign, the Hittite armies campaigned throughout Anatolia and met strong resistance, especially in the west. After claiming victory, Hattusilis turned his attention to the east, crossed the Taurus Mountains, and defeated the kingdom that controlled all of northern Syria from its capital (located at the site of the modern city of Aleppo). In 1595 BCE, Hattusilis and his son Mursilis I marched south along the Euphrates River as far as Babylon and sacked the city. But the occupation of Mesopotamia left the homelands exposed to domestic feuding and overstretched his army. With rebellion brewing in Anatolia, the Hittite forces soon withdrew to their plateau bastions, leaving a power vacuum in southern Mesopotamia.

It took almost two centuries for the Hittites to recover the strength that had enabled them to attack and destroy Babylon in 1595 BCE. Under the leadership of the great king Suppilulimua I (r. 1380–1345 BCE), the Hittites returned to their former glory and became one of the major powers of Southwest Asia. After conquering the small kingdoms to the southwest, the Hittites extended their control all the way to the Euphrates in the east and Syria in the south, where at Qadesh they met the Egyptians in a battle involving a vast number of chariots. The Hittites controlled much of the middle ground between Mesopotamia and the Nile, and thus the kingdom's rulers were crucial in maintaining the region's balance of power.

THE IRANIAN PLATEAU AND THE ELAMITES

As environmental conditions turned warmer and drier, the early part of the second millennium BCE saw extensive movements of people on the Iranian plateau. The people living in the valley of the Halil River, whose trade in precious stones and metals in the third millennium BCE had linked the peoples from North Africa to South Asia (see "Global Connections & Disconnections" in Chapter 2), gradually abandoned their heartland regions, some moving to the north and others to the west. During this time, the Elamites with their capital in the upland valley of modern Fars in the southwest formed into a cohesive polity that incorporated various transhumant peoples of the Zagros Mountains. When the catastrophic drought hit the Iranian plateau, some of the Elamites and the peoples of the Zagros Mountains migrated further south and westward into Mesopotamia, ultimately bringing down the Third Dynasty of Ur in 2004 BCE (see below). A century or so later, the Elamites and the Amorites were at the center of newly formed dynasties in southern Mesopotamia.

Gradually, pastoral nomads entered the Iranian plateau from the steppes of inner Eurasia. Perhaps the Kassites, who would come to rule southern Mesopotamia during the second half of the second millennium BCE, began their journey from there. Certainly the Indo-Iranian-speaking Medes and the Persians, who rose to prominence in the first millennium BCE, started their movement onto the Iranian plateau at this time. Transhumant peoples continued to dominate the lands of the Zagros Mountains and on occasion to threaten their settled neighbors to the west.

MESOPOTAMIA

The period of drought that brought down the Old Kingdom of Egypt near the end of the third millennium BCE was as damaging to Mesopotamia and the Iranian plateau. Harvests were small, the price of basic goods rose, and the social order broke down. Already short of agricultural produce, the towns of southern Mesopotamia were invaded by transhumant peoples coming from the Zagros Mountains to the east and from the Syrian Desert to the west. These herding peoples, who did not use horses or chariots, were looking for new grazing lands to replace those swallowed up by the growing deserts. As elsewhere in Afro-Eurasia, environmental changes altered the human landscape. A millennium of intense cultivation, combined with a period of severe drought, seriously damaged the productivity of the land. The rich arable soil was increasingly depleted of nutrients; at the same time, salt water from the Persian Gulf was spreading into the marshy deltas and contaminating the water table. As the main branch of the Euphrates River shifted to the west, large areas of previously arable land were no longer sufficiently watered for cultivation. As a result, many of the ancient cities lost access to their fertile agrarian hinterlands and slowly withered away. Other agrarian belts were developed along which new cities appeared. All these alterations pushed the center of political and economic gravity northward, away from the silted, marshy deltas of the southern heartland. North of Uruk and farther up the Euphrates River, Amorite pastoralists founded the city of Babylon (near current-day Baghdad) in 1830 BCE. Its establishment marked the end of the era of Sumer and Akkad and the beginning of the Old Babylonian era.

NOMADIC AND TRANSHUMANT MIGRATION TO MESOPOTAMIAN CITIES   Mesopotamian urbanites called the transhumant herders from the Arabian Desert Amorites, from the Akkadian word for "west," *Amurru*. Technically speaking, the term *Amorites* does not refer to a single tribe; it was a general label for all transhumant groups who had their roots in

the western desert. City dwellers looked down their noses at these rustic folk, as the scorn in the following poetry makes clear. The Amorite is

> a tent-dweller, [buffeted] by wind and rain, [who offers no] prayer,
> He who dwells in the mountains, [knows not] the places [of the gods];
> A man who digs up mushrooms at the foot of the mountain, who knows no submission,
> He eats uncooked meat,
> In his lifetime has no house,
> When he dies, he will not be buried;
> My girlfriend—why would you marry Martu?!
> (Klein, "The Marriage of Martu," 89)

Transhumant herders may have been "foreigners" in the cities of Mesopotamia in the sense that they did not make their homes there, but they were not strangers to them. They had always played an important role in Mesopotamian urban life and were familiar with the culture of Mesopotamian city-states. During the winter, these rural folk spent their time in villages close to the river (their lowland pastures) to water their animals, which grazed on fallow fields. In the scorching summer, they retreated to the cooler highlands. Their flocks provided the various wools for the vast textile industries of Mesopotamia, and the herders supplied the leather, bones, and tendons that were used in other craft productions. Conversely, they admired and purchased those products created by sedentary craftworkers as well as agricultural goods. Moreover, they paid taxes, served as warriors, and labored on public works projects. Yet despite being part of the urban fabric and benefiting economically from the connection, they had few political rights within city-states.

As scarcities mounted, transhumant peoples began to press the settled communities more closely. Finally, in 2004 BCE, Amorites from the western desert joined forces with the Elamites and other allies from the Iranian plateau to bring down the Third Dynasty of Ur that had controlled all of Mesopotamia for more than a century. As in Egypt, a century of political instability followed the demise of the old city-state models of the third millennium BCE. But here, too, it was pastoral folk who finally restored order, taking the wealth of the regions they conquered and helping the cultural realm to flourish. They also expanded trade and founded new kinds of political communities: territorial states with dynastic ruling families and well-defined frontiers.

RESTORED ORDER AND CULTURE   Restored order and prosperity enabled new kings to nourish a vibrant intellectual and cultural milieu. Public art and works projects were commissioned, and institutions of learning thrived. The court supported workshops for skilled artisans such as jewelers and sculptors, and it also established schools for scribes, the creators and transmitters of an expanding literary culture.

→ *What was the impact of the interactions triggered by the drought on the organization of societies?*

Culturally, Babylonians inherited and reproduced the achievements of earlier Mesopotamia. To rid themselves of the image of being rustic foreigners and to show their familiarity with the core values of the region, they studied the oral tales and written records of the earlier Sumerians and Akkadians. Scribes transcribed the ancient texts and preserved their tradition. Royal hymns, for instance, continued to be composed in the Sumerian language that had not been spoken for centuries but that was used for this form of literature. These hymns portrayed the king as a legendary hero whose status was quasi-divine.

Heroic narratives about ancient founders, which were based on a cycle of traditional stories concerning the legendary rulers of ancient Uruk, served to establish the legitimacy of the new rulers. These great poems were written not in Sumerian but in the contemporary Babylonian dialect of the Semitic Akkadian language and constituted the first epic narratives of purely human—as opposed to godly—achievement. They helped identify the history of a people with their king, constructing stories intended to circulate widely and to unify the kingdom. The most famous was the elaboration of the *Epic of Gilgamesh.*

Mesopotamian kings invested in cultural production because it enlightened them, unified their people, and distinguished their subjects from peoples in other kingdoms. Literature, the arts, and science helped delimit the kingdom's reach—beyond which lay other cultures and other polities.

TRADE AND THE RISE OF A PRIVATE ECONOMY

With restored prosperity also came a decisive shift away from economic activity dominated by the city-state and toward autonomous private ventures. The new rulers designated private entrepreneurs rather than state bureaucrats to collect taxes. People paid their taxes in the form of commodities, which the entrepreneurs exchanged for silver that they passed on to the state after taking a percentage for their profit. The result was both more private activity and wealth and more revenues flowing into state coffers.

At the same time, a reliance on labor from state impressments was giving way to contracted work. Palace and temple officials, as well as private agents, began hiring individuals on daily contracts: workers were taken on as needed and were no longer maintained year-round. While cheaper for the state in the short run, this piecework approach—mirrored in agriculture, where tenant farmers began renting land and giving a portion of their crop back to the landowners, a system known as sharecropping—did not provide for all of the needs of the workers. The result was a large destitute and disenfranchised underclass that ultimately threatened the existence of the state.

Mesopotamia was a crossroads for overland caravans leading east and west. Merchants organized donkey caravans to transport goods over long distances. When the region was peaceful and well-governed, the trading community flourished. Their ability to move exotic foodstuffs, valuable minerals, textiles, and luxury goods across Southwest Asia won Mesopotamian merchants and entrepreneurs a privileged position as they connected producers with distant consumers. Merchants also used sea routes for trade with the Indus Valley. Before 2000 BCE, mariners had

Gilgamesh. This terra-cotta plaque in the Berlin Museum is one of the very few depictions of Gilgamesh (on the left wielding the knife) and his sidekick, Enkidu. It illustrates one of the episodes in their shared adventures, the killing of Ḫumwawa, the monster of the Cedar Forest. The style of the plaque indicates that it was made during the Old Babylonian period, between 2000 and 1600 BCE.

THE EPIC OF GILGAMESH

Gilgamesh, an early ruler of the ancient city of Uruk, was the supreme hero of Mesopotamian myth and legend. He and his deeds were the subject of epic poems composed and revised over two millennia. He was a larger-than-life figure—a successful ruler, boastful and vain, as well as a courageous adventurer and a devoted friend to his companion Enkidu. The Gilgamesh epic, constructed in the early second millennium BCE from a number of independent stories, is the oldest piece of world literature still extant. It portrays the hero as a tragic figure who is obsessed with fame and glory and whose quest for immortality necessarily ends in failure. The following excerpt from tablet X tells of his anguish on his long and ultimately fruitless journey to gain immortal life. He is speaking to an alewife (a woman who keeps an alehouse) as he continues to refuse to accept his humanity and embrace the inevitability of death.

The alewife spoke to him, to Gilgamesh,
"If you are truly Gilgamesh, that struck down the Guardian,
Destroyed Humbaba, who lived in the Pine Forest,
Killed lions at the mountain passes,
Seized the Bull of Heaven who came down from the sky,
    struck him down,
Why are your cheeks wasted, your face dejected,
Your heart so wretched, your appearance worn out,
And grief in your innermost being?
Your face is like that of a long-distance traveler,
Your face is weathered by cold and heat . . .
Clad only in a lion skin you roam open country."
Gilgamesh spoke to her, to Siduri the alewife,
"How could my cheeks not be wasted, my face not
    dejected.
Nor my heart wretched, nor my appearance worn out,
Nor grief in my innermost being,
Nor my face like that of a long-distance traveler,
My friend whom I love so much, who
Experienced every hardship with me,
Enkidu, whom I love so much, who experienced every
    hardship with me—
The fate of mortals conquered him! Six days and seven
    nights I wept over him,
I did not allow him to be buried, until a worm fell out of
    his nose.

I was frightened and . . .
I am afraid of Death, and so I roam open country.
The words of my friend weigh upon me.
I roam open country for long distances; the words of my
    friend
Enkidu weigh upon me.
I roam open country on long journeys.
How, O how, could I stay silent, how O how could I keep
    quiet
My friend whom I love has turned to clay:
Enkidu my friend whom I love has turned to clay.
Am I not like him? Must I lie down too,
Never to rise, ever again?"

→ *What does this passage from* Gilgamesh *tell us about human relationships and human nature during this period? What does it tell us about rulers and their relationship with their gods? How should historians view a work such as* Gilgamesh *that was passed on via oral tradition for many centuries before it was written down? Is it a legitimate historical source?*

SOURCE: Stephanie Dalley, *Myths from Mesopotamia: Creation, The Flood, Gilgamesh and Others* (New York: Oxford University Press, 1991), pp. 100–101.

charted the waters of the Red Sea, the Gulf of Aden, the Persian Gulf, and much of the Arabian Sea. During the second millennium BCE, shipbuilders figured out how to produce larger and larger vessels and to rig them with towering masts and woven sails—creating seaworthy craft able to carry bulkier loads to remote ports. Building ships of course required wood, particularly cedar from Phoenicia, as well as wool and other fibers from the pastoral hinterlands for the sails. Such reliance on imported materials was part of a more general trend of growing regional economic specialization and increasing interaction across western Afro-Eurasia.

Doing business in Mesopotamia was profitable but also very risky. If harvests were poor, cultivators and merchants were unable to meet their tax obligations and thus incurred heavy debts. The frequency of such misfortune is evident from the profusion of royal edicts that annulled certain kinds of tax debts as a gesture providing relief for weary subjects. Moreover, traders and goods had to pass through many lands, some of whose rulers were hostile and unwilling to protect the caravans. Taxes, duties, and bribes had to be paid along the entire route. If goods reached their final destination, they yielded large profits; if disaster struck, as often happened, investors and traders had nothing to show for their efforts. As a result, merchant households seeking to lower their risks experimented with various instruments. They formalized commercial rules, established early insurance schemes, and used extended kinship networks (relying on trusted family or clan members living in cities along trade routes and handled the family's interests there) to ensure strong commercial alliances and gather intelligence. They also cemented their ties with political authorities—indeed, the merchants who dominated the ancient city of Assur on the Tigris pumped revenues into the coffers of the local kingdom in the hope that wealthy dynasts would look out for the merchants' interests in the rough-and-tumble world of early Mesopotamian commerce.

> *Control over military resources was necessary to gain dominance but was no guarantee of success: the ruler's charisma also mattered.*

MESOPOTAMIAN KINGDOMS The new rulers of Mesopotamia changed not only how trade was conducted but also how the state was organized. Where city-states had once prevailed, rulers from pastoral nomadic stock fashioned kingdoms that ruled over large territorial expanses. These herders-turned-urbanites hybridized their own social organization with that of the city-states to create the structures necessary to support territorial states. The basic social organization of the Amorites was tribal, dominated by a ruling chief. Tribal polities, even those extending over wide areas, were divided into clans; each claimed descent from a common ancestor, and thus drew a line between itself and all who were not kin, yet the clans were open to incorporate and exchange new members through marriage and adoption. Even the many Amorites who had given up nomadic ways and settled in the cities remained conscious of their genealogical roots. The new territorial polities were rooted in identification with the clan and tribe, with the line between own group and others now drawn on a larger scale.

The emergence of ruling cliques from among the nomadic chieftains who took power in Mesopotamia gave way to a new model of statecraft in three stages. In the first major transformation, chieftains became kings. Second, these new Mesopotamian kings turned their authority—which in the tribe had been based on their prowess on the battlefield—into an alliance with merchant magnates in exchange for revenues and for elite support. Finally, royal status became hereditary, a practice of sucession that replaced the old tribal system according to which leaders were elected by influential members of the community. Yet even in this new system, kings could not rule without the support of nobles and merchants.

Over the centuries, powerful kings continued to push out the borders of their territories. They subdued weaker neighbors, coaxing or forcing them to become vassals—allies required to pay tribute in the form of luxury goods, raw materials, and manpower as part of a broad confederation of Mesopotamian polities under the king's protection. Control over military resources—access to metals for weaponry and eventually to herds of horses used to pull vast numbers of chariots—was necessary to gain dominance but was no guarantee of success: the ruler's charisma also mattered. This emphasis on personality explains why Mesopotamian kingdoms tended to be strong for certain periods, but vulnerable to ambitious rivals and neighbors when the king was weak or vacillating. It also distinguished them fundamentally from Middle Kingdom Egypt and Hittite Anatolia, territorial states in which power was much more institutionalized and durable.

The most famous of the Mesopotamian rulers of the second millennium BCE was Hammurapi (or Hammurabi), who ascended the throne as the sixth king of Babylon's First Dynasty in 1792 BCE and ruled until 1750 BCE. Continuously engaged in conflicts with powerful neighbors, he sought to centralize state authority and to create a new legal order. He used both diplomatic and military skills to become the strongest king in Mesopotamia, making Babylon the capital of his kingdom and calling himself "the king who made the four quarters of the earth obedient." After subduing his rivals, he implemented a new system to secure his power, appointing regional governors to manage outlying provinces and to deal with local elites.

Hammurapi's image as ruler was borrowed from that of the Egyptian pharaohs of the Middle Kingdom. The king was shepherd and patriarch of his people, responsible for the proper preparation of the fields and irrigation canals and for the well-being of his followers. Such an ideal recognized that being king was a delicate balancing act. While he had to curry favor among the realm's powerful merchants and elites, he was also expected to attend to the needs of the poor and disadvantaged—in part to keep from gaining a reputation for cruelty but in part to gain a key base of support should the elites become dissatisfied with his rule.

Hammurapi converted this balancing act into an art form, encapsulated in a grand legal structure—Hammurapi's Code. The code began and concluded with the rhetoric of paternal justice. For example, he concludes the code by describing

The Code of Hammurapi. The inscription on the shaft of the Code of Hammurapi is carved in a beautiful rendition of the cuneiform script. Because none of the laws on the Code were recorded in the thousands of judicial texts of the period, it is uncertain if the Code of Hammurapi presented actual laws, or only norms for the proper behavior of Babylonian citizens.

himself as "the shepherd who brings peace, whose scepter is just. My benevolent shade was spread over my city, I held the people of the lands of Sumer and Akkad safely on my lap."

The Code of Hammurapi was in fact a compilation of more than 300 edicts addressing crimes and their punishments, listing the behaviors that could bring legal sanction. One theme rings loud and clear: governing public matters was man's work, and upholding a just order was the supreme charge of rulers. Whereas the role of the gods in ordering the world was distant, the king was directly in command of ordering the relations between people. Accordingly, the code elaborated in exhaustive detail social rules that were supposed to ensure the peace of the kingdom through its primary instrument, the family, carefully outlining the rights and privileges of fathers, wives, and children. The father had the duty of treating his kin as the ruler would treat his subjects, with strict authority and care. Adultery, which represented the

supreme violation of this moral code, was considered a female crime. Any woman found with a man not her husband was bound and thrown into the river, as was her lover.

Hammurapi's order both pacified the region and stratified society. His code divided the Babylonian kingdom into three classes—each member was either a freeman (*avilum*), a dependent man (*mushkenum*), or a slave (*wardum*), and each had an assigned value and distinct rights and responsibilities.

By the end of his reign, Hammurapi had reconfigured the political map of Southwest Asia. He had established Babylon as the single great power in Mesopotamia and had reduced competitor kingdoms to mere vassals. Following his death, his sons and successors struggled to maintain control over a shrinking domain lands for another 155 years in the face of internal rebellions and foreign invasions. In 1595 BCE, Babylon was sacked by the Hittite king Hattusilis I.

KASSITE RULE As a crossroads for Afro-Eurasia, Mesopotamia continued both to benefit from and to be threatened by the arrival of nomadic and transhumant neighbors and immigrants. The Kassites, for instance, who came from the eastern Zagros Mountains, had entered southern Mesopotamia from the Iranian plateau. They began arriving in the river valley as agricultural laborers as early as 2000 BCE and gradually integrated themselves into Babylonian society by becoming bureaucrats associated with the temple. Already deeply entrenched in society, they were well placed to fill the power vacuum left when the Hittites destroyed the First Dynasty of Babylon. By 1475 BCE, Kassite rulers had reestablished order in the region; over the next 350 years they brought all of southern Mesopotamia under their control, creating one of the great territorial states within an emerging latticework of states from North Africa to South Asia.

STATES OF SOUTHWEST ASIA AND NORTH AFRICA, 2000–1200 BCE

Middle Kingdom Egypt	2040–1640 BCE
The Old Hittite Kingdom	1800–1600 BCE
Hammurapi's Babylonia	1792–1750 BCE
New Kingdom Egypt	1550–1070 BCE
The New Hittite Kingdom	1400–1200 BCE
Kassite Rule	1475–1125 BCE
Community of Major Powers	1400–1200 BCE

The Kassites presided over a golden age that was based not on militaristic expansion but on trade in such precious commodities as horses, chariots, and lapis lazuli, which they exchanged for gold, wood, and ivory. Like other immigrant communities who had come to this ancient land before them, the Kassites absorbed the traditions and institutions of Mesopotamia. Even more vigorously than their predecessors, they strove to preserve the past and transmit its institutions to posterity. Very little of their own language and customs, apart from their personal names, has been preserved. With an unrivaled thoroughness and dedication, Kassite scribes translated much of the older Sumerian literature into Akkadian. They revised and compiled texts into standard editions, from which scholars have recovered a Babylonian creation myth called the Enuma Elish. In their determination to become even more Babylonian than the Babylonians, the Kassites saved a treasure trove of historical literature and artifacts for later generations.

THE COMMUNITY OF MAJOR POWERS (1400–1200 BCE)

By the fifteenth century BCE, societies in Southwest Asia and North Africa had recovered from environmental upheaval and invasion. The five great territorial states that emerged, occupying the area between the Aegean Sea and the Iranian plateau, ultimately established an interregional system based on the concept of a balance of power. Over the course of two centuries, these major powers learned how to settle their differences through treaties and diplomatic negotiations rather than on the battlefield. Only in Syria and Palestine, where the edges of major powers met, did lesser states centered on single cities continue to exist. Jerusalem, Byblos, Damascus, Ugarit, and Aleppo were all capitals of little kingdoms tightly squeezed between the large states to the north, south, and east. Although small in size, each of these vassal kingdoms played an important role in maintaining the balance of power and thus keeping the region peaceful.

The leaders who created this international system pioneered a form of international diplomacy that would inspire rulers across the centuries. Each state, large and small, knew its place in the political pecking order of the broader interregional system. It was an order that depended on constant communication—the foundation of what we now call diplomacy. A remarkable cache of more than 300 letters discovered at Tell el-'Amârna, the capital city of the New Kingdom under the pharaoh Akhenaten, offers intimate views of these complex interactions. Most are letters from the Egyptian king to his vassals in the small tributary states of Palestine, but others were sent from Akhenaten and his father to the Babylonian, Mitanni, Middle Assyrian, Kassite, and Hittite kings. Many of these letters were written in a dialect of Akkadian, used by the Babylonian bureaucrats, that served as the diplomatic language of the era. This correspondence reveals a delicate balance, constantly shifting, between competing kings who were intent on maintaining their status and who knew that winning the loyalty of the small buffer kingdoms was crucial to political success.

Formal international treaties, although rare and usually signed only at the conclusion of serious military conflicts, re-inforced diplomatic contacts. Diplomacy more commonly took the form of marriages and the exchange of specialized personnel who would reside at the court of foreign territorial states. Gifts also strengthened the peaceful relations between the major powers and signaled a ruler's respect for his neighbors. They had to be acknowledged by reciprocating gifts of equal value; anything less risked a potentially dangerous slight. At the same time, gifts introduced raw materials into regions that otherwise lacked them. According to the letters, Egypt was the sole source of gold, which it exchanged for horses and lapis lazuli from the Kassites, who certainly obtained these goods from further east. Copper came from Alashiya (the ancient name for Cyprus), and ivory and craft goods were sent from the small vassal states in Syria and Palestine.

Although each of the major powers and the vassal kingdoms had its own social order, their close-knit international relations led to the creation of an elite cosmopolitan merchant and political class. Use of the Babylonians' Akkadian dialect soon separated these elites from the lower classes. Like the royal courts on which they depended, they drew on their

Akhenaten. The pharaoh Amenhotep IV changed his name to Akhenaten to reflect his deep devotion to Aten, the god of the sun disk. The art of the period of his reign, like his religion, challenged conventions. In it, the faces of the king and queen, as well as their bodies, were extremely elongated and distorted. Some scholars think that this distortion reflects a condition that the king himself suffered from.

great fortunes to erect buildings, decorate their tombs, and consume goods in a conspicuous way that marked their special status. Supporting these elites were specialists, bureaucrats, scribes, and craftworkers. Military men also enjoyed high status, especially the charioteers. Standing armies provided the foundation of royal power.

The foundations of power were not always durable, however. Building the state system was ultimately the task of those at the bottom of the social pyramid, and the reliance of the ruling classes on the least privileged for their power and political authority was an intrinsic weakness of these regimes. Commoners remained tied to the land, which sometimes was owned by communities or institutions, not individual families. They paid taxes to the state, performed corvée labor (that is, labor conscripted by the state for public works such as irrigation or building projects), and served as foot soldiers. The hefty taxes and conscription were needed to sustain the state. The collapse of the international age had many causes, but one factor contributing to its demise was the disintegration of the social fabric as workers could not pay their taxes or fled their communities rather than fight in the armies of the rulers.

NOMADS AND THE INDUS RIVER VALLEY

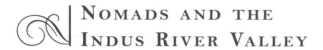

> → *How did Vedic migrations influence South Asia?*

Drought at the end of the third millennium BCE ravaged the Indus River valley as it did other regions. By 1700 BCE, the population of the old Harappan heartland had plummeted. Around 1500 BCE, the Vedic people, who originally came from the steppes of inner Eurasia, crossed from the northern highlands of Central Asia through the Hindu Kush and entered the fertile lowlands of the Indus River basin. (See Map 3-3.) As they moved into the Indus Valley, these nomads changed and adapted to their new environment.

The Vedic people called themselves Aryans, or "respected ones." Like other nomads who had arrived from the northern steppe into Southwest Asia, they spoke an Indo-European language—in this case Sanskrit, which literally means "perfectly made." They brought with them domesticated animals—especially horses, which they used to draw chariots and which thus were crucial to establishing their military superiority—as well as elaborate rituals for worshipping gods, which they actively used to distinguish themselves from the indigenous populations. The Vedic people did not doubt that their chief god, Indra, the deity of war, was on their side. But, as was true of so many Afro-Eurasian migrations, the arrival of outsiders led to as much fusion as conflict. While the native-born peoples eventually adopted the language of the newcomers, the new-

Indra with Buddha. The Vedic people worshipped their gods by sacrificing and burning cows and horses and by singing hymns and songs, but they never built temples or sculptured idols. Therefore we do not know how they envisioned Indra and their other gods. However, when Buddhists started to make images of Buddha in the early centuries CE, they also sculpted Indra and Brahma as attendants of the Buddha. Indra in Buddhist iconography evolved into Vajrapani, the Diamond Lord. In this plate, the one on the left holding a stick with diamond-shaped heads is Indra/Vajrapani.

comers soon took up the techniques and rhythms of agrarian life. In adapting to local conditions, the Vedic steppe people developed their own world.

The Vedic people used the Indus Valley as a staging area for migrations throughout the northern plain of South Asia. As they mixed agrarian and pastoral ways and borrowed technologies such as ironworking from further west, their population grew, and they began to look for new resources. With horses, chariots, and iron tools and weapons, they marched south and east. By 1000 BCE, they reached the southern foothills of the Himalayas and gradually began to settle in the Ganges River valley. Five hundred years later, they had settlements as far south as the Deccan plateau.

Each wave of occupation was accompanied by violence, but the invaders did not simply dominate the indigenous peo-

Primary Source

VEDIC HYMNS TO THE CHARIOT RACE OF THE GODS

The Vedic people did not leave us accounts of their horse chariot races and festivals, despite the centrality of these events to their culture. However, they have left us their religious hymns praising the chariot races of gods. As we see from the following hymn, the Maruts, the storm gods under the direction of Indra, were viewed as particularly good charioteers.

1. The Maruts charged with rain, endowed with fierce force, terrible like wild beasts, blazing in their strength, brilliant like fires, and impetuous, have uncovered the (rain-giving) cows by blowing away the cloud.

2. The (Maruts) with their rings appeared like the heavens with their stars, they shone wide like streams from clouds as soon as Rudra, the strong man, was born for you, O golden-breasted Maruts, in the bright lap of Prisni.

3. They wash their horses like racers in the courses, they hasten with the points of the reed on their quick steeds. O golden-jawed Maruts, violently shaking (your jaws), you go quick with your spotted deer, being friends of one mind.

4. Those Maruts have grown to feed all these beings, or, it may be, (they have come) hither for the sake of a friend, they who always bring quickening rain. They have spotted horses, their bounties cannot be taken away, they are like headlong charioteers on their ways.

5. O Maruts, wielding your brilliant spears, come hither on smooth roads with your fiery cows (clouds) whose udders are swelling; (come hither), being of one mind, like swans toward their nests, to enjoy the sweet offering.

6. O one-minded Maruts, come to our prayers, come to our libations like (Indra) praised by men! Fulfil (our prayer) like the udder of a barren cow, and make the prayer glorious by booty to the singer.

7. Grant us this strong horse for our chariot, a draught that rouses our prayers, from day to day, food to the singers, and to the poet in our homesteads luck, wisdom, inviolable and invincible strength.

8. When the gold-breasted Maruts harness the horses to their chariots, bounteous in wealth, then it is as if a cow in the folds poured out to her calf copious food, to every man who has offered libations.

→ *What kind of gods are the Maruts? What is their heavenly job when racing on horse chariots? Why did the Vedic people try to please the Maruts by offering libations?*

SOURCE: Mandala II, Hymn 34, in Vedic Hymns, translated by Hermann Oldenberg, in vol. 32 of *Sacred Books of the East,* edited by F. Max Müller (1897; reprint, New Delhi: Motilal Banarsidass, 1979), pp. 295–96.

ples; indeed, the confrontation was a catalyst for change. Although the Vedic people despised the local rituals, they were in awe of the inhabitants' farming skills and knowledge of seasonal weather. They therefore adapted even as they

Gandhara Grave Site. Gandharan Grave Culture, an archaeological assemblage named after cemeteries and settlements in Timargarh, Pakistan, testifies that the migration to South Asia lasted more than a thousand years. The people who are buried there show many different physical types. The early graves were complete burials of bodies. Cremation, the practice of Vedic people, appeared after the fourteenth century BCE.

HOW LANGUAGES SPREAD: THE CASE OF
NOMADIC INDO-EUROPEAN LANGUAGES

Language arose independently in a number of places around the world. All languages change with time, and related tongues with a common ancestral origin are grouped as "language families"; members of the same family diverged from one another at different times, varying with each family, but share grammatical features and root vocabularies.

While technically more than a hundred language families exist in the world, a much smaller number have influenced vast geographic areas. For example, the Altaic languages spread from Europe to Central Asia. The Sino-Tibetan language family includes Mandarin, the most widely spoken single language in the world. The Uralic family, which includes Hungarian and Finnish, is found mainly in Europe. The Afro-Asiatic language family contains several hundred languages spoken in North Africa, sub-Saharan Africa, and Southeast Asia, Hebrew and Arabic among them.

The family of languages that has received the most attention from linguists, and the one with the largest number of speakers, is Indo-European; it was first identified by scholars who recognized the similarities in grammar and vocabulary among classical Sanskrit, Persian, Greek, and Latin. Living languages in this family include English, Irish, German, Norwegian, Portuguese, French, Russian, Persian, Hindi, and Bengali. For the past 200 years, comparative linguists have sought to reconstruct Proto-Indo-European, the parent of all the languages in the family. They have drawn some conclusions about its grammar (hypothesizing a highly inflected language, with different endings on nouns and verbs depending on how they are used) and its vocabulary. For example, after analyzing regular patterns of linguistic change, scholars have suggested that the basic Indo-European root that means "horse"—in Sanskrit, *aśva*; Persian, *aspa*; Latin, *equus*; and Greek, *hippos* (ἵππος)—is *ekwo-.

Attempts have also been made to locate the homeland of the original speakers of Proto-Indo-European. These efforts have relied heavily on the reconstructed vocabulary, which contains words for "snow," "mountain," and "swift river," as well as for animals not native to Europe, such as "lion," "monkey," and "elephant"; such terms are then mapped onto a matching geography. Other words describe agricultural practices and farming tools that date back as far as 5000 BCE. Many believe that nomadic and pastoral peoples of the Eurasian steppes took this language as well as their horses and chariots to the borderlands of what is now Afghanistan and eastern Iran.

We know that the early speakers of Indo-European languages used chariots, and they also had specific terminology for "wheel," "yoke," and "axle." The earliest pictures of horse-drawn chariots, marked on stone, are found in the region between two lakes, Van (in modern-day Turkey) and Urmia (in modern-day Iran). The chariot was the literal vehicle for cultural mingling, as reflected in the spread of the language of the people who used them. In this way, migrations of populations from distant regions created new cultural convergences.

The reasons that languages move over vast areas and alter over time are complex, and scholars argue over the importance of such factors as invasions, migrations, climatic changes, the availability of natural resources, and ways of life (hunter-gatherer vs. agriculturalist). Even within one language, the import of words changes through generations of use—for example, the original sense of the English word *nice* was "foolish, stupid"—and words from a common Indo-European root could take on very different meanings while remaining quite similar phonetically. Thus *aśura* means "demonic creature" in Sanskrit, whereas the Persian *ahura* means "Supreme God."

The study of language families and their history throughout the world can be quite revealing. The geographic, material, climactic, and demographic details of their use and penetration into different countries clearly indicate the importance of language in how cultures intermingled throughout time.

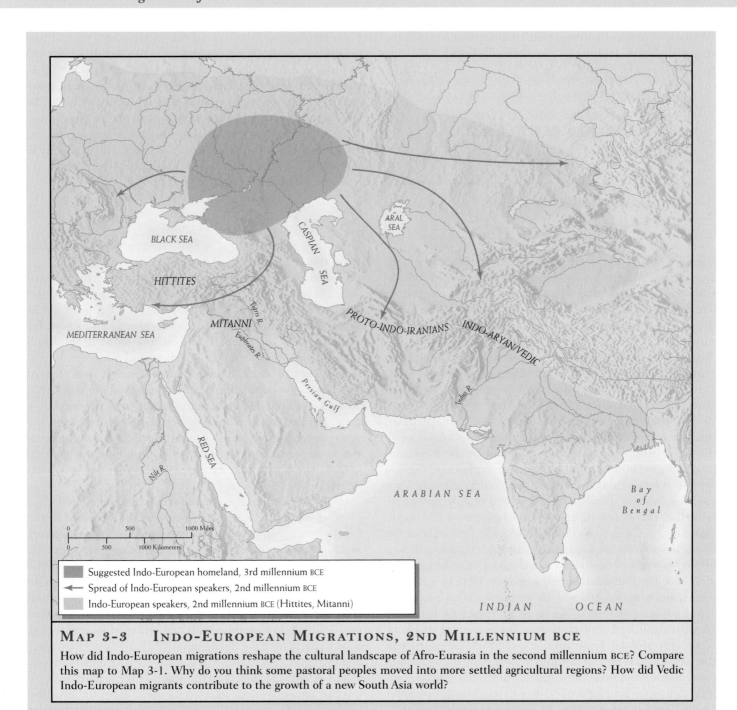

MAP 3-3   INDO-EUROPEAN MIGRATIONS, 2ND MILLENNIUM BCE

How did Indo-European migrations reshape the cultural landscape of Afro-Eurasia in the second millennium BCE? Compare this map to Map 3-1. Why do you think some pastoral peoples moved into more settled agricultural regions? How did Vedic Indo-European migrants contribute to the growth of a new South Asia world?

continued to expand their territory. They moved into huts constructed from mud, bamboo, and reeds. They refined the already highly developed production of beautiful carnelian stone beads, and they further aided commerce by devising standardized weights. In addition to raising domesticated animals, they planted wheat and rye on the Indus plain, and they learned to plant rice in the marshy lands after they had settled in the Ganges Valley. Eventually they mastered the use of plows with iron blades, an innovation that transformed the agrarian base of South Asia.

The turn to settled agriculture was a major shift for the pastoral Vedic people, whose staple foods were dairy products and meat and who traditionally measured their wealth in livestock—horses were valued most highly, and cows worth more than sheep. Horses were prized for their ability to draw chariots but could not be bred in South Asia's semi-tropical climate; the need to import them from central and western Asia helped support a brisk trade. But as they became an agrarian folk, the Vedic people learned from the local agriculturists among whom they now lived. In the process, they created polities and cultures that combined traits from the steppe lands with indigenous ways. We will pick up their story again in the next chapter.

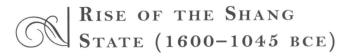

RISE OF THE SHANG STATE (1600–1045 BCE)

> → *What methods did the Shang state employ to maintain its rule?*

Climatic change at the end of the third millennium BCE affected East Asia much as it had central and western Asia. As Chapter 2 detailed, this was a time of cultural integration among agricultural communities along the Yellow and Yangzi rivers. Chinese lore maintains that in this era the Xia dynasty was founded by the mythological Yu the Great. While evidence for such a kingdom is sketchy, archaeological and other evidence does confirm the later emergence, around 1600 BCE, of a territorial state called the Shang dynasty, located in northeastern China. (See Map 3-4.)

Like the ruling families in the Southwest Asian societies, the Shang handed down their own foundation myths to unify the state. Stories supposedly written on bamboo strips and later collected into what are known as the authentic "Bamboo Annals" tell of a time at the end of the Xia dynasty when the sun was dimmed, frost and ice appeared in July, and heavy rainfall and flooding were followed by a long period of drought. According to Chinese mythology, Tang, the first ruler of the Shang dynasty, defeated a cruel and despotic Xia king and then offered to sacrifice himself so that the long drought would finally end. Tang survived, however, and proved to be a just and moral ruler who strengthened his state and unified his people.

The Shang state was not as well defined by fixed and clearly established borders as were the territorial kingdoms of Southwest Asia. To be sure, it faced threats—but not in the form of rival territorial states encroaching on its peripheries. It had little need for a strongly defended central complex, though its heartland was called Zhong Shang, or "center Shang." Its capital moved as its frontier expanded and contracted. This relative security can also be seen in the Shang kings' highly personalized style of rule, as they traveled regularly around the country to meet, hunt, and conduct military campaigns with those who owed allegiance to them. Yet, like the territorial kingdoms of Southwest Asia, the Shang state had a ruling lineage (that is, a line of male sovereigns descended from a common ancestor), which was eventually set down in a written record. Like the kings of other early territorial states, Shang rulers used metallurgy and writing to reinforce their rule, as well as ancestor worship, divination, and other rituals. At the heart of their power, however, was their keen awareness of the importance of promoting agricultural growth and controlling the precious metals that could be used to wage war. All of these efforts cumulatively laid the foundation for future state formation in East Asia, shaping a system in which one regime would be dominant, surrounded by (not always happy) satellites. For the time being, spared the intense scramble for territorial control, the Shang regime had relatively little motivation to assert its hegemony, especially in comparison with contemporary Southwest Asian states.

STATE FORMATION

One of the first kingdoms of East Asia, the Shang state built upon the small agricultural and riverine village cultures of the Longshan peoples, who had set the stage for a centralized state, urban life, and a cohesive culture at the end of the third millennium BCE. The Shang state did not grow out of urban polities such as those in Mesopotamia and Egypt, for the abundant supply of food from the agriculturally rich lands in the areas around the Yellow and Yangzi rivers enabled China to maintain a more decentralized local form of life. But as the population began to grow and the number of villages multiplied, interactions—and conflicts—inevitably grew. Because of the increase in trading networks and the greater need for mechanisms to settle disagreements between towns, larger and more centralized forms of control were required. The Shang state emerged to play that larger governmental role.

Four fundamental elements that were instrumental in forming the Shang state had already been introduced by the Longshan peoples: a metal industry based on copper, pottery making, standardized architectural forms and walled towns, and divination using animal bones. To these foundations, the Shang dynasty added a lineage of hereditary rulers whose hold on power was based on their relation to their ancestors and the gods, written records, tribute, and elaborate rituals that enabled them to commune with ancestors and foretell the future. In particular, the Shang promoted large-scale metallurgy and the development of writing, major components in the advance of Chinese society in the second millennium BCE.

The Shang dynasty derived its name from the location where, over the course of several centuries, a royal ancestral temple, a city, and finally the dynasty itself were established. To expand and protect their borders, the Shang fought with neighboring states and with pastoral nomads from the central Asian steppes. Horses imported from central Asia helped the Shang dominate northern and central China. Moreover, the Shang copied the chariots of the nomads they encountered, improving them by adding bronze fittings and harnesses; this new technology gave the warriors devastating range and speed. The importance of such chariots to military victories highlights the impact of nomadic contacts across Afro-Eurasia. Here, as in Southwest Asia, chariot aristocracies emerged.

↦ *What methods did the Shang state employ to maintain its rule?*

Several other large states also developed in East Asia between 1500 and 1300 BCE, formed both by relatively urban and wealthy southeastern peoples and by more rustic peoples bordering the Shang. The latter interacted with and traded with these other groups, whom they called the Fang, their label for those who lived in non-Shang areas. Other kingdoms in the south and southwest also had independent bronze industries, with casting technologies comparable to those of the Shang.

Though the Shang dynasty arose in part because greater centralization of power was needed, it was never as fully centralized a state as its contemporaries in Southwest Asia and North Africa, such as the New Kingdom in Egypt or Hammurapi's Babylonian kingdom. It did not control surrounding vassal states or even, as noted above, have a fixed capital. Sima Qian (c. 145–86 BCE), the greatest historian of ancient China, claimed that the Shang state moved its capital six

times, adding that the final and most important move to Yin (Anyang in present-day Henan) in 1350 BCE led to the dynasty's golden age. Its rulers may have moved in search of metal resources, as copper and tin were the basis of the bronze industry and thus of wealth and power for those who controlled them.

The Shang state reached its zenith around 1200 BCE. At Yin, the Shang erected massive palaces, royal neighborhoods, and bronze foundries. In workshops surrounding the palace, craftworkers decorated jade, stone, and ivory objects; wove silk on special looms; and produced bronze weapons and bronze ritual objects and elaborate ceremonial drinking vessels from which the Shang dynasts, ancient accounts say, imbibed strong drink. Based on the local abundance of metal ores, artisans were able to organize large numbers of workers into workshops where they mass-produced the large bronze vessels. The levels of urbanization reached at Yin make it

MAP 3-4   SHANG DYNASTY IN EAST ASIA

Why were there no clear territorial boundaries for the Shang state? Why do you think that control of copper and tin sources was important to Shang rulers? Compare this map to Map 3-2. How was the Shang state different from territorial states in Western Asia?

SIMA QIAN ON THE RULER'S MANDATE

Sima Qian was the first great historian in ancient China; he later had as much influence in East Asia as Herodotus, the first Greek historian, had in Greece and Rome. The excerpt below presents the Xia-Shang dynastic transition as an example of the transfer of the ruler's mandate.

After Emperor K'ung-chia was enthroned, he delighted in following ghosts and spirits and engaging in licentious and disorderly actions. The prestige of the Hsia-hou Clan declined and the feudal lords rebelled against him.

Heaven sent down two dragons, a male and a female. K'ung-chia was not able to care for them and he lost the support of the Huan-lung (Dragon Raising) Clan. The Yao-t'ang Clan was already in decline, [but] among their descendants one Liu Lei learned the technique of taming dragons from the Huan-lung Clan and thus obtained service with K'ung-chia. K'ung-chia bestowed on him the *cognomen* Yü-lung (Dragon Tamer) and conferred on him the people descended from the Shih-wei [Clan]. The female dragon died and Liu Lei fed it to The Hsia-hou, The Hsia-hou sent [someone] to demand [more of it], and, fearing [that he would be punished], Liu Lei moved on.

When K'ung-chia passed away, his son Emperor Kao was enthroned. When Emperor Kao passed away his son Emperor Fa was enthroned. When Fa passed away, his son Emperor Lu-k'uei was enthroned. He was known as Chieh.

From K'ung-chia's time to the time of Emperor Chieh, the feudal lords had revolted many times against the Hsia. Chieh did not engage in virtuous [government] but in military power and [this] hurt the families of the hundred cog-nomens. The families of the hundred cognomens were not able to bear him.

Chieh then summoned T'ang and jailed him in Hsia-t'ai. After a while he freed him. T'ang cultivated his virtue and the feudal lords all submitted to T'ang. T'ang then led troops to attack Chieh of Hsia. Chieh fled to Ming-t'iao and subsequently was exiled and died there. Before he died he said to someone, "I regret failing to kill T'ang in Hsia-t'ai; that is what has brought me to this."

T'ang then ascended the throne of the Son of Heaven and received the world's homage in The Hsia's place. T'ang enfeoffed the descendants of the Hsia. In the Chou dynasty they were enfeoffed at Ch'i.

→ *Does Sima Qian's first-century BCE account confirm the existence of the Xia [Hsia] dynasty in the third millennium BCE? What role did morality play in Sima Qian's description of the transfer of the Xia ruler's mandate to the Shang dynasty?*

SOURCE: "The Hsia, Basic Annals" 2, in *The Grand Scribe's Records*, edited by William H. Nienhauser, Jr., translated by Tsai-fa Cheng, Zongli Lu, William H. Nienhauser, Jr., and Robert Reynolds, vol. 1 (Bloomington: Indiana University Press, 1994), pp. 37–38.

clear that the Shang also collected tribute from their agrarian heartlands and used these resources to support the city's nobles, priests, and dependent artisans and metalworkers. The Shang state simultaneously promoted both the writings of elite scribes and the productions of common artisans.

METALWORKING, AGRICULTURE, AND TRIBUTE

Small-scale metalworking first emerged in northwestern China; pre-Shang sites such as Erlitou reveal that casting techniques were being used as early as 1800 BCE. Because both copper and tin were accessible from the North China plain, only short-distance trade was necessary to obtain the resources needed by a bronze culture. Access to copper and tin and to the new technology that used them to make bronze war and ritual objects gave the Shang unprecedented power as they dealt with their neighbors. The Shang used an alloy of copper, lead, and tin to produce bronze, from which they made weapons, fittings for chariots, and ritual vessels. They created hollow clay molds into which they poured the molten metal alloy and then removed the desired bronze objects after the liquid metal had cooled and solidified. Casting modular components that could later be combined made possible huge increases in production and fueled the extravagant uses of bronze vessels by royal elites for burials. For example, in 1975 archaeologists found a tomb at Anyang that held a bronze vessel weighing 1,925 pounds that was produced in the Shang workshops around 1200 BCE. Another Anyang tomb from the same period contained 3,500 pounds of cast bronze.

The bronze industry in the second millennium BCE shows the high level in ancient China not only of material culture—that is, the actual physical objects produced—but also of cultural development. The Shang metalworking that emerged around 1500 BCE in the Yellow River valley required extensive mining (and thus a large labor force), efficient casting, and a reproducible artistic style. The extraction of the resources was separated from their conversion into goods. And while highly valuing its artisans, the Shang state treated its copper miners as lowly tribute laborers.

By closely controlling access to tin and copper and to the production of bronze, the Shang kings managed to prevent their rivals from forging bronze weapons and thus increased their own power and legitimacy. With their metal weapons, Shang armies could easily destroy armies equipped with wooden clubs and stone-tipped spears. Moreover, the ruler

also enhanced his power by hiring artisans to record his feats for posterity. Shang workers produced large and small bronze vessels that they then delicately inscribed with images of important events, particularly those in which the ruler played a significant role, such as a battle, a wedding, the birth of an heir, or an astrological sighting.

The Shang dynasts also understood the importance of agriculture to winning and maintaining power and did much to promote agrarian development. The activities of local governors and the masses revolved around agriculture. The rulers controlled their own farms, which supplied food to the royal family, craftworkers, and army. New technologies enabled food production to rise. Farmers opened up previously untilled land by draining low-lying fields or clearing forested areas so that they could expand the cultivation of millet, wheat, barley, and possibly some rice. Farm implements included stone plows, spades, and sickles. In addition, farmers cultivated silkworms and raised pigs, dogs, sheep, and oxen. To best use the land and increase production, they tracked the growing season. And to record the seasons, the Shang

Bronze. At the height of the Shang state, circa 1200 BCE, its rulers erected massive palaces at the capital of Yin, which required bronze foundries for its wine and food vessels. In these foundries, skilled workers produced bronze weapons and ritual objects and elaborate ceremonial drinking and eating vessels.

Bronze Head. Other large states such as Sanxingdui emerged in East Asia between 1500 and 1300 BCE, showing that the Shang rulers were not unique. These kingdoms in the south and southwest had their own metallurgy and casting technology. From Sanxingdui in particular we have spectacular gold masks and bronze sculptures that present unprecedented human—as opposed to purely graphic—forms.

developed a twelve-month, 360-day lunar calendar; it contained leap months inserted as necessary to maintain the proper relationship between months and seasons. The calendar also relieved fears about seemingly anomalous events such as solar and lunar eclipses by rendering them predictable.

As in other Afro-Eurasian states, the ruler's wealth and power depended on tribute from elites and allies. Elites supplied warriors and laborers, as well as horses and cattle. Allies sent foodstuffs, soldiers, and workers and "assisted in the king's affairs"—perhaps hunting, burning brush, or clearing land—in return for such help as providing defense against invaders and predictions about the harvest. Commoners sent their tribute to the elites, who held the land as fiefs from the king. Farmers transferred their surplus crops to the elite landholders (or to the ruler himself if they worked on his personal landholdings), making payments in kind on a regular schedule. Commoners also made labor (corvée) payments: some became workers attached to the royal workshops that produced vast quantities of bronze ritual vessels as well as bronze armaments, such as dagger-axes, arrowheads, spearheads, helmets, shields, and chariot fittings; others labored to drain fields, clear land, build palaces, excavate tombs, or construct walls to protect towns or the capital.

Tribute could also take the form of turtle shells and cattle scapulas, which the Shang used for divination. The ability to divine the future was a powerful way to legitimate royal power—and then to justify the right to collect yet more trib-

ute. By placing themselves symbolically and literally at the center of all exchanges, Shang kings reinforced their power over others.

SHANG SOCIETY AND BELIEFS

Both metalworking and agriculture contributed to the wealth of the state and supported a complex social structure. The organizing principle of Shang society was a patrilineal ideal: descent was traced back through the generations to a common male ancestor. Grandparents, parents, sons, and daughters lived and worked together. Their property was held in common, and male family elders took precedence. Women from other patrilines married into the family, winning honor when they became mothers, particularly of sons.

The social hierarchy was also reflected in the death ritual, which involved sacrificing humans to accompany the deceased in the next life. A member of the royal elite was often buried with his full entourage, including his wife, consorts, servants, chariots, horses, and drivers. The inclusion of personal slaves and servants indicates a belief that the familiar social hierarchy would continue to exist in the afterlife. Modern Chinese historians have described the Shang as a "slave society," but its economy was not primarily based on owning slaves and using their labor. Instead, the driving force was the tribute labor of the commoners who made up most of society, particularly as delivered in metalworking and farming.

The Shang state can best be described as a patrimonial theocracy: the ruler at the top of the hierarchy was believed to derive his authority from the guidance from ancestors and gods. Rulers therefore had to find ways to communicate with ancestors and foretell the future, and they relied mainly on divination. When diviners applied intense heat to the shoulder bones of cattle or to turtle shells, they cracked. Diviners would then interpret those cracks as an auspicious or inauspicious sign from the ancestors regarding royal plans and actions. Scribes subsequently inscribed the queries they had asked of the ancestors on these so-called oracle bones to confirm that the cracks had been understood. Thus, Shang writing began as a dramatic ritual performance in which the living responded to their ancestors' oracular signs.

In Shang theocracy, the ruler was also head of a unified clergy; and because the Shang theocratic ruler simultaneously embodied religious and political power, no independent priesthood emerged to challenge the power of the royal family as happened in Egypt and Mesopotamia. Diviners and scribes were subordinated to the ruler and the royal pantheon of ancestors he was thought to represent: unlike in the regimes of Mesopotamia and Egypt, diviners were never entrusted with independent action. Ancestor worship sanctified Shang control and legitimized the lineage of rulers, ensuring that all political and religious power was held by the ruling family.

Primary Source

THE ORACLE BONE

About 3,000 years old (c. 1200 BCE), the oracle bone below dates from the Shang dynasty reign of King Wu Ding, the husband of Lady Fu Hao. Oracle bones enabled diviners to access the other world and provided the ruler with important information about the future. Because Shang kings wished to plan ahead, they often relied on divination to predict the weather and make current political or military decisions or justify future ones.

A partial translation of the left-hand side of this oracle bone reads

[Preface:] Crack making on *gui-si* day, Que divined:

[Charge:] In the next ten days there will be no disaster.

[Prognostication:] The king, reading the cracks, said, "There will be no harm; there will perhaps be the coming of alarming news."

[Verification:] When it came to the fifth day, *ding-you*, there really was the coming of alarming news from the west. Zhi Guo, reporting, said, "The Du Fang [a border people] are besieging in our eastern borders and have harmed two settlements." The Gong-fang also raided the fields of our western borders.

→ *Why did Shang kings rely on oracle bones? With whom were the diviners communicating through the medium of oracle bones?*

SOURCE: This translation follows, with slight modifications by Bryan W. Van Norden, David N. Keightley, *Sources of Shang History* (Berkeley: University of California Press, 1978), p. 44.

Because the Shang gods were ancestral deities, all the Shang rulers were deified when they died and ranked in descending chronological order. Thus, the primary Shang deity was Di, the High God (Shangdi), who was the founding ancestor of the Shang royal family. The Shang ruler who became a god was closer to the world of humans than the supreme Egyptian and Mesopotamian gods, and he served to unite the world of the living with the world of the dead. Much as the Egyptian pharaohs were thought to be born of human mothers and godlike fathers, who had ascended into heaven after their deaths, so the Shang kings moved into a parallel other world when they died.

THE DEVELOPMENT OF WRITING IN CHINA

Although Shang scholars did not invent writing in East Asia, they certainly perfected it. Oracle bones, which were so central to political and religious authority, are our primary evidence of early writing in China. Archaeologists have found oracle bones with inscriptions of Chinese script dating from the Shang dynasty, around 1300 to 1200 BCE. Divinations were inscribed on an imperishable material, bones. Other early written records may have been committed to materials that did not survive through the centuries. Thus accidents of preservation may explain the major differences between the ancient texts in China (primarily divinations) and in the Southwest Asian societies that impressed cuneiform on clay tablets (primarily economic transactions, literary and religious documents, and historical records).

The extant inscriptions on oracle bones and bronzes leave no doubt that the Shang surpassed the other states and peoples in northwestern China in their ability and determination to leave records; their governmental institutions and religious rituals were more complex and sophisticated than those of the peoples living nearby. But in comparison with Mesopotamia and Egypt, here the transformation of record keeping (for example, questions and answers to ancestors, lineages of rulers, or economic transactions) to literature (for example, mythological tales about the founding of states) was slower.

As noted above, Shang kings used writing to reinforce their position at the top of the hierarchy of royal families. Priests used writings on the oracle bones to address the other world and gain information about the future. Because the North China climate entered a warmer and wetter phase in the twelfth and eleventh centuries BCE, their divinations were often aimed at predicting rainfall for the sustenance of crops—particularly the Shang staple of millet, often mentioned on the oracle bones. The priests presented the living Shang ruler as the religious pivot between Di, the High God (who controlled the ever-important rain cycles), the ancestors, and their royal descendants.

In addition, like the Babylonian dynasts, later Shang rulers organized a wide range of ceremonial and bureaucratic routines that depended on detailed written records to integrate their urban capital with tributary states and peoples. In these records, the court kept track of foods, wines, bronze vessels, and livestock, thereby demonstrating that a centralized "royal household" had emerged. During this period, the original archaic script evolved into the preclassical script used on many of the bronze vases discussed above, which in turn was the precursor to the formal character-based system that has endured among elites to the present day and that sets apart the later Chinese, Japanese, Korean, and Vietnamese societies in East Asia from the cultures in Mesopotamia and the Mediterranean that rely on syllable- and alphabet-based writing.

THE SOUTH PACIFIC (2500 BCE–400 CE)

> → *How did Austronesian migrations affect the South Pacific?*

As Eurasian populations grew, and migration and trade brought cultures together, some of the peoples of East Asia left the mainland and took to the waters in search of opportunities or refuge. By comparing the vocabularies and grammatical similarities of languages spoken today by the tribal peoples in Taiwan, the Philippines, and Indonesia, we can trace the ancient Austronesian-speaking peoples back to their origins in coastal South China in the fourth millennium BCE. Apparently that first migration, which reached the islands of Polynesia, was followed by another from Taiwan around 2500 BCE, which then extended into the South Pacific. By 2000 BCE these peoples had replaced the earlier inhabitants of the East Asian coastal islands, the hunter-gatherers known as the Negritos. The latter had migrated south from the Asian landmass around 28,000 BCE, during an ice age when the coastal Pacific islands were still connected to the Asian mainland.

Using their remarkable double-outrigger canoes, which were 60 to 100 feet long and bore huge triangular sails, the early Austronesians successfully crossed the Taiwan Straits and colonized the key islands in the Pacific. Their vessels represented a major advance beyond the earlier simple dugout canoes used in inland waterways. In good weather, double-outrigger canoes could cover more than 120 miles in a day. The invention of a stabilization device for deep-sea sailing sometime after 2500 BCE triggered further Austronesian expansion into the Pacific. By 400 CE, these nomads of the sea had reached most of the South Pacific except for Australia and New Zealand.

Their seafaring skills enabled the Austronesians, like the Phoenicians in the eastern Mediterranean during the middle of the first millennium BCE, to monopolize trade wherever they went. Among their specialized craftworkers were potters, who produced a distinctive kind of pottery called Lapita ware on offshore islets or in coastal villages. We know from archaeological finds that these canoe-building people also served as inter-island traders in New Guinea after 1600 BCE. By four hundred years later, according to the evidence of Lapita potsherds and remains of animals typically domesticated by the Austronesians—pigs, dogs, and chickens—they had also made their way to Fiji, Samoa, and Tonga.

Pottery, stone tools, and domesticated crops and pigs characterized Austronesian settlements throughout the coastal islands and in the South Pacific. These unique cultural markers reached the Philippines from Taiwan. By 2500 BCE, according to archaeologists, the same cultural features had spread to the islands of Java, Sumatra, Celebes, Borneo, and Timor. Austronesians arrived in Java and Sumatra in 2000 BCE; by 1600 BCE they were in Australia and New Guinea, although they failed to penetrate the interior, where descendants of the indigenous peoples still survive. The Austronesians then ventured further eastward into the South Pacific, apparently arriving in Samoa and Fiji in 1200 BCE and on mainland Southeast Asia in 1000 BCE. (See Map 3-5.)

Because the lands along the equator in the South Pacific have a tropical or subtropical climate and, in many places,

MAP 3-5   AUSTRONESIAN MIGRATIONS

How did Austronesian speakers migrate to these various locations? How have historians traced this migration across time and space? Why, unlike other migratory people during the second millennium, did Austronesian settlers in Polynesia become a world apart?

rich soils left by the ash from volcanoes, Austronesians successfully cultivated dry land crops (yams, and sweet potatoes), irrigated crops (yams, which grew more prolifically in paddy fields or on land where water was supplied by rainfall or by supplemental irrigation), and tree crops (breadfruit, bananas, and coconuts). In addition, the areas that were colonized off the Asian landmass, such as the islands of Indonesia, provided the inhabitants and newcomers with labyrinthine coastlines rich in maritime resources, including coral reefs and mangrove swamps full of wildlife. Island hopping certainly led the adventurers to encounter new food sources, but the shallow waters and reefs teemed with sufficient fish and shellfish for their needs.

In the South Pacific, the Polynesian descendants of the early Austronesians shared a common culture, language, technology, and stores of domesticated plants and animals. These later Polynesian seafarers came from many disparate island communities (hence the name *Polynesian,* or "belonging to many islands"), and after they settled down their numbers

grew. Their crop surpluses allowed more densely populated communities to support craft specialists and soldiers. The size of the island and its resources determined how much specialization the islanders required. Most settlements created ceremonial buildings to promote local solidarity and forts to provide defense. On larger islands, communities often cooperated and organized workforces to enclose ponds for fish production and to build and maintain large irrigation works for agriculture. Politically, Polynesian communities ranged from tribal or village units to multi-island alliances that on occasion invaded other areas.

The Austronesians reached the strategically located Marquesas Islands in the central Pacific around 200 CE; over the next few centuries, some moved on to Easter Island to the south and Hawaii to the north. The immense thirty-ton stone structures on Easter Island, for example, represent the monumental Polynesian architecture produced after their arrival. In separate migrations they traversed the Indian Ocean, heading westward, and arrived at the island of Madagascar by

Austronesian Canoe. Early Austronesians crossed the Taiwan Straits and colonized key islands in the Pacific using double-outrigger canoes from sixty to one hundred feet long equipped with triangular sails. In good weather, such canoes could cover more than 120 miles in a day.

the sixth century CE; along the way, they transmitted crops such as the banana to East Africa.

The expansion of East Asian peoples throughout the South Pacific and their trade back and forth did not, however, integrate the archipelagos of islands closely into the mainland culture. Expansion south and east could not overcome the underlying tendency of these societies, physically dispersed across a huge ocean, toward fragmentation and isolation.

Easter Island. By the fifth century BCE the Austronesians had reached Easter Island to the south of the Marquesas. The thirty-ton stone structures on Easter Island represent the monumental Polynesian architecture produced after the arrival of the Austronesians.

THE AEGEAN IN THE SECOND MILLENNIUM BCE

> → *How did long-distance trade influence the Aegean world?*

In the region around the Aegean Sea, the islands and the mainland of what is now Greece, no single power emerged before the second millennium BCE. Settled agrarian communities developed into local polities linked by trade and culture but not by an integrated central government. Fragmentation was the norm, perhaps as a consequence of the landscape itself, which lacked a single riverine axis or common plain. In this sense, the island world of the eastern Mediterranean initially resembled that of the South Pacific.

One unintended benefit of the lack of centralization was that there was no single regime to collapse when the droughts ushered in the new millennium. Thus, in the second millennium BCE, peoples of the eastern Mediterranean did not struggle to recover lost grandeur. Rather, they enjoyed a remarkable though gradual development, making advances that drew on the many influences that they absorbed from Southwest Asia, Egypt, and Europe both by land and by sea. It was a time when the people of such islands as Crete and Thera engaged in extensive trade with the Greek mainland and with Egypt and the Levant. It was also a time of the migration and movement, sometimes peaceful but sometimes violent, of peoples from the region of the Danube and central Europe into the Mediterranean. Groups of these peoples moved into settlements in mainland Greece in the centuries after 1900 BCE; modern archaeologists have named them "Mycenaeans," after the famous palace at Mycenae that dates to this era. Once settled in their new environment, the Mycenaeans quickly turned to the sea to look for resources and interaction with their neighbors.

SEABORNE TRADE AND COMMUNICATION

At the outset, the dominant influence on the Aegean world came from the east by sea. As the institutions and ideas that

had developed earlier in Southwest Asia moved westward, they found a ready reception along the coasts and on the islands of the Mediterranean. Like the ships and the trade products that preceded them, these innovations followed the sea currents in the eastern Mediterranean, moving counterclockwise up the eastern seaboard of the Levant, then to the island of Cyprus and along the southern coast of Anatolia, and finally westward to the islands of the Aegean Sea and to Crete. Trade was the main bearer of eastern influences—and the sea-lanes were busy, with vessels carrying cargoes from island to island and up and down the commercial centers along the coast. (See Map 3-6.)

The islands in the Mediterranean were important meeting points that brought together the mainland peoples of western

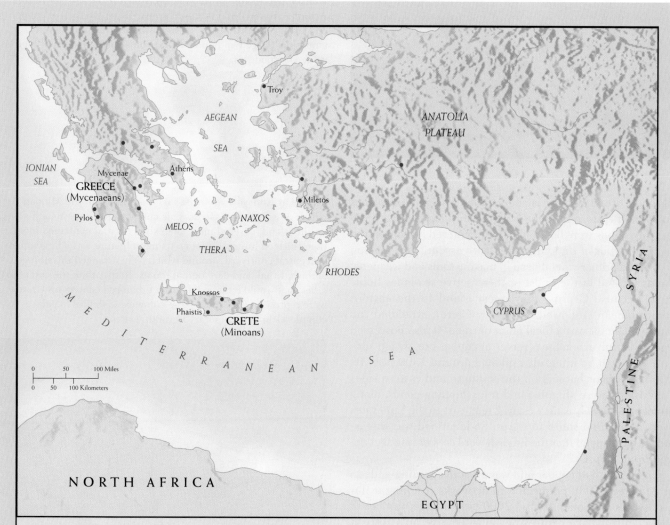

MAP 3-6 THE AEGEAN SEA WORLDS

What does the distribution of the Aegean Islands tell us about how trade most likely developed? Given their geographic locations, why do you think that the Mycenaeans eventually conquered the Minoans? If an Egyptian trade item reached Mycenae, what do you think was the most likely route it took?

Seaborne Trade. The size of the seaborne trade is revealed most spectacularly in the shipwrecks recovered by underwater archaeologists. One of these ships, sunk off the southern coast of Anatolia around 1325 BCE, was transporting ten tons of copper in 354 oxhide-shaped ingots, as well as more than a hundred amphorae (large two-handled jars) containing all kinds of high-value commodities.

Asia and Europe with the islanders, thereby serving as places from which eastern influences spread into Europe. By 1500 BCE, the islands were booming. Trade centered heavily on the precious metals of tin and copper, both essential for making bronze, the primary metal used in making tools and weapons. Islands located in the midst of these active sea-lanes flourished. Because Cyprus, the largest island in the eastern Mediterranean (followed closely by Crete), straddled the main sea-lane, it was a focal point of trade. It also possessed large and easily workable reserves of copper ore, which suddenly began to be intensely exploited around 2300 BCE. By 2000 BCE, major harbors on the southern and eastern sides of the island were shipping and transshipping goods, along with copper ingots, as far west as Crete, east to the Euphrates River (Mari), and south to Egypt. So identified was this island with the metal that the English word *copper* is in fact derived from "Cyprus."

Crete, too, had copper and was an active trading node in the Mediterranean, connected to networks reaching as far east as Mesopotamia. Around 2000 BCE, a large number of independent palace centers began to emerge on Crete, at Knossos and elsewhere. Modern scholars have named the people who built these elaborate centers the Minoans, after the legendary King Minos, said to have ruled Crete at this time. The Minoans sailed back and forth across the Mediterranean, and by 1600 they were planting colonies around the

Palace at Knossos. An artist's reconstruction of the Minoan palace at Knossos on Crete. This complex, the largest such center on the island, covered more than six acres and contained more than thirteen hundred rooms. Its main feature was a large open-air central courtyard, around which were arranged the storage, archive, ritual, and ceremonial rooms. Rather than the complex cities that would emerge later, the urbanized centers on Crete were represented by these large complexes, similar to palace complexes in contemporary Levantine sites.

LINEAR A AND B—WRITING IN THE EARLY MEDITERRANEAN WORLDS

On the island of Crete and on the mainland areas of Greece, documents of the palace-centered societies were written on clay tablets in two scripts that, unlike the Cretan pictographs of c. 2000 BCE, were linear. These were first discovered on Crete in 1900 by the British archaeologist Arthur Evans. Linear A script, apparently written in Minoan, has not yet been deciphered. Linear B was first deciphered by Michael Ventris, a brilliant young British architect and freelance scholar, in the early 1950s. In the process he discovered that contrary to the assumptions of almost all classical scholars, these tablets were inscribed by speakers of Mycenaean, an early form of Greek. Massive numbers of these records, kept on clay tablets by palace scribes, have survived. Carefully noting every detail of the goods and services managed by the palace bureaucracy, they contain lists short and long of persons or things—about as interesting as modern grocery or laundry lists. The following tablet from the Pylos on the Greek mainland notes how much seed grain the bureaucrats were distributing to rural landholders who were dependent on the ruler.

The plot of Qelequhontas: this much seed: 276 l. of wheat

R. slave of the god, holds a lease: so much seed: 12 l. of wheat

W. the priest holds a lease: so much seed: 12 l. of wheat

Thuriatis, female slave of the god, dependant of P. the old man: so much seed: 108 l. of wheat

The plot of Admaos, so much seed: 216 l. of wheat. . . .

T. slave of the god, holds a lease: so much seed: 32 l. of wheat

The plot of A . . .eus, so much seed: 144 l. of wheat. . . .

The plot of T. slave of the god, holds a lease: 18 l. of wheat

The plot of R., so much seed: 138 l. of wheat. . . .

The plot of Aktaios, so much seed: 384 l. of wheat. . . .

→ *What does this document suggest is the function of writing in these societies? What does this kind of information tell us about these societies? What doesn't it tell us?*

SOURCE: M. Ventris and J. Chadwick, *Documents in Mycenaean Greek*, 2nd ed. (Cambridge: Cambridge University Press, 1973), doc. 116.

An example of the earlier Linear A writing, used to write the non-Greek language of the Minoans. This script was used for record keeping, but it was used only on Crete and is therefore closely connected solely with the early Minoan palatial centers on the island. This example was found at the small palace site at Hagia Triada.

This is a typical Linear B document inscribed on clay with linear signs representing syllables and signs. The clay tablet was dried and stored in a palace archive. This particular tablet was found in the excavations of the Mycenaean palace at Pylos on the mainland of Greece.

islands of the Aegean that became trading and mining centers. The Minoans' wealth soon became a magnet for the Mycenaeans, their mainland competitors, who took over Crete around 1400 BCE.

MINOAN CULTURE

Although they were connected to the people of Southwest Asia, these far-flung islands and coastal communities had their own distinctive cultural elements. To be sure, the monumental architecture so characteristic of Southwest Asia found small-scale echoes in the Aegean world, notably in the Minoan palace complexes built between 1900 and 1600 BCE; the largest and most impressive of these palaces was at Knossos. But religion was a prime example of cultural differences.

Worship on the islands focused on a female deity, the "Lady," but the communities have left no traces of the large temple complexes that were common in Mesopotamia, Anatolia, and Egypt. Nor, apparently, was there any priestly class of the type so central to running the temple complexes of Southwest Asian societies. Scholars disagree about whether these societies had full-time scribes. Moreover, significant regional diversity existed even within this small Aegean world. The most intense and complex developments were found on islands. On Thera, for example, archaeologists have uncovered a splendid trading city in which large private houses contained bathrooms with toilets and running water and were decorated with exotic wall paintings. One such painting depicted a flotilla of pleasure, trading, and naval vessels. On the

island of Crete, the palace-centered communities were civil societies of a high order of refinement, confident in their wealth and power. None of the large palaces was fortified or even built in a locale with natural defenses. They were light, airy, and open to their surrounding landscapes.

MYCENAEAN CULTURE

Migrating to Greece from central Europe, the Mycenaeans brought with them their Indo-European language along with their horse chariots and their metalworking skills. Their move to Greece was gradual, lasting from about 1850 to 1600 BCE, but they came to dominate the indigenous population. Known for their exceptional height, they maintained their dominance with their powerful weapon, the chariot, until 1200 BCE, and horse chariots remained important in their mythology and cultural tradition. The battle chariots and festivities of chariot racing described in the epic poetry of Homer, which date from a time after the collapse of Mycenaean societies, contain memories of the importance of chariots that echo similar stories in Vedic legends, told among the speakers of another Indo-European language who had settled in South Asia.

The population centers on the Mycenaean Greek mainland were much more oriented toward war and conflict than were the Minoan centers. In this respect, they resembled settlements of the Southwest Asian mainland kingdoms. The Mycenaeans possessed a less refined material culture than that of the Minoans: it emphasized displays of weaponry, por-

Aegean Fresco. This is one of the more striking wall paintings, or frescoes, discovered by archaeologists in the 1970s and 1980s at Akrotiri on the island of Thera (Santorini) in the Aegean Sea. Its brilliant colors, especially the blue of the sea, evoke the lively essence of Minoan life on the island. Note the houses of the wealthy along the port and the flotilla of ships that reflects the seaborne commerce that was beginning to flourish in the Mediterranean in this period.

Mycenaean Sword. The hilt and engraved gold pommel of a sword from the regal burials at the site of Mycenae. The presence of this weaponry, both depicted in the art of the period and preserved in artifacts buried with the dead, was typical of a violent society with a warrior elite. The riveted hilt and the bronze sword blade are of a kind found widely distributed in the Mediterranean, following the patterns of Mycenaean trade routes.

traits of armed soldiers, and illustrations of violent conflicts. The main palace centers at Tiryns and Mycenae were the hulking fortresses of warlords, who surrounded themselves with huge rough-hewn stone walls and lived on the top of large rock outcroppings. The Mycenaeans amassed an amazing amount of wealth and carried some of it with them to their graves. Their tombs contain many gold vessels and decorations; most ostentatious were the gold masks. The many amber beads found by archaeologists indicate that the warriors had contacts with inhabitants of the coniferous forest regions in northern Europe.

Southwest Asian economic and political structures shaped the coastal sites where the Mycenaeans settled, such as Tiryns and Pylos. Massive stone fortresses and fortified palaces dominated these urban hubs. A preeminent ruler (*wanax*) stood atop a complex bureaucratic hierarchy run by various officials; he was aided by a large number of subordinates, some of whom were slaves. At the heart of the palace

society were the scribes, who kept records of the goods and services that the palace organizations allotted to local communities of farmers, shepherds, and metalworkers, among others.

Mycenaean expansion eventually reached and overwhelmed the Minoans; as noted above, they ultimately occupied Crete. The Mycenaeans also sought to create colonies and trading settlements, reaching as far as Sicily and southern Italy. In this fashion, "Greek" trade and language created a veneer of unity linking the dispersed worlds of the Aegean Sea.

At the close of the second millennium BCE, the eastern Mediterranean faced large-scale internal and external convulsions that brought an end to the flourishing heyday of these exotic micro-societies. Most notably, a series of sometimes violent migrations of peoples from central Europe moved through the whole of southeastern Europe, Anatolia, and the eastern Mediterranean between 1250 and 1150 BCE (see Chapter 4). The invasions, as destructive as they were, did not extinguish but rather reinforced the creative potential of this frontier area. Following the upheaval at the close of the millennium, yet another new kind of social order emerged, destined to have an even greater brilliance and influence. Because theirs was a closed maritime world—in comparison with the wide-open Pacific—the Aegean peoples quickly reasserted a dominance in the eastern Mediterranean that Austronesians could not match in Southeast Asia or Polynesia.

EUROPE—THE NORTHERN FRONTIER

→ *Why did politics remain small-scale in Europe?*

The transition to settled agriculture and the raising of domesticated animals proved to be an altogether slower and more arduous process in the western flank of Afro-Eurasia than in the rest of the landmass. It took two millennia, from 5000 to 3000 BCE, before settled agriculture became the dominant economic form in Europe. In large areas of the continent, hunters and gatherers were reluctant to give up their traditional ways. Even this frontier, however, was visited by peoples driving horse chariots during the second millennium BCE.

The northern area of the far western stretches of Europe, dominated by cold and forbidding evergreen forests, remained thinly populated and was slow to implement any of the new ways. The new agricultural communities appeared first as frontier settlements in which pioneers struggled to break new land. Surrounded by hunting and foraging communities, these innovators lived hard lives in harsh environments, overcoming their isolation only by creating regional alliances. They were unstable and too weak to initiate or sustain long-distance trade. These were not fertile grounds for creating powerful kingdoms.

The early European cultivators adopted the techniques for controlling plants and animals pioneered in Southwest Asia; but rather than establishing large, hierarchically organized and centralized societies they used them to create self-sufficient communities. They did not incorporate the other cultural and political features that characterized the societies of Egypt, Mesopotamia, and the eastern Mediterranean. Innovations such as the working of metal (initially, copper), the manufacture of pottery, and the use of the plow occurred sporadically and had little impact on local conditions. Throughout this period, Europe was hardly a developed cultural center. Instead, it was a wild frontier in which new agriculturalists struggled, often unsuccessfully, to open up new lands, in the process undoubtedly engaging in violent confrontations with each other and with the indigenous inhabitants.

Two significant changes were decisive in the northern frontier zone: the domestication of the horse and the emergence of wheeled chariots and wagons. Both became instruments of war and enabled humans to adapt to the expanses of steppe lands across the southern face of inner and central Europe, a vast open zone where pasturing animals in large herds proved profitable. The success of this horse culture created several frontiers, including those bearing the kinds of agriculturally self-sustaining communities discussed above.

These new agriculturalists seeking to cultivate the land faced constant challenges not just within Europe but also eastward, as they looked toward the rolling grasslands that stretched across central Eurasia. Their attempts to enter this zone were usually countered successfully by men on horseback, who could rapidly marshal an overpowering mobile force. The inhabitants of the great flat steppelands north of the Black Sea gradually shifted from a primitive agriculture to an economy based on the mobile herding of animals. In this zone, the domestication of the horse encouraged the development of a highly mobile culture in which whole communities moved on horseback or by the use of large wheeled wagons. These pastoral nomads in the east were constantly attracted to the richer agricultural lands in central Europe, producing a source of constant hostility between the two worlds. Although in most cases agricultural communities could defend themselves when these nomadic raiders looked to Europe, its agricultural heart continued to draw their attacks. The constant struggles between settlers, hunter-gatherers, and nomadic horse riders created cultures with a strong warrior ethos at their core. The fullest development of this mounted horse culture is found in the centuries after 1000 BCE, when the Scythian peoples in the steppelands engaged in rituals like the drinking of blood, in which male warriors forged bonds of blood brotherhood that were central to their

aggressive and violent behavior. This rough-and-tumble frontier gave its people an appetite to borrow more effective means of waging war. Europeans desired the nomadic people's weaponry, and over time, their interactions with the horsemen included trade as well as violence. As a result of these trading contacts with nomadic steppe peoples to the east, Europeans adopted horses and finer metalworking technologies from the Caucasus. Of course, such trade only made their battles even more lethal. And while the connections between this northern frontier zone and other parts of the Afro-Eurasian world began to multiply, it was still too dispersed and unruly a region to give rise to integrated kingdoms. At a time when the rest of Afro-Eurasia was developing, Europe was still a land of warmaking small chieftainships. Politics there remained a small-scale, rivalrous affair.

EARLY STATES IN THE AMERICAS

> → *How did the ecology of the Central Andes influence early state systems?*

Across the Americas, river valleys and coasts filled in with villages and towns drawing their sustenance from the rich resources in their hinterlands. But without beasts of burden or domesticated animals able to carry loads or plow fields, local communities could produce only limited surpluses. Trade from one community to the next was therefore restricted to luxuries and symbolic trade goods, such as shells, feathers, hides, and precious metals and gems.

In the Central Andes, however, archaeologists have found evidence of early state systems that transcended local communities to create "confederations," or alliances of towns. These were not as well integrated as many of the territorial states of Southwest Asia, the Indus Valley, and China; they more closely resembled settlements in Europe and the eastern Mediterranean, where towns engaged in a form of trade in basic goods, and in some cases joined together to defend themselves against outside aggressors.

Facilitating the development of Central Andean confederations was the region's ecological mix. Along the arid coast of what is now Peru, fishermen learned to exploit the currents that teemed with large and small fish; they brought in good hauls of a basic staple that could be dried to make it less perishable and more easily transported. The rivers that flowed down the Andean mountains cut through the desert, often creating basins suitable for agriculture. And as the mountains rose from the Pacific, rainfall and higher altitudes favored the creation of extensive pasturelands, known as *puna*, used by wild ruminants such as llamas and alpacas—difficult to use as beasts of burden but valuable for the wool that was needed for textile production. Such ecological diversity within a relatively limited area promoted greater trade between subregions and towns, and the interchange of manioc, chili peppers, dried fish, and wool created the commercial networks that could support political ones.

Communities on the coast, in the riverbeds, or in the mountain valleys were not large but they were numerous. They took shape around central plazas, most of which had large platforms with special burial chambers built for elders and persons of importance, surrounded by clusters of dwellings. Much of what we know about political and economic transactions between communities—and the confirmation of longer-distance trade and statecraft—comes from the offerings and ornaments left in these burial chambers. Painted gourds, pottery, and fine textiles illustrate the degree to which complex cultures were increasingly in contact with each other, and often bound in alliances. Marriage, for instance, between noble families of scattered communities, was a common means of strengthening a pact or confederation.

One early site known as Aspero reveals how a local community had evolved into a form of chiefship, with a political elite and diplomatic and trading ties with neighbors. The large temple at the center was heavily ornamented, temples straddled the top of the raised platform, and there is plenty of evidence that smaller communities around Aspero sent crops (like fruits) and fish (especially anchovies) as part of an intercommunity system of mutual dependency. But not all politics among the valley peoples of Peru consisted of trade and diplomacy. In the Casma Valley, some 300 feet from the Pacific coast, excavation of a clay and stone architectural complex at Cerro Sechín has revealed a much larger sprawl of dwellings and plazas, dating back to 1700 BCE. The community's central structure was surrounded by a wall composed of hundreds of massive stone tablets, carved with ornate etchings of warriors, battles, prisoners, executions, and many human body parts. Warrior clothing was simple and rustic, and the main weapon appears to have been nothing more than a club. Clearly, the first expressions of statecraft in the Americas were accompanied by warfare.

CONCLUSION

The second millennium BCE was an unprecedented era of migrations, warfare, and the building of territorial kingdoms in Afro-Eurasia. Emerging riverine societies had marked the fourth and third millennia BCE in Mesopotamia, Egypt, and the Indus Valley, but in the second millennium BCE humans confronted the dire ecological challenges that droughts and deserts posed for their agricultural and pastoral economies.

The drought would trigger large-scale migrations across Afro-Eurasia. In their search for arable land and water sources, transhumant herders first entered into the riverine societies and thereby changed the social and political fabric of these communities. Soon following, and for similar reasons, were horse-riding nomads from steppe communities in inner Eurasia; they conquered and settled in the agrarian states, bringing with them a number of key innovations. Chief among them were the horse chariots, which became an irresistible military catalyst sparking the evolution from smaller states and polities to larger-scale kingdoms that linked crowded, endangered cities to their vast hinterlands. These nomads and transhumant herders did not simply impose their ways on those they conquered, but instead adopted many of the beliefs and customs of the settled people. Land and sea nomads also created zones of interaction in which long- distance trade by sea and land linked agrarian societies.

The Nile Delta, the basin of the Tigris and Euphrates rivers, the Indus Valley, and the Yellow River basin were worlds apart before 2000 BCE. Through trade and conquest, nomadic groups provided means of bringing these early societies into closer contact, sometimes for the first time. The result was a political transformation and the makings of the first territorial states. The alliance of farmers and warriors united agrarian wealth and production with political power to create and defend boundaries around communities living under common laws and customs. The new arrangements overshadowed the historic role of nomads as predators and enabled them to become military elites at the top of social hierarchies that ruled territorial states.

This unique partnership created armies of foot soldiers and elite charioteers who protected and spurred the expansion of farmers' villages. Through their taxes and drafted labor, the villagers repaid their rulers for local security and state-run diplomacy. Their symbiotic relationship with warrior elites fostered trade and commerce. Their cooperation, not always voluntary, with the ruling elite made possible the first great territorial states and kingdoms of Afro-Eurasia.

The rhythms of state formation differed where regimes were not as closely packed together. In East Asia, one state was coming into its own, but the absence of strong rivals allowed the Shang to accumulate strength more gradually. Where landscapes had much sharper divisions, whether in the island archipelagos of the South China Sea, in Europe, or elsewhere, the political arrangements were much more decentered, as people lived in what resembled a tapestry of micro-states. This was true above all in the Americas, where the lack of wheeled vehicles and horses made long-distance communication and movement much more challenging—and therefore inhibited the territorial ambitions of rulers. Here, too, micro-states were the norm during the second millennium. But we must recall that fragmentation is not the same as isolation. Even peoples on the fringes and the subjects of micro-states were not absolutely secluded from the increasing flows of technologies, languages, goods, and migrants.

STUDY QUESTIONS

WWNORTON.COM/STUDYSPACE

1. Explain the differences between nomadic pastoral and transhumant migrations. How did each shape Afro-Eurasian history during the second millennium BCE?
2. Analyze the impact of the domestication of horses on Afro-Eurasia during the second millennium BCE. How did this development affect both nomadic and settled societies?
3. Define the term *territorial state*. Where in Afro-Eurasia did this new form of political organization emerge and thrive?
4. Compare and contrast political developments in Mesopotamia and Egypt during the second millennium BCE. To what extent did outside groups influence each region?
5. Identify the five great territorial states of western Asia and North Africa during the second half of the second millennium BCE and describe their relationships with each other. How did they pioneer international diplomacy?
6. Compare and contrast Austronesian and Indo-European migrations. What impact did each people have on the regions it settled?

7. Describe the Shang state in East Asia. How was it similar to and different from the territorial states of western Afro-Eurasia?
8. Compare and contrast the islands of the South Pacific to those in the eastern Mediterranean during the second millennium BCE. Why were societies in the South Pacific more fragmented and isolated than those in the eastern Mediterranean?
9. Explain why state structures were smaller and less integrated in Europe and the Central Andes than the territorial states that arose elsewhere during the second millennium BCE. How similar and different were state structures in both regions?

FURTHER READINGS

Allan, Sarah, *The Shape of the Turtle: Myth, Art and Cosmos in Early China* (1991). Explains the roles of divination and sacrifice in artistic representations of the Shang cosmology.

Allen, James P., *Middle Egyptian: An Introduction to the Language and Culture of Hieroglyphs* (2000). An introduction to the system of writing and its use in Ancient Egypt.

Arnold, Dieter, *Building in Ancient Egypt: Pharaonic Stone Masonry* (1996). Details the complex construction of monumental stone architecture in ancient Egypt.

Chronology

	MAJOR TRENDS	2000 BCE	1900 BCE	1800 BCE	1700 BCE	1600 BCE	1500 BCE	1400
NORTHERN AFRICA	Global warming and drying cycle beginning 2000 BCE	Middle Kingdom in Egypt, 2010–1640 BCE						
		Development of chariot technology, 2000 BCE				Hyksos rule in Egypt, 1640–1550 BCE		
				New Kingdom in Egypt, 1550–1070 BCE				
SOUTHWEST ASIA		Kassite, Median, and Persian migration begins, 2000 BCE						
				Old Hittite Kingdom in Anatolia, 1800–1600 BCE				
				Hammurapi's Babylonia, 1792–1750 BCE				
						Kassite rule, 1475–1125 BCE		
						New Hittite Kingdom in Anatolia, 1400–1200 BCE		
SOUTH ASIA							Vedic migration into Indus River valley begins, 1500 BCE	
EAST ASIA						Shang State emerges, 1600 BCE		
THE AEGEAN		Minoan culture, 2000–1600 BCE						
			Mycenaean culture, 1850–1200 BCE					
SOUTH PACIFIC		Austronesian migration to East Asian coastal islands begins, 2500 BCE						
EUROPE					Frontier zone with Southwest Asia and horse culture in Eastern Europe emerge		Rise of small chieftai	
CENTRAL ANDES					Emergence of small-scale political confederations, 1700 BCE			

Baines, John, and Jaromir Málek, *Atlas of Ancient Egypt* (1980). Useful compilation of information on ancient Egyptian society, religion, history and geography.

Beal, Richard H., *The Organization of the Hittite Military* (1992). A detailed study based on textual sources of the world's first chariot-based army.

Bogucki, Peter, and Pam J. Crabtree (eds.), *Ancient Europe 8000 BC–AD 1000: Encyclopedia of the Barbarian World*, 2 vols. (2004). An indispensable handbook on the economic, social, artistic, and religious life in Europe during this period.

Bruhns, Karen Olsen, *Ancient South America* (1994). The best basic text on pre-Columbian South American cultures.

Castleden, Rodney, *The Mycenaeans* (2005). One of the best current surveys of all aspects of the Mycenaean Greeks.

Chadwick, John, *The Decipherment of Linear B*, 2nd ed. (1968). Not only a retelling of the story of the decipherment of the Linear B script but an introduction to the actual content and function of the tablets themselves.

Cline, E. H., *Sailing the Wine-Dark Sea: International Trade and the Late Bronze Age Aegean* (1994). An excellent account of the trade and contacts between the Aegean and other areas of the Mediterranean, Europe, and the Near East during the late Bronze Age.

Cunliffe, Barry, *Facing the Ocean: The Atlantic and Its Peoples, 8000 BC–AD 1500* (2001). An in-depth, highly useful treatment of western Europe during this period.

Cunliffe, Barry (ed.), *Prehistoric Europe: An Illustrated History* (1997). A state-of-the-art treatment of first farmers, agricultural developments, and material culture in prehistoric Europe.

Davis, W. V., and L. Schofield, *Egypt, the Aegean and the Levant: Interconnections in the Second Millennium* BC (1995). A discussion of the complex interactions in the eastern Mediterranean during the "international age."

Doumas, Christos, *Thera: Pompeii of the Ancient Aegean* (1983). A study of the tremendous volcanic eruption and explosion that destroyed the Minoan settlement on the island of Thera.

Drews, Robert, *Coming of the Greeks: Indo-European Conquests in the Aegean and the Near East* (1988). A good survey of the evidence for the "invasions" or "movements of peoples" that reconfigured the world of the eastern Mediterranean and Near East.

Finley, M. I., *The World of Odysseus*, 2nd rev. ed. (1977; reprint, 2002). The classic work that describes what might be recovered about the world of the social values and behaviors of men and women in the period of the so-called Dark Ages of early Greek history.

Frankfort, Henri, *Ancient Egyptian Religion: An Interpretation* (1948; reprint, 2000). A classic study of Egyptian religion and culture during the pharaonic period.

Keightley, David N., *The Ancestral Landscape: Time, Space, and Community in Late Shang China, ca. 1200–1045 B.C.* (2000). Provides insights into the nature of royal kinship that undergirded the Shang court and its regional domains.

1300 BCE	1200 BCE	1100 BCE	1000 BCE	900 BCE	100 BCE	1 CE	100 CE	200 CE	300 CE	400 CE	500 CE

Vedic migration into Ganges River valley begins, 1000 BCE

Austronesian migration to Samoa and Fiji, 1200 BCE

Austronesian migration to Southeast Asia, 1000 BCE

Austronesian migration to Madagascar, 500 CE

Austronesian migration to Polynesia, 200 CE

Kemp, Barry J., *Ancient Egypt: Anatomy of a Civilization* (2006). A definitive presentation of the history, culture, and religion of ancient Egypt.

Klein, Jacob, "The Marriage of Martu: The Urbanization of 'Barbaric' Nomads," in *Mutual Influences of Peoples and Cultures in the Ancient Near East,* ed. Meir Malul (1996).

Kristiansen, Kristian, *Europe Before History* (1998). The finest recent survey of all the major developmental phases of European prehistory.

McIntosh, Jane, *Handbook to Life in Prehistoric Europe* (2006). Highlights the archaeological evidence that enables us to re-create the day-to-day life of different prehistoric communities in Europe.

Preziosi, Donald, and L. A. Hitchcock, *Aegean Art and Architecture* (1999). One of the best general guides to the figurative and decorative art produced both by the Minoans and Mycenaeans and by related early societies in the region of the Aegean.

Quirke, Stephen, *Ancient Egyptian Religion* (1992). A highly readable presentation of ancient Egyptian religion that summarizes the roles and attributions of the many Egyptian gods.

Ratnagar, Shereen, *Understanding Harappa: Civilization in the Greater Indus Valley* (2001). A cogent and meaningful summary from one of the leading archaeologists of Harappan society.

Robins, Gay, *The Art of Ancient Egypt* (1997). The most comprehensive survey to date of the art of pharaonic Egypt.

———, *Women in Ancient Egypt* (1993). An interesting survey of the place of women in Ancient Egyptian society.

Romer, John, *Ancient Lives: Daily Life in Egypt of the Pharaohs* (1990). A discussion of the economic and social lives of everyday ancient Egyptians.

Sandars, N. K., *The Sea Peoples: Warriors of the Ancient Mediterranean* (1985). A readable discussion of a very complex period of Levantine history.

Simpson, William Kelly (ed.), *The Literature of Ancient Egypt: An Anthology of Stories, Instructions, and Poetry* (1972). A compilation of the most important works of literature from Ancient Egypt.

Thorp, Robert L., *China in the Early Bronze Age: Shang Civilization* (2005). Reviews the archaeological discoveries near Anyang, site of two capitals of the Shang kings.

Warren, Peter, *The Aegean Civilizations: From Ancient Crete to Mycenae,* 2nd ed. (1989). An excellent textual and pictorial guide to all the basic aspects of the Minoan and Mycenaean societies.

Wilson, John A., *The Culture of Ancient Egypt* (1951). A classic study of the history and culture of pharaonic Egypt.

Yadin, Yigael, *The Art of Warfare in Biblical Lands in the Light of Archaeological Discovery* (1963). A well-illustrated presentation of the machinery of war in the second and first millennium BCE.

Chapter 4

First Empires and Common Cultures in Afro-Eurasia, 1200–350 BCE

Sennacherib—the ruler of the vast Assyrian Empire, which at the height of its power at the beginning of the seventh century BCE ruled over much of Southwest Asia—tells us in his annals that at the end of his successful campaign against Hezekiah, the king of Judah, he took "200,150 people great and small, male and female, horses, mules, asses, camels and sheep, without number, I brought away from them and counted them as spoil." Similarly, he forced other peoples whom he had conquered and who would not submit to his rule, especially the Arameans who lived in the Levant, to leave their lands and to migrate to Assyria. With such people, Sennacherib rebuilt and greatly expanded his capital city of Nineveh and developed immense irrigation works to open up new agricultural lands.

From early on, Assyrian kings' policy of moving large numbers of people over great distances was a foundation of their rule. The Assyrians pushed the establishment of power a step further than previous regimes: whereas their predecessors had annexed

141

territory, they redistributed populations to create more homogeneity within their territory and to settle more productive regions of the dominion. Those they had uprooted were assimilated into the social fabric as the equals of Assyrian citizens. In small rural communities, these new inhabitants increased the agricultural potential of the empire and populated new cities. They were a source of manpower for the army, and many became elite troops. Their numbers included not only military men and laborers but also scribes and skilled craftworkers. Through these practices, the Assyrian rulers both punished those who were not subservient and integrated their enormous and diverse populations.

While nomadic pastoralists and transhumants moved between pasturelands, most agrarian people at the end of the second millennium BCE remained in the same place for all of their lives. Yet further climatic change and political conquests spurred the migration—in effect, mass resettlements—of people who might otherwise have never left their lands. From the Mediterranean region, some people traveled by sea to the Levant, Egypt, and Anatolia, spreading before them disruption and political upheaval. Similarly, transhumant herders from the Syrian Desert moved on land toward the riverine cities in Mesopotamia in search of water and pastures for their animals. And in China, as in the Assyrian Empire, conquerors from beyond the borders took aim at obstinate local elites and forced them to submit—or move. The new rulers relocated valued workers such as metalworkers skilled in making bronze so that their special knowledge could be applied to building a new imperial capital. Throughout Afro-Eurasia, large-scale population movements were becoming part of the regional integration of new imperial states.

FORCES OF UPHEAVAL AND THE RISE OF EARLY EMPIRES

> → *What were the agents of change that facilitated the rise of culturally integrated early empires?*

Beginning around 1200 BCE, another warming phase gripped the Afro-Eurasian landmass. As had happened a thousand years earlier, in some areas prolonged drought brought about social upheavals and human migration. In other regions, population growth and the exhaustion of marginal soil forced many people to leave their homes in search of food and fertile land. (See Map 4-1.) These renewed migratorial incursions overturned urban societies as fierce warriors attacked capitals and cities and destroyed the administrative centers of kings, priests, and dynasties, leaving the way open for new states. Some of these states became the world's first empires, precursors of the giant empires we will encounter in later chapters.

Invaders came from loosely organized peripheral societies rather than from neighboring states. Marauders from the Mediterranean and from the Syrian Desert attacked the territorial kingdoms of the Levant, Egypt, Anatolia, and Mesopotamia, upsetting the diplomatic relations among these states and disrupting the elaborate system of international trade that had linked this area. In East Asia, rugged nomadic people from the steppes of Inner Eurasia tangled with Shang

Focus Questions   FIRST EMPIRES AND COMMON CULTURES IN AFRO-EURASIA

→ *What were the agents of change that facilitated the rise of culturally integrated early empires?*

→ *What distinguished the Neo-Assyrian Empire from earlier territorial kingdoms?*

→ *In what ways was the Persian Empire similar to the Neo-Assyrian Empire, and in what ways was it different?*

→ *How did the growth of the first empires in western Afro-Eurasia affect societies in the Levant and the Aegean? What influence did they have on the broader region?*

→ *How did South Asia become more socially and culturally integrated despite the absence of an imperial state?*

→ *To what extent was the Zhou state similar to contemporary empires in western Afro-Eurasia in its structure and its impact on its neighbors?*

WWNORTON.COM/STUDYSPACE

authorities in the Yellow River valley and eventually overwhelmed the regime in the eleventh century BCE. In the Indus Valley, waves of nomadic invaders likewise pressed down from the northwest, lured by the wealth of the fertile lands to the south. Once there, they discarded their nomadic ways and became an agrarian folk. This was a process that took centuries, but by the time of Alexander the Great (see Chapter 6), the splendor of India had become legendary.

The resultant intermixing and intermingling of these nomadic and urban societies impelled many rulers to expand beyond the old territorial kingdoms; warrior kings deployed troops that conquered independent and culturally distinct kingdoms and subjugated their people. With these conquests, different regions became more integrated, connected by a common language (or by individuals fluent in multiple languages), joint political structures, and shared religious beliefs. Local worlds were beginning to converge. But convergence did not yield homogeneity, as local customs, languages, and gods persisted even as common administration, laws, calendars, and ritual practices were instituted. In a few places, the prophet emerged as an important new agent of social change but prophets like Jesus and Mohammed and the universalizing religions that followed them would not appear until the beginning of the next millennium, and would take nearly another millennium to be fully established across all of Afro-Eurasia.

Some regions, like South Asia, were united less by shared political systems than by shared cultures and beliefs about the gods and ritual practices. Other regions had no political integration but were instead connected through extensive trade; for example, coastal cities such as Byblos and Tyre had commercial and cultural tentacles that reached as far as, and sometimes farther than, the empires' military conquests. There remained a great deal of variation within and across worlds.

In a few places, the prophet emerged as an important new agent of social change.

The rise of empires in the first millennium BCE depended on the expanded use of pack camels and ships for trade, iron tools for cultivation, and iron weapons for conquest. Innovations involving iron production were thus a major catalyst for change. The first millennium empires were highly centralized and militarized states that successfully expanded their boundaries by using force and the threat of force to absorb the wealth of neighboring states. They were based on the interaction and integration of the conquerors with their conquered peoples.

The role of iron was crucial in these advances. Although far more abundant and widely distributed in nature than are the tin and copper used to make bronze, iron is a harder substance to mold and hammer into shape. To make iron implements, metalworkers learned to apply intense heat to soften the ore and to remove its impurities. A further breakthrough occurred when they discovered how to add carbon to the iron, thereby making an early form of steel. When the technology to smelt and harden iron advanced, iron tools and weapons rapidly replaced those made in bronze. The new ability to use iron—a cheap and highly durable metal accessible to all—was a technological breakthrough that quickly leaped across territorial and cultural borders.

Iron also contributed to a shift in agrarian techniques—one that produced an agrarian revolution analogous to the leap forward earlier stimulated by irrigation engineering. Innovators learned to tip their plowshares with edges of forged iron that could be shaped and resharpened with ease. With the aid of the iron-tipped plow, for instance, cultivators could clear the dense jungle of the Ganges plain and repeatedly till the topsoil to keep it clear of weeds and to enhance its quality. Increasingly, farmers did not have to rely on regular floods to restore layers of rich loess soil to their fields for planting; they could break the sod and turn it over to bring up fertile subsurface soils. The effects of this transformation are easy to miss, but together they drove the agrarian frontier far beyond the traditional floodplains of riverine settings. Agricultural developments thus provided the technological underpinning to support larger, more integrated societies linked by roads and canals.

The camel became the chief overland agent of change during this period. Employed as a beast of burden since around 1700 BCE, the animal was now used to open up new overland trade routes across the Syrian and the Arabian deserts. The domestication of the camel, which is able to carry heavy loads over long distances, contributed significantly to the growth of overland trade—especially across deserts. The fat stored in camels' humps helps them survive long journeys and the harsh conditions of deserts, and thick pads under their hoofs enable them to walk smoothly over sand. First to be domesticated, around 4000 BCE, was the one-humped and more streamlined-looking camel called the *dromedary*, or Arab camel, native to the Sahara Desert. Other peoples, probably in central Asia, independently domesticated the bigger, two-humped Bactrian camel sometime before 2500 BCE. A stockier and hardier animal, it was better able than the dromedary to survive the scorching heat of northern Iran and the frozen winters along the route from China that would become the Silk Road (so named because silk was one of the major products carried along this route).

The final developments driving change were innovations in military and administrative control. The expansion of the first empires was based on military might. For example, using a standing army equipped with the most advanced weapons and armor, the Assyrian king led annual campaigns to establish and reinforce his absolute control over the countryside.

NORTH SEA

BALTIC SEA

URAL MOUNTAINS

EUROPE

Dnieper R.

Dniester R.

Volga R.

ARAL SEA

Danube R.

BLACK SEA

CASPIAN SEA

CENTR

E U

I

O

ANATOLIA

MYCENEANS • Troy
AEGEAN
SEA
Tiryns
CRETE

CYPRUS

HITTITES • Nineveh
MITANNI
• Ashur

ELAMITES ZAGROS MTS.

IRANIAN PLATEAU

Tigris R.

Euphrates R.

Babylon •

SOUTHWEST ASIA

A F R

MEDITERRANEAN SEA

SYRIAN DESERT

LEVANT

Tyre •
Jericho
Jersualem

NORTH AFRICA

A
F
R

El Amarna •

EGYPT

• Thebes

Persian Gulf

ARABIAN PENINSULA

S A H A R A

RED SEA

Nile R.

Sub-Saharan periphery:
Increased population
and gradual adoption
of agriculture

NUBIA

Niger R.

S U B -
S A H A R A N   A F R I C A

Tropical woodlands:
Yams and palm nuts
cultivated

*ATLANTIC
OCEAN*

Congo R.

*Lake
Victoria*

■ (dark)	Urban cores
■ (light)	Vedic settlement by 900 BCE
←	Nomadic incursions (sea peoples)
←	Nomadic incursions (pastoralists)
▪	Destroyed site
•	City

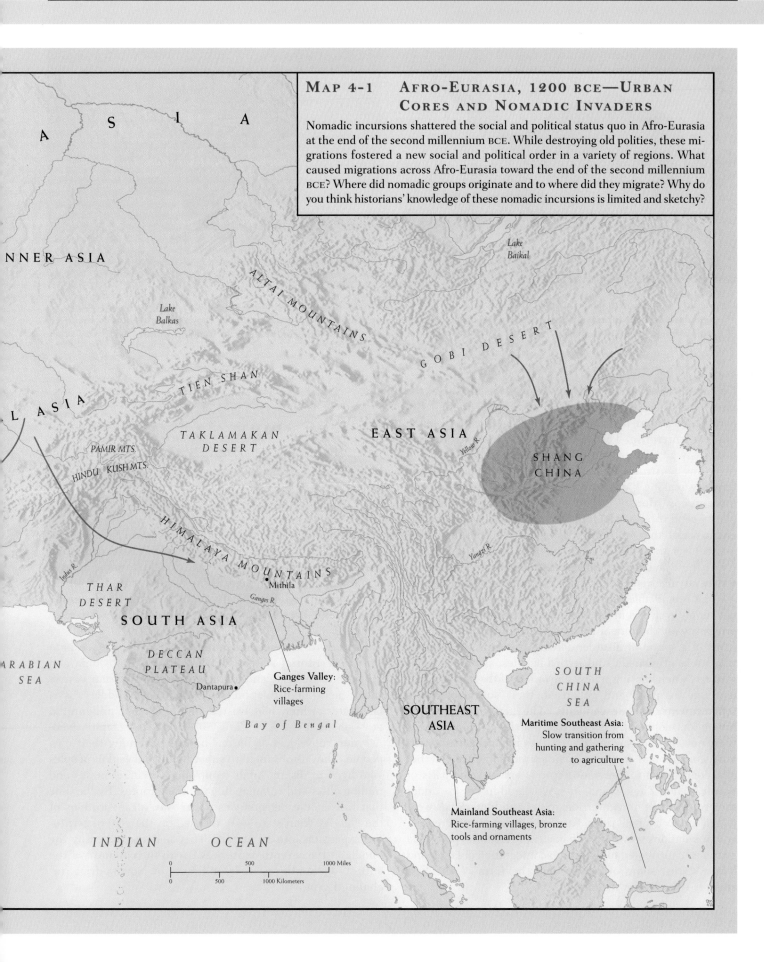

MAP 4-1   AFRO-EURASIA, 1200 BCE—URBAN CORES AND NOMADIC INVADERS

Nomadic incursions shattered the social and political status quo in Afro-Eurasia at the end of the second millennium BCE. While destroying old polities, these migrations fostered a new social and political order in a variety of regions. What caused migrations across Afro-Eurasia toward the end of the second millennium BCE? Where did nomadic groups originate and to where did they migrate? Why do you think historians' knowledge of these nomadic incursions is limited and sketchy?

ASIA

INNER ASIA

Lake Baikal

ALTAI MOUNTAINS

Lake Balkas

GOBI DESERT

TIEN SHAN

L ASIA

TAKLAMAKAN DESERT

EAST ASIA

Yellow R.

SHANG CHINA

PAMIR MTS.

HINDU KUSH MTS.

HIMALAYA MOUNTAINS

Indus R.

THAR DESERT

Mithila

Ganges R.

Yangzi R.

SOUTH ASIA

DECCAN PLATEAU

Dantapura

Ganges Valley: Rice-farming villages

ARABIAN SEA

Bay of Bengal

SOUTHEAST ASIA

SOUTH CHINA SEA

Maritime Southeast Asia: Slow transition from hunting and gathering to agriculture

Mainland Southeast Asia: Rice-farming villages, bronze tools and ornaments

INDIAN OCEAN

0   500   1000 Miles
0   500   1000 Kilometers

Dromedary Camels. Dromedary camels look neat and tidy. They are good draft animals for travel and domestic work in the deserts of Arabia, Afghanistan, and India.

Two-hump Camels. Two-hump camels are much bigger and messier than dromedary camels. They are more suited to the extreme dry and cold weather in Iran and Central Asia.

Deportations were another strategy regularly used to break the unity of resisters. They also served to provide slave labor to parts of the empire in need of manpower and to integrate the imperial enterprise. Throughout the 300 years of Assyrian hegemony, an infrastructure of roads, garrisons, and relay stations was constructed throughout the entire expanse of the territory, making it easier to communicate information and move troops. Moreover, the Assyrians required subject peoples to send tribute, which they used to build imperial cities and to enrich the royal coffers, as well as to bolster their dominance over those they had conquered. In the coming centuries, these practices would become common among empires, widely varying degrees of brutality used as a method of control.

This remarkable period of integration and interaction did not simply evolve from the kingdoms of the previous age. The prosperity and bounty of the first millennium BCE were the fruits of a spasm of disorder across Afro-Eurasia caused by migrations of nomadic and settled peoples, as well as by invasions by neighboring states. The orders of the previous millennium trembled and collapsed; their successors were replacements, not descendents. The key factor shaping human development was now war, not the environment. As these new hybrid societies formed, they produced fresh, written ideologies and doctrines, some sacred, some secular, that also contributed to integration in this era in Vedic parts of South Asia, in Zhou China, in Assyria, and in Persia. Under the protection of fierce warriors, cities and hinterlands were joined under a single ruler. Farming yields again increased, and populations grew. The expansion of territorial power via conquest contributed to the regional integration of larger and larger states, some of which took the form of the first empires—the bigger, the better.

THE NEO-ASSYRIAN EMPIRE

> → *What distinguished the Neo-Assyrian Empire from earlier territorial kingdoms?*

When stability returned to Southwest Asia and North Africa, around 950 BCE, the societies were entirely restructured, and the balance among many large and small powers soon gave way to a regional superpower. The Neo-Assyrian Empire directly dominated or more indirectly affected all the area's populations, even those living in the Mediterranean. (See Map 4-2.)

The third and second millennia BCE had seen expansionary territorial states, such as those of Babylonia and Egypt, but the scale and extent of the Neo-Assyrian state—"new" (neo-) in distinction to the "Old" and "Middle" Assyrian states, which had existed in the second millennium BCE—made it the Afro-Eurasian world's first empire. Neo-Assyrian rulers had ambitions beyond governing their own people. They also wanted to subordinate and exploit peoples who lived in distant lands, controlling their resources and trading cities and commanding the trade routes. By the time that full-scale expansion was under way, all institutions of the Neo-Assyrian state were focused on the goal of territorial expansion into an empire. They had succeeded by the middle of the seventh century BCE with the conquest of the entirety of Southwest Asia and parts of North Africa, including Egypt.

→ *What distinguished the Neo-Assyrian Empire from earlier territorial kingdoms?*

EXPANSION INTO AN EMPIRE

The Neo-Assyrian Empire lasted for three brutal centuries. It became legendary for its ruthless efficiency and particularly for its reliance on terror (through harsh punishments, such as the cutting off of ears, lips, and fingers; castration; and mass executions), large-scale deportations, and systematic intimidation to crush its adversaries.

The heartland of Assyria was a small area centered on the ancient cities of Ashur and Nineveh on the upper reaches of the Tigris River. Unlike the surrounding regions, during the disturbances of the eleventh century BCE Middle Assyria had managed to fend off the invading peoples, kept at bay by trained warriors loyal to the royal house. By the ninth century BCE, the turmoil had subsided, and soon the Assyrians renewed their westward expansion. By 824 BCE, the Assyrians again dominated the land and inhabitants all the way to the shores of the Mediterranean and thus controlled trade and tribute from these areas.

The Assyrians had several advantages. Their armies were made up of well-trained and ruthlessly disciplined professional troops led by officers who, in the empire's later years, rose high in the ranks because of their merit, not their birth. They perfected the combined deployment of infantry and cavalry (horse-mounted warriors equipped with iron weapons) together with horse-drawn chariots that were armored with iron plates and carried archers. They were also siege warriors par excellence, using iron to build massive wheeled siege towers and to cap their battering rams. No city walls could stand against them for long. Finally, Assyrian armies were massive. At the height of their power in the ninth century BCE, the rulers sent 120,000 soldiers on the annual campaign to the west. Chinese armies would not reach this scale for another 500 years.

In the first stage of imperial expansion, the king himself participated in the annual campaigns. Not surprisingly, such pressure provoked fierce opposition, particularly from the small independent states in the west, but the resisting populations were devastated —they were relocated through forced deportations, their lands annexed. The Assyrian state grew even more ambitious when a talented military leader usurped the throne. Naming himself Tiglath Pileser III (r. 745–728 BCE), after an

MAP 4-2 THE NEO-ASSYRIAN EMPIRE

The Neo-Assyrians built the first strong regional empire in Afro-Eurasia. In the process of building their state, they faced the challenge of promoting order and stability throughout their diverse realm. Where did the Neo-Assyrian empire expand? Which parts of the Neo-Assyrian Empire were "the Land of Ashur" and which were "the Land under the Yoke of Ashur"? How did the Assyrian state govern each of these areas? Why do you think expansion after 720 BCE led to the destruction of the empire?

earlier reform-minded Assyrian king, he completely reorganized the Assyrian state in order to centralize power in royal hands and thus prepared the empire for a second phase of imperial expansion and consolidation. He took away the rights of the nobility to own and inherit land and other wealth. He abolished the old system of hereditary provincial governors, whom he replaced with officials who were annually appointed and directly controlled by the center of the empire. He reinstated the practice of aggressive, expansionary annual military campaigns. But the destruction and mass deportations carried out by his armies intensified the conquered peoples' hatred of the Assyrians. While they occasionally employed diplomacy in their dealings with other peoples, the Assyrians increasingly relied on state-sponsored terror in governing their empire.

In the final phase of the Neo-Assyrian Empire (721–612 BCE), the state's expansion far exceeded its ability to maintain effective control, given the limits that its infrastructure—particularly the roads and means of transportation available—imposed on its integration. The empire's collapse came swiftly and without warning.

Tiglath Pileser III. The walls of the Assyrian palaces were lined with stone slabs carved with images of the victories of the king. This fragmentary slab from the palace of Tiglath Pileser III originally decorated the wall of his palace at Nimrud. It shows in two registers the inhabitants and their herds being forced to leave after the defeat of their town by the Assyrians. Below is Tiglath Pileser III, shaded by his royal umbrella, in his war chariot.

INTEGRATION AND CONTROL OF THE EMPIRE

The idea of conquest was not new. We have seen episodes of warfare and expansion before. But the Neo-Assyrian Empire was distinguished from earlier territorial kingdoms and nascent empires by its idea of conquest and subjugation of other peoples. Conquered peoples were forced to obey and to pay tribute to their new imperial masters, as they were integrated into a cohesive empire. This system was based in part on the rulers' ability to employ brutality to break the will of defeated peoples, destroying their identity by removing them from their homes through mass deportations. It also depended on elaborate propaganda that equated Assyrian might with the maintenance of the cosmic order under the national god Ashur.

STRUCTURE OF THE EMPIRE The Assyrian rulers divided their empire into two parts that were ruled in different ways, a strategy used by empires in later centuries. The core, the Land of Ashur, included the lands between the Zagros Mountains and the Euphrates River. The king's appointees governed these interior lands, whose inhabitants were responsible for supplying food for the temple of the national god Ashur, manpower for the residence of Ashur in the city of Ashur, and officials to carry out the business of the state.

The other area, known as "the Land under the Yoke of Ashur," lay outside of Assyria proper. While dominated by the Assyrians, these lands and the people who occupied them were not Assyrians. Their local rulers continued to hold power, but as vassals of Assyria. Instead of supplying agricultural goods and manpower, vassal states had the much greater burden of delivering exorbitant amounts of tribute, as specified in treaties, in the form of gold and silver. This wealth went not to the god Ashur and his temple but to the king, who used it to pay for his extravagant court and ever-increasing military costs. After the reforms of Tiglath Pileser III, more and more lands were incorporated into the Land of Ashur proper. While such incorporation eliminated the oppressive need to pay tribute, the programs of forced Assyrianization were harshly administered.

DEPORTATION AND FORCED LABOR In the early years of the empire, the army was made up of Assyrians who went to war on annual campaigns during the summer months. Later, when the demands of campaigning became year-round, the army grew to several hundred thousand men mobilized to protect and extend the vast imperial holdings. These later forces included not only Assyrians but also men from the conquered peoples. By the seventh century BCE, different ethnic groups under Assyrian rule were assigned to specialized military functions. The Phoenicians from the Levant provided the ships and sailors for battle in the Mediterranean; the Medes,

Capture of an Egyptian City. This stone panel from the palace in Nineveh shows warriors scaling walls with ladders during Ashurbanipal's campaign against Egypt (mid-seventh century BCE).

Defeat of Arab Tribes. In Room L of the North Palace of Ashurbanipal at Nineveh, the wall slabs were carved with three registers showing the defeat of rebellions in various parts of the realm. This slab shows with great artistry and detail the defeat of the Arab tribes who resisted the Assyrian war machine in the very south of Mesopotamia. The Arabs, like the Amorites and the Arameans before them, arrived in the riverine valley from the western desert. They were a formidable foe as they conducted war from the back of dromedary camels.

from the Iranian plateau, served as the king's bodyguards; and charioteers from Israel fought against rebellious western provinces.

In order to accomplish its goals, the Assyrian state had to organize huge labor forces for agricultural work and for enormous building projects. Since so many Assyrians went into the army, most of the agricultural and construction workers were recruited from conquered peoples, who often had to be relocated to the areas where their labor was needed. During the three centuries of the Neo-Assyrian Empire, the state moved more than 4 million people, a practice that not only supported work projects but also undermined local resistance efforts.

ASSYRIAN IDEOLOGY AND PROPAGANDA The Neo-Assyrian Empire, like all others, had a propaganda machine that promulgated an imperial ideology to support and justify its system of expansion, exploitation, and pervasive inequality. Even in the late second millennium BCE, when Assyrian expansion was first beginning, Assyrian inscriptions and art projected a strong sense of divinely determined destiny that drove the regime to swell westward toward the Mediterranean Sea. According to the state ideology, the national god Ashur commanded all Assyrians to support the endless and forcible growth of the empire, whose goal was to establish and maintain order and keep an ever-threatening cosmic chaos at bay. Only the god Ashur and his agent, the king, could bring universal order out of the cosmic chaos. The king as the *sangu,* or priest, of Ashur conducted holy war to transform the entire known world into the well-regulated Land of Ashur, and he intensified his campaign of terror and territorial aggrandizement with elaborate and far-reaching propaganda. This state

propaganda, based on a detailed historical record of countless military and political victories, assured the people that Assyria's triumph was inevitable. It was directed primarily at the nobles, whose complete devotion to and support of the king and the empire were crucial. Both verbal and visual programs were developed to reinforce their loyalty to the empire.

The rulers devised three distinct but mutually reinforcing varieties of propaganda campaign. First, as in Egypt and China, elaborate architectural complexes serve to stage ceremonial displays of pomp and power. Second, many different types of texts were composed that glorified the king and the empire. These were spoken at state occasions, inscribed on monumental surfaces, written in annals that detailed the military campaigns and achievements of the Assyrian kings, and buried at propitious places in public buildings, where they could be viewed only by the eyes of the god Ashur. Finally, visual images glorifying the king and the might of the Assyrian army were placed on palace walls. They graphically depicted the overwhelming force of the Assyrian army, showing all who resisted being smashed into submission—their towns burned; their men killed, impaled on stakes, or flayed for all to see; and their women and children taken into captivity and physically deported to faraway lands with any male survivors.

The commitment to "accurately" depict the triumphal events of the regime was visible not only on palace walls but also in the refinement of a particularly Assyrian literary form

Primary Source

THE BANQUET STELE OF ASSURNASIRPAL II

From the third millennium BCE onward, the rulers of Mesopotamia used architecture as one of the most effective means of signaling their power to their subjects. When a change of dynasty or other fundamental reorganization of power took place, rulers would build new palaces; sometimes they would even move their capital city. In the ninth century, Assurnasirpal II established Assyria as an imperial power that intended to expand and consolidate its economic and political control of surrounding peoples. After moving the capital and building a new palace and royal precinct, he called all of the people of the empire to a celebration to mark the transformation of the polity; it lasted for ten days. This remarkable event was commemorated by an inscribed stele that he erected in the chamber next to the throne room.

(102) When Ashur-nasir-apli, king of Assyria, consecrated the joyful palace, the palace full of wisdom, in Kalach (and) invited inside Ashur, the great lord, and the gods of the entire land; 1,000 fat oxen, 1,000 calves (and) sheep of the stable, 14,000 . . . -sheep which belonged to the goddess Ishtar my mistress, 200 oxen which belonged to the goddess Ishtar my mistress, 1,000 . . . -sheep, 1,000 spring lambs, 500 *ayalu*-deer, 500 deer, 1,000 ducks (*iṣṣū rū rabûtu*), 500 ducks (*usū*), 500 geese, 1,000 wild geese, 1,000 *qaribu*-birds, 10,000 pigeons, 10,000 wild pigeons, 10,000 small birds, 10,000 fish, 10,000 jerboa, 10,000 eggs, 10,000 loaves of bread, 10,000 jugs of beer, 10,000 skins of wine, 10,000 containers of grain (and) sesame, 10,000 pots of hot . . . , 1,000 boxes of greens, 300 (containers of) oil, 300 (containers of) malt, 300 (containers of) mixed *raqqatu*-plants, 100 (containers of) *kudimmus*, 100 (containers of) . . . , 100 (containers of) parched barley, 100 (containers of) *ubuḫšennu*-grain, 100 (containers of) fine *billatu*, 100 (containers of) pomegranates, 100 (containers of) grapes, 100 (containers of) mixed *zamrus*, 100 (containers of) pistachios, 100 (containers of). . . , 100 (containers of) onions, 100 (containers of) garlic, 100 (containers of) *kunipḫus*, 100 bunches of turnips, 100 (containers of) *ḫinḫinu*-seeds, 100 (containers of) *giddū*, 100 (containers of) honey, 100 (containers of) ghee, 100 (containers of) roasted *abšu*-seeds, 100 (containers of) roasted *šu'u*-seeds, 100 (containers of) *karkartu*-plants, 100 (containers of) *tiatu*-plants, 100 (containers of) mustard, 100 (containers of) milk, 100 (containers of) cheese, 100 bowls of *mīzu*-drink, 100 *stuffed oxen*, 10 homers of shelled *dukdu*-nuts, 10 homers of shelled pistachios, 10 homers of . . . , 10 homers of *ḫabbaququ*, 10 homers of dates, 10 homers of *titip*, 10 homers of *cumin*, 10 homers of *saḫūnu*, 10 homers of . . . , 10 homers of *andalšu*, 10 homers of *šišanibu*, 10 homers of *simberu*-fruit, 10 homers of *ḫašū*, 10 homers of fine oil, 10 homers of fine aromatics, 10 homers of . . . , 10 homers of *naṣṣabu*-gourds, 10 homers of *zinzimmu*-onions, 10 homers of olives; when I consecrated the palace of Kalach, 47,074 men (and) women who were invited from every part of my land, 5,000 dignitaries (and) envoys of the people of the lands Suhu, Hindanu, Patinu, Hatti, Tyre, Sidon, Gurgumu, Malidu, Hubushkia, Gilzanu, Kumu, (and) Musasiru, 16,000 people of Kalach, (and) 1,500 *zarīqū* of my palace, all of them – altogether 69,574 (including) those summoned from all lands and the people of Kalach – for ten days I gave them food, I gave them drink, I had them bathed, I had them anointed. (Thus) did I honour them (and) send them back to their lands in peace and joy.

➤ *Compare the use of such display with the architectural practices of Egypt, ancient China, and the polities of the New World. What techniques, as reflected in the text of the Banquet Stele, did Assurnasirpal use to build loyalty among his subjects?*

SOURCE: *Assyrian Royal Inscriptions, Part 2: From Tiglath-pileser I to Ashur-nasir-apli II,* compiled and translated by Albert Kirk Grayson, vol. 2 of Records of the Ancient Near East, edited by Hans Goedicke (Wiesbaden: Otto Harrassowitz, 1976), pp. 175–76.

The Annals of Ashurbanipal. This baked clay faceted cylinder carries a portion of the annals of Ashurbanipal. It was found at Nineveh along with thousands of other tablets preserved in his famous library. The annals of Ashurbanipal were detailed, almost novelistic accounts of his military and civic achievements. Unlike earlier annals, there is first-person discourse, indirect discourse, flashbacks, and lively description of events and places. These annals are invaluable for our understanding of the Assyrian Empire.

called *annals.* A major milestone in human history, these documents illustrate the ways in which communication and writing served state formation from a very early stage. The annals were inscribed in cuneiform, both across carved stone slabs and on tablets and clay cylinders. The scribes of the Assyrian court entered a record of each successful campaign (and all were by definition successful) into the yearly report of the achievements of the Assyrian king. These written compositions, like the images, never gave any indication that the Assyrians did or could lose a battle in the struggle to extend and maintain their control of the land.

ASSYRIAN SOCIAL STRUCTURE AND POPULATION

The iron-fisted rule of the Assyrians rested on a rigid social hierarchy. Alone at the top was the king, who as the sole agent of the god Ashur conducted war to expand the Land of Ashur. Beneath the king were seven powerful officials who executed the king's commands and ensured the smooth functioning of the state. The governors of the provinces were originally members of ancient Assyrian families, and the office was passed down from father to son. For a time, nobles vied with the monarch for control over resources and power. But this competition ended with the reforms of Tiglath Pileser III.

The state handsomely rewarded its military elites who surrounded the king for their service, plying them with land grants, silver, and exemptions from royal taxes. Over time, they became the noble class and intimates of the king, replacing the older landed elites who had lost their hold on resources after Tiglath Pileser III reorganized the empire's landholdings. Elites often controlled vast estates that included both the land and the local populations who worked the fields and orchards. The bulk of the population consisted of peasants owned by the throne or by elites. These workers fell into different categories, with different privileges. Those who were enslaved because of an inability to pay their debts were allowed to marry free partners, engage in financial transactions, and even own property with other slaves attached. In contrast, foreigners enslaved after being captured in war had no rights; they were forced to undertake hard manual labor constructing the state's monumental building projects. Those forcibly relocated were not slaves but they became attached to the new lands that they were required to work. The little evidence we have indicates that families were small and lived on small plots of land, where they raised vegetables and planted vineyards.

Women in Assyria were far more restricted and controlled than their counterparts in the earlier periods of Sumerian and Old Babylonian Mesopotamia. Under the patriarchal social norms of the Assyrians, women had almost no control over their lives. Because all inheritance in the Assyrian system passed through the male line, it was crucial that a man be certain of the paternity of the children borne by his wives. As a result, all interactions between men and women outside of the family were highly restricted. The Middle Assyrians introduced the practice of veiling in the thirteenth century BCE, requiring it of all respectable women. Indeed, the veil was expressly forbidden to prostitutes who serviced the men of the army and worked in the taverns, so that their revealed faces and hair could signal their disreputable status to all. Any prostitute found wearing the veil would be taken to the top of the city wall, stripped of all of her clothing, and flogged. In certain circumstances, she could even be killed.

The queens of Assyria were bound by the same social norms, but their lives were more comfortable and varied than those of commoners. They dwelled in a separate part of the palace and were served by women or by eunuchs, whose role throughout the Assyrian court became increasingly important. Though Assyrian queens rarely wielded genuine power, they usually enjoyed respect and recognition, especially in the role of mother of the king. A queen could serve as a regent for her son, however, if the king died while the heir to the throne was still a child. Such was the case of Sammuramat, a queen who served as regent from 810 to 806 BCE, successfully ruling the empire until her son came of age.

THE INSTABILITY OF THE ASSYRIAN EMPIRE

At their high point, the Assyrians had conquered most of the lands stretching from Persia to Egypt. This was an awesome feat, but the empire was also unstable. Imperial expansion brought political headaches. Assyrian commanders had to position occupying armies far and wide to keep subjects in line. The propaganda machine ramped up, but so did the discontent among the regime's nobility. To compound the internal unrest, subject peoples also rose up—often using the iron weapons on which their tormentors had relied. Once a successful rebellion had challenged the Assyrian worldview of invincibility, the empire's fall was inevitable. Although successor states would temporarily fill the Assyrian political vacuum, the three-millennia-long culture of Mesopotamia was essentially dead. In 612 BCE, the Neo-Assyrian Empire collapsed as Nineveh was conquered.

 # THE PERSIAN EMPIRE

> → *In what ways was the Persian Empire similar to the Neo-Assyrian Empire, and in what ways was it different?*

The Assyrians were not the only people to push territorial states to their limits. Nor were they alone in feeling the pressures of nomadic incursions, which both shook up the existing system and gave its successors access to new resources, especially military and other technologies. The Persians were one of the nomadic groups speaking an Indo-Iranian language who arrived on the Iranian plateau from central Asia during the last centuries of the second millennium BCE. The Medes before them had settled on the central plateau and formed a large polity that stretched from the Zagros Mountains in the west to at least as far east as the modern city of Tehran. The Persians arrived in the region of Pars in the southwestern part of the Iranian plateau during the early centuries of the first millennium BCE. For many years, both the Medes and the Persians had warred with and paid tribute to the Assyrians, and later the Neo-Babylonians. Expert horsemen, they shot arrows with deadly accuracy while on horseback. Until Cyrus the Great (r. 559–529 BCE) took the reins of power, the Medes had dominated the Persians. But Cyrus

united the Persian tribes and defeated the Medes, incorporating them and their lands in Anatolia into his empire. In 546 BCE, his armies defeated the Lydians in southwestern Anatolia and took over their gold mines, land, and trading routes; he next gained ascendancy over the Greek city-states on the Aegean coast of Anatolia.

Cyrus's conquests set the stage for a vast and multicultural empire that spread from Europe to South Asia. His capture and incorporation of Babylon changed the nature of empire. In place of the Assyrians' reliance on brutal control, the Persians created a political system that used persuasion to impose their will on subject populations—though they kept the threat and reality of physical coercion close to hand. And because their ancestors were pastoralists, the Persians had no highly developed urban tradition of their own to draw on. Instead, they adapted the ideology and institutions of the Elamites, the Babylonians, and the Assyrians, modifying them to better fit their own customs. They thereby created the Persian institutions that formed the basis of the new empire, which would last until the arrival of Alexander the Great in 331 BCE.

THE INTEGRATION OF A MULTICULTURAL EMPIRE

Cyrus, the founder of the Persian Empire, traced his ancestry back to a legendary king, Achaemenes, and used his heritage to legitimate his empire-building campaign. By defeating the Median and Babylonian kings, Cyrus assumed control of much of Southwest Asia. From their base on the Iranian plateau, over the next 200 years the Persian rulers expanded their domain into an enormous empire that extended from the Indus Valley to northern Greece, and from Central Asia to the south of Egypt. (See Map 4-3.)

Cyrus was a benevolent ruler who liberated his subjects from the oppression of their own kings. He pointed to his victory in Babylon as a sign that the city's gods had turned against its king, Nabonidus, as a heretic. According to the cuneiform text known as the Cyrus cylinder, the Babylonians greeted him "with shining faces." At the same time, as will be discussed below, Cyrus released the Jews from their fifty-year captivity in Babylon. They, too, considered him a savior who, having freed them on the orders of their God, allowed them to return to Jerusalem and to rebuild their temple, and they acclaimed him as the Lord's anointed (see Isaiah 45:1). Even the Greeks, who later defeated the Persians, saw Cyrus as a model ruler.

Following the death of Cyrus on the battlefield, Darius I (r. 521–486) put the nascent empire on a solid footing. In his first two years of rule, Darius put down revolts across the lands, recording this feat on a monumental rock relief at Beisitun on the road to his capital city, Persepolis. Then he conquered territories held by seventy different ethnic groups,

MAP 4-3 THE PERSIAN EMPIRE, 550–479 BCE

Starting in the sixth century BCE, the Persians succeeded the Assyrians as rulers of the large regional empire of Southwest Asia and North Africa. Compare the Persian Empire's territorial domains to those of the Neo-Assyrian Empire in Map 4-2. Geographically, how did the Persian Empire differ from the Neo-Assyrian state? How does this map help explain Persian strategies for promoting order and stability in their empire? Which groups proved most resistant to Persian rule?

stretching from the Indus River in the east to the Aegean and Mediterranean seas in the west, from the Black, Caspian, and Aral seas in the north to the Nile River in the south. To manage this huge domain, Darius introduced innovative and dynamic administrative systems that enabled the empire to flourish for another two centuries. The Persian Empire brought together people of many different cultures, languages, and backgrounds in its new bureaucracy, which successfully combined central and local administration to exploit the strengths of local tradition, economy, and rule—rather than attempting to force Persian tradition and customs on subject people via rigid central control in the manner of the Assyrians.

This empire was both centralized and multicultural. The Persians believed that all subject peoples entered it on an equal footing; the only demand on them was that they give the king their loyalty and pay tribute—which was considered an honor, not a burden. The Persians' lack of administrative

experience and urban traditions may have contributed to their political flexibility. When they came to power, the Persian ruling classes simply adapted the bureaucratic practices of the peoples whom they conquered.

Local Persian administrators used local languages: thus in Iran, the authorities employed Elamite; in Babylon, they used Akkadian; and in Egypt, they used Egyptian, written in hieroglyphs and demotic scripts. In time, Aramaic, a dialect of a Semitic language long spoken in Southwest Asia, became the empire's lingua franca because many of its literate scribes came from Mesopotamia. Aramaic was written on parchment or papyrus in an alphabetic script, and its use spread quickly throughout the empire. The language of the emperors, Old Persian, was now written down for the first time. Monumental inscriptions were usually recorded in three languages, Elamite, Akkadian, and Old Persian; by order of Darius, the last was rendered in a script known as alphabetic cuneiform.

Cyrus the Great. This great Genius with four wings was preserved in the doorjamb of Gate R at the palace of Cyrus the Great at Pasargadae. When Cyrus forged the Persian Empire from Media, Assyria, Babylonia, and Egypt, there was no coherent imperial imagery to represent the new political entity. His court artists borrowed freely from the realms that he had brought into his empire. The image is a combination of features borrowed from Egypt (the headdress), Assyria (low relief representation on a stone slab and the four wings), and Babylonia (the long garment).

Much like Tiglath Pileser III of Assyria, Darius understood that the empire could not be expanded without reorganization and centralization. His method for ensuring that the wealth of the provinces came to the imperial center was to establish a system of provinces, or satrapies, each ruled by a satrap (a governor) who was a relative or an intimate associate of the king. The local bureaucrats and officials who ran the government and administration were closely monitored by military officers, tax collectors from the center, and spies (the so-called eyes of the king) who enforced the satrap's loyalty. Further, Darius put in place a system of fixed taxation and formal tribute allocations; when needed, he instituted economic reforms. Moreover, he promoted trade throughout the empire by building roads, establishing a standardized currency including coinage, and introducing standard weights and measures.

ZOROASTRIANISM, IDEOLOGY, AND SOCIAL STRUCTURE

Like the Assyrians, the Persians established their ideology of kingship on religious foundations. The supreme god, Ahura Mazda, was believed to have appointed the monarch as ruler over all the people and lands of the earth and charged him with maintaining a perfect order on earth from which all would benefit. Thus, according to Darius, one reason Ahura Mazda made him king was that the earth "was in commotion" and Darius "put it down." Unlike their Mesopotamian neighbors, the Medes and the Persians drew their religious ideas from their pastoral and tribal roots, which reflected the same traditions of warrior and priestly classes as those preserved in the Vedic texts of the Indus Valley. The effects of the Persian Empire's religious ideas would be powerful and lasting. As was true of so much else in this age of increasing integration,

Darius's Relief at Beisitun. At Beisitun, high above the Royal Road through the Zagros Mountains, Darius carved a relief on the face of the cliff commemorating his victories over Gaumata (the false Smerdis) and nine rebel kings. The kings are roped together at the neck, and Baumata lies under Darius's feet. Above the rebels is a figure of a winged disk, probably the god Ahuramazda. Darius had his scribes develop a version of cuneiform script to represent Old Persian. In a trilingual inscription (Old Persian, Elamite, and Babylonian), he recorded in detail this victory, which allowed him to consolidate and expand the empire founded by Cyrus. This inscription, which was copied between 1835 and 1847 by Sir Henry Creswicke Rawlinson, provided the key for the decipherment of Babylonian cuneiform.

Primary Source

BEISITUN INSCRIPTION

To commemorate his consolidation of power over the Persian state, Darius I commissioned a pictorial relief of himself as victor high above the main road leading from Mesopotamia to Ecbatana. The images are surrounded by a long text, inscribed in three languages—Old Persian, Akkadian, and Elamite. This is the earliest Old Persian inscription; it is written in a version of the cuneiform script that Darius had devised specially for this occasion.

4.31–2. Saith Darius the King: These IX kings I took prisoner within these battles.

4.33–6. Saith Darius the King: These are the provinces which became rebellious. The Lie made them rebellious, so that these (men) deceived the people. Afterwards Ahuramazda put them into my hand; as was my desire, so I did unto them.

4.36–40. Saith Darius the King: Thou who shalt be king hereafter, protect thyself vigorously from the Lie; the man who shall be a Lie-follower, him do thou punish well, if thus thou shalt think, "May my country be secure!"

4.40–3. Saith Darius the King: This is what I did; by the favor of Ahuramazda, in one and the same year I did (it). Thou who shalt hereafter read this inscription, let that which has been done by me convince thee; do not thou think it a lie.

4.43–5. Saith Darius the King: I turn myself quickly to Ahuramazda, that this (is) true, not false, (which) I did in one and the same year.

4.45–50. Saith Darius the King: By the favor of Ahuramazda and of me much else was done; that has not been inscribed in this inscription; for this reason it has not been inscribed, lest whoso shall hereafter read this inscription, to him what has been done by me seem excessive, (and) it not convince him, (but) he think it false.

4.50–2. Saith Darius the King: Those who were the former kings, as long as they lived, by them was not done thus as by the favor of Ahuramazda was done by me in one and the same year.

4.52–6. Saith Darius the King: Now let that which has been done by me convince thee; thus to the people impart, do not conceal it: if this record thou shalt not conceal, (but) tell it to the people, may Ahuramazda be a friend unto thee, and may family be unto thee in abundance, and may thou live long!

4.57–9. Saith Darius the King: If this record thou shalt conceal, (and) not tell it to the people, may Ahuramazda be a smiter unto thee, and may family not be to thee!

4.59–61. Saith Darius the King: This which I did, in one and the same year by the favor of Ahuramazda I did; Ahuramazda bore me aid, and the other gods who are.

4.61–7. Saith Darius the King: For this reason Ahuramazda bore aid, and the other gods who are, because I was not hostile, I was not a Lie-follower, I was not a doer of wrong---neither I nor my family. According to righteousness I conducted myself. Neither to the weak nor to the powerful did I do wrong. The man who cooperated with my house, him I rewarded well; whoso did injury, him I punished well.

4.67–9. Saith Darius the King: Thou who shalt be king hereafter, the man who shall be a Lie-follower or who shall be a doer of wrong---unto them do thou not be a friend, (but) punish them well.

4.69–72. Saith Darius the King: Thou who shalt hereafter behold this inscription which I have inscribed, or these sculptures, do thou not be destroy them, (but) thence onward protect them; as long as thou shalt be in good strength!

→ *Do you think that all imperial states must go through similar stages of reorganization to preserve themselves? Throughout the millennia, local and imperial rulers on the Iranian plateau used rock reliefs such as the Beisitun inscription to project their power and to mark boundaries. Often these were high and completely inaccessible. Who would see these monuments, and what messages would they receive? What other methods did rulers use to inscribe their political power?*

SOURCE: Roland G. Kent, *Old Persian: Grammar, Texts, Lexicon*, 2nd rev. ed. (New Haven: American Oriental Society, 1953), pp. 131–32.

those ideas came not from the urban cores of ancient kingdoms but from the hinterlands.

Zoroaster (also known as Zarathustra), who is thought to have taught sometime after 1000 BCE in eastern Iran, was most responsible for crystallizing the region's traditional beliefs into a formal religious system. The eastern tribes of the Iranian plateau spread the ideas of Zoroastrianism to the Iranian peoples living in the west, and Zoroastrianism became the religion of the Persian Empire. (The archaeological record is too sketchy to give us a clear sense of how this came about.) The main source for the teachings of Zoroaster is the Avesta, a compilation of holy works transmitted orally by priests for more than a millennium before they were written down in the sixth century CE. It has much in common linguistically with the Vedic texts of the people of the Indus Valley, even though deities with the same names played different roles when they were worshipped in different parts of the world.

Zoroaster's teachings endeavored to wean the Iranian faithful away from their earlier animistic nomadic beliefs. He was radical for the age and place in promoting belief in one god, Ahura Mazda, who had created the world and all that was good. Though rare, monotheism was also found during this time in Judah; it had briefly been the official religion of Egypt, when Akhenaten (r. 1375–1350 BCE) had imposed

Sasanian Coin. Fire worship is central to the Zoroastrian faith. On the reverse of a coin of the Sasanian king Shapur II, two images of kings flank a fire altar. Fire altars of this shape are known from as early as the seventh century BCE in Iran.

worship of Aten, the sun, on his subjects during the New Kingdom period. This initial effort to impose monotheism on Egyptians failed primarily because the people remained devoted to their old gods, and because the new religion lacked a single key component: the attraction of an afterlife. Persians came to believe that the universe was fundamentally dualistic: Ahura Mazda was good and capable only of good, whereas his adversary, Ahiram, was deceitful and wicked. These two forces were engaged in a cosmic struggle for the universe. Ahura Mazda was destined to save the earth from darkness, to deliver Ahiram to the dark place (akin to hell), and to enable the dead to rise for their final judgment.

Unlike the fatalistic religions of Mesopotamia, Zoroastrianism treated humans as independent actors, capable of choosing between good and evil and of engaging in good works or sinful acts. Their choices had consequences—rewards or punishments in the afterlife. Strict rules of behavior determined the fate of each individual. For example, because animals were good, they deserved to be treated well. Intoxicants, widely used in tribal religions, were strictly forbidden. The treatment of the dead was carefully prescribed. To prevent the sacred elements of earth, fire, and water from being contaminated by death, it was forbidden to bury, burn, or drown the dead. Instead, corpses were exposed to the elements to be devoured by beasts and birds of prey. Apparently, this practice was borrowed from the Median priestly class, known as the Magi. These priests enjoyed great prestige throughout the region; indeed, the reported appearance of *magoi apo anatolōn* (the "wise men from the east" of Matthew 2:1) to honor the newborn Jesus was viewed by Christians as evidence that he was the messiah.

Persian kings enjoyed absolute authority. But in return, they were expected to exercise power according to moral and political tenets that reflected Zoroastrian notions of ethical behavior. As the embodiment of the positive virtues that made them fit to hold power, they were to be just rulers, fair in bestowing rewards and in meting out punishments, displaying insight and the ability to distinguish right from wrong so that they might preserve justice and maintain social order. In addition, kings were required to demonstrate physical superiority that mirrored their moral standing. Kings had to be awe-inspiring horseman and peerless in wielding bows and

Panel from the Palace of Darius. The Palace of Darius at Susa was elaborately decorated with glazed bricks. This panel shows human-headed winged lions in a heraldic seated posture. Above them is a winged disk with tendrils and a human bust. This symbol, which borrows from Assyrian and Egyptian imagery, is thought to represent the Zoroastrian god Ahuramazda.

spears. These were qualities valued by all Persian nobles, who continued to prize the virtues of their nomadic ancestors. The ancient Greek historian Herodotus tells us that Persian boys were taught three things only: "to ride, to shoot with the bow, and to tell the truth."

Persians divided their social order into four large and quite diverse groups: priests, nobles, and warriors; scribes/bureaucrats and merchants; artisans; and peasants. Members of each contributed to the welfare of the state by paying taxes and performing their required duties. Surrounding the king was the powerful Persian hereditary nobility, whose support was crucial to the success of the empire. These men had vast landholdings and often served the king as satraps or advisers. Also close to the king were wealthy merchants who orchestrated trade across the vast empire. The king's obligations to them required that he take his wives only from their families and grant them exemptions from certain taxes. But in order to consolidate his hold on the throne, Darius diminished the real political power of aristocrats; by exerting direct control over all appointments, he ensured that the nobles would be his puppets. At the same time, he allowed them to maintain their high status in a society in which birth and royal favor counted for everything.

Royal gifts solidified the relations between king and nobles, reinforcing the king's place at the top of the political pyramid. Vessels of gold, elaborate textiles, and jewelry were presented in public ceremonies designed to reward the recipient's loyalty and underscore his dependence on the crown. Most often these gifts were specially made in the court workshops from gold and silver obtained through tribute, and they reminded those to whom they were given of their continual obligation to the ruler. Any kind of failure would result in the king withdrawing his royal favor; should such failures be serious or treasonous, the offenders faced torture and death.

PUBLIC WORKS AND IMPERIAL IDENTITY

Given the enormous size of the empire, good roads and a system of rapid and dependable communication were absolute necessities. A key element in unifying the land was the Royal Road, which followed age-old routes 1,600 miles, from Sardis in western Anatolia to Susa at the heart of the empire in southwestern Iran. It continued to the east along the traditional route across the northern reaches of the Iranian plateau and beyond into central Asia. The Royal Road was used by traders and by the Persian army (and later by other warriors), as well as by those taking tribute to the king and by couriers carrying messages from the king to his satraps and imperial armies. As the Assyrians had done, the Persians placed way stations with fresh mounts and provisions for the messengers along the route at regular intervals.

In addition to the Royal Road, the Persians also built other infrastructures to connect the far reaches of the empire with its center in southwestern Iran. Under Darius, a canal was built that was some 150 feet wide and more than 50 miles long and linked the Red Sea to the Nile River. One of the most ingenious contributions of the Persians was the invention of *qanats,* underground tunnels through which water, vital for irrigation and society, could flow for long distances without evaporating or being contaminated. Later adopted by many cultures, this system is still used today to

Persepolis. In the highland valley of Fars, the homeland of the Persians, Darius and his successors built a capital city and ceremonial center at the site of Persepolis. On top of a huge platform, there were audience halls, a massive treasury, the harem, and residential spaces. The building was constructed of mudbrick. The roof was supported by enormous columns with bull protome capitals.

The King and His Courtiers. Leading to the Apadana (reception hall) are two monumental staircases that are faced with low-relief representations of the king and his courtiers, as well as all of the delegations bringing tribute to the center of the empire. The lion attacking the bull is a symbolic rendering of the forces of nature. Above the central plane is the winged disk of Ahuramazda and the human-headed lion griffins.

move water across arid lands. These feats of engineering were by and large built by laborers from the local populations, who worked on them as their civic obligation.

Until Cyrus's time, the Persians had been nomadic pastoralists and had no traditions of monumental architecture, visual arts, or written literature or history. Cyrus began to define a Persian court style, which drew on the talents of his subjects. It was Darius, however, who was most responsible for forging visual and physical expressions that were uniquely Persian.

The vast capital at Persepolis was the clearest expression of this new imperial identity. On the highland plain of Fars, near the capital of Cyrus the Great at Pasargadae, Darius built an immense complex that complemented the administrative center at Susa in the lowlands. Skilled craftworkers were gathered from all over the empire to work on the complex, and their distinct cultural influences were melded into a new Persian architectural style. He erected his city, designed for celebrations and ceremonies, on a monumental terrace that covers more than thirty acres. Into the cliffs behind it, Darius and his successors cut their eternal resting places from the rock. Persepolis was also an important administrative hub, where archaeologists have found more than 30,000 tablets; written in Elamite cuneiform script, they describe in meticulous detail the bureaucracy and the activities of the great empire.

For their monumental architecture, Persians borrowed from the Urartians (in modern Armenia) and the Medes the use of grand columned halls. These huge open spaces provided reception rooms for thousands of representatives arriving from all over the empire and bringing tribute to the Persian king. Not only did this central place serve as the treasury for the court, but it also helped integrate disparate peoples by connecting them all to one imperial authority located at the center of the realm. In the palace, three of the columned halls were placed on raised platforms that were reached through monumental processional stairways, lined with endless repeating images of the peoples of the empire taking gifts and tribute to the king. This elaborate architectural decoration was a highly refined program of visual propaganda. The carved relief images showed the Persian Empire not as a homogenized state but as a rich conglomeration of gladly obedient peoples. The carvings on the great stairway of Persepolis offer a veritable ethnographic museum frozen in stone. Each group carries its own distinctive tribute—the Armenians bringing precious metal vessels, the Lydians from Anatolia bringing gold armlets and bowls, the Egyptians bringing exotic animals, and the Sogdians from Central Asia bringing horses. Gateway figures and protective relief images copied from the palaces of Assyria represented the grandeur of the occasion and the power of the king—but the borrowings in this visual propaganda underscore the contrast with their originals. While both the Persians and the Assyrians aspired to and realized their dreams of creating substantial empires, the methods they used for achieving their goals were quite different.

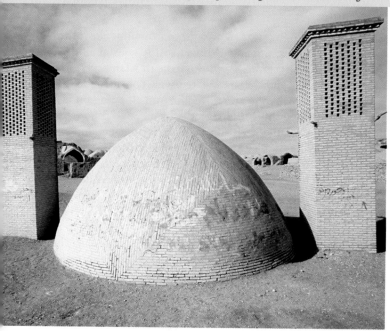

enabled them to rule over large expanses of land, the apparatus of empire did not eradicate differences. In fact, the very smallness and intimacy of communities on the fringes of the big empires enabled them to project their own kind of power and influence.

MIGRATIONS AND UPHEAVAL

Demographic upheavals and migrations around 1200 BCE enhanced the ability of the smaller fringe communities to wield an influence perhaps out of proportion to their size. In earlier millennia, influences and ideas had moved rapidly up the Danube River basin into Central Europe, provoking a shift to an economy based on agriculture (see Chapter 3). Among the consequences of these east-to-west communications were a rapid rise in population and advances by the peoples of Central Europe to develop their own natural resources, including an advanced metallurgy in a new metal, iron. At the end of the second millennium, this surplus population armed with its new metal weapons moved in large groups back down the river highway of the Danube into southeastern Europe, the Aegean, and the eastern Mediterranean. Advancing quickly over southwestern Asia and the Mediterranean, the invaders threw the existing societies into turmoil. These huge movements considerably weakened the power of empires and regimes in the region, increased the value of mobility and communication as peoples vied for resources, and opened

Persian Water-Moving Technique. The Perisans perfected the channeling of water over long distances through underground channels called "qanats." This technique, an efficient way to move water without evaporation, is still used today in hot, arid regions. In this example near Yazd, in central Iran, the domed structure leading to the underground tunnel is flanked by two brick towers called "badgir," an ancient form of air conditioning that cools the water using wind (*bad* in Persian).

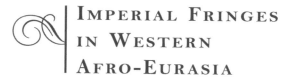

IMPERIAL FRINGES IN WESTERN AFRO-EURASIA

→ *How did the growth of the first empires in western Afro-Eurasia affect societies in the Levant and the Aegean? What influence did they have on the broader region?*

Although the first empires of Southwest Asia proclaimed their control over vast territories, their power was never as total or as far-reaching as their propagandists claimed. Peoples living on the edges of the empires or well beyond their reach in western Afro-Eurasia and around the northern and southern shores of the Mediterranean Sea were equally dynamic actors, often intruding on the empires themselves. More important, they developed their own political and cultural systems. Their powerful neighbors greatly affected their societies, yet they retained their own languages, belief systems, and local arrangements for ruling themselves. Despite establishing large bureaucracies, priestly classes, and armies that

The Naval Battle against the Sea Peoples. The walls of Egyptian temples were covered with images in sunk relief, a technique that allows them to stand out in the bright sunlight. On the temple of Ramses III at Medinet Habu at Thebes, the North Wall is covered with scenes of the naval battle against the Sea Peoples. The Sea Peoples invaded both Egypt and the cities of the Levant during the last centuries of the second millennium BCE.

Mycenaean Arms and Armor. A Mycenaean vase that illustrates the central role of arms and war to the societies on mainland Greece in the period down to 1200 BCE. The men bear common suits of armor and weapons—helmets, corsets, spears, and shields—most likely supplied to them by the palace-centered organizations to which they belonged. Despite these advantages, they were not able to mount a successful defense against the land incursions that destroyed the Mycenaean palaces toward the end of the thirteenth century BCE.

new spaces in which smaller, more innovative communities could gain sway.

These invasions brought about the collapse of even the most highly developed societies in the region. The first of the big states in the region to fall were the Hittites, who had once dominated the central lands of what is today Turkey (see Chapter 3); they could not retain power in the face of violence and social chaos.

Once they reached the Mediterranean, migrants from the north appeared to have adopted boats as their primary means of transportation, hugging the coasts of the Aegean and the eastern Mediterranean seas. For this reason, these communities on the move are sometimes known as the Sea Peoples. The Egyptians knew them as the Peleset, and it was only by marshalling all the resources of their land that the pharaohs Merneptah in the 1220s BCE and Ramses III in the 1180s BCE managed to repel them, thereby securing the traditional order of Egyptian society for several more centuries. Still, Egypt's survival was achieved at considerable cost. And outside Egypt, the former major states and kingdoms suffered heavily from the ravages of these violent freebooters. Settling along the southern coast of the Levant, where they became known as the Philistines, the Sea Peoples considerably weakened local Canaanite communities—and that weakness allowed another tribe from the fringes of empire, the Israelites, to move in and settle the interior of the country.

From 1100 to 900 BCE, a prolonged economic downturn unsettled the major kingdoms, as well as the coastal cities of the eastern Mediterranean and the Aegean islands. During this time, artistic representation, large-scale construction, the development of urban centers, trading and shipping on any significant scale, writing and record keeping, and much else disappeared; societies were now characterized by smaller-scale, technically simpler, materially impoverished, illiterate, and certainly more violent rural communities.

In the Mediterranean, the intrusions of the Sea Peoples shook up the social order of the Minoans on the island of Crete and of the Mycenaeans in mainland areas of Greece. Agricultural production declined, and populations moved to other islands in the Aegean and to southwestern Anatolia. The basis of the complex social order of the second millennium—the large palace-centered bureaucracies and priesthoods, which maintained elaborate written records—vanished, and a more violent society, reliant on the iron weapons used by the newcomers, emerged. This was the culture of individual warrior-heroes that was evoked in the *Iliad,* an epic poem about the Trojan War composed centuries after the events it purports to describe. Like many retrospective accounts, the *Iliad* reflected concerns of later years, but it was based on oral tales passed down and embellished for generations. The Greeks told these stories about a hazily recalled war that may have occurred around 1200 BCE at Troy, a city in Anatolia, during a time of seismic political and social upheaval.

For the long-established kingdoms and states of Southwest Asia and the Mediterranean, these rapid transformations were destructive and traumatic. But they were also creative: they shattered long-established ways of doing things, wiping the social slate clean. Violent change was the first step toward completely new patterns of human relations.

PERSIA AND THE GREEKS

The contact between empires and peoples on their fringe sometimes led to coexistence, sometimes to conflict. But contact always created a political borderland between the imperial cores and emerging regimes on the periphery. It was in such zones of contact that great shifts in the political centers of gravity were most keenly felt. Consider the example of the western fringe of the Persian Empire, where by the sixth century BCE, the influence of the urban cultures of Anatolia and Mesopotamia had waned, replaced by stronger associations with the people of the Mediterranean. The peoples known as Greeks are a good example of these borderland dynamics. In the area of contact with the Persian empire, Greek-speaking people in different cities sometimes cooperated with the Persians, even borrowing their ideas and styles, but sometimes strongly resisted them.

In 499 BCE, some Greek city-states joined with others in the eastern Mediterranean in a revolt against the Persians in Anatolia. The struggle went on for five years until the Per-

WAR IN HOMER'S *ILIAD*

The great epic poem, more than 15,500 lines long, called the Iliad—about the war that took place at Ilium, a Greek name for the city of Troy—was attributed by the later Greeks to a single poet named Homer. The written text that we have, however, is actually the end result of generations of oral singers who composed different versions of this story in the ninth and eight centuries BCE. The story of the Iliad takes place during just three days of fighting on the plains in front of the city of Troy. It is the story of a war, but it focuses on a few prominent individual warriors—men such as Achilles and Odysseus on the side of the Achaeans and Hector and Paris on the Trojan side. There have been many debates among historians about the historical reality of the story in the Iliad, but almost all agree on the site of the ancient city it describes.

        Antiphus hurled at *him*—
the son of Priam wearing a gleaming breastplate
let fly through the lines but his sharp spear missed
and he hit Leucus instead, Odysseus' loyal comrade,
gouging his groin as the man hauled off a corpse—
it dropped from his hands and Leucus sprawled across it.
Enraged at his friend's death Odysseus sprang in fury,
helmed in fiery bronze he plowed through the front
and charging the enemy, glaring left and right
he hurled his spear—a glinting brazen streak—
and the Trojans gave ground, scattering back,
panicking there before his whirling shaft—
a direct hit! Odysseus struck Democoon,
Priam's bastard son come down from Abydos,
Priam's racing-stables. Incensed for the dead
Odysseus speared him straight through one temple
and out the other punched the sharp bronze point
and the dark came swirling thick across his eyes—
down he crashed, armor clanging against his chest.
And the Trojan front shrank back, glorious Hector too
as the Argives yelled and dragged away the corpses,
pushing on, breakneck on. But lord god Apollo,
gazing down now from the heights of Pergamus,
rose in outrage, crying down at the Trojans,
"Up and at them, you stallion-breaking Trojans!
Never give up your lust for war against these Argives!
What are their bodies made of, rock or iron to block
your tearing bronze? Stab them, slash their flesh!
Achilles the son of lovely sleek-haired Thetis—
the man's not even fighting, no, he wallows
in all his heartbreak fury by the ships!"
        So he cried
from far on the city's heights, the awesome god Apollo.
But Zeus's daughter Athena spurred the Argives on—
Athena first in glory, third-born of the gods—
whenever she saw some slacker hanging back
as she hurtled through the onset.
        Now Amarinceus' son
Diores—fate shackled Diores fast and a jagged rock
struck him against his right shin, beside the ankle.

Pirous son of Imbrasus winged it hard and true,
the Thracian chief who had sailed across from Aenus . . .
the ruthless rock striking the bones and tendons
crushed them to pulp—he landed flat on his back,
slamming the dust, both arms flung out to his comrades,
gasping out his life. Pirous who heaved the rock
came rushing in and speared him up the navel—
his bowels uncoiled, spilling loose on the ground
and the dark came swirling down across his eyes.
        But Pirous—
Aetolian Thoas speared *him* as he swerved and sprang away,
the lancehead piercing his chest above the nipple
plunged deep in his lung, and Thoas, running up,
wrenched the heavy spear from the man's chest,
drew his blade, ripped him across the belly,
took his life but he could not strip his armor.
Look, there were Pirous' cohorts bunched in a ring,
Thracians, topknots waving, clutching their long pikes
and rugged, strong and proud as the Trojan Thoas was,
they shoved him back—he gave ground, staggering, reeling.
And so the two lay stretched in the dust, side-by-side,
a lord of Thrace, a lord of Epeans armed in bronze
and a ruck of other soldiers died around them.
        And now
no man who waded into that work could scorn it any longer,
anyone still not speared or stabbed by tearing bronze
who whirled into the heart of all that slaughter—
not even if great Athena led him by the hand,
flicking away the weapons hailing down against him.
That day ranks of Trojans, ranks of Achaean fighters
sprawled there side-by-side, facedown in the dust.

→ *What does this selection reveal about the style of combat used in this period? What does it tell us about the weapons used? What can we surmise about the cultures from which these soldiers come?*

SOURCE: Homer, *The Iliad*, translated by Robert Fagles (1990; reprint, New York: Penguin, 1998), pp. 160–63.

sian coalition gained mastery over the rebellious Greek cities. In this same struggle, however, there were Greek communities that sided with the Persians and were condemned by other Greeks as "Medizers"—Greeks who sided with the Medes or Persians. On the mainland, further away from the contact zone, most Greek cities exhibited a more hostile attitude, actively resisting the Persian king's authority. So, in 492 BCE, Darius sent his fleet to subdue Athens and Sparta, the two big city-states on the mainland, but the ships were destroyed in a storm. Two years later, Darius and his vast army invaded mainland Greece but were soundly defeated by the much smaller force of Athenians at Marathon, just to the northeast of Athens. The Persians wisely retreated to nurse their wounds, waiting another decade before daring to hit their western foe again. Meanwhile, Athens emerged as a major sea power.

Under the leadership of Themistocles in the 480s BCE, Athens became a naval power whose strength was in the fleet of its triremes, or battleships. This great shift was fundamental to the future relationship between the Greeks and the Persians and to the rise of Athens as a great power. When the two militaries met again in 480 BCE, the Persians were able to burn Athens but lost the pivotal naval battle of the invasion at Salamis. A year later, they were decisively defeated on land and eventually lost the war. But in a way that was typical of the close and intertwined relationships between the two cultures, Themistocles, the hero of Salamis, later finished his career in the service of the Persian king.

The major Persian defeats changed the balance of power, and for the next 150 years Persia continually lost ground to the Greeks, who gradually regained territory in southeastern Europe and western Anatolia. During this time, palace intrigues and ongoing rebellions throughout the empire preoc-

cupied the Persian court. The Greek historian Xenophon wrote that "whereas the king's empire was strong in that it covered a vast territory with large numbers of people, it also was weak because of the need to travel great distances and the wide distribution of its forces, making it vulnerable to a swift attack." In the end, the fatal blow against Persian rule would come from the most remote of the Greek outposts in the eastern Mediterranean, Macedonia; its armies, led by Alexander the Great, would range as far as India in their quest for empire (see Chapter 6).

THE PHOENICIANS

The effects of integration on the fringes went beyond resistance. Some peoples who lived on the borderlands of empire, such as the Phoenicians, seized opportunities to coexist with and to flourish under imperial rule—and to create their own autonomous dominions. Particularly successful were those living on the western edges of the emerging Assyrian and later Persian empires. (See Map 4-4.)

Engaging in trade and retaining their autonomy, albeit as imperial vassals, were the people who called themselves the Chanani—called "Canaanites" in the Bible, but better known by the name that the Greeks gave them, probably because they manufactured and widely traded throughout the Mediterranean an expensive purple dye: the Phoenicians, or literally the "Purple People." These Phoenicians were a mixture of the local population and the Sea Peoples who had arrived in recent centuries. As traders, they were more socially opportunistic than politically ambitious; they preferred opening up new markets and new ports to subduing frontiers. Their coastal cities made the Phoenicians ideally situated to develop trade in the whole of the Mediterranean basin. Inland from their cities was an extraordinary forest of massive cedars—perfect timber for making large, seaworthy craft and a highly desirable export to the treeless heartlands of Egypt and Mesopotamia.

Innovations in shipbuilding and seafaring enabled the Phoenicians to sail as far west as present-day Morocco and Spain, carrying huge cargoes of such goods as timber, dyed cloth, glassware, wines, textiles, metal ingots, and finished goods, as well as carved ivory. They established trading colonies all around the southern and western rim of the Mediterranean, including Carthage in modern-day Tunisia on the North African coast. The Phoenician cities were full-scale trading ports that attracted goods from their respective interiors that were then shipped throughout the Mediterranean.

During the height of Assyrian power in the eighth and seventh centuries BCE, the Phoenicians supplied the empire with special commercial services and were able to continue their business without Assyrian interference. They accommodated their powerful neighbors rather than resisting them. Phoenician kings signed treaties with the Assyrian

The Sea Battle at Salamis. A modern artist's reconstruction of the sea battle at Salamis in which the Greek ships led by Athens defeated a large invading fleet commanded by King Xerxes of Persia. The trireme—so-called because of its three banks of oars—was the state-of-the-art battleship of the time. Drawing on their long experience of sailing on the Mediterranean and using the fleet of triremes built under Themistocles, the Athenians gained a critical victory over the Persians and asserted ascendancy over the eastern Mediterranean.

→ *How did the growth of the first empires in western Afro-Eurasia affect societies in the Levant and the Aegean?*

MAP 4-4   THE LEVANTINE BORDERLAND, 1000–400 BCE

Peoples on the borderlands of the great regional empires of Southwest Asia and North Africa demonstrated strong influence beyond their borders, despite their political marginalization. Though politically dwarfed by the Neo-Assyrian and Persian empires in the first millennium BCE, various groups in the Levant displayed strong cultural and economic power. Why are the Phoenicians and Judeans of the Levant called *borderland communities*? What kind of relationship did they have with the large regional empires and with other peoples of western Afro-Eurasia? How did they contribute to the cultural integration of the wider region?

kings that required the Phoenicians to pay tribute with luxury goods in return for some political autonomy. Phoenician merchants and citizens established and colonized port cities along the Mediterranean coasts and sent ships to the colonies full of goods from the east. On their return trips, they carried new goods that would meet the demands of the Assyrian elites for exotic luxuries. At precisely the same time, Greek merchants were spreading eastward and establishing colonies on the northern rim of the Mediterranean. As the two groups competed and interacted intensely, many ideas of the advanced cultures of Southwest Asia were transferred across the Mediterranean.

The Phoenicians were part of the larger Mesopotamian culture, whose shared gods, laws, units of measurement, and science all proved useful to their entrepreneurship. But the Phoenicians themselves developed a groundbreaking innova-

tion that revolutionized communication and commerce between and within societies: the alphabet, first introduced in the second millennium BCE in the western Levant, where it provided a simplified record of spoken languages. Around 800 BCE, this new method of writing was transmitted to the west, probably through Greek traders who lived and worked in Phoenician centers. The alphabet made it possible for educated men to communicate directly with each other, dramatically reducing the need for the professional scribes of Western Afro-Eurasian societies.

ISRAEL AND JUDAH

To the south of the mountains of Lebanon (the homeland of the Phoenicians), in an area that extended to the borders of Egypt, lay southern Canaan, the land that would become the nations of Israel and Philistia. The origins of Israel are disputed, but ultimately unknown. According to the biblical account, the Israelites entered the land from Egypt in approximately 1400 BCE, killing all the native inhabitants. In fact, Egypt controlled southern Canaan in 1400, and there is no evidence that a new population group arrived during this period. More recently, scholars have hypothesized that the Israelites arrived in the 1200s, or that they were originally Canaanites who moved into the central hill country (the heart of biblical Israel) during the late 1200s. However they arrived, the people who would eventually call themselves Israel gradually spread outward from their base in the central hills, until by 1000 BCE they had established a kingdom under the rule of David.

Around 1100 BCE, the Sea People, possibly natives of Cyprus, arrived on the southwest coast of Canaan, where they became known as the Philistines. Though later famous as the birthplace of Judaism, a religion already taking shape in this period, around 1000 BCE Israel was just another small frontier kingdom, intermittently controlled for much of the period by the Assyrian and Persian empires. This micro-region was a borderland that became the center of yet another way of understanding the world.

Israel did not have the special status of the trader-state Phoenicia, but it did figure as one of the micro-states on the borderlands of the Assyrian system. Israel was not a source of irrepressible resistance, as were the Greek borderlands. It was in essence a hybrid society, for it merged aspects of the Mesopotamian states with its own distinctive traits—uneasily surviving on the fringes of Assyrian power. A centralized monarchy emerged under David (r. 1000–960 BCE) and his son Solomon (r. 960–931 BCE), who used their military skill and creative diplomacy to unify the local populace. The size and importance of Israel under David and Solomon are impossible to reconstruct; biblical narrative portrays heroes whose achievements were grand, but archaeological remains suggest a kingdom of more modest size and wealth.

The Phoenician Alphabet. The first alphabet was written on clay tablets using the cuneiform script. It was developed by Phoenician traders who needed a script that was easy to learn and could represent their form of west Semitic language. This tablet was found at the port town of Ugarit (Ras Shamra) in Syria and is dated to the fourteenth century BCE.

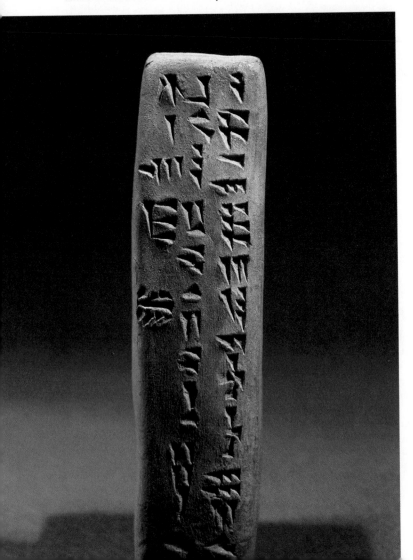

PHENICIAN	ANCIENT GREEK	LATER GREEK	ROMAN

Comparative Alphabets. The forms of the letters in the Phoenician alphabet of the first millennium BCE are based on signs used to represent the Aramaic language. These Phonenican letters were then borrowed by the ancient Greeks. Our alphabet is based on that used by the Romans, who borrowed their letter forms from the later Greek inscriptions.

The kingdom founded by David proved short-lived. By 925 BCE, civil war had split the nation into the rival kingdoms of Israel in the north and Judah in the south. By the middle of the ninth century BCE, both kingdoms had come under the control of the Neo-Assyrian Empire. After successive attempts at rebellion, the northern kingdom was destroyed by the Assyrians, with much of its population dispersed throughout the Assyrian Empire. Judah, the southern kingdom, had remained loyal to Assyria, and so remained an Assyrian vassal until shortly after the fall of Nineveh in 612 BCE, when it became a vassal of Assyria's successor, Babylon. Judah, however, soon rebelled against its new overlords, and in 587 BCE the Babylonian forces of Nebuchadrezzer destroyed Jerusalem. The Babylonians deported large numbers of Judeans from Jerusalem and other cities to exile in Babylon. Later, following the collapse of Babylon, when in 539 Persians under Cyrus the Great swept into Mesopotamia, many Judeans straggled home, where they rebuilt their ancient temple and began the process of reuniting and restoring their society in what is known as the Postexilic or Second Temple period.

The origins of the Judeans' religious beliefs are closely tied to these historical developments. What we can piece together from the Hebrew Bible (Old Testament) and archaeological evidence suggests that Israelite religion, in a period spanning well over half a millennium, underwent a tumultuous transformation: during this time, it would establish its own identity as one of the world's earliest and most enduring monotheistic religions. The early Israelites, like their neighbors, had worshipped many gods, including their national god, Yahweh. By the period of the Babylonian exile, however, they had clearly moved into a stage of monolatry, in which most people worshipped Yahweh alone, without denying the existence of other gods.

From an early period, Israelite prophets urged the people to worship only Yahweh, as well as announcing that Yahweh demanded justice, especially for the poorest members of the society. Unlike diviners who could be hired to forecast the future, the prophets whose words are recorded in the Hebrew Bible were primarily concerned with the moral well-being of the people.

The Israelites saw Yahweh as both the all-powerful creator of the universe and a personal god who expected his followers to subscribe to moral precepts, rituals, and taboos. The moral precepts at their broadest level were outlined in the Ten Commandments, which included injunctions against murder, adultery, and lying. The Bible also prescribes ritual requirements, such as not working on the seventh day of the week. These laws for proper living would be further specified and codified in the coming centuries. Ultimately, religious leaders compiled them into a set of religious scriptures and teachings known as the Torah (literally, "Law" or "Instruction"), which would become the central text of Judaism.

Through their lengthy period of oppression by and resistance to the Neo-Assyrians, which began in the ninth century BCE, and the Babylonian captivity, which ended in the sixth century BCE, Judeans did not turn away from Yahweh. Instead, they elevated his standing to that of the one true God, beside whom all others were false. Their turn toward monotheism and their striking of a covenant with Yahweh—in which he promised deliverance to them in exchange for their devotion and adherence to his "Law"—helped them to survive as a people and to establish a strong identity during this extended period of suffering.

From the practice of this small and otherwise insignificant borderland community, the idea of worshipping a single

Phoenician Inscription. This detail of a basalt slab carries an inscription written in the Phoenician alphabetic script that recounts how Eshumanazar and Amashtarte (servant of Astarte) built the temples to the gods of Sidon.

god spread over the rapidly developing Mediterranean world. Soon, one omnipotent god would take the place of the pantheons of gods in religions across much of Afro-Eurasia.

FOUNDATIONS OF VEDIC CULTURE IN SOUTH ASIA (1500–400 BCE)

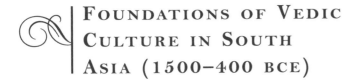

> → *How did South Asia become more socially and culturally integrated despite the absence of an imperial state?*

The origins of Vedic culture in South Asia do not follow the patterns found in Southwest Asia and the Mediterranean lands, where nomads pressed on older civilizations. In Southwest Asia, nomads adapted to metropolitan ways as they created integrated states and sometimes imperial systems. The polities of Mesopotamia built on earlier cultural and technological achievements, military machinery, laws, religions, and trading networks. By contrast, rulers in the region stretching from the Indus River to the Ganges plain did not have previous polities to draw on; the earlier Harappan urban centers in the Indus River valley had been pushed into decline by floods and earthquakes and ultimately died out, vanishing several hundred years before the nomads arrived from the northwest. When nomadic charioteers (who called them-

selves Aryans), speaking their Indo-European languages, gradually entered South Asia through passes in the Hindu Kush Mountains around 1500 BCE, they neither encountered states to conquer nor were united.

Like the Persians, the new migrants lacked an urban tradition. And because the Harappan urban centers had long since disappeared, they had no existing cities to emulate. But they did bring with them many of the cultural traits that characterized Indo-European nomadic communities living on the Inner Eurasian steppe lands and in central Asia. The early Aryan settlers were herders who measured their wealth by the number of cattle they had, and cattle raids often led to conflicts. Rituals were extremely important to them; they attached great significance to the formal sacrificing of cattle, horses, and sheep to their numerous gods, gathering together at festivities to sing hymns, make animal sacrifices, burn *ghee* (clarified butter) for the gods, and share a meal. Priests conducted the ceremonies (for which they received payment in cows). Moreover, they composed rhymes, hymns, and explanatory texts called the Vedas (literally, "wisdom," "knowledge") as part of their rituals. The Vedas were initially passed on orally. Because the newcomers did not develop a writing system for at least 800 years, the Vedas became their most sacred religious works. They were eventually written down in Sanskrit, in which form they have survived into modern times. Because the Vedas became the cultural authority for these new migrants to South Asia, historians call this group of Indo-Europeans the Vedic peoples.

Although they did not find states or urban centers when they first arrived in the Indus Valley, the migrants did encounter indigenous people—a number of whom were likely the descendants of the Harappans—who lived in agricultural settlements or were herders like themselves. The migrants allied with some of the indigenous people who showed them how to live and prosper in their new environment; they made enemies of others, with whom they fought for territory and dominance. As they encountered people speaking different languages and following different cultural practices, the Vedic people held on to their own language and rituals to their gods but also absorbed local vocabulary into their language and deities into their pantheon. Accepting Vedic culture—a culture modified in the South Asian environment—was the price paid by both allies and defeated enemies who were absorbed into their society. By the middle of the first century BCE, the Vedic peoples covered all of what is now northern India, and their language and rituals had become dominant in the area.

In occupying the Indus Valley and later migrating into and settling on the Ganges plain, the newcomers mingled among local farming people, who came to adopt their rituals and their gods as well as their language. Yet while the Vedic migrants changed the social geography and culture of the region, they did not give it greater political coherence, as they did not create a single, unified regional kingdom. To the extent that this world grew more integrated, it did so because of a shared culture: its inhabitants adhered to a set of basic principles and norms inscribed in the Vedas. In contrast, political affairs brought Southwest Asian societies together by imposing political practices and institutions.

Initially, the material culture of Vedic society was very rudimentary. Even the chiefs and elite warriors enjoyed few luxuries. Early trade was based not on importing sumptuous goods but rather on obtaining horses, which could not be bred or trained in the lands newly settled by the Vedics. These former nomads still highly prized horses, and their importation from the northwest beyond the Hindu Kush—from *asvika* "the country of horses"—never ceased to be a major preoccupation of the ruling elite. It eventually drove the creation of the long-distance route across the North Indian plain that stretched from the Khyber Pass to the lower Ganges. Moreover, while engaging in the horse trade in the northwest, the Vedic people encountered the Persians, who by the end of the sixth century BCE had extended their suzerainty all the way to the upper Indus.

As the Vedic people entered the fertile river basins, they gradually settled down and gave up their roaming ways. They cultivated the land and kept herds of animals. Their turn to agriculture was made easier because from peoples to the west they had gained access to the iron plow, which was crucial for tilling the Ganges plain in the east and transforming the Deccan plateau into croplands. The word for plow (*lāngala*), however, is not Indo-European in origin. In other words, Vedic people learned agricultural practices from locals but applied them with new, more effective tools. In the drier north, they cultivated wheat, barley, millet, and cotton, while wet rice paddies filled the lowlands; farmers also produced such tropical staples as sugarcane and spices (pepper, ginger, and cinnamon). Over time, the agrarian frontier filled in, and regions that had been sparsely populated became crowded.

As farming became the dominant way of life, and urban settlements spread across the region, overland and riverine trade also blossomed. Trade between urban settlements developed as the agricultural surpluses grew. Grain was transported to towns to feed their residents; sugarcane was pressed into sugar in the cities, then sold back to people in the agricultural villages.

SPLINTERED STATES

The region's social and economic integration offered a stark contrast to its persistent political disintegration. In the process of fanning out from the Punjab, the region of the five tributaries of the Indus River, and settling along the Ganges

> *As much as the Vedic people fought with the indigenous peoples, they fought even more fiercely among themselves.*

River, the Vedic peoples created regional oligarchies and chieftainships. And as much as they fought with the indigenous peoples, they fought even more fiercely among themselves. Such aggression reinforced the importance of warriors and of Indra and Agni, the gods of war and fire respectively. As in the Mycenaean societies, the tribal societies of the Iranian plateau, and the society of Zhou China, the warriors were the elite, battling each other and the farmers for land and other resources.

Their chieftainships eventually became fragmented kingdoms, grounded in kin and clan structures. Inhabitants were bound to each other through lines of descent from a common ancestor, tracing that lineage through blood ties, marital alliances, and, in many cases, invented family affinities. The earliest Vedic society was divided into two main lineages: the Chandravamsha, or the lunar lineage, and the Suryavamsha, or the solar lineage. Each had its own creation myth, ancestors, language, and rituals. The lineages included many clans, ordered in a hierarchy determined by seniority. The Vedic people absorbed many of the clans of the indigenous people into their lineages. Clans that adopted their culture were made part of the lineage (through marriage or fictive ties) and were considered insiders; clans that had other languages and rituals were considered outsiders, beyond the pale of so-called civilized people. Roughly contemporaneous parallels to this notion of the civilized versus uncivilized could be found in Zhou China.

These lineages ceased to be the basis of the social structure with the rise of urban society and states, but they continued to live on in two major epics that recounted tales of the Vedic people: the *Mahabharata*, which relates the last phase of the lunar lineage, and the *Ramayana,* which focuses on a hero of the solar lineage. Later rulers would continue to exploit the memory of these two ancient lineages, legitimizing their regimes by claiming blood links with them.

Nomadic communities on the steppe lands of Inner Eurasia attached more importance to kinship than to landed territory. This heritage lived on in their lineage systems, in which some clans had higher status than others and senior members of a clan enjoyed higher individual status. Such individuals became the chiefs of the clans, and in the more unified Vedic regimes chiefs (*rajas*) took on the characteristics of kings, bequeathing their authority to their offspring.

The senior clan of a lineage was called *Rajanya,* meaning "the group of brilliant ones," and the lesser clans were known as *Vis*. *Rajanya* were protectors of the entire lineage, while *Vis* herded cattle. As the Vedic society expanded from the Punjab to the Upper Ganges, the clans of the solar lineage tended to stay together in the same geographical area. In contrast, the clans of the lunar lineage split into many branches, as some migrated east to the Ganges River valley and others south to the northern Deccan plain. Though separated by distance, the dispersed groups maintained their relationship through marriage. Within kin-bound clan structures, hierarchies and divisions established each member's location in the political and social order.

CASTES IN A STRATIFIED SOCIETY

When the Vedic peoples first spread out across South Asia, their herding societies were quite homogeneous. But as these herders settled down and created state structures, more complex and stratified arrangements became the norm. Thus, the development of settled agriculture after 1000 BCE led to an increasing discrepancy between those who controlled land and those who worked it—and the differences were represented in castes (inherited social classes) that were associated with specific lineages. Dominant clan members became Kshatriyas, who had power and controlled the land (originally the warrior caste). Meanwhile, lesser clan members became Vaishya, householders whose obligation was to work the land and tend the livestock. Moreover, as rice production expanded and labor-intensive paddy cultivation took hold, households often supplemented the family workforce by hiring laborers and using slaves. Such workers and slaves came from outside the Vedic lineages and were known as Shudras, literally "the small ones." They constituted the lowest caste.

In this way, the late Vedic social system came to consist of four strata, or castes, known as *varna*: the Kshatriyas, who controlled the land and were the ruling caste; the Vaishyas, who were agrarian commoners; and finally the Shudras, who were servants and menial laborers. The Shudras included those who had no lineage, as defined by Vedic society; they were outsiders who joined households as hired or enslaved laborers. The fourth layer was above the Kshatriyas: the priests or Brahmans, who performed rituals and communicated with gods. Some of them continued to function as priests for the chiefs and some were *rishi*, sages who chose to live as ascetics in forests, where they discussed philosophical questions with their students. Their ability to communicate with the heavens, the most coveted of skills, elevated them to the apex of the social pyramid. As communicators with the deities, ritual experts, and Vedic intellectuals, the Brahmans guided a society in which the proper relationship with the forces of nature as represented by the deities was seen as the cornerstone of prosperity. As agriculture became more and more important, Brahmans acted as agents of Agni, the god of fire, to purify the new land for cultivation.

In settling down, the Vedic people created stratified societies that bore little resemblance to those of their egalitarian, pastoral ancestors. Powerful monarchies emerged around hereditary kings (*rajas*), who ruled in conjunction with councils of elders. Kings were also aided by Brahmans, who turned the customary social sanctions and practices into formal legal codes. Much later (c. 100 BCE–100 CE), one or several sages, using the collective name of Manu (Sanskrit for "human being"), gathered these laws into a single text (see Chapter 8 for full discussion). Unlike Hammurapi's code, which was a creation of the ruler, the Laws of Manu and numerous similar documents compiled before and after it were the handiwork of Brahmans. These legal books served both to guide the king and to regulate the behavior of the king's subjects.

VEDIC WORLDS

A Vedic culture, transmitted by the Brahman caste, unified what political rivalries had divided. Belief in Indra and other gods, a common language (Sanskrit), and shared cultural symbols linked the communities dispersed across the northern half of the region and gave the Vedic peoples a collective sense of destiny. Though Sanskrit was an imported tongue, it was the language in which the Vedas were orally transmitted. The Vedas contained the sacred knowledge of the people—prayers and hymns praising gods and goddesses and fixing the rules for making sacrifices to them—and the Sanskrit language, with its beautiful rhythms and rhymes, was thus the means of passing on the people's culture.

As the priests of Vedic society, the Brahmans were responsible for memorizing every syllable and tone of the Vedic works. During the time when the Vedic people had evolved from being predominantly pastoral nomads into a society of settled agriculturists, the Brahmans had compiled numerous commentaries on the older sacred works. Before long, the Brahman priests and scholars had developed a new set of rules and rituals, which became a full-scale theology that explained their new settled, farming environment. In addition to promoting cultural unity and pride through common ritual practices and support for hereditary *raja* kingdoms, the Brahmans did not neglect the non-Sanskrit-speaking peoples, many of whose beliefs and farming practices were incorporated into the Vedas. The *Atharva Veda*, the last and latest of the four Vedas, is full of charms and remedies from indigenous traditions. Although the Vedic period of South Asian history has not left impressive buildings and artifacts, it created a wealth of thinking about cosmology and human society, thereby laying the foundations of the religion for coming generations.

The main corpus of Vedic literature includes the four Vedas: the Rig-Veda (the earliest), Yajur-Veda, Sama-Veda, and Atharva-Veda (the most recent). These foundational literatures consist of hymns recited at sacrificial rituals to the gods, as well as formulas and spells dealing with calamities and diseases. The Sanskrit-speaking people worshipped and sacrificed to a large number of gods. A strict oral tradition required every word and sound to be learned by heart so that recitations would be errorless.

Primary Source

BECOMING A BRAHMIN PRIEST

When the Vedic people became farmers, many of them started to question the validity of sacrificing cows, the draft animals valued for their use in cultivation. Around the seventh century BCE, some thinkers abandoned Vedic rituals and chose to live simply in forests as they debated the meaning of life and the structure of the universe. Those sages were Brahman rishis, highly respected priests in their society. However, not every one of the famous Brahmans was born a Brahman.

1. Satyakâma, the son of Gabâlâ, addressed his mother and said: 'I wish to become a Brahmakârin (religious student), mother. Of what family am I?'

2. She said to him: 'I do not know, my child, of what family thou art. In my youth when I had to move about much as a servant (waiting on the guests in my father's house) I conceived thee. I do not know of what family thou art. I am Gabâlâ by name, thou art Satyakâma (Philalethes). Say that thou art Satyakâma Gâbâla.'

3. He going to Gautama Hâridrumata said to him, 'I wish to become a Brahmakârin with you, Sir. May I come to you, Sir?'

4. He said to him: 'Of what family are you, my friend?' He replied: 'I do not know, Sir, of what family I am. I asked my mother, and she answered: "In my youth when I had to move about much as a servant, I conceived thee. I do not know of what family thou art. I am Gabâlâ by name, thou art Satyakâma," I am therefore Satyakâma Gâbâla, Sir.

5. He said to him: 'No one but a true Bráhmana would thus speak out. Go and fetch fuel, friend, I shall initiate you. You have not swerved from the truth.'

Having initiated him, he chose four hundred lean and weak cows, and said: 'Tend these friend.'

He drove them out and said to himself. 'I shall not return unless I bring back a thousand.' He dwelt a number of years (in the forest), and when the cows had become a thousand.

➤ *Satyakama became a well-known Brahman teacher after his study. Judging from this story, which section of the society was he from? At that time, was membership in the Brahman caste strictly exclusive?*

SOURCE: *The Upanishads*, translated by F. Max Müller, vol. 1 of *Sacred Books of the East*, edited by F. Max Müller (1900; reprint, New Delhi: Motilal Banarsidass, 1981), pp. 60–61.

During the middle of the first millennium BCE, thinkers felt that the Vedic rituals were no longer adequate for their fast-changing society; the result was a collection of works known as the Upanishads, or the supreme knowledge. The Upanishads, which take the form of dialogues between disciples and a sage, record explorations and discussions of questions of deep concern to the people of that time. Out of these conversations came a set of didactic lessons that offered insights into the fundamentals of the social order. Indeed, the social order and the religious order were fully intertwined; the term *Brahma* refers to a universe composed of the earth, the sky, and the heavenly bodies beyond the sky. In this universe, an eternal being, *atman*, exists everywhere, in the smallest creature as well as in the entire universe. In the Upanishads, the term *atman* does not name a supreme

deity. While all living creatures are destined to die, the *atman* never perishes but is reborn when it transmigrates into another life. Reincarnation was therefore a cornerstone of the late Vedic belief system. According to one philosophical school, the Vedanta (literally, "the end of the Veda"), people did not die but simply appeared in different life forms, governed by the eternal cosmic order.

These unique Vedic views of life and the universe were transmitted as principles of faith, bringing spiritual unity to the northern half of South Asia. The peoples of the Indus Valley and Ganges plain would follow a different path forward than those in the societies of Southwest Asia and North Africa. Here in this array of localized kingdoms, the common Vedic culture rather than larger-scale polities would be the unifying bond.

Global Connections & Disconnections

PROPHETS AND FOUNDING TEXTS—
COMPARING JEWISH AND VEDIC SOURCES

Reliance on sacred texts is one of the defining traits of religious movements. Writing helped make possible the transmission of beliefs from generation to generation. The stories, historical material, and parables contained in religious texts contributed to forming belief systems that have become the backbone of religious identity for many of the major faiths. In many faiths, we find one core immutable text, such as the Bible, for Jews and Christians; or the Vedas, for Hindus; or the Koran, for Muslims. In addition, we also often find supplementary texts that discuss, clarify, or expand on the ideas expressed in the core texts. In the Jewish tradition, such textual exegesis is known as *midrash.*

Like many other religions, Judaism is based on a revealed scripture, thought to have been transmitted directly from God to his prophets. These were the core works over whose interpretation rabbis argued for centuries; their discussions were passed on orally through their students. Judaism is thus built on a series of texts that include debates about the Bible by generations of scholars.

The name *Bible* was not originally used by Jews themselves; instead, a common term was *Tanakh,* an acronym derived from the Hebrew titles of the text's three major parts:

1. Torah (literally, "Instruction"). The Torah is usually referred to as the law of the Jewish people; it encompasses five books, also called the Pentateuch, whose authorship was traditionally ascribed to Moses.

2. Nevi'im (Prophets). This term is associated with texts ascribed to various prophets who preached and warned the people about how to live their lives in accordance with the law.
3. Ketuvim (Writings). It includes the Psalms and Proverbs.

According to Jewish tradition, the Tanakh consists of twenty-four books: five in the Torah, eight in the Nevi'im, and eleven in the Ketuvim. They took their canonical written form gradually, beginning with the Torah in the sixth century BCE. Determined to ensure their religion's survival and restoration in Jerusalem, priests in exile in Babylon combined and finalized writings that had begun to be recorded in the tenth century BCE. The entire canon was not closed until the first or second century CE, at a time when Jewish scholars again felt that their religion was imperiled, now by the enormous social and religious upheaval that followed the destruction of the second temple in Jerusalem by the Romans in 70 CE. The huge compilation of oral law, the Talmud, was finally written down (in two versions) around the fifth and sixth centuries BCE. Taken together, these texts express the ability of the Jewish community to adapt and persevere, turning to the written word to determine how to respond and shape their lives when historical conditions changed.

Vedic culture also had foundational texts at its core, and developed traditions for their use in religious rituals. There are four Vedic texts: the Rig-Veda, Sama-Veda, Yajur-Veda, and Atharva-Veda. The Rig-Veda, the earliest text in the

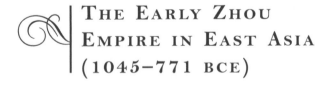

THE EARLY ZHOU EMPIRE IN EAST ASIA (1045–771 BCE)

> → *To what extent was the Zhou state similar to contemporary empires in western Afro-Eurasia in its structure and its impact on its neighbors?*

China also felt the effects of incursions from nomadic neighbors. Around the same time that western Afro-Eurasian states

and societies went through a cycle of upheaval and reconsolidation, invasion and warfare were setting the stage for a reconfiguration of the political and social map of East Asia. The Zhou initially swore allegiance to the Shang and allied with them in their fight against nomadic incursions on the western borderlands. But they eventually turned against the Shang, assembling superior military forces in the northwest and using chariots and archers to defeat them in about 1045 BCE.

According to Korean and Chinese legends, a disgruntled Shang prince refused to cede power to the Zhou when Anyang, the capital city, fell. He led remnants of the Shang garrisons east toward modern-day Pyongyang and established corpus, is a collection of hymns praising the gods, including Indra (god of war), Agni (god of fire), and Varuna (god of water). Though every major god receives attention, Indra stands out as the most powerful and important, as he is the one who set the order of the universe and made life possible. Priests would recite hymns from the Rig-Veda during sacrifices in which hundreds of cows and several horses were slaughtered and clarified butter was burned in the name of the gods. The Sama-Veda is a textbook of songs to be performed by the priest at a sacrifice; most of their stanzas had already appeared in the Rig-Veda. The Yajur-Veda is a prayer book for the priest who conducted rituals for chariot racing, horse sacrifices, or the king's coronation. The Atharva-Veda, the most recently composed of the four, includes charms and remedies for major and minor difficulties; many address problems related to agriculture, a central aspect of life.

Brahmans, the priests and intellectuals of Vedic society, composed works—the Brahmanas and Aranyakas—to explain how and when the hymns and chants of the Vedas should be recited, during the ritual performances and to elucidate the rituals' secret meanings. However, as Vedic peoples embraced settled agriculture and abandoned the lifeways of herding nomads by the middle of the first millennium BCE, some thinkers seriously doubted the validity of Vedic sacrificial rituals that were based on gods driving chariots and began to reflect on the meaning of life and the universe. Scholars then composed the Upanishads, mystic speculative works whose concepts of life and death,

time and space, geography and the cosmos laid the foundations for most, if not all, of South Asia's later schools of thought, including Buddhism and Jainism.

Vedic literature, both hymns and rules for rituals, long remained an oral tradition. Brahman masters taught their pupils to recite and remember every syllable. Even after Buddhists started to write down texts in the late first millennium BCE, Brahmans resisted the temptation to make copies of the Vedas, fearing that they would lose exclusive control of their sacred works. It is possible that sometime after the beginning of the common era, Brahmans started to copy Vedic passages onto palm leaves, which soon decay in the tropical climate of South Asia, only to aid their memory: they still considered oral teaching the most reliable. When Brahmanism was reborn as Hinduism during the first half of the first millennium CE, a host of new deities became objects of cults of worship and gave rise to new genres of Sanskrit literature, such as Puranas (stories of the past) and epics. The Vedas are still considered the final authority of Hinduism, though most Hindus find their contents incomprehensible and of little relevance to their lives.

In both Jewish and Vedic traditions, the pressures of a changing world, and especially the inability to carry out sacrificial rituals in traditional ways, created a new relationship between oral culture, texts, and interpretation. Though their old systems of religious practice were abandoned, Jewish and Vedic worshippers continued to interpret sacred texts as they made sense of their lives, passing from religions of oral tradition to those of the written word.

the first Korean kingdom. According to Sima Qian's much later but well-researched account, the son of the last Shang ruler declared his allegiance to the new Zhou ruler. In return, he received the title of the Prince of Yin and was permitted to retain nominal control of Yin, the Shang capital where he could continue to perform rituals in honor of his ancestors. In fact, he remained a thorn in the side of the Zhou regime and eventually joined a rebellion against the Zhou ruler, only to be killed in the fighting. With that victory, the Zhou consolidated their military power and also ensured their cultural supremacy over the Shang, thereby becoming the dominant kingdom in East Asia at the end of the second millennium BCE. (See Map 4-5.)

When the Zhou took over power from the Shang, China was not yet a fully integrated empire. Like Vedic South Asia, China under the Zhou dynasty was at first a decentralized polity split into regional powers; but as we will see, China's political substructure gave it more unity. The Shang dynasty had exerted control in northeastern China from its capital at Anyang or Yin. The unifying dynastic institutions that it created were emulated by the Zhou: a patrimonial state centered on ancestor worship, as the rulers' power was transmitted through genealogies (from their ancestors and, ultimately, the gods). The Zhou also continued and expanded on the Shang state's tribute system, under which allied regional leaders paid tribute to the Shang, including the provision of warriors and laborers, in

MAP 4-5 THE ZHOU DYNASTY, 2200–256 BCE

Toward the end of the second millennium BCE, the Zhou state supplanted the Shang dynasty as the most powerful political force in East Asia. Using the map above, compare and contrast the territorial reach of the Zhou state with that of the Shang. What factors account for the Zhou state's larger geographic influence? How effectively did the Zhou state control the various groups living in all of this territory? Compared to the large regional empires in western Eurasia during the first millennium, to what extent did the Zhou politically integrate the peoples of East Asia?

return for land, divinations, and protection from the incursions of nomads or other states. On such a foundation—notably absent in Vedic South Asia—an integrated and remarkably durable political structure could gradually be built. In some respects, the creation of integrated war-making regimes, more productive modes of agriculture, and common legal norms re-

sembled the Assyrian and Persian models. But China was not a crossroads for invaders, and thus the Chinese under the Zhou never faced the kinds of rivals or powerful neighbors that would eventually bring down the Assyrian and Persian states.

Able to adopt the local political organization of the Shang and spared the assaults and intrigues of rivals, the Zhou began

Zhou Chariots. After swearing allegiance to the Shang, the Zhou assembled superior military forces in the northwest, in part by emulating Shang chariots. The Zhou subsequently used their own chariots and archers to defeat the Shang in about 1045 BCE. The regional lords who owed allegiance to the Zhou king distinguished themselves in the aristocratic hierarchy by using chariots for travel and battle.

the extended process of integration that formed "China proper" in East Asia. Bit by bit, without a decisive conquest, regional aristocracies joined into a hierarchical system under a single ruler. It was a balancing act between a dynastic central ruler and powerful local lords, however. Using cultural symbols and the art of statecraft rather than religion, the Zhou peoples in the north established a single dynasty, one with broad geographic influence but with limited power over its regional states. This was integration, but not quite unification.

ZHOU SUCCESSION AND POLITICAL FOUNDATIONS

The rise of the northwestern neighboring state of the Zhou and the demise of the Shang distinguished Chinese political successions from western Afro-Eurasia's conquest model of outsiders taking power. Emerging from west of the Shang heartland in the valley of the Wei River, which flowed into the Yellow River as it entered the North China plain, the Zhou

may have had ties to the bronze-producing peoples in the northwest who had preceded the Shang. For many years, the Zhou and Shang peoples lived side by side, westerners and easterners trading and interacting. Indeed, as noted above, they often allied to fend off raiders from the far west. Though initially less advanced in writing and technology than the Shang, the Zhou learned and borrowed from them. And when the Zhou became strong enough, they overcame the Shang.

The Zhou rulers sought to legitimize their takeover of Shang wealth and territories by claiming moral superiority. The rich array of textual and material evidence uncovered from this period indicates that a powerful ruler, commanding wide cultural respect and political loyalty, established Zhou control in northwestern China and also expanded north toward what is now Beijing and southward toward the Yangzi River valley. Under the Shang, the regional lords had been princes of preexisting states who gave their allegiance to the Shang ruler; now the Zhou ruler held the allegiance both of the lords of older states and of new lords whom he installed in new states in the east and north that had been annexed and colonized over time. Rewarding his relatives and key followers with lands that they could pass on to their descendents was an important means of exerting control over strategic areas. Often, the new colonies consisted of a garrison town (containing what they called the "people of the state," or the Zhou colonizers) surrounded by fields containing the local inhabitants (the "people of the field," or the farmers). As under the Shang, Zhou regional lords were required to supply military forces as needed, to pay tribute, and to appear at the imperial court to pledge their continuing allegiance to the king.

THE ZHOU "MANDATE OF HEAVEN" AND THE LEGITIMATION OF POWER

To establish their superiority over the vanquished Shang and their theocratic state, the Zhou dynasts elaborated an ideology to support a morally correct transfer of power, which they called the "mandate of heaven." At first the mandate of heaven (*tianming*) was a religiously based compact between the Zhou people and their supreme god in heaven, known as *tian* (literally, the "sky god"), but it evolved in the first millennium BCE into a fundamental Chinese political doctrine. The Zhou argued that since worldly affairs were supposed to align with those of the heavens, heavenly powers conferred legitimate rights to rule on their chosen representative. The ruler was then duty-bound to uphold heaven's principles of harmony and honor. Any ruler who lapsed from this duty, who let instability creep into earthly affairs, or who let his people suffer would lose his "mandate." In this conception of politics, it was the prerogative of spiritual authority to withdraw support from wayward dynasts and find another, more worthy agent. Thus the Zhou sky god legitimated regime change.

ZHOU SUCCESSION STORY

The early Zhou dynasty is often glamorized in Chinese lore as an era of sage rulers such as King Wu and the Duke of Zhou. The Shangshu (Book of History) account, however, shows that the transition of power from the founder King Wu to the Duke of Zhou was fraught with difficulty, as was often the case in early states. It reveals how the Duke of Zhou tried simultaneously to protect his reputation as regent to King Wu's young son and to preserve Zhou rule. This document also represents one of the first major efforts in Chinese history to provide a historical narrative of events.

After he had completed the conquest of the Shang people, in the second year, King Wu fell ill and was despondent. The two lords, the duke of Shao and Tai-kung Wang, said, "For the king's sake let us solemnly consult the tortoise oracle." But the duke of Chou [King Wu's younger brother, named Tan] said, "We must not distress the ancestors, the former kings?"

The duke of Chou then offered himself to the ancestors, constructing three altars within a single compound. Fashioning one altar on the southern side facing north, he took his place there, holding a jade disc and grasping a baton of jade. Then he made this announcement to the Great King, to King Chi, and to King Wen, his great grandfather, grandfather, and father, and the scribe copied down the words of his prayer on tablets:

"Your chief descendant So-and-so [King Wu's personal name is tabooed] has met with a fearful disease and is violently ill. If you three kings are obliged to render to Heaven the life of an illustrious son, then substitute me, Tan, for So-and-so's person. I am good and compliant, clever and capable. I have much talent and much skill and can serve the spirits. Your chief descendant has not as much talent and skill as I and cannot serve the spirits! . . . "

Then he divined with three tortoises, and all were auspicious. He opened the bamboo receptacles and consulted the documents, and they too indicated an auspicious answer. The duke of Chou said to the king, "According to the indications of the oracle, you will suffer no harm."

[The king said,] "I, the little child, have obtained a new life from the three kings. I shall plan for a distant end. I hope that they will think of me, the solitary man."

After the duke of Chou returned, he placed the tablets containing the prayer in a metal-bound casket. The next day the king began to recover.

[Later, King Wu died and was succeeded by his infant son, King Ch'eng. The duke of Chou acted as regent and was slandered by King Wu's younger brothers, whom he was eventually forced to punish.]

In the autumn, when a plentiful crop had ripened but had not yet been harvested, Heaven sent great thunder and lightning accompanied by wind. The grain was completely flattened and even large trees were uprooted. The people of the land were in great fear. The king and his high ministers donned their ceremonial caps and opened the documents of the metal-bound casket and thus discovered the record of how the duke of Chou had offered himself as a substitute for King Wu. The two lords and the king then questioned the scribe and the various other functionaries, and they replied, "Yes, it is true, But his lordship forbade us to speak about it."

The king grasped the document and wept. "There is no need for us to make solemn divination about what has happened," he said. "In former times the duke of Chou toiled diligently for the royal house, but I, the youthful one, had no way of knowing it. Now Heaven has displayed its terror in order to make clear the virtue of the duke of Chou. I, the little child, will go in person to greet him, for the rites of our royal house approve such action."

When the king came out to the suburbs to meet the duke of Chou, Heaven sent down rain and reversed the wind, so that the grain all stood up once more. The two lords ordered the people of the land to right all the large trees that had been blown over and to earth them up. Then the year was plentiful. (*Chin t'eng.*)

→ *Why was the Duke of Zhou [Chou] willing to die in place of his older brother, King Wu? Why did King Wu's son and successor suspect that his uncle, the Duke of Zhou, coveted the throne himself? What do the direct speeches tell us about the place of religion and divination in Zhou politics?*

SOURCE: Translated in Burton Watson, *Early Chinese Literature* (New York: Columbia University Press, 1962), pp. 35–36.

In using this creed to justify their overthrow of the Shang, the Zhou rulers had to acknowledge that any group of rulers, themselves included, could be ousted as illegitimate if they lost the mandate of heaven because of their illicit and improper practices. By breaking the Shang line of succession in the eleventh century BCE, the Zhou made the full-scale deification of rulers problematic. Henceforth, dynastic legitimacy depended on ruling in accordance with the principles of good governance and upright behavior. China's rulers, unlike the theocracies of Southwest Asia and the later emperor system of Japan, created political and ideological tools that favored a secular empire based more on politics, military power, and morality than on religious legitimacy.

The early Zhou kings contended that heaven had favored their triumph over "all under heaven" (*tianxia*) because the last Shang kings had been evil men whose policies had brought pain to the people. Thereafter, the mandate became a political tool. The mandate of heaven was a compelling way to defend continuity of political structures, if not rulers, in the name of preserving a natural order. It helps explain why the break from the Zhou to the Shang did not result in an abrupt overhaul of political and cultural institutions.

The Shang had employed writing to communicate with the divine world, and the Zhou continued this practice. But the Zhou also expanded the use of writing, recording matters from royal divinations (omens, predictions, and questions for the gods) to a variety of political practices, such as kingly speeches, grants of official offices, and rewards that we can tie directly to the early Zhou state. Other texts—notably the *Zhouli* (*Rituals of Zhou*), which described the organization and administration of government, and the *Yi Li* (*On Ceremonies and Rituals*)—were said to have been prepared by the Duke of Zhou but were actually from a much later period. They thus cannot be taken as proof of how effectively the Zhou used writing to legitimate their power by providing a basis for government and a guide to behavior.

When King Mu (r. 956–918 BCE) put in place a more formal system of bureaucratic governance, restructuring the court and military by appointing officials, supervisors, and military captains who were not related to him and instituting

Zhou Wine Vessel and Sword. Under the Zhou, bronze metallurgy depended on a large labor force. Many workers initially came from Shang labor groups, who were superior to the Zhou in technology. The use of bronze, such as for this wine vessel and sword, exemplified dynastic continuity between the Shang and Zhou.

a formal legal code, writing became even more essential: bureaucratic records, including archives of appointments and legal verdicts, had to be kept. Increasingly, a pool of scribes and scholars joined the entourage of royal diviners, using their mastery of writing to find patrons at court and among regional powers. Using powerful rhetoric, they tied many of the new changes to the early Zhou founding myth.

One of the duties and privileges of the king was to create a royal calendar, which defined times for undertaking agricultural activities and celebrating rituals. The calendar also served as an impartial gauge of the ruler's success or failure. Anomalies such as unpredicted solar eclipses or natural calamities threw into question the ruling house's authority. Since they claimed that their authority was derived from heaven, the Zhou rulers believed it important to gain accurate knowledge of the stars and to perfect the astronomical system on which the calendar was based. By creating a calendar that improved on the Shang's version, they enhanced their public legitimacy. Advances in astronomy and mathematics enabled Zhou astronomers to precisely calculate the length of a lunar month (29.53 days) and measure the length of the solar year (365.25 days). But a year of twelve lunar months is 354.36 days long; to resolve the discrepancy, the Zhou occasionally inserted a leap month. Scribes dated the reigns of kings by days and years within a repeating sixty-year cycle, which was said to match the cosmological interaction between heaven and earth.

Zhou legitimacy also derived indirectly from Shang material culture—that is, from the use of bronze ritual vessels, statues, ornaments, and weapons. The Zhou emulated the Shang's large-scale production of ceremonial bronzes, which they employed in announcements of official appointments, gift-giving, and rituals. The Zhou's extensive bronze metalworking depended on a large force of tribute labor. Many of its members were Shang, who long maintained their superiority to the Zhou in technology, written language, and sociopolitical organization, if not on the battlefield. These Shang craftworkers were sometimes forcibly transported to new Zhou towns to produce the bronze ritual objects.

Such continuity was not merely an uncritical clinging to old ways. The Zhou revered their predecessors and devised elaborate rituals to underscore the importance of inheritance and thereby justify their power. Ancestor worship was a critical component of political life, which celebrated the resilient influence of the past on the present.

SOCIAL STRUCTURE AND ECONOMIC TRANSFORMATION

Accompanying the consolidation of an integrated order was greater social differentiation within Chinese society. Directly under the Zhou ruler and his royal ministers were the hereditary nobles, divided into five ranks (*gong, hou, bo, zi,* and

Zhou Cooking Vessel. Zhou bronze workers began by using Shang decorative designs, such as those that highlighted dragon and animal motifs.

nan, somewhat but not exactly equivalent to the later English titles duke, marquis, earl, viscount, and baron, respectively). These regional lords had landholdings of different sizes, with the largest being held by overlords or dukes. They all owed allegiance to the Zhou king, and they supplied warriors to fight in the king's army and laborers to clear land, drain fields, and do other work as needed. They periodically appeared at court and took part in complex rituals to reaffirm their allegiance to the king. Below the regional lords were a number of high officers at the Zhou court, as well as ministers and administrators who were supposed to supervise the work of the people. A military caste, the *shi,* consisted of aristocratic warriors at the bottom of the noble hierarchy during the first centuries of Zhou rule.

Initially, most of the population worked as farmers on fields owned by great landholding families. Some commoners were artisans, such as those who produced valuable bronze vessels used in rituals, or weavers who spun delicate silk textiles. Over time, according to contemporary accounts, an elaborate ladder of occupational strata appeared, dividing people by function into landholders who produced grain, growers of plants and fruit trees, woodsmen, breeders of cattle and chickens, artisans, merchants, weavers, servants, and those with no fixed occupation. These same sources claimed that this system was held together by the central government, which supposedly controlled how each group did its work—for example, telling landholders what crops to plant, when to harvest, and when to irrigate their lands. To be sure, these efforts to burnish the Zhou's image as a well-organized state by applauding its success as China's integrator overstated the true reach of the early government. Still, the Chinese state played a major role in pulling the region and its diverse peoples together in ways attempted by none of Eurasia's other great regimes.

One of the important methods of integration was the political and legal use of family structures. In their patrilineal society, the Zhou perpetuated an elite organized around kinship principles, which established strict hierarchies for both men and women. The filial son who honored his parents was celebrated in both art and literature. Men and women played out different roles in family and ceremonial life. On landholdings, men farmed and hunted, while women produced silk and other textiles and made them into clothing. Wealth increasingly trumped gender and class distinctions, however. In particular, rich women who were highly placed in the Zhou aristocracy were likely to be permitted a greater range of actions than others of their sex. Wealthy merchants in emerging cities challenged the hegemony of local lords.

What has been remarkable about China throughout history is how its integration progressed in small steps, not in a single, triumphal bound. Zhou achievements likewise were incremental, rooted in a transformation of the countryside. Both princes and peasants began the process of expanding

Shang-Zhou Axe Head. The Zhou dynasty was one of the first empires in the first millennium BCE that expanded its territory by relying on new weaponry, in addition to monopolizing trade and creating new institutions. The Shang-Zhou axe head shown here represents the important role that bronze weaponry played in the invasions and warfare that set the stage for reconfiguring the political and social map of East Asia after 1045 BCE.

the agrarian frontier inland. Wooden and, much later, iron plows enabled farmers to break the hard sod of lands beyond the river basins, and in due course cultivators learned the practice of field rotation to prevent the nutrients in their soils from being exhausted. A great advance occurred in the middle of the first millennium BCE as regional states organized local efforts to regulate the flow of the main rivers. They built long canals to promote communication and trade, and dug impressive irrigation networks to convert arid lands into fertile belts. Some of these systems remain in use today. A slow-motion agrarian revolution enabled the Chinese population to soar—reaching perhaps 20 million by the late Zhou era. Thus already this region was arguably the world's most densely populated.

Over the course of the first millennium BCE, under the Zhou dynasty, landowners and rulers organized the construction of dikes and irrigation systems to control the floodplain of the Yellow River. They particularly concentrated their efforts in the Wei River valley surrounding the Zhou capital at Chang'an (present-day Xi'an), transforming it into a fertile area for the cultivation of crops. For centuries, peasants labored over the floodplain of the Yellow River and its tributaries—building dikes, digging canals, and raising levees as the river flowed to its destination in the sea. When their work was done, the bottom of the floodplain looked like a latticework of rich, well-watered fields, with carefully manicured terraces rising in gradual steps to higher ground. This enormous undertaking was the work of many, many generations. Eventually, irrigation works grew to such a scale that they could be managed only by powerful territorial rulers, the Zhou dynasts centered in the Wei River valley, and by their skilled engineers. The engineers also designed canals that connected rivers and facilitated commerce and internal exchanges. Such canals were dug by tens of thousands of corvée workers, paying their tribute to the state in the form of labor. Other dynasties in Afro-Eurasia similarly provided the resources for massive building works. We have seen in Chapters 2 and 3 how both Egypt and Mesopotamia depended on the labor of thousands to tame the Nile and the Tigris and Euphrates rivers so that their peoples might survive and flourish.

Increasingly, the canals linked China's two breadbaskets: the fields of wheat and millet in the north and the rice fields in the south. The Yangzi River in the south, which also fell under the dynasty's reach, was likewise controlled by engineers. So wealthy was China that its influence was even starting to be felt in the distant steppe lands to the north and west. Nomads living on the edge of Zhou frontiers or in mountainous areas within the Zhou lands, who often engaged in conflict with the Zhou ruler and his regional lords, were now becoming dependent on their trade with the fertile heartlands. In return for the pastoral produce they provided to the Zhou, they received textiles, metal tools and weapons, and luxury items.

LIMITS AND DECLINE OF ZHOU POWER

At its center, the Zhou state had great influence, but its power outside its immediate domains was limited. The rulers' control of their allies in the Yellow River should not be exaggerated. The Zhou state was powerful, but unlike Assyria and Persia it never evolved into a superpower. The dynasty relied instead on culture (its bronzes) and statecraft (the mandate of heaven) to maintain its leadership role among competing powers and lesser principalities. Rather than having absolute control of an empire, the Zhou state was first among many regional economic and political allies.

The Zhou dynasty ruled over a much larger expanse than did the Shang dynasty, but its government displayed little increase in centralization. It relied on local authorities—the regional lords, who in this regard resembled Persian satraps—to hold provinces in line. Military campaigns continued to be fought by the Zhou rulers seeking to expand into new lands or to maintain their holdings when attacked by enemy peoples (often labeled "barbarians," simply because they were not part of the Zhou state). Rulers attempted to keep neighbors and allies in line by giving them power, by protecting them from others' aggression (especially the repeated incursions from the steppe lands), and by the tried-and-true method of intermarriage between Zhou dynastic family members and local nobles. The Zhou's subordinates had more than autonomy; they had genuine resources that they could turn against dynasts at opportune moments.

The power of the Zhou royal house over its regional lords declined in the ninth and eighth centuries BCE. In response, the Zhou court at its impressive capital at Chang'an introduced ritual reforms. The earlier Zhou family rituals that had focused on small sets of ritual bronzes were replaced by grandiose ceremonies performed by specialists employing large bronze vessels, newly standardized. Yet this assertion of centralized control of rituals and of bronze metalworking did nothing to address the regime's growing political weakness in dealing with its steppe neighbors and internal regional lords. For the most part, the Zhou court became a theater state, hoping that impressive rituals would conceal its lack of military might.

The facade began to crumble as wars, their attendant social dislocations, and changes in landholding shook the system's social and political foundations. The Zhou dynasts managed to cling to their authority over their vast domains until 771 BCE, when northern steppe invaders forced the Zhou to flee their western capital at Chang'an. The Zhou dynastic period, like the Shang, was later idealized by historians such as Sima Qian. He portrayed this period as a golden age of wise kings and sage officials. Even more than the Shang, the Zhou model of government, culture, and society became the standard for later generations. As a result, a tradition emerged in China of upholding political continuity and social stability; the regime's fundamental legitimacy was seen as resting on the moral bonds between ruling families, who were at the top of a carefully managed social pyramid, and those in the orderly layers beneath them. Though the Mesopotamian and Persian superpowers were capable of greater expansion during this period, China was sowing the seeds of a more durable state.

CONCLUSION

Upheavals in the territorial states of Afro-Eurasia led to the emergence of more extensive political powers—in Egypt, Mesopotamia, and China—during the first half of the first millennium BCE. For a total of seven centuries, both the Assyrian Empire based in Mesopotamia and the Persian Empire based in Iran stood as superpowers whose reach continued to grow. These first empires pioneered ways of expanding territorial states beyond their "ethnic" or linguistic

Chronology

	1100 BCE	1000 BCE	900 BCE
SOUTHWEST ASIA AND NORTH AFRICA			▪ *Neo-Assyrian Empire, 950–612 BCE*
THE MEDITERRANEAN			
SOUTH ASIA		▪ *Vedic migrations* ▪ *Development of settled agriculture after 1000 BCE* ▪ *Emergence of caste system after 1000 BCE*	
EAST ASIA	▪ *Zhou state, 1045–771 BCE (Western Zhou)*		

homelands, and eventually provided means for parts of Afro-Eurasia to intensify their interactions and exchanges. Driving these changes were the incursions of nomadic people, new weaponry, trade, and new administrative strategies and institutions.

The Assyrian and Persian empires marked a new stage in the history of the world's polities. Despite the numerous borrowings by their rulers, they differed fundamentally from the previous city-states and territorial states that had flourished in this area earlier. Assyrians and Persians created ideologies, political institutions, economic ties, and cultural ways that facilitated their unceasing territorial expansion across very large regions. They also established more forceful control over outlying regions than their predecessors had achieved; their strong imperial institutions permitted the systematic exploitation of the human and material resources at great distances from the imperial centers.

We should not treat the Assyrian and Persian empires as models of durable integration, however. In this regard they differed from the gradual and sustained evolution of cultural continuity in South Asia or the slow development of dynastic statecraft in China. For all their majesty and power, these first empires tended to be highly unstable, because they created enormous concentrations of power and ruthlessly extracted resources from local populations. The study of world history suggests that the rise of empires can follow distinct trajectories. In the most common, illustrated by Assyria and Persia, an initial period of expansion is followed by a radical administrative restructuring of institutions in order to further territorial expansion and consolidate control over dispersed dominions. Next, the polities undergo a period of decline, occasioned by problems within the core of the regime that are aggravated by external shocks. As time passes, what is remembered is an age of imperial grandeur.

The empires of Assyria and Persia had distinctive features, but they shared core ideological and institutional characteristics. A single absolute ruler, claiming legitimacy from a supreme divine being, lay at the heart of their imperial ideologies. Both saw the link between the god and the ruler as unique and irrevocable; the ruler maintained imperial order to secure cosmic well-being, a task mandated by the god. These imperial enterprises were founded on moral imperatives: both the ruler and his subjects deemed the state's success to be an unmitigated good, and resistance to empire to be always bad.

But there were other models of expansion that did not yield political empires—at least at first. Core beliefs and principles did not everywhere encourage political integration. In the Vedic world of the Indus Valley and Ganges plain, commonality of values and revered texts did not lead even to a single state. The unparalleled degree of integration across northern South Asia was cultural and economic rather than political. Centuries would pass before a regime would layer a state over this shared cultural world.

In China as well, a core of cultural and political beliefs developed. As in Persia and the Indus Valley and Ganges plain, shared ideas and values circulated across a wide geographic area. But unlike in Vedic South Asia, a powerful political system emerged in China when the Zhou dynasts sought to integrate their empire. It could not last, however; although the Zhou transformed China in many ways, they could not overcome the power of local nobles or fully protect the western frontier from nomadic predators—and thus the regime could never command military and fiscal powers as great as those that characterized the empires of southwestern Afro-Eurasia. But Zhou efforts had the longer-term consequence of establishing the foundations of a political and ruling culture that would serve the ambitions of later imperial dynasts.

Empire building was not occurring around the globe at this time. Indeed, the vast majority of the world's people lived in smaller polities. Sub-Saharan Africa and the Americas—which were worlds apart from the first empires of Afro-Eurasia—aside, those expanding empires left many Afro-Eurasian areas completely untouched. Nor did the might of Assyria and

800 BCE	**700** BCE	**600** BCE	**500** BCE
			▮ *Persian Empire, 550–479* BCE
▮ *Phoenician colonization, 8th and 7th centuries* BCE			
Greek colonization ▮		*Greek/Persian battles, 499–480* BCE ▮	

Persia necessarily crush all who came into contact with imperial rulers, soldiers, and traders; the nomadic peoples who lived in the northern steppes and in southern desert locations throughout the Afro-Eurasian landmass continued to enjoy their autonomy.

Significant political developments were taking place among peoples living in Vedic Indus Valley and Ganges plain, the river valleys of China, and around the eastern Mediterranean shore. Here, men and women developed their own sophisticated state structures in relative isolation from Assyria and Persia. The new state structures of China, Vedic South Asia, and the Mediterranean did not leave as many impressive monuments as did the Assyrian and Persian empires. But they promoted the agrarian revolutions in China and Vedic South Asia and the precocious commercial life of the Mediterranean, which served to make their worlds more integrated.

The peoples living on the eastern Mediterranean shore, in the Vedic society in South Asia, and in the Zhou kingdom in China made distinctive and enduring contributions to the cultural and religious history of humanity. A budding monotheism sprouted from the land of Judah, the concept of cyclic universal time in the form of rebirth or reincarnation developed in late Vedic South Asia, and an ideal of statecraft and social order took shape in late Zhou China. All evolved into powerful cultural forms that in time spread their influences well beyond their sites of origin.

Thus, in the first millennium BCE a crucial transformation occurred. Even as Assyrians and Persians were erecting monuments to political centralization, southwestern Asia clearly was becoming less central to world history. Up to the first millennium BCE, much of recorded human history was concentrated in Mesopotamia and its environs. But by the close of the first millennium BCE, many other, fully independent sources of writing, science, and legal and spiritual thought had emerged, based near the Yellow River and in the Ganges plain, and scattered over the hills of Judah and the Greek islands of the eastern Mediterranean. We thus can see the ongoing tension within and between worlds as they came together, while also standing apart. Moreover, the Afro-Eurasian world was breaking out of a very long cycle in which urban culture was synonymous with a couple of great river systems in Mesopotamia and Egypt. As the next chapter shows, small-scale but innovative places of human discovery were proliferating around the globe.

STUDY QUESTIONS

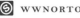 WWNORTON.COM/STUDYSPACE

1. Explain how migrating populations paved the way for greater cultural integration across Afro-Eurasia after 1200 BCE. Where did migrants come from, and where did they invade?

2. Analyze the extent to which political integration in the form of regional empires led to cultural integration in western Afro-Eurasia in the first millennium BCE. What other factors contributed to cultural convergence?

3. Compare and contrast the statecraft of the Neo-Assyrian and Persian empires. How did each strive to integrate their multicultural realms?

4. Analyze the role of the peripheral societies in the Aegean and Levant in western Afro-Eurasia during the first millennium BCE. How did they contribute to cultural integration and expansion during this time?

5. Explain the role of clans and castes in Vedic society in South Asia during the first millennium BCE. To what extent did these social institutions sustain a culturally integrated and distinct world in the absence of political unity?

6. Compare and contrast the Zhou state to the regional empires in western Afro-Eurasia in the second millennium BCE. What legacies did each leave to their respective regions?

7. Compare and contrast the process of regional integration in East Asia, South Asia, and western Afro-Eurasia. What primary agents encouraged these processes in each region? How important to regional integration was the role played by states?

FURTHER READINGS

Ahlström, Gosta W., *The History of Ancient Palestine from the Paleolithic Period to Alexander's Conquests* (1993). An excellent survey of the history of the region by a renowned expert, with good attention to the recent archaeological evidence.

Allen, J. P., *Middle Egyptian: An Introduction to the Language and Culture of Hieroglyphs* (2000). An introduction to the system of writing and its use in Ancient Egypt.

Arnold, Dieter, *Building in Ancient Egypt: Pharaonic Stone Masonry* (1996). Details the complex construction of monumental stone architecture in ancient Egypt.

Aubet, Maria Eugenia, *The Phoenicians and the West,* 2nd ed. (2001). The basic survey of the Phoenician colonization of the western Mediterranean and Atlantic, with special attention to recent archaeological discoveries.

Baines, John, and Jaromir Málek, *Atlas of Ancient Egypt* (1980). A useful compilation of information on ancient Egyptian society, religion, history, and geography.

Briant, Pierre, *From Cyrus to Alexander: A History of the Persian Empire*, trans. Peter T. Daniels (2002). A complex and comprehensive history of the Persian Empire by its finest modern scholar.

Bright, John, *A History of Israel,* 4th ed. (2000). An updated version of a classic and still very useful overview of the whole history of the Israelite people down to the end of the period covered in this chapter.

Cook, J. M., *The Persian Empire* (1983). An older but still useful, and highly readable, standard history of the Persian Empire.

Falkenhausen, Lothar von, *Chinese Society in the Age of Confucius (1000–250 BC): The Archaeological Evidence* (2006). A timely reassessment of early Chinese history that compares the literary texts on which it has traditionally been based to the new archaeological evidence.

Frankfort, Henri, *Ancient Egyptian Religion* (1948). A classic study of Egyptian religion and culture during the pharaonic period.

Frye, Richard N., *The Heritage of Persia* (1963). This classic study of ancient Iran gives the political and literary history of the Persians and their successors.

Grayson, A. K., "Assyrian Civilization," in *Cambridge Ancient History*, vol. 3, pt. 2, pp. 194–228. The Assyrian and Babylonian empires and other states of the Near East, from the eighth to the sixth centuries BCE.

Isserlin, Benedikt J., *The Israelites* (1998). A very well-written and heavily illustrated history of all aspects of life in the regions of the Levant inhabited by the Israelites, equally good on the latest scholarship and the archaeological data.

Kemp, Barry J., *Ancient Egypt: Anatomy of a Civilization* (1989). A definitive presentation of the history, culture, and religion of ancient Egypt.

Lancel, Serge, *Carthage: A History*, trans. Antonia Nevill (1997). By far the best single-volume history of the most important Phoenician colony in the Mediterranean (the first three chapters are especially relevant to materials covered in this chapter).

Lemche, Niels Peter, *Ancient Israel: A New History of Israelite Society* (1988). A quick, readable, and still up-to-date summary of the main phases and themes.

Lewis, Mark Edward, *Writing and Authority in Early China* (1999). A work that traces the changing uses of writing to command assent and obedience in early China.

Markoe, Glenn E., *Phoenicians* (2000). A thorough survey of the Phoenicians and their society as it first developed in the Levant and then expanded over the Mediterranean, with excellent illustrations of the diverse archaeological sites.

Matthews, Victor H., and Don C. Benjamin, *Social World of Ancient Israel, 1350–587 BCE* (1993). A thematic overview of the main occupational groups and social roles that characterized ancient Israelite society.

Oates, Joan and David, *Nimrud: An Assyrian Imperial City Revealed* (2001). A fine and highly readable summary of the state of our knowledge of the Assyrian Empire from the perspective of the early capital of Assurnasirpal II.

Oded, Bustenay, *Mass Deportations and Deportees in the Neo-Assyrian Empire* (1979). A detailed textual examination of the deportation strategy of the Assyrian kings. Good for in-depth research of the question.

Potts, D. T., *The Archaeology of Elam: Formation and Transformation of an Ancient Iranian State* (1999). The definitive study of the archaeology of western Iran from the Neolithic period through the Persian Empire.

Quirke, Stephen, *Ancient Egyptian Religion* (1992). A highly readable presentation of ancient Egyptian religion that summarizes the roles and attributions of the many Egyptian gods.

Robins, Gay, *The Art of Ancient Egypt* (1997). The most comprehensive survey to date of the art of pharaonic Egypt.

———, *Women in Ancient Egypt* (1993). Interesting survey of the place of women in ancient Egyptian society.

Romer, John, *Ancient Lives: Daily Life in Egypt of the Pharaohs* (1990). A discussion of the economic and social lives of everyday ancient Egyptians.

Shaughnessy, Edward L., *Sources of Western Zhou History: Inscribed Bronze Vessels* (1992). Detailed work on the historiography and interpretation of the thousands of ritual bronze vessels discovered by China's archaeologists.

Simpson, W. K. (ed.), *The Literature of Ancient Egypt: An Anthology of Stories, Instructions, and Poetry* (1972). Compilation of the most important works of literature from ancient Egypt.

Thapar, Romila, *From Lineage to State* (1984). The only book on early India that uses religious literature historically and analyzes major lineages to reveal the transition from tribal society to state institutions.

Tubb, Jonathan N., *Canaanites* (1998). The best recent survey, well illustrated, of one of the main ethnic groups dominating the culture of the Levant.

Wilson, John A., *The Culture of Ancient Egypt* (1951). A classic study of the history and culture of pharaonic Egypt.

5

WORLDS TURNED INSIDE OUT, 1000–350 BCE

he sixth century BCE was an age of violent conflicts. Regional lords attacked other regional lords; communities fought neighbors. The struggle for power and territory gripped societies from China to Africa. In the midst of this mayhem, Master Kong Fuzi of China gathered his disciples and instructed them on how best to govern, saying: "Guide them by edicts, keep them in line with punishments, and the people will stay out of trouble but will have no sense of shame. Guide them by virtue, keep them in line with the rites, and they will, besides having a sense of shame, reform themselves" (Confucius, *The Analects*, II, 3). Master Kong, better known to us by his Latinized name, Confucius (c. 551–479 BCE), represented a new breed of highly influential leaders—teachers and thinkers, not nobles, kings, warriors, or priests—who relied on words and ideas to persuade and mobilize large numbers of people. They sought to instruct rulers on how to govern in an orderly and just way, and tried to teach ordinary individuals how to live an ethical life. Instead of fighting wars of conquest, they conducted wars of ideas. In doing so, they began to integrate regional worlds with shared identities and beliefs, not just institutions or rulers. In this process, regional cultures distinguished themselves from others—so as regions grew more integrated, they also became more self-conscious of their difference from other regions.

How did teachers and prophets reshape the world? As paradoxical as it might seem, thinkers emerged from a world in which unremitting warfare fostered first political conflict and then large-scale integration. China's Eastern Zhou king had no real power—his primary function was to enact rituals and lead ceremonies. Genuine power was wielded by regional lords, who took what they wanted, paying only lip service to morality or the welfare of the common people. Many of them made sacred covenants that they broke at a whim, willing to bribe, to betray, and to kill anyone (including relatives) who got in their way or displeased them. Armed conflict was endemic, and the common people saw the land they farmed pillaged during times of both war and peace. As the states fought for territory and competed for economic resources, the larger states often annexed their smaller neighbors. Warfare shook up societies. Nobles among the ranks of the defeated—like Confucius himself—fell to the bottom of the aristocratic hierarchy, while upward mobility proved a boon to many commoners. As the bonds of servitude that had tied them to their local lords were broken, the former peasants became independent, taxpaying farmers whose sons served in the vast infantries of their regional lords. A new political and social order was emerging; in many parts of the world, societies were being turned inside out.

> *Thinkers emerged from a world in which unremitting warfare fostered first political conflict and then large-scale integration.*

A teacher and an aspiring official (he hoped to attain an appointment as a minister to a regional lord), Confucius wanted to end the chaos of the times and restore order by promoting education, moral behavior, and the performance of ritual. He thought that cooperation rather than conflict, ethical behavior rather than reckless actions, merit rather than heredity, and concern with the welfare of the others rather than self-aggrandizement should be the basis of society and government. The good life was, in effect, an ethical one, pursued to protect the welfare of the family and society. This was an age in which great sages—philosophers and teachers in a range of societies—expressed many similar concerns as they explored what it meant to live an ethical life. For example, in the Greek city-state of Athens, Socrates not only questioned the political order but also challenged people to justify what they claimed to know. Rather than accepting the status quo, he called on individuals to reform their own moral world by constantly examining their lives and their values. These new ideas were the product of a turbulent world; but by providing new ways of viewing the world, they were intended to lead societies out of that turbulence. Beginning in this age, philosophers would change humanity, not immediately, of course, but forever. This chapter is about how an age of political turmoil in many places of the world was also an era of great intellectual and cultural creativity. From this ferment emerged a new global cultural geography of regions from Mesoamerica to China that developed shared notions and beliefs and became more aware of the differences between themselves and others.

Focus Questions   WORLDS TURNED INSIDE OUT

→ *How did "second-generation" cultures expand the social, political, and cultural options available to men and women?*

→ *In what ways did scholars propose ending the incessant warfare and chaos of China's Spring and Autumn and Warring States periods?*

→ *How did political and social transformations encourage new beliefs and dissident thinkers in South Asia?*

→ *How did cultural integration develop in the Andes and Mesoamerica in the absence of political unity?*

→ *How did the spread of iron smelting shape the social landscape of sub-Saharan Africa?*

→ *In what ways did city-states integrate the geographically dispersed settlements of the Mediterranean?*

 WWNORTON.COM/STUDYSPACE

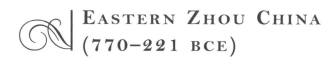

ALTERNATIVE PATHWAYS AND IDEAS

> → *How did "second-generation" cultures expand the social, political, and cultural options available to men and women?*

During the first millennium BCE, societies along the peripheries of regional empires started to follow their own innovative paths, defying the ways of the dynastic regimes they often envied. (See Map 5-1.) They tinkered with new types of political and social organization, new ideas, and new ways of fighting and expanding borders. Such innovation occurred, for example, in Eastern Zhou China, where nearly constant warfare and power struggles culminated in the formation of several large and powerful territorial states. Radical changes also took place in Greece and in the Levant, where the period of chaos and economic decline caused by the onslaught of the Sea Peoples was followed by the emergence of city-states.

In regions as far apart as the great river valleys of East and South Asia, the Caribbean coast of Mexico, and the coasts of the Mediterranean, new complex societies arose. These societies developed cultural and political ideas that were radically different from those of the large regional empires of Southwest Asia. As they did so, the communities of China, the Indus Valley, the Americas, and the Mediterranean demonstrated that they could rely more on their own innovations than on patterns inherited from such older, well-established societies as those of Egypt and Mesopotamia. In the Indus Valley, for example, new complex societies were based on sacred categories (especially caste, which determined every individual's status, occupation, and spouse) and new religious experiences. These communities revolved around small-scale monarchies and urban oligarchies dominated by elite families. In China, small polities held by regional lords under the Zhou king gave way to powerful and ever more centralized and belligerent states. In the Americas, the Olmecs in Mesoamerica and the Chavín peoples of the Andes ordered their lives around dispersed settlements that relied on simple agricultural technology, but they produced complex and increasingly hierarchical social orders. Around the Mediterranean Sea, new social forms were taking shape in independent cities. Some elements in these new communities were borrowed from the older complex societies, but more often, they developed in place to match their environments.

These new communities were not just extensions of old lifeways. In each, dramatic innovations in how inhabitants expressed cultural and religious beliefs expanded the social, political, and cultural options available to men and women. Although the cultures were clearly different from one another, we might call these all "second-generation" societies, simultaneously building on their predecessors and representing a departure from ancient legacies. They were marked by a competitiveness in which literary warfare and battles of ideas produced political and social innovations and encouraged intellectual curiosity. The new communities harbored bold thinkers who devised new ways of looking at politics and society. They were present in China during the time of Confucius (who looked to the past but transformed its meaning) and in the Ganges Valley during the age of the Buddha (who questioned the dominance of kings and priests), and their ideas have reverberated down through the ages. The Greek city-states produced a generation of skeptical and questioning philosophers who influenced later Western political, moral, and scientific thinkers, as well as many Muslim scholars. The new cultural centers in Afro-Eurasia encouraged probing and reflective inquiries into who human beings were, how human behavior was to be explained, and to what end it was directed. Their theological and philosophical questions, and their answers, are still relevant today.

The new engagement with ideas by no means bred consensus: the age of great ideas was in fact characterized by magnificent disputes over what was best for humanity. For instance, thinkers disagreed over the very political and moral status of the individual. In Greece, they worried about the possibility of gaining and transmitting true or reliable knowledge of the world. Their new and more skeptical forms of thinking led them to doubt the permanence of the social order and ponder the relationship between humans and the cosmos. In Eastern Zhou China, beset by constant warfare, they debated how best to restore order; some advocated engagement while others urged withdrawal from government. In the Ganges Valley, philosophers questioned the rituals of the Brahmans and sought new ways of exhibiting moral behavior and attaining enlightenment. Whereas many Greek philosophers endorsed skepticism for its own sake, thinkers in Eastern Zhou China and in the Ganges Valley at the time of the Buddha tended to debate the issues in the name of ultimate truths that would end all controversy and yield a unitary vision of state and society.

EASTERN ZHOU CHINA (770–221 BCE)

> → *In what ways did scholars propose ending the incessant warfare and chaos of China's Spring and Autumn and Warring States periods?*

The first millennium BCE was a time of political and cultural innovation in China, as it was in the Ganges Valley and the Mediterranean. But unlike the South Asian and Greek

NORTH AMERICA

ROCKY MOUNTAINS

NOMADIC HUNTERS

Great Lakes

Mississippi R.

St. Lawrence R.

ATLANTIC OCEAN

Gulf of Mexico

OLMEC

MESOAMERICA

• La Venta
Monte Alban

WEST INDIES

CELTIC PEOPLES

Rhine

IBERIANS

Latin-cities

Cartha

SAHARA

SAHARAN PEOPLES

SAHEL

Niger R.

NC

PACIFIC OCEAN

CHAVÍN

ANDES MOUNTAINS

NOMADIC HUNTERS

Amazon R.

SOUTH AMERICA

Legend:
- Persian Empire
- Zhou China
- South Asian states
- Nubia
- Kush
- Nok
- Olmec
- Chavín
- Mediterranean colonies
- • City
- NOK State
- *SLAVS* People

0   1000   2000 Miles
0   1000   2000 Kilometers

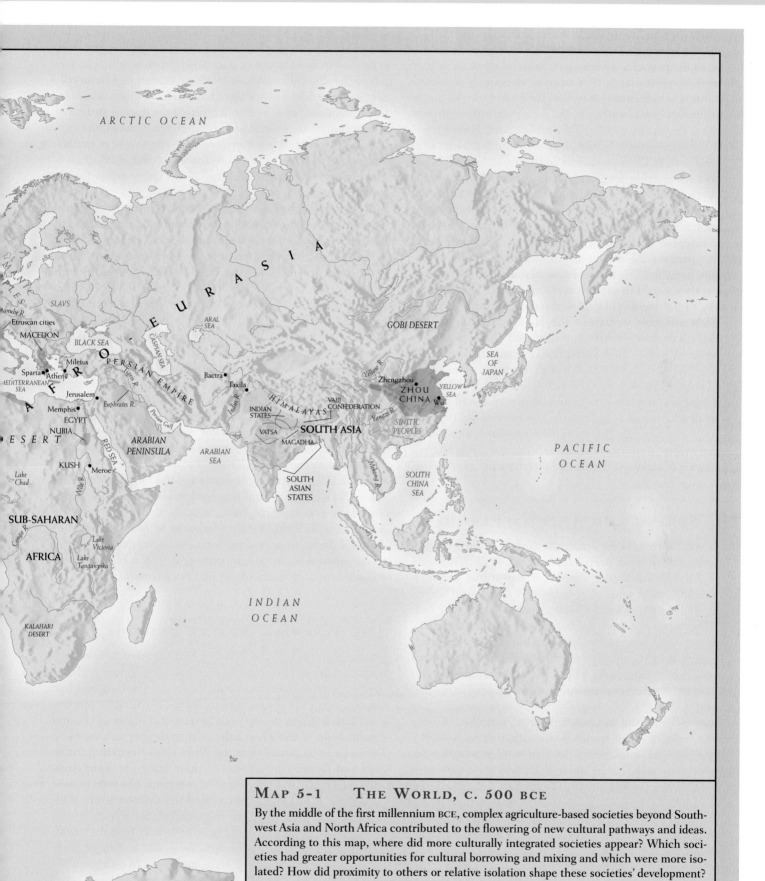

MAP 5-1   THE WORLD, C. 500 BCE

By the middle of the first millennium BCE, complex agriculture-based societies beyond Southwest Asia and North Africa contributed to the flowering of new cultural pathways and ideas. According to this map, where did more culturally integrated societies appear? Which societies had greater opportunities for cultural borrowing and mixing and which were more isolated? How did proximity to others or relative isolation shape these societies' development?

intellectuals, the new Chinese leaders and thinkers did not rise up to challenge the old cultural orthodoxy. Instead, they looked to the past as a golden age that could show them how to govern complex states; they stressed elaborately regulated court protocol and ritual, as well as the importance of maintaining hierarchies of authority and deference within families and the state. By the middle of the millennium, however, political innovations were taking place on a much broader geographical scale in China and involved larger numbers of people than did comparable developments in the Mediterranean, or even in the Indus Valley. As Chapter 4 noted, their defeat by northern steppe invaders forced the Zhou to flee their western capital at Chang'an. The beginning of the Eastern Zhou dynasty, centered on Luoyang, was known as the Spring and Autumn period (722–481 BCE); it was marked by great competition, fierce fighting among regional states and their ruling lords as they sought to acquire land and expand their borders, and the beginning of political and social transformations. A chronicle allegedly written at this time by Confucius, expressing his despair over the demise of high Zhou ideals, gave the period its name. The Eastern Zhou dynasty ended with the Warring States period (403–221 BCE), when seven major regional states consolidated their power into territorial states. The result was a multistate system that manifested revolutionary developments in agriculture, government, politics, and society, including new transportation networks, changes in landownership, universal military service, and the growth in importance of scholar-officials and merchants.

THE SPRING AND AUTUMN PERIOD

China was far from being politically unified: at the outset of the Spring and Autumn period, there were 148 Zhou tributary states. Though many were simply garrison towns and their surrounding lands, some were quite large and powerful. The central states on the North China plain clustered on or near the Yellow River and were the bastions of Zhou culture. The peripheral states were more aggressive than the central states and eagerly sought control of neighboring Zhou states as well as non-Zhou borderlands, where the cultural outsiders or "barbarians" lived; they therefore engaged in nearly constant warfare.

During the Spring and Autumn period, anarchic violence led to a series of major transformations in politics and society. The regional states, which wielded more power than the Zhou ruler, forged alliances and met at interstate conferences under a *ba* (a hegemon or "senior one," who led the alliance); new administrative units were formed in the countryside to conscript men for fighting and to collect taxes; landownership was no longer based on a tribute system, in which the regional lords had their holdings legitimated by the Zhou king; the rulers of the states were advised by ministers who gained their positions through their merit and wile rather than ties

of kinship; and the southern states of Chu, Wu, and Yue came to recognize Zhou culture. Throughout the dynasty, the major states competed for power and land, but they still acknowledged the Zhou dynasty's mandate of heaven and nominally accepted the authority of the Zhou ruler. In effect, the fractured political system in China inverted the normal pattern of strong central states with weaker satellites. Instead, the central states served as a buffer zone between the large peripheral states to which they were forced to swear allegiance. They became the battlefields on which larger states fought for dominance.

Increasing political anarchy coincided with technological breakthroughs. As new smelting techniques to remove metallic impurities from iron were devised and became known across China, bronze weaponry gave way to stronger iron swords and armor. Zhou kings tried hard to monopolize iron production and to maintain control of stockpiles, but to no avail. The spread of cheaper and more lethal weaponry accelerated the shift in influence away from the central government to local authorities. Indeed, the regional states became so powerful that they were able to engage in large-scale projects that earlier had been feasible only for empires. As regional states undertook the construction of dikes and of drainage and irrigation systems, they brought greater areas of land under cultivation. New canals linked rivers, and the networks spurred transformation. For example, in 486 BCE the regional lord of the Wu state began to build what would eventually become the thousand-mile-long Grand Canal, tying the Yellow River in the north and the Yangzi River in the south. Stretching several hundred miles, Wu's canal functioned as an artificial Nile, making it possible for the economies of all the states to begin to be more highly integrated. Like all the grand infrastructure projects of this era, it was constructed by peasants whom the Zhou regional lords pressed into corvée labor in lieu of tax payments.

THE WARRING STATES PERIOD

By the beginning of the Warring States period, seven large territorial states had come to dominate the Zhou world in a multistate system; several smaller states on the Central Plain remained part of the sphere of influence of the major powers. (See Map 5-2.) All of these states were still under the formal overlordship of the Zhou ruler, although they continued to have more real power than the Zhou king. Beginning in the fifth and fourth centuries BCE, their vying for dominance would devour the Zhou dynasty from within. The wars of conquest of the seven major states and the shifting political alliances among them involved the mobilization of huge armies and resources unprecedented in scale anywhere in the world, far surpassing the Assyrian armies at the height of their power. Qin was the greatest state, and it would ultimately replace the Zhou dynasty in 221 BCE.

→ *In what ways did scholars propose ending the chaos of China's Spring and Autumn and Warring States periods?*

The Warring States alternatively formed bonds or fought with each other; they engaged in diplomacy or battle, depending on which seemed to further their interests at the moment. Thus statecraft emerged, similar to that which developed between major states in Southwest Asia in the second millennium BCE (see Chapter 3). Trained diplomats traveled on missions to persuade rulers of other states to ally with the ruler they represented, and if dismissed by their first employer they would offer their services to another. The Warring States sought to maintain a balance of power and would re-form their coalitions if one state appeared to be becoming too powerful. Moreover, impersonal legal codes, which established uniform punishments based on the specific crime committed rather than the social status of the perpetrator, enhanced the rulers of these states at the expense of the remaining aristocratic elites. There can be little doubt that intrigues, alliances, and wars of conquest were also instrumental in the emergence of the large-scale states that dominated China during the Zhou decline.

Overall, the conception of central power changed dramatically in the Warring States era, as royal appointees replaced hereditary officeholders. Moreover, by the middle of

MAP 5-2   ZHOU CHINA IN THE WARRING STATES PERIOD

The Warring States period initially witnessed a fracturing of the Zhou dynasty into a myriad of states, followed centuries later by the emergence of even more durable and enduring dynasties. What about this map tells us why diplomacy was so important during this period? What does this map tell us about the relationships between "civilized" and "barbarian" peoples in East Asia? How do you think so many smaller polities could survive when surrounded by three large and powerful states (Qin, Qi, and Chu)?

the fourth century BCE, power was so concentrated in the hands of the rulers of the major states that each began to call himself "king," a title formerly held only by the Zhou ruler. Despite the incessant warfare, scholars, soldiers, merchants, peasants, and artisans were able to thrive in the midst of an expanding agrarian economy and interregional trade. At the same time, major innovations, largely begun during the Spring and Autumn period, were taking place in government, warfare, culture, economy, and society. Despite the warfare and chaos—or perhaps because of them—many of the fundamental beliefs, values, and philosophies that would become the foundation for later dynasties were formulated during this period. By the middle of the first millennium BCE, China's political activities and innovations were involving larger numbers of people, spread over a much broader area, than comparable developments in South Asia and the Mediterranean.

INNOVATIONS IN STATE ADMINISTRATION

Beginning in the Spring and Autumn period, many of the states reorganized their administrative structure to concentrate central power in the hands of the ruler, to obtain natural resources and men for their armies, and to oversee conquered areas; this trend continued in the Warring States period. The major states created administrative districts, each with stewards, sheriffs, and judges; a system of registration of peasant households was instituted to facilitate both tax collection and the provision of conscripts for the ruler's armies. Keeping such records enabled officials to closely monitor the rural population and punish those who did not comply with their obligations. The officials were drawn from the *shi,* who under the Western Zhou had been knights but were now bureaucrats in direct service to the ruler. Confucius and other classical masters called them "gentlemen," or "superior men" (*junzi*), and considered them partners of the ruler in state affairs. Officials were paid in salaries of grain and sometimes received gifts of gold and silver, as well as titles and seals of office, from the ruler.

Of all the ministers who aimed at enhancing the power and size of central government, none was more successful than Shang Yang of Qin. The ministerial reforms that he carried out after he arrived in Qin in 361 BCE expanded the power of the Qin domain and positioned it to become the dominant state of its time. He divided the state into administrative *xian* (districts) and appointed their magistrates, vice magistrates, military commanders, and overseers, thereby extending the ruler's authority into the hinterland and using the districts for universal military recruitment. He divided the land into blocks that would be farmed by individual households, and he introduced a capitation, or head tax, ensuring that households containing two or more adult sons would pay more in taxes than families with only one adult son. He rewarded those who distinguished themselves in war (as determined by the number of enemy killed in battle) with titles and land; conversely, nobles who failed to distinguish themselves in war lost their status. He introduced a harsh penal code that stressed collective responsibility. For example, those who harbored criminals had their bodies cut in two. The legal code applied to both government officials and peasants, with severe punishments for violent crimes, theft, use of nonstandard weights and measures, or wrongdoing in office. Paradoxically, Shang Yang was later trapped by his own regulations when his ruler charged him with sedition; he tried to flee Qin, but he was captured and executed.

INNOVATIONS IN WARFARE

The most powerful and successful states in China ruled over millions of people, and by 221 BCE, they were able to boast of million-man armies. The contrast with Athens, which at the height of its ascendancy in the fifth century BCE was the largest and most powerful city-state in the Mediterranean, is obvious: with a whole population of 250,000, it could field an army of just 20,000 men. Only Rome, just beginning to assert itself in the Mediterranean at around this time and later to become a mega-state, could possibly compete with China's scale. With administrative reform came reforms in military recruitment and warfare. As noted above, one purpose of registering the rural population was to guarantee their military service. During the Spring and Autumn period, rulers began to rely on men from the countryside to expand their armies, recruiting some into corps of personal bodyguards. During the Warring States period, as such practices persisted, the conscription of peasants provided rulers with ever larger military organizations.

In earlier battles, the nobles had shot arrows from chariots while some peasants from their lands stood and fought beside them. But the Warring States relied instead on massed infantries of peasants bearing iron lances, who fought fiercely and to the death, unconstrained by their relationships with nobles. Rather than 30,000 nobles fighting from chariots, war was now waged by huge state armies reported to contain as many as one million commoners in the infantry, supported by 1,000 chariots and 10,000 bow-wielding cavalrymen. During the Spring and Autumn period, one state's entire army would be massed against another state's; now, armies could be divided into separate forces and fight several battles simultaneously.

Vast campaigns involving hundreds of thousands of replaceable peasant soldiers led by a professional officer corps were common. Armies also contained elite professional troops who wore heavy iron armor and helmets, carried iron weapons, and were trained to use the recently invented crossbow. The crossbow's tremendous power, range, and accuracy, with its ingenious trigger mechanism, enabled archers to eas-

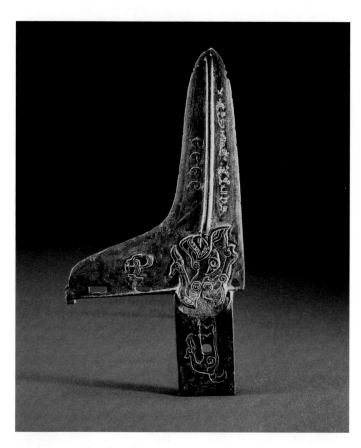

Bronze Spearhead. Although bronze weaponry gave way to stronger iron swords and armor during the Warring States era, stylized bronze spearheads were still prized by Zhou kings and regional lords.

ily kill lightly armored cavalrymen or charioteers at a distance. The technology of siege warfare also advanced in response to the growing importance given to defensive walls along frontiers and around towns. Enemy armies used counterweighted siege ladders (called "cloud ladders" by the Chinese) to scale urban walls or dug tunnels under them; those defending their city often pumped smoke into the tunnels to thwart the attackers. The rhythms of warfare also changed; rather than lasting a season, campaigns could stretch over a year or even longer. As commanders of armies seeking conquest plotted their strategies (determining which troops should be placed where, the kind of terrain best suited for battle, and how to outmaneuver opposing armies), military action and thought became ever more sophisticated.

ECONOMIC, SOCIAL, AND CULTURAL CHANGES

Rather than being a drain on the economy, the incessant warfare of both the Spring and Autumn period and the Warring States period spurred China's economic growth to remark-

able heights. A veritable agricultural revolution on the North China plain along the Yellow River made possible rapid population growth, and the inhabitants of the Eastern Zhou reached approximately 20 million—the largest number of people then living in a single state in the world. These dramatic demographic changes affected the environment, however; greater numbers of people required more fuel, and the deforestation that resulted as trees were cut down to supply it led to erosion of the fields. In addition, many animals were hunted to extinction; others, like the elephant, found their open range sharply curtailed.

Economic changes began in the Spring and Autumn period when rulers of some of the states gave peasants the right to their land in exchange for paying taxes and providing military service. Because the peasants could enjoy the benefits of their labor, their productivity increased. Innovations in the technologies of agriculture also raised productivity: crop rotation was introduced (millet and wheat in the north, and rice and millet in the south), and farmers began using iron plowshares harnessed to oxen to prepare their fields.

With larger harvests and advances in bronze and iron casting came trade in surplus grain and in pottery and ritual objects, and thus the beginning of a market economy. Grain and goods were shipped along roads, rivers, and canals. Peasants continued to rely on barter as they exchanged goods, but minted coins began to circulate among elites and rulers. Early coins were made of bronze, and were formed in a variety of shapes, some resembling spades. Private traders and merchants also appeared during this time.

During the Warring States period, these changes continued. The new bargain with the peasants—allowing them private ownership of land in exchange for their taxes and military service—undergirded the economies of all the Warring States. A strong emphasis on the military aided the polities more broadly. Infrastructure benefited directly, as roads and walls, forts and towers were built to defend against invading armies.

Knife Coin. Zhou dynasty coins, like the later Han coin shown here, were made of bronze and produced in a variety of shapes, some resembling spades and knives, depending on the region. Each of the Warring States had its own currency.

In addition, rulers and administrators applied the skills gained in organizing the military to devising public projects: powerful states undertook large-scale irrigation projects, built canals and dikes, and drained low-lying lands, which opened up more acreage for agriculture. Moreover, military conscripts worked on these large-scale municipal and irrigation projects during periods when they were not needed for fighting.

Economic growth helped the rulers attain a high level of cultural sophistication, as reflected in their magnificent palaces and burial sites. At the same time, social relations became more fluid during the Warring States period as commoners gained power and aristocrats lost it. In Qin, for example, as noted above, peasants who served in the ruler's army were rewarded for killing enemy soldiers; their military success fueled their advance through the ranks, and could win them land, houses, and slaves, and a change in status. Officials were also rewarded with lands and gifts that enhanced their status and wealth. Officials, ministers, and diplomats traveled far and wide during this period, but peasants were required to stay in their fields and villages, leaving them only to fight in the ruler's army.

While class relations had a revolutionary fluidity, gender relations became more inflexible for elites and nonelites alike as the value ascribed to male-centered kinship groups grew. The resulting separation of the sexes and heightened male domination within the family naturally affected the position of women. An emphasis on monogamy, or at least the primacy of the first wife over additional wives (concubines), also emerged. Relations between the sexes were increasingly ritualized and were marked by heavy moral and legal sanctions against any behavior that appeared to threaten the purity of authoritarian male lineages.

Recently discovered archaeological evidence about the daily lives of people of the time reveals that commoners and elites were both concerned with restoring order and stability in their lives through religion, medicine, and statecraft. Rites of divination to predict the future and medical recipes to heal the body among elites were paralleled by commoners' use of ghost stories and astrological almanacs to understand the meaning of their lives and the significance of their deaths. Elites recorded their political discourses on wood and bamboo slips that were tied together to form scrolls. They also prepared military treatises, the arts of persuasion, ritual texts, geographic works, and poetry this way. Moreover, social changes were occurring. Even commoners could now purchase bronze metalwork, for example, when previously only Zhou rulers and aristocrats could afford to do so.

NEW IDEAS AND THE "HUNDRED MASTERS"

As states came and went under the Eastern Zhou dynasty during both the Spring and Autumn and the Warring States pe-

Pendant. Gender relations became more inflexible because of male-centered kinship groups. Relations between the sexes were increasingly ritualized and were marked by heavy moral and legal sanctions against any behavior that appeared to threaten the purity of powerful lineages. This pendant depicts two women who formed a close relationship with each other in the "inner chambers" of their homes.

riods, the losers among the political elites sought to replace their former aristocratic advantages with status gained through new types of service—not just political but also social and intellectual. In this fashion, political conflict was conducive to intellectual creativity, and important teachers emerged, each with disciples attracted to what was presented as an independent school of thought. The most prominent of the "hundred masters" of the age was Confucius; other masters either expanded on Confucian thought or formulated opposing ideas about human nature and the role of government. Their philosophies are now known as the Hundred Schools of Thought.

Confucius taught hundreds of students, but historian Sima Qian claims that during his lifetime he had seventy-seven core disciples. Like the Greek philosopher Socrates, Confucius left no writings of his own; the followers of each sage—in Confucius's case, working anonymously—compiled and transmitted his teachings after his death. *The Analects,* which collected Confucius's ethical teachings and cultural ideals, had an extraordinary influence on many of the leading scholar-officials who came after him. In his effort to persuade society to again embrace what he saw as the lost ideals of the early Zhou, Confucius set forth a new moral framework, stressing correct performance of ritual (*li*), responsibility and loyalty to the family (*xiao*), and perfection of moral character to become a "superior man" (*junzi*)—that is, a man defined by *ren* (benevolence, goodness) rather than by the pursuit of profit. Confucius believed that government should be the purview of these superior men; in such a society, coercive laws and punishment would not be needed to achieve order. He taught these concepts to those who were highly intelligent and willing to work, whether their backgrounds were noble or humble; thus any man could gain the education needed to become a gentleman of the ruling class. This was a dramatic departure from past centuries, when only nobles were believed to be capable of ruling. Nonetheless, Confucius's clear distinctions between gentlemen-rulers and commoners continued to support a society based on social hierarchy, though

Iron Spoon Stamp. Zhou courtiers used geomancy (*fengshui*) to determine sites for burials and palaces. Elites and commoners also used geomancy to site their homes and graves. As the image proudly heralded on this modern stamp reveals, by the third century BCE, the Chinese had discovered that an iron spoon on a bronze surface would always point south, the cardinal direction for the Zhou king and his regional lords. Such a "compass" served as a reliable siting device for what we might call a "spiritual ecology."

Chinese Calendar. This Han period calendar for 63 BCE is formed from sixteen slips of wood with handwritten characters; each begins with day one, day two, and so on; the calendar is to be read from right to left.

an individual's position in that hierarchy might rest more on education than on birth.

One competing school of thought, later called Mohism, derived from the teachings of Mozi, also known as Mo Di (c. 479–438 BCE). This writer and craftsman-builder lived after Confucius, just before the Warring States period; he believed that each man should feel obligated and responsible to all other people, not just to his own family and friends. Thus, whereas ritual or art or music was associated with Confucianism, he instead emphasized practical concerns of good government; in his view, government should promote social order, material benefits for its people, and population growth. He opposed wars of conquest, arguing that they wasted life and resources and interfered with productivity and fair distribution. His relatively utilitarian philosophy appealed mainly to city dwellers, and he recognized the need for strong urban defenses to keep out marauders.

Another philosophy that took shape during this time was Daoism, which distinguished itself sharply from the credo of Confucius and his followers, scorning what was seen as the Confucian emphasis on rigidly prescribed rituals and social hierarchies. Its ideas were first formulated by someone known to us as Master Lao (Laozi, literally, "Old Master"), who—if he actually existed—may have been a contemporary of Confucius. His sayings were collected in writings titled *The Daodejing,* or *The Book of the Way and Its Power* (c. third century BCE). His book was then elaborated by Master Zhuang (Zhuangzi, c. 369–286 BCE). Daoism stressed the *dao* (the

Primary Source

WARRING IDEAS: CONFUCIANISM VERSUS DAOISM

Normally historians who compare the influence of Confucianism and Daoism focus on their strictures for individuals—moralist and laissez-faire, respectively. Though Daoists and Confucians similarly viewed the world of political power as perilous, their competing teachings also offered regional Chinese rulers a choice in political philosophies.

Initially, Confucius's call for moral rigor had little appeal to those in power. But some saw the attractions of his humanistic beliefs after they realized that a tyrannical government that punished its citizens harshly could be brought down by a peasant rebellion.

In one exchange with a student, Confucius described the core foundations of government:

> Zigong asked about government. The Master said, "Sufficient food, sufficient military force, the confidence of the people." Zigong said, "If one had, unavoidably, to dispense with one of these, which of them should go first?" The Master said, "Get rid of the military." Zigong said, "If one had, unavoidably, to dispense with one of the remaining two, which should go first?" The Master said, "Dispense with food: Since ancient times there has always been death, but without confidence a people cannot stand." (*Analects* 12.7)

Many who sought power were drawn more to Daoism, whose teachings warned that the state was easily ruined by overly assertive rulers. Thus, the *Daodejing* (*The Book of the Way and Its Power,* c. third century BCE), a famous Daoist work attributed to Master Lao (Laozi), argued that long-term rule should be based on "doing nothing" (*wuwei*):

If one desires to take the empire and act on it,
I say that he will not succeed.
The empire is a sacred vessel,
That cannot be acted upon.
In being acted upon, it is harmed;
And in being grasped, it is lost.
For among living things some move ahead and others follow,
Some breathe easily and others hard,
Some are strong and others are weak,
Some rise up and others are brought low.
Thus the sage rejects the excessive, the extravagant, the extreme.

(*The Book of the Way and Its Power,* Vol. 1, p. 86)

→ *Why did Confucius think that culture trumped politics and the military in government?*
→ *Why did he believe that a cruel tyrant could not remain in power for very long?*
→ *Why did the Legalists find Daoism more appealing than Confucianism as a practical political philosophy?*

SOURCE: Wm. Theodore De Bary and Irene Bloom, comp., *Sources of Chinese Tradition,* 2nd ed. (New York: Columbia University Press, 1999).

Way) of nature and the cosmos: the best way to live was to follow the natural order of things. Its main principle was *wuwei,* "doing nothing"—what mattered was spontaneity, noninterference, and acceptance of the world as it is rather than attempting to change it by entering politics and government. In Laozi's vision of politics, the ruler who interfered least in the natural processes of change was the most successful. Zhuangzi focused on the enlightened individual, who lived spontaneously and in harmony with nature, free of ethical rules and laws as defined by society and viewing life and death as simply different stages of existence.

Legalism, or Statism, another major way of understanding how best to live an orderly life, grew out of the writings of Master Xun (Xunzi, 310–237 BCE), who lived toward the end of the Warring States period. He believed that men and women were innately bad, and therefore required moral education and authoritarian control. In the decades leading up to the Qin victory over the Zhou, the Legalist thinker Han

Fei, Han state minister and Xunzi disciple (280–233 BCE), agreed that human nature was primarily evil. He imagined a state with a ruler who followed the Daoist principle of *wuwei*, detaching himself from everyday governance but only after setting an unbending standard—strict laws, accompanied by harsh punishments—for judging his officials and people. For Han Fei, the establishment and uniform application of these laws would ensure that the evil nature of all people would be kept in check. As we will see in Chapter 7, the Qin state, before it became the dominant state in China, was particularly draconian in enforcing its laws, as it systematically followed the Legalist philosophy.

The inseparability of scholars and the state, so vital a feature of Chinese society through many centuries, began in this age. Scholars became state functionaries dependent on the patronage of rulers. In return, the rulers recognized the expertise of scholars in matters of punishment, ritual, astronomy, medicine, and divination. Because philosophers and priests in Greece and South Asia did not exclusively serve the state and its rulers and had no interest in justifying the existence of a particular ruler, they felt free to speculate on a wide range of issues; they also tended to see the world as constantly changing. In Zhou China and later dynasties, in contrast, philosophical deliberations focused on the need to maintain order and stability by preserving the state and tended to view the world as static. The close bonds that rulers forged with their scholarly elites distinguished governments in Warring States China from the other Afro-Eurasian polities of this period.

The growing importance of scholars as bureaucrats and philosophers promoted the use of writing as a fundamental tool of statecraft and philosophical discourse. Indeed, even though the evolving Chinese script was not standardized until 221 BCE, its use in the philosophical debates that raged between various schools across many states and regions helped foster cultural unity at a time of intellectual pluralism, a diversity of thinking inspired not by skepticism but by a vision of empire and unity. Scholar-diplomats and scribes in each of the Warring States debated and attacked each other in clear and forceful prose, as they argued over how to create a stable and harmonious society; some nine to ten thousand graphs or signs became required for writing. The active participation in these debates by men holding high political office—scholar-bureaucrats—set China apart from other societies of this period.

Over the coming centuries, the ideas of Confucianism, Daoism, and Legalism gradually merged into a unified story about the crucial role that the ancient sage-kings had played in empire building. This account invoked the concept of the mandate of heaven (see Chapter 4), but scholars embellished it with details of how the dynastic cycle of history worked. The Qin imperial victors—Statists who at first relied on raw military power and strictly applied Legalist approaches to running the state and achieving order—drew on the discourses of their rivals, the Daoists, whom they had scorned for simply "leaving things alone," and the Confucians, whom they derided as overly concerned with ritual and "preachy." This new formulation of history described the evolution of state power as a natural process, as small states grew into a unified empire, and thus gave the chaotic Warring States period a coherent shape and a virtuous, moral purpose aiming toward unity.

THE NEW WORLDS OF SOUTH ASIA

> → *How did political and social transformations encourage new beliefs and dissident thinkers in South Asia?*

Following their gradual migration into South Asia around 1500 BCE, the Vedic peoples fought with the indigenous population as well as with each other as they established and sought to enlarge new states. Around 1000 BCE, they began to expand eastward from the Indus River valley into the mid-Ganges plain, where they created new polities. Here, as in Eastern Zhou China and in the Mediterranean, warfare and expansion led to political, social, and ideological transformations in the first millennium BCE. At the same time that scholar-officials in Zhou China were developing theories about the role of government, conceiving new ways of administering states, and devising economic and social innovations, the Vedic peoples were also forging new political institutions, new economic activities, and new ways of viewing the natural and supernatural worlds. In Vedic societies, these transformations were driven by warriors and upper-class intellectuals, with kin groups and caste organizations the primary agents of social transformation.

THE RISE OF NEW POLITIES

Significant political and social transformations in South Asia began about 600 BCE, after the Vedic peoples had expanded eastward into the mid-Ganges plain—around the same time that major changes were occurring in Zhou China and the Mediterranean. The leading force in reclaiming the new lands in the east were the Brahmans, an upper class of priests and scholars. The area into which the Vedic peoples migrated was a monsoon region where abundant rainfall made the land suitable for cultivating rice in paddies; in contrast, the appropriate crops in the Indus River valley were wheat and barley. The migrants cleared the land by setting fire to the forests and using iron tools—fashioned from the abundant supplies of iron ore in the mid-Ganges plain—to remove what was left of the jungle.

Gradually, between 1000 and 600 BCE, settlements and towns evolved into small territorial states; as in China, it was a time of constant feuding. Sixteen polities known as *mahajanapadas* (great countries) quarreled for territory and dominance and gave their name to the era: the Sixteen State period. None could completely overpower the others to establish a unified state. (See Map 5-3.) It was also a time marked by new thinking—most dramatically, the rise of Buddhism as a challenge to the authority of Vedic sacrifices and the leadership of the Brahmans.

There were two major kinds of states in the mid- and lower Ganges plain: those ruled by hereditary monarchs and those ruled by a small, elected elite, or oligarchies. One such oligarchy was the Vrijji Confederacy, also called *ganasangha,* meaning "a gathering of a large number." As described in Chapter 4, the South Asian city-states were led by a class of warriors and officials called the Kshatriya. The rulers of kingdoms assumed the title *raja,* a word usually translated "king." But in the oligarchic communities, which were ruled collectively, each adult freeborn male head of a family was called a *raja.* Nonetheless, the Kshatriya aristocracy alone controlled the land and other resources in the ganasangha states. At regular gatherings in their meeting halls, they both performed religious rituals and discussed and made decisions on important issues.

Powerful as they were, the *rajas* in the kingdoms often came from low-status clans that gained power with their military strength. Their land and wealth made it unnecessary for them to claim Ksha-

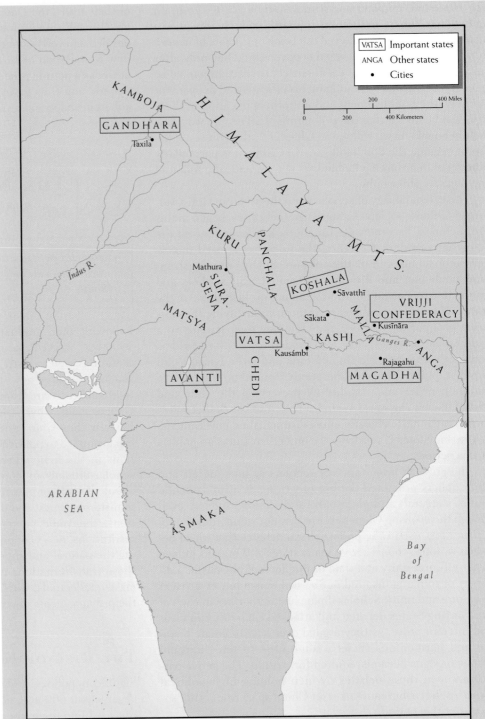

MAP 5-3   SIXTEEN STATES IN THE TIME OF THE BUDDHA IN SOUTH ASIA

South Asia underwent profound social, cultural, and political transformations in the first millennium BCE that reflected growing urbanization, increased commerce, and the emergence of two types of states. Where did new states and cities appear? What regional features encouraged social and cultural integration? According to this map, what other regions had influence on South Asia, and where might South Asian culture spread?

triya status as the basis of their authority. Such a *raja* would often elevate his status by marrying a woman from a high-status clan. For example, according to the *Jatakas*, a Buddhist text, Pasenadi, the ruler of Koshala, sought to gain status by marrying a princess of the prestigious Shakya family. Although unhappy at the prospect of a daughter marrying beneath her station, the Shakya feared offending their powerful neighbor. But one man came up with an ingenious plan: his daughter born to a slave woman (hence not a real princess) could be married to Pasenadi, thereby preserving both the honor and safety of the Shakya. Unfortunately for them, Vidudabha, the prince born of this marriage, learned the truth of his mother's birth on a visit to her homeland, where the elders failed to accord him the respect due a prince. Outraged, he returned home, only to encounter more humiliation when the people of Koshala learned that his mother was slave-born. He later usurped the throne of Koshala and took his revenge on the Shakyas, organizing four military expeditions against the small mountainous state—which the young Koshala king eventually destroyed.

EXPANSION OF THE CASTE SYSTEM

Though the kingdoms and oligarchic republican cities had different political structures, they shared many social features, including the caste system. As they migrated eastward, the Vedic peoples brought elements of the caste system into the Ganges plain. The traditional *varna* scheme of Brahmans (scholars and priests), Kshatriyas (warriors), Vaishyas (commoners), and Shudras (laborers and servants) expanded in an economy centered on farms that were worked by extended families. Many more Shudras, clans outside the Vedic lineages, joined the agricultural economy as *jatis*, or subcastes of laborers. Cows were no longer the main draft animals because they could not work in rice paddies and therefore were replaced by water buffaloes; some plows required six or eight animals to pull them. Moreover, cultivating rice paddies was highly labor-intensive, since water had to be constantly supplied to the fields from distant rivers through elaborate irrigation canals that needed constant maintenance.

Households therefore came to rely on hired workers and slaves, who probably differed little in their status and economic conditions. Either as tenants of the householders or as cultivators of small pieces of land, Shudra peasants now appeared as a distinct status group. While men in the three *varnas* above them—Brahmans, Kshatriyas, and Vaishyas—were "twice-born" by virtue of having experienced a second, ritual birth around age twelve, this ceremony—together with the status it brought—was denied to Shudras, who therefore remained outsiders in the Brahman-dominated society. The Shudras then invented their own social hierarchy based on kinship and religious rituals. When the Vedic landowners incorporated them into the farming economy as laborers, ten-

ants, or cultivators, they joined the communities as a unit and maintained their communal structure by marrying inside their group. Such a group became known as a *jati* (literally, "born"—that is, the group into which a person was born). The *jatis* became the lower orders (the "subcastes") of an expanding caste system. A further expansion of the caste system occurred as the booming agricultural economy generated more labor specialization. Carpenters and ironsmiths were needed to make the tools for tilling the land, to build irrigation systems, and to fashion utensils for daily life. Carpenters were usually residents of the villages, while ironsmiths as a rule traveled. Those specialists formed their own *jatis*

Brahman Recluse. When Buddhists started to tell their stories in sculptures and paintings, Brahmans were included when appropriate. This character in Gandharan Buddhist art probably represents a Brahman who lived as a recluse, instead of as a priest. He is not shaved or dressed, but his expression is certainly passionate.

through marriage networks. Although ironsmiths were essential to the economy, even Shudra peasants looked down on them as itinerant craftsworkers.

There were also *jatis* of traders and artisans, who were viewed as Vaishya or commoners, in the Brahmans' *varna* scheme, but the relative ritual status among these *jatis* varied by their profession. Traders were usually considered "purer" than artisans, while those engaged in making gold utensils had a higher status than those who made copper or iron ones. But as they gained wealth, even these subcastes began to monopolize skills and resources by banning intermarriage with outsiders, thus preventing the leak of knowledge—a significant change in the highly stratified Vedic society.

NEW CITIES AND AN EXPANDING ECONOMY

Supported by rice agriculture, around 500 BCE cities began to emerge on the Ganges plain. These cities became centers of commercial exchange. Some, such as Shravasti and Rajagriha, also thrived as artisanal centers. Others in the northwest, like Taxila—not far from present-day Peshawar, on the border between Pakistan and Afghanistan—engaged in trade with Afghanistan and the Iranian plateau.

As agricultural production increased, surplus grain, sugarcane, and rice became available for trade with towns and cities over longer distances. Farmers needed markets in which to sell their products and to purchase manufactured wares from the cities. Specialized goods were produced in some of the new towns and cities, and trade in these goods expanded beyond the local area in which they were produced.

In the middle of the first millennium BCE, cities in northern India grew as their commercial activities flourished, but they arose with little planning. Alleys leading from the main streets zigzagged between houses built with pebbles and clay. Yet though development was haphazard, civic authorities showed great interest in sanitation. Garbage bins were placed in squares all over the city, and dirty water was channeled deep underground. Streets were graded so that they could be cleaned by rainfall. Because most of the cities settled during this period have been continuously inhabited, they are difficult sites in which to conduct archaeological digs. Taxila, destroyed in the fifth century CE, is an exception: it was excavated in the twentieth century, providing much of our knowledge of urban life in early South Asia.

These new cities opened up exciting opportunities for the adventurous. Rural householders who moved into them prospered by importing rice and sugarcane from villages to sell in the markets; they then transported such processed and manufactured goods as sugar, salt, and utensils back to their villages. Those who already possessed capital became bankers, financing trade and industry. The less affluent turned to craftwork, fashioning textiles, tools such as needles, fine pottery,

Taxila. *Top:* Taxila became the capital of Gandhara at the time that it was occupied by the Persian Empire in the fifth century BCE. Dharmarajika was one of the most important monasteries. The walkway around the stupa was covered with glass tiles, and the stupa itself was decorated with jewels. *Bottom:* This corner of a stupa exhibits a variety of the architectural styles that prevailed in Gandharan art at its height. Both square and round columns are covered by Corinthian capitals. The right arch gate shows the style of Sanchi, the famous stupa in central India.

copper plates, ivory decorations, and gold and silver utensils. Traders and artisans formed guilds (associations of people with similar interests) to regulate competition, prices, and wages; to provide support for destitute members and their families; and to set standards to which all members had to comply. To protect their trading and manufacturing monopolies, guilds required their members to marry within their organizations. By following this practice, the guilds were eventually transformed into *jatis*.

The leaders of traders' guilds wielded financial influence over the new urban communities. Even kings had to heed their advice when deciding on issues as important as war and peace. Coins came into use at about the same time that they appeared in Greece and China. Traders and bankers established municipal bodies that issued the coins and vouched for their worth. Made of silver, they had irregular shapes but specific weights, which determined their value; they were punched-marked, or stamped with symbols of authority on one side.

Cities generated many new professions: they supported physicians, launderers, barbers, cooks, tailors, and entertainers. Complex financial transactions necessitated accountants and professional scribes to keep accurate records, but unfortunately no writing from this period has survived; kings had yet to learn to have their achievements inscribed on stone, while religious teachers taught orally.

The new cities were melting pots that allowed considerable social mobility despite the rigidity of the caste system, as the story of the famous physician Jivika illustrates. Jivika lived during the time of the Buddha, whose good friend he became, in the mid–sixth century BCE. His mother was a courtesan in the great city of Rajagriha in the lower Ganges Valley, beautiful and highly accomplished in dancing, singing, and playing the lute; her fame spread far and wide, attracting business to the city. When she found herself pregnant, she hid away until the baby was born; then, under cover of darkness, she had her maid carry the infant in a basket to a trash dump. The next morning, the baby's crying attracted the attention first of a crowd and then of a prince named Abhaya, who sent a servant to find out the reason for the uproar. When he learned that the newborn boy was alive, he adopted the child as his own and named him Jivika, meaning "alive." Prince Abhaya did raise the boy like a son, but after learning of his low birth Jivika decided to earn his own livelihood. From his hometown of Rajagriha, Jivika set out for Taxila. He traveled more than 800 miles along the Ganges River, journeying from city to city—a long journey well worth the effort, for Taxila was widely known as a center of learning. There Jivika received the best training available in medicine, and after he returned to Rajagriha his knowledge and skill soon earned him a brilliant reputation in all of northern India.

The opportunities provided by the new cities and states did not ensure success for everyone. Royal warfare expanded polities but disrupted lives. Many who lost their land and livelihood entered cities in search of work, and some fared better than others. Householders who turned to commerce and finance risked losing everything. As a whole, the society had more material wealth, but individual lives were far more

Indian Coins. Coinage appeared in India at about the same time as in the Greek world and China. Although standard in weight, the silver punch-marked coins were not regular in shape.

uncertain. In addition, the demands of urban life created a new status of person: those who did the dirtiest jobs, such as removing garbage and sewage, and were therefore viewed as physically and ritually impure. They were thought to be so polluting that a daughter of a decent householder was expected to go home to wash her eyes after seeing one of these outcastes, known as "untouchables." Even though their work kept the cities clean and healthy, they were forced to live in shantytowns outside the city limits.

Yet some among these untouchables were dissatisfied with the lot assigned to them. In times of rapid change, when thinkers were putting all varieties of authority into question, some of them joined dissident sects to protest their oppression. The turbulence and ferment in the new cities affected even the most abject of their inhabitants. Residents of the dynamic and cosmopolitan cities would offer those challenging the Vedic rituals and Brahman priests their most receptive audiences.

BRAHMANS, THEIR CHALLENGERS, AND NEW BELIEFS

The South Asian wise men found urban life in the fast-changing society to be profoundly unsettling. Traditional priests viewed cities as dirty and polluting places, where castes mixed indiscriminately, where lowborn persons were able to raise their status by acquiring wealth or skill, and where the oral traditions that they had monopolized were threatened by writing. These Brahmans were not happy when an alphabetic script appeared around 600 BCE, for it undermined their ability to control the definition of right and wrong and thus weakened the moral legitimacy of the order they dominated. Because all of Vedic literature had been memorized, only the brightest of the Brahmans, free from the need to do productive labor, could master the tradition. The newer, simpler writing made sacred knowledge more accessible. To the Brahmans, nothing about the cities seemed good.

Frightened by these chaotic conditions, Brahmans sought to strengthen their relationships with the rajas by establishing the idea of a king endowed with divine power. Kingship had been unnecessary according to Brahman writings in a long-ago golden age; but over time the world deteriorated, until "fish ate fish" and the pure mixed with the impure. Then the gods decided that people on earth needed a king to maintain order. The gods selected just such a king, calling him Manu—literally, "Man"—but Manu did not want to accept the difficult job. To win his consent, the gods promised him one-tenth of the grain harvest, one-fiftieth of the cattle, one-quarter of the merits earned by the good behavior of his subjects, and the most beautiful woman in his domain. In this account of how kingship began, royal power has a divine origin: the gods chose the king and protected him. Moreover, priests and Vedic rituals were essential to royal power, since it was validated through ceremonies carried out by Brahman priests.

This emphasis on divine kingship created tensions within Vedic South Asian society.

> *Since land could not be cultivated without killing insects, the extreme nonviolence of Jainism automatically excluded peasants.*

The Brahmans' claim to moral authority came to be resented by many of the Kshatriyas—especially those in the oligarchic republics, whose leaders did not claim divine power through sacrificial rituals. Merchants and artisans, as members of subcastes in growing cities, also came to chafe at the power and superiority of the Brahmans, whose performance of rituals served only the kings. Such resentments provoked members of these other groups to challenge the Brahmans' domination. Some thinkers in South Asia, like those in China and in the Greek cities experiencing similar upheavals around this time, believed that they were in an age of acute crisis because their culture's ancient harmony had been lost. And like many contemporary scholars and philosophers elsewhere, a new group of South Asian scholars and religious leaders took on the new challenges by developing their own answers to questions about human existence.

DISSIDENT THINKERS   As the Brahmans had feared, the spread of writing led to questioning of the order over which they presided. Dissident South Asian thinkers challenged the religious foundations of the Brahmans' worldview by refusing to recognize the gods that populated the Vedic world. Some of these rebels sprang from inside of the Vedic tradition; though Brahmans, they rejected the idea that sacrificial rituals pleased the gods. Their discussions and teachings about the universe and life resulted in the collection called the Upanishads (see Chapter 4). Others, from non-Vedic cultural traditions, challenged the Brahmans more directly, though some adopted and developed ideas expressed in the Upanishads.

MAHAVIRA AND JAINISM   Jainism and Buddhism were the two most influential schools that set themselves against the Brahmans. The doctrines of Jainism, which emerged in the seventh century BCE, were popularized in the sixth century BCE by Vardhamana Mahavira (c. 540–468 BCE), who drew on the teachings from the Upanishads but emphasized interpretation for everyday human life rather than trying to provide deeper understanding of the fundamentals of the social order of the universe. Born into the Kshatriya caste in an oligarchic republic, Mahavira left home when he was thirty years old to seek the truth about life; he spent twelve years as an ascetic, meaning one who denies themselves of material possessions and physical pleasures, wandering around the Ganges Valley before reaching enlightenment. He taught his disciples that the universe obeys its own everlasting rules and could not be affected by any god or other supernatural being. Meanwhile, he believed that the purpose of life was to purify one's soul through asceticism, or *ahimsa*, and to attain a state of permanent bliss. The Jains' religious doctrines emphasize asceticism over knowledge: strict self-denial enables one to avoid harming other creatures and thereby purify the soul. Moreover, the doctrine of ahimsa—literally, "no hurt"—held that every living creature has a soul. Killing even an ant would incur demerits and thus an unfavorable rebirth and further away from permanent bliss. Therefore, believers had to watch every step to avoid inadvertently becoming a murderer.

Since land could not be cultivated without killing insects, the extreme nonviolence of Jainism automatically excluded peasants from its devotees; it became a religion of traders and other city dwellers whose occupations allowed them to follow its precepts. The teachings of Mahavira were originally transmitted orally by his followers; but around the fifth century CE, a thousand years after his death, his followers wrote down his teachings. The strictly nonviolent doctrine, though originally intended only for followers of Jainism, has profoundly affected the thinking of inhabitants of South Asia down to modern times.

BUDDHA AND BUDDHISM   The most direct challenge to traditional Brahman thinking came from Siddhartha Gautama (c. 563–483 BCE), usually called the Buddha (the Enlightened One), a contemporary of Mahavira as well as of Confucius in China. The Buddha not only objected to the traditional Brahman rituals and sacrifices; he also denied the elaborate cosmology described by the Brahmans and the preference for

→ *How did political and social transformations encourage new beliefs and dissident thinkers in South Asia?*

kingship so important to the power of the priestly class. His teachings provided the peoples of South Asia and elsewhere with alternatives to established traditions that eventually themselves became established. In this respect, Buddhism in South Asia functioned much as did Confucianism in China.

Known as the wise man of Shakya, the Buddha came from a small Kshatriya community in the foothills of the Himalayas; in this oligarchic republic, his father was one of the *rajas* (though he may have been elected to head the oligarchs of his state, he was not a king). Like many other thinkers, Siddhartha was dismayed at the misery and political carnage of his age, and he left home at the age of twenty-nine in search of truth and enlightenment. Traveling through the Ganges region, he lived first as a beggar and then as a hermit, and finally, according to legend, meditated for forty-nine days until he understood how to eliminate suffering from the world.

His wanderings and ascetic life led him to create a new credo. He delivered his first sermon at Sarnath, or the Deer Garden, near Banaras. His teachings can be summarized as the Four Truths: first, life, from birth to death, is full of suffering; second, all sufferings are caused by desires; third, the only way to rise above suffering is to renounce desire; and fourth, it is only through adherence to the Noble Eightfold Path that individuals can rid themselves of desires and the illusion of separate identity and thus reach a state of contentment, or *nirvana*. The elements of the Eightfold Way can be grouped into three overarching categories: wisdom (right views and right intentions), ethical behavior (right conduct, right speech, and right livelihood), and mental discipline (right effort, right thought, and right meditation). Because these principles were simple and clear, the Four Truths of the Buddha had a powerful appeal. Like the teachings of Mahavira, the doctrines of the Buddha left no space for the supernatural, which was a prominent feature in classical Brahmanical thinking. His logical explanation of human suffering and his guidelines for renouncing desire appealed to many—though, not surprisingly, Brahman potentates frowned on this disturbing new development.

For people outside South Asian culture, the major barrier to accepting the Buddha's teachings was the concept of *nirvana*—literally, "nonexistence." For people not familiar with the Indian conception of life and death, nirvana at its most simplistic level could be interpreted as the end of life, or nonexistence, which implicates death. Just as unappealing was Buddha's pessimistic belief that life is bad and that we must endure cycles of endless suffering and deaths in order to ultimately liberate our souls. Buddhism's appeal becomes more understandable in the context of a belief in reincarnation of the soul. If life itself is suffering, and death leads simply to rebirth into another life, then the cycle of time brings endless suffering. Attaining *nirvana*, a state reached only after accumulating many merits, was the sole means of achieving a final liberation from life's troubles.

Like the other dissident thinkers of this period who challenged the authority of the Brahmans, Buddha delivered his message in Pali, a colloquial dialect of Sanskrit that all could understand. He soon attracted many followers, who formed a community of monks called a *sangha* (literally, "gathering"). Unlike the Brahmans, the Buddha and his followers preferred cities, wandering from one to another on the Ganges plain. The cities provided larger audiences for his preaching as well as the alms needed to sustain his expanding *sangha*. It is not surprising that the Buddha's most influential patrons were urban merchants. And in struggles between the oligarchs and kings, the Buddha sided with the oligarchs—reflecting his upbringing in an oligarchic republic. He inevitably aroused the opposition of the Brahmans, who favored monarchical government. While the Buddha himself did not seek to erase the *varna* hierarchy, the Buddhist *sangha* provided an escape

The Buddha's Footprints. Before his followers came to regard Buddha as a god, they were reluctant to make an idol of him—the footprints were an early representation of Buddha. They were carved in a limestone panel in a first-century BCE stupa in India.

WARRING IDEAS: THE BUDDHA VERSUS THE BRAHMANS

Great Election

This passage is from one of the earliest Buddhist texts, Dialogues of the Buddha. Here the Buddha explains to one of his disciples, Vāseṭṭha, how the state and king came into being. Early in our existence, human beings were pure, but they became greedy and chaotic. As a result they elected one person, typically someone capable and handsome, as king to maintain order. The one chosen is rewarded with a share of their rice.

When they had ceased rice appeared, ripening in open spaces, without powder, without husk, pure, fragrant and clean grained. Where we plucked and took away for the evening meal every evening, there next morning it had grown ripe again. Where we plucked and took away for the morning meal, there in the evening it had grown ripe again. There was no break visible. Enjoying this rice, feeding on it, nourished by it, we have so continued a long long while. But from evil and immoral customs becoming manifest among us, powder has enveloped the clean grain, husk too has enveloped the clean grain, and where we have reaped is no re-growth; a break has come, and the rice-stubble stands in clumps. Come now, let us divide off the rice fields and set boundaries thereto! And so they divided off the rice and set up boundaries round it.

Now some being, Vāseṭṭha, of greedy disposition, watching over his own plot, stole another plot and made use of it. They took him and holding him fast, said: Truly, good being, thou hast wrought evil in that, while watching thine own plot, thou hast stolen another plot and made use of it. See, good being, that thou do not such a thing again! Ay, sirs, he replied. And a second time he did so. And yet a third. And again they took him and admonished him. Some smote him with the hand, some with clods, some with sticks. With such a beginning, Vāseṭṭha, did stealing appear, and censure and lying and punishment became known.

Now those beings, Vāseṭṭha, gathered themselves together, and bewailed these things, saying: From our evil deeds, sirs, becoming manifest, inasmuch as stealing, censure, lying, punishment have become known, what if we were to select a certain being, who should be wrathful when indignation is right, who should censure that which should rightly be censured and should banish him who deserves to be banished? But we will give him in return a proportion of the rice.

Then, Vāseṭṭha, those beings went to the being among them who was the handsomest, the best favoured, the most attractive, the most capable and said to him: Come now, good being, be indignant at that whereat one should rightly be indignant, censure that which should rightly be censured, banish him who deserves to be banished. And we will contribute to thee a proportion of our rice.

And he consented, and did so, and they gave him a proportion of their rice.

Chosen by the whole people, Vāseṭṭha, is what is meant by Mahā Sammata; so Mahā Sammata (the Great Elect) was the first standing phrase to arise [for such an one]. Lord of the Fields is what is meant by Khattiya; so Khattiya (Noble) was the next expression to arise. He charms the others by the Norm—by what ought (to charm) —is what is meant by Rāja; so this was the third standing phrase to arise.

The Duties of a King

Unlike their legal codes, such as the Laws of Manu, the Brahmans' early law was not very specific about daily duties of a monarch. Gautama, a Brahman thinker, nevertheless made clear that "the king is master of all, with the exception of Brahmanas." His main duties include sponsoring Brahmans to carry out rituals and maintaining the hierarchy of castes.

Chapter XI

1. The king is master of all, with the exception of Brâhma*n*as.

2. (He shall be) holy in acts and speech,

3. Fully instructed in the threefold (sacred science) and in logic,

4. Pure, of subdued senses, surrounded by companions possessing excellent qualities and by the means (for upholding his rule).

5. He shall be impartial towards his subjects;

6. And he shall do (what is) good for them.

7. All, excepting Brâhma*n*as, shall worship him who is seated on a higher seat, (while they themselves sit on a) lower (one).

8. The (Brâhma*n*as), also, shall honour him.

9. He shall protect the castes and orders in accordance with justice;

10. And those who leave (the path of) duty, he shall lead back (to it).

11. For it is declared (in the Veda) that he obtains a share of the spiritual merit (gained by his subjects).

12. And he shall select as his domestic priest (purohita) a Brâhma*n*a who is learned (in the Vedas), of noble family, eloquent, handsome, of (a suitable) age, and of a virtuous disposition, who lives righteously and who is austere.

13. With his assistance he shall fulfil his religious duties.

14. For it is declared (in the Veda): 'Kshatriyas, who are assisted by Brāhma*n*as, prosper and do not fall into distress.'

15. He shall, also, take heed of that which astrologers and interpreters of omens tell (him).

16. For some (declare), that the acquisition of wealth and security depend also upon that.

17. He shall perform in the fire of the hall the rites ensuring prosperity which are connected with expiations (sânti), festivals, a prosperous march, long life, and auspiciousness; as well as those that are intended to cause enmity, to subdue (enemies), to destroy (them) by incantations, and to cause their misfortune.

18. Officiating priests (shall perform) the other (sacrifices) according to the precepts (of the Veda).

19. His administration of justice (shall be regulated by) the Veda, the Institutes of the Sacred Law, the Aṅgas, and the Purâ*n*a.

20. The laws of countries, castes, and families, which are not opposed to the (sacred) records, (have) also authority.

21. Cultivators, traders, herdsmen, money-lenders, and artisans (have authority to lay down rules) for their respective classes.

22. Having learned the (state of) affairs from those who (in each class) have authority (to speak he shall give) the legal decision.

23. Reasoning is a means for arriving at the truth.

24. Coming to a conclusion through that, he shall decide properly.

→ *The Buddha and Brahmans gave different explanations of how states arose in late Vedic India.*

→ *Why did the Buddha suggest that the first king was elected by people to end the chaos?*

→ *Why did the Brahman lawmakers make the king the masters of everyone but themselves?*

Source: *Dialogues of the Buddha, Part iii*, vol. 4 of *Sacred Books of the Buddhists*, translated by T. W. Rhys David and C. A. F. Rhys David (London: Oxford University Press, 1921), pp. 87–88; *The Sacred Laws of the Âryas as Taught in the Schools of Âpastamba, Gautama, Visishtha, and Baudhâyaa*, translated by Georg Bühler, vol. 2 of *The Sacred Books of the East*, edited by Friedrich Max Müller (1879; reprint, Delhi: Motilal Banarsidass, 1975), pp. 234–37.

PROPHETS AND THE FOUNDING TEXTS: COMPARING CONFUCIUS AND THE BUDDHA

Throughout history, universalizing religions have been defined not just by their sacred texts but also by central figures whose lives inspired and shaped movements and long-lasting traditions. Stories about them and their religious experience have often become a primary method of transmitting beliefs. In Confucianism and Buddhism, we find key leaders who inspired the faiths that were subsequently named for them.

Although famous for claiming that as a thinker he was a "transmitter who invented nothing," Confucius was one of ancient philosophy's great innovators. Born in China near the northern city of Qufu, he elaborated a code of behavior that put the highest value on individual performance of traditional rituals and on governmental morality based on correct social relationships, sincerity, and justice. Seeing division and war between rival states, he wished to restore the mandate of heaven to the declining Zhou dynasty and reunify China, but peace and prosperity would not come to the region until long after his death.

Though Confucius never held a high government post himself, over the centuries both the method and substance of his teaching, with many revisions, became the mainstream ideology of imperial China. His idea that the state should be modeled on the patriarchal family—that is, the ruler should respect the heaven as if it was his father, and protect his subjects as if they were his children—became the foundation of Chinese political theory. His philosophy of teaching could be summarized in three statements: "I teach whoever wants to learn with no regard to his birth," "The best educated men should serve the government," and "Those who work with their mind should rule, and those who work with their manual labor should be ruled." In short, each man was perfectible if he received the proper training. Confucius wanted people to perform the rituals bequeathed by the early Zhou and to emulate the actions of the great men who had ordered the world according to principles of civility and culture.

These ideas directly affected his immediate disciples and prominent Chinese philosophers of later generations, who did not always agree on how they should be interpreted. One school of Confucianists was represented by Mencius (372–289 BCE), who held that while recognizing the tendency of people to be led astray by worldly appetites and ambitions, Confucius believed in the inherent goodness of human nature. To recover that innate goodness required moral training. But according to Xunzi, Confucius saw humans as evil and lacking an innate moral sense. They therefore had to be controlled by education, ritual, and custom—an argument that later would be embraced by the founders of Legalism. Xunzi's pessimistic understanding seemed to better fit the experience of those who lived through the Warring States period and its imperial aftermath, the rise and fall of the short-lived Qin Empire.

Nevertheless, both Mencius and Xunzi embraced—though for different reasons—Confucius's dictum that the people were perfectible by being educated and by practicing the proper rules of conduct. All Confucians, whether pessimists or optimists, viewed the moral cultivation of the individual through education as the heart of the Confucian civilizing process, and they ensured that his ideas remained a vital force throughout Chinese history. Confucius's teachings, innovative and new during his life, in-

---

from the oppressive *varna* system and the tremendous prestige that it afforded the Brahman caste.

Thus, in South Asia as in China, the first millennium BCE was a time of innovation as well as warfare. Until the fourth century BCE, South Asia remained a confusing mass of warring territorial states. But out of the competition between these states came social transformations, including expansion of the caste system, the rise of cities and trade, and new philosophies and religions. Political unification would eventually follow in 321 BCE, followed by the conversion of the most powerful emperor of the new empire to Buddhism (see Chapter 6).

COMMON CULTURES IN THE AMERICAS

> → *How did cultural integration develop in the Andes and Mesoamerica in the absence of political unity?*

For many thousands of years, the original inhabitants of the Americas lived in small groups and villages as they engaged in hunting, gathering, and farming. Having wiped out the influenced all Chinese, both high and low, to focus on bettering their lives in this world through education and cultural pursuits. To become a "Confucian" meant to put into daily practice the civilized ideals of the past in order to achieve a vision of the highest good.

Though Buddhism cannot match Confucianism's long incorporation into state ideology, the teachings of the Buddha, like those of Confucius, had a far-reaching influence. The two thinkers were roughly contemporary, and both formulated their ideas in response to what they perceived as social chaos and degeneration. The Buddha, who had grown up in an oligarchic republic whose leaders (*rajas*) did not claim their authority to rule as divinely sanctioned by the Brahmans' rituals, presented a vision of society that challenged the Brahmanical order, although that order—in the form of caste hierarchy and monarchical polities—continued to thrive in South Asia. Indeed, Buddhist *sangha*, or communities of monks, had nearly vanished from the subcontinent after the first millennium CE. Nevertheless, Buddhism shaped the views of life and death and the scheme of time and space of the universe in South Asia. It also had a profound impact on peoples outside the region and even replaced Confucianism as the dominant religion in China for a few hundred years.

The Buddha offered a logical approach in the form of a unified system underlying the universe, instead of invoking divine intervention, to understanding the universe and social life at a time of rapid political development. As the Upanishads taught, he believed that the universe and individual lives all go through eternal cycles of birth, death, and rebirth, and the Buddha focused on and elaborated the concept of *karma* (literally, "fate" or "action"), a universal principle of cause and effect. The birth of every living being, human or animal, reflects actions taken in his or her past lives. Karma embodies the sins and merits of each individual, establishing his or her status in the current life—and deeds in the current life, in turn, affect that karma and thus determine suffering and happiness in the next life. Buddhist believers therefore focused not on pleasing gods who threatened punishment for misdeeds but on the consequences of their own actions: through their own behavior, they could attain better future lives. The Buddha's teachings, recorded as his dialogues with disciples in the vernacular dialect of Pali, were collected in *Nikayas* (*Collections*) and *Vinayas* (*Disciplines*). Several centuries later, when Buddhists rewrote his teachings in Sanskrit, the more poetic rhetoric obscured many of his original ideas.

Confucianism and Buddhism, much like the Vedic, Brahmin, and Judaic faiths discussed in Chapter 4, emerged during periods of great turmoil and change. All four faiths are undoubtedly products of their historical circumstances, and all were initially transmitted orally; later adherents created a written record of their teachings so that they might spread more widely. From their inception to the present, the basic principles and teachings of each have been debated by their believers. But Buddhism and Confucianism differ from the other two faiths in that they have founders whose identification with their belief systems remains their single most defining characteristic. We will see this phenomenon again with the rise of Christianity (from the teachings of Jesus) and Islam (from the teachings of Muhammad) as we continue our discussion of universalizing religions.

digenous large animals—not just the woolly mammoth but proto-camels and horses as well—the first Americans lacked domesticable animals; unlike members of early Afro-Eurasian societies, they could not mount horses, yoke oxen, or herd sheep. They therefore also lacked any impetus to invent a working wheel that an animal could pull to transport heavy loads. The result, quite apart from the obvious divergence in lifeways between American and the Afro-Eurasian peoples, was that basic communications between settlements in the Americas relied on human feet for locomotion on land; on water, they relied on canoes. These restrictions limited the distances that individuals traversed and the cargoes that they could haul.

There was some evidence for seaborne contact among native Americans dating from 1500 BCE. Buoyed in canoes, they paddled up and down the shorelines of the Pacific Ocean and the Gulf of Mexico. Strikingly similar chambered tombs, for instance, appear from the Pacific coast of Mexico, where the earliest instances have been found, all the way down to South America to coastal Peru. Early clothing, ceramic bottles, and other common items with shared features are likewise scattered across the Pacific coast of the Americas. For the most

El Lanzón. The Chavín excelled at elaborate stone carvings with complex images of their deities. This image of El Lanzón is a good example. At the center of one of the Chavín peoples' greatest temples is this massive gallery with a giant monument in the middle, etched with images of snakes, felines, and humans combined into one hybrid supernatural form. Observe the hands and feet with claws and the eyebrows that turn into serpents.

part, however, communications were intermittent, though recent excavations suggest that settlements may have been established on the coast of present-day Ecuador by colonists from western Mexico. Regional diversity, influenced by only sporadic long-distance communication and exchange, dominated the lifeways of the inhabitants of the Americas.

THE CHAVÍN IN THE ANDES (1400–200 BCE)

In this world of extreme localization and diversity, the steep mountainsides and deep fertile valleys of the Andes Mountains became the home of a distinctive people called the Chavín. In what is now northern Peru, farmers and pastoralists began to share a common belief system around 1400 BCE. With time, their artistic influence and spiritual principles touched a broad expanse of Andean folk. Like the peoples of South Asia and others in Afro-Eurasia, the Chavín peoples were united by culture and faith much more than by any political structure.

The Chavín peoples literally organized their societies vertically. Communities and households spread their trading systems up the mountainsides: valley floors yielded tropical and subtropical produce, further up the mountains maize and other crops were grown, and in the highlands, potatoes became a staple, and llamas were domesticated to produce wool

and dung (as fertilizer and fuel) and eventually to serve as beasts of burden. But because llamas could not transport humans, the Chavín migratory and political reach remained limited: no empire would emerge in the Andes for another millennium. The ecological diversity of the vertical societies of the Chavín enabled them to find all necessities close at hand, but they did undertake some long-distance trade, restricted mainly to dyes and precious stones, like obsidian. By 900 BCE, the Chavín were erecting elaborate stone carvings, using advanced techniques to weave fine cotton textiles, and making gold, silver, and copper metal goods. Scholars have found evidence that by 400 BCE, trade in painted textiles, ceramics, and gold objects spanned the Pacific coast, the Andean highlands, and the watershed eastward to the tropical rainforests of the Amazon basin. But these networks were not extensive and restricted themselves to conveying light precious goods.

There was a great deal of heterogeneity and fragmentation among the Chavín. But unifying their communities was a shared artistic tradition motivated by devotion to powerful deities; their spiritual capital was at the central temple complex of Chavín de Huántar, in modern Peru's northeastern highlands. The temple boasted a U-shaped platform, whose opening to the east surrounded a sunken, circular plaza; from its passageways and underground galleries, priests could suddenly emerge during ceremonies. The priests took hallucinogenic drugs, which were believed to enable them to become jaguars—the largest and most dangerous of the predators in the region—and to commune with the supernatural. Pilgrims brought tribute to Chavín de Huántar, where they worshipped and feasted together.

The Chavín drew on influences from as far away as the Amazon and the Pacific coast as they created devotional cults that focused on wild animals as representatives of spiritual forces. Carved stone jaguars, serpents, and hawks, baring their large fangs and claws to remind believers of the powers of nature, dominated the spiritual landscape. The "Smiling God" at Chavín de Huántar, El Lanzón, shaped from a slab of white granite fifteen feet high, had a human form but a fanged, catlike face, hair made of snakes, feet ending with talons, and hands that bristled with claws. This supernatural image was set on an awe-inspiring stage: dimly lit from above so that his face would glow from the reflection of polished

mirrors, the god stood over a canal, and the vibrations and deep rumbling sounds of the rushing water below helped convey a sense of the spiritual forces in the world. Though they borrowed from neighbors and refined existing sculptural techniques, the Chavín created the first great art style of the Andes; their cult finally gave way around 400 BCE to multiple local cultural heirs. Still, elements of it survived, taken up by successor religions adopted by stronger states further south.

THE OLMECS IN MESOAMERICA

Further to the north, in Mesoamerica, the first complex society emerged around 1500 BCE in the region between the highland plateaus of central Mexico and the Gulf Coast around modern-day Veracruz. (See Map 5-4.) The Olmecs

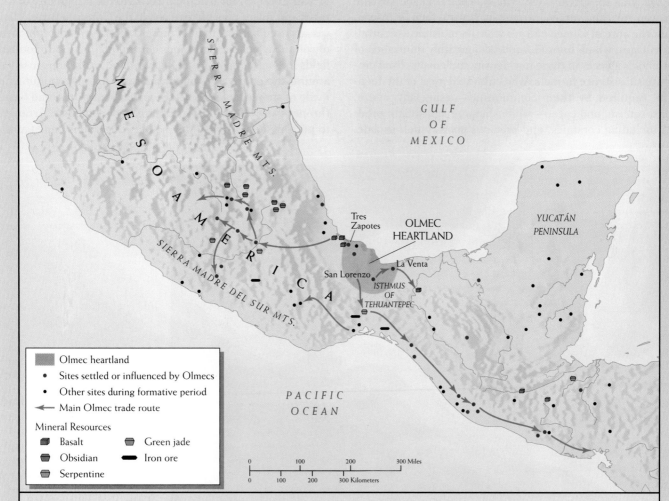

MAP 5-4   THE OLMEC WORLD

The Olmecs had a strong impact on Mesoamerica's early cultural integration. According to this map, how did they influence people living beyond the Olmec heartland? What factors limited the extent of Olmec influence? Why do you think the Olmec never became a politically unified regional empire?

provide an example of a first-generation small-scale community endeavoring to create new political and economic institutions while trying to answer the most profound questions about the nature of humanity and the world beyond.

Unlike the territorial states of Mesopotamia, these native American peoples had no preexisting high cultures from which to draw inspiration. Rather, the Mesoamerican cultures were something new, created out of local village roots. The peoples of this region formed themselves into a loose confederation of villages, scattered from the coast to the highlands and in large part nestled in river valleys and along the shores of swampy lakes. Their residents traded with each other, shared a common language, and worshipped the same gods. These were the Olmecs, a name meaning "inhabitants in the land of rubber"—one of their basic staples exported from the lowlands. Around 1500 BCE, the residents of hundreds of hamlets began to integrate themselves into a single culture and to spread elements of their beliefs, artistic achievements, and social structure far beyond their heartland.

At the core of Olmec culture were its multiple decentralized villages, which housed hundreds, possibly thousands of households apiece. In these low-density settlements lived productive subsistence farmers, who cultivated most of the foodstuffs required by their communities—especially maize, beans, squash, and cacao—while shipping lightweight products including ceramics, and precious goods (such as jade,

obsidian, or quetzal feathers, obtained from outlying areas and used to create masks and ritual figurines) to other villages. Most of these highly valued objects were intended for religious purposes rather than everyday consumption. The Olmecs also forged a network of exchange of sacred ritual objects among fellow believers.

CITIES AS SACRED CENTERS Despite their dispersed social landscape, the Olmec peoples created shared belief systems, a single language, and a priestly class who ensured that villagers adhered to highly ritualized practices. Their primary cities, including San Lorenzo, La Venta, and Tres Zapotes, were not large compared to the urban centers of Afro-Eurasia, but they were religious and secular hubs that bound together the surrounding agrarian hamlets. They were built around specialized buildings that featured massive earthen mounds, platforms, palaces, and capacious plazas. The rulers of San Lorenzo, for instance, constructed a high city of terraces and ridges on a plateau above the Chiquito River. Their vassals used baskets to haul more than 2.3 million cubic feet of soil to lay out the enormous central platform, two football fields in length, upon which palaces and workshops rose. All around the courtyards and paths were massive monuments made of stone—colossal heads, jaguar sculptures, and basalt thrones—as well as clusters of large wooden busts. Arranged to portray scenes, these vast sculpture gardens depicted the

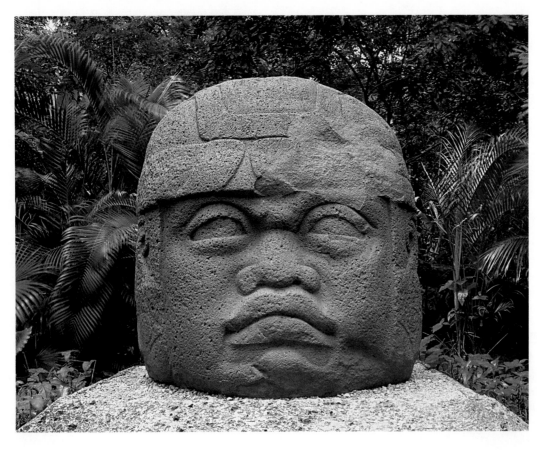

Olmec Head. At La Venta, in Tabasco State in Mexico, four colossal heads rest on the ground, remnants of a field of monumental figures that once ornamented this Olmec site. Nine feet high and weighing up to twenty tons, the giant helmeted heads are the source of much speculation. Carved from single boulders, they are thought to be portraits of great kings or legendary ballplayers. Each head bears distinctive elements in homage to its subject.

Primary Source

OLMEC ART AS IDEOLOGY

Olmec ideology put great emphasis on the ties between the natural, supernatural, and the human worlds. It was also an ideology crafted to influence and possibly convert the Olmecs' neighbors. Known for their great monumental architecture and artwork, Olmec craftsworkers also made portable objects, icons, and miniature figures that unify their belief systems and that could be transported long distances to convey a religious message to non-Olmecs and bring them into their cultural sphere of influence. Such works were designed to expand the spiritual frontier of Olmec belief throughout Mesoamerica.

Consider one of the most famous of these surviving portable spiritual icons, called "Young Lord" by some archaeologists and "Slim Jim" by others because of his elongated figure. Although most icons represent a single deity or power, Young Lord combines many of the basic elements of Olmec belief into a single, beautiful figurine. Standing about two feet tall, Young Lord was a diplomatic artifact, intended to spread the influence of a complex belief system far and wide.

Look closely at the photograph of Young Lord. He is fierce. Holding two scepters against his chest, and himself carved in the form of a scepter, he is meant to con-

vey power and influence—but the power and influence of what?

See if you can "read" the delicate incisions around his body. Note his pose: rigid and tall, like a ruler who is the axis mundi, the turning point who joins the earthly and the supernatural worlds. The images you see represent ceremonial practices—rituals that Young Lord oversees, and that enable him to exercise his shamanic powers over believers. His face, for instance, is covered by a mask that evokes classic Olmec shamanic images; his mouth snarls like a jaguar's and his nose resembles an eagle's beak. The mask and its carvings suggest that this lord is capable of transforming into a jaguar or an avian hunter to conduct sacrificial rites, a surmise confirmed by the extensive incisions over his body.

Bloodletting and human sacrifice dominate the cicatrices and underscore the importance of the scepters, used to draw blood. These sacrifices were intended to please the forces of the supernatural world, which would reward believers with rain. Notice the arms and hands, covered with images of ritual performers and victims. His legs are adorned with figures of serpentlike creatures, monsters with gaping jaws, fangs, and forked tongues.

The statue as a whole is divided horizontally into three, signifying the three layers of the cosmos—the supernatural, the terrestrial, and the underworld—which Young Lord has the power to travel between as he brings messages to believers and nonbelievers alike. This is a powerful image, one meant to drive home the authority of Olmec rulers to their subjects and neighbors.

→ *What kind of power and influence does Young Lord represent?*

→ *What do the various symbols on his statue tell us about various spiritual aspects of Olmec society?*

→ *What kinds of spiritual objects would Christians, Muslims, or Buddhists draw on to propagate their faith, as the Olmecs did with Young Lord?*

human rulers and deities to whom the Olmecs paid homage and offered sacrifice. Artificial lagoons and channels criss-crossed the precinct. Beneath these mounds archaeologists have found axes, knives made of sharpened obsidian, other tools, and simple yet breathtaking figurines made most often of jade, buried as tokens for those who dwelled in the super-natural world. San Lorenzo was not a capital city, with a large permanent population whose rulers made laws throughout Olmec territorial dominions. Rather, it was a devotional cen-ter, the influence of whose monumental architecture and art was felt throughout the Olmec hinterlands.

Paying homage to their gods and rulers was part of the Olmecs' daily life. While devotional activity took place on the shores of lakes, in caves, on mountaintops, and in other nat-

Olmec Ballplayer. Ball-playing was an important ceremonial and athletic activity among the Olmec. Games were occasions for human competitors to display their skills to deities, and also against the gods themselves. Playing the sport was intimately tied to fertility. This figure exemplifies the Olmec's skill at refined stone carving.

ural settings, it occurred above all in the primary cities. In La Venta, huge pits (one was thirteen feet deep and seventy-seven feet wide) contained the devotees' massive offerings of hundreds of tons of serpentine carved blocks. Olmec art speaks to the powerful influence of devotion on creativity. Many images were dominated by representations of natural and supernatural entities—not just animals such as snakes, jaguars, and crocodiles but also certain humans called *shamans,* who were believed to have special powers to com-mune with the supernatural and the ability to transform themselves wholly or partly into beasts (as also seen in im-ages at Chavín sites). A common figurine, for instance, is of the "were-jaguar," a being that was part man, part animal. Shamans representing jaguars invoked the Olmec rain god, a jaguarlike being, to bring rainfall to the land and thereby se-cure its fertility. The ceremonial life of the Olmecs revolved around agricultural and rainfall cycles. Throughout the Olmec heartland, we see evidence of a distinct and shared iconography—an integrated culture that transcended eco-logical niches.

The Olmecs' major cities were not just centers of pure de-votion. They were also athletic hubs where victorious teams paid homage to their deities. Intricate ball courts made room on the sidelines for fans to applaud and jeer at the sweating contestants, who struggled to bounce hard rubber balls off parallel side walls and their bodies and into a goal. Noble players, bearing helmets and heavy padding, could touch the six-pound rubber ball only with their elbows, hips, knees, and buttocks, and were honored when they knocked the ball through the stationary stone hoop. Massive sculptures of hel-meted heads carved out of volcanic basalt suggest that famous ballplayers gained more renown by being monumen-talized. At La Venta, a huge mosaic made out of greenstone served as an elegant ball court; at its center was a portal that was thought to open out into the otherworld. Olmec archae-ological sites are now filled with the remains of game equip-ment and of the trophies awarded to the victors. Some trophies were buried in the tomb of a dead ruler so that he could play ball with the gods in the otherworld. Ritual ball games, for all their entertainment value, were integral to Olmec devotional culture. It was in honor of the powerful rain god that players struggled to win.

What added to the thrill of the ball court was that they were dangerous yet fecund places associated with water and agricultural fertility, for an equally important aspect of devo-tional culture was the practice of human sacrifice. Indeed, it is likely that athletics and sacrifice were blended in the same rituals. Many monuments depict a victorious and costumed ballplayer (sporting a jaguar headdress or a feathered serpent helmet) atop a defeated, bound human, though it is not known whether the losers were literally executed. Rainmak-ing rites also included other forms of human sacrifice. Captives—we do not know how they were selected or seized —were executed and dismembered. There is increasing evidence that the Olmecs practiced ritual warfare to supply rulers with humans whose death and torture was meant to ensure that the soil would be fertile and the rains would continue. At El Manatí, select offering sites alongside a spring and the shore of a boggy lake are filled with the bones of children slaughtered for the gods. Across the artistic landscape of the Olmecs are representations of human victims fed to the gods and to the rulers who embodied them.

MAN, NATURE, AND TIME The Olmec cosmology also assumed a basic relationship between the natural and supernatural worlds, with the latter dictating the motions of the former. Olmec culture is saturated with belief in the power of supernatural forces and with tales of shamans controlling the supernatural. But the Olmecs were hardly a simple, superstitious folk; indeed, their conviction that the supernatural pervaded the natural world drove them to learn more about nature so that they might know with more certainty what the gods wanted. By systematically observing the natural world, they might discover godly meanings. There was no hard-and-fast line between what we now consider the separate arenas of "faith" and "science." The way that rulers reckoned time reflects this belief system, for they were convinced that the gods defined calendric passages, and therefore seasons and rainfall patterns that so decisively shaped the livelihoods of agrarian peoples. Priests, charting celestial movements, devised a complex calendar that marked the passage of seasons and generations. As in China and Mesopotamia, a flowering of culture encouraged priests and scholars to study the world around them—and the heavens—so that they might accurately chart the rhythms of the terrestrial and celestial worlds.

A WORLD OF SOCIAL DISTINCTIONS It is easy to forget, as we consider all the remarkable effigies, artwork, and evidence of early scientific observation and writing, that Olmec centers were also communities where people went about their daily business. Daily labor kept Olmecs busy. The vast majority worked the fertile lands as part of household units, children and parents alike toiling in the fields with wooden tools, fishing in streams with nets, and hunting turtles and other small animals. Most Olmecs had to juggle the needs of their village neighbors, their immediate families, and the taxes imposed by rulers.

The Olmecs present us with an enigma. We often think of dispersed and decentralized agrarian cultures as simple and egalitarian. Increasingly, however, archaeologists of the Olmecs are finding the reverse. Not only did the Olmecs have an elaborate cultural system, they had many tiers of social rankings. The priestly class, raised and trained in the palaces at La Venta, San Lorenzo, and Tres Zapotes, directed the exchanges of sacred ritual objects between farming communities. Because these exchanges involved immense resources, the engagement of the ruling families was necessary and their involvement with these objects buttressed their claim to be

The Las Limas Monument. The were-jaguar was an important figure in the pantheon of Olmec deities. This sculpture, known as the Las Limas monument, represents a youth holding a limp were-jaguar baby. We do not know what these figures represented exactly—most likely they refer to spiritual journeys. Some have argued that this monument harkens to child sacrifice. Notice the faces of supernatural forces incised on the knees and shoulders of the youth, common Olmec motifs.

descended from divine ancestors. At the same time, their control of the commerce in precious secular goods added to their fortunes. In this fashion, dominant families blurred the line between the everyday and the religious, the profane and the sacred heritages, and thereby legitimized their domination of their subjects.

Alongside the priestly elite, a secular one emerged composed of chieftains who supervised agrarian transactions among farmers, oversaw a class of artisans, and accepted tribute from inhabitants of their villages. They set up specialized workshops, managed by foremen who answered to them,

La Mojarra Stela. This monument bears the inscription of the Long Count Olmec calendar. It is called "Long Count" because it is nonrepeating and vigesimal (base-20, in contrast to our decimal system). It also relied on the use of a zero as a place-holder, represented by a small glyph, one of the earliest uses of the concept of zero. We still have only partial knowledge of how the Olmec kept temporal records, but their system was the basis of future calendric systems across Mesoamerica. The calendar is part of a narrative about astronomy, rituals or accession, warfare, and bloodletting.

where craftsworkers carved, created pots, painted, sculpted, and wove; stones and gems were imported from surrounding villages. Those at the top of the hierarchy of chieftainships could command villages scattered over the approximate area of a territorial state. The larger the domain, the greater the ability to ship the produce of workshops and fields to the chiefs' centers or priests' capitals.

The combination of an integrated culture and a complex social structure gave the Olmecs a degree of cohesion unprecedented in the Americas. With this cohesion and the ability to transmit goods and services up the social ladder, rulers at the top had access to vast resources. Olmec influence radiated well beyond their heartland. Without an urge to con-

quer or colonize, the Olmecs nonetheless shaped the social development of much of Mesoamerica. As their population centers grew and their arts expanded, their demand for stones such as obsidian and jade, seashells, plumes, and other precious goods drove them to find suppliers at an ever greater remove. Nor were the Olmecs merely importers. They exported rubber, cacao, pottery, ceramics, figurines, refined jaguar pelts, and crocodile skins, all of which found purchasers throughout Mesoamerica. Importing and exporting were probably in the hands of a merchant class—about whose size and wealth we know little. What is more, as the evidence of the Young Lord suggests (see Primary Source box), the Olmecs also conveyed their belief system to neighbors, if not to convert them, at least to influence them and reinforce a sense of superiority.

THE LOSS OF CENTERS   The breakdown of the Olmec culture is shrouded in mystery. The decline was uneven, abrupt in some centers and protracted in others. At La Venta, for instance, the altars and massive basalt heads were defaced and buried—the ultimate ignominy for the people and gods they were meant to represent, indicating a dramatic shift. And yet, there is little evidence of a spasm of war, a peasant uprising, a demographic cataclysm, or civil conflict between factions of the ruling classes. Indeed, in many parts of the Olmec heartland, the religious centers that had once served as the hubs of the Olmec world were abandoned but not destroyed. Much of the Olmec hinterland remained heavily populated and highly productive.

The machinery for drawing resources into Olmec capitals eventually failed. As the bonds between rulers and their subjects weakened, so did the networks of exchange of ritual objects that had enlivened the Olmec centers and made them magnets for obedience and piety. Olmec hierarchies then collapsed. Without a sacred elite to transmit the cosmology, it too faded. What was left of the Olmec heritage passed on to other Mesoamericans—especially those of the central plateaus and the tropical lowlands of the Yucatán peninsula, where new centers of power eventually arose that bore traces of their Olmec predecessors.

COMMON CULTURES IN SUB-SAHARAN AFRICA

> → *How did the spread of iron smelting shape the social landscape of sub-Saharan Africa?*

Africa's most significant historical development in the first millennium BCE was the continued desiccation of the northern and central parts of the landmass, and the emergence of the

↝ *How did the spread of iron smelting shape the social landscape of sub-Saharan Africa?*

great Sahara Desert, the largest desert on the planet, as its primary geographical and population barrier. (See Map 5-5.) Large areas that had once supported abundant plant and animal life, including human settlements, now became more sparsely populated. Moreover, the peoples living in Africa began to coalesce in a few locations; the most important of these was the Nile Valley, which may have held more than half of the landmass's population at this time. Climatic change divided the whole of Africa from the Equator northward to the Sahara Desert roughly into four distinct geographical and human zones. Moving from north to south, the first zone was the Sahara Desert itself, which never completely emptied out, despite its extreme heat and aridity. Its oases supported pastoral peoples, like the ancestors of the modern Tuareg tribal communities, who raised livestock and promoted contacts between the northern and the western parts of Africa. Further south of the Sahara was the Sahel, literally the coast (Arabic *sahil*) of the great ocean of sand. In time, some of Africa's great commercial cities, like Timbuktu, would arise in this zone; but in the first millennium BCE no city of great size had yet made its appearance.

The next zone was the Sudanic savanna region, an area of high grasslands stretching all the way from present-day Senegal along the Atlantic Ocean in the west to the Nile River and the Red Sea in the east. Many of West Africa's kingdoms emerged there, since the area was free of the tsetse fly, which was as lethal to animals as to humans, killing off livestock, including cattle, horses, and goats. The fourth and final ethnogeographical zone was the

western and central African rain forests, a region characterized by small-scale societies. In this period, it was sparsely populated.

Although there was contact across the Sahara, Africa below the Sahara was markedly different in many ways from

	Nubia
	Kush
	Nok
	Mediterranean colonies
	Persia
•	City
NOK	State
←	Trans-Saharan trade route
▲	Spread of iron making from 6th century BCE to the 2nd century BCE

MAP 5-5 AFRICA, 500 BCE

The first millennium BCE was a major period of social, cultural, economic, and political integration for North and sub-Saharan Africa. What effect did the presence of the Greek and Phoenician colonies have on Africa? What main factor integrated Nubia and Egypt? Does the map reveal a relationship between the rise of Sudanic culture and the spread of iron-working? If so, what is it?

North Africa and Eurasia. It did not develop a plough agriculture; its farmers depended on hoes. Also, in most parts of sub-Saharan Africa, except for densely populated regions, land was held communally and never regarded as having as much value as labor. African peoples could always move into new locations. They had more difficulty finding workers to till the soil.

Distinctive ways of life that were to become associated with these areas from 1000 CE onward were only beginning to appear during the first millennium BCE. In the savanna area, millet and sorghum were the primary food crops; in the rain forests, yams and other root crops dominated. Relatively large populations were confined mainly to the Sudanic savanna region, the sole area for which substantial historical records for this period exist. Here, in fact, a way of life that can be called Sudanic began to crystallize.

These peoples of the first millennium BCE were not completely dependent on their feet to get around, as were their counterparts in the Americas. They had domesticated several animals, including cattle and goats, and even possessed small horses (about the size of today's ponies). Although their communities were scattered widely across Africa, some 4,000 miles from west to east, they had much in common. They all tended to adhere to a cosmology dominated by a high god, and their polities were led by sacred kings; servants were buried alongside their rulers in the belief that the rulers would be resurrected in the afterlife and would need to be served by those who had been loyal to them in this life. They were skilled cultivators and weavers of cotton, which they had domesticated from a wild plant indigenous to the area. At

first, archaeologists and historians believed that these Sudanic peoples had borrowed their institutions, notably their sacred kingships, from their Egyptian neighbors to the north; but linguistic evidence and especially their custom of burying servants along with the rulers make it clear that the Sudanic communities had developed these practices on their own.

MEROE: BETWEEN SUDANIC AFRICA AND PHARAONIC EGYPT

Without doubt, the most highly developed of these Sudanic sacred kingdoms was the state of Meroe, located in what is now Sudan. Meroe arose in the southern part of an area known historically as Nubia, a region lying between the first Nile cataract (located at the present-day city of Aswan) and the sixth and last cataract (just north of present-day Khartoum, where the Blue and the White Nile come together). From at least the fourth millennium BCE onward, and perhaps earlier, peoples in this region were in contact with both the northern and southern parts of the African landmass. It was one of the few parts of sub-Saharan Africa known to the outside world. The Greek poet Homer described its inhabitants as "the remotest nation, the most just of men; the favorites of the gods." Nubia's historical connection to Egypt was obvious: it was Egypt's corridor to sub-Saharan Africa; a source of ivory, gold, and slaves; and an area that expansionist Egyptian monarchs wanted to dominate. The best known of the conquerors from Egypt was Rameses II, who left his imprint on the culture of this area with his magnificent monuments at

The Temple of Ramses II. The temple of Ramses II at Abu Simbel was constructed during the reign of Ramses II between 1304 and 1237 BCE. It was cut out of the rock and featured four colossal statues of the king, each of which was twenty meters high. When the Aswan High Dam was built in the 1960s, the monument had to be cut into large stone slabs and moved to higher ground so that it would not be submerged under the waters of Lake Nasser, which the High Dam formed.

Primary Source

WRITING THE HISTORY OF PRELITERATE AFRICAN PEOPLES

Traditionally, historians have relied on written records and have had difficulty reconstructing the history of preliterate societies. Hence, African history has come of age only in recent times as scholars devised new techniques for uncovering past narratives.

The sources used in African history are varied and in many ways unconventional. They include art, pottery, linguistic analysis, oral traditions, and many other elements that most historians have not commonly worked with. Here are two such vital but unusual historic sources. The first is Nok terra-cottas. These terra-cottas were discovered just before and during World War II in the middle belt region of modern-day Nigeria. The figurines themselves probably were created in the common era, but they are part of a vibrant culture that dates back to the fifth century BCE.

The second source comes from the kingdom of Meroe, located between the fifth and sixth Nile cataracts. Meroe flourished for nearly a millennium, from the fifth century BCE to the fifth century CE. Though in close contact with Egypt, it lay within sub-Saharan Africa. The Egyptian influences were profound and obvious—for example, the use of the term *pharaoh* to refer to the king, borrowed religious beliefs, and the use of hieroglyphics. The African influences were more subtle and less easily discerned, but important nonetheless.

Nok figurine.

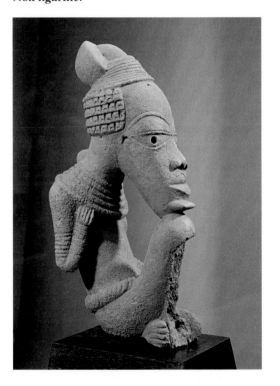

Burial pyramids at the Royal Necropolis of the ancient kingdom of Kush.

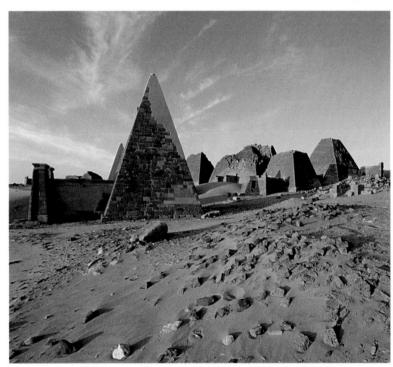

→ *How do the Nok figures help scholars understand the very ancient culture of West Africa?*
→ *Do they provide insight into the artistic abilities of the people living in this region?*

→ *What can they tell us about how people dressed and how they looked?*
→ *Can you see the Egyptian influence in the photograph of the Kush burial pyramids?*

Abu Simbel. Such connections with Egypt have long been stressed by historians, especially Egyptologists, but only recently have scholars become aware of just how deeply the peoples and states in Nubia were influenced by the cultures of sub-Saharan Africa.

Building on the earlier foundations of kings that had ruled Nubia, the Meroe kingdom came into being in the fourth century BCE and flourished until 300 CE. The rulers of Meroe were much influenced by the pharaonic culture, even to the point of adapting hieroglyphs, erecting pyramids in which they buried their rulers, viewing their kings as divine, and worshipping the Egyptian god Amun. But Meroe was equally a part of the Sudanic way of life that flourished across Africa's savanna lands. In order to assert their autonomy from the powerful Egyptians to the north, the rulers of Meroe moved their capital city about 300 miles upstream (to the south), where it commanded the whole of the Nile region between the fifth and sixth Nile cataracts.

Meroe soon became a thriving center of production and commerce. The residents of the city were especially skilled in iron smelting and the manufacture of textiles, and their products were widely circulated throughout Africa. The capital city itself covered a square mile; at its center was a royal city, surrounded by a rectangular wall 300 yards long and half as wide. The royal city featured monumental and highly decorated buildings, which were built, according to the custom of this area, not in stone but in mud bricks.

WEST AFRICAN KINGDOMS

Meroe was not the only sacred kingship in the Sudanic savanna lands of Africa. Similar polities thrived in West Africa, among peoples living in the Senegal River basin and among the Mande peoples living inland around the western branch of the Niger River. They established settlements at such places as Jenne and Gao, which would expand to become large trading centers. In these areas, artisans smelted iron ore and wove textiles, and merchants engaged in long-distance trade.

Even more spectacular was the Nok culture, which arose in the sixth century BCE in an area that is today the geographical center of Nigeria. Though slightly south of the Sudanic savanna lands of West Africa, it was (and still is) in regular contact with that region. At a place called Taruga, near the present-day village of Nok (which gave this cultural system its name), early iron smelting occurred in 600 BCE. Taruga may well have been the first place in western Africa where iron ores were smelted. Undeniably ironworking was significant for the Nok peoples, who made the move from using stone materials directly to iron, bypassing the customary intermediate stage of working in bronze and copper. They made iron axes and hoes, iron knives and spears, and luxury items that could be traded. Ironworking had spread east toward Egypt and Nubia and south to the Congo River by 300 BCE. Moreover, Bantu-speaking people from Nok migrated southward into the equatorial rain forests, where they cleared land for farming; from there, some moved on to southern Africa. Yet Nok is famous not for its iron-smelting prowess but rather for its magnificent terra-cotta figurines, discovered only in the 1940s in the tin-mining region of central Nigeria. These naturalistic figures, with features that are striking in their resemblance to modern inhabitants of the region, date back to at least 500 BCE. They were altarpieces, produced in connection with a cult associated with the fertility of the land. Placed next to new lands that were being brought into cultivation, they were believed to have the power to bless the soil and to enhance its productivity.

During the first millennium BCE, sub-Saharan Africa remained a highly diverse area ecologically and culturally, with many different peoples living in a wide variety of climates and ecologies. Simple hunting and gathering peoples dwelled in the tropical forests at the same time that Bantu people from sophisticated farming societies cleared land to grow millet and sorghum; raised cattle, sheep, and goats; organized themselves into clans with chiefs; conducted complex religious rituals; and engaged in extensive trade within and across regions. Perhaps the most telling development in sub-Saharan Africa in this period was the widespread improvement in iron-smelting techniques. It would be these advances in metalworking that would enable larger settled communities to develop. With better and stronger tools made with iron, settled communities could improve their farming techniques—and as a result, they had more food and could sustain larger communities. Indeed, in the period between 400 BCE and the new millennium, the estimated population of sub-Saharan Africa shot up from 3.5 million to more than 11 million people. This would be the first of many major population explosions that would transform sub-Saharan Africa and its inhabitants.

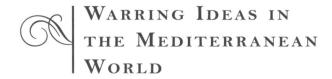

WARRING IDEAS IN THE MEDITERRANEAN WORLD

> → *In what ways did city-states integrate the geographically dispersed settlements of the Mediterranean?*

The tortuous and widespread movements of peoples that convulsed large parts of southern Europe and Southwest Asia around 1200 BCE (see Chapter 4) also brought marauding armed bands into the well-settled regions of the Mediterranean. The combined impact of large population movements and social destruction radically transformed the existing social organizations and cultures throughout the region. Thus, as in Eastern Zhou China and Vedic South Asia, the first millennium BCE in the Mediterranean was a time of political, economic, and social changes, as well as of new ideas.

The violent upheavals at the end of the second millennium BCE had a great impact on the borderland areas west of the highly developed societies of Southwest Asia. As noted in Chapter 4, these areas comprised the northern region of the Levant (approximately the area of modern-day Lebanon), the coastal lands of Anatolia (in modern-day Turkey), the islands of the Aegean and Mediterranean seas, and mainland Greece. The inhabitants of these regions had always been in contact with the most highly developed societies in Southwest Asia, and they had experienced the power of the Assyrians and Persians. But the disorder and chaos of the time freed them from the domination of those large regional states. More on their own than ever before, these communities were now able to experiment with new cultural ideas and new types of social and political organization. Thus, around 1000 BCE, the peoples in these lands (many of whom were new settlers from the north and west) not only absorbed the rapidly changing cultural and technical knowledge but also devised new and challenging ways of organizing their societies—creating what could be considered second-generation societies, hybrids that mix the old and the new.

The seaborne peoples from all around the Mediterranean Sea basin—Phoenicians, Greeks, Cretans, Cypriots, Lydians, Etruscans, and many others—shared common characteristics. As they sailed through the Mediterranean, they carried with them not just trade goods but also new ideas about the virtues of self-sufficient cities in which power was shared more widely (even more democratically) than before. Inventions that proved valuable in one place, such as the use of money and the alphabet in trading transactions, usually spread rapidly throughout the entire region; the result was an uncommonly high degree of intercommunication, drawing together the diverse communities of the region.

Increased knowledge and refinements in maritime technology were crucial to the expansion of trade and the rapid, large-scale population movements that took place in the first millennium BCE. In the ninth and eighth centuries BCE, improved design and construction of ships, better deployment of sail and rowing technology, and, above all, better practical knowledge of winds, currents, and shorelines made it possible for sailing peoples to transform the seaborne world of the Mediterranean.

Homer's *Odyssey* (composed in the eighth century BCE about events that had occurred centuries earlier) was the epic

> *The stories of Odysseus and Hanno reflect the new kinds of mobility and transforming encounters that people from Mediterranean communities enjoyed in the first millennium BCE.*

tale of the wanderings of Odysseus as he sailed through the Mediterranean on his way back to his island home of Ithaca after the siege of the city of Troy. It tells of his encounters with pirates, traders, adventurers, witches, monsters, powerful barons, and wealthy and exotic kings and queens, and suggests that the Greeks were premier seafarers. Yet the Greeks were far from being the first, the only, or even the best masters of the seas. Around 800 BCE, the Phoenicians began sailing westward in the Mediterranean in search of metals and trade (see Chapter 4). Some historians even believed that Phoenician sailors had circumnavigated Africa around 600 BCE. Even if this claim was an exaggeration, it is certain that as early as 750 BCE Phoenicians *had* sailed across the Mediterranean and had ventured into the Atlantic Ocean—and that they had also sailed through the Red Sea and down the eastern coast of Africa. Hanno, a general from the Phoenician city of Carthage in the western Mediterranean (near present-day Tunis), is said to have set sail from Carthage in 500 BCE with a fleet of sixty-seven fifty-oared ships filled with a large number of men and women. His mission was to explore and settle the Atlantic coast of Africa, and he reports finding elephants, gorillas, and wild people along the way. The stories of Odysseus and Hanno reflect the new kinds of mobility and transforming encounters outside their own sphere that people from Mediterranean communities enjoyed in the first millennium BCE.

A NEW WORLD OF CITY-STATES

In the ninth and eighth centuries BCE, order was reestablished and the population returned to levels that had been achieved in earlier periods. But when these larger numbers of people began to congregate in more concentrated settlements, they did not revive the old palace and temple organizations of the Mycenaeans and Minoans. Instead, they created something quite novel: the independent, self-governing city-state. These city-states were characterized by intense competition both between them and inside them. Furthermore, they became commercial centers managing exchange and trade, and they established colonies throughout the Mediterranean.

SELF-GOVERNMENT AND DEMOCRACY The self-governing city-state was a new political form that had a profound impact on the whole of the Mediterranean. First found among the Phoenicians (see Chapter 4) and in their settlements in the western Mediterranean like Carthage, but ultimately associated most strongly with the Greeks, these new urban communities had multiplied throughout the

Mediterranean by the sixth century BCE. This new urban entity that we call a city-state—known by the Phoenicians as a *qart*, the Greeks as a *polis*, and the Romans as a *civitas*—is perhaps best understood by what it was *not*. Unlike the great urban centers in the empires of Southwest Asia, the new city-states were not organized by a critically important class of scribes or run by directives issued by high priests, monarchs, or their subordinates. Record keeping and the administration of goods and services by a central authority were very minor, often unimportant elements in their day-to-day operation.

The new principles of rulership were revolutionary. Ordinary residents or "citizens" of these cities—cities such as Athens, Thebes, Sparta, or Corinth among the Greeks, Caere and Rome on the Italian peninsula among the Etruscans (and later among the Romans themselves), or Carthage and Gadir (modern-day Cádiz in Spain) among the Phoenicians—governed themselves and selected their leaders. Their self-government took various forms. One kind was rule by a popularly approved political head of the city, called a *tyrannis* (tyrant) by the Greeks. Another was rule by a restricted number of wealthy and powerful citizens—the "few" or *oligoi,* as the Greeks called them (hence the modern concept of "oligarchs" and "oligarchies"). The most inclusive type of government involved all free adult males in a city—in Greek, a *dēmokratia* (democracy; see below). The wealthiest landowners often formed the power elite in these new city-states, but farmers, craftsworkers, shopkeepers, merchants, soldiers, and traders were the backbone of the citizenry. The inhabitants of the burgeoning number of new Mediterranean communities ran the city's affairs, decided when they would go to war, and set their own priorities for the development of their communities. This approach contrasted with that in Mesopotamia, where the much smaller number of cities of the second millennium BCE had been administered from the top down: the power of kings largely determined whether new cities were founded and how they grew.

The new cities of the Mediterranean basin were made up of communities of adult male citizens, other free persons (including women, who could not vote or hold office), foreign immigrants, and large numbers of unfree persons (including slaves and Sparta's helots, people tied to the land who could not vote or fight for the polis). Those enjoying full citizenship rights—the adult freeborn males—in each community were able to decide for themselves what was to be done (what tasks would be undertaken by the city-state) and how it was to be done (what kind of government and laws would be adopted by the city-state). Consequently, these cities differed markedly from one another.

FAMILIES AS THE FOUNDATIONAL UNITS Within all these cities the small family unit, called an *oikos* (household) by the Greeks and a *familia* by the Romans, was the single most important social unit. Indeed, thinkers like Aristotle regarded the state as a natural outgrowth of the household. To

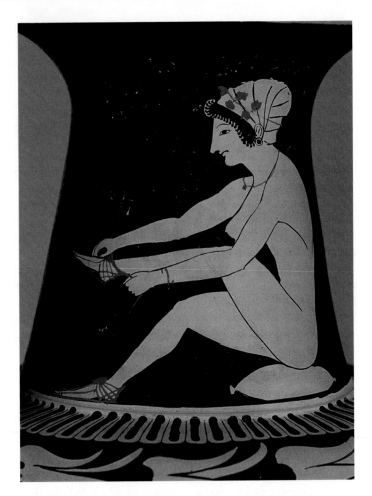

Hetaira. The painting on this vase by the artist Oitos is of a "companion" woman—called by the Greeks an *hetaira*—putting a sandal on her foot. Proper Greek women were protected and enclosed within their households; they were modest and always fully clothed. Women who were so bold as to be out in public, talking and otherwise associating with men—like the woman portrayed here—were deemed immoral. The artist therefore had no problem portraying this *hetaira* in the nude.

Aristotle, the *oikos* embodied the fundamental power relationships found in cities, where free men and citizens were lords over their wives and children, and masters of their slaves. The free adult male was head of the household and fully entitled to engage in the city's public affairs.

In contrast, adult women of free birth were permanently enclosed within the private world of the family and had no standing to debate policy in public, vote, or hold office. Women who did carry on intelligent conversations with men in public about public matters were castigated as *hetairai* (courtesans—literally, "female companions"). Spartan women were a partial exception to all of these rules, and their unusual behavior, such as exercising in the nude in public (as did men) or holding property in their own right, evoked humor and hostility from men in the other Greek city-states.

COMPETITION AND ARMED WAR   Because centralized governments exerted little control over the actions and thoughts of the inhabitants of these new city-states, they were comparatively freewheeling and competitive places, sometimes bloodily so. Their histories are filled with violent rivalries between individuals, social classes, and other groups. Among the larger Greek city-states, only Sparta avoided most of this internal strife, achieving greater calm by a radical and rigorous program of social discipline and military organization that cut the city and its people off from many external influences. The Spartans rejected coined money and chattel slavery (see below), thereby avoiding what they saw as the "corruption" of cities with more mercantile interests. However successful it was as a military state, Sparta was widely viewed by the other Greeks as a very unusual polis.

Competition for honor and prestige—a "good strife," as the Greek poet Hesiod called it—was one of the moral values that shaped the behavior of individuals in the city-states. Such an extreme competitive ethic, which might easily take bad forms such as murder and feuds, could find a benign outlet in organized sporting events, or *agōnes* (struggles). Almost from the moment that Greek city-states emerged, athletic contests sprang up—both on a small scale, as an essential part of life in all cities, and in large, centralized events in which all Greeks could participate. The greatest of these competitions were the Olympic Games, which were staged for the first time in 776 BCE at Olympia in southern Greece.

Greek Boxers. Greek athletic contests or struggles (*agones*) were less games in our sense than all-out attempts to decide who was superior in a given competition, such as this one between two boxers. Since the point was to decide on a winner, there were no rounds and few restrictions regarding the level of violence. The men simply hit each other as hard as possible until one went down or gave up. The winner received glory, fame, and material rewards.

Hoplites. Most battles between Greek city-states took place on land between massed formations of infantrymen, or "hoplites" [*hoplon* meaning shield]. Serving the community in this way defined one's right to citizenship or membership in the city. Since hoplites wore the same armor and contributed equally to the battle line, the nature of hoplite warfare helped to define the democratic ethos of the individual citizen.

This competitive spirit existed not just between individuals on the athletic field but also between communities, where it took the more dangerous and destructive form of armed conflicts over borderlands, trade, minerals, religious shrines, prestige, and other valuable resources. Wars of one sort or another were characteristic of city-state relations, as they were of relations between states in Eastern Zhou China and Vedic South Asia during the same period. Almost no year enjoyed complete peace, and the incessant battles fueled new developments in military equipment, such as the heavy armor that gave its name to the hoplites, or infantrymen, and in tactics, such as the standard blocklike configuration (called a *phalanx* by the Greeks) in which the regular rank and file fought.

These wars were so destructive that they threatened to destabilize the world of the city-states. The bigger the states and the more resources that they had, the more likely their embroilment in warfare, even to the detriment of their own people. The longest and most famous of these conflicts was the Peloponnesian War (431–404 BCE), fought between Athens and Sparta, the two largest and most powerful of the Greek city-states. It dragged on for decades, eating away the resources of both of these great polities and the numerous cities that allied themselves with one side or the other; Athens never fully recovered from its defeat. On the other hand, the superiority in land warfare developed in the course of the persistent clashes between the Greek city-states enabled them to defend themselves successfully against external enemies who outnumbered them, sometimes against considerably larger armies. Earlier in the fifth century BCE, the Greek cities, led by Athens, had managed to defeat Persians Darius I and Xerxes, though the kings mounted huge expeditions against Greece that spanned more than a decade (see Chapter 4).

ECONOMIC INNOVATIONS AND POPULATION MOVEMENT

Besides novel political structures, the Mediterranean communities also created economic innovations, such as the alphabet, coins, and the central marketplace, which facilitated trade and were well adapted to the fragmented and yet interconnected human ecology of the Mediterranean. As a result, city-states entered into a period of accelerated economic growth in the ninth and eighth centuries BCE. Even more spectacular than the obvious signs of expansion, such as population growth and rapid urbanization, was the speed with which these city-states began to establish colonies throughout the Mediterranean, wherever they found resources and trade. Their superior military technology, developed and tested in intense conflicts among themselves, enabled them to easily defeat any local resistance to their land takeovers. Moreover, in the course of trade and colonization, the

Mediterranean peoples also came to buy or capture as slaves the inhabitants of frontier communities to the north. The labor of these slaves further contributed to the city-states' wealth and growth.

FREE MARKETS AND MONEY-BASED ECONOMIES Since they were not living within a top-down bureaucratic and administrative structure, the residents of the new cities of the Mediterranean had to devise new ways to run their own affairs. They developed open trading markets and a system of money that enabled buyers and sellers to know the precise value of commodities so that exchanges worked quickly and efficiently. The Greek historian Herodotus, who journeyed widely throughout the eastern Mediterranean and Southwest Asia in the mid–fifth century BCE, observed that the new city-states had at their center a marketplace (*agora*), a large open area in which individuals bought and sold commodities. He found no such public commercial spaces set aside in Egypt or the cities of Babylonia.

Soon most transactions involving goods required money rather than barter or gift exchange; coins also were used to buy services, and such payment may have been used at first mainly to hire mercenary soldiers. In the absence of large bureaucracies to manage commerce, the new Mediterranean cities relied on money to connect the producers and buyers of goods and services with each other, often over long dis-

The Agora. The agora, or central open marketplace, was one of the core defining features of Mediterranean city-states. At its center, each city had one of these open-air plazas, the heart of its commercial, religious, social, and political life. When a new city was founded, the agora was one of the first places that the colonists measured out. The large rectangular-shaped open area in this picture is the agora of the Greek colonial city of Cyrene (in modern-day Libya).

Mediterranean Coins. From the sixth century BCE onward, money in the form of precious metal coins began spreading through the city-states of the Mediterranean, beginning with the Greek city-states in the western parts of what is today Turkey, then spreading to the other Greek *poleis* and beyond. On the left here is the classic tetradrachm (four-drachma piece) coin of Athens with its owl of the goddess Athena; on the right is a silver coin of shekel weight produced by the city of Carthage in the western Mediterranean.

tances. By the end of the fifth century BCE, a striking variety of coins was being issued by Greek city-states, and the use of coins spread to non-Greek peoples nearby, including the Phoenicians, Etruscans, and Persians. During the same period, around 500 BCE, money was independently developed and also came into common use in Vedic South Asia and in Eastern Zhou China.

TRADE AND COLONIZATION   The search for high-value commodities, especially such metals as silver, iron, copper, and tin, drove the first traders westward across the Mediterranean. Early Greek traders and settlers were attracted to the western coast of Italy by its iron deposits.

By about 500 BCE, the Phoenicians, Greeks, and others who had set sail from their homes in the eastern Mediterranean had planted new city-states around the shores of the western Mediterranean and the Black Sea; historians and archaeologists have identified dozens attributable to the Phoenicians and hundreds that were Greek. Once established, these offshoots became completely independent entities, and their independence enabled them to spread rapidly. These colonial communities transformed the coastal world. City-based life became common everywhere, from southern Spain and western Italy to the Crimea on the Black Sea.

With amazing speed, seaborne communications helped create a Mediterranean-wide urban culture embraced by the wealthy and powerful elites across the region. This cultural movement witnessed the spread of material elements from the east to cover the whole of the Mediterranean. Found among the local elites of Tartessos in southern Spain, among Gallic chiefs in southern France, and among the Etruscan and Roman nobles of central Italy, the new shared aristocratic culture featured similar public displays of wealth—richly decorated chariots, elaborate armor and weapons, high-class dining ware, elaborate houses, and public burials. From one end of the Mediterranean to the other (and also around the Black Sea), we can see the gradual emergence not just of city-state communities but also of a culture founded on alphabetic scripts, market-based economies, and private property.

HUMANS FOR SALE: SLAVES AND SLAVERY   The explosion of buying and selling that accompanied the rise of the city-state and the expansion of trade and colonization also produced an ethos in which all the different things that the city dwellers needed, even human beings, were given a monetary value. Turning men, women, and children into objects of commerce, bought and sold on a large scale in markets, created something novel—a new form of slavery called *chattel slavery*, as human beings were treated as property. This

Prisoners of War. Constant warfare both among the Greek city-states and with their "barbarian" neighbors produced prisoners of war. The Greek convention was to permit the ransoming of fellow Greeks—as in this illustration of Spartans captured by the Athenians in the Peloponnesian War. Prisoners taken from "barbarians," however, were almost inevitably sold into slavery.

chattels for the next 2,000 years. This trade in humans was immensely profitable. Indeed, it was one of the most profitable businesses of the entire Mediterranean.

ENCOUNTERS WITH FRONTIER COMMUNITIES   The forces creating the new world of the Mediterranean cities obviously changed the lives of the people living in them and in the rural lands immediately around them, as the new identity of the individual citizen and his family took shape. But these same forces significantly affected those much further away, in the lands of northern and central Europe, whose inhabitants lived in ethnic groups. Whether they wished it or not, peoples as diverse as the Celts and Germans in western Europe and the Scythians to the north of the Black Sea became integrated into the expanding cities' networks of violence, conquest, and trade.

In the rural lands and mountainous regions surrounding this mosaic of urban communities scattered around the Mediterranean Sea was a different world of tribes and ethnic groups. In these frontier communities, people lived in roaming nomadic bands, in isolated settlements, or in small villages. By this time, most of Europe—including Spain in the west, most of France, and the lands along and north of the Danube River—had created a culture based on bronze- and ironworking technologies. Kinship and cooperation held these communities together, but they were just as likely to resort to violence to settle their differences as were the cities of the Mediterranean. Here, change took place much more slowly, impeded by the densely wooded forests, mountainous terrain, and inhospitable climates that challenged easy movement and communications by land—and also hindered by pervasive illiteracy.

Increasingly drawn to the wealth of the city-states and wanting what the city-states produced—money, wine, ornate clothing, weapons—the tribal peoples often became an armed threat to the core societies of the Mediterranean, as they sometimes tried to acquire the desired commodities through force rather than through trade. These frontier peoples convulsed the settled urban societies of the Mediterranean in repeated wavelike incursions that fell most severely between 2200 and 2000 BCE, then again between 1200 and 1000 BCE, and finally between 400 and 200 BCE. Called "barbarians" (*barbaroi*), a mocking name given by the Greeks to foreigners unable to speak their language, the invaders in fact were not much different from the Phoenicians or Greeks who themselves had sought new homes and a better future by large-scale migrations. In colonizing the Mediterranean, they too had violently dispossessed the original inhabitants. The Celts, Gauls, Germans, Scythians, and other northerners came to the Mediterranean first as conquerors. Later, when Mediterranean empires grew more powerful and could successfully keep them at bay, they were imported as slaves. Because the Greeks and the western Phoenicians regarded these external peoples with whom they came into contact as uncivilized and savage, the lands of these outsiders could be seized and col-

commercial type of slavery spread quickly. Where additional labor was needed, especially for dangerous and exhausting tasks like mining, slave laborers were purchased and owned by the freeborn citizens. The proportion of slaves in different places could vary considerably: in Athens, the largest and most economically powerful of the Greek city-states, slaves may well have formed a fifth, or even a quarter, of the whole population. But whatever their absolute or relative numbers, slaves were essential to every one of the new city-states, providing manual and technical labor of all kinds and producing the agricultural surpluses that supported the urban population.

The new seaborne communications networks of the Mediterranean greatly enhanced the ability to acquire and to transport the slaves that the urban economies demanded. At this time, supply lines were first established to what would become the main sources for slaves, especially the lands around the Black Sea—zones that would furnish human onized. And these "barbarians" (as they regarded them) could be captured and sold as commodities in the new marketplaces of the Mediterranean.

NEW IDEAS

As we have already seen, new ways of thinking about the world emerged from the competitive atmosphere found inside each Greek city-state, as well as from the rivalries between them. Moreover, since the Mediterranean city-states imposed very few top-down controls, such as existed in the kingdoms of Southwest Asia, their citizens had to devise methods for managing and directing their own affairs. In the absence of monarchical or priestly rule, ideas and beliefs were free to arise, circulate, and clash. Individuals seeking to establish the validity of their thinking about the nature of the gods, the best state, what is good, or even whether or not to go to war, argued publicly with those holding other and sometimes strongly opposing views. In these cities, there was no final authority—whether a god-king, a holy priest, or a huge bureaucracy—to give any particular idea a final stamp of approval and force its general acceptance.

NATURALISTIC SCIENCE AND REALISTIC ART Given these new opportunities, some curious and daring persons in the new city-states developed novel ways of perceiving the cosmos and representing the environment. Rather than seeing everything around them as the handiwork of all-powerful deities, they took a naturalistic view of humans and their

The Human Form. The human body as it appeared naturally, without any adornment of clothing or accessories, became the ideal set by Greek art. Even gods, as perfect beings, were portrayed in this same natural nude human form. These are two divine portraits produced by Praxiteles: a statue of the god Dionysos and the child Hermes (*left*) and one of the god Apollo (*right*). Such bold nude portraits of humans and gods were sometimes shocking to other peoples.

WARRING IDEAS: PLATO VERSUS ARISTOTLE

Great debates raged among Greek thinkers during the fifth and fourth centuries BCE *over the essence of the world that we live in and how we can have knowledge of it. They began by rejecting religious explanations that posited the existence of creator gods and goddesses, and instead began to seek explanations elsewhere. Some looked to the material world (in primary substances like water), while others turned to abstractions. For example, Pythagoras suggested that numbers were at the basis of everything—a far more revolutionary notion then than it might seem today. Some later thinkers, most notably Plato, took this line of argument further and argued that all existence, and therefore all human knowledge, is based on absolute concepts that are like numbers, existing independent of time and place. Each of them he called an idea, a word whose meanings in Greek include "shape," "form," and "appearance" (its root is the verb "to see").*

In a number of Plato's dialogues, his teacher, Socrates, tries to explain this theory:

Socrates: I am going to try to explain to you the theory of causes that I myself have thought out. . . . I assume that you admit the existence of absolutes like "beauty" and "good" and "size" and the rest. If you admit that these absolutes exist, then I can hope with their help to show you what causes are. . . . I remain obstinately committed . . . to the explanation that the one thing that causes a thing to be "beautiful," for example, is the existence in it of "the beautiful" or its sharing in "the beautiful"[;] . . . and so, is it not also the case that things that we call "big" are big because they share the idea of "bigness" and similarly that things that we call "small" are small because they share in the idea of "smallness"? [Socrates then goes on to dismiss the claim that in calling things "tall" or "small" we are simply describing them in relation to other things.]

Phaedo: I believe that Socrates has persuaded us of these matters and that we have agreed that these different ideas do exist; and he has also persuaded us that the reason why specific things in our world are named after these ideas is that they share in the existence of the specific idea. (Phaedo 99d–102b)

Still other thinkers drew on some of the very first Greek *philosophoi* (knowledge lovers, philosophers) in the sixth century BCE to argue that the basis of all existing things was, quite simply, other things. They rejected the proposal that all the things that we feel, see, hear, and otherwise perceive with our senses are poor copies of permanent ideas of them that exist in a separate, unchangeable sphere of existence. Human knowledge was in fact acquired through the careful observation of existing things and through the

place in the universe. Evidence for this concept of the world comes from their art, which placed an ideal form of the natural world as perceived by human eyes at its center. Artists increasingly attempted to picture the world in a more "natural" way, representing humans, objects, and landscapes not in hyperreal, abstract, or formal ways but rather more or less as they appeared to the human eye of the time in these cities. Even gods increasingly were portrayed as being more or less like humans. Later, these more objective and natural views of humans and nature were themselves turned into ideals, the highest of which was the unadorned human figure: the nude became the centerpiece of Greek art. The public display of the uncovered human body, both in artistic representations and in everyday life (notably in men's athletic training and competition, which normally took place in the nude) signaled

the sharp break between the moral codes of the older traditional societies of the east and those of the revolutionary cities of the Mediterranean. Vase painters such as Exekias (sixth century BCE), spurred on by a desire to be famous, signed their works and became known as individual artists. Sculptors like Praxiteles (mid–fourth century BCE) became famous as artists in their own right. But no less assertive were creative writers, such as the poets Archilochus (fl. c. 700 BCE) and Sappho (born c. 612 BCE), who wrote individual lyrics exploring their own emotions.

Perhaps nothing more vividly evokes this new sense of the individual cut free of the restraints of an autocratic state or a controlling religious system than these poems of Sappho and her peers. In them we see the individual human expressing nothing but his or her own self.

meticulous collection of data about them. Thus in the following passage, in a fundamental statement of his purpose, Aristotle rejects Plato's concept of ideas:

> For the moment, we can simply dismiss the followers of Pythagoras. It is good enough that we have dealt with them briefly. As for the followers of Plato who claim that "ideas" (or "shapes") are the causes or origins of all things, this too is objectionable. First of all, in their struggle to find causes for things that exist in our world of sense perceptions, they simply introduce as many new things into the equation as they are attempting to explain[;] . . . so their "ideas" are as many . . . as the things whose causes they are seeking to explain and for which reason they were led to invent these ideas. They must do this because they must create an idea to match every substance that exists in our real everyday world . . . and also one in the realm of the eternal heavenly entities. Not one of the arguments by which they try to demonstrate that these ideas actually exist can demonstrate or prove their claim. From some of their arguments, indeed, no real conclusions follow. From other arguments of theirs it only follows that there must be ideas of things for which they themselves hold no such ideas can exist. (*Metaphysics* 1.9, 990a–b)

In other works Aristotle further contested Plato's claims and put forth his own views about how humans could gain reliable knowledge of the world in which they lived:

> All teaching and learning by means of rational argument is based on our existing knowledge and observations; . . . and I think that we have reliable knowledge of each thing . . . when we think that we have found the cause because of which that thing exists—what is the cause of that thing and of nothing else, with the result that this thing or this fact cannot be other than it is. That this is real knowledge of something is very clear—just look at those people who falsely claim to know [i.e., the followers of Plato and others] as opposed to those who possess real knowledge. . . . We know what we do by demonstration, by showing that it is true. By demonstration I mean an argument that produces real knowledge, . . . all of which is based on a knowledge and observation of facts and things . . . of these things the most important are the prior ones. By prior I mean those objects that are closer to human sense perceptions which are better known to us. . . . But I also say that not all real knowledge can in fact be demonstrated or proved. (*Posterior Analytics* 1.1–3, 71a–72b)

→ *What factors in the makeup of these Mediterranean city-states encouraged such debates over fundamental values and concepts?*

→ *Other than the philosophical debates themselves, what provoked Plato and Aristotle to advance such different concepts of knowledge?*

→ *Might such factors be linked to other major developments of the time, occurring not just in the Greek city-states but elsewhere (in South or East Asia, for example)?*

SOURCE: Plato, *Phaedo*, 99d–102b; Aristotle, *Metaphysics*, 1.9 = 990a–b; *Posterior Analytics*, 1.1-3 = 71a–72b. All translations are by Brent Shaw.

NEW THINKING AND GREEK PHILOSOPHERS These new thinkers, however, were deeply influenced by existing ideas on the gods, the environment, and the cosmos developed in Southwest Asia. Not surprisingly, the first generation of new thinkers came from eastern Anatolia, a contact zone in which Greeks had the greatest exposure to ideas from the Persian Empire. Armed with their own ideas and with this borrowed knowledge, thinkers in cities such as Miletus and Ephesus did not accept the earlier explanations of how and why things came to be the way they were in the universe. Rather than focusing on the role of the gods, they looked to nature itself, which many held to be made up of some fundamental substance (usually one of the traditional elements: earth, air or breath, fire, or water). Thales (c. 636–546 BCE), the earliest known theorist of these ideas, believed that water was the primal substance from which all other things were created. He was also said to have predicted the eclipse of the sun on May 28, 585 BCE.

As each thinker competed to outdo his peers in offering persuasive and comprehensive explanations, the theories became ever more radical. Men like Xenophanes (c. 570–480 BCE), from the city of Colophon, even came to doubt the very existence of gods as they had been portrayed and, rather, asserted that there was only one general divine aura that suffused all creation. He pointed out that each ethnic group in fact produced images of gods that were more or less like themselves. Ethiopians made representations of their gods with dark skins and broad noses, while Thracians depicted their gods as blue-eyed redheads. Such variation in human beliefs about the attributes of the divinities suggested that the gods existed only in the human imagination.

Some of the new thinkers proposed that the real world had some physical and tangible basis. Among them was Democritus (c. 460–370 BCE), who claimed that everything that humans saw was made up of small and ultimately indivisible particles. Since the particles were indivisible, Democritus called them *atoma* (uncuttables), or atoms (a word that we have come to use in a similar sense). Even more radical were thinkers like Pythagoras from Samos, who held that a wide range of physical phenomena in the world, from masks to music, were in fact based in numbers; thus in a sense he foreshadowed the modern-day digital revolution. He devoted himself to studying numbers, though the famous "Pythagorean theorem" attributed to him was already known to Babylonian priests and mathematicians—and was borrowed from them, along with other eastern ideas.

Such thinkers may in some respects appear eerily modern, but in many others they remained men of their time. Although Democritus did produce a primitive atomic theory, he did not view the cosmos with the eyes of a scientist of today: like other ancient theorists, he regarded it as a single great huge organism, living and breathing. And most still considered the particles and elements of nature to be suffused with profound divine powers. Yet they challenged commonly accepted values and ideas, including traditional religious beliefs. Very soon these new ideas spread far from their birthplace in the eastern Aegean through the web of Greek and Phoenician city-states to the whole of the Mediterranean.

The competition between ideas led to a more aggressive mode of public thinking. The Greeks called this new speculation *philosophia* (love of wisdom), and the professional thinkers who were good at it *philosophoi* (philosophers). Some of the earliest recorded debates dealt with the nature of the cosmos, the environment, and the physical elements of human existence. But by the fifth century BCE, philosophers were focusing on humans and their place in society. These debates were lively dialogues—a term that itself derives from a Greek verb meaning "to speak alternately"—deeply informed by the identities of those engaged in them: autonomous human beings, who were almost always adult male citizens of a city-state. They argued about the fundamental questions of human existence much as they debated civic policy in their political assemblies.

In the early fourth century BCE, the prolonged and unremitting conflicts between the major city-states created greater economic difficulties: poverty became more widespread, cities had fewer resources for benefits for their citizens, and social discontent and civil violence were on the rise. Responses to these social and economic problems varied, but the crisis provoked skepticism about the political viability of independent cities. What *was* to be done?

Some thinkers tried to describe an ideal city, possessing harmonious relationships among all of its parts and therefore free from corruption and political decline. Socrates (469–399 BCE), a philosopher in Athens, asked questions designed to encourage people to reflect on ethics and morality; he stressed the importance of honor and integrity as opposed to wealth and power, as had Confucius in Eastern Zhou China and the Buddha in Vedic South Asia. Plato (427–347 BCE) was a student of Socrates who presented Socrates' philosophy in a series of dialogues (much as Confucius's students had

Chronology

	1500 BCE	1400 BCE	1300 BCE	1200 BCE	1100 BCE	1000 BCE
THE AMERICAS	▌Olmec culture emerges and diffuses throughout Mesoamerica, 1500–400 BCE					
		▌Chavín culture flourishes in Central Andes of South America, 1400–400 BCE				
SUB-SAHARAN AFRICA						
SOUTH ASIA					Sixteen State period, 1000–600 BCE ▌	
					Vedic migrations ▌	
THE MEDITERRANEAN					Migration of Sea Peoples ▌	
EAST ASIA						

written down his thoughts). In *The Republic*, Plato described his vision of a perfect city that would be ruled by philosopher-kings. He thought that if fallible humans could imitate this model city more closely, they could create polities less susceptible to the decline and decay that affected the Greek city-states of his own day. This belief was an outgrowth of his more general theory of "ideas"—eternal archetypes that are only imperfectly copied by their instantiations in the real world. For the followers of Socrates and Plato, these perfect conceptions provided a guide to pursuing not just state and government affairs but all forms of human knowledge. The more closely that faulty and error-prone human constructions could be made to match these eternal, perfect, and unchanging models, the better.

In the next generation, Plato's most famous pupil answered the same question differently. Aristotle (384–322 BCE) was deeply interested in the natural world; he believed that by collecting all the ascertainable facts about a given thing—no matter how imperfect they might be—and studying them closely, it was possible to achieve a better understanding of the general patterns in the world around him. Those patterns could reveal what ways of living were most successful both in nature and in culture. Following this inductive approach, Aristotle collected evidence from more than 150 Greek city-states, and in *The Politics* he described the institutional responses and codes of moral conduct that he believed would enable urban communities to function better. Neither Plato nor Aristotle, however, was able to promote and preserve the city-state as the exemplary civilized society. Indeed, during their lives, the world of the independent city-state was to change dramatically, as new forms of bigger states emerged and later became dominant.

CONCLUSION

Afro-Eurasia's four great river basin areas—the Tigris-Euphrates, the Nile, the Yellow and Yangzi, and the Indus—were still important in the first millennium BCE. But their time as centers of world cultures, the hubs of pioneering civilizations, was passing. They had to yield some of their leadership to regions that had previously been on the fringes of their worlds. In those peripheral regions, smaller-scale polities came into being; and the increased face-to-face contacts fostered by these city-states (in the Mediterranean world), smaller territorial states (in China), and smaller kingdoms and oligarchies (in Vedic South Asia) created great social dynamism. In time, the new polities were destined to expand and be incorporated into massive empires. The Mauryan Empire, later established by the Magadha kingdom (see Chapter 6), would grow out of the turbulent political competition in northern India and eventually spread over almost the whole of South Asia. The Warring States of China prepared the way for the later Qin and Han empires.

The later developments in each region can be traced back to small beginnings in this period. Thinkers came to the fore with perspectives quite different from those that had dominated the great river basin civilizations. The Greek philosophers put forward new views about nature, about their political world, and about human relations and values, all based on secular rather than religious ideas. They introduced new concepts captured in a new vocabulary, as the terms *democracy*, *philosophy*, and *politics* became part of this new discourse. In South Asia, dissident thinkers challenged the prevailing Brahmanic

'00 BCE	800 BCE	700 BCE	600 BCE	500 BCE	400 BCE	300 BCE	200 BCE

■ *Nok culture in West Africa (early iron smelting), 600 BCE*
Meroe kingdom in Nubia, 4th century BCE–3rd century CE ■

■ *Cities emerge on Ganges plain, 500 BCE*
■ *Vardhamana Mahavira (540–468 BCE) popularizes Jainism*
■ *Siddhartha Gautama (c. 563–483 BCE) develops Buddhist principles*

■ *Phoenician settlements and trade networks emerge, c. 800 BCE*
■ *Greek and other city-states flourish*
Socrates, Plato, and Aristotle teach in Athens, 5th and 4th centuries BCE ■   ■ *Peloponnesian War, 431–404 BCE*

■ *Eastern Zhou dynasty, 770–221 BCE*   ■ *Mozir, c. 479–438 BCE*
■ *Spring and Autumn period of Eastern Zhou dynasty, 722–481 BCE*   ■ *Zhuangzi, c. 369–286 BCE*
Laozi (founder of Daoism), c. 605–520 BCE ■   *Warring State period, 403–221 BCE* ■   ■ *Xunzi, fl. 298–238 BCE*
■ *Confucius, c. 551–479 BCE*   *Han Fei, 280–233 BCE* ■

spiritual and political order, and the Buddha, the region's leading religious figure, created a new belief system, much less hierarchical than its Vedic predecessor. In China, the political instability of the Warring States gave scholars like Confucius an opportunity to insert themselves into the political debate, where they promoted a political and social philosophy that stressed respect for social hierarchy.

Around the world, distinctive regional cultures defined by shared faiths, texts, and the teachers and prophets who recited them were on the rise. Even where the contacts with other societies were much less intense, as in the Americas and sub-Saharan Africa, a great deal of innovation and trail blazing occurred. Indeed, in this period we see the origins of many social developments to come. In the Americas, the Olmecs came to terms with their environment by developing a view of the world in which angry gods had to be appeased through human sacrifice and elaborate temples were erected to allow the peoples of a vast region of villages to pay homage to the same deities. In sub-Saharan Africa as well, pockets of settled peoples began to devise complex cultural foundations for community life that would extend well beyond local districts. The Mediterranean and Egyptian cultures continued to expand their influence up the Nile through the Nubian corridor into sub-Saharan Africa. The most spectacular example of a sub-Saharan and Egyptian synthesis was the polity and culture of Meroe. There pharaonic influences mixed with those of tropical Africa. There, too, merchants intensified contacts with North Africa and other parts of Sudanic Africa. In addition, the Nok peoples of West Africa promoted interregional trade and cultural contact, as the peoples of sub-Saharan Africa, like those living in Eurasia and North Africa, expanded their geographical horizons.

The world was being carved up into culturally distinct regions. All these ideas newly forged in Afro-Eurasia, the Americas, and sub-Saharan Africa were to long endure. In whatever region of the world they were created, they had a continuing and powerful impact on the societies that later emerged.

STUDY QUESTIONS

Ⓢ WWNORTON.COM/STUDYSPACE

1. Explain how small states created new cultural and social pathways and ideas in Afro-Eurasia in the first millennium BCE. What alternative approaches to philosophy, economics, and religion emerged in East Asia, South Asia, and western Afro-Eurasia?

2. Explain the "war of ideas" that occurred during the first millennium in China. How did Legalism, Confucianism, and Daoism influence political developments during the Warring States period?

3. Analyze the impact of commerce and urbanization on the Vedic belief system in South Asia during the first millennium

BCE. Why were urban audiences more receptive to Buddhist and other challenges than to Vedic concepts?

4. Compare and contrast Buddhist and Confucian philosophies. What problems and issues did they address, and what solutions did they propose?

5. Explain the broad cultural features that united Olmec and Chavín society in the Americas in the first millennium BCE. To what extent did each cultural group leave an imprint on their respective regions?

6. Analyze the extent to which the diverse peoples of sub-Saharan Africa were connected to each other and the larger world during the first millennium BCE. What processes brought various groups together, and what kept them apart?

7. Describe the political and economic innovations in the Mediterranean world in the first millennium BCE. What impact did these ideas have on peoples living on the periphery of that world?

8. Analyze how the use of coins shaped economic systems in Afro-Eurasia during the first millennium BCE. Which regions adopted this practice?

9. Compare and contrast the Greek philosophers Socrates, Plato, and Aristotle with Confucius in China and the Buddha in South Asia. What was similar and what was different in their proposals for creating a better world?

FURTHER READINGS

Adams, William Y., *Nubia: Corridor to Africa* (1977). The authoritative historical overview of Nubia, the area of present-day Sudan just south of Egypt and a geographical connecting point between the Mediterranean and sub-Saharan Africa.

Aubet, Maria Eugenia, *The Phoenicians and the West*, 2nd ed. (2001). The basic survey of the Phoenician colonization of the western Mediterranean and Atlantic, with special attention to recent archaeological discoveries.

Barker, Graeme, and Tom Rasmussen, *The Etruscans* (1998). The most up-to-date introduction to this important pre-Roman society in the Italian peninsula, with strong emphasis on broad social and material patterns of development as indicated by the archaeological evidence.

Burkert, Walter, *Greek Religion*, trans. John Raffan (1985). The best one-volume introduction to early Greek religion, placing the Greeks in their larger Mediterranean and Near Eastern contexts.

Burns, Karen Olsen, *Ancient South America* (1994). A very useful overview of recent debates and conclusions about pre-Columbian archaeology in South America, including both the Andes and the lowland and coastal regions.

Cartledge, Paul (ed.), *The Cambridge Illustrated History of Ancient Greece* (2002). An excellent history of the Greek city-states down to the time of Alexander the Great.

Chakravarti, Uma, *The Social Dimensions of Early Buddhism* (1987). A description of the life of Buddha drawn from early Buddhist texts.

Cho-yun, Hsu, *Ancient China in Transition* (1965). An account of the political, economic, social, and intellectual changes that occurred during the Warring States period.

Coarelli, Filippo (ed.), *Etruscan Cities* (1975). A brilliantly and lavishly illustrated guide to the material remains of the Etruscans: their cities, their magnificent tombs, and their architecture, painting, sculpture, and other art.

Coe, Michael, et al. (eds.), *The Olmec World: Ritual and Rulership* (1996). A collection of field-synthesizing articles with important illustrations, based on one of the most comprehensive exhibitions of Olmec art in the world.

Confucius, *The Analects (Lun Yü)*, trans. D. C. Lau (1979). An outstanding translation of the words of Confucius as recorded by his major disciples. Includes valuable historical material needed to provide the context for Confucius's teachings.

Garlan, Yvon, *Slavery in Ancient Greece*, trans. Janet Lloyd (1988). A treatment of the emergence, development, and institutionalization of chattel slavery in the Greek city-states.

———, *War in the Ancient World: A Social History*, trans. Janet Lloyd (1976). A discussion of the emergence of the forms of warfare, including male citizens fighting in hoplite phalanxes and the development of siege warfare, that were typical of the Greek city-states.

Finley, M. I., and H. W. Pleket, *The Olympic Games: The First Thousand Years* (2005). A fine description of the most famous of the Greek games; it explains how they exemplify the competitive spirit that marked many aspects of the Greek city-states.

Iliffe, John, *Africans: The History of a Continent*, 2nd ed. (2007). A first-rate scholarly survey of Africa from its beginnings, with a strong emphasis on demography.

Kagan, Donald, *The Peloponnesian War* (2004). A vivid description of the major war that pitted the major Greek city-states, including Athens and Sparta, against each other over the latter half of the fifth century BCE.

Lancel, Serge, *Carthage: A History*, trans. Antonia Nevill (1997). By far the best single-volume history of the most important Phoenician colony in the Mediterranean.

Lewis, Mark Edward, *Sanctioned Violence in Early China* (1990). An analysis of the use of sanctioned violence as an element of statecraft from the Warring States period to the formation of the Qin and Han empires in the second half of the first millennium BCE.

———, *Writing and Authority in Early China* (1999). A revisionist account of the central role of writing and persuasion in providing models for the invention of a Chinese world empire.

Lloyd, G. E. R., *Early Greek Science: Thales to Aristotle* (1970). An especially clear and concise introduction to the main developments and intellectuals that marked the emergence of critical secular thinking in the early Greek world.

Lloyd, G. E. R., and Nathan Sivin, *The Way and the Word: Science and Medicine in Early China and Greece* (2002). A comprehensive rethinking of the social and political settings in ancient China and city-state Greece that contributed to the different views of science and medicine that emerged in each place.

Murray, Oswyn, *Early Greece*, 2nd ed. (1993). One of the best introductions to the emergence of the Greek city-states down to the end of the archaic age.

Osborne, Robin, *Archaic and Classical Greek Art* (1998). An outstanding book that clearly explains the main innovations in Greek art, setting them in their historical context.

———, *Greece in the Making, 1200–479 BC* (1999). The standard history of the whole early period of the Greek city-states characterized by an especially fine and judicious mix of archaeological data and literary sources.

Pallottino, Massimo, *The Etruscans,* rev. ed., trans. J. Cremona (1975). A fairly traditional but still classic survey of all aspects of Etruscan history, political and social institutions.

Redford, Donald B., *From Slave to Pharaoh: The Black Experience of Ancient Egypt* (2004). A description of Egypt's twenty-fifth dynasty, which was made up of Sudanese conquerors.

Schaberg, David, *A Patterned Past: Form and Thought in Early Chinese Historiography* (2002). A comprehensive study of the intellectual content of historical anecdotes by the followers of Confucius collected around the fourth century BCE.

Schaps, David, *The Invention of Coinage and the Monetization of Ancient Greece* (2004). A new analysis that offers a broad overview of the emergence of coined money in the Near East and the eastern Mediterranean and its effects on the spread of money-based markets.

Sharma, J. P., *Republics in Ancient India, c. 1500 B.C.–500 B.C.* (1968). Relying on information from early Buddhist texts, this book first revealed that South Asia had not only monarchies but also alternative polities.

Shaw, Thurston, *Nigeria: Its Archaeology and Early History* (1978). An important introduction to the early history of Nigeria by one of that country's leading archaeologists.

Shinnie, P. L., *Ancient Nubia* (1996). An excellent account of the history of the ancient Nubians, who, we are discovering, had great influence on Egypt and also on the rest of tropical Africa.

Snodgrass, Anthony, *Archaic Greece: The Age of Experiment* (1981). A good introduction to the archaeological evidence of archaic Greece.

Taylor, Christopher, Richard Hare, and Jonathan Barnes, *Greek Philosophers* (1999). A fine, succinct one-volume introduction to the major aspects of the three big thinkers who dominated the high period of classical Greek philosophy: Socrates, Plato, and Aristotle.

Torok, Laszlo, *Meroe: Six Studies on the Cultural Identity of an Ancient African State* (1995). A good collection of essays on the most recent work on Meroe.

Welsby, Derek A., *The Kingdom of Kush: The Napatan and Meroitic Empires* (1996). A fine book on these two important Nubian kingdoms.

6

SHRINKING THE AFRO-EURASIAN WORLD, 350 BCE–250 CE

In the burning August heat of 324 BCE, at a town on the Euphrates River that the Greeks called Opis but the local Babylonians called Upî (not far from modern Baghdad), Alexander the Great's crack Macedonian troops declared that they had finally had enough. They had been fighting away from their homeland, in northern Greece, for more than a decade. They had marched from the Mediterranean, forded wide rivers, traversed great deserts and vast plains, trudged over the high mountain passes of present-day Afghanistan, and slogged through the rain-drenched forests of South Asia. Along the way, they had defeated large armies, including those armed with fearsome war elephants. Some had taken wives from the cities and tribes of the vanquished, and the army soon became a giant swarm of ethnically mixed families. This was an army like no other. It did more than just defeat neighbors and rivals—it forcefully connected entire worlds, bringing together peoples and lands.

But conquering in the name of building a new world was not what the soldiers had bargained for. They loved their leader, but many thought that he had gone too far. They had lost companions and grown weary of war. Some had mutinied at Hyphasis, a tributary of the Indus, halting Alexander's advance into South Asia. At Opis, they threatened to desert him altogether. They wanted to return to their families and their homeland. Plucking up their courage, they voiced these resentments to their supreme war commander. Alexander's response was immediate and inspired. In persuading his rebellious troops not to desert him, he evoked the great military triumphs and history-making achievements that he and they had accomplished—his personal rule, stretching from Macedonia to the Indus Valley. It was a monumental achievement to bring together such dispersed places. This grand new far-reaching and landmass-uniting political vision came to an sudden end with Alexander's death at Babylon a year later, in June of 323 BCE, when he was only thirty-two. But even in his own short lifetime, he set in motion cultural and economic forces that would transform Afro-Eurasia.

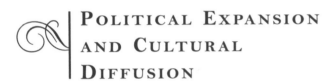

POLITICAL EXPANSION AND CULTURAL DIFFUSION

> → *How did political expansion enable a variety of exchanges between different parts of the Afro-Eurasian world?*

Alexander's armies, linked to Greek population movements throughout Afro-Eurasia, ushered in an age of thinking and practices that transformed Greek achievements into a common portable culture that is called "Greek-based," or Hellenistic. While this cultural movement did not eradicate local cultures, its influence spread outward from Greece to all shores of the Mediterranean, into parts of sub-Saharan Africa, and across Southwest Asia and through the Iranian plateau into central and south Asia; it even had echoes in China. As a cultural system that linked widely removed areas and forced other cultural systems to respond to its unifying aspirations, Hellenism was a new phenomenon. By diffusing well beyond its homeland, Hellenism brought worlds together; it did not lead to a single common culture, but it did provoke shifts and adjustments in the cultures it contacted. In that process, many of the world's regions, from China to Africa, became more internally integrated.

What Alexander did, along with conquering, was to lay the foundations for state systems and introduce some institutional stability for, and protection and patronage of, trading systems. Instead of plundering, governments promoted trade. With their fear of attack reduced, cities could thrive. And increasingly, states encouraged the use of money and a common language for contracts, both innovations that aided commercial transactions. In effect, the early passageways that carried small bands of traders were replaced by major commercial arteries. Political expansion became an important enabling condition for all kinds of exchanges, among them commercial, between different parts of the Afro-Eurasian world. One consequence was the emergence of what is called the Silk Road, an artery that for nearly a thousand years would serve as the primary commercial network linking East Asia and the Mediterranean world.

It is impossible to make sense of Alexander and this Hellenistic movement without acknowledging the importance of some underlying ways in which the distinct parts of the world were already in contact and in some places converging. In-

Focus Questions SHRINKING THE AFRO-EURASIAN WORLD

> → *How did political expansion enable a variety of exchanges between different parts of the Afro-Eurasian world?*
>
> → *How did the spread of Hellenism reshape the Mediterranean world?*
>
> → *How did Hellenistic and pastoral nomadic cultures influence central and South Asia?*
>
> → *In what ways did the transformation of Buddhism represent cultural integration in South Asia?*
>
> → *How did long-distance exchanges alter the cultural geography of Eurasia and North Africa?*
>
> → *What factors contributed to the growth of the Indian Ocean sea trade?*

WWNORTON.COM/STUDYSPACE

deed, political expansion driven by military conquest followed a period of extensive migration, trade, and technological diffusion over very long distances. Alexander's conquests did not take arbitrary pathways; long-distance trading and cross-cultural exchanges had laid the trails for him. Yet cross-cultural contacts were limited by the weakness of institutional ties. In the absence of armies, legal codes, and governors to integrate vast regions, cultural and economic influences lacked protection and promotion, and thus could not spread over long distances. Such expansion would accelerate with the emergence of a powerful—if fleeting—center that would unite parts of Asia and Africa. Slowly a new idea took hold: the world's parts could be integrated by common cultures and shared commodities. Political expansion occurred from Macedonia in northern Greece to the Buddhist worlds of South Asia, first under the Persians and then under Alexander. And just as Hellenistic influences followed on the heels of Alexander's conquests, so Buddhist influences followed the conquests of the Mauryan dynasty in South Asia. Backed by a major dynasty, with its belief systems carried outward by powerful armies and legions of magistrates and monks, Buddhism spread far and wide. From the corners of South Asia, Buddhism now became the world's most expansive religious system.

From the corners of South Asia, Buddhism now became the world's most expansive religious system.

The interconnections of trade and cultural diffusion therefore enhanced regional integration, which unfolded in specific political contexts—marking a shift to territorial kingdoms (states ruled by powerful monarchs). The changes were mutually reinforcing: the Persian, Macedonian, and Mauryan conquests were made possible by some existing links across long distances, and the political shakeups and political integration they caused created immense opportunities for other ways of absorbing societies, notably trade, migration, and religious conversion. Conquests yielded to new kinds of contacts and stimulated old ones, as traders, moving goods by sea and land, quickly took advantage of the institutional links forged across long distances. The first long-distance caravan trading, and even fleets, began to ply regular trade routes, setting up commercial hubs that would crisscross the landmass from China to the Mediterranean. Merchants joined with monks and administrators in helping to tie disparate parts of Afro-Eurasia into a more interconnected whole, thereby enabling busy sea-lanes and the Silk Road to flourish.

This chapter examines how peoples from the western end of Afro-Eurasia sent shock waves east, and how the Hellenistic movement created new ways of imagining societies in far-flung regions. Its influences, both direct and indirect, were enormous. A few centuries after his conquests, the world looked very different from the realms Alexander had traversed.

THE EMERGENCE OF A COSMOPOLITAN WORLD

→ *How did the spread of Hellenism reshape the Mediterranean world?*

The armed campaigns of a minor Greek people, the Macedonians, and their leader, Alexander the Great, began a drive for empire from the west. Alexander's rapid and novel use of new kinds of armed force in a series of lightning attacks on the Persian Empire broke down earlier barriers between the Mediterranean world and the rest of Southwest Asia. The massive transfers of wealth and power that resulted from his conquests sped up the development of the Mediterranean into a new, more unified world of common economic and cultural exchanges. The whole period and the cultural movement associated with it are called Hellenistic (a term derived from the Greeks' name for themselves, *Hellēnes*). Alexander's ambition drove Hellenistic influences as far as Vedic South Asia and contributed to the flourishing of a new power, the Mauryan Empire, which united the smaller warring states in South Asia.

CONQUESTS OF ALEXANDER THE GREAT

The story of Alexander the Great has been recounted by many historians and biographers, yet it remains one of the most fascinating in world history. Alexander, who came from the small frontier state of Macedonia, to the north of Greece, was a pathbreaking conqueror who transformed the Mediterranean world. For a dozen years, between 334 and 323 BCE, he commanded a compact and highly mobile force that was armed with the advanced military technologies developed in the incessant warfare between Greek city-states.

Under Alexander's predecessors—especially his father, Philip II—Macedonia had developed into a large ethnic and territorial state. Philip had unified Macedonia and then gone on to conquer neighboring states, one of which had gold mines that he used to finance new military technology and a disciplined, full-time army. Heavily armored infantry in closely arrayed phalanxes, allied with the large-scale shock cavalry formations from his native land, were paid for not just with the huge income from the local gold mines but with the enormous profits of a slave trade that passed directly through Macedonia. By the early 330s BCE, Philip had crushed the old

NORTH SEA

GERMANIC PEOPLES

BALTIC PEOPLES

C E L T I C   P E O P L E S

STEPPE

SCYTHIAN

ARAL SEA

CASPIAN SEA

CONQUESTS OF ALEXANDER THE GREAT, 323 BCE

GREEK CITY STATES

GREEK CITY STATES

GREEK CITY STATES

BLACK SEA

CAUCASIAN PEOPLES

Massilia

Rome

Pella

MACEDONIA

Byzantium

Ancyra

Gordium

Sardis

Troy

Delphi

Athens

Sparta

Samarkand

Bukhara

Merv

Bactr

Herat

Kandahar

Carthage

CARTHAGE

Syracuse

MEDITERRANEAN   SEA

RHODES

Antioch

Tigris R.

Euphrates R.

Gaugamela

Ecbatana

SELEUCID EMPIRE

Tyre

Seleucia

Babylon

Susa

Jerusalem

Persepolis

Persian Gulf

Alexandria

Memphis

Siwa Oasis

PTOLEMAIC EMPIRE

A R A B S

ARABIAN PENINSULA

Nile R.

RED SEA

KUSH

SAHARA   DESERT

SAHARAN PEOPLES

Niger R.

ARABIAN

SUB-SAHARAN

AFRICA

NOK

ATLANTIC OCEAN

Congo R.

B A N T U

INDIAN

MADAGASCAR

KALAHARI DESERT

| 0 | 500 | 1000 Miles |
| 0 | 500 | 1000 Kilometers |

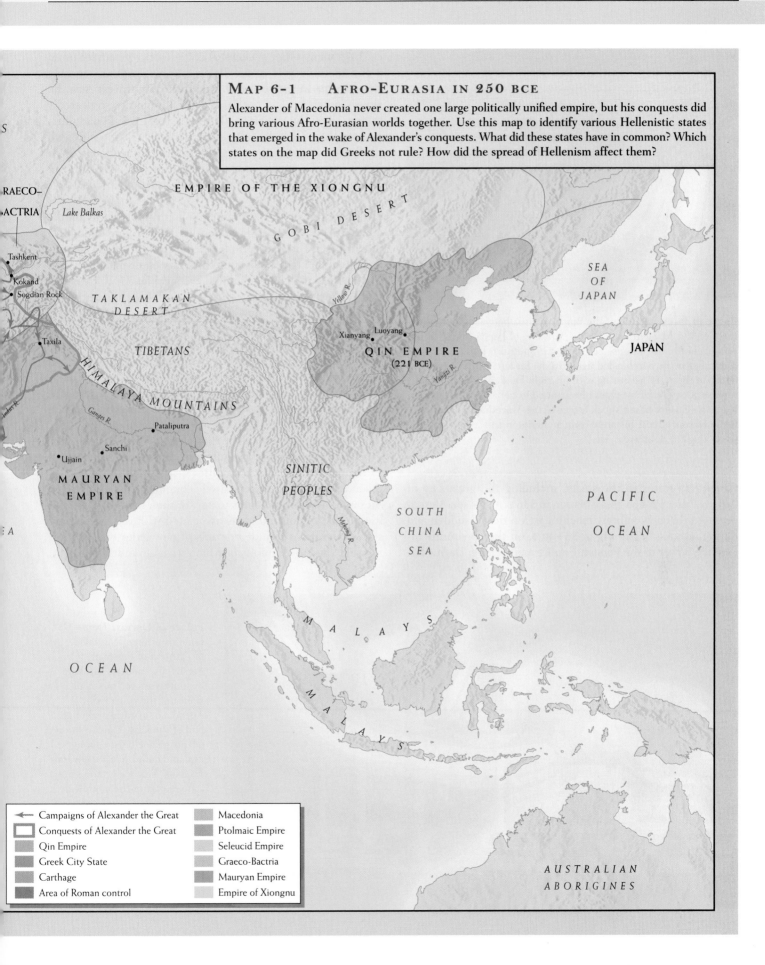

MAP 6-1   AFRO-EURASIA IN 250 BCE

Alexander of Macedonia never created one large politically unified empire, but his conquests did bring various Afro-Eurasian worlds together. Use this map to identify various Hellenistic states that emerged in the wake of Alexander's conquests. What did these states have in common? Which states on the map did Greeks not rule? How did the spread of Hellenism affect them?

EMPIRE OF THE XIONGNU

GRAECO-
BACTRIA

Lake Balkas

GOBI DESERT

Tashkent

Kokand

Sogdian Rock

TAKLAMAKAN
DESERT

Yellow R.

SEA
OF
JAPAN

Taxila

Xianyang   Luoyang

TIBETANS

QIN EMPIRE
(221 BCE)

JAPAN

HIMALAYA MOUNTAINS

Yangzi R.

Ganges R.

Pataliputra

Sanchi

SINITIC
PEOPLES

PACIFIC

Ujjain

MAURYAN
EMPIRE

OCEAN

SOUTH
CHINA
SEA

Mekong R.

SEA

OCEAN

M A L A Y S

M A L A Y S

M A L A Y S

Campaigns of Alexander the Great   Macedonia

Conquests of Alexander the Great   Ptolmaic Empire

Qin Empire   Seleucid Empire

Greek City State   Graeco-Bactria

Carthage   Mauryan Empire

Area of Roman control   Empire of Xiongnu

AUSTRALIAN
ABORIGINES

Battle of Issus. Mosaic of the Battle of Issus between Alexander the Great of Macedon and Darius, the king of Persia (found as a wall decoration in a house at Pompeii in southern Italy). Alexander is the bareheaded figure to the far left; Darius is the figure to the right, gesturing with his right hand. The men represent two different types of warfare. On horseback, Alexander leads the cavalry-based shock forces of the Macedonian Greeks, while Darius directs his army from a chariot in the style of the great kings of Southwest Asia.

Greek city-states to the south, including the great city of Athens. After Philip's assassination in 336 BCE, his son Alexander used this new military machine in a series of sudden and daring attacks, beginning in 334 BCE, on the apparently invincible power of the Persian Empire and its king, Darius III.

Like many other successful conquerors, Alexander owed a considerable part of his success to his readiness to take risks. In his initial series of forays into Southwest Asia, he simply outpaced and outflanked his adversaries, repeatedly taking them by surprise. Through these rapid assaults, he brought under the rule of his Greek-speaking elites all the lands of the former Persian Empire that extended from Egypt and the shores of the Mediterranean to the interior of what is now Afghanistan as well as to the Indus River valley.

The result of this lightning, violent rampage was hardly an empire, given that Alexander did not live long enough to put in place the institutions needed to hold these distant lands together. But Alexander's military campaigns smashed the barriers that had separated the peoples on the eastern and western ends of Afro-Eurasia. Indeed, the conqueror modeled himself as a new universal figure, a bridge between distant cultures. He epitomized this vision in his choice of wife, Roxana, the daughter of a Bactrian chief from Central Asia, and turned Balkh into a center of operations for two years, reinforcing the long-term importance of the new kingdoms of the Kushan rulers, who would emerge as powerful brokers in the new east-west axis between Asia and the Mediterranean.

Alexander opened a door that changed Afro-Eurasia forever. His conquests exposed Syria, Palestine, Egypt, and Mesopotamia to the commodities of the Mediterranean, to the development of money-based economies (both Philip and Alexander issued gold coins to pay for their invasions), and to the bundle of cultural ideas associated with the Greek city-states. Alexander founded dozens of new cities named after himself, the most famous of which was Alexandria in Egypt.

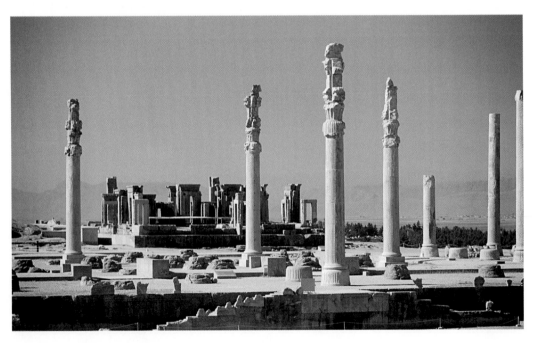

Palace of Darius. The remains of the great palace of Darius I of Persia at Persepolis, modern Tatchara in southwestern Iran. This is part of the so-called Appadana, or royal audience hall of the king. Construction of this palace began about 520 BCE and continued for several decades. This view shows only a small part of the complex, which covered dozens of acres and included hundreds of rooms in addition to the grand stairways and royal reception rooms. The palaces of Near Eastern monarchs physically represented the huge extent of their power.

→ *How did the spread of Hellenism reshape the Mediterranean world?*

Primary Source

CLASH OF EMPIRES: THE BATTLE OF GAUGAMELA (331 BCE)

The following passage, taken from the Greek historian Arrian, delineates the makeup of the army of Darius as it marshaled to confront Alexander and his forces. In describing the size of the army—much larger than that of the largest Greek city-state, Athens—Arrian mentions the various ethnic groups of the Persian Empire that contributed troops to it. Arrian is as reasonably trustworthy a writer as we can get on these matters, even though he was writing more than four centuries after the events in question. Note that army contingents come from lands as far-flung as Bactria (near modern-day Afghanistan), Scythia (in the broad geographical area from Ukraine to Kazakhstan), Armenia, Cappadocia (in east-central Turkey), and Caria (what is today southwestern Turkey), as well as from lands close to the Red Sea.

Darius's army was so large because it had been reinforced with Sogdians, with Bactrians, and with Indian peoples from the borderlands of Bactria, all under the command of Bessus, the satrap [i.e., the regional governor] of Bactria. There were also units of the Sakai—who were part of the Scythians who are found in Asia. They owed no loyalty to Bessus, but were still allies of Darius. These soldiers were mounted bowmen commanded by one Mauaces. The Arachotoi and the hillmen from India were commanded by Barsaentes, the satrap of Arachosia. The Areioi were commanded by their satrap, Satibarzanes; the Parthians, the Hyrcanians, and Tapeiroi, all cavalrymen, were commanded by Phrataphernes. The Medes, to whom were attached the Kadousioi, the Albanoi, and Sakesinai, were commanded by Atropates the Mede. All the units from the lands near the Red Sea were commanded by Orontobates, Ariobarzanes, and Orxines. The Ouxioi and Sousianoi were commanded by Oxathres, son of Aboultius. The men from Babylon, to whom were attached the Siracenioi and Carians, were commanded by Boupares—these Carians had been resettled in the empire by a mass transfer of their people. The Armenians were commanded by Orontes and

Mithraustes; the Cappadocians, by Ariaces. The Syrians from Hollow Syria [i.e., the Bekáa Valley in modern Lebanon] and from Mesopotamia were commanded by Mazaeus. The total number of men in the army of Darius was reported to be 40,000 cavalry, 1,000,000 infantry, 200 scythed chariots [i.e., war chariots with blades mounted on both ends of the axle], and some war elephants—the Indians who came from this side of the Indus River had about fifteen of them.

→ *Does the ability of both Xerxes, in the early fifth century BCE, and Darius, in the late fourth century BCE, to command ethnic loyalties across the huge landmass of Southwest Asia tell us something important about the nature of communications across this immense area?*

→ *Do you think that the mobilizing of military force on this scale by a large empire contributed in important ways to these commnications?*

→ *Do you think that it also contributed to transfers of types of knowledge beyond what pertains to military concerns?*

SOURCE: Arrian, *The History of Alexander* 3.8; translated by Brent Shaw.

While it is true that some of these new colonial cities had little long-term impact, the linkage of Afro-Eurasian societies from East Asia to the Mediterranean world was never again to be broken.

One of Alexander's most significant acts was to seize the accumulated wealth stored by the Persian kings in their im-

mense palaces, especially at Persepolis, and to disperse it into the money economies of the Mediterranean city-states. This massive redistribution of wealth, like the post-Columbian exploitation of the Americas, in turn fueled a huge economic expansion in the Mediterranean (along with price inflation, the downside of such rapid expansion).

ALEXANDER'S SUCCESSORS AND THE TERRITORIAL KINGDOMS

Alexander died in Babylon at the age of thirty-two—struck down by massive overconsumption of alcohol and other physical excesses of a piece with his larger-than-life personality and the war culture of the Macedonian male. His death in 323 BCE brought on the collapse of the regime he had personally held together. The conquered lands fragmented into large territories over which his generals fought incessantly for control.

Alexander's generals became his successors. Seleucus, Ptolemy, Antigonus, Lysimachus, and others did not think of themselves as citizens, even very important ones, of a Greek city-state, but rather modeled themselves on the regional rulers whom they had defeated. The emergence of kingdoms created by these men in the Eastern Mediterranean worlds not only imported Alexander's predilection for absolute rulership into the region but also unified large blocks of territory under the control of single, powerful rulers.

One effect of powerful families placing themselves in charge of whole kingdoms was that a few women were now able to hold great power, a prospect that had been completely closed to them in the democracies of the city-states. Queens in Macedonia, Syria, and Egypt, whether independent or co-regents with their husbands, established new public roles for women. Berenice of Egypt (c. 320–280 BCE) was the first of the powerful royal women who helped rule over the kingdom of the Nile; the line was to end with the most famous of them all, Cleopatra, in the 30s BCE.

The old city-states of the Mediterranean, such as Athens and Corinth, still continued to thrive, but they now had to function in a world dominated by much larger power blocs. In the eastern Mediterranean, three large territorial states overshadowed this new Greek world: Syria, ruled by the Seleucids (the dynasty established by Seleucus); Macedonia, ruled by the Antigonids (the dynasty established by Antigonus); and Egypt, ruled by the Ptolemies (the dynasty established by Ptolemy). In the interstices between these larger states, middle-sized kingdoms emerged—for example, Pergamum, in the northwestern part of what is today Turkey. Elsewhere, polities banded together in order to survive in this new world; on mainland Greece, larger confederations like the Achaean League or the Aetolian League now forced the previously independent city-states to join with them.

In general, therefore, political states became bigger and began to coalesce into larger operating units that displayed a uniformity unknown in the governments of the earlier city-states. The impulse to standardization during this period can be seen not just in its politics but in every aspect of ordinary daily life. Unlike the first empires we described in Chapter 4, which sought to prevail over neighbors by subordinating them as colonies or tribute states, these kingdoms expanded their frontiers by integrating neighboring peoples as fellow sub-

Berenice. Portrait head of Berenice, wife and consort of Ptolemy I, the first Macedonian king of Egypt after its conquest by Alexander the Great. Berenice was one of the women who, as queens of huge empires, wielded power and commanded wealth in their own right.

jects. They believed, unlike their predecessors, that they possessed cultural assets that could be disseminated across much broader geographic areas. They were Alexander's successors in their certainty that their culture could transcend the place where it was born and make all peoples within a vast state the worthy subjects of powerful monarchs.

Competition in war remained an unceasing fact, even in the new world of expanding states. But the wars between the kingdoms established by the successors of Alexander were bigger in size and more complex in organization than ever before. The adversaries fought some of the largest-scale battles that the Mediterranean was ever to witness. At the same time, the relative parity in strength of each of the large states meant that warfare never achieved much. Every big state had access to much the same advanced military technology. Rulers simply went out into the marketplace and acquired the highly trained soldiers, mercenaries, generals, and military advisers required to run their armies. After battles that killed tens of thousands, and severely injured and wounded hundreds of thousands, the three major kingdoms, and even the minor ones, remained largely unchanged.

The great powers therefore settled into a prolonged centuries-long game of carefully watching each other and balancing threats with alliances. What emerged was a fierce competition that dominated international relations, with diplomacy and endless treaty making replacing actual fighting—an equilibrium reminiscent of the first international age in the second millennium BCE (see Chapter 3). Long periods of peace began to exist between the extremely violent and destructive wars waged by the new kingdoms.

HELLENISTIC CULTURE

Just as large-scale uniformity in politics and war trumped the small size and diversity of the old city-state, so too the individuality of the cultures of the earlier city-states now gave way to a new uniform culture that stressed the common identity of all who embraced Greek ways. This homogenized culture emphasized the common denominators of language, style, and politics to which anyone, anywhere in the Afro-Eurasian world, could have access.

Following already existing commercial networks, Greek culture spread rapidly through the whole of the Mediterranean basin. It was an alluring package, and ruling elites in all the regions that came into contact with it were strongly attracted to its powerful modes of thinking and behaving. This Greek city-state culture included secular disciplines from history to biology, philosophical and political thinking, popular entertainment in theaters, competitive public games, and secular art for art's sake in all kinds of media. No other society at the time had such a complete package of high culture: hence its obvious appeal and its diffusion into distant corners. Archaeologists have found a Greek-style gymnasium and theater in the town of Aï Khanoum in modern Afghanistan and adaptations of Greek sculptures made at the order of the Vedic king Sandrakottos (better known as Chandragupta); we know of Carthaginians in North Africa who became "Greek" philosophers, and Gallic and Moorish chieftains, from the far west of France and Morocco, who had fine Greek drinking vessels buried with them.

Hellenistic cultural forces provoked varying responses in different parts of the Afro-Eurasian world as they came into contact with preexisting cultures and ruling groups. Hellenism had its most decisive impact and produced its strongest reactions in the home territory of the Greeks, the Mediterranean. A segment of the Jewish population of the region then called Judea resisted it violently, seeing it as a lethal threat to the identity of their culture and to their religious beliefs. The inhabitants of the rising city of Rome, in contrast, regarded the mastery of Greek ways as a vehicle for advancing the status of Rome throughout the Mediterranean. And the Carthaginians took the new Greek influence in stride, promoting its spread throughout the larger Mediterranean world and seeing it as an aid to their economic and cultural well-being.

COMMON LANGUAGE A common language had widespread appeal, for it replaced the numerous idiosyncratic dialects of Greek, each with relatively few speakers, found in the world of the early city-states with a new, everyday form of Greek that could be understood anywhere. Known as "common," or *koine,* Greek, it became the international language of its day.

Most of the peoples who came into contact with this language, and with the culture accompanying it, accepted the benefits of Greek language and culture in expanding a wide network of communication and exchange. Peoples living in Egypt, Judea, Syria, and Sicily, who all had their own languages and cultures, were now able to communicate more easily with each other, to worship Greek deities such as Dionysus, and to enjoy the same dramatic comedies in their theaters and new common forms of art and sculpture. But—as would generally be the case throughout history—cultural dominance was not achieved without considerable local resentment and resistance. As noted above, some of the Jews in Judea rejected the push to "become Greek": local Jewish religious leaders rebelled against Hellenism's common language, music, gymnasia, nudity, public art, and secularism, believing that the new culture was deeply immoral and threatening to local beliefs. Yet despite pockets of resistance, overall the Hellenizing movement was remarkably successful in spreading a shared Greek culture throughout the Mediterranean and into Southwest Asia.

COSMOPOLITAN CITIES Much as Athens had been the model city of the age of the Greek city-state, the city of Alexandria in Egypt became exemplary in the new age. Whereas fifth-century BCE Athens had zealously maintained an exclusive civic identity, Alexandria was a multiethnic city that was built from scratch by immigrants, who rapidly totaled half a million as they streamed in from all over the Mediterranean and Southwest Asia in search of new opportunities. Members of its huge and dynamic population, representing dozens if not hundreds of Greek and non-Greek peoples, communicated with each other in the new common language, which supplanted their original dialects. A new urban culture emerged to meet the needs of so diverse a population.

The culture of the Hellenistic movement supplanted local art forms. In the previous city-state world, comic playwrights had written plays for their city and its culture, basing their art on local languages, local foibles and problems, and local well-known politicians; in this new connected world, however,

Primary Source

THE COSMOPOLITAN CITY OF ALEXANDRIA

According to legend, Alexander both selected the site of Alexandria and named the city after himself. As a result of Alexander's personal influence and its strategic location, Alexandria quickly grew into a megalopolis that attracted an immense and diverse immigrant population from the entire Mediterranean world. In the following description of the city, the Greek geographer Strabo, who was writing in the time of the first two Roman emperors, Augustus and Tiberius (between about 25 BCE and 20 CE), emphasizes the city's function as an enormous entrepôt for trade and commerce across Eurasia. (Entrepôts are ports that had become transshipment centers where cargoes were unloaded from seafaring vessels and then sent elsewhere, by sea or by land.) By Strabo's time, it was the second-largest city in the Mediterranean, surpassed only by Rome itself. Alexandria's commercial reach was enormous. From the upper regions of the Nile in what is now Sudan it received ivory, slaves, and animal skins, many of which its merchants transported to other Mediterranean locations in North Africa, Europe, and Southwest Asia.

As for the Great Harbor at Alexandria, it is not only wonderfully well closed in and protected by artificial levees and by nature, it is also so deep that even the largest ships can be moored right at the stairs along its quayside. This Great Harbor is divided up into several minor harbors. . . . Even more exports are handled than imports. Anyone who might happen to be at Alexandria and at Dichaiarchia [the large Italian port on the Bay of Naples] would easily see for himself that the cargo ships sailing from here are bigger and more heavily laden. . . . The city itself is crisscrossed by streets that are wide enough for riding horses and driving chariots, and intersected by two main roads very much broader than the others. Its streets and avenues cut across each other at right angles. The city also boasts exceedingly beautiful public parks and its royal quarters take up a quarter, perhaps even a third of the whole city. . . . In earlier times, not even twenty ships would dare to go as far as the Arabian Gulf and manage to get a look outside its straits. But now large fleets of ships are sent out as far as India

and to the furthest lands of the Ethiopians, from which the most valuable cargoes are brought to Egypt and then sent out again to other regions of the world. Double charges are collected on these shipments—both when they come in and when they go out—and the duties are especially high on luxury goods . . . for Alexandria alone does not just receive trade goods of this kind from all over the world, but it also furnishes supplies to the whole of the world outside.

→ *If you consider the historical circumstances of the city's foundation by Alexander the Great, what factors might have led to the sudden, even explosive, growth in its size and population?*

→ *Looking at the city's location on a map, can you think of other factors connected with communication, travel, trade, and supply that would have further encouraged the city's tremendous expansion?*

SOURCE: Strabo, *Geography* 17.1.6, 7, 8, 13; translated by Brent Shaw.

entertainment had to appeal to bigger audiences and had to be accessible to a wider variety of people. Plays were now staged in any city where Greek influence existed, and they were understood in any environment. Distinctive regional humor or local characters gave way to dramas populated by stock characters with whom a vast Afro-Eurasian audience

could identify: the miser, the old crone, the jilted lover, the golden-hearted whore, the boastful soldier, the befuddled father, the cheated husband, and the rebellious son. Such plays could be performed anywhere in the Mediterranean, and the laughter would be just as loud in Syracuse on the island of Sicily as in Scythopolis in the Jordan Valley of Judea.

The Theater at Syracuse. The great theater in the city-state of Syracuse in Sicily was considerably refurbished and enlarged under the Hellenistic kings. It could seat 15–20,000 persons. Here the people of Syracuse attended plays written by playwrights who lived on the far side of their world, but whose works they could understand as if the characters were from their own neighborhood. In the common culture of the Hellenistic period, plays deliberately featured typecast characters and situations, thereby broadening their audience.

Ways of thinking changed to match this newly unified world. The new ideas took into account that individuals were no longer citizens (*polites*) of a particular city (*polis*): they were the first "cosmopolitans," belonging to the whole world or "universe" (*kosmos*). The new political style was relentlessly cosmopolitan, radiating out of cities not just into local hinterlands but also to distant (and often rivalrous) cities.

Kingdoms and states had become so big that individuals could relate to it only through the personality of kings or rulers and their families. Rulership was personality, and personality and style bound together large numbers of subjects. For example, Demetrius Poliorcetes, the ruler of Macedonia, wore high-platform shoes and heavy makeup, and he decorated his elaborate, flowing cape with images of the sun, the stars, and the planets. In the presence of a powerful and solitary sun king like Demetrius, ordinary individuals felt small, inconsequential, and personally isolated. In response, an obsessive cult of the self arose, as Hellenistic religion and philosophy increasingly focused on the individual and his or her place in the larger world.

PHILOSOPHY AND RELIGION This new concern with the individual self was expressed in many different ways. One was personified in Athens by the philosopher Diogenes (c. 412–323 BCE), who was originally from Sinope on the Black Sea. He sought self-sufficiency and freedom from the laws and customs of society, rejecting all the cultural norms of his society as human-made inventions not in tune with nature and therefore false. He masturbated in public in order to "relieve himself" (it was, after all, a "natural need"), as well as to show his disdain for the artificial sexual mores of the city. He lived with no clothing in a wooden barrel in the public square, or agora, of Athens, with his female companion in her barrel beside him. Other teachers were also rejecting the values of the city-state, although with more finesse and less contentiousness than Diogenes. Nonetheless, all recognized that a new orientation was required now that the old world of the city-state, with its face-to-face relationships, had vanished. In a world turned larger and more threatening, many sought answers within the individual.

The self was similarly emphasized by the teacher Epicurus (c. 341–279 BCE), the founder of a school in Athens that he called The Garden. He set out his ideal of a community centered on The Garden and stressed the importance of sensation, saying that pleasurable sensations were good and painful sensations were bad. Epicurus was seen as a personal savior (*sōtēr*) and his students were taught to pursue a life of contemplation and ask themselves, "What is the good life?" The Epicureans struggled to develop a sense of "not caring" (*ataraxia*) about things in their life and to view them as not mattering, so as to find peace of mind. In Epicurus's cult, none of the social statuses of the old city-state had more value than any other: women, slaves, and others in the underclass were equally welcome in The Garden as worshippers.

Epicurus and his followers acquired adherents throughout the Mediterranean, but they were hardly alone. Unrestrained by the controls of any one city-state, other new cults and schools of philosophy emerged. Of these, Stoicism was perhaps the most widespread and effective. It was initiated by a man named Zeno (c. 334–262 BCE), from Citium on the island of Cyprus, and a large number of other cosmopolitan figures across the Hellenistic world—from Babylon in Mesopotamia to Sinope on the Black Sea—developed its beliefs; their mission was to make individuals better able to understand their place in the cosmos. Zeno taught his ideas in the Stoa Poikilē, a decorated roofed colonnade that opened onto the central marketplace of Athens and gave his followers their name. For the Stoics, everything was grounded in nature itself, which was held to be the ultimate, permanent world. Cities and kingdoms were human-made things, important but transient. Being in tune with nature and living a good life required understanding the rules of the natural order and being in control of one's passions and thus indifferent to pleasure or pain.

Greek colonial control of other lands and cultures transformed long-established religions, which were then reexported to cities throughout the Mediterranean. The Greeks in Egypt drew on the cult of Osiris and his consort Isis, once a vital element in pharaonic temple rituals, to fashion a new narrative, employing the story of Osiris's death and rebirth to represent personal salvation from death. Isis became a supreme goddess whose lists of "excellencies" or "supreme virtues" encompassed the powers of dozens of other Mediterranean gods and goddesses. Believers experienced personal revelations and out-of-body experiences (*exstasis*, "ecstasy").

A ritual of dipping in water (*baptizein*, "to baptize") marked the transition of believers, "born again" into lives devoted to a "personal savior" who produces an understanding of a new life by direct revelation. These new religious beliefs, like the worship of Isis, emphasized the spiritual concerns of humans as individuals, rather than the collective worries of towns or cities.

HELLENISM AND THE ELITES Once high Greek culture coalesced, its appeal to elites in widely dispersed communities along the major communication routes became almost irresistible. Social elites in such communities believed that they could enhance their position by adopting Hellenistic culture, the only culture that had standing above the level of local values. This attitude was taken by Syrian, Jewish, and Egyptian elites in the eastern Mediterranean, as well as by Roman, Carthaginian, and African elites in the western Mediterranean. The later Roman high culture was itself a form of Greek culture. Of the Romans' extensive borrowings from the Greeks, not the least important was a belief—unusual at that time—in the value of a written history. They, too, began writing about contemporary events and their past. Secular plays, philosophy, poetry, competitive games, and art followed, all based on Greek forms or on local imitations of them. North African kings, ruling polities located in the area

The Painted Stoa. An artist's reconstruction of the Stoa Poikilē, or "Painted Stoa," in the city-state of Athens of the fourth century BCE. In the manner of a modern-day strip mall, this business and administrative center ran along the northern side of the agora, or central business and marketplace of the city. Philosophers and their students would hang out at the Stoa, lounging in the shaded areas under the colonnade as they debated the ideas flowing into Athens from all over the Hellenistic world. The painted wall decoration behind the columns (from which the Stoa received its name) depicts the Battle of Marathon.

of present-day Algeria and Tunisia, similarly decked themselves out in Greek dress, built Greek-style theaters, imported Greek philosophers, and wrote history. Now they, too, had "culture."

The Hellenistic influence penetrated deeply into sub-Saharan Africa, where the kingdom of Meroe (see Chapter 5), while decisively influenced by pharaonic forms, displayed many of the characteristics of Greek culture. Both Meroe and its rival, Axum, located in the Ethiopian highlands, used Greek stelae to boast of their military exploits. Not surprisingly, Greek influences were extensive among the Meroe, whose continuous interaction with the Egyptians exposed its people to the world of the Mediterranean. Herodotus mentions that the citizens of Meroe "worshipped Zeus and Dionysus alone of the gods, holding them in great honor. There is an oracle of Zeus there, and they make war according to its pronouncements, taking from it both the occasion and the object of their various expeditions." The rulers of Meroe, understanding the advantages of the Greek language, employed many Greek scribes to record the accomplishments of the kings on the walls of Greek-Egyptian temples. In this way, the kingdom and culture of Meroe provided a remarkable mix of Greek, Egyptian, and African cultural and political elements. Of all of the archaeological finds in Meroe, perhaps the most stunning is the bronze head of the Roman emperor Augustus that was discovered in front of the royal temple in the capital city of Meroe and frequently has been used to illustrate books on Nubia.

JEWISH RESISTANCE TO HELLENISM

The Jews in Judea, a small land squeezed between Egypt to the south and the superstates of Mesopotamia to the north and east, offer a striking case of resistance to the universalizing forces of Hellenistic culture. The focal point of all Jewish culture was the temple in Jerusalem. The people of Judah had first been unified under King David in the early tenth century BCE. And it was his son and successor, King Solomon, who masterminded the building of the new temple, designed by a Phoenician architect, as well as an even more elaborate royal palace. These two structures were in the new city of Jerusalem, where a high priesthood ordered the affairs of the single supreme deity of the whole people, who in effect defined themselves in opposition to all of the powers impinging on their small world. After the seventh century BCE, however, Judah and the Jews were almost constantly subject to one or another of the major powers dominating the region—first the Assyrians and then the Babylonians, who finally destroyed the city and its temple in 587 BCE. The Jews therefore had a long schooling in surviving and resisting foreign rule. The defeat of Babylon by the Persians was followed by a royal edict of restoration issued by the Persian monarch Cyrus in 538 BCE and the subsequent integration of what was now a province, Judea, into the Persian Empire. As the Jews who had been forced to move to Babylon returned to Judea, the process of rebuilding Jerusalem began.

The reconstruction of the temple was finally completed in 516 BCE. It was under the aegis of Nehemiah, a Jewish eunuch in the Persian court of Artaxerxes I, that permission and resources were given to rebuild the fortification walls around the city (440–437 BCE). Around this same time, the physical rebuilding of Jerusalem was complemented by a restoration of the religious community, with stricter adherence than ever before to the cultural and ritual regulations that defined the Jewish people (for example, no marriage with "outsiders") and to the laws of their God. Yet all of this rebuilding of local Jewish society occurred within the confines of another great Southwest Asian empire, that of the Achaemenids, where Persian toleration of local customs and beliefs supported the restoration of Jewish tradition. It took Alexander's lightning defeat of the Persian Empire in the 330s BCE to suddenly make possible the transformation of political relationships and a new and shocking openness to the cultural innovations of the Mediterranean world. Hellenism came in the wake of Alexander's sweep through the region.

Some parts of the ruling elite of Jewish society began to adopt Greek ways—to wear Greek clothing; to introduce the culture of the gymnasium, with its cult of male nudity; to produce images of gods as art. When a full-scale armed revolt, led by the family of the Maccabees, broke out in 166 BCE after the Syrian overlords issued edicts forbidding the practice of Judaism and deliberately profaned the temple, the rebels consciously rejected the imported culture of the Hellenists. Though they succeeded in establishing an independent Jewish state centered on the temple in Jerusalem, they did not entirely overcome the impact of the new universal culture. By the beginning of the first century BCE, descendants of the Maccabees were calling themselves kings, were minting coins with Greek legends, and were presiding over a largely secular kingdom. Moreover, a huge Jewish society that existed outside Judea in the new Hellenistic city of Alexandria in Egypt fully embraced the new culture; there scholars produced a Bible in koine Greek, and historians, like Jason of Cyrene, and philosophers, like Philo of Alexandria, wrote in Greek, imitating Greek models.

ROMAN HELLENISM AND THE BEGINNINGS OF THE ROMAN EMPIRE

Other cities were less reluctant than Jerusalem to follow Hellenistic ways. Early on, the Romans saw the Greek model as offering them opportunities to increase their importance in the Mediterranean world. In the 330s and 320s BCE, when Alexander's conquests were uniting the whole of the eastern Mediterranean, a city-state on the Tiber River in central Italy took the first critical military actions to unify Italy; eventually, it would bring together the rest of the Mediterranean and parts of Southwest Asia. Rather than beginning as a kingdom like Macedonia, Rome mutated from a Mediterranean city-state into a large territorial state. In this transformation, it adopted, bit by bit, many of the elements of the new uniform Hellenistic culture: Greek-style temples, elaborately decorated Greek-style pottery and paintings, and an alphabet based on that of the Greeks, all of which had appeared in the fifth and fourth centuries BCE.

Romans saw immersion in Greek culture and language as enabling them to appear to the rest of the world as "civilized." Yet this notion was not accepted by the Roman elites without struggle, resistance, and much worry and debate. The Roman senator Cato the Elder (234–149 BCE), one of the best-known figures in this transitional age, reveals the extreme tensions and adaptations that these changes required. Although he was devoted to the Roman past, the Latin language (his extant prose works are among the oldest that survive in Latin), and the ideal of small-scale Roman peasant farmers

Roman Mosaic. Although this colorful mosaic comes from a later period of Roman history (third-century CE Gaul; it was found at Saint-Germain-en-Laye in modern-day France), it shows a constant theme of Mediterranean history—the annual cycle of hard work required of Roman peasants. Here the peasants are ploughing the land in the spring—the farmer to the right is driving the pair of oxen drawing the plough—and seeding the crop—the farmer to the left is throwing seed from a wicker basket into the furrows made by the plough.

and their families, he embraced many of the new Hellenistic influences. He wrote a standard how-to manual for the new economy of slave plantation agriculture (discussed below), invested in shipping and trading, learned Greek rhetoric (both speaking and writing the language), added the genre of history to Latin literature, and much more. In some ways, Cato blended an extreme devotion to tradition and the solid and unchanging Roman past, manifest in his public statements, with bold innovations in most aspects of his day-to-day life.

CARTHAGE

In contrast to Rome, whose inhabitants assimilated Greek ways to elevate their status in the larger Mediterranean world, cities that were prosperous and well integrated into the world economy welcomed Hellenistic culture because it facilitated communication and exchange. The ideas and new economic forces that the Romans and Cato experienced so powerfully in the second century BCE spread throughout the Mediterranean; when they reached the great city of Carthage in present-day Tunisia, they were adapted without great fanfare but with much success. Not only did Carthage's merchants trade with other Phoenician colonies in the western Mediterranean, but its ruling families assumed direct control over western Sicily and Sardinia. Remains of pottery and other materials unearthed by archaeologists demonstrate that the Carthaginians' trading contacts extended far beyond other Phoenician settlements to towns of Etruscans and Romans in Italy, to the Greek trading city of Massilia (modern Marseilles) in southern France, and to Athens in the eastern Mediterranean. In addition, the Carthaginians expanded their commercial interests into the Atlantic, moving north along the coast of Iberia and south along the coast of West Africa—which, as noted in Chapter 5, a great Carthaginian commander, Hanno, explored and colonized. Pushing their influence along the littoral, they even established a trading post at the island of Mogador, more than 600 miles down the Atlantic coast of Africa.

Carthaginian culture—or Punic culture, to use the Romans' name for the people with whom they would soon be embroiled in warfare—also shared important parts of the common Hellenistic culture of the time. Carthaginians went to Athens to become philosophers. The design of their sanctuaries, temples, and other public buildings reveals a marriage of modes and styles: Greek-style pediments and columns mixed with Punic designs and measurements, and local North African motifs and structures were added to the mix. The fine jewelry worn by Phoenician women reflected influences and styles coming from Egypt. The finest tableware and pottery were imported from Etruscans in Italy, and coinage and ideas came from the Greek city-states.

Aerial View of Punic Carthage. Carthage was located on a promontory in the Bay of Tunis. In the lower foreground of this artist's reconstruction is a rectangular area of water and above it a circular-shaped one. These were the two major harbors of Carthage—the rectangular one was the commercial port and the circular one was the military harbor. Above these harbors are the main market square and the high central point named the Byrsa. To the left is the twenty-mile-long wall that defended the city on its land side.

ECONOMIC CHANGES AND MEDITERRANEAN UNITY: PLANTATION SLAVERY AND MONEY-BASED ECONOMIES

Perhaps the fundamental economic innovation that accompanied the unification of the Mediterranean world was the use of very large numbers of slaves in agricultural production, especially in Italy, Sicily, and the regions of North Africa close to Carthage. The conquests of Alexander and the political rise of Rome produced unprecedented wealth for a small elite living in the Mediterranean cities. These men and women, in turn, used their riches to acquire huge tracts of land and to purchase slaves—either individuals who had been kidnapped or peoples conquered in warfare—on a scale and with a degree of detailed managerial organization never seen before.

The slave plantations, wholly devoted to the production of surplus crops for profit, became one of the engines driving a new Mediterranean economy. The estates created vast wealth for their owners, though at a heavy price to others. Reliance on slave labor forced the free peasants who previously had worked the fields into overcrowded cities where employment was hard to find. The results of the sudden importing of such large numbers of slaves and working them in such harsh conditions should have been anticipated but were not. Between 135 and 70 BCE, authorities on the island of Sicily and in southern Italy were challenged by three massive slave uprisings against owners, led by the religious seer and prophet Eunus in 130 and the slave gladiator Spartacus in the late 70s. These were among the greatest slave wars known in world history.

The circulation of money reinforced the effects of forced labor. With more cash in the economy, wealthy landowners, urban elites, and merchants could more easily do business. The increasingly widespread adoption of Greek-style coins to pay for goods and services, in place of a barter system, promoted the importation of such cultural commodities as wine from elsewhere in the Mediterranean region. As coined money became more and more available, it was increasingly used as the main means for facilitating commercial exchanges. The forced transfer of precious metals to the Mediterranean from Southwest Asia by Alexander's conquests actually caused the price of gold to fall. In the west, Carthage now began to mint coins of its own on a large scale, at first mainly in gold but later in other metals. Rome moved to a money economy at the same time. By the 270s and 260s BCE, the Romans created their first major issues of coins and then moved decisively toward the

Early Roman Coin. Coins like this one were the standard means by which the state paid its expenditures, and they later were widely used in ordinary commercial dealings. This coin features the prow of a ship with its "evil eye" decoration and armed beak for ramming other ships. The legend ROMA stamped on the bottom signals that Rome is a state with the power and autonomy to have its own money.

Roman Slaves. One of the most profitable occupations for peoples living beyond the northwestern frontiers of the Roman Empire, in what was called Germania, was that of providing bodies for sale to Roman merchants. In this relief from Roman Moguntiacum on the Rhine River (modern-day Mainz), we see chained German prisoners whose fate was to become slaves in the empire. This stone picture supported columns in front of the headquarters of the Roman fortress at Mainz-Kästrich.

general use of money under the pressures of their first full-scale war with Carthage (264–241 BCE). By the end of the third century, even borderland peoples such as the Gauls in their kin-based kingdoms had begun to mint coins, using the galloping-horse images found on Macedonia's gold coins issued by Philip II. So, too, did the kinship-based African kingdoms in North Africa, where the coins of the kings Massinissa and Syphax were imprinted with the same Macedonian royal imagery. By the end of this period, inhabitants of the whole of the Mediterranean basin and of the lands immediately around it were using coins to buy and sell all manner of commodities.

To pay for the goods made desirable by their newly acquired tastes, Celtic chieftains in the regions covered by modern France were willing to sell their own people in the expanding slave markets of the Mediterranean. Slavery and slave trading also became central to the economies of the

Iberian Peninsula, especially in the hinterlands of large river valleys like the Ebro, where local elites founded urban centers imitating Greek styles and forms in the fourth and third centuries BCE. If Alexander's more immediate triumphs were the broadcast of political and, especially, military influences from the Hellenistic world, the more influential aftershocks were economic and cultural. From North Africa to South Asia and beyond, Hellenistic influences and the very idea of a universal culture that might incorporate all urban, settled peoples reverberated across Afro-Eurasia.

CONVERGING INFLUENCES IN CENTRAL AND SOUTH ASIA

> → *How did Hellenistic and pastoral nomadic cultures influence central and South Asia?*

The mountains of what is today known as Afghanistan are formidable but permeable. Their passes, between the high plateau of Iran to the west and the towering ranges of Tibet to the east, are pinched like the narrow neck of an hourglass —but they offer the shortest route through the mountains.

By crossing those passes Alexander's armies opened a route between two worlds, the eastern and western portions of Afro-Eurasia, fashioning a new land bridge that has remained open to this day. It created avenues for an unprecedented sort of cross-cultural exchange that eventually remapped whole regions. Conquerors moving from west to east, like Alexander, and from east to west, like the later nomads from central Asia, were drawn southward, through the mountains, into the rich plains of the Indus and Ganges River valleys. South Asian trade and, above all, South Asian religions moved northward toward the trade routes that ran from west to east along what became known as the Silk Road. As a result, the politics, economics, and cultures of Afro-Eurasia, between China and the eastern regions of the empire of Alexander, were profoundly influenced by the incorporation of central Asia and South Asia into this east-west axis. The new links set the stage for exchanges that would first touch and penetrate North Africa, and then over time work their way into East Africa and parts of sub-Saharan Africa.

INFLUENCES FROM THE MAURYAN EMPIRE (321–184 BCE)

Alexander's occupation of the Indus Valley, though it lasted only two years (327–325 BCE), helped pave the way for

The Bolan Pass. The formidable Bolan Pass separated India from the highland of Baluchistan. It was both an artery for transportation and a strategic military spot.

India's most powerful and durable polity before the Common Era. Previous to the arrival of Alexander's forces, India had been a conglomerate of small warring states. This political instability came to an abrupt halt when, in 321 BCE, an ambitious young man named Chandragupta Maurya ascended the throne of the Magadha kingdom and launched a series of successful military expeditions in what is now northern India. Magadha, located on the lower Ganges plain, held great advantages over other states. It contained rich iron ores and fertile rice paddies. On the nearby northeast Deccan plateau, ample woods supported herds of elephants, the mainstay of the potent Magadha cavalries. The Mauryans did not start out as a distinguished ruling family in north India, but economic strength and military acumen elevated them over their rivals. The retreat of Alexander created a momentary political vacuum: it was an opportunity for the

shrewd Mauryans to extend the dynasty's claims to the northwest areas of South Asia, the region previously controlled by the Persian Empire.

Chandragupta's expanding regime, called the Mauryan Empire by late historians, constituted the first large-scale empire in the history of South Asia and served as a model for later Indian empire builders. This empire was known to the contemporary Greek world as "India," the country stretching from the Indus River eastward. Indeed, the Mauryan regime began to etch out the territorial contours of what would many centuries later become modern India. Chandragupta, who ruled from 321 to 297 BCE, used his military resources to reach beyond the Ganges plain to the northwest into the Punjab, pushing up to the border with the Seleucid kingdom, the largest successor kingdom of Alexander's ephemeral empire. Its king, Seleucus Nicator, fretted about his neighbor's challenge and invaded Mauryan territory—only to run into Chandragupta's impregnable defenses. Soon thereafter, a treaty between the two powers gave a large portion of Afghanistan— including Kandahar, one of the Alexandrias—to the Mauryan Empire. The territory that the Mauryans wrested from the Seleucids, especially Kandahar, remained Greek-speaking for centuries, and some urban locations developed from garrison towns into genuine Greek-style poleis. The treaty yielded a round of gift exchanges and diplomacy. One of the daughters of Seleucus went to the Mauryan court at Pataliputra, accompanied by a group of Greek women. Seleucus also sent an ambassador, Megasthenes, to Chandragupta's court. Megasthenes lived in India for years, and he gathered his observations of Indian life in a book titled *Indica*. In return, Mauryans sent Seleucus many Indian valuables, including hundreds of elephants, which the Greeks soon learned to use in battles.

The Mauryan Empire reached its height during the reign of the third king, Aśoka (ruled 268–231 BCE), Chandragupta's grandson. Aśoka's lands comprised almost the entirety of South Asia, including the Deccan plateau; the tip of the peninsula alone remained outside his control. In 261 BCE, the eighth year of his long reign, Aśoka waged the dynasty's last campaign: the conquest of Kalinga, a kingdom on the east coast of the Indian peninsula. It was a gruesome and despicable operation. The Mauryan army triumphed but at a high price. About 100,000 soldiers died in battle, and many more perished in its aftermath; some 150,000 people were uprooted and forcibly relocated. Aśoka himself, when he learned of the devastation, was shocked and appalled at his own handiwork, and in a fit of guilt issued a famous edict renouncing his brutal ways.

Aśoka was a faithful follower and patron of Buddhism. Indeed, the Kalinga campaign redoubled his fealty to Buddhism, which informed his peaceable edict. All over his domain he built stupas, or Buddhist dome monuments, which marked the burial sites of relics of the Buddha. In the Kalinga edict, he claimed to rule over his subjects according to

AŚOKA'S KALINGA EDICT

After the Kalinga war, Aśoka issued an edict to express his regret at the miseries it had caused his people. From this edict, we can tell that Aśoka knew that he was ruling a country of many different cultures and religions.

Beloved of the Gods, is that those who dwell there, whether brahmans, *śramaṇas*, or those of other sects, or householders who show obedience to their superiors, obedience to mother and father, obedience to their teachers and behave well and devotedly towards their friends, acquaintances, colleagues, relatives, slaves, and servants—all suffer violence, murder, and separation from their loved ones. Even those who are fortunate to have escaped, and whose love is undiminished [by the brutalizing effect of war], suffer from the misfortunes of their friends, acquaintances, colleagues, and relatives. This participation of all men in suffering weighs heavily on the mind of the Beloved of the Gods. Except among the Greeks, there is no land where the religious orders of brahmans and *śramaṇas* are not to be found, and there is no land anywhere where men do not support one sect or another. Today if a hundredth or a thousandth part of those people who were killed or died or were deported when Kaliṅga was annexed were to suffer similarly, it would weigh heavily on the mind of the Beloved of the Gods.

The Beloved of the Gods believes that one who does wrong should be forgiven as far as it is possible to forgive him. And the Beloved of the Gods conciliates the forest tribes of his empire, but he warns them that he has power even in his remorse, and he asks them to repent, lest they be killed. For the Beloved of the Gods wishes that all beings should be unharmed, self-controlled, calm in mind, and gentle.

The Beloved of the Gods considers victory by *Dhamma* to be the foremost victory. And moreover the Beloved of the Gods has gained this victory on all his frontiers to a distance of six hundred *yojanas* [i.e., about 1500 miles], where reigns the Greek king named Antiochus, and be-

yond the realm of that Antiochus in the lands of the four kings named Ptolemy, Antigonus, Magas, and Alexander; and in the south over the Colas and Pāndyas as far as Ceylon. Likewise here in the imperial territories among the Greeks and the Kambojas, Nābhakas and Nābhapanktis, Bhojas and Pitinikas, Andhras and Pārindas, everywhere the people follow the Beloved of the Gods' instructions in *Dhamma*. Even where the envoys of the Beloved of the Gods have not gone, people hear of his conduct according to *Dhamma*, his precepts and his instruction in *Dhamma*, and they follow *Dhamma* and will continue to follow it.

What is obtained by this is victory everywhere, and everywhere victory is pleasant. This pleasure has been obtained through victory by *Dhamma*—yet it is but a slight pleasure, for the Beloved of the Gods only looks upon that as important in its results which pertains to the next world.

This inscription of *Dhamma* has been engraved so that any sons or great grandsons that I may have should not think of gaining new conquests, and in whatever victories they may gain should be satisfied with patience and light punishment. They should only consider conquest by *Dhamma* to be a true conquest, and delight in *Dhamma* should be their whole delight, for this is of value in both this world and the next.

→ *Aśoka promised to rule his people with Dhamma (Dharma in Sanskrit). Is this Dhamma the Buddhist doctrine or a general moral standard for all religious and ethnic communities?*

SOURCE: Romila Thapar, *Aśoka and the Decline of the Maurya*, 2nd ed. (Delhi: Oxford University Press, 1973), 255–57.

dhamma, or a general set of moral regulations that applied to all—including the priestly Brahmans, Buddhists, and members of other religious sects, and even the Greeks. To explain and implement this *dhamma,* Aśoka regularly issued decrees, which he had displayed on stone pillars and boulders

in every corner of his domain; occasionally, he also issued edicts to explain his own Buddhist faith. All were inscribed in local languages. While most of his decrees were written in dialects of Sanskrit, those published in northwestern regions were in Greek or in Aramaic, the administrative script of old

Persia. Aśoka's legal pronouncements helped give legitimacy to the Greek-speaking population that had entered the country with Alexander and now resided in Greek-style towns.

The works of art created under Aśoka's patronage celebrated the copious cultural and economic exchanges between the Greeks, Persians, and Indians. The most famous monument of this kind was the edict pillar that Aśoka erected in Sarnath at the Deer Garden, where the Buddha gave his first sermon. Atop the pillar, four lions sat facing four directions. Beneath the four lions, four wheels representing universal rule were separated by a bull, a horse, elephants, and another lion. The majestic images of lions, animals not found in the Ganges plain, represented an Indian version of the Persian royal symbol. Its technique displayed Greek influence as well, in vivid, animated style.

Lion Pillar. Aśoka had his edicts carved on this kind of pillar all over India. The majestic lion as the capital of the pillar shows the influence of Persian art, in which the lion was the symbol of royalty.

The Stupa at Sarnath. Buddhist legend claims that Aśoka placed relics of the Buddha into the many stupas he had built. The stupa at Sarnath is the best-preserved one from the time of Aśoka.

THE SELEUCID EMPIRE AND GREEK INFLUENCES

Alexander's Asian military thrust reached as far as the Punjab (literally "Five Rivers," the area around the upper stream of the Indus where four tributaries joined it); there, he defeated several rulers of Gandhara in 326 BCE. In the course of this campaign, he planted many garrison towns. Their highest concentration was in eastern Iran, northern Afghanistan, and the Punjab, where many encampments were needed to protect his easternmost new territory. A large number of these eastern outposts, such as those at Ghazni, Kandahar, Kapisi, and Bactra (modern Balkh), became major Hellenistic cities, sporting the characteristic features of a Greek polis—a colonnaded main street lined by temples to patron gods or goddesses, a theater, a gymnasium for education, a palace administration center, a marketplace.

After the death of Alexander, Seleucus Nikator (358–281 BCE), the ruler of the Hellenistic successor state in this area, built more Greek garrison towns throughout the region. Seleucus, who also controlled Mesopotamia, Syria, and Persia, named sixteen cities Antioch after his father, five Laodiceas after his mother, nine Seleucia after himself, three Apamea after his wife Apama, and Stratonicea after another wife. Though many of these towns or cities, especially those located in Iran, have vanished without a trace, the remains of several have been found in modern-day Afghanistan, the easternmost corner of the Hellenistic world. These cities were originally stations for soldiers, but they soon also became centers of Hellenistic culture.

Most of the Greek invaders integrated themselves into the local societies. Once the soldiers realized that they would be spending their lives in a country far from their homeland, they married local women and started families. They brought their ways to the local populations and established the institutions familiar to them from the polis. Greek was the official language, but because local women used their native tongues in daily life, subsequent generations were bilingual. The traditional Greek institutions, and especially Greek language and writing, survived many political changes and much cultural assimilation in a long strip of land stretching from the Mediterranean to South Asia, providing a common basis of engagement for many different lands and people across several centuries.

THE KINGDOM OF BACTRIA AND THE YAVANNA KINGS

Hellenistic influences were even more pronounced in the successor regimes of central Asia of the late third century BCE. The Seleucid state took over the entire Achaemenid Persian realm, including its central Asian and South Asian territory. The Hellenistic kingdom of Bactria, located west of the Hindu Kush in modern-day Afghanistan and Uzbekistan, broke away from the Seleucids to establish a strong state, which included the Gandhara region in modern Pakistan, around 200 BCE. As Mauryan power receded from the northwestern region of India, the Bactrian rulers extended their conquests into this area, drawn by the prospects of obtaining even more fertile territories. Because the cities that the Bactrian Greeks founded included a substantial number of Indian residents, and thus were a mix of cultural influences, they have been called "Indo-Greek." Those in Gandhara incorporated familiar features of the Greek polis, but inhabitants kept a reverence for Indian patron gods and goddesses.

Hellenistic Bactria served as a bridge between South Asia and the Greek world of the Mediterranean. Among the many goods that the Bactrians sent west were elephants, which were vital to the Greek armies. The Greeks' fascination with Indian war elephants is demonstrated by their frequent appearance in Greek art. The Greek king Demetrius invaded India around 200 BCE and had himself portrayed on his coins as wearing an elephant cap (i.e., a headdress with an elephant's trunk). In the following decades, Bactrian Greek in-

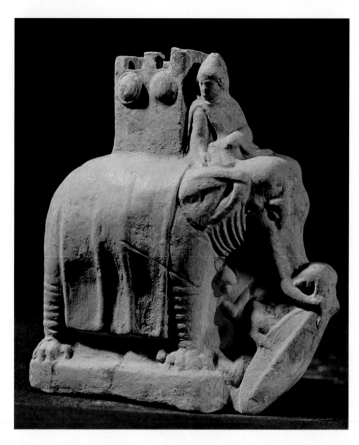

Elephant Cavalry. As shown by this terra-cotta statuette from 200 BCE, elephant cavalry was an important component of the Greek military. In their exchanges with India, Hellenist states demanded numerous elephants for their army.

vaders not only revived the cities in India left by Alexander but also founded several new Hellenistic cities in the Gandhara region. Demetrius entrusted the extension of his territorial empire in northern India to his generals, many of whom became independent rulers after his death. In Sanskrit literature, these Greek rulers were known as the Yavana kings— a word derived from Ionia, a region of western Asia Minor whose name was extended to all those who spoke Greek or came from the Mediterranean.

Remains of a Greek garrison town, unearthed under the site of ancient city of Samarkand in Uzbekistan, attest to the strength of Hellenistic influences even in cities far removed from the Greek homelands. In the 1960s, archaeologists working at Aï Khanoum on the Oxus River (now the Amu) in present-day Afghanistan were stunned to find the ruins of nearly an entire Greek city, largely undisturbed. Miraculously, Aï Khanoum had avoided the reconstructions and devastations that had befallen so many other Hellenistic cities in this region. We do not know its Greek name, but it was certainly an administrative center, if not the capital city, of the Bactrian state. The Greek-style architecture and inscriptions indicate that the original residents of the garrison city were soldiers from Greece. They followed the typical pattern: they married local women and stayed, but they also established the fundamental institutions of a Greek polis.

Aï Khanoum had many characteristic Greek structures: a palace complex, a gymnasium, a theater, an arsenal, a citadel on the acropolis, several temples, and elite residences. Built with marble columns with Corinthian capitals, the palace contained an administrative section, storage rooms, and a library. Though far from Greece, the elite Greek residents read poetry and philosophy. The baths in the palace had a mosaic floor made of colored pebbles,which were readily available from the nearby riverbank. At the city's theater, Greek dramas were performed. Grape cultivation made possible a festival of wine drinking, associated with the god Dionysus. The main temple housed a gigantic marble statue of an unknown deity; only its huge marble foot has survived the ravages of time. The remains of various statues make clear that the residents not only revered the Greek deity Athena and the demigod Heracles but also paid homage to the Zoroastrian religion and worshipped the gods of Mesopotamia.

Thus, Alexander's Asian conquests implanted Greek culture in what is modern Uzbekistan, Afghanistan, and northern India, connecting settlements there with communities in the Mediterranean basin. Although the residents of these Asian Hellenistic cities often worshipped different patron gods and were fluent in local languages, they too were influenced by the ideals of the Greek polis. Most men and women spoke and wrote some Greek, often as a second language.

The Hellenistic cities tried to maintain Greek culture by educating young people in gymnasia and by performing Greek dramas in their theaters. Their temples housed various deities —some Greek in origin, some not. Because Greek religious practices were inclusive, temples were suitable places for cultural assimilation; there, local deities donned Greek garb to protect the city. When Greeks moved into the new areas, they planted crops familiar to them from their homeland, and vineyards and olive orchards flourished. A material culture, such as tableware associated with wine drinking, also thrived. Cities and kings issued coins with Greek inscriptions, or legends, in the standard weights of the Greek world. Perhaps the most adept at mingling Greek and Indian influences was Menander, the best-known of the Yavana city-state kings in India in the mid–second century BCE and ruler over a large area stretching from Mathura on the Yamuna River to the Gulf of Khambhat (Cambay), located on the Indian Ocean. Using images and legends on coins to promote both traditions among his new subjects, Menander claimed his legitimacy as an Indian ruler but also cultivated Greek cultural forms. On the face of his coins, he had his regal image surrounded by the Greek words *Basileus Sōtēr Menandros* (King, Savior, Menander). The reverse side of these coins featured the Greek goddess Athena; her image was accompanied by the king's title in the local Pakrit language, written in Karoshthi letters (the alphabetic script developed in northwest-

ern India). These legacies, some obvious and others more subtle, persisted long after the collapse of the Hellenistic regimes. Greek language, letters, and coinage remained essential elements in the communication and trade around the Indian Ocean rim until at least the third century CE.

NOMADIC INFLUENCES OF PARTHIANS, SAKAS, AND KUSHANS

A wave of invasions and migrations from central Asia during the last three centuries BCE weakened Hellenistic influences in Iran and central Asia but did not completely eradicate them. The Seleucid state in Iran, having lost control of Bactria, now came under relentless pressure from the nomadic peoples living on the steppes to the north. The first to prey on them were the Parthians, a horse-riding people, who pushed southward around the middle of the second century BCE and wiped out the Greek kingdoms in Iran. The Parthians extended their power all the way to the Mediterranean, where they would ultimately encounter the expanding Roman Empire in Anatolia and Mesopotamia.

The original heartland of the world's first cities was becoming a borderland between the emerging powers of the Mediterranean and West Asia. Parthia and Rome were both strong, expansionist states and became archenemies: they confronted each other in Mesopotamia for nearly four centuries, until the Sasanian kings replaced the Parthians as the rulers of Iran in 224 CE. Because the Parthians probably did not have their own writing system when they became rulers of settled agricultural communities, their empire left no historical record; it is known to us only through the descriptions of Greek observers who had remained in central Asia after the retreat of Greek powers. According to these sources, the Hellenistic caravan cities on the eastern frontier of the Roman Empire continued to trade with the east in spite of the conflicts between the Romans and the Parthians. From the eastern shore of the Mediterranean all the way to Afghanistan, Greek was still the lingua franca for commercial activities.

During a second major wave of invasions after the Parthians invaded in the middle of the second century BCE, nomadic peoples swept out of Mongolia and central Asia into India around 130 BCE. They filled some of the vacuum left by the disintegration of Alexander's and Aśoka's empires, infusing the societies of South Asia with the nomadic and equestrian values of the steppe. In the process, they blended both Hellenism and Buddhist religious thought with a culture that glorified nomadic and pastoral ways and institutions. A modified Hellenistic culture and the Greek language became even more vital than before; even as its connections to Greece became more attenuated, its influence over Buddhism and other South Asian cultures grew. The famous Gandharan Buddhist art of this period clearly demonstrates a Hellenistic imprint.

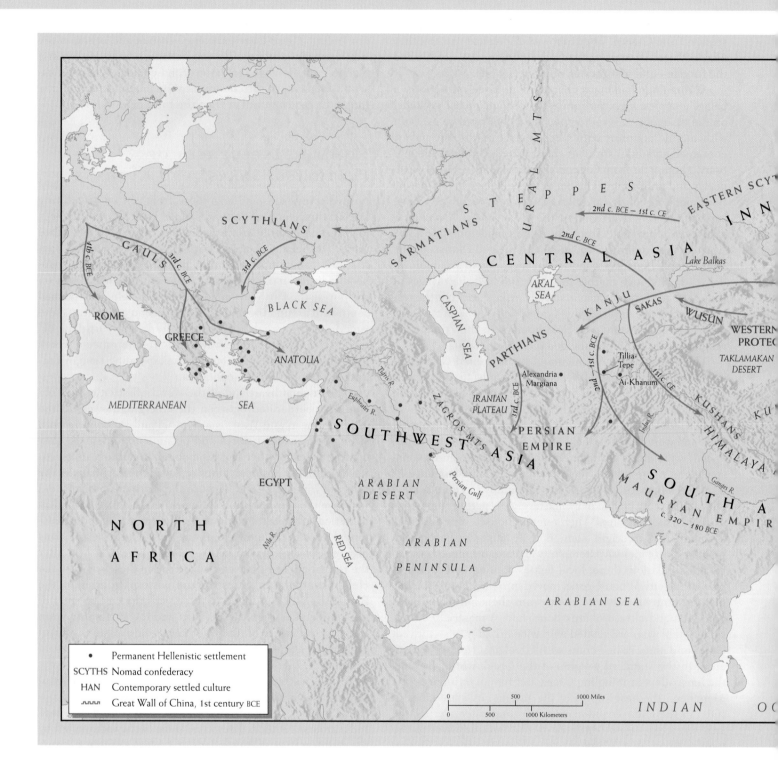

The new rulers came down from the dry northern steppe in waves, each driving its predecessor before it in search of new tribal domains. In the second century BCE, a vast tribal confederacy called the Xiongnu emerged as a dominant force in the east Asian steppe lands. While consolidating their power, the Xiongnu forced many other pastoral groups out of their homelands. One of these groups, the Saka tribes, moved toward the southwest into India; they conquered the area from Mathura to the western coast of India and gradually es-tablished many states. Meanwhile, the Parthians, who had supplanted the Greek Seleucids in Iran, also entered the Indus Valley—from the northwest, through the mountain passes of Baluchistan.

India's new Central Asian rulers were proud horse-riding peoples, possessing different cultural and linguistic back-grounds than the indigenous inhabitants. Like the Parthians, all lacked their own system of writing. Once they entered Bactria and the Indus Valley, they imitated the sedentary

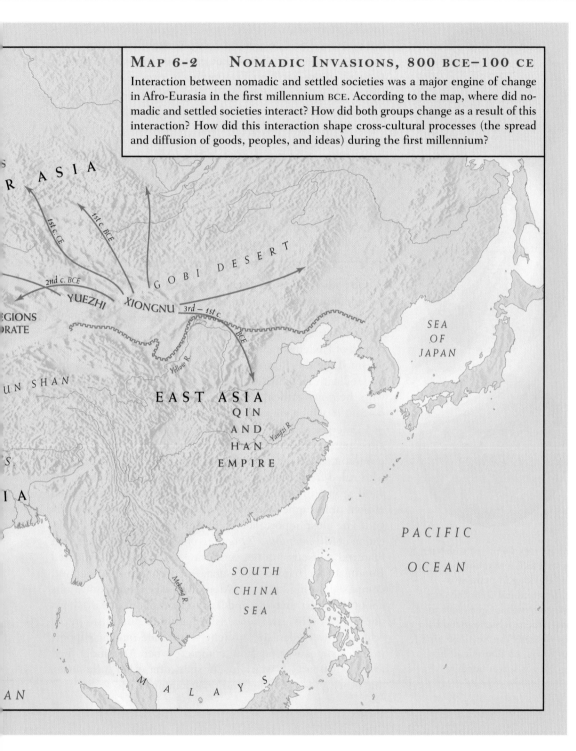

MAP 6-2   NOMADIC INVASIONS, 800 BCE–100 CE

Interaction between nomadic and settled societies was a major engine of change in Afro-Eurasia in the first millennium BCE. According to the map, where did nomadic and settled societies interact? How did both groups change as a result of this interaction? How did this interaction shape cross-cultural processes (the spread and diffusion of goods, peoples, and ideas) during the first millennium?

surrounded by the same legend—but here in the script of northwestern India.

The most dynamic and powerful of all of the northern nomadic groups to migrate into South Asia were the Yuezhi-Kushans, who arrived in 50 CE, about 150 years after the Yuezhi had entered Bactria. Led by their chief, Kujula Kadphises, the Yuezhi unified all the tribes of the region and immediately set up the Kushan dynasty. The Kushans' empire embraced a large and diverse territory and played a critical role in the formation of the Silk Road.

Like the Sakas and the Parthians, the Kushans were an illiterate people, but they adopted Greek as their official language. The face of a gold coin of Wima Kadphises (the second Kushan king to rule South Asia) features the king's bust, surrounded by Greek legends. The reverse side of the coin contains the image of the Hindu god Shiva, with his cow. Up to the end of the Kushan Empire in the early third century CE, Greek letters continued to be displayed on Kushan coins, sometimes on both sides but always on the face. The Kushan rulers kept alive the influence of Hellenism in Afghanistan and northwestern India in an area strategically located on the Silk Road, even though by this time few Greek speakers were left in the population. Mediterranean traders arrived in the Kushan markets to purchase silks from China, as well as Indian gemstones and spices; they carried out their transactions in Greek. The coins they used—struck to Roman weight standards (themselves derived from Greek coinage) and inscribed with Greek inscriptions—answered their needs perfectly.

rulers such as Menander, issuing coins, collecting taxes, and facilitating trade. The legends and images on the coins vividly demonstrate how these nomadic chiefs used the Hellenistic cultures of their conquered subjects. For example, one of the silver coins issued by the Saka ruler Maues, dated around 100 BCE, carries an image of Zeus, surrounded by the Greek inscription ΒΑΣΙΛΕΩΣ ΒΑΣΙΛΕΩΝ ΜΕΓΑΛΟΥ ΜΑΥΟΥ (King of Kings, the Great Maues). The reverse side of the coin shows the image of the Greek goddess Nike (Victory),

The coming of the many nomadic groups did not undermine local cultural traditions or the Hellenistic heritage, but it brought in a powerful new cultural ingredient: equestrianism.

Three Coins. *Top*: Wearing an elephant cap, Demetrius of Bactria titled himself the king of Indians as well as Greeks. On the other side of the coin is Hercules. *Middle*: The king Menander is remembered by Buddhists for his curiosity about their theology. His image appears on one side of the coin with a Greek legend of his name and title. On the other side, Athena is surrounded by Kharoshthi script, an Indian writing. *Bottom*: The Scythian king Maues used Greek to claim "King of Kings" on one side of his coin. On the other side, the goddess Nike is surrounded by Kharoshthi letters.

The Sakas and Kushans were proud nomads, who carried their horse-riding skills into India. In spite of the hot climate, the Sakas and Kushans continued to wear cone-shaped leather hats, knee-length robes, trousers, and boots as a way to set themselves off from the indigenous inhabitants. Since the time of the Vedic invaders (see Chapter 3), horses had been valued imports into the region—and with the advent of the Kushans, they became the most prestigious status symbol of the ruling elite. At the same time, the Kushans began consuming exotic goods that arrived from as far east as China and as far west as

the Mediterranean, as they enjoyed a highly diversified material culture. Their successful rule also stabilized the trading routes through central Asia that stretched from the steppes in the east to the Parthian Empire in the west. This would become one of the major segments of the Silk Road.

THE TRANSFORMATION OF BUDDHISM

> → *In what ways did the transformation of Buddhism represent cultural integration in South Asia?*

While India was undergoing noteworthy political and social change caused by the incursions of nomadic tribes, it was also experiencing dramatic cultural change in the religious sphere. Perhaps the most surprising repercussion of the spread of Hellenism after Alexander was the mutation of Buddhism. Like the Romans, the Indians were profoundly impressed with Hellenistic thought, and they sought to blend it with their own ethical and religious traditions—the most important of which was Buddhism.

A merger of belief systems began first among the Yavana city-states in the northwest, where Buddhism's sway was most pronounced. Here, for example, Menander, the Yavana king who ruled from Mathura on the Ganges plain, went far beyond promoting the belief that the Buddha was an inspired ethical philosopher: he held instead that the Buddha was a god. The most important step in this direction was the publication of *Milindapunha* (*Questions of King Milinda*), a text that featured a discussion between the king and a sophisticated Buddhist sage named Nagasena. According to this account, composed during his reign, Menander asked many questions about Buddhist theology and Nagasena explained away all his doubts. Nonetheless, the transformation of Buddhism into a religion with Hellenistic influences and wide-ranging support in other states was far from complete when Menander died around 130 BCE. It would occur only after other influences, and other gods and beliefs, were accommodated.

INDIA AS A SPIRITUAL CROSSROADS

Hellenism spread through many lands and cultures, but it was not the sole cultural movement to make a virtue of reaching out to other cultures, if only to subdue or transform them. Hellenism disrupted traditional political institutions and threatened existing religions wherever it went. In India, the nomads added another layer to this transformation, as did Arab and other seafarers whose mastery of the monsoon trade winds opened the Indian Ocean to commerce (see below) and made

> *In what ways did the transformation of Buddhism represent cultural integration in South Asia?*

Primary Source

THE QUESTIONS OF KING MILINDA

> *The Indo-Greek king Menander is a famous patron of Buddhism, as described in the* Questions of King Milinda. *The book, written in Pāli, begins with a description of the kingdom of Milinda, the Pāli name for Menander. The country is Yonakas (the Pāli name for Greeks, derived from Ionia, a region in western Asia Minor). This kingdom, according to the following passage from* The Questions of King Milinda, *is a center of prosperous trade and people of many different creeds, with a city whose glory rivals that of "the city of the gods."*

Thus hath it been handed down by tradition—There is in the country of the Yonakas a great centre of trade, a city that is called Sâgala, situated in a delightful country well watered and hilly, abounding in parks and gardens and groves and lakes and tanks, a paradise of rivers and mountains and woods. Wise architects have laid it out, and its people know of no oppression, since all their enemies and adversaries have been put down. Brave is its defence, with many and various strong towers and ramparts, with superb gates and entrance archways; and with the royal citadel in its midst, white walled and deeply moated. Well laid out are its streets, squares, cross roads, and market places. Well displayed are the innumerable sorts of costly merchandise with which its shops are filled. It is richly adorned with hundreds of almshalls of various kinds; and splendid with hundreds of thousands of magnificent mansions, which rise aloft like the mountain peaks of the Himâlayas. Its streets are filled with elephants, horses, carriages, and foot-passengers, frequented by groups of handsome men and beautiful women, and crowded by men of all sorts and conditions, Brahmans, nobles, artificers, and servants. They resound with cries of welcome to the teachers of every creed, and the city is the resort of the leading men of each of the differing sects. Shops are there for the sale of Benares muslin, of Kotumbara stuffs and of other cloths of various kinds; and sweet odours are exhaled from the bazaars, where all sorts of flowers and perfumes are tastefully set out. Jewels are there in plenty, such as men's hearts desire, and guilds of traders in all sorts of finery display their goods in the bazaars that face all quarters of the sky. So full is the city of money, and of gold and silver ware, of copper and stone ware, that it is a very mine of dazzling treasures. And there is laid up there much store of property and corn and things of value in warehouses—foods and drinks of every sort, syrups and sweetmeats of every kind. In wealth it rivals Uttara-kuru, and in glory it is as Âlakamandâ, the city of the gods.

> *The city Sâgala is in the country Yonakas, that of the Greeks. Judging from the references to elephants, horses, and the Himalayas, where approximately would it have been located?*
> *What kind of people lived there?*

SOURCE: *The Questions of King Milinda*, translated by T. W. Rhys Davis (1890; reprint, Delhi: Motilal Banarsidass, 1975), 2–3.

India the hub for long-distance ocean traders and travelers. All land and sea roads seemed to lead to India. Not surprisingly, during this era the region became a melting pot of ideas and institutions, from which a powerful and expansionist new spiritual synthesis emerged. Taken together, these influences—Hellenism, nomadism, and Arab seafaring culture—profoundly transformed one of India's most characteristic and indigenous spiritual and philosophical systems, Buddhism.

The Kushans, as rulers from the steppe, courted the local population by patronizing local religious cults. In so doing, they accommodated to the ways of their vanquished subjects. For example, in Bactria, where they encountered the shrines of many different gods, the Kushan kings had the images of various deities cast on the reverse side of their coins. They further demonstrated their acceptance of local belief systems by donating generously to shrines of Zoroastrian, Vedic, and particularly Buddhist cults. Around Kushan political centers, religious shrines mushroomed, and sculptural works reached a high artistic level. Kushan kings also had royal dynastic shrines built, beside which they placed statues of themselves, as patrons of the deities honored. Governors and generals followed their example of patronizing religions, as did traders, artisans, and other urbanites. Wealth flowed into religious institutions, especially Buddhist monasteries.

As a result, Buddhism changed dramatically from the days in the sixth and fifth centuries BCE when the Buddha walked from city to city preaching to his community of followers (*sangha*). In the first century CE, under the Kushan rule of northwestern India, the Buddhist *sangha* grew so rich because of India's growing commercial prosperity that monks began to live in elegant monastic complexes. The center of each was a stupa decorated with sculptures depicting the life and teachings of the Buddha. Such monasteries provided generously for the monks' well-being, with halls in which they gathered and worshipped and rooms in which they meditated and slept. During this age, Buddhist monasteries also opened themselves up to the public as places for worship.

THE NEW BUDDHISM: THE MAHAYANA SCHOOL

The mixing of new ways—nomadic, Hellenistic, Persian, and Mesopotamian—with traditional Buddhism produced a spec-

Stupa Staircase. These risers from the staircase of a large stupa in the Gandhara region display scenes from Buddhist stories. The upper one shows men in nomads' clothing playing music, including the Greek-style lira. On the middle one, men and women in Greek clothing drink and make merry. The people on the lower riser wear little clothing but are as happy as those on the other two panels.

Buddhist Cave Temple at Ajanta. Buddhists excavated cave temples along the trade routes between ports on the west coast of India and places inland. Paintings and sculptures from Ajanta became the models of Buddhist art in Central Asia and China.

tacular spiritual and religious synthesis. A new Buddhist school of theology, Mahayana, appeared at this time, marking a new stage in the evolution of the religion. For at least a hundred years, Buddhist learned men had debated the question of whether the Buddha was a god or a wise human being. The Mahayana Buddhists resolved this dispute in the first two centuries of the Common Era with a ringing affirmation: the Buddha was, indeed, a deity. This deification merged older Buddhist doctrines with Hellenism and cultural influences imported from the northern steppes. Mahayana Buddhism was at once worldly and accommodating, a spiritual pluralism that positioned Indian believers as a cosmopolitan, open people—welcoming contacts with peoples from other parts of Afro-Eurasia and laying the spiritual foundations for a region that had emerged as a crossroads of world cultures.

The religious appeal of Mahayana Buddhism was greater among lay followers than had been the earlier form of Buddhism, which had stressed that life was full of suffering and that people had to renounce desire to end their suffering and achieve *nirvana*. Indeed, as we saw in Chapter 5, the appeal of *nirvana* was difficult to understand for those without a belief in reincarnation. Newcomers such as migrants or traders were unlikely to embrace the nonexistence offered by *nirvana*, since they saw no need to escape painful cycles of birth, growth, death, and rebirth. In the vision of the Mahayana Buddhists, bodhisattvas (enlightened demigods who were ready to reach *nirvana* but delayed so that they might help others attain it) prepared "buddha-lands" and heavens—spiritual halfway points, like the Western Pureland of Amitabha—to

welcome deceased devotees not yet ready to let go of desires and enter *nirvana*. The universe of the afterlife in Mahayana Buddhism thus was colorful and pleasant, promising an attractive variety.

Mahayana—literally, "Great Vehicle"—Buddhism was so named because it was viewed as enabling all individuals, the poor and powerless as well as the rich and powerful, to move from a life of suffering into a happy existence. Yet to suffering devotees, the Buddha, who was now considered a god and had moved on to *nirvana*, could provide little relief. Mahayana

Stone Frieze from Ajanta. The figures flanking the Buddha should be bodhisattvas. However, the iconography of bodhisattvas was not clearly established at the time that this frieze was carved.

Buddhism featured a religious world peopled by bodhisattvas, still living in the world, whose primary purpose was to help all ranks of the human race. One of these bodhisattvas, Avalokiteshvara, proclaimed his willingness to stay in this world to guide people out of trouble, especially those who traveled in caravans and had the misfortune of running into robbers or those who had to navigate ships through storms.

The new image of the Buddha and the bodhisattvas also appeared in a new genre of Buddhist literature: Sanskrit Buddhist texts. Aśvaghosa (80?–150? CE), a great Buddhist thinker and also the first known Sanskrit writer, wrote a biography of the Buddha. In this work, known as the Buddhacarita, Aśvaghosa set the life story of the Buddha within the Kushan Empire instead of in the Shakya republic in the foothills of the Himalayas, where he had actually lived. Aśvaghosa said that the Buddha was born as a prince into a life of extreme luxury, becoming aware of human suffering only after heavenly revelations. To escape his mundane life, the young prince left home in the middle of the night, riding on his white horse. This new, largely fictive, version of the Buddha's life story quickly became canonical, spreading throughout India as well as to other countries in which people accepted Buddhism. Aśvaghosa's foundational spiritual text gave Buddhist beliefs more uniformity across South Asia.

CULTURAL INTEGRATION

Sanskrit Buddhist texts of the first centuries CE created a colorful set of images that gave rise to a large repertoire of Buddhist sculptural art and drama. On Buddhist stupas and shrines, artisans carved scenes of the Buddha's life, figures of bodhisattvas, and statues of patrons and donors. Buddhist sculptures from the northern part of Kushan territory, fashioned from gray schist rock, are called Gandharan art, and those from the southern part are called Mathuran art, created mainly from the local red sandstone. Gandharan Buddhist art shows strong Greek and Roman influences, whereas the sculptural style of the Buddha and bodhisattvas in the Mathura region evolved from the carved idols of folk gods and goddesses.

In spite of their stylistic differences, the schools shared themes and cultural elements. Both took the bold step, inspired by Hellenistic art and religious tradition, of sculpting the Buddha and bodhisattvas in realistic human, rather than symbolic, form, such as a bodhi tree. The Buddha of the Gandharan artists took on a Greek look, while the Buddha of Mathura appeared more Indic, yet both were serene. Though the Buddha wore no decorations, since he had cut off all his links to the world of endless death and rebirth, bodhisattvas were dressed as princes because they were still in this world, generously helping others. What was important was bringing the symbolic world of Buddhism closer to the people.

Bronze Buddha. This bronze Buddha often strikes viewers as a Jesus Christ. Greco-Roman influence on the iconography of Buddha was probably responsible for the Gandharan-style attire and facial expression of Buddhas and bodhisattvas.

Buddhist art depicted a society of diverse populations, as befit a spiritual system that appealed to peoples of many different cultural backgrounds. Take, for example, the clothes of the patron figures. For men and women alike, the garments represented were simple and well adapted to tropical climates. Those indigenous to the semi-tropical land dressed in a fashion that left their upper bodies nude; their lower bodies were covered by a wrapping akin to the modern dhoti, or loincloth. Jewelry adorned the headdresses and bodies. By contrast, their cone-shaped leather hats, knee-length robes, trousers, and boots made it easy to spot the nomadic peoples and identify their traditional garb. Figures with Greek clothing demonstrate continuing Hellenistic influence, and the appearance of Roman togas makes clear that imperial Rome's influence had reached the Indian subcontinent. In fact, the loose toga-like robes that adorn many statues of the Buddha suggest a mix-

Mathuran Buddha. This Mathuran Buddha of Gupta times is more refined than the Buddhas of the Kushan era. The robe is so transparent that the artist must have had very fine silk in mind when sculpturing.

ing of Roman and Buddhist themes. The jumble of different clothing styles makes visible the appeal of Buddhism to peoples of diverse backgrounds, who could share a faith while retaining their ethnic or regional differences.

The many peoples who lived under Kushan rule, Buddhist or not, had important cultural traits in common. They preferred Hellenistic or pseudo-Hellenistic architecture, particularly favoring columns, and they reveled in Greek music and dance. Although we do not know the songs that they sang at their festivals, we can recognize many of their musical instruments: the lira (a small version of the harp), the flute, the cymbal, the drum, and the xylophone. They were wine drinkers, and celebrated wine's intoxicating pleasures by using grape and grape-leaf motifs in their carvings. Carvings in the vicinity of Buddhist shrines often highlight festive drinking scenes. The horse was also celebrated in the story of

the Buddha. Under the Kushans, Buddhist monasteries were cosmopolitan organizations, where Greco-Roman, Indic, and steppe nomadic cultural themes blended together.

Long-distance and regional trade contributed to the transformation of Buddhism as well. Traders brought incense and jewels, which adorned bodhisattvas and stupas. Mahayana texts describe how these commodities became sacred to Buddhism. At the same time, monastic organizations became hospitable to traders who converged on India over mountain passes or from the Indian Ocean.

THE FORMATION OF THE SILK ROAD

→ *How did long-distance exchanges alter the cultural geography of Eurasia and North Africa?*

By 300 BCE, Afro-Eurasia was in the throes of a major transformation. Traders, migrants, and marauders, as well as conquerors, took to the roads and waterways with unprecedented zeal. They forged connections between distant areas, transporting products and ideas that would alter societies.

Overland routes, focusing on the spice trade (the trade in frankincense and myrrh from the Arabian Peninsula) and on the exchange of metals (copper, tin, and iron) and precious commodities (precious stones and textiles), had been traveled by merchants and traders in earlier periods, but they now expanded to link the lands from South Asia to the Mediterranean. In the first century BCE, early overland trade routes stretching from China to central Asia and then from central Asia to the Mediterranean would be joined in what was later labeled the Silk Road—though many commodities flowed back and forth on caravans, it was silk that came to exemplify the commercial integration of the Afro-Eurasian world. Traders would travel specific segments of the route, passing their goods on to others who would take the goods further along the road and, in turn, pass them on.

Also effective in promoting long-distance trade were waterways. The Egyptians had used the Nile River to transport goods and to trade for thousands of years, and coastal trade between ports thrived from very early times. Sea routes arose, following the coastlines of Iran, the Persian Gulf, and the Arabian Sea into the Red Sea, stretching down the shore of East Africa. Initially, mariners relied on land-based markers to orient themselves; but toward the end of the first millennium BCE, as navigational techniques improved and larger, more seaworthy craft were built, Arab traders ventured out into the Indian Ocean, and trade expanded. Once a large body of water such as the Indian Ocean could safely be crossed, the possible connections, exchanges, and accumulated knowledge

Legend:

— Silk Road
— Other trade routes
SCYTHS Nomad group
— Boundary of empires, states, and kingdoms
• Port/trading town
ᗧᗧᗧ Great Wall of China

Traded Goods

A/D Aromatics and drugs
Cu Copper
○ Coral
Everyday textiles
Fine cotton/garments
Fine stone and metal vessels
Furs
G Glassware
Gems
Gold
Grain
H Horses
I Incense
Ivory

○ Jewelry and cut gems
Laquerware
LF Luxury foods
LT Luxury textiles
Peacocks
Pearls
Silk
Slaves
S Spices
Statuary
Sn Tin
Tortoiseshell
Wine
Wood

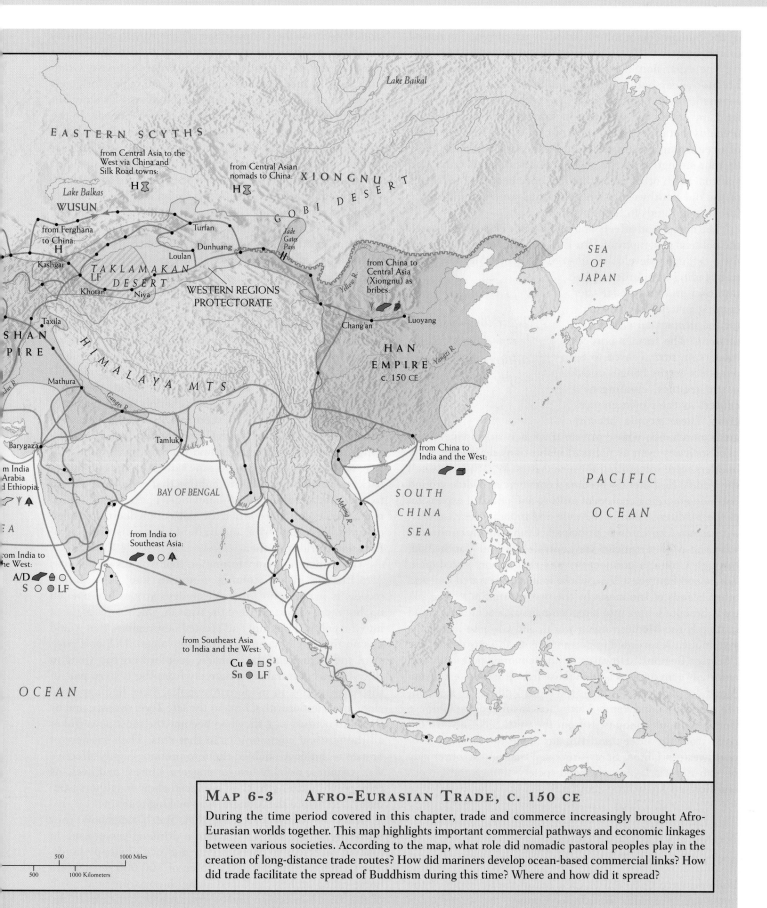

MAP 6-3 AFRO-EURASIAN TRADE, C. 150 CE

During the time period covered in this chapter, trade and commerce increasingly brought Afro-Eurasian worlds together. This map highlights important commercial pathways and economic linkages between various societies. According to the map, what role did nomadic pastoral peoples play in the creation of long-distance trade routes? How did mariners develop ocean-based commercial links? How did trade facilitate the spread of Buddhism during this time? Where and how did it spread?

of the human communities linked by its currents increased dramatically.

The expansion of commerce and contacts between the Mediterranean and South Asia built on and then reinforced a frenetic rise in commercial activity within each region. Over land and across the seas, traders loaded textiles, spices, and precious metals onto the backs of camels and into the holds of oceangoing vessels destined for distant markets. Trade thereby strengthened the ongoing political, intellectual, and spiritual shift: other areas that had once been on the fringes of the old Southwest Asian heartlands were coming to the fore as heartlands in their own right.

The compound effects of long-distance exchanges altered the political geography of Afro-Eurasia. The former cradles of the most highly developed cultures, Egypt and Mesopotamia, were fading as sources of innovation and knowledge, becoming instead a crossroads for the peoples on either side of them. The former borderlanders, in turn, ceased to be outsiders on the fringes of dynastic regimes, creating new centers as their own empires grew. These people became great merchants, whose private trade networks helped connect societies even as political institutions devised by state builders were integrating those societies. What we now call the Middle East literally became a commercial middle ground between emerging centers of culture and political expansion of the Mediterranean in the west and India in the east.

Eastern Afro-Eurasia, principally China, finally connected with the Mediterranean via central Asia and South Asia; through China, a connection was then made with Japan, Korea, and Southeast Asia, whose traders penetrated Bali and other islands of Indonesia by the first century BCE. The silk trade brought China into direct contact with central Asia and indirectly the Mediterranean world, and Chinese historians systematically recorded important events and customs of the "Western Regions." However, China remained politically and culturally a mysterious land to those from the Mediterranean. Alexander had gotten as far as the Indus Valley, to be sure, but the Himalayas and Pamir Mountains insulated the Chinese from ambitious conquerors from the west. Silk—a word derived from the Greek and Roman name for the people of northwestern China, *Sēres*—revealed that on the other side of Afro-Eurasia lay an advanced society, though the Greeks and Romans knew little about it.

NOMADS, FRONTIERS, AND TRADE ROUTES

Long-distance trade routes grew out of the activities of the horse-riding nomads from Inner Eurasia, the steppe lands stretching from the Caspian Sea all the way to present-day Mongolia, accustomed in the course of their migrations to carry supplies over great distances in order to survive. Gradually, they learned to trade goods from one region for goods produced elsewhere. They were the pioneers of a slow but powerful commercial transformation of Afro-Eurasia. In the second millennium BCE, as noted in Chapter 3, the arid central Asia homelands of the nomadic horsemen became deserts, and they sent out conquering armies. These so-called foreign barbarians played a vital role in history and in trade, for they alone traversed the entire region and had an impact on all the peoples living there.

One other advantage proved crucial to the nomads' interactions with other populations. Because of their movements from place to place, they were exposed to—and thus acquired resistance to—a greater variety of microbes than did sedentary peoples. Their relative immunity to disease aided the launch of early overland trade routes across Afro-Eurasia in the middle of the second millennium BCE, at the time when chariots first appeared in central Asia and pastoral groups began to link the North China plain to Turkestan (Xinjiang) as well as to Mongolia and Manchuria. Around 600 BCE, nomads on the steppe became skillful archers on horseback, gaining an advantage in fighting that emboldened them to range farther from their homelands. These long-distance marauders eventually learned the skills of mediating between cultures, blending terror and traffic to bring disparate Afro-Eurasian worlds together.

> *These long-distance marauders eventually learned the skills of mediating between cultures, blending terror and traffic to bring disparate Afro-Eurasian worlds together.*

The commercial transformation that would sweep across Afro-Eurasia in the coming centuries had political antecedents in the routes that Alexander's armies had opened up, but more important were the ways in which nomads raced into the political vacuum and created new regimes that would link northwest China and the Iranian plateau. The most powerful and intrusive of the nomadic peoples were the Xiongnu (Hsiung-nu) pastoralists, originally from the eastern part of the Asian steppe in modern Mongolia. They had appeared along the frontier with China in the late Zhou dynasty, and by the third century BCE they had become the most powerful of all the pastoral communities in that area. Their mastery of bronze technology enabled them to produce highly effective war weapons, notably bronze daggers, knives, and axes. As they grew in strength, they menaced their neighbors, and many fled before the Xiongnu war-making machine.

After the Xiongnu attacked their Yuezhi neighbors, they made the Yuezhi king's skull into a drinking vessel used in making sacrifices to the supreme god of the steppe lands. The humiliated Yuezhi, still a force of 100,000 to 200,000 horse-riding archers, galloped along the pastoral land north of the Tianshan Range until they reached the banks of the

Oxus. Their desire for revenge on the Xiongnu was tempered by their fear of yet more carnage. Besides, from their camp along the river they could see the fertile Bactrian plain dotted with Hellenistic cities. The Yuezhi continued their retreat westward, into Bactria and then into South Asia proper, where they would form the mighty Kushan Empire. As described above, the Kushans, occupying a large and diverse territory in northern and western India, played a key role in creating the infrastructure of the Silk Road during the first century CE and thus providing the key link between supply in the east and the rising market demand of the Roman Empire in the west.

What emerged was a political bridge that brought parts of Afro-Eurasia together. Both the land routes linking the Roman trading depot of Palmyra to central Asia and the sea routes carrying ships from the Red Sea to ports on the western coast of India had to pass through the territory of the Kushan Empire. At the eastern end of this chain of political and commercial contacts, the Chinese state was also beginning to protect trading outposts and frontiers, thereby enabling caravans to move about more easily. Chinese silk textiles were reaching the Roman market, and glassware from the Mediterranean, incense from the Arabian Peninsula, and precious stones from India were reaching China. The Silk Road connected the Mediterranean and Pacific coasts.

EARLY OVERLAND TRADE AND CARAVAN CITIES

As nomads moved southward, exposing new regions to their trading and migrating habits, they pushed the axis of commerce further south, beyond the original overland routes of central Asia—into the valleys and across the mountain passes east and west of India. The result was a new set of networks, parallel to and south and west of the original systems.

With this surge in trade came a new kind of commercial hub: the caravan city, established at strategic locations—often at the edges of deserts, or in oases—where vast trading groups would assemble before beginning their arduous journeys. Some of these caravan cities in the mountains and deserts of Southwest Asia, having begun as Greek garrison towns, became centers of Hellenistic culture, displaying such staples of the polis as public theaters. Even those depots founded by Arab traders had a Hellenistic tinge, as local traders often admired Greek culture and in any case had frequent commercial interactions with the Mediterranean world. They wrote in Greek, sometimes speaking it in addition to their native tongues.

A number of important caravan cities emerged at the northern end of a route that led through the deserts of Arabia. At the extreme southwestern tip of the Arabian Peninsula, in what is now known as Yemen, was a land watered by the same rains responsible for the annual flooding of the Nile. The area was a wonder of its own, a vivid patch of green at the end of 1,200 miles of desert. Its prosperity was in part due to its role as a major gathering place both for long-distance spice traders about to transport frankincense and myrrh north through the Arabian Desert and for sailors, whose ships early on traveled the Red and the Arabian Seas, and later crossed the Indian Ocean.

The southern Arabian Peninsula had long been famous for its frankincense and myrrh, products used by Greeks and Romans to make perfume and incense; they reached their buyers via an overland route sometimes called the Incense or Spice Road. The Sabaeans, who lived in southern Arabia, became fabulously wealthy from these sales and from the Indian Ocean spice trade. The traders who transported the spices and fragrances to the Mediterranean were another Arabic-speaking people: the Nabataeans, sheepherders who eked out a living in the Sinai Desert and the northwestern Arabian Peninsula.

Because the Greeks and later the Romans needed large quantities of incense to burn in worshipping their gods, the trade passing through this region was extremely lucrative. But the camel caravans had a difficult journey through the rock ravines stretching from the Dead Sea to the Red Sea's Gulf of Aqaba. Here, Nabataean herders had learned to cut cisterns out of solid stone to catch rainwater and to provide themselves with cave shelters. Nabataeans profited by supplying water and food to the travelers. In one of the valleys through which travelers frequently passed, in what is now southwest Jordan, the Nabataeans built their capital—a rock city called Petra ("rock" in Greek is *petros*)—which displayed abundant Greek influences. Many of the houses and shrines were cut out of the mountains. Their colonnaded facades and tombs, constructed for common people as well as the nobles, projected Hellenistic motifs. The most striking building of this kind was the vast theater. The entire structure—the stage

Petra. This beautiful building is known as El-Khaznah, or The Treasury, at Petra, the capital of the Nabataean kingdom, located in the southern part of modern-day Jordan. The wealth created by the region's long-distance trade is manifest in the magnificent buildings at the center of the city. Both the face of the building and its interior are cut out of the sandstone rock that forms the cliffs surrounding Petra.

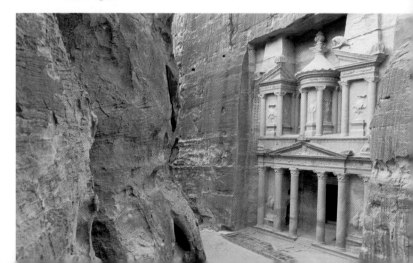

Primary Source

THE CARAVAN CITY OF PETRA

Petra was a city cut out of the pink rock cliffs in the valley between the Dead Sea and the Red Sea. The Nabataeans, an Arabic-speaking people, built the city to host traders from west and east; from here, caravans were sent to trading entrepôts in the Mediterranean and on the Iranian plateau. Petra was totally dependent on the spice and perfume trade, and its good fortune ran out under the Roman Empire when the silk trade favored another caravan city, Palmyra. Yet even today, the rock structure of the city shining in the sun is an imposing sight.

Much has already been written about Petra and I do not wish to repeat what has already been said. I am tempted almost to liken the city to some wonder from the *Arabian Nights*. When one descends into the valley from the surrounding heights towards the place where the river has cut for itself a passage between the dark-red rocks, one seems to be gazing at some large and fantastic excrescence—a piece of reddish-mauve raw flesh set between the gold of the desert and the green of the hills. It is a most extraordinary sight, which becomes even more extraordinary when the cavalcade slowly descends into the river valley, and the rocky walls of the ever-narrowing gorge tower up to the right and left, speckled with red, orange, mauve, grey, and green layers. Wild and beautiful they are, with their contrasts of light and shade; the light blinding, the shadows black. And there is seldom even anything to remind the visitor that this gorge served for centuries as a main road, trodden by camels, mules, and horses, and that along it rode Bedouin merchants who must have felt like ourselves its horror and its mystic fascination. Yet suddenly one may be confronted with the façade of a tomb-tower

with dog-tooth design, or with an altar set high up on one of the vertical walls, bearing a greeting or prayer to some god, inscribed in the Nabataean tongue. Our caravan advanced slowly along the gorge, until an unexpected bend disclosed to us an apparition sparkling pinky-orange in the sun, which must once have been the front of a temple or tomb. Elegant columns joined by fascinating pediments and arches form the frames of the niches in which its statues stand. All this rose up before us dressed in a garb of classicism yet in a style new and unexpected even by those well acquainted with antiquity. It was as though the magnificent scenery of some Hellenistic theatre had appeared, as though a Pompeian wall-painting, not of the fourth but of the second period, had been chiselled in the rock.

→ *What specific features in the description of the gorge leading to Petra and the monuments in and around the city remind you of the* Arabian Nights?

SOURCE: M. Rostovtzeff, *Caravan Cities* (Oxford: Clarendon Press, 1932), 42–43.

---

platform, orchestra, and forty-five rows of seats—was carved out of the sandstone terrain and could accommodate an audience of 6,000 to 10,000 people (up to one-third of the city's population). Plays were at first invariably performed in Greek, and later in Latin, for being cosmopolitan required participating in the language of high culture.

Petra's power and wealth, at its height from the mid–second century BCE to the early second century CE, outlasted the Hellenistic Seleucids' control of the region. The Greek language persisted as the lingua franca critical to Petran mer-

chants seeking to maintain their trading ties. The caravan traders, the ruling elite of the rock city, controlled the supply of spices and fragrances from Arabia, North Africa, and India to the ever-expanding Roman Empire. During these years, Nabataean caravan traders based in Petra traveled throughout the eastern Mediterranean, erecting temples wherever they established their trading communities. Yet the glory of this commercial people dimmed with the coming of the Romans, who took over the province of Arabia—and with it, the profitable Spice Road trade.

THE WESTERN END OF THE SILK ROAD: PALMYRA

As central Asia became dotted with overland trading hubs, these new commercial cities thrived in Southwest Asia as well. Indeed, they soon came to overshadow the older political or religious capitals. With Petra's decline during the Roman period, another settlement took its place as the most important caravan city at the western end of the Silk Road: Palmyra. (Palmyra's local name was Tadmor, which means "palm.") Rich citizens of Rome relied on the Palmyran traders to procure luxury goods for them, importing Chinese silks for women's clothing and incense for the worship of their gods, as well as gemstones, pearls, and many other precious items.

Administered by an oligarchy composed of the chiefs of local tribes, Palmyra was able to maintain a great deal of local autonomy, even under formal Roman control. Although the Palmyrans used a Semitic dialect in daily life, state affairs and business were conducted in Greek. Their merchants had learned the language when the region came under Seleucid rule, and it remained useful to them when they did business with caravans from afar, long after the political influences of Hellenism had waned. Palmyran traders handled many kinds of textiles, including cotton from India and cashmere wool that originated in Kashmir or nearby in the highlands of central Asia. The many silk textiles that archaeologists have discovered at this site were produced in Han China (see Chapter 7), providing material evidence that the Silk Road had, by the first century CE, reached the Mediterranean. While the oli-

garchs retained some of the exquisite silks for themselves, most were shipped on to the more profitable markets in the Mediterranean. The Romans not only purchased silk cloth but also started to have silk woven to order in eastern Mediterranean cities such as Beirut and Gaza. Silk yarns and dyes have also been found at Palmyra.

The earnings from this lucrative trade enabled the people of Palmyra to build a splendid marble city in the desert. A colonnade, theater, senate house, agora, and major temples formed the metropolitan area of the city. The Palmyrans worshipped many deities, both local and Greek, but they seemed most concerned about their own afterlife. Like Petra, Palmyra had a cemetery as big as its residential area, and the marble sculptures on the tombs depicted the life of the city. Many tombs showed the master or the master and his wife reclining on a Greek-style couch, holding drinking goblets in their hands. The clothes on those marble statues appear more Iranian than Greek: robes with wide stripes whose hems were decorated with exquisite designs. Sculptures of camel caravans and horses tell us that the deceased were caravan traders in this world and were looking forward to continuing their rewarding occupation in the afterlife.

Left alone to conduct its business, Palmyra rapidly grew into a commercial powerhouse. The city not only provided supplies and financial services to passing caravans but also hosted self-contained trading communities, or *fondûqs*—complexes of hostels, storage houses, offices, and often temples. Palmyra achieved its golden age at the same time that the Silk Road in central Asia was flourishing as the major

Palmyran Tomb Sculpture. This relief was part of the tomb sculptures for a wealthy trader from Palmyra. The camel to the left of the men—a dromedary, a one-humped camel renowned for its speed—was truly the ship of the desert, able to haul huge loads of commercial goods over the big trade routes of Southwest Asia. Merchants, like these two men, became wealthy from the transcontinental exchange of luxury goods.

Palmyran Tomb Sculpture. This tombstone relief sculpture shows a wealthy young Palmyran, attended by a servant—probably a household slave. Palmyra was at the crossroads of the major cultural influences traversing southwestern Asia at the time. The style of the clothing—the flowing pants and top—and the couch and pillows reflect the trading contacts of the Palmyran elite, in this case with India to the east. The hairstyle and mode of self-presentation signal influences from the Mediterranean to the west.

route for the shipment of silk and other luxuries from China to the eastern rim of the Indian Ocean. Some of the goods went across the Iranian plateau, reaching the Mediterranean by way of Syria's desert routes. Another major artery went via Afghanistan, the Indus, and the west coast of India, then across the Indian Ocean to the Red Sea. Aiding the success of the Silk Road was the pervasive shared culture of Hellenistic influences, lingering centuries after Greek political power had vanished from this region.

REACHING CHINA ALONG THE SILK ROAD

The Chinese economy was growing rapidly at the eastern end of the trans-Afro-Eurasian networks of commerce. Chinese artisans produced the most sought-after commodity of long-distance trade: silk. The country grew rich from the Silk Road and the ships that plied the South China Sea. Silkworms, carefully bred, produced silk, which was China's most valuable export. It was also used to conduct diplomacy with the nomadic kingdoms on the western frontiers and to underwrite its armies. Chinese rulers used silk to pay off neighboring nomads and borderlanders, buying both peaceful borders and horses with the fabric. During the Zhou dynasty, it served as a precious medium of exchange and trade. Silk has always been highly valued as a material for clothing—

while cloth made from hemp, flax, and other fibers tends to be rough, silk looks and feels rich. Moreover, it was both cool against the skin in hot summers and warm in the winter. Silk also had immense tensile strength, useful for bows, lute strings, and fishing lines; spun into a tight fabric, it could be made into light body armor or light bags to transport liquids (particularly useful for long-distance traders, who traveled across arid expanses). Before the invention of paper by the Chinese sometime after 100 CE, silk was widely used as writing material, more durable than bamboo or wood. Brush writing on silk was the medium of choice for correspondence, maps, and illustrations, and important texts written on silk often joined other funerary objects in the tombs of aristocratic lords and wealthy magnates. No wonder it was such a prized commodity!

Thousands of bales of silk made their way to Indian, central Asian, and Mediterranean markets, where they became extraordinarily valuable trade goods—an exotic luxury that could be obtained only from China. The ultimate prestige commodity of the ruling classes from India to the Mediterranean, silk naturally gave its name to the trade route along which its precious bales traveled. Pliny the Elder noted: "The *Seres* [the Chinese] are especially well known for a wool-like substance in their trees. After soaking it in water, they comb a white-colored substance from the down of the leaves. . . . The work involved is so complex, and the goods sought out from a place so distant in our world, all so that Roman women can appear in public in transparent clothing" (*Natural History* 6.20.54; trans. Brent Shaw).

Economic life in ancient China had centered on the agricultural manors of rich and powerful landowners. After 300 BCE, however, independent farmers increasingly produced commercial crops for the expanding marketplaces now scattered across the landscape along key land routes as well as rivers, canals, and lakes. As the market economy grew, merchants organized themselves into influential family lineages and specialized occupational guilds. Increasingly, power shifted away from older agrarian elites and into the hands of urban financiers and traders. They benefited from the improvement in roads and waterways, which eased the transportation of local products such as grain, hides, horses, and silk from the villages to the new towns and cities. By the second century BCE, wealthy merchants such as the Fan family were ennobled as local magnates and wore the clothing that marked their official status. Bronze coins of various sizes and shapes (such as the spade-shaped money of a number of semi-autonomous Warring States; see photo in Chapter 5), as well as cloth and silk used in barter, also aided the growth in long-distance trade. As commerce expanded, regional lords opened local customs offices to extract a share of the money and products for themselves.

Chinese and other merchants expanded trade across the Silk Road and the South China Sea. Local tollgates and customhouses sprang up to tax this commerce along land routes

→ *How did long-distance exchanges alter the cultural geography of Eurasia and North Africa?*

and waterways, but facilitating trade was also a key concern of the state. To protect traders, the merchant ships were joined by military boats, able to cover some seventy-five miles in a day and carry fifty soldiers and supplies for a three-month voyage. Though China still had little intellectual interaction with the rest of Afro-Eurasia, its commercial exchanges skyrocketed. Southern silk was only the first of many Chinese commodities that reached the world beyond the Taklamakan Desert. China also became an export center for lacquer, hemp, and linen. From Sichuan came iron, steel, flint, hard stone, silver, and animals, while jade came from the northwest. At the same time, China was importing Mediterranean, Indian, and central Asian commodities.

Despite its early development of commerce, China still had no major ports on the east coast that might compare to Palmyra. Internal, interregional trade predominated; it eventually fed into the emerging Silk Road through much more decentralized networks. Cities in the landlocked north were usually administrative centers where farmers and traders gathered to take advantage of the regional states' political and military protection. The larger ones had gates that were closed between sunset and sunrise, and during the night, mounted soldiers patrolled the streets. Newer towns along the seacoast in the southeast still looked upriver to trade with inland agrarian communities, which also produced the silk that made it to the Mediterranean via Central Asia. Later, China would become the site of massive trading centers.

The Chinese people and the Chinese state remained little affected by Hellenism and Mahayana Buddhism, the intellectual globalizing influences so important elsewhere in Afro-Eurasia during this period. China went about dealing with its own crises, laying the foundations for the magnificent Han Empire that eventually expanded into the Silk Road in the middle of the first century BCE (see Chapter 7). But through trade, the emergence of long-distance exchange and increasingly globalized contacts did powerfully influence the

Silk Texts. Before the invention of paper, silk was widely used as writing material because it was more mobile and durable than bamboo or wood for correspondence, maps, illustrations, and important texts included as funerary objects in the tombs of aristocrats. The Mawangdui silk texts shown here are from a Hunan tomb that was closed in 168 BCE and opened in 1973. Daoist philosophical texts and medical works were found in the tomb.

Zhou Coins. The diversity of bronze coinage during the late Zhou represented the growing autonomy of the Warring States from the declining Zhou dynasty. Not until the Qin unification would a centralized government again issue a unified bronze currency.

region. The booming trade that rippled through China would reshape its social and political structures.

THE SPREAD OF BUDDHISM ALONG THE TRADE ROUTES

Conquest and commerce brought the edges of Afro-Eurasia together. The pathways that took shape with the migrations of nomads, and had become the routes followed by armies, now were secured, enabling merchants to expand their business. But more than just commercial opportunity coursed through the trade arteries. Monks also plied these roads to spread the word of new religions to far-flung peoples. The chief expansionist faith in this period came out of India, inspired in part by the successful spread of Hellenism (which had, for the most part, diffused itself through secular institutions) and taking advantage of the great new trade links that crisscrossed Afro-Eurasia. The Buddha was no longer just a sage departed to the state of *nirvana*, but was also a god who could be worshipped like any Greek deity.

Under Kushan patronage during the first centuries CE, Buddhism reached out from India to China and central Asia,

following the Silk Road. Commercial networks became the channels for spreading religious beliefs. Monks from the Kushan Empire accompanied traders to Luoyang, the eastern capital of the Han Empire. There they started to translate Buddhist texts into Chinese, aided by Chinese converts who were mostly also traders. Buddhist ideas were slow to gain acceptance, however. It took several centuries, and a new wave of nomadic migrations, for Buddhism to take root in China.

Buddhism fared less well when it tried to follow the same commercial arteries westward. Although Buddhists did make efforts to gain followers in the Parthian Empire—indeed, some early Buddhist preachers in China were Parthians—the religion never became established on the Iranian plateau and made no further headway toward the Mediterranean. The main barrier to its westward movement was Zoroastrianism, which had been a state religion in the Achaemenid Empire during the fifth and fourth centuries BCE; by the time Buddhism's aspirations took a global form, it had long been well established in Iran. Iranian Hellenism had done little to weaken the power of Zoroastrianism, whose adherents, like their Buddhist counterparts, formed city-based religious communities affiliated primarily with traders. Following the Silk Road, Zoroastrian traders traveled both eastward to China and westward to the coast of the Mediterranean and were another impediment to the westward spread of Buddhism.

TAKING TO THE SEAS: COMMERCE ON THE RED SEA AND INDIAN OCEAN

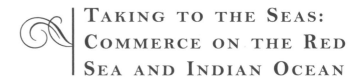

> → *What factors contributed to the growth of the Indian Ocean sea trade?*

Land routes were the tried-and-true avenues followed by migrants, traders, and wayfarers. But they carried only what could be borne on the backs of humans and animals; travel on them was slow, and they were vulnerable to marauders. With time, some risk takers found ways of moving about on waterways and thereby connecting regions together—eventually on an unprecedented scale and with an ease unimaginable to earlier merchants. These risk takers were Arabs, from the commercial middle ground of the emerging Afro-Eurasian trading system.

Arab traders had long carried such spices as frankincense and myrrh to the Egyptians, who used them in religious and funerary rites, and later to the Greeks and Romans. Metals such as bronze, tin, and iron were carted by traders over land routes from Anatolia, as were gold, silver, and chlorite from

THE WORLDS OF *PERIPLUS*

A particularly revealing periplus that has survived was written in Greek by an Egyptian sailor and trader toward the end of the first century CE. *Periplus Maris Erythraei,* or *Periplus of the Red Sea,* was much more than a guide to the Red Sea trade. Its author, a shrewd businessman, keen observer, and experienced navigator, described the whole world of commerce of the Red Sea, the Mediterranean, and the Indian Ocean. He catalogued the navigable routes and listed the various goods that were available and marketable in the ports; starting from the Red Sea, he moved southward along East Africa's coast and then eastward all the way to India. The result is the first historical record of the city-states existing along the coast of East Africa and one of the earliest accounts of Africa south of the Sahara. Throughout, he supplied data on currencies, customs, and the political regimes that controlled the ports and radiated into their hinterlands.

The author's voyage began from Berenice. After leaving this Red Sea port, he encountered tribal countries on his right hand, the coastal lands of today's Sudan and Eritrea. The *Periplus* named the region Barbaria, the land of barbarians, and identified its inhabitants with such labels as "eaters of fish" and "eaters of wild animals." Further south, the author noted the coastal area of a former Ptolemaic Egyptian colony that had fallen into decline and now exported only tortoise shells and ivory. On the other side of the Red Sea lay the coast of Arabia, where the waters were so calm that ships did not need to be anchored but where pirates from the Nabataean tribes preyed on passing ships.

Once it sailed out of the narrow strait, the ship entered the Gulf of Aden, famed as the land of frankincense and myrrh. The author of the *Periplus* dubbed the northern coast of modern Somalia "the Far-side Country." Beyond the territory from which incense was exported, traders brought ivory, tortoise shells, and slaves to the markets. The Somalia ports received cargoes of staple goods from India such as rice and ghee (clarified butter), sesame oil, cotton textiles, and sugar. The southernmost port along the east coast of Africa known to the author was Rhapta, somewhere near modern Dar es Salaam and nearly 3,000 miles from Berenice. This region had fallen under the influence of Arabs—specifically, the Sabaeans— through intermarriage and trade.

The trading ships left the southern Arabian coast with the monsoon winds behind them, heading for the entrepôts of India. With the emergence of long-distance trade, entrepôts became a new kind of urban hub on the social landscape. Barbaricum, at the mouth of the Indus, was the first Indian port reached from the west. On their arrival there, traders unloaded linen textiles, red coral, glassware, wine, and money from the Mediterranean and Egypt, as well as frankincense and storax, aromatic gum resins from Southwest Asia that the traders had purchased on their journey. These cargoes were shipped to the upper Indus region of the Punjab and Gandhara. While at harbor in India, traders loaded their ships with treasures from the east: fragrances or spices from the Himalayas and India, such as costus root and bdellium, turquoise from Khorasan in Iran, lapis lazuli from Badakhshan in Afghanistan, indigo dye and cotton textiles from India, furs from central Asia, and silk textiles and yarn from China.

The most important Indian port at the time of the *Periplus* was Barygaza on the Gulf of Khambhat (Cambay), near the modern city of Broach in Gujarat, but its harbor was very difficult to navigate. The coast was rugged, the sea bottom was uneven, and the tidal waves were high and variable. Local fishermen under the king's service came out to guide foreign ships to the harbor. In fact, the entire northwestern and western parts of India were connected to the Mediterranean through Barygaza. Here the descriptions in the *Periplus* concentrate on the abundance of Greek influences. For example, the author noted that in the market of Barygaza old drachmas of the Indo-Greek kings Apollodotus and Menander, inscribed with Greek letters, were still circulating. Although he often garbled the names of places and people, his general point was clear enough: Greek culture played a critical role in the long-distance trade of India.

Map of the Periplus.

Arab seafarers led the way into the Indian Ocean, forging the links that joined East Africa, the eastern Mediterranean, and the Arabian Peninsula with India, Southeast Asia, and East Asia. Such voyages involved longer stays at sea and were far more dangerous than sailing in the Mediterranean. Yet by the first century CE, Arab and Indian sailors were transporting Chinese silks, central Asian furs, and fragrances from the trees of the Himalayas across the Indian Ocean. The city of Alexandria in Egypt soon emerged as a key transit point between the Mediterranean Sea and the Indian Ocean. Boats carried the main Mediterranean exports of olives and olive oil, wine, drinking vessels, glassware, linen and wool textiles, and red coral up the Nile, stopping along the river at Koptos and other port cities from which camel caravans took the goods to the Red Sea ports of Myos Hormos and Berenice. For centuries, Mediterranean merchants considered the Arabian Peninsula to be the end of the Spice Road. But after Alexander's expedition and the establishment of numerous colonies between Egypt and Afghanistan, they began to appreciate the wealth and opportunities that lay along the shores of the Indian Ocean.

Arab sailors who ventured into the Indian Ocean took advantage of new navigational techniques, especially celestial bearings (using the position of the stars to determine the position of the ship and the direction to sail). They used large ships called *dhows*, whose sails were rigged to easily capture the wind; these were the forerunners of modern cargo vessels, capable of long hauls in rough waters. Beginning about 120 BCE, mariners came to understand the seasonal rain-filled monsoon winds, which blow strongly from the southwest be-

the Iranian plateau. Gold, ivory, and other goods from northern India passed through Taxila (the capital of Gandhara) and the Hindu Kush Mountains into Persia as early as the sixth century BCE. Following the expansion of the Hellenistic world, however, ships increasingly engaged in long-distance trade by sea, sailing down the Red Sea and across the Indian Ocean as they carried goods between the tip of the Arabian Peninsula and the ports of the Indian subcontinent.

Chronology

	400 BCE	300 BCE	200 BCE
SOUTHWEST ASIA AND NORTHERN AFRICA		▪ *Conquests of Alexander the Great, 334–323 BCE* ▪ *Emergence of Hellenistic "successor kingdoms" beginning in 323 BCE* ▪ *Parthian kingdom, 240 BCE–224 CE*	
THE MEDITERRANEAN		▪ *Roman expansion in the Italian Peninsula beginning in 330s and 320s BCE* ▪ *Roman-Carthage war (continued Roman territorial expansion), 264–241 BCE*	
CENTRAL ASIA		▪ *Conquests of Alexander the Great, 334–323 BCE* ▪ *Bactrian kingdom, 250–130 BCE*	
SOUTH ASIA		▪ *Mauryan Empire, 321–184 BCE* *Yavana kings emerge around 200 BCE* ▪	*Saka invasions* ▪ *Han expands into the Silk Road* ▪
EAST ASIA	▪ *Warring States period, 403–221 BCE*	*Xiongnu Confederacy in the Mongolian steppes, 2nd or 3rd century BCE* ▪ *Unification of China under the Qin dynasty, 221 BCE* ▪ *Emergence of Han Empire, 206 BCE* ▪	

tween October and April and then from the northeast between April and October—knowledge that gave a huge impetus to the maritime trade connecting the Mediterranean with the Indian Ocean.

The new sailing knowledge was reflected in the books—each called a *periplus,* or a "sailing around"—in which sea captains recorded the landing spots and ports between their two destinations. The revolution in navigational techniques and knowledge dramatically reduced the cost of long-distance shipping and multiplied the ports of call around large bodies of water such as the South China Sea, the Indian Ocean, and the Mediterranean Sea. Some historians have argued that there were now two Silk Roads: one by land and one by sea.

 ## CONCLUSION

Alexander's bloody campaigns, which reached the frontiers of South Asia, had effects more profound than any military or political regime that had preceded them. To be sure, the regime created by his conquests depended so much on Alexander himself that it fragmented almost immediately after his death. Nevertheless, the political, social, and cultural significance of those conquests was lasting, for they ultimately helped transform Afro-Eurasia culturally and economically. Alexander's military forces carried with them Greek institutions and culture, and they promoted the establishment of Greek-speaking communities across Eurasia and North Africa. For at least five centuries after the breakup of Alexan-

der's short-lived rule, Hellenistic culture reverberated from Rome in the west all the way to the Ganges in the east. Appropriately, the Hellenistic cultural movement was most strongly represented by the Greek language, which was linked to Greek culture, institutions, and trade. We should not lose sight of the fact, however, that many of the Greek-speaking peoples and their descendants who stayed on in parts of Southwest and Central Asia integrated cultural practices and traditions with their own Greek ways creating a series of diverse and rich cultures. The influences of culture flowed both ways. The economic story is equally a complex one. Let us remember that we should not give all the credit to Alexander and his successors. In many respects, they followed pathways long established by previous kingdoms and empires. If anything, Alexander's successors helped strengthen and expand the existing trade routes and centers of commercial activity, which ultimately led to the formal creation of the Silk Road.

Although this cultural movement that we call Hellenistic lasted longer than most cultural systems and had a wider appeal than any previous set of philosophical and spiritual ideas, it did not sweep away everything before it. Indigenous cultures made their accommodations with this movement or fought against it with all their might, fearing the loss of their own cultural identities. Others took from it what they liked and discarded the rest. The citizens of Rome admired its achievements and steeped themselves in it while fashioning their own Latin-based culture. Eventually, they created an imperial polity that outdistanced Alexander's in expanse, depth, and durability. In North Africa, the culturally sophisticated and commercially talented Carthaginians saw some

100 BCE	1 CE	100 CE	200 CE

■ *Transformation of Buddhism, 1st century* CE
■ *Kushan kingdom, 1st–3rd centuries* CE *(established 60* CE*)*

of these Greek means of expression as advantageous and useful for new elites of the Mediterranean like themselves.

Of all the peoples brought under the sway of Hellenistic thinking, the South Asian peoples produced the most varied responses because Hellenism struck a region that was already riddled with a multitude of cultures. Once opened to the external influences of Macedonian invaders, steppe nomads, and Arab seafarers, South Asia became the confluence of the currents that were moving so swiftly and decisively across Afro-Eurasia. The most telling of the South Asian responses took place in the realm of spiritual and ethical norms, where the doctrines of a compelling teacher of the sixth and fifth centuries BCE, the Buddha, evolved in the direction of a full-fledged world religious system, which in turn spread through the commercial networks that crisscrossed Afro-Eurasia.

Greater political integration helped fashion highways for commerce. Nomads left their steppe lands and exchanged wares across great distances. As they continued to find greater opportunities for business, their trade routes shifted further south, radiating out of the oases of central Asia. Eventually merchants, rather than the trading nomads, created new ventures and seized the opportunities provided by new technologies, especially in sailing and navigation. These commercial transformations connected distant parts of Afro-Eurasia. Accompanying the spread of Greek ways—indeed, fueling the diffusion of Hellenism—was the opening of trade. Alexander's campaigns had followed some of the trade routes east, and his conquests opened up the channels of exchange permanently. In the wake of conquests, the Silk Road and proliferating sea-lanes connected ports and caravan towns from North Africa to South China, creating new social classes, producing new urban settings, and ultimately supporting the emergence of powerful new polities. In this sense, long-distance trade began the process of bringing distant parts of the world together and fostering awareness of other cultures. The paradox of the era discussed in this chapter is that although growing trade and migration encouraged greater contact between the regions of Afro-Eurasia, it also ushered in the beginnings of new universalist ideas of a "people" bound by customs and faith, if not by loyalty to a leader. As people began to adopt these varying creeds, they also became increasingly aware of their differences.

STUDY QUESTIONS

◎ WWNORTON.COM/STUDYSPACE

1. Analyze the impact of Alexander's conquest on the Afro-Eurasian world. How did his military pursuits, and those of his successors, bring together various worlds?

2. Describe the influence of Hellenism on societies outside the Greek homeland during this time period. What aspects of Hellenistic culture held broad appeal for diverse groups?

3. Compare and contrast Judean, Roman, and Carthaginian responses to Hellenistic influences. How receptive was each society to Greek cultural influences?

4. Explain how South Asia (or India) became a melting pot for the intellectual, political, and economic currents sweeping across Afro-Eurasia between 350 BCE and 250 CE. How did this development affect Buddhist doctrine?

5. Analyze the extent to which long-distance trade routes connected societies across Afro-Eurasia during this time period. Which societies were involved in these exchanges? How did commercial linkages affect those societies involved?

6. Analyze the influence of nomadic pastoral societies in Afro-Eurasia during this time period. What role did they play in integrating cultures and economies?

7. Explain how interregional contacts transformed Buddhism during this time period. How did Buddhism expand across a variety of cultures?

8. Explain how art, architecture, and other forms of material culture in various Afro-Eurasian societies reflected broader patterns of cultural, political, and economic integration during this period. In particular, how did caravan cities along long-distance trade routes reflect new cultural configurations?

FURTHER READINGS

Bradley, Keith, *Slavery and Rebellion in the Roman World, 140 B.C.–70 B.C.* (1989). A description of the rise of large-scale plantation slavery in Sicily and Italy, and a detailed account of the three great slave wars.

Browning, Iain, *Palmyra* (1979). A narrative of the history of the important desert city that linked eastern and western trade routes.

Casson, Lionel, *The Periplus Maris Erythraei* (1989). An introduction to a typical ancient sailing manual, this one of the Red Sea and Indian Ocean.

———, *Ships and Seamanship in the Ancient World* (1995). The classic account of the ships and sailors that powered commerce and war on the high seas.

Colledge, Malcolm, *The Art of Palmyra* (1976). A well-illustrated introduction to the unusual art of Palmyra with its mixture of eastern and western elements.

Fowler, Barbara H., *The Hellenistic Aesthetic* (1989). How the artists in this new age saw and portrayed their world in new and different ways.

Green, Peter, *Alexander to Actium: The Historical Evolution of the Hellenistic Age* (1990). The best general guide to the whole period in all of its various aspects, and well illustrated.

Habicht, Christian, *Athens from Alexander to Antony*, trans. Deborah L. Schneider (1997). The authoritative account of what happened to the great city-state of Athens in this period.

Holt, Frank L., *Thundering Zeus: The Making of Hellenistic Bactria* (1999). A basic history of the most eastern of the kingdoms spawned by the conquests of Alexander the Great.

Hopkirk, Peter, *Foreign Devils on the Silk Road* (1984). A historiography of the explorations and researches on the central Asian Silk Road of the nineteenth and early twentieth centuries.

Juliano, Annette L., and Judith A. Lerner (eds.), *Nomads, Traders and Holy Men Along China's Silk Road* (2003). A description of the travelers along the Silk Road in human terms, focusing on warfare, markets, and religion.

Lane Fox, Robin, *Alexander the Great* (1973). Still the most readable and in many ways, the sanest biography of the world conqueror.

Lewis, Naphtali, *Greeks in Ptolemaic Egypt* (1986). An account of the relationships between Greeks and Egyptians as seen through the lives of individual Greek settlers and colonists.

Liu, Xinru, *Ancient India and Ancient China* (1988). The first work to connect political and economic developments in India and China with the evolution and spread of Buddhism in the first half of the first millennium.

Long, Antony A., *Hellenistic Philosophy: Stoics, Epicureans, Sceptics*, 2nd ed. (1986). One of the clearest guides to the main new trends in Greek philosophical thinking in the period.

Martin, Luther H., *Hellenistic Religions: An Introduction* (1987). An introduction to the principal new Hellenistic religions and cults that emerged in this period.

Mendels, Doron, *The Rise and Fall of Jewish Nationalism* (1992). A sophisticated account of the various phases of Jewish resistance in Judah to foreign domination.

Miller, James Innes, *The Spice Trade of the Roman Empire, 29 B.C. to A.D. 641* (1969). A first-rate study of the spice trade in the Roman Empire.

Pomeroy, Sarah B., *Women in Hellenistic Egypt: From Alexander to Cleopatra* (1990). An highly readable investigation of women and family in the best-documented region of the Hellenistic world.

Ray, Himanshu P., *The Wind of Change, Buddhism and the Maritime Links of Early South Asia* (1994). Ray's study of Buddhism and maritime trade stretches from the Arabian Sea to the navigations between South Asia and Southeast Asia.

Rosenfield, John, *The Dynastic Art of the Kushans* (1967). Instead of focusing on the Gandharan Buddhist art itself, Rosenfield selects sculptures of Kushan royals and those representing nomadic populations in religious shrines to display the central Asian aspect of artworks of the period.

Rostovtzeff, Michael Ivanvovich, *Caravan Cities*, trans. D. and T. Talbot Rice (1932). Though published more than seven decades ago, this small volume contains accurate descriptions of the ruins of many caravan cities in modern Jordan and Syria.

——, *The Social and Economic History of the Hellenistic World* (1941). A monumental achievement. One of the great works of history written in the twentieth century. An unsurpassed overview of all aspects of the politics, social and economic movements of the period. Despite its age, there is still nothing like it.

Schoff, Wilfred H. (ed. and trans.), *The Periplus of the Erythraean Sea* (1912). An invaluable tool for mapping the names and places from the Red Sea to Indian coastal areas during this period.

Shipley, Graham, *The Greek World after Alexander, 323–30 B.C.* (2000). A more up-to-date survey than Peter Green's work (above), with more emphasis on the historical detail in each period.

Tarn, W. W., *Greeks in Bactria and India* (1984). The most comprehensive coverage of Greek sources on Hellenistic states in Afghanistan and northwest India.

Thapar, Romila, *Ashoka and the Decline of the Mauryas* (1973). Using all available primary sources, including the edicts of Ashoka and Greek authors' accounts, Thapar gives the most authoritative analysis of the first and the most important empire in Indian history.

Vainker, Shelagh, *Chinese Silk: A Cultural History* (2004). A work that traces the cultural history of silk in China from its early origins to the twentieth century and considers its relationship to the other decorative arts. The author draws on the most recent archaeological evidence to emphasize the role of silk in Chinese history, trade, religion, and literature.

Wood, Francis, *The Silk Road: Two Thousand Years in the Heart of Asia* (2004). Illustrated with drawings, manuscripts, paintings and artifacts to trace the Silk Road to its origins as far back as Alexander the Great, with an emphasis on its importance to cultural and religious movements.

Young, Gary K., *Rome's Eastern Trade: International Commerce and Imperial Policy, 31 BC–AD 305* (2001). This study examines the taxation and profits of eastern trade from the perspective of the Roman government.

7

HAN DYNASTY CHINA AND IMPERIAL ROME, 300 BCE–300 CE

In the third century BCE, the Eastern Zhou state of Qin absorbed the remaining Warring States in China and set the stage for the vast empire of the succeeding Han dynasty. The chief minister of the Qin state, Li Si, urged his king to take actions based on the pragmatic notions of power politics. He tried to press on the king the need to seize opportunities: a man who aimed at great achievements must relentlessly exploit the advantages offered to him. With the armed might of the Qin and his own virtues, the king could sweep away his regional rivals as if he were removing the dust from a kitchen stove—he could annihilate them all. In this way he could establish a truly imperial rule and unify the whole world. "This is the one moment in ten thousand ages," Li Si advised. The king listened carefully and acted.

We have already seen in Chapter 5 how the Qin state emerged as the dominant "warring state" in Zhou China because of its unprecedented military power and strong agrarian economy. Now, seizing that "one moment in ten thousand ages," the Qin king relied on his massive army of conscripted peasant farmers to make himself China's First Emperor. Thus, in 221 BCE, the Qin emerged as the dominant power over the other Warring States and created a new political structure for a new era. No longer a mere regional power, the Qin became the first great land-based empire in East Asia. But the Qin Empire quickly collapsed in 207 BCE, and soon the Han Empire took its place. Following the Qin model for imperial power—as did all subsequent Chinese dynasties—the Han defeated other regional groups and established the first long-lasting Chinese empire.

The cultural identity of the Han dynasty became synonymous with "China" as the "Middle Kingdom." A subject of Han felt he or she was participating in an ideal society whose four estates of land-holding literati elites, millions of free farmers, trained artisans, itinerant traders, and urban merchants were all part of a new era that emulated the statecraft ideals of antiquity, unlike the pragmatic and cruel Qin. To be "Han Chinese" meant that elites shared a common written language based on the Confucian classics, which qualified them for public office. It also meant that commoners from all walks of life shared with those elites a common cultural framework based on family-organized ancestor worship, ritual practices in which an appropriate decorum and dress reigned for each estate, and a view that the Han as an agrarian-based empire was organically a microcosm of the entire cosmos. Those who lived beyond the pale of the Han were uncivilized peoples whose pastoral ways and primitive beliefs marked them as outsiders.

At the other end of Afro-Eurasia, another great state, imperial Rome, similarly met its rivals in war, ultimately emerging victorious and consolidating its power over the lands around the Mediterranean into an empire. The Romans achieved this feat of political unification by the use of violent force on a scale hitherto unseen in their part of the globe. The result was a state of huge size, astonishingly unified and stable. Living in the Roman Empire in the mid-70s CE, a man of middle rank, Pliny the Elder, could write glowingly about the unity of the imperial state that he served. Praising its communications network, he noted that not just people but even plants moved around the empire, traveling through the whole of the Roman world as they were taken from their orig-

inal regions to be transplanted in new ones. As he saw it, all of this was for the general welfare of humankind. In Pliny's eyes, all of the benefits that flowed from the unimpeded movement of humans, animals, and even plants were owed to the boundless greatness of a peace that joined diverse peoples, beliefs, and customs under one benevolent emperor. He fervently prayed that this gift of the gods might last forever. The gods, he thought, seemed to have intended the Romans as a gift to all humans, to shine, as it were, as a second sun for them.

Just as in China, the expansion of empire changed what it meant to be a Roman. In the beginning, being a Roman was just like belonging to any other city-state in the Mediterranean. Like "being an Athenian," it meant having citizenship in a city and sharing in that urban community's language and culture. So in the fifth century BCE, being a Roman meant being a member, a citizen, of the city of Rome, speaking Latin—the regional language of central Italy of the time—and eating and dressing like Latin-speaking people. By the end of the second century BCE, however, as the Roman state had expanded its control over Italy and parts of the Mediterranean, the concept of citizenship was also expanded to include not just members of the city of Rome, but anyone who had been granted formal membership in the new larger territorial state that the Romans were building. By the beginning of the third century CE, even this bigger view was no longer true. Now being a Roman meant simply being a subject of the Roman emperors. This even more general idea of who a Roman was became so deeply rooted that when the western parts of the empire disintegrated in the fifth century CE, the inhabitants of the eastern parts of the empire that survived, who had no connection with the city of Rome, who did not speak Latin, and who did not dress or eat like the original Romans, still considered themselves to be "Romans" (or *Rhomaioi*, in the Greek language that they spoke). In this way, the creation of a huge territorial empire had created a new and very much larger idea of what it was to be Roman.

Put very simply, the mere existence of these two states, much larger than any that had existed before, mattered a great deal. At least one out of every two human beings living in Afro-Eurasia fell directly under the control of China or

Focus Questions HAN DYNASTY CHINA AND IMPERIAL ROME

→ *How did the Roman and Han empires differ from earlier large states?*

→ *What policies did the Qin leaders use to integrate their empire?*

→ *How did Han leaders promote peace and stability?*

→ *Were the policies and institutions involved in integrating the Roman Empire similar to those of the Han dynasty in China?*

 WWNORTON.COM/STUDYSPACE

Rome, and still more fell under their influence. In addition, these empires made it possible for their subjects to live more predictable and peaceful lives than anyone had known before. The long period of several centuries of settled conditions established by the Roman Empire, for example, is rightly known as the *Pax Romana,* or "the Roman peace." So it is natural that by Pliny's time, further large-scale expansion of the Roman Empire mattered less than did the rational use of force and administration to maintain stable conditions of existence for the empire's subjects. Moreover, the general patterns of imperial expansion were broadly similar both in East Asia and in the Mediterranean. The Roman Empire in western Eurasia and the Han Empire in East Asia fully exploited the ecological limits of their agrarian base and human resources. They then became more interested in consolidating power within these limits than in expanding beyond them. In effect, each empire brought the provinces of their dominions together into regimes of unprecedented scale, and therefore enhanced the integration of local worlds into a common legal (and eventually cultural) framework, and had economic effects even further afield. They were big. They were, for a long time, indomitable. But they were not yet like the empires that would step on to the global stage after 1300, empires that pulled distant overseas lands under one roof.

> *At least one out of every two human beings living in Afro-Eurasia fell directly under the control of China or Rome, and still more fell under their influence.*

CHINA AND ROME: HOW EMPIRES ARE BUILT

> → *How did the Roman and Han empires differ from earlier large states?*

The massive new empires in the Mediterranean and East Asia emerged toward the end of the first millennium BCE, rising out of preexisting territorial kingdoms and states located on the edges of Eurasia. Though there had been regional empires before them, the Roman and the Han empires represented a different scale and quality of empire building. And they left huge imprints that lasted for centuries after their demise. Did common ecological factors, such as increasing population growth and expanding long-distance trade, feed these impulses to empire building? Or was the concurrent emergence of two great imperial systems just a coincidence? Whatever the causes, the most salient characteristic of these new empires was their sheer size.

The scale of the Han dynasty was unprecedented. A land survey made by the imperial government in 2 CE revealed a registered population of 12,233,062 households, or a grand total of around 58 million people. These households paid taxes, provided recruits for the military, and produced laborers for public works. At its height, the Han Empire covered some 3 million square miles of land in China proper and, for a while, another 1 million square miles in Central Asia. The extent of the system of the two big rivers—the Yellow River and the Yangzi River—dominated by the Han Empire was similarly unprecedented, as each was almost as long as the Nile. The Yellow River was nearly 3,500 miles long and drained an area of a third of a million square miles in the north, while the Yangzi River drained a basin of three- quarters of a million square miles in the south as it flowed almost 4,000 miles from Central Asia to the East China Sea.

The new empires of Asia and the Mediterranean united huge landmasses and extraordinarily diverse populations. The Roman Empire governed an area and a population that were as great as those of Han China. These new states were empires in the sense that we usually think of empires today: superstates of enormous size and power that are wholly dominant in their own worlds. The Han and Roman empires achieved new heights of cultural, economic, and administrative control over vast numbers of people whom they made subjects of their rule.

Despite their similarities, the Roman and Han empires had separate patterns of development and different representative types of public servants: the civilian magistrate and the bureaucrat were typical of the Han Empire, while the citizen, the soldier, and the military governor stood for the Roman Empire. Their ideals of the best kind of government were also different. In China, dynastic empires were constructed according to the models of past empires. The Chinese envisaged imperial culture as an ideal from the past that had to be emulated. By contrast, Rome began as a collectively ruled city-state—a "republic," as the Romans called it—and pursued a pragmatic road to the domination of its world. Only by a long, sometimes violent process of trial and error did the Romans finally work their way to a political system of one-man rule by emperors. Nonetheless, they, like the Chinese, were strongly traditional. They also idealized their ancestors, or *maiores.* But they were less fascinated with the earlier major powers of their world. What characterized Roman expansion and empire building was a process of continual experimentation, innovation, and adaptation.

Both empires created indelible ideas of what it was to be an empire and to behave imperially. Although the Han Empire collapsed in the third century CE and the Western Roman Empire disintegrated in the fifth century CE, they survived as models, displacing earlier large states from the center of political and cultural debates and discourse about empire. Successor states in the Mediterranean sought to become the Second Rome. And, after the Han dynasty fell, as a people the Chinese always identified themselves and their language simply as "Han." Both empires enabled people throughout Afro-Eurasia to elevate their idea of what life could be to a new level—now they saw that they could share a common identity on a much larger scale than ever before. It was a vision that would never be lost, even if the empires were.

THE QIN DYNASTY

> → *What policies did the Qin leaders use to integrate their empire?*

The Qin and the Han were the dynasties that established the groundwork to make China a unified state. (See Map 7-1.) They created the political, social, economic, and cultural structures that would thereafter characterize imperial China. Through conquest and a strong bureaucracy, the Qin managed to forge a central state that was far more powerful than the Zhou state had been even at its most potent. The administrative organizations and laws, and standardized measures and procedures, put in place by the Qin rulers would last well beyond their own rule.

King Zheng of Qin succeeded in defeating the remaining Warring States between 230 and 221 BCE, thereby ending one of the most violent periods in Chinese history. With the help of able ministers and generals and with a large conscripted army, as well as a system of taxation that provided revenues to finance all-out war, he assumed the mandate of heaven from the Zhou and unified the states into a centralized empire, declaring himself Shi Huangdi (First August Emperor)—much as the first emperor of Rome was also to call himself Augustus. He took the title of emperor (*di*) to distinguish himself from both the Zhou ruler and the rulers of the states, all of whom had been referred to as kings (*wang*). To further consolidate his power, he forced the defeated states' rulers and their families to move to Xianyang, the capital of Qin, where he could assure himself that they were not gathering armies to rebel against him. As noted at the start of this chapter, the Qin ruler also had a clearer and more ruthless vision of empire building than did his more conservative enemies.

Qin Warriors. As part of the tax quota, all able-bodied males were expected to serve in the army and to build border walls, roads, canals, and palaces. Terra-cotta warriors were buried with the Qin emperor in the expectation that they would join in his military campaigns in the next life.

MAP 7-1   EAST ASIA, 206 BCE–220 CE

Both the Qin and the Han dynasties consolidated much of the population of East Asia into one large regional empire in the last two centuries of the first millennium BCE. According to the map, what physical features imposed an ecological limit to this territorial expansion? What impact did the pastoral Xiongnu have on each empire's effort to consolidate a large territorial state? How did each respond? Why did the Han leaders expand their imperial influence further west than the Qin?

ADMINISTRATION AND CONTROL

After securing the loyalty of the rulers from the defeated states, the First Emperor proceeded to systematically divide up China so that the new dynasty could effectively rule the massive new state. Ultimately, the emperor parceled China into thirty-six provinces, called commanderies (*jun*), which

he then subdivided into counties (*xian*). Each commandery had a civilian and a military governor, both of whom answered to an imperial inspector. Importantly, the regional and local officials also answered directly to the emperor, who could dismiss them whenever he pleased. Civilian governors would not serve in their home areas and would be frequently reassigned to new posts, policies designed to prevent them from building up their own power. Clerks registered the common people in order to observe, to control, and to punish them. Registration, required of all males when they reached maturity (at age sixteen or seventeen, and five feet in height), provided the lists from which men were taxed and conscripted. All able-bodied males were expected to serve in the army and to provide labor for public works: to build border walls, imperial roads, water canals, and huge palaces in the capital. Imperial rule was harsh, and censorship was rife. Unauthorized books were banned, and allegedly many scholars were executed in an effort to eliminate criticism of the government. Social order and control were reestablished after nearly two and a half centuries of warfare and chaos.

To further unify the divergent systems that had survived from the time of the Warring States, the Qin emperor also established standard weights and measures, and a standard currency: circular coins with square holes in the center replaced the coins shaped like miniature spades or knives that had been used in different states.

The Qin began to extend China's boundaries in the northeast to the Korean Peninsula, in the south to present-day Vietnam, and in the west into Central Asia. Han Fei, a minor official from the state of Han, first voiced the notion of a "grand unity" that the Qin rulers and ministers embraced as their guiding political idea. The chief minister of the Qin Empire, Li Si, used it to justify the harsh measures that he enacted to join the various states of the Central Plain into an empire and to establish a centralized administrative structure.

Both Han Fei and Li Si subscribed to the principles of Legalism developed during the Warring States period of the previous Zhou dynasty (see Chapter 5). This philosophy accorded the highest value to written law codes, administrative regulations, and set punishments rather than to rituals and ethics (as emphasized by the Confucians) or spontaneity and the natural order (as stressed by the Daoists). They were both disciples of the Confucian Xunzi, a moralist who had favored solutions based on rational statecraft over the unpredictable vagaries of human nature (see Chapter 5). They believed that strict laws and punishments would lead to stability and order in a turbulent society. They therefore enacted unambiguous laws and regulations, as well as harsh punishments (including beheading, mutilation by cutting off a person's nose or foot, tattooing, shaving off a person's beard or hair, hard labor, and loss of office and rank) that applied to anyone who violated the law, regardless of rank or wealth. They registered people in groups of five and ten, and made all of them responsible for each other and hence subject to punishment for a crime committed by any one of them.

The Qin also devised systems to make communication more efficient. They built roads connecting the Qin capital to all parts of the new empire. These were immense thoroughfares, 115 feet wide and divided into three lanes to accommodate vehicles, pedestrians, animals, and, most importantly, soldiers. Their thick embankments of soil were reinforced with metal poles and planted with pine trees to check erosion. Officials required vehicles to have a standard axle length so that all wheels would fit in the same dirt ruts.

Just as crucial to bringing unity to the empire was the Qin effort to standardize the diverse forms of writing used in the Warring States period. Regional variants in written characters had appeared in different states under the Eastern Zhou dynasty, but the Qin banned these alternative versions. In their place, scribes and ministers throughout the empire were required to adopt the "small seal script"; its characters, smaller and simpler than those used previously, eventually evolved into the less-complicated clerical style of bureaucratic writing prominent during the Han dynasty.

The new, standardized script helped the Qin disseminate their idea of the state and eliminate the competing political ideas that had been so prominent during the Warring States era. It made uniform the style of writing employed by regional elites and clerks, who now served as bureaucratic intermediaries transmitting oral and written communications between the imperial capital and local government. Standardization also eliminated aberrant ideas that might disturb the new imperial unity. In 213 BCE, a Qin decree ordered officials to confiscate and to burn all books in residents' private possession (technical works dealing with medicine, divination, and agriculture were exempt). In addition, the court prosecuted teachers who used the newly outlawed classical books, including some of Confucius's works that could be used to criticize the Qin regime. Education and learning were now entrusted exclusively to state officials.

Qin Coin. After centuries of distinctive regional currencies, the Qin unified the currency as part of its general unification policy. Thereafter bronze or copper cash was the standard imperial currency in China.

Roof Tiles. Roof tiles (*wadang*) with molded designs were manufactured beginning in the late Zhou. The use of stylized characters as architectural ornaments began during the Warring States Period and continued during the Qin and Han dynasties.

A QIN LEGAL DOCUMENT: MEMORIAL ON THE BURNING OF BOOKS

When the first emperor of Qin came to power, his minister, Li Si, devised a cultural policy to enhance state power by creating a unified political ideology. Any traditions of learning that differed from the Qin orthodoxy were thus considered heterodox and targeted for elimination. The most serious threat to Qin power came from the Five Classics, *said to have been compiled by Confucius, which contained teachings that urged the importance of moral rectitude, personal character, and political responsibility while holding office. Such texts were an affront to imperial power, Li thought, and should therefore be destroyed, and the scholars who defended such teachings in public should be executed.*

In earlier times the empire disintegrated and fell into disorder, and no one was capable of unifying it. Thereupon the various feudal lords rose to power. In their discourses they all praised the past in order to disparage the present and embellished empty words to confuse the truth. Everyone cherished his own favorite school of learning and criticized what had been instituted by the authorities. But at present Your Majesty possesses a unified empire, has regulated the distinctions of black and white, and has firmly established for yourself a position of sole supremacy. And yet these independent schools, joining with each other, criticize the codes of laws and instructions. Hearing of the promulgation of a decree, they criticize it, each from the standpoint of his own school. At home they disapprove of it in their hearts; going out they criticize it in the thoroughfare. They seek a reputation by discrediting their sovereign; they appear superior by expressing contrary views, and they lead the lowly multitude in the spreading of slander. If such license is not prohibited, the sovereign power will decline above and partisan factions will form below. It would be well to prohibit this.

Your servant suggests that all books in the imperial archives, save the memoirs of Qin, be burned. All persons in the empire, except members of the Academy of Learned Scholars, in possession of the *Classic of Odes*, the *Classic of Documents*, and discourses of the hundred philosophers should take them to the local governors and have them indiscriminately burned. Those who dare to talk to each other about the *Odes* and *Documents* should be executed and their bodies exposed in the marketplace. Anyone referring to the past to criticize the present should, together with all members of his family, be put to death. Officials who fail to report cases that have come under their attention are equally guilty. After thirty days from the time of issuing the decree, those who have not destroyed their books are to be branded and sent to build the Great Wall. Books not to be destroyed will be those on medicine and pharmacy, divination by the turtle and milfoil, and agriculture and arboriculture. People wishing to pursue learning should take the officials as their teachers.

→ *Why did Qin fear the teachings of Confucius about gentlemen of moral purpose and proper behavior?*
→ *Why were writings dealing with medicine, pharmacy, and agriculture exempt from this policy of book burning?*

SOURCE: *Sources of Chinese Tradition*, vol. 1, *From Earliest Times to 1600*, compiled by Wm. Theodore de Bary and Irene Bloom, 2nd ed. (New York: Columbia University Press, 1999), pp. 209–10.

ECONOMIC AND SOCIAL CHANGES

The Qin rulers expanded their agrarian empire through conquest. During the Warring States period, landownership had shifted from the great aristocratic clans to a new Chinese peasantry, who were now free of the burden of paying tribute—in money, commodities, and services—to regional lords. An agrarian bonanza created wealth that could be taxed by the state, and increased tax revenues supplied the resources that enabled the central state to impose order on the country. Government support for agriculture continued under the Qin Empire; the government established rules on working the fields (with severe penalties for failure to follow its regulations), taxed individual households that farmed the land, and conscripted laborers to build irrigation systems and canals in order to provide even more land that could be cultivated. Whereas the Greek city states and the Roman Empire relied heavily on slave labor, the Qin and later the Han dynasties championed free farmers and successfully conscripted able-bodied sons into their huge armies. Free to work their own land, and required to pay only a relatively small portion of their crops in taxes, peasant families were the economic foundation of the Chinese empires.

The Qin dynasty's consolidation of central power was accompanied by major economic changes: self-sufficient local royal manors increasingly were replaced by farms producing goods for exchange in the marketplace and buying necessities from merchants. As production rose, landowners—some of them peasants—began to focus on profiting from their surpluses. Increasingly, public royal domains and private employers used contracts and money to strike bargains with laborers and with each other. A similar shift toward a reliance on contracts occurred more generally in Chinese society and government. Previously, ties of blood had been all-important, but with the growth in trade and commercial ways, nonroyal newcomers such as farmers and traders were coming to dominate public and private business.

Agricultural surpluses fueled long-distance commerce—yet another source of wealth and revenues. The growth of a money economy gave rise to a class of merchants in China's cities, which became market centers rather than fortresses and created a new world of region-based networks. Merchants handled foodstuffs as well as weapons, metals, horses, dogs, hides, furs, silk, and salt. They traded specialized goods produced in different regions of the empire. Moreover, the new roads and canals between rivers not only aided the movements of soldiers but also promoted commerce, carrying both goods and the tax revenues sent from the commanderies throughout the empire. Nonetheless, the central government, believing that trade produces nothing of lasting value, continued to value and encourage the production of crops and goods over trade, and imposed ever-higher taxes on goods in transit and in the markets.

THE XIONGNU AND THE QIN ALONG THE NORTHERN FRONTIER

Both the Qin dynasty and later the Han dynasty grappled not only with the problems of governing their empires but also with the need to expand and defend their borders. During the last centuries of the Warring States period, states along the northern border had enlarged their domains by conquering nomadic frontier peoples (see Chapter 6). When the Qin dynasty united the states into an empire and sought to further extend its borders to the north and west, it faced direct contact with nomadic warrior peoples—especially the Xiongnu, the dominant people in the Asian steppe regions. Like the Qin, the Han faced the same ecological limits. Despite its huge financial resources, the Han dynasty's identity as an empire of sedentary farmers who tilled the soil in thousands of permanent villages petered out on the Asian steppe where the

Xiongnu and their migrating herds of horses and sheep were in their element.

The Xiongnu were horse-riding pastoral nomads who traveled within a large zone of the Inner Eurasian steppe in search of pastures for their herds. Their warrior elites fought for pasturelands with other nomadic tribes and strove to protect those lands from the northern Zhou states and then from the conscripted armies of the Qin Empire. Yet archaeological evidence indicates that they also engaged in trade and diplomacy with the people of China's Central Plain, the Yellow River valley (see Chapter 6). Thus, during the fourth century BCE the nomads exchanged their horses, cattle, sheep, and furs for gold necklaces, beads of precious stones, sculpted silver animals, and coins from the settled population. The rich burial sites of the Xiongnu that have been excavated contain hundreds of gold and silver objects and reveal a society sharply divided by social distinctions, for it was only the aristocratic rulers who were entombed with precious goods.

A precarious balance existed between these nomadic peoples of the steppe and the Chinese until 215 BCE, when the newly founded Qin Empire expanded north into the middle of the Yellow River basin. At that time, the First Emperor sent troops against the Xiongnu in the north in order to seize their pasturelands for his empire. To make these new lands more secure for settlement, the Qin officials built a road between the frontier and the nearest city. They also used conscripts and criminals sentenced to hard labor to build a massive defensive wall along the northern border (the beginnings of the Great Wall of China, though considerably to the north of the current wall, which was constructed more than a millennium later). As a result of these imperial efforts, in 211 BCE the Qin settled 30,000 colonists in the steppe lands of Inner Eurasia.

The Xiongnu ultimately regrouped; in response to the expansion of Qin imperial power into the steppe and the economic crisis created by the loss of their pasturelands, they

Qin Crossbow. This is a reproduction of one of the formidable crossbows carried by the Qin terra-cotta kneeling archers. The bronze arrowhead and trigger mechanism in this reproduction were found with the terra-cotta army.

Primary Source

THE "FAULTS OF THE QIN" BY JIA YI

After the Qin dynasty disintegrated in 207 BCE, Confucians sought reasons to explain the fall of so strong a military power that had unified China just fourteen years before. In one notable account, Jia Yi tied the Qin dynasty's collapse to its autocratic rule and mean-spirited policies. Rather than blame the imperial system itself, Jia blamed the immorality of the Qin penal code and the first Qin emperor's totalitarian policies for his loss of the mandate of heaven. If the empire had been ruled according to Confucian teachings and ritual guidelines, he contended, it would have endured.

[Later] when the First Emperor ascended [the throne] he flourished and furthered the accomplishments of the six generations before him. Brandishing his long whip, he drove the world before him; destroying the feudal lords, he swallowed up the domains of the two Zhou dynasties. He reached the pinnacle of power and ordered all in the Six Directions, whipping the rest of the world into submission and thus spreading his might through the Four Seas. . . . He then abolished the ways of ancient sage kings and put to the torch the writings of the Hundred Schools in an attempt to keep the people in ignorance. He demolished the walls of major cities and put to death men of fame and talent, collected all the arms of the realm at Xianyang and had the spears and arrowheads melted down to form twelve huge statues in human form—all with the aim of weakening his people. Then he . . . posted capable generals and expert bowmen at important passes and placed trusted officials and well-trained soldiers in strategic array to challenge all who passed. With the empire thus pacified, the First Emperor believed that, with the capital secure within the pass and prosperous cities stretching for ten thousand *li*, he had indeed created an imperial structure to be enjoyed by his royal descendants for ten thousand generations to come.

Even after the death of the First Emperor, his reputation continued to sway the people. Chen She was a man who grew up in humble circumstances in a hut with broken pots for windows and ropes as door hinges and was a mere hired field hand and roving conscript of mediocre talent. He could neither equal the worth of Confucius and Mozi nor match the wealth of Tao Zhu or Yi Dun, yet, even stumbling as he did amidst the ranks of common soldiers and shuffling through the fields, he called forth a tired motley crowd and a mob of several hundred to turn upon the Qin. Cutting down trees to make weapons, and hoisting their flags on garden poles, they had the whole world come to them like gathering clouds, with people bringing their own food and following them like shadows. These men of courage from the East rose together, and in the end they defeated and extinguished the House of Qin.

Actually, the Qin empire was by no means small and weak, having always been secure within the pass in Yongzhou. Moreover, Chen She's position was far below the level of respect commanded by the rulers of Qi, Chu, Yan, Zhao, Han, Wei, Song, Wei, and Zhongshan. His weapons made of farm implements and thorny tree branches were no match in battle against spears and halberds, his roving conscripts in no way compared to the armies of the nine states. In matters of strategy and tactics, and other military arts, Chen was no match for the men of the past. . . . Qin, from a tiny base, had become a great power, ruling the land and receiving homage from all quarters for a hundred-odd years. Yet after they had unified the land and secured themselves within the pass, a single common rustic could nevertheless challenge this empire and cause its ancestral temples to topple and its ruler to die at the hand of others, a laughingstock in the eyes of all. Why? Because the ruler lacked humaneness and rightness; because preserving power differs fundamentally from seizing power.

→ *How was the mandate of heaven used to justify the defeat of the Qin by rebels?*

→ *Why did Jia Yi seek to preserve the imperial government that the Qin had created, even while he attempted to eliminate the Legalist ideology informing its political policies?*

SOURCE: *Sources of Chinese Tradition*, vol. 1, *From Earliest Times to 1600*, compiled by Wm. Theodore de Bary and Irene Bloom, 2nd ed. (New York: Columbia University Press, 1999), pp. 229–30.

Qin Archer. This kneeling archer was discovered in the tomb of the First Emperor. Notice his breastplate. The wooden bow he was holding has disintegrated.

founded a state in 209 BCE in the form of a loose confederacy among various steppe tribes. When the Qin fell in 207 BCE and civil war broke out, the new Xiongnu confederacy pushed across the defensive lines and reconquered their old pasturelands. They continued to threaten the Han rulers who would emerge as leaders of a new empire.

In their warfare, the sedentary Chinese and the nomadic warriors exhibited a dynamic symbiotic relationship that was both political and ecological; that is, the locally fixed agrarian villages of the Chinese peasants contrasted with the vast steppe grasslands traversed by the Xiongnu (see the section on the Han Empire, below). This pattern persisted for centuries, until later nomads challenged the hegemony of the Chinese dynastic system along the frontiers of the Inner Eurasian steppe and agricultural settlements connected to the Yellow River valley. Thereafter, long-term trade relations and diplomatic contacts between the Chinese and the nomads were frequently punctuated by armed hostilities.

THE QIN DEBACLE

For all of its military power, the Qin dynasty collapsed quickly. Qin rule weighed heavily on taxpayers because of constant warfare, which required not just massive tax revenues but also huge numbers of corvée and forced laborers, the latter drawn from petty criminals. Dissension at court became apparent: Chief Minister Li Si was implicated in a conspiracy and executed. When desperate conscripted workers mutinied in 211 BCE, they were joined by descendants of the nobles from the Warring States, local military leaders, and influential merchants. The rebels gained thousands of supporters with their call to arms against the "tyrannical" Qin. Shortly before the First Emperor died in 210, even the educated elite, who had grown tired of Qin social and cultural repression, joined with former lords and regional vassals in revolt. The second Qin emperor was forced to commit suicide early in 207, and his weak successor promptly surrendered to the leader of the Han forces later that year.

In the aftermath of the fall of the Qin, the leader of the insurgents, Xiang Yu, tried to restore the Zhou system of powerful regional states that had existed before the Qin dynasty, establishing nineteen feudal states. In the ensuing civil war between them, an unheralded commoner and former policeman named Liu Bang (ruled 206–195 BCE) declared himself the prince of his home area of Han. In 202 BCE, after Xiang Yu committed suicide, Liu declared himself the first Han emperor.

Emphasizing his peasant origins, Liu demonstrated his initial disdain for intellectuals by urinating into the hat of a court scholar. But Liu quickly learned that power would be kept only with better manners. Confucian scholars loyal to the Han were employed to justify Liu Bang's victory by depicting his Qin predecessors as cruel and oppressive dynasts and as ruthless despots. They painted the Qin in dark colors to exaggerate the purity of the succeeding Han. The Han court and its officials denied any link to the Qin. Instead, they affirmed the Confucian idea of the moral and cultural foundations of state power. In his essay titled "The Faults of the Qin," the scholar Jia Yi (c. 200–168 BCE) argued that the Qin had fallen "because the ruler lacked moral values." Under the cover of receiving the mandate of heaven, the Han construed the Qin as evil, even as they adopted the Qin's bureaucratic system. In reality—as we can see from the cache of Qin penal codes and administrative ordinances, written on some 1,000 bamboo slips, that was discovered in 1978—Qin laws were not especially any more cruel or arbitrary than those of the later Han. Punishments suited the crimes, and the laws themselves actually closely resembled the later Han penal code.

THE HAN DYNASTY

→ *How did Han leaders promote peace and stability?*

The Han dynasty, which lasted from 206 BCE to 220 CE, became China's formative empire. (See Map 7-2.) Han armies had some 50,000 lethal crossbowmen, who fought with mass-produced weapons made from bronze and iron. Armed with the crossbow, foot soldiers and cavalry (mounted archers) extended Han imperial lands in all directions. Following the Qin practice, the Han relied on a huge conscripted labor force for special projects such as building canals, roads, or defensive walls. State revenues came from state lands and a land tax, though the latter was reduced to gain the peasants' support for the dynasty.

MAP 7-2 *PAX SINICA*: THE HAN EMPIRE IN THE FIRST CENTURY BCE

Agriculture, commerce, and industry flourished in East Asia during the first century BCE under Han rule. According to the map, what Han policies contributed to this period of peace and prosperity? How did the Han organize their vast domains? How did they integrate them economically?

The 400 years of Han rule were characterized by both change and continuity. The first part of the Han dynastic cycle, known as the Western (or Former) Han dynasty (206 BCE–9 CE), was marked by economic prosperity and the expansion of the empire, especially under Emperor Wu or Wudi, who was known as the "Martial Emperor" because of his many military campaigns (ruled 140–87 BCE). After Wu's reign, however, poor harvests, heavy taxes, and increased debt forced many peasants to sell their land to the wealthy, and social tensions grew. A usurper who tried to introduce land reforms took power from 9 to 23 CE, but he was overthrown by a coalition of landowners and peasants who restored the Han dynasty to power. Liu Xiu reconsolidated the Han Empire as the Eastern (or Later) Han dynasty, which lasted from 25 to 220 CE. He moved the capital eastward from its former location, Chang'an, to Luoyang on the North China plain. Out of the experience of the Han, the Chinese produced a political narrative known as the dynastic cycle. Dynasties rose and fell, and heaven could, potentially, grant its mandate to anyone who unified the empire. Indeed, the imperial continuity established by the Han was extraordinarily long-lasting, enduring more than 2,000 years, until 1911.

FOUNDATIONS OF HAN POWER

The Han and Roman empires, like all subsequent big imperial states, relied on political institutions, ideological supports, and control of economic assets to maintain power. Yet they differed in the places assigned to civil bureaucracy, the military, and the ideologies designed to ensure the consent of the governed. The Han Empire was distinguished by the tight-knit alliance that existed between the imperial family and the new elite—the scholar-gentry class—who united in their determination to impose order on the rank and file of the Chinese population. Economic and social supports, as well as a strong military and bureaucratic administration, also contributed to the strength, expansion, and longevity of the Han Empire.

POWER AND ADMINISTRATION The first Han emperors were compelled to compromise with the aristocratic groups who had helped overthrow the Qin. To win their favor, Liu Bang provided land grants to his military supporters as well as to his relatives. His brothers and sons became regional lords, and military leaders and selected high officials were set up as local lords. Initially, two-thirds of the land in the empire was governed by royal relatives or supporters, and only one-third was directly administered by the emperor's officials.

Power emanated from the ruling family, whose dynasts combined the decentralized aristocratic institutions of the Zhou with the centralized bureaucratic system of the Qin. Kin of the imperial family were made nobles and were given lands over which they had direct power, while governors ap-

Emperor Wudi. This idealized representation of Emperor Wudi (156–87 BCE, ruled 141–87 BCE) welcoming a man of letters was one of a series of seventeenth-century silk paintings of Chinese emperors.

pointed by the emperor administered the commanderies that remained under central control. A "grand counselor," chosen by the emperor, headed a civil bureaucracy whose members were drawn from educated men representing powerful local communities. At the outset of the Han dynasty, the central government refrained from interfering with regional communities. The court followed the same flexible policy toward border peoples, using marriage alliances to gain control over their territories. Han administration was therefore marked by complex compromises between the ruling household and the rest of the Chinese population. The emperor, his family, and the court represented a strong centralized, hierarchical, and autocratic monarchy. But practical considerations always restrained the ruler's power.

The Han state developed a more highly centralized bureaucracy than did Rome, and that structure became the source of its enduring power. As under the Qin, the bureaucracy affected individuals through requirements that all males register, pay taxes, and serve in the military. At first, regional officials seldom intervened at the local level, simply supervising the local officials and making sure that they sent tax revenues and army conscripts. But the Han court was quick to tighten its control over regional administration. From 177 to 155 BCE, the court successively removed several pow-

Primary Source

HAN LEGAL PHILOSOPHY FROM DONG ZHONGSHU

The Qin legal system was presented as more brutal than its predecessors in its application of uniform punishments against criminals. It had allegedly not allowed for any extenuating circumstances whatsoever. Scholars claimed that all crimes under the Qin were punished equally, regardless of the accused's motive or social status. Under the Han emperor Wudi, Dong Zhongshu devised an ingenious way to humanize such laws in the Han penal code using Confucian philosophy, so that the social statuses of those involved in litigation and the personal motives behind allegedly criminal behavior could be considered. In essence, Dong as a Confucian argued that the spirit of the law took precedence over its letter when true justice was the goal.

At the time, there were those who questioned the verdict saying: "A had no son. On the side of the road, he picked up the child B and raised him as his own son. When B grew up, he committed the crime of murder. The contents of the accusation [against B] included [the fact that] A had concealed B [after the crime]. What should be the judgment regarding A?"

Tung Chung-shu passed judgment saying: "A had no son. He restored [B] to life and raised him [as his own son]. Although B was not A's natural son, who would think of seeing [B] as anyone but [A's] son? The *Poetry* [*Classic*] says: 'The mulberry-tree caterpillar has little ones, but the wasp raises them.' According to the intent of the *Annals*, a father must cover up for his son. A accordingly concealed B. The verdict: A does not deserve to be punished."

→ *Why did the Han state maintain a penal code that drew on the Qin legal system?*

→ *How could the penal code serve the ritual needs of the new Han dynasty?*

SOURCE: Pan Ku, *Han-shu* 3:1714 (*chüan* 30); quoted in Benjamin A. Elman, *Classicism, Politics, and Kinship: The Ch'ang-chou School of New Text Confucianism in Late Imperial China* (Berkeley: University of California Press, 1990), p. 262.

---

erful princes, crushed rebellions, and took over the areas controlled by regional lords. As princes lost power, regional officials came to govern these aristocratic enclaves as commanderies of the empire. The empire, according to arrangements put in place in 106 BCE by Emperor Wu, was made up of thirteen provinces under imperial inspectors, who each oversaw between four and ten commanderies. Governors-general were appointed during emergencies such as floods or famine.

A civilian official and a commandant for military affairs administered each commandery. The responsibilities of such officials were immense, far exceeding the duties of their counterparts in the Roman Empire. The total populations of commanderies, which covered vast landmasses and were inhabited by diverse ethnic groups, ran into millions of people. These officials, like their Roman equivalents, were responsible for political stability and for the regular and efficient collection of taxes. But in light of the immense numbers that came under their jurisdiction and the heavy duties that fell on them, the local administrative staff was skeletal and in many respects inadequate.

Government schools that promoted the scholar-official ideal became a major source for the recruitment of local officials. To provide an adequate number of educated officials to fill the many positions in the bureaucracy, the Han established formal institutions of learning. Emperor Wu founded a college for classical scholars in 136 BCE and soon expanded it into the Imperial University. It had 30,000 members by the second century CE, completely dwarfing the number of students in even the largest of Roman schools. Not only did they study the classics, but Han scholars were also naturalists and inventors, making important medical discoveries, inventing the magnetic compass and developing high-quality paper, which replaced silk, wood, and bamboo strips as the most

The Wuliang Shrine. This rubbing of a Wuliang Shrine stele depicts Han scholars sitting on mats on the floor. Chairs were not used until late medieval times.

convenient medium for communicating laws, ideas, rituals, and technical knowledge.

Officials selected students on the basis of recommendations and exempted them from corvée labor, military service, and the poll tax so that they could concentrate on their studies. At graduation, the young men began their careers in the lower ranks of the bureaucracy. The Han state school system was a precursor of the later civil examination system. Increasingly, local elites encouraged their sons to become masters of the classical teachings in Confucianism. This practice not only became one of the most widely accepted ways of entering the ruling class but also made the Confucian classics the heart of the imperial state.

Gradually a bureaucratic political culture emerged that balanced the interests of the authoritarian emperor and his officials, without whom he could not rule. The court tried to control its elites. At the same time, the elites brazenly used the government to enhance their social status and economic assets. Rather than exercising absolute despotic power, the Han rulers ended up by creating a remarkable partnership between the imperial government and China's educated and economic elites—a collaboration emulated by all later dynasties that ruled China.

CONFUCIAN IDEOLOGY AND LEGITIMATE RULE The Han used Confucian thought as the primary ideological buttress of the empire. According to official Han political philosophy, the welfare of the people was the foundation of legitimate rule. When the Confucian scholar and official Jia Yi wrote that "the state, the ruler, and the officials all depend on the people for their mandate," he was describing the role that "the primacy of the people" played in affirming the mandate of heaven. Claims like these promoted devotion to classical political principles of civilizing the people as well as supporting local elites. Such principles did *not* imply, as they did in the Greek-city states, that the people actually chose their own leaders. The only power given to the people was that of turning away from rulers who failed to promote general well-being.

By 50 BCE, Han officials made the Confucian ideals of honoring tradition, respecting the lessons of history, and emphasizing the emperor's responsibility to heaven the official doctrine of the empire. Confucians now tutored the princes, and the grand historian Sima Qian provided a historical vision of good and evil Shang and Zhou rulers for the Han dynasty to mark the lessons of the past. By embracing Confucian political ideals, the Han rulers established a polity based on the mandate received from the people and created a careful balance between two arms of government—the emperor and his officials—that enabled the officials to provide a counterweight to the emperor's autocratic strength. Of course, when the interests of the court and the bureaucracy clashed, the will of the emperor was paramount. But classical political teachings empowered officials to criticize bad government and even to impeach corrupt leaders.

THE NEW SOCIAL ORDER AND THE ECONOMY The Han Empire slowly established a new imperial order. The genius of the Han was their ability to win the support of diverse social groups that had been in conflict for centuries. They did so by working with them and by forming alliances with key leaders. The Han allowed some aristocratic survivors of the Qin collapse to reacquire some of their former power and status. They also encouraged enterprising peasants who had worked the lands of nobles to become local leaders in the countryside. Successful merchants were permitted to extend their influence in cities or towns, and in local areas scholars became de facto masters when their lords were removed.

A massive agrarian base provided the Han with tax revenues and labor for military forces and public works. The Han court also relied on revenues from special state-owned imperial preserves, mining, and mints; tribute from outlying domains; household taxes on the nobility; and additional contributions of surplus grains from wealthy merchants who sought noble ranks, official appointments, or a decrease in their tax burdens. Emperor Wu established state monopolies in salt, iron, and wine to fund his expensive military campaigns. He supported policies that encouraged growth in silk

"RESPONSIBILITIES OF HAN RULERSHIP" BY DONG ZHONGSHU

In the early Han dynasty, officials sought to enhance the legitimacy of the imperial government by replacing the Legalist defense of an autocratic state with a Confucian notion that presented the ruler as the moral and cosmological foundation of the government. Thus the philosopher Dong Zhongshu provided a new theory of legitimation for the Han dynasty, while criticizing the Qin's mismanagement of the imperial government. Under the guidance of Confucian officials, Dong argued, the imperial system would nourish the people and promote upright officials who would maintain the Han dynasty's mandate to govern, rather than ruling through fear and intimidation.

He who rules the people is the foundation of the state. Now in administering the state, nothing is more important for transforming [the people] than reverence for the foundation. If the foundation is revered, the ruler will transform [the people] as if a spirit. If the foundation is not revered, the ruler will lack the means to unite the people. If he lacks the means to unite the people, even if he institutes strict punishments and heavy penalties, the people will not submit. This is called "throwing away the state." Is there a greater disaster than this? What do I mean by the foundation? Heaven, Earth, and humankind are the foundation of all living things. Heaven engenders all living things, Earth nourishes them, and humankind completes them. With filial and brotherly love, Heaven engenders them; with food and clothing, Earth nourishes them; and with rites and music, humankind completes them. These three assist one another just as the hands and feet join to complete the body. None can be dispensed with because without filial and brotherly love, people lack the means to live; without food and clothing, people lack the means to be nourished; and without rites and music, people lack the means to become complete. If all three are lost, people become like deer, each person following his own desires and each family practicing its own customs. Fathers will not be able to order their sons, and rulers will not be able to order their ministers. Although possessing inner and outer walls, [the ruler's city] will become known as "an empty settlement." Under such circumstances, the ruler will lie down with a clod of earth for his pillow. Although no one endangers him, he will naturally be endangered; although no one destroys him, he will naturally be destroyed. This is called "spontaneous punishment." When it arrives, even if he is hidden in a stone vault or barricaded in a narrow pass, the ruler will not be able to avoid "spontaneous punishment."

One who is an enlightened master and worthy ruler believes such things. For this reason he respectfully and carefully attends to the three foundations. He reverently enacts the suburban sacrifice, dutifully serves his ancestors, manifests filial and brotherly love, encourages filial conduct, and serves the foundation of Heaven in this way. He takes up the plough handle to till the soil, plucks the mulberry leaves and nourishes the silkworms, reclaims the wilds, plants grain, opens new lands to provide sufficient food and clothing, and serves the foundation of Earth in this way. He establishes academies and schools in towns and villages to teach filial piety, brotherly love, reverence, and humility, enlightens [the people] with education, moves [them] with rites and music, and serves the foundation of humanity in this way.

If these three foundations are all served, the people will resemble sons and brothers who do not dare usurp authority, while the ruler will resemble fathers and mothers. He will not rely on favors to demonstrate his love for his people nor severe measures to prompt them to act. Even if he lives in the wilds without a roof over head, he will consider that this surpasses living in a palace. Under such circumstances, the ruler will lie down upon a peaceful pillow. Although no one assists him, he will naturally be powerful; although no one pacifies his state, peace will naturally come. This is called "spontaneous reward." When "spontaneous reward" befalls him, although he might relinquish the throne and leave the state, the people will take up their children on their backs and follow him as the ruler, so that he too will be unable to leave them. Therefore when the ruler relies on virtue to administer the state, it is sweeter than honey or sugar and firmer than glue or lacquer. This is why sages and worthies exert themselves to revere the foundation and do not dare depart from it.

➤ *Why was the emperor so important in Dong Zhongshu's vision of Han political culture after the fall of the Qin?*
➤ *What role did public officials play in transmitting the policies of the state to the people so that they could live out their lives in peace and prosperity?*

Source: *Sources of Chinese Tradition*, vol. 1, *From Earliest Times to 1600*, compiled by Wm. Theodore de Bary and Irene Bloom, 2nd ed. (New York: Columbia University Press, 1999), pp. 299–300.

Wuzhu Coin. This copper coin was issued by Emperor Xuandi during the Western Han Dynasty, 73–49 BCE. *Wuzhu*, which means "five grains," refers to the weight of the coin (1 wuzhu = 5 grains = 4 grams). The wuzhu was in circulation until 621.

production and iron production—especially iron weapons and everyday tools—and sought to control profiteering by instituting central price controls. He also minted standardized copper coins and exacted stiff penalties for counterfeiting. All these efforts were undertaken to expand the Han economy and to support the emperor's imperial ambitions.

Later Chinese monarchs took their cue from the Han, using government monopolies to undercut the independence of merchants. Merchants in this way became partners of the rulers, responsible for the management of peasants and artisans and for the transfer of agrarian and industrial products to the state, yet they never submitted entirely to state policy. They used their financial resources to become officials and secured state protection for their wealth and property. That wealth was often displayed in their lavish urban homes.

Laid out in an orderly grid, Han cities—particularly capitals—mainly reflected their political functions. Markets were strategically placed south of the palace complex and served as the only public areas. The palaces of the court became forbidden inner cities, off-limits to all but those in the imperial lineage or in the government. Monumental architecture in China was associated with the palaces and tombs of rulers rather than with sites of mass entertainment, like the Colosseum in Rome.

Wealthy families lived in houses of several stories built with richly carved crossbeams and rafters. They covered their floors with embroidered cushions, wool rugs, and mats. Fine embroideries hung as drapes, and screens in the rooms secured privacy for the inhabitants. Women and children were cloistered in inner quarters, as the patriarchal gender ideology encouraged lineage heads to protect their mothers, wives, and children from the harsher society at large. Elite women were often literate and managed to win respect for their talents as teachers and managers within the family while their husbands served as officials away from home. Women who were commoners led less-protected lives; many worked in the fields, and some joined troupes of entertainers to sing and dance for food at the open markets.

Silk was abundant and worn by members of all classes, though in winter only the rich wore furs, while everyone else was dressed in woolens and ferret skins. The rich were also distinctive in their footwear, clad in slippers inlaid with leather or lined with silk. No longer were wine and meat reserved only for festivals, and critics decried the prodigal and indecorous ways of the well-to-do. In the cooked-meat stalls in the markets, those who could afford them pushed and shoved to buy their piglets, dog cutlets, or chopped liver. Such tasty victuals were served to the wealthy on vessels fashioned with silver inlay or golden handles. Carriages transported rich families up and down the wide avenues, and they paid dearly for the privilege: keeping a horse required as much grain as a family of six could consume.

Entertainment for those who could afford it included performing animals, tiger fights, and foreign dancing girls. Some gambled, betting for high stakes at *liubo*, a board game that involved shaking bamboo sticks out of a cup. Music was fre-

Han Man with Fish. A terra-cotta sculpture of a chef or fishmonger during the Han Dynasty.

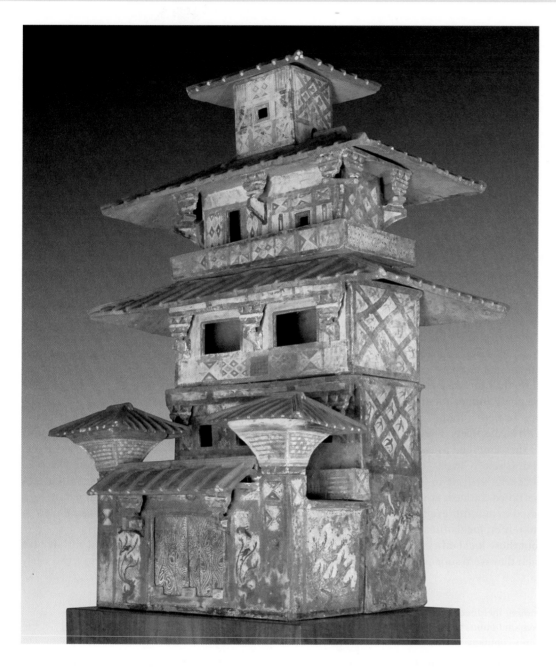

Model of a Han House. Elite families in Chang'an and other Han cities typically lived in two-story houses with carved crossbeams and rafters and enclosed courtyards. The floors were covered with embroidered cushions, wool rugs, and mats for sitting. Screens were used for privacy. Women and children were cloistered in the inner quarters.

quently played at homes, and rich families kept their own orchestras, complete with bells and drums. Such events during the Zhou dynasty were tied to formal, ritual occasions; now, Han elites called on the gods for their own earthly happiness. Funerary rites were still taken very seriously, however; the finest wood was used for the coffins of the rich, and the poor managed to have at least their coffin lids painted.

At the base of Han society was a free peasantry—farmers who owned and tilled their own land. The Han court held to an agrarian ideal: peasants were honored for their productive labors, while merchants were subjected to a range of controls, including regulations on luxury consumption, and were belittled for not engaging in physical labor. For their own reasons, Confucians and Daoists supported this hierarchy, but we will

see below that the Daoists later challenged the status quo. The Confucians, for instance, envisioned scholar-officials as working hard for the ruler to enhance a moral economy in which the profiteering of merchants would be kept to a minimum. In reality, however, the first century of Han rule perpetuated powerful elites. At the apex were the imperial clan and nobles, followed, in order, by the high-ranking officials and scholars, the great merchants and manufacturers whose wealth placed them on an equal level with nobles, and a regionally based class of local magnates. Below these elites, lesser clerks, medium and small landowners, free farmers, artisans, small merchants, poor tenant farmers, and hired laborers eked out a living. The more destitute became government slaves and relied on the state to supply their food and clothing. At the

The Wuliang Shrine. This rubbing of a stele from the Wuliang Shrine shows musicians performing on typical Han Dynasty stringed instruments.

bottom was a thin layer of convicts and private slaves, who made up less than 1 percent of the total population.

Between 100 BCE and 200 CE, scholar-officials whose Confucian learning encouraged them to seek civil service appointments emerged as the empire's most loyal and most formidable social group, the ultimate bulwark of imperial authority and legitimacy. At first, they used their political clout and cultural prestige to complement the power of landlords and large clans, but over time they increased their political and economic autonomy, gaining independent wealth as they acquired private property. In their official capacity, they linked the imperial center with local society. Their power survived the fall of the Han, and they emerged as the dominant aristocratic clans in post-Han China.

In the long run, the imperial court's struggle to limit the power of local lords and magnates failed. Indeed, any central ruler would have been hard-pressed to monitor every corner of so huge a realm; dynasts had to rely on local officials to legitimate and enforce their rule, but those local officials could rarely stand up to the powerful men they were supposed to be governing. And when central rule proved too onerous for local elites, they always had the option of rebelling. Local uprisings against the Han that began in 99 BCE forced the court to relax its measures and left landlords and local magnates as dominant powers in the empire's provinces. Below these privileged strata, increasingly disenfranchised agrarian groups turned to Daoist religious organizations to provide the organizational framework that crystallized into potent cells of dissent and revolt.

RELIGION AND OMENS   Under Wu, Confucianism slowly took on religious overtones. Dong Zhongshu, Wu's chief minister, advocated a new and more powerful view of Confucius, promoting texts that turned Confucius into a man who possessed aspects of divinity. An apocryphal treatise on Confucius's *Spring and Autumn Annals* portrayed him not as a humble teacher but as an uncrowned monarch, and even as a demigod and a giver of laws.

Classical learning was not just state orthodoxy—it also informed popular religion. Although the world of the early

Han Entertainment. Han entertainment included dancing, particularly by foreign girls, and acrobatics, for which the Chinese remain famous today. Music was often played at the homes of rich families, who kept their own orchestras complete with bells and drums.

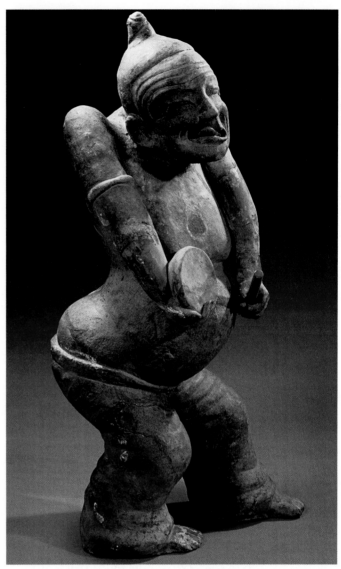

Han Musicians. Musical events became so popular, for both the entertainers (note the faces in these Han statues) and the entertained, that performances ceased being only somber ritual occasions.

Han was dominated by social elites, religion was the universal element that linked scholars and officials to the peasantry. Classical learning remained the orthodox monopoly of the Confucians at court, but many in local communities practiced forms of a remarkably dynamic popular Chinese religion.

Imperial cults, magic, and sorcery reinforced the court's interest in astronomical omens such as the appearance of a nova (a suddenly bright star), solar halos, and meteors, in addition to periodic lunar and solar eclipses. Celestial events that imperial officials could not predict, as well as earthquakes and famines, were portents that pointed to the emperor's lack of virtue, and powerful ministers exploited them to restrain and to intimidate their ruler. A cluster of calamities, prodigies, and heavenly omens was usually taken to mean that the emperor had lost the mandate of heaven. Similarly, witchcraft was taken very seriously; believed to manip-

ulate natural events and to interfere with the will of heaven, it was feared by high and low alike.

EXPANSION OF THE EMPIRE AND THE SILK ROAD

Empires cannot be maintained by shared political and cultural beliefs alone. They invariably survive by force, and the Han Chinese, like their Roman counterparts, created a powerful, even ruthless military machine that expanded the borders of the empire and created stable conditions that permitted the safe transit of goods by caravans over the Silk Road. Emperor Wu did much to transform the military forces and set them on the path of territorial conquest. Following the Qin precedent, he again made military service compulsory. Most conscripts served in their own local areas. The

Reconstruction Drawings of Composite Ritual Hall in the Suburbs of Chang'an. After taking the throne in 9 CE, Wang Mang rebuilt the Ritual Hall in the former Han palace by following the six cardinal directions (N-S, E-W, Up-Down), which enabled the building and its rooms to correspond to the tenets of popular religion and elite philosophy. The court's interest in astronomical omens and natural disasters also meant that the Ritual Hall represented the cosmological confluence of heaven and earth.

number of men under arms at any one time was stunning: some 100,000 crack troops formed the Han Imperial Guard and were stationed in the capital, and the standing army totaled more than a million. In contrast, the armies of Athens, the largest of the Greek city-states, rarely exceeded 20,000 men; the Hellenistic kingdoms that arose later were sometimes able to field double these numbers but still nowhere near as many soldiers as the Chinese. Even the Roman field armies rarely exceeded 30,000 men. The Han simply created armies on an entirely different scale.

EXPANDING BORDERS Like all large empires, the Han dynasty used military force to expand its frontiers. During the reign of Emperor Wu, between 138 and 111 BCE, power struggles among the Yue people, then living in the Yangzi delta in southeastern China, enabled the Han to absorb several kingdoms in this region. Han control thereafter extended from southeastern China to northern Vietnam. Because of similar strife in the northeast, pro-Han-dynasty Koreans could appeal for Han help against their rulers in their internal squabbles. Emperor Wu sent an expeditionary force that defeated the Korean king, and four Han commanderies were set up in northern Korea in 108 BCE. Incursions into Sichuan and the southwestern border areas were less successful, as the Han armies were hampered both by the mountainous terrain and by malaria, which was endemic to the region. Much like the steppe horsemen of later invasions, the Han infantry and cavalry moved easily from east to west. But because of their lack of resistance to semitropical "miasmas," the viral infections prevalent in more southerly latitudes wrought havoc when they ventured into those areas. Nevertheless, a commandery was established in southern Sichuan in 135 BCE, and it opened trading routes to S. E. Asia.

THE XIONGNU, THE YUEZHI, AND THE HAN DYNASTY For the Han, the most serious military threat came from the nomadic peoples living in the north, especially from the Xiongnu. The Han inherited from the Qin a symbiotic relationship with the nomads outside the defensive wall along the northern frontier. As under the Qin, mutual dependence between the Xiongnu and the Han Empire brought silk cloth and thread, bronze mirrors, and lacquerware to the nomadic chiefs, and furs, horses, and cattle to China's settled farming communities. It also took Chinese textiles to the west along the Silk Road.

At the beginning of the Han dynasty, the battles against the Xiongnu intrusion were defensive, and the Han often suffered humiliation at the nomads' hands. Under Emperor Wu, however, the Han Empire started offensive campaigns against the Xiongnu. In addition to sending military expeditions to the Mongolian steppe to push the nomadic raiders from the frontier, Wu also looked for allies on the steppe. To the west of the Xiongnu territory of central Mongolia, a Turkic nomadic people called the Yuezhi roamed on pastoral lands. The Yuezhi people had long had friendly relationships with the farming societies in China. They had supplied jade from Khotan, a Taklamakan Desert oasis, to Shang rulers (who preferred jade even to gold), as well as large, strong horses for the horse chariots and cavalry of the northern Warring States. The Yuezhi detested the Xiongnu and had frequent armed clashes with them. In 177 BCE, the Xiongnu invaded their lands; in 162 BCE, the Yuezhi were soundly defeated and their chief killed. Humiliated, the 100,000 to 200,000 Yuezhi horse-riding archers left the area; as described in Chapter 6, they eventually reached the bank of the Oxus River, on the border between present-day Afghanistan and Tajikistan.

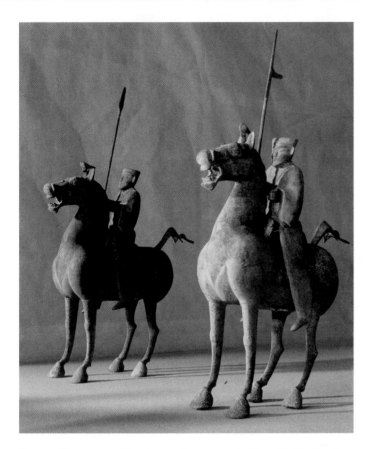

Bronze Horsemen. Two bronze horsemen holding *Chi*-halberds from the Later Han Dynasty, circa second century CE. These statues were excavated in 1969 in Gansu along the Silk Road. Note the size and strength of these Ferghana horses from Central Asia.

Between 129 and 124 BCE, the Han repelled several Xiongnu invasions. In campaigns from 123 to 119 BCE, Han forces of more than 100,000 men penetrated deep into Xiongnu territory, reaching as far as the northern Mongolian steppe. Eventually, the Han armies split the Xiongnu tribes in half. The southern tribes surrendered, but the northern Xiongnu tribes moved westward away from Han forces, toward the Mediterranean, where they were eventually to threaten the stability of the eastern flank of the Roman Empire.

THE CHINESE PEACE: TRADE, OASES, AND THE SILK ROAD The military expansion of the Han Empire resulted in the submission or retreat of the Xiongnu and other nomadic peoples and made the years from 149 to 87 BCE the most peaceful and prosperous of the entire Han epoch. China achieved a *Pax Sinica* that had many of the same features as the *Pax Romana* in the west. Long-distance trade flourished, cities increased in size, material standards of living rose, and the population grew, although not everyone benefited from the expansion of the empire and trade. As a result of their military campaigns, Emperor Wu and his successors became

monarchs enjoying tribute from vassal peoples far outside Han territories. Normally, the Han did not intervene in the domestic policy of vassal states unless they rebelled. Instead, the Chinese preferred to rely on trade and markets to induce their vassals to work within the tribute system and become prosperous satellite states within the Han political sphere of influence.

The clash of cultures between the nomadic Xiongnu and sedentary Chinese farmers frequently led to local conflict. But even more often, Chinese-outsider tributary relations in the borderlands produced benefits for both sides. Han expansion coincided with the flourishing of the Silk Road during which the Xiongnu nomads served as necessary middlemen. In the first century BCE, trade along the eastern half of the Silk Road enabled the Chinese to export silk in exchange for Central Asian horses, furs, and jade.

When the Xiongnu were no longer a threat on the northern border of the empire, Wu decided to extend his territory to reach the exotic products from further west. By 100 BCE, he had the northern defensive wall extended along the corridor between the Tianshan Mountains and the Gobi Desert. Along the wall were stationed signal beacons to send emergency messages, and it contained gates that opened periodically for trading fairs. The westernmost gate was called the Jade Gate, since jade from the Taklamakan Desert passed through it. Wu also had a series of garrison cities built at oases to protect the trade routes through the region; the farthest west of these garrisons was Dunhuang, which would later become a famous polyglot center of Buddhist culture.

Han Crossbow. The Han created huge armies to maintain and expand its borders. Between 138 and 111 BCE, Emperor Wu used his archers and cavalry to absorb kingdoms from southeastern China to northern Vietnam to Central Asia. At its height, the Han had about fifty thousand crossbowmen.

The Jade Gate Pass. From the Jade Gate Pass, the most significant pass on the Silk Road, foods, fruits, and religions of the "Western Regions" were introduced into central China during the Han Dynasty. Chinese inventions, such as paper during the Later Han and then the compass and gunpowder, traveled in the opposite direction.

To maintain a strong military force in such a remote and barren country was expensive. Wu thus initiated the practice, followed by many later Chinese rulers, of establishing military and farming settlements in the semi-desert region. Soldiers were encouraged to bring their families to settle on the frontier. As warfare in these territories was then relatively infrequent, soldiers could spend much of their time digging wells, building canals, and reclaiming wastelands. The government gave the soldiers seeds, tools, and technical support.

Soon after its military power had expanded outside the Jade Gate, the Han government set up a similar system of oases on the rim of the Taklamakan Desert. With irrigation, agriculture on the oases developed and attracted many more settlers. Traders now could find food and fodder for their animals in the oases along what was increasingly becoming the Silk Road as the Xionghu fled westward. As trade routes passing through deserts and oases took shape, they became safer and more reliable than the steppe routes, which they gradually replaced. These new desert routes would continue to flourish for another century, until the distant Han frontiers were challenged by fierce Tibetan Qiang tribes in the second and third centuries CE. Local tribes and magnates filled the power vacuum, and Chinese power and influence in Central Asia became dormant for a span of six centuries.

SOCIAL CONVULSIONS AND THE USURPER

Emperor Wu's dramatic military expansions required that Han soldiers be stationed in large garrisons stretching all the way from Central Asia to the Pacific and from Korea to Vietnam. But further conquests failed to add new wealth to the state coffers, and the huge expenditures required to maintain a standing army of over a million men exhausted the reserves of the imperial treasury. Wu raised taxes, which put a strain on the small landholders and peasants, who were the foundation of the empire. The strains continued after his death, and by the end of the first century BCE, the Chinese empire was drained financially. In this epoch, large segments of the population experienced a dramatic economic decline, as natural disasters led to crop failures. These further exacerbated the plight of poor farmers, whose taxes were based not on their crop yield but on the size of their holdings. Unable to pay their taxes, many free peasants fell into debt and were consequently forced to sell their land to large landholders; they became tenant farmers and sometimes even slaves. As local landlords rebuilt their power and their landholdings, they accumulated even more wealth, which enabled them to obtain classical educations and begin careers as government officials. As a fast-growing population confronted the shortage of land in the countryside, the social fabric of Han society finally tore. In desperation, the ever-increasing number of dispossessed peasants turned to rebel movements.

This crisis led Wang Mang (ruled 9–23 CE), who had served as a Han minister and then regent to a child emperor, to take over the throne and establish a new dynasty, as he believed that the Han had lost the mandate of heaven. After usurping power, Wang Mang attempted to enact reforms to help the poor. He tried to foster economic activity by confiscating gold from wealthy landowners and merchants and by depreciating the value of state coinage so that peasants would have more money to pay their taxes and their debts. He sought to break up large estates, placing limits on the amount of land each family could own, and even prohibited the purchase and sale of land. His goal was to redistribute excess land equitably among the people on the basis of an ancient ideal of a "well-field" land system: all families would work their own parcels of land and also share in cultivating a communal plot whose crops would be set aside as tax surplus for the state. Wang Mang imposed higher taxes on artisans, hunters, fisherman, and silk weavers in order to pay for a storehouse system that was intended to help alleviate grain shortages, and he forbade slavery. Unfortunately, his reforms did not succeed.

NATURAL DISASTER AND REBELLION

Wang Mang was unseated by a violent upheaval that united peasants and large landholders against central authority. Bad luck also played a part in his fall. Up to 5 million Chinese lived along the great northern plain south of the Yellow River—whose course, unluckily for Wang, changed greatly soon after he assumed power. In 11 CE, the river broke its dikes; rather than bending northward on the Central Plain, it now flowed due south toward the Yellow Sea. This demographic catastrophe, which plunged the entire region into famine and banditry, would be played out several more times in Chinese history. Each time it changed its course from north to south and then back again, "China's Sorrow," as the Yellow River was called, unleashed enormous flooding that caused mass death and vast migrations outside the region. Peasant impoverishment and revolt followed with chilling regularity. Researchers estimate that these floods affected some 28 million Chinese, or half of China's population. The recorded population in China declined from 58 million in 2 CE to 49 million in 140 CE, the next time we have reliable figures.

Not surprisingly, Wang Mang's reforming regime proved incapable of coping with a cataclysm of such a magnitude. Rebellious peasants, led by Daoist clerics (who ministered to peasants in their religious communities in the countryside), used the disaster as a pretext to march on Wang's capital at Chang'an. The peasants painted their foreheads red and called themselves Red Eyebrows in imitation of demon warriors, who were believed to have red eyelids. Their leaders spoke to them through inspired religious mediums. By 23 CE, they had overthrown Wang Mang, whom they considered a usurper.

Wang's enemies attributed this natural disaster to the emperor's unbridled exercise of power. They created a history of legitimate Han dynastic power that Wang Mang had illegitimately overturned, and soon Wang was cast as the model of the evil usurper. The fall of Wang Mang also brought an end to his reformist policies, as the statecraft tradition of the first half of the Han was forgotten. Instead, a conservative ethos emerged during the Later Han dynasty that favored the hereditary privileged elite, who used Wang Mang's sudden fall to justify their own social and political status and power.

THE LATER HAN DYNASTY (25–220 CE)

The Later Han dynasty restored Han rule by accepting existing social, political, and economic inequalities. After Wang Mang's fall, these problems fatally diluted the central power of the emperor and the court. As a result, the Later Han followed a hands-off economic policy that enabled large landowners and merchants to amass great wealth and more property. Decentralizing the regime was also good for local business and long-distance trade, as international trade along the Silk Road continued to grow. Chinese silk became familiar to people as far away as the Roman Empire. In return, China received glass, jade, horses, precious stones, tortoiseshells, and fabrics.

By the second century CE, landed elites were enjoying the fruits of their success in manipulating the Later Han tax system, which granted them so many land and labor exemptions that the government never again firmly controlled its human and agricultural resources as Emperor Wu had. As the court refocused on the new capital in Luoyang, local power devolved into the hands of great aristocratic families, who concentrated even more privately owned land in their own hands and turned free peasants into tenants.

This kind of prosperity was accompanied by greater social inequity, creating a new source of turmoil. Pressure grew on tenants to pay high rents, on free peasants to pay most of the taxes, and on poor migrant workers—called by the Chinese the "floating population"—to provide laborers. As the Later Han state's political arm weakened, its ritual tasks became more formalized (a similar symbolic compensation for the loss of real power had also occurred under the Eastern Zhou dynasty). The tensions between large landholders and peasants, who had briefly been mollified by Wang Mang's reforms, erupted in a full-scale rebellion in 184 CE. Popular religious groups such as the Red Eyebrows, who had helped overthrow Wang Mang, championed new ideas among commoners and elites during the Later Han dynasty. Confucius was replaced as the exemplary figure: the new models were a mythical Yellow Emperor, who was extolled as the inventor of traditional Chinese writing and medicine, and the Daoist sage Master Laozi, who was presented as the voice of naturalness and spontaneity. Laozi was now treated as a god. Although scholars denigrated folk cults and magical practices, these beliefs persisted in rural communities among both the common people and local magnates.

At this propitious moment, Buddhist clerics arrived in northern China from Central Asia, preaching a new religion of personal enlightenment for the elite and millennial salvation for the masses. Their message was warmly welcomed by an increasingly disaffected population. The rise of Buddhism

Jade Burial Shroud. Shown here is the jade burial suit of Princess Tou Wan, late second century BCE.

in China thus parallels the rise of Christianity in Roman Empire in the Mediterranean world. Yet the most powerful challenge to the Later Han came not from the Buddhists but from Daoists. Idiosyncratic Daoist masters challenged Confucian ritual conformity, advancing their ideas in the name of a theocracy that would redeem all people. Officials who were unhappy with Wang Mang's usurpation and other political outcasts who had retreated to local areas became leaders of strong dissident groups. They eventually formed local religious movements. Under their leadership, religious groups such as the Yellow Turbans—so called because of the yellow scarves that they wrapped around their heads—emerged across the empire and championed Daoist millenarian movements.

Proclaiming the Daoist millenarian belief in a "Great Peace" in the future, the Yellow Turbans demanded fairer treatment by the Han state and, more importantly, an equal distribution of all farm lands. When agrarian conditions further deteriorated, widespread famine ensued, a catastrophe that, in the view of the Daoist rebels, demonstrated the emperor's loss of the mandate of heaven. The economy disintegrated when the people refused to pay taxes or to provide forced labor, and internal wars engulfed the Han dynasty. After the 180s CE, three competing states replaced the Han: the Wei in the northwest, the Shu in the southwest, and the Wu in the south. A unified empire did not return until three centuries later with the emergence of the Tang dynasty in 618 CE. Unlike the post-Roman world in Europe, with its multitude of small kingdoms and states, East Asia clung to the ideal of a united, powerful empire. The Chinese viewed the waxing and waning of empires as inevitable. In the words of the opening line of the fourteenth-century classical novel *Romance of the Three Kingdoms,* which depicted this post-Han period, "Long united, the empire must divide. Long divided, the empire must unite." Bigger remained better.

THE ROMAN EMPIRE

> → *Were the policies and institutions involved in integrating the Roman Empire similar to those of the Han dynasty in China?*

The other large empire of the time was found at the other end of Eurasia. There, Rome had established itself as a great power ruling 60–70 million subjects. The Roman Empire at its height encompassed lands from the highlands of what is now Scotland in the northwest to the lower reaches of the Nile River in what is today Egypt and part of Sudan in the southeast, from the borders of the Inner Eurasian steppe in what is today Ukraine and the Caucasus in the northeast to the Atlantic shores of North Africa in what is today Morocco

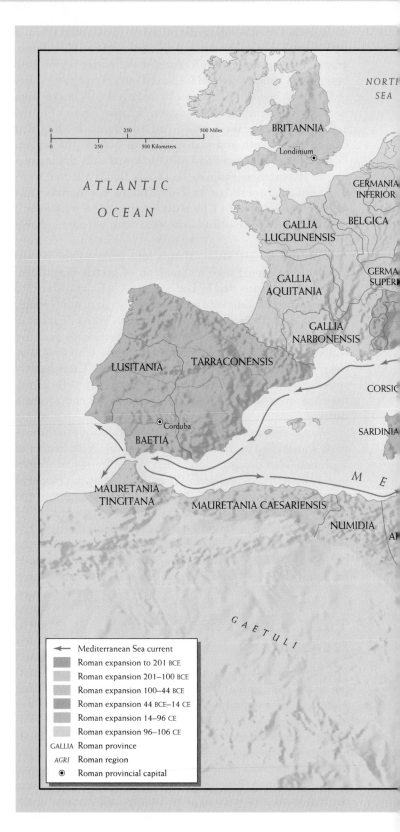

in the southwest. (See Map 7-3.) It was comparable in size and scale to Han dynasty China.

Centered on the Mediterranean, the world's largest inland sea, the Roman Empire dominated lands around the sea;

→ *Were the policies and institutions involved in integrating the Roman Empire similar to those of the Han dynasty in China?*

MAP 7-3 ROMAN EXPANSION TO 120 CE

Roman expansion continued for several centuries before reaching its peak in the second century CE. What factors contributed to Rome's conquest of the Mediterranean world? Why did Romans not expand their empire further into eastern Europe or Southwest Asia? What were the ecological limits to Rome's expansion?

China, in contrast, dominated an enormous continental landmass. But like Han China, the Romans had relied on an unprecedented exercise of violence to acquire command over their world. Through their almost unceasing wars waged against their neighbors, by the first century CE the Romans were able to forge an unparalleled number of ethnic groups and minor states into a single large political state. This achievement was so unusual and so striking that the Jewish historian and general Josephus, writing in the 90s CE, saw the empire as the unchallengeable work of God on earth. We can easily see how the Latin word that the Romans used to designate their power of command over their subjects—*imperium*—became the source for the English words *empire* and *imperialism*.

FOUNDATIONS OF THE ROMAN EMPIRE

The emergence of the Romans as a world-dominating power was a surprise. Although the Romans might have looked to the Persians or to Alexander the Great to provide imperial models, they did not. Unlike the Han, in their own world in the western Mediterranean, the Romans had no great imperial ancestors on whose shoulders they could stand. Down to the 350s BCE, the Romans were just one of a number of Latin-speaking communities in Latium, a small region south of the Tiber River in the center of the Italian peninsula. Not much was exceptional about them. Although Rome was already one of the largest urban centers on the Italian peninsula, it was still only a city-state, and one that had to ally itself with about thirty other Latin-speaking towns for the purposes of self-defense. Beginning in the middle of the fourth century BCE, however, Rome suddenly began an extraordinary phase of military and territorial expansion; by 265 BCE, it had taken control of most of the Italian peninsula. At least two factors contributed to this achievement. One, a migration of foreign peoples, had little to do directly with the Romans. The other consisted of the military and political innovations created by the Romans themselves.

POPULATION MOVEMENTS Between 450 and 250 BCE, great movements of peoples in northern and central Europe brought large numbers of Celts from the north to settle in lands in the Mediterranean. They convulsed the northern face of the Mediterranean, staging armed forays into lands from what is now Spain in the west to present-day Turkey in the east.

One of these large movements in the late fifth and early fourth century BCE involved dozens of different Gallic peoples in a series of violent incursions into northern Italy that ultimately—around 390 BCE—led to the seizure of the city of Rome. The important result for the Romans was not the capture of their own city, which was temporary and brief (the Gauls were paid to go away), but the permanent destruction and dislocation that the invading Gauls inflicted on the city-

> *Beginning in the middle of the fourth century BCE, Rome suddenly began an extraordinary phase of military and territorial expansion; by 265 BCE, it had taken control of most of the Italian peninsula.*

states of the Etruscans, who until that time were the dominant people in the Italian peninsula. The Etruscans did survive and, with great effort, finally succeeded in driving the invading Gauls north back into the Po Valley. But the Etruscan cities never recovered their ability to dominate other peoples in Italy, including the Romans. This great population movement, over which the Romans had no control, removed one of the most formidable roadblocks to their growth and expansion in Italy.

MILITARY INSTITUTIONS AND CONQUESTS To grasp the full nature of the unparalleled expansion of Rome, we must also understand the military and political institutions developed by the Romans themselves. In brief, the Romans were more successful and more efficient in killing other humans than were any other people in their part of the world. They created their unassailable military power by organizing the communities that they conquered in Italy into a system that provided huge and unprecedented reservoirs of manpower for their army. This development began decisively in the years between 340 and 335 BCE, when the Romans faced a concerted attack by their fellow Latin city-states. By then, the Latins had come to see Rome not as a brotherly ally in a system of mutual defense but as a growing threat to their own independence. After overcoming the nearby Latins, the Romans went on to defeat one community after another in Italy. The main demand that the Romans made of their defeated enemies was to provide men for the Roman army every year. The result was a snowball-like accumulation of military manpower: with each new community that the Romans conquered on the Italian peninsula, they automatically increased the size of their army.

By 265 BCE, Rome controlled the Italian peninsula. It next turned outward, entering into a series of three wars with the Carthaginians, the major power located in the region of present-day Tunisia. The First Punic War (264–241 BCE) was a prolonged naval battle over the island of Sicily. With their victory, the Romans acquired a dominant position in the western Mediterranean. But the Second Punic War, beginning in 218 BCE, revealed the real strength and might of Roman arms. The great Carthaginian general Hannibal had the insight that if the Carthaginians were to have any hope of victory, the Italian peninsula itself would have to be attacked. But the new Roman military system made a Roman victory almost certain. Whereas the resources of Carthage were those of a large city-state, like classical Athens, the resources of Rome had taken on a qualitatively different character. Like a modern nation-state, Rome could draft military manpower from a huge population. Hannibal moved his foot soldiers and his cavalry from southern Spain, which Carthage had conquered, toward the Italian peninsula. After the heroic feat of crossing the Pyrenees and the Alps mountain ranges with his war elephants, Hannibal entered Italy in the spring of 217 BCE with a force of about 20,000 men. Because of the innovative system of recruiting that Rome had developed in Italy, it could draw on reserves of more than three-quarters of a million men for its armed confrontation with Hannibal. With those numbers, Roman commanders could afford to lose battles—which they proceeded to do, suffering casualties of about 60,000 to 80,000 dead in three great encounters with the able Carthaginian general—and still win the war. They finally did so in 201 BCE. In the end, not even a strategic and tactical genius like Hannibal could prevail against them.

In addition to enjoying an overwhelming advantage in manpower, the Romans cultivated an unusual war ethos among their male citizens. Roman adult males were driven by a heightened sense of honor to push themselves into battle again and again, and never to accept defeat. They were educated to imitate the example of such soldiers as Marcus Sergius. Wounded twenty-three times in battle, Sergius was crippled in both hands and both feet. In the war with Hannibal, he lost one hand but continued to serve in the military, using a false right hand made out of iron. He was twice taken prisoner by Hannibal, each time managing to escape despite being kept in chains. Going into action four times with his artificial hand tied to the stump of his arm, Sergius helped to rescue major Roman cities from siege by the Carthaginians—

and twice the horse that he was riding was cut out from under him. Such men set a high standard of commitment to war. What also controlled and formed Roman soldiers was an unusual regime of training and discipline, which held that minor infractions of duty were punishable by death (in Greek armies, misconduct merely drew fines). Disobedience by a whole unit led to a savage mass execution called decimation, in which every tenth man was arbitrarily selected and killed. For men like Sergius, the annual campaign in the spring of every year, in the month dedicated to Mars (still called March today), the Roman god of war had an almost biological rhythm to it.

Displaying an unrelenting compulsion to war, the Romans continued to draft, train, and put into the field extraordinary numbers of men. The percentage of young men that they pressed into army service in western Afro-Eurasia was not matched until the later modern mass drafts of Napoleon in France in nineteenth-century Europe. In the late Republic, in the centuries after 220 BCE, about 10 percent of the whole adult male population (about one-fifth of all adult male citizens) was drafted into service. Soldiers, conscripted at age seventeen or eighteen, could expect to serve for periods of up to ten years at a time. Since such large numbers of young men were devoted to war for such long spans, the ethos of battle became deeply embedded in the ideals of every generation. It was this successful war machine that was unleashed on the kingdoms of the eastern Mediterranean after 200 BCE—with devastating results. In one year, 146 BCE, Romans achieved the final extermination of what was left of the city of Carthage in the west and the parallel obliteration of the great Greek city-state of Corinth in the east: their monopoly

War Elephants. There are no contemporary illustrations of the elephants that Hannibal brought when he invaded Italy in 217 BCE. Hannibal was influenced by the Hellenistic armies in the east who had borrowed the idea of war elephants, and the elephants themselves, from Indian rulers. This painting, by an artist from the school of the Renaissance painter Raphael, highlights the terrifying aspect of the elephants and reduces the human warriors to bit players. In fact, the elephants were not decisive in the winning of any major battle in Italy in the Second Roman-Carthaginian War. Hannibal won them all by superior generalship.

EMPIRES, ALLIES, AND FRONTIERS

Both the Han and the Roman empires faced threats on their frontiers, and both relied on allies as much as on their own military prowess to counter such threats. Keeping good relations with frontier allies was essential to the statecraft of empires. It could also yield important intelligence for rulers in capitals.

Consider first the ways in which the Han dealt with their enemies, the Xiongnu. Emperor Wu decided to send a special envoy to the Yuezhi, whom he thought would be willing to ally with him against the Xiongnu. His emissary was Zhang Qian, who had volunteered to undertake the journey into the unknown and dangerous steppe. In 139 BCE, Zhang set out with a group of 100 people; one was a former slave from the steppe, Ganfu, who proved invaluable, guiding the travelers and using his bow to kill wild animals when they ran out of food. Aware of the envoy's purpose, the Xiongnu chief detained the group when they tried to pass through his territory. The Xiongnu kept Zhang Qian for ten years, during which time he married a Xiongnu woman and had children. Zhang learned much of steppe life and geography, but he did not forget his mission; together with Ganfu, he eventually managed to escape. At last, they reached the Yuezhi camp on the northern bank of the Oxus River.

Unfortunately, Zhang Qian did not succeed in enlisting the support of the Yuezhi. Their surviving leaders had little inclination to return to the steppe to again battle the fierce Xiongnu, especially as they could see before them the fertile Bactrian plain dotted with Hellenistic cities (see Chapter 6). Zhang Qian accompanied the Yuezhi court in crossing the Oxus and touring the land of Bactria. After consuming a year in futile negotiations with the Yuezhi leaders, Zhang set out for home, bearing much information about the cultures and products of Bactria and regions beyond, including India and Persia. On his way back, he was again captured by the Xiongnu. One year later, the Xiongnu chief died, and as the camp was thrown into chaos, Zhang was able to slip away. He finally reached Chang'an, the Han capital, together with his family and Ganfu, thirteen years after beginning his expedition. Although he had failed in his diplomatic mission, Zhang had collected invaluable information for Wudi about the frontier areas in central Asia, and the emperor was pleased by his report, which told of all the wonders he had seen and heard in his journey to the Western Region.

The Romans also had to deal with their frontiers; to the north, they contended with "barbarians," and to the east, they ran up against the powerful kingdoms of the Parthians and the Sasanians (discussed below). But the Romans did have occasional contacts with kingdoms far to the east of the empire. For example, in the reign of the first emperor, Augustus (ruled 27 BCE–14 CE), an embassy came from Poros, a king in India. In a letter carried by his ambassadors, Poros described himself as the king over 600 other kings, and he offered any help that the emperor Augustus might want of him. With the letter, according to Strabo, came gifts carried by eight slaves, naked except for their scented loincloths: a "freak," a number of large snakes, a huge turtle, and a partridge larger than a vulture.

Although embassies of this sort did bring information from far afield, Rome knew little of communities outside the empire to the east except for the peoples and provinces of the Parthian and Sasanian empires, which were closest to its frontiers. And most of this knowledge was very local in nature, gained not through formal channels but in contacts between the two states over specific military or territorial problems or from merchants and other travelers passing between the two regions. Diplomacy did exist—emperors from Nero (ruled 59–68 CE) to Justinian (ruled 527–565 CE) intervened to manage affairs within the kingdom of Armenia—but the Roman empire had nothing like a modern diplomatic service and certainly had no centralized bureaucratic office to collect and manage intelligence reports.

Still, that diplomacy of some kind did exist raises the question of how much contact the Romans and Han had via their intermediaries. The evidence is scant. It is reported by the Roman historian Florus that once an ambassador of the Seres (i.e., the Han Chinese) made it all the way to Rome in the reign of Augustus. More important than the practice of statecraft were exchanges along the Silk Road that regularly brought news, rumors, and impressions of distant empires. The Chinese were the source of the single most expensive item in the Roman Empire: the greatly desired and highly valued commodity silk. But in Roman eyes, the Chinese were still very remote, unknown, and therefore barbaric, as Pliny the Elder wrote: "Though mild in character, the Chinese still resemble wild animals in that they shun the company of the rest of humankind, and wait for trade to come to them." Although connected, the two empires that so dominated their own worlds were still worlds apart.

THE ROMAN EMPIRE | **303**

→ *Were the policies and institutions involved in integrating the Roman Empire similar to those of the Han dynasty in China?*

of power over the whole of the Mediterranean basin was now unchallenged.

During the last centuries BCE, the prodigious war capabilities of the Romans both overwhelmed the organized and highly structured city-states of the Mediterranean and systematically pulverized the warrior-based societies along the periphery of the empire, such as those in Iberia and Gaul. Roman military forces were led by men who knew they could win not just glory and territory for the state but also enormous personal rewards. They were talented men driven by burning ambition, from Scipio Africanus (d. 183 BCE) in the 200s BCE, the conqueror of Carthage—a man who claimed that he personally communicated with the gods—to Julius Caesar, the great general of the 50s BCE. A man of prodigious abilities, the greatest orator of his age, and a writer of boundless persuasion, Julius Caesar (100–44 BCE) allegedly was able to dictate seven letters simultaneously to his secretaries while attending to other duties. He was also a mass killer who kept an exact body count: he knew that he had killed precisely 1,192,000 men in his wars. And that number did not include his fellow citizens, whose murders during civil war he refused to acknowledge or add to the total. The eight-year-long cycle of his wars in Gaul—that is, modern-day France and the Rhine valley—between 58 and 50 BCE was one of the most murderous of his expeditions. By Caesar's own estimation, his army killed more than 1 million Gauls and enslaved another million. War on this scale had never been witnessed in the Western world; it had no equal anywhere, except in China.

POLITICAL INSTITUTIONS AND INTERNAL CONFLICT   The conquest of the Mediterranean placed new and unprecedented power and wealth into the hands of a few men in the Roman social elite. The rush of battlefield successes, one following another, had kept Romans and their Italian allies constantly preoccupied with the demands of army service overseas. Once this process of territorial expansion slowed, social and political problems that had been lying dormant back home in the Italian peninsula began to resurface. Following the traditional date of its foundation in 509 BCE, the Romans had lived in a state that they called the "public thing" or *Res publica* (i.e., republic), in which policy and rules of behavior were determined by the Senate—a body of permanent members, 300 to 600 of Rome's most powerful and wealthy citizens—and by popular assemblies of the citizens. The Republic was to remain the only form of Roman government for the next five centuries. Every year the citizens voted to elect the officials of state, principally two consuls who held power for a year and commanded the armies. In addition, the people annually elected ten men who, as tribunes of the plebs (literally, "the common people"), had the special task of protecting their interests against those of the rich and the powerful. In severe political crises, the Romans sometimes chose one man to hold absolute power over the state, a man whose words, or *dicta*, were law—so he was called a *dictator*. But

Julius Caesar. This full-size statue represents Caesar as a high-ranking Roman army commander and conveys some of the power and influence that a charismatic military and political leader like Caesar had over both soldiers and citizen voters. Caesar belonged to a generation of Roman politicians who were immensely attentive to their public images.

ordinarily he could hold those powers for no longer than six months. The problems with using these institutions, originally devised for a city-state, to rule a Mediterranean-sized empire became glaringly apparent by the second century BCE.

Rome's power elite seized the influx of wealth that poured into Italy from Rome's Mediterranean conquests to acquire huge tracts of land in Italy and Sicily, and then imported enormous numbers of slaves from lands all around the Mediterranean to work them. This process drove the poorer free citizen farmers, the backbone of the army, off their lands and into the cities. The result was a severe agrarian and recruiting crisis. In 133 and 123–21 BCE, two tribunes, the brothers Tiberius and Gaius Gracchus, attempted to institute land reforms that would guarantee to all of Rome's poor citizens a basic amount of land that would qualify them for army service. Both men were assassinated by their political

Roman Farmers and Soldiers. In the late Republic most Roman soldiers came from rural Italy, where small farms were being absorbed into the land holdings of the wealthy and powerful. In the empire, soldiers were recruited from rural provincial regions. They sometimes worked small fields of their own and sometimes worked the lands of the wealthy—like the domain in the Roman province of Africa (in modern-day Tunisia) that is depicted in this mosaic.

enemies. From this point onward, poor Roman citizens increasingly looked not to the established institutions of the state but rather to army commanders, to whom they gave their loyalty and support, to provide them with land and a decent income. These generals thus became increasingly powerful in their own right and began to compete directly with each other, ignoring the Senate and the traditional rules of politics. As they sought control of the state and their supporters lined up on opposite sides, a long series of civil wars began in 90 BCE: the tremendous resources built up during the conquest of the Mediterranean were now turned inward by the Romans on themselves. These civil wars were of a scale and ferocity that threatened to tear the empire to pieces from the inside.

EMPERORS, AUTHORITARIAN RULE, AND ADMINISTRATION

It is perhaps strange that the most violent and warlike of all the ancient Mediterranean states was responsible for creating the most pervasive and long-lasting peace of its own time—often called the *Pax Romana* (Roman Peace). Worn out by half a century of savage civil wars, by the 30s BCE the Romans, including their warlike governing elite, were ready for basic changes in their fundamental values. The Romans were now prepared to embrace the virtues of peace.

But political stability came with its own price: authoritarian one-man rule. Peace depended on the power of one man

who possessed enough authority to enforce an orderly competition among Roman aristocrats. Ultimately, Julius Caesar's adopted son, Octavian (63 BCE–14 CE), would reunite the fractured empire by the year 30 BCE and emerge as the new undisputed master of the whole Roman world. Octavian concentrated most of the state's surplus wealth, the most important official titles, and positions of power in his own hands. To signal the transition to a new political order in which he and he alone would control the army, the provinces, and the political processes in Rome, in 27 BCE he assumed a new name, Augustus (the Revered One). He also assumed a series of titles: *imperator,* or "commander in chief" (compare the English word *emperor*), *princeps* or "first man" (whence the English *prince*), and *caesar* (pronounced "kai-sar" in Latin and the source of the words *tsar* in Russian and *kaiser* in German). Augustus had become the first of dozens of men who, over the next five centuries, were to rule the Roman empire as emperors.

Rome's subjects always tended to see and to cultivate these emperors as heroic or semi-divine beings in life, and to think of the good ones among them as becoming gods on their death. This propensity to deify good emperors prompted the Emperor Vespasian's famous deathbed joke: "Dear me, I think I'm turning into a god!" Yet emperors were always careful to present themselves as civil rulers whose power ultimately depended on the consent of Roman citizens and the power of the army. They deliberately contrasted themselves with the image of the "king," or absolute tyrannical ruler, whom the Romans for centuries had been taught to detest. The powers possessed by emperors were nevertheless im-

THE ROMAN EMPIRE | **305**

→ *Were the policies and institutions involved in integrating the Roman Empire similar to those of the Han dynasty in China?*

mense. Moreover, quite a few of them deployed those powers arbitrarily and whimsically, thereby exciting a profound fear of emperors in general. One such emperor was Caligula (ruled 37–41 CE), who presented himself as a living god on earth, engaged in casual incest with his sister, and kept books filled with the names of persons whom he wanted to kill. His violent behavior was so erratic that he was thought to suffer from serious mental disorders; those who feared him called him a living monster.

Being a Roman emperor was a delicate high-wire act that required finesse and talent, and few succeeded at it. Of the twenty-two emperors who held power in the most stable period of Roman history—between the first Roman emperor, Augustus, and the beginning of the third century—fifteen met their end by murder or suicide, a sign of their failure at this difficult task. As powerful as he might be, no individual emperor could alone govern an empire of such great size and population, encompassing a multitude of different languages and cultures. He needed institutions and competent people to help him. In terms of sheer power, the most important institution was the army. The emperors, beginning with Augustus, systematically transformed the army into a full-time professional force. Men now entered the imperial army not as citizen volunteers for a limited (albeit lengthy) span but rather as paid experts who signed up for life and swore loyalty to the emperor and his family. And it was part of the emperor's image to present himself as a victorious battlefield commander, inflicting defeat on the "barbarian" peoples who threatened the frontiers of the empire. Such a warrior emperor, like Trajan, was a "good" emperor.

For most emperors for most of their time, however, governance was a long daily chore of listening to complaints, answering petitions, deciding court cases, and hearing reports from civil administrators and military commanders. By the second century CE, the empire was divided into more than forty provinces or administrative units; as in Han China, each was headed by a governor personally appointed or approved by the emperor. In turn, these governors depended on lower-ranking officials to help them. Compared with the Chinese imperial state, however, with its ranks of senior and junior officials, the Roman empire of this period was relatively underadministered by its central government. The emperor and his provincial governors had to depend very much on local help, sometimes aided by elite slaves and freedmen (ex-slaves) who served as government bureaucrats. With these few full-time assistants and with an entourage of amateur friends and acquaintances, the governor would be expected to guarantee peace and collect taxes for his province. But for many essential tasks, especially the collection of imperial taxes, even these helpers were not sufficient: the state had to rely on private companies to perform these necessary governmental functions, setting up a constant tension between the profit motives of the publicans—the men in the companies that took up government contracts—and expectations of fair and just government among the empire's subjects.

TOWN AND CITY LIFE

Above all, the emperor had to count on the local elites of the empire to see him as a presence that guaranteed the stability of their world and their personal well-being. Because of the unusual concentration of wealth made possible by imperial unity, core areas of the empire—central Italy, southern Spain,

Symbols of Roman Power. Roman power was conveyed to people as much by symbols as by actual words. In this piece of sculpture from Santo Omobono in Rome dating to the third century BCE, we see symbols of imperial power. The winged figures to the left and right of the military shield represent the idea of Victory; the eagle on the shield, holding bundles of lightning bolts in its claws, represents brute power; and the garland around the top of the shield represents the wealth and rewards of empire. These powerful images have been copied by many modern states in the West.

A Roman Municipal Charter. This bronze tablet inscribed in Latin is part of a group of six bronze tablets discovered in 1981 at the Roman town of Irni, near modern Molino del Postero, in southern Spain. Charters like this one, set up for public display in the forum or central open area of the town, displayed regulations for the conduct of public life in a Roman town, from rules governing family inheritance and property transfers to the election of town officials and definitions of their powers and duties. For some of these rules, see the Primary Source box on the facing page.

northern Africa, and the western parts of what is today Turkey—had surprising densities of urban settlements. Perhaps up to one in every twenty persons in these regions lived in a town. To the extent that these towns imitated Roman forms of government, they provided the backbone of local administration for the empire. This world of municipalities was to be one of the permanent legacies left by Roman govern-

A Roman Town. Roman towns featured many of the standard elements of modern towns and cities. Streets and avenues crossed at right angles; streets were paved; sidewalks ran between streets and houses. The houses were often several stories high and had wide windows and open balconies. All these elements can be seen in this street from Herculaneum, nicely preserved by the pyroclastic flow that ran down the slopes of nearby Mount Vesuvius when its volcano erupted in August of 79 BE, burying the town and its inhabitants.

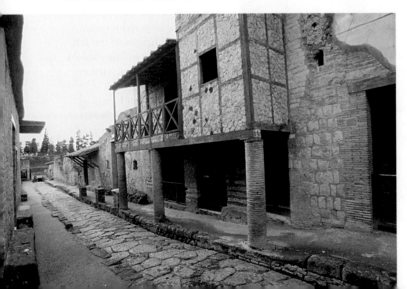

ment to the Western world. Some of our best records of how these towns were run come from Spain, later to become one of the great colonial powers that exported Roman forms of municipal life to the Americas.

Some of the best physical records of such towns are offered by Pompeii and Herculaneum in southern Italy, which were almost perfectly preserved by the ash and debris that buried them in the explosion of a nearby volcano, Mount Vesuvius, in August 79 CE. Their excavation by archaeologists has provided us with a great deal of information. Towns would often be walled, and inside those surrounding walls, streets and avenues ran at regular right angles. A large, open-air, rectangular area called the *forum* dominated the center of the town. Around it were arranged the town's main public buildings: the markets, the main temples of the principal gods and goddesses, and the building that housed the city administrators. Residential areas featured regular blocks of houses, usually tiled with bright red roof tiles, closely packed together and fronting directly on the streets. Larger towns like Ostia, the port city of Rome, contained large apartment blocks that were not much different from the four- and five-story buildings in any modern city. In the smaller towns, sanitary and alimentary conditions were usually reasonably good. Human skeletons discovered at Herculaneum in the 1970s revealed people in good health, with much better teeth than many people have today—a difference explained largely by the lack of sugar in their diet.

The great imperial metropolis of Rome was another matter. With a population of well over a million inhabitants, it was an almost grotesque exaggeration of everything good and bad in Roman city life. The only other urban centers of com-

MUNICIPAL CHARTER OF A ROMAN TOWN

Towns in the Roman Empire gradually came to be governed according to standard sets of rules and regulations that were developed during the Roman conquest of Italy. These uniform sets of laws were sometimes imposed on and sometimes voluntarily adopted by cities and towns in the provinces of the empire, and determined how they were to run their affairs. One of the most detailed copies of these town regulations was discovered in 1981, in southern Spain at Molino del Postero (a place called Irni in Roman times). The rules on administering the town, publicized by the Roman governor of Spain in 81 CE, were incised on ten plates of bronze that were publicly displayed in the town's forum. Only six of the original ten tablets have been recovered, but they reveal how the lives of people in the municipality of Irni were regulated. By following these rules, the indigenous people of a Spanish community learned how to behave like Romans.

[19] ON AEDILES: The aediles [the two town business managers] . . . are to have the right and power of managing the grain supply, the sacred buildings, the sacred and holy places, the town and its roads and neighborhoods, the drains and sewers, the baths, the marketplace, and of checking weights and measures; and also of setting a night watch if the need arises.

[20] CONCERNING THE RIGHT AND POWER OF QUAESTORS: The quaestors [the two town financial officers] . . . are to have the right and power of collecting, spending, storing, administering, and managing the common funds of the municipality at the discretion of the *duumviri* [the two town mayors]. And they are allowed to have the public slaves belonging to the municipality to help them.

[21] HOW ROMAN CITIZENSHIP IS ACQUIRED IN THE MUNICIPALITY: When those who are senators, decurions [town councillors], or conscripted town councillors who have been or are chosen as town magistrates according to the terms of this law, have completed their term of office, they are to become Roman citizens, along with their parents and wives and any children who have been born out of legal marriages and who are in the power of their parents, and likewise grandsons and granddaughters born to a son. . . .

[28] CONCERNING THE FREEING OF SLAVES BEFORE THE MAYORS: If any citizen of the municipality of Flavian Irni . . . in the presence of a *duumvir* [mayor] of that municipality in charge of the administration of justice sets free his male or female slave from slavery into freedom or orders him or her to be free . . . then any male slave who has been manumitted or ordered to be free in this way is to be free, any female slave who has been manumitted or ordered to be free in this way is also to be free. . . . Someone who is under twenty years of age may manumit his or her slave only if the number of town councillors necessary for decrees passed under this law to be valid decides that the grounds for said manumission are proper.

→ *What are some of the characteristics of the typical Roman town or municipality?*
→ *What different types of persons are assumed to be part of the normal social structure?*
→ *In what ways did inhabitants of towns such as Irni become Roman citizens?*
→ *Why would making small towns uniform in design and function be important to the Roman Empire?*

SOURCE: J. González, "The *Lex Irnitana*: A New Copy of the Flavian Municipal Law," *The Journal of Roman Studies* 76 (1986): 147–243; translated by Brent Shaw.

parable size at the time were Chang'an and Luoyang, the Han capitals, each with a population of between 300,000 and 500,000. Rome's inhabitants were privileged, because there the power of the emperor and the wealth of the empire assured them of a basic food supply. Thirteen huge and vastly expensive aqueducts provided the city with a constant and dependable supply of water, sometimes brought from very great distances. A basic amount of wheat (and, later, olive oil and pork) was given regularly to many of its adult citizens—about a quarter of a million of them at the height of these

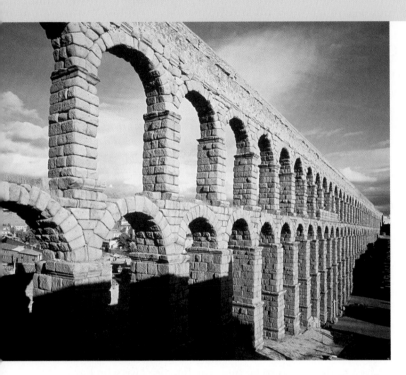

Aqueduct. The Romans built aqueducts to transport to Rome the huge amounts of water needed to sustain the city's population of over a million. The idea soon spread to the provinces, where these expensive structures were built to bring water to Roman-style cities developing in the peripheral regions of Roman rule. This aqueduct at Segovia in modern Spain is one of the best preserved.

free distributions. But living conditions were often appalling, with large numbers of people jammed into ramshackle high-rise apartments that threatened to collapse on their renters or go up in flames. And Romans constantly complained of rampant crime and violence. Worse than all of these problems, however, was the city's terrible lack of sanitary conditions—despite the sewage and drainage works that were wonders of their time. Like most premodern cities in early-modern Europe, Rome was disease-ridden; its inhabitants died from infection at a fearsome rate—malarial infections were particularly bad—and so the city required a constant input of a large number of immigrants every year just to maintain its population.

MASS ENTERTAINMENT

Every self-respecting Roman town had at least two major entertainment venues. One of these was an adoption from Hellenistic culture—a theater devoted to staging plays, dances, and other kinds of popular entertainments. The other was a Roman innovation that combined two horseshoe-shaped theaters in the form of a more elaborate structure called an amphitheater—literally, a "surround theater." A much larger seating capacity than in a regular theater surrounded the oval performance area at its center. The emperors Vespasian and

Titus completed the Flavian Amphitheater in Rome and dedicated it in 80 CE. It is the vast structure that today is known as the Colosseum, after the colossal statue of the emperor Nero that formerly stood beside it. It was a state-of-the-art entertainment facility whose floor area, the arena, could be used to put on elaborate hunts of exotic wild animals, such as giraffes and elephants. The arena area could also be flooded to stage naval battles in which hostile fleets attacked each other, to the delight of the audience, or it could provide a venue for a Roman invention, gladiatorial games: expensive public entertainments in which heavily armed and well-trained men—most of them slaves and prisoners of war, but sometimes even free men who volunteered—fought each other, wounding or killing for the enjoyment of the huge crowds of appreciative spectators. People from the West tend to think of these structures for public entertainment as ordinary and normal. Seen from a contemporary Chinese perspective, however, they look strange and unusual. Among the Han, local elites and the imperial family created gigantic palace complexes across the empire, complete with hunting parks to impress and to amuse themselves, not the general

North African Amphitheater. After the original Colosseum was built in Rome under the Flavian emperors in the 70s CE, the idea that an important Roman town anywhere in the empire must have an amphitheater took hold. This huge amphitheater is in the remains of the Roman city of Thysdrus in North Africa (the town of el-Jem in modern-day Tunisia). The wealth of the Africans under the empire enabled them to build colossal entertainment venues that competed with the one at Rome in scale and grandeur.

Roman Gladiators. In this brilliant mosaic from Rome, we see two gladiators at the end of a full combat in which Astacius has killed Astivus. The Greek letter theta, or "th" (the circle with crossbar through it), beside the names of Astivus and Rodan indicates that these men are dead—*thanatos* being the Greek word for "death."

public. In contrast, the public entertainment facilities of a Roman town were there precisely because of the distinctive cultural and political developments that stressed the importance of the citizen public in town life.

SOCIAL AND GENDER RELATIONS

Political forums and game venues were just two key constituent elements of a Roman community. Even more significant were the personal relations that linked the rich and powerful with the mass of average citizens in these towns. Men and women of wealth and high social status acted as "patrons," protecting dependents or "clients" of a lower class. From the emperor at the top to the local municipal man at the bottom, these popular relationships were reinforced by generous distributions of food and entertainments made by wealthy men to their people. The bonds that linked these two groups in each city were formalized in legal definitions of the responsibilities of patrons to clients; at the same time, the informal social code raised expectations that the wealthy would engage in do-gooding as public benefactors. For example, a senator, Pliny the Younger, constructed for his hometown of Comum a public library and a bathhouse, and supplied the money needed to furnish and run them both; supported a teacher of Latin; and established a fund to support the sons and daughters of former slaves. The emperors at the very top were no different. Augustus documented the

scale of his gifts to the Roman people in his autobiography, gifts that exceeded hundreds of millions of sesterces in expenditures made out of his own pocket. A later emperor, Trajan (ruled 98–117 CE), under whose rule the empire reached its greatest extent, was responsible for establishing a social scheme for feeding poor Roman citizen children in Italy—a benefaction that he advertised on coins and in pictures on dramatic arches in Beneventum and other towns.

But the essence of Roman civil society was less the informal system of patronage than the presence of formal relationships governed by Rome's system of laws and courts. Disputes were brought to the public courts, and decisions were made by judges and sometimes by large juries. By the last century BCE, the Roman state's complex legal system featured not only a rich body of written law but also institutions for settling legal disputes and a growing number of highly educated men who specialized in the interpretation of the law. The apparatus of Roman law eventually appeared in every town and city of the empire, creating a deeply entrenched civil culture that affected the lives of most ordinary subjects. It is no surprise that this legal infrastructure of empire persisted long after the empire's bigger political and military institutions had disappeared.

Municipal charters and the civil laws—as well as secular philosophers and, later, Christian writers—placed the family at the very foundation of the Roman social order. In its purest ideal, the authoritarian *paterfamilias* (father of the family) headed the family. Legally speaking, he had near total power

Primary Source

BIRTHDAY INVITATION OF CLAUDIA SEVERA

The ability to write in Latin became widespread under the Roman Empire; even its distant frontier areas could boast some level of basic literacy. The discovery at the Roman army base at Vindolanda, in northern England, of a large cache of documents written on thin sheets of wood has revealed the normal use of Latin writing for a very wide range of day-to-day activities in the last decades of the first century CE. Roman women married to officers on the base were as skilled in writing as the men. One of these elite women, Claudia Severa, sent a letter to a good friend of hers (whom she addresses affectionately as her "sister"), inviting the woman to her birthday party. The elegant handwriting found on several of these documents is almost certainly that of Claudia Severa herself. The second letter is a reply by her friend, Sulpicia Lepidina.

Claudia Severa to her Sulpicia Lepidina. Greeting.

My sister, I am sending an invitation to you to attend my birthday festivities on the third day before the Ides of September [September 11 in our calendar]—just to make sure that you come to visit us. Your presence will make the day all the more enjoyable for me. Please convey my greetings to your Cerialis [i.e., Lepidina's husband]. My Aelius and our little son send him their warmest greetings.

I await your arrival, my sister.

I bid you goodbye, my sister, my dearest soul. Be well. [Address on the outside:] To Sulpicia Lepidina, wife of Cerialis, from Severa.

[Sulpicia Lepidina to Claudia Severa] Greeting.

Just as I had told you, my sister, and had promised that I would ask your Brocchus [i.e., Claudia Severa's husband, Aelius Brocchus] for permission to come to visit you, he replied to me that I was, of course, always most welcome to come. . . . [I shall try] to come to you by whatever way I can, for there are certain things that we must do . . . on which matter you will receive a letter from me so that you will know what I am going to do. . . .

Farewell, my sister, my dearest and most-desired soul . . .

→ *What does the very existence of these letters tell us about Roman women?*

→ *What does the writing of letters in Latin at this far edge of the empire at this time tell us about Roman culture?*

→ *Does the ordinariness of the letters—a birthday invitation and its reply—tell us anything about the extent and nature of written communications in the Roman world?*

SOURCE: Alan K. Bowman and J. David Thomas, with contributions by J. N. Adams, *The Vindolanda Writing-Tablets (Tabulae Vindolandenses II)* (London: British Museum Press, 1994), nos. 291 and 292, pp. 256–62. Translated by Brent Shaw.

over his dependents, including his wife, children, grandchildren, and the slaves whom he owned. Imperial society heightened the importance of the basic family unit of mother, father, and children in the urban centers, whose growth it fostered. As in Han dynasty China, the Roman state regularly undertook a detailed census, rigorously counting the inhabitants of the empire and assessing their property for tax purposes—a process that more clearly than ever defined the family as the core unit of society.

In this Roman system, women might seem to be under the domineering rule of fathers and husbands. That is certainly the picture presented in the repressive laws that Roman men drafted and in the histories that Roman men wrote. But compared with women in most Greek city-states,

THE ROMAN EMPIRE | **311**

→ *Were the policies and institutions involved in integrating the Roman Empire similar to those of the Han dynasty in China?*

Roman women, even those of only modest wealth and status, had much greater freedom of action and much greater control of their own wealth and property. Thus Terentia, the wife of the Republican senator Cicero, bought and sold properties of some scale on her own, made decisions regarding her family and wealth without so much as consulting her husband (much to his chagrin—he later divorced her), and apparently fared perfectly well following her separation from Cicero. Her behavior, so far as we can see, was normal for a woman of her status: she was well educated, literate, well connected, and in control of her own life—despite what the laws and ideas of Roman males might suggest. The daily lives of ordinary women that are well documented in the papyrus documents from the Roman province of Egypt, for example, show them buying, selling, renting, and leasing with no sign that the constraints written into laws that tried to subject them to male control had any significant effect on their dealings.

Terentia reminds us of Ban Zhao, the younger sister of the historian Ban Gu (32–92 CE). She became the first female Chinese historian and lived her life relatively unconstrained. After marrying the local resident, Cao Shishu, at the age of fourteen, she was called Madame Cao at court. Subsequently, she completed her elder brother's *History of the Former Han Dynasty* when he was imprisoned and executed in 92 for dealings with the dowager empress's family. In addition to completing the first full dynastic history in China, Ban Zhao also wrote a work entitled *Lessons for Women*, in which she described the status and position of elite women in society and presented the ideal woman in light of her virtue, her type of work, and the words she spoke and wrote.

ECONOMY AND NEW SCALES OF PRODUCTION

At the most basic level, families and the state depended for their existence on the workings of the economy: production and consumption. Although Rome never transformed economic relations in the Mediterranean sufficiently to create a modern industrial economy, it did achieve staggering transformations of scale in the production of agricultural, manufactured, and mined goods. Public and private demand for metals, for example, led the Romans to mine lead, silver, and copper in Spain in operations so massive that traces of the air pollution they generated can easily be detected today in ice core samples taken in far distant Greenland. The evidence from Mediterranean shipwrecks similarly indicates that goods were transported by sea in the Mediterranean on a scale never seen before. The area of land carefully surveyed and brought under cultivation rose steadily throughout this period, as Romans reached into arid lands on the periphery of the Sahara Desert to the south, and opened up heavily forested regions in present-day France and Germany to the north. (See Map 7-4.)

The Romans also built an unprecedented number of roads to connect the various parts of their empire. Although many of these roads did not have the high quality—flagstone paving and excellent drainage—exhibited by the major highways in Italy, such as the Via Appia, many of them were systematically marked, for the first time in this part of the world, with milestones that indicated to travelers their precise location and the distance to the next town. Also for the first time, complex land maps and itineraries were prepared on which all of the major roads and distances between towns were specified. Adding to the roads' significance was their deliberate coordination with the sea routes of the Mediterranean to support the flow of traffic, commerce, and ideas through the empire on land and at sea more smoothly and safely than had previously been possible.

The mines produced the valuable metals—copper, tin, silver, and gold—out of which the Roman state and its agents produced the most massive coinage known in the Western world before early modern times. Coinage greatly facilitated the exchange of commodities and services, which could now be assigned standard values. Throughout the Roman Empire, from small towns on the edge of the Sahara Desert to army towns along the northern frontiers, goods were appraised, purchased, and sold in coin denominations. Taxes were assessed and hired laborers were paid day wages in coin. Although not fully money-based in a modern sense, the

Roman Roads. Like Qin and Han China, the Roman Empire was characterized by large-scale road building, which began as early as the late fourth century BCE. Roads eventually connected most land areas and larger urban centers in the empire, considerably easing ordinary travel, as well as trade and commerce. Here we see part of the Via Appia, the great highway that connected Rome with the southern parts of Italy.

economy of the empire in its leading sectors functioned more efficiently because of the government's production of coins on an immense scale—indeed, on a scale paralleled only by Han dynasty China and its successors.

Roman mining, as well as other sizable operations, relied significantly on chattel slaves—human beings purchased as private property. The unprecedented concentration of wealth and slaves at the center of the Roman world led to the first large-scale commercial plantation agriculture, along with the first technical handbooks on how to run such large operations for profit. These *latifundia* (literally, "broad estates") as they were called, specialized in products destined for the

big urban markets: cash crops such as wheat, grapes, and olives, as well as cattle and sheep raised on a huge scale. And all these economic developments rested on a bedrock belief that private property and its ownership were sacrosanct. Indeed, the Roman senator Cicero argued that the defense and enjoyment of private property were the basic reasons for the existence of the state. Roman law more clearly defined and more strictly enforced the rights of the private owner than had any previous legal system. The enormous extension of the private ownership of land and other property to regions that previously had little or no knowledge of it—Egypt in the east, Spain in the west, the lands of

MAP 7-4 · *PAX ROMANA*: THE ROMAN EMPIRE IN THE SECOND CENTURY CE

The Roman Empire enjoyed remarkable peace and prosperity in the second century CE. Economic production increased and Roman culture expanded throughout the realm. According to the map, what Roman policies contributed to these conditions? Where did threats to the empire's peace exist? With what groups did Romans trade beyond their empire? How did the *Pax Romana* promote the spread of Christianity?

Coin Hoard. The use of coins for a wide spectrum of economic exchanges became common in the Roman Empire. Looking at the batches that people buried for safekeeping gives us some idea of the range of coins in circulation at any one time. This coin hoard was found near Didcot in Oxfordshire, England. Buried about 165 CE, it contained about 125 gold coins minted between the 50s and 160s CE and represents the equivalent of about eleven years' pay for a Roman soldier. Gold coins were used only for very expensive transactions or to store wealth. Most ordinary purchases or payments were made with silver or brass coins.

western Europe—was one of the most enduring, if less visible, effects of the Roman Empire.

RELIGIOUS CULTS AND THE RISE OF CHRISTIANITY

The political unification of the Mediterranean under one empire also suggested that the beliefs of its peoples might be unified. The world of gods, spirits, deities, and demons remained hugely important, even as the region had experienced the general spread of new religions as part of the Hellenistic movement. Indeed, the municipal charters of Roman towns required the local town councilors to institute and maintain the support of a wide variety of official and semi-official cults of different gods and goddesses.

But if there was any religion of empire, it was Christianity, whose spread followed the geopolitical movement of the other big Mediterranean-wide religious cults. Its foundations lay in the specific context of a direct confrontation and dialogue with Roman imperial authority: the trial of Yeshua ben Yusef (Joshua son of Joseph), who had preached the new doctrines of what was originally a sect of Judaism and who is known to us today by the Greek form of his name, Jesus. Jesus was tried by a Roman governor, Pontius Pilatus, in a typical form of Roman provincial trial; found guilty of sedition; and executed, along with two bandits, by a standard Roman penalty—crucifixion.

We know of Jesus only after his death. No reference to him survives from his own lifetime. Two years after his crucifixion, Jesus was believed by Paul of Tarsus, a Jew and a Roman citizen from a city in southeastern Anatolia, to have appeared to him in full glory outside the city of Damascus. Paul and the communities to whom he preached between 40 and 60 CE were the first to call Yeshua "Jesus." They also referred to him as "the Christ"—*ho Christos*—or the Anointed One (i.e., the Messiah), and thought of him as a god.

Paul had not been one of Jesus' original disciples. Only much later did four of those men—Matthew, Mark, Luke, and John—attempt to write about his life and to record his sayings in accounts that came to be called the Gospels, an early English word that directly translates their name in the original Greek, *Evangeliai* (Good News). While they varied greatly, they had in common the need to tell the world not what Jesus had said, but who he had been. They were written as answers to the question that Jesus was reported to have asked his disciples a few months before he died: "Who do people say that I am?" (Mark 8:27).

Jesus' preachings could not have been more Jewish. God is the father of his people—a people of sinners, who are always liable to fall away. But God is like a good shepherd to them. Scrambling down dangerous ravines, the good shepherd seeks those who have gone astray, carrying home with joy on his shoulders even a single lost lamb (see John 10:1–18). We have already met the ancient image of the great king as shepherd of his people in both Egypt and Mesopotamia (see Chapter 3). This image also passed through the Psalms and the books of the prophets of Israel (Psalm 23:1, Isaiah 40:11). With Jesus, this ancient image took on a new intimacy. Not a distant monarch but a preacher, Jesus had set out, on God's behalf, to gather a new, small flock. Jesus' teachings—like the teachings of the Buddha—comforted people who lived at a distance from power, such as scholars, merchants, and farmers.

To his followers, Jesus was a man who had slowly revealed to them an awesome, hidden identity. Jesus was crucified not for what he had preached but for what he (or others) claimed that he was. Through the preaching of Paul in Greek and the textual portraits carefully painted in the Gospels, also in Greek, this image of Jesus rapidly spread beyond the local confines of Palestine—where Jesus had preached to Jews only and only in the local language, Aramaic—and entered the religious bloodstream of the Mediterranean.

Just half a century after his crucifixion, the followers of Jesus saw in his life not the wanderings of an amiable Jewish charismatic but a moment of head-on conflict between "God" and "the world." Jesus had "overcome" the "world." He had even broken the boundaries of the human condition: he had been raised by God from the dead. This was the chief thing that Paul wished his followers in Corinth and elsewhere to know about Jesus: "If Christ has not been raised, your faith is futile [and] we are truly to be pitied" (1 Corinthians 15:17,

CICERO ON THE ROLE OF THE ROMAN STATE

Greek thinkers debated ethics and morals, the role of the good life, the nature of the universe, and how we know things, but it is perhaps natural to expect the Romans, given their more pragmatic attitudes and their possession of a huge empire, to have deliberated more about the nature of government and the role of the state. In the following passage, Marcus Tullius Cicero, one of the leading politicians in Rome from the 60s to the 40s BCE, discusses how the politician—the man who holds public office in the state (in this case, the Roman state)—has a fundamental duty to defend the state's main function.

That man who undertakes responsibility for public office in the state must make it his first priority to see that every person can continue to hold what is his and that no inroads are made into the goods or property of private persons by the state. It was a bad policy when Philippus, when he was tribune of the plebs [about 104 BCE], proposed an agrarian reform law. When his law was defeated, he took the defeat well and was moderate in his response. In the debates themselves, however, he tried to curry popular favor and acted in a bad way when he said, "In our community there are not more than two thousand men who have real property." That speech ought to be condemned outright for attempting to advocate equality of property holdings. What policy could be more dangerous? It was for this very reason—that each person should be able to keep his own property—that states and local governments were founded. Although it was by the leadership of nature herself that men gathered together in communities, it was for the hope of keeping their own property that they sought the protection of states. . . . Some men want to become known as popular politicians and for this reason they engage in making revolutionary proposals about land, with

the result that owners are driven from their homes and money lent out by creditors is simply given free to the borrowers with no need for repayment. Such men are shaking the very foundations of the state. First of all, they are destroying that goodwill and sense of trust which can no longer exist when money is simply taken from some people and given to others [by the state]. And then they take away fairness, which is totally destroyed if each person is not permitted to keep what is his own. For, as I have already said, it is the peculiar function of the state and of local government to make sure that each person should be able to keep his own things freely and without any worry.

→ *According to Cicero, what is the main function of the Roman state?*

→ *How does the very important role given to the protection of private property rights of individuals determine the claims that citizens had on their rulers?*

→ *And how does this differ from the role of the state as envisioned in contemporary Han dynasty China?*

SOURCE: *De Officiis (On Duties)*, 2.21.73, 22.78; translated by Brent Shaw.

19). Thus, the preaching that the followers of Jesus brought to confront this world was no longer the preaching of a man. It was the message of a god—a god who, for thirty years, half a century before, had moved (largely unrecognized) among human beings. And the followers formed a church, an *ekklēsia*: a permanent gathering committed to the charge of leaders chosen by God and by their fellow believers. For these leaders and their followers, death—death for Jesus—was the hallmark of their faith. In dying they witnessed for the faith. Indeed, the central defining experience for Christians remained that of the Roman trial and the idea of "witnessing" to God. The Greek word *martus* means a witness in a trial. From this came the English term *martyr* and the concept of martyrdom.

The persecutions of Christians were sporadic and intensely local in nature. Like imperial power itself, they were a series of responses to local concerns. Not until the emperor Decius, in the mid-third century CE, was a formal empire-wide attack on Christians directed by the state as a whole. And that attempt failed in its objective. Decius died within the year and Christians, not unnaturally, interpreted the death of their persecutor as evidence of the hand of God in human affairs. By the last decades of the third century, Christian communities of various kinds, reflecting the different strands of their movement through the Mediterranean as well as the background of local cultures into which they settled, were present in every local society in the empire.

THE LIMITS OF EMPIRE

The empire both defined and labeled outsiders as those whom it excluded. A crucial part of that process was the successful exercise of force in extending its borders. (See Map 7-5.) Thus the limitations of that force determined who belonged in the empire and was subject to it, and who was outside it and therefore excluded. For two of the four phases of the empire, there was not much question about such deter-

minations. To the west, the Romans pushed their authority to the shores of the Atlantic Ocean, and to the south they drove it to the edges of the Sahara Desert. In both cases, they extended their control to its ecological limits: in those directions, little further land was available that the empire could dominate to its own profit. To the east and north, however, things were different.

On Rome's eastern frontiers, powerful Romans such as Marcus Licinius Crassus in the mid-50s BCE and Mark

MAP 7-5   POPULATION OF ROMAN WORLD IN 362 CE

Roman frontiers at the northern and eastern limits of the empire were persistent sources of anxiety and concern for imperial leaders. While not as densely populated as the Roman Empire, these regions contained large population centers as well. Name some of the major groups of peoples that lived just beyond Roman rule in the areas of eastern Europe and Southwest Asia. What kinds of political and social organization did these societies develop? Why were Roman armies never able to subdue these neighboring peoples?

Wooden Tablet Letter. This wooden tablet from Vindolanda in northern England contains a text, not in neat Latin print but in the natural longhand writing of the time. On the tablet is a letter from two men, Niger and Brocchus, to their friend Cerialis. They wish him success in all that he is about to do. The large cache of letters found at Vindolanda has expanded our vision of the role and place of writing in distant parts of the empire.

Antony in the early 30s BCE wished to imitate the achievements of Alexander the Great and conquer the arid lands beyond Judea and Syria. But they failed miserably, stopped by a barrier that would limit the ability of any Mediterranean state to extend its influence east of the Mediterranean periphery: the empire of the Parthians, who had moved south from present-day Turkmenistan and settled in the region covered by the modern-day states of Iraq and Iran. Unlike the Persians before them, the Parthians were a people whose social order was founded on nomadic pastoralism and whose war power was based on the technical advances in mounted horseback warfare made on the great plains of Inner Eurasia. Reliance on horses made their style of fighting highly mobile,

and it was ideally adapted to the arid plains and deserts. They perfected the so-called Parthian shot: the arrow shot from a bow with great accuracy, at long distance, and from horseback at a gallop. On the flat, open plains of Iran and Iraq, the Parthians had a decisive advantage over the slow-moving, cumbersome Roman mass infantry formations that had been developed for war in the Mediterranean.

The Sasanians, who in the mid-220s CE succeeded the Parthians as the major power in this region, improved on and expanded these same technical advantages. King Shapur I (Shabuhr), their greatest monarch (ruled 240–272 CE), was able to exploit the weaknesses of the Roman Empire in the mid–third century, even capturing the Roman emperor Valerian in 260 CE. On the other hand, as successful as Parthians and Sasanians were in fighting the Romans, they could never equal the Romans' sway. Their relatively different political structure—built up out of modular units, mainly of local ethnic groups—set limits of a different kind on their empires. And though the Parthian and Sasanian militaries were very successful in their own desert environment, they were ill-suited to fighting around the Mediterranean. Thus these states, centered in the arid lands to the east, never posed a serious threat of long-term military domination over the Mediterranean world to the west.

In the lands across the Rhine and Danube, to the north, the limits imposed on empire were largely determined by ecological conditions. The long and extremely harsh winters, but excellent soil and growing conditions, produced hardy populations clustered densely across vast distances. They formed illiterate, kin-based agricultural societies that had changed little since their emergence in these regions over the first millennium BCE. And because their warrior elites still engaged in armed competitions, it is hardly surprising that war and vio-

Chronology

	400 BCE	300 BCE	200 BCE	100 BCE
THE MEDITERRANEAN		▮ *Roman city-state expansion in Italian peninsula, 350–265 BCE* *Rome defeats Carthage in three Punic Wars and* ▮ *incorporates Carthaginian territory, 265–146 BCE*		*Civil wars divide Romans, 90–30 BCE*
SOUTHWEST ASIA			*Parthian Empire established in Southwest Asia, 129 BCE* ▮	
EAST ASIA		*Qin Empire, 221–207 BCE* ▮ *Han dynasty, 206 BCE–220 CE* ▮ *Western (Former) Han, 206 BCE–9 CE* ▮ *Expansion of Han Empire under Emperor Wu, 140–87 BCE* ▮ *Zhang Qian leads western expedition in a failed attempt to form a Han alliance with Yuezhi tribes, 139 BCE* ▮ *Imperial University founded, 136 BCE* ▮		

Soldier versus Barbarian. On the frontiers of the empire, the legionary soldiers faced the non-Roman 'barbarians' from the lands beyond. In this piece of a stone-carved picture from the northwestern frontier, we see a civilized and disciplined Roman soldier, to the left, facing a German 'barbarian'—hair uncut and unkempt, without formal armor, his house a thatched hut. Frontier realities were never so clear-cut, of course. Roman soldiers, often recruited from the 'barbarian' peoples, were a lot more like them than was convenient to admit; and the 'barbarians' were influenced by and closer to Roman cultural models than this picture indicates.

lence characterized their connections with the empire. As the Roman Empire fixed its northern armed frontiers along the Rhine and Danube rivers, the relationship of the empire to the large populations of Germans and Goths north of the rivers was determined by two factors. First, these small kinship-based societies had only one major commodity for which the empire was willing to pay: human bodies. The slave trade out of the land across the Rhine and Danube was immense, and gold, silver, coins, wine, arms, and other luxury items of high value flowed in one direction in exchange for slaves in the other. Second, their wars were unremitting, as it came to be expected of every emperor that he would deal harshly with these northern tribal peoples whom the Romans considered to be "barbarians." These fundamental connections, involving arms and violence, were to enmesh the Romans ever more tightly with the northern tribal societies. Indeed, they overlapped, as the internal conflicts within the Roman Empire prompted increasing recourse to the use of "barbarians" as soldiers and officers who served the empire.

CONCLUSION

China and Rome were similar in their construction of empires of immense and unprecedented scale and duration. In many ways, however, they were fundamentally different. Having initially less numerous and, more important, a less dense population than China, Rome relied on slaves and "barbarian" immigrants to expand and to diversify its workforce. While about 1 percent of the Chinese population was enslaved, more than ten times this proportion were slaves in the Roman Empire. The Chinese rural economy was based

	1 CE	100 CE	200 CE	300 CE
Julius Caesar conquers Gaul, 58–50 BCE				
		Jesus preaches in Judea, 1st century CE		
	Augustus reigns as first Roman emperor, 27 BCE–14 CE		Christianity expands to broader Roman Empire by 2nd and 3rd centuries CE	
		Roman Empire reaches greatest territorial extent under Emperor Trajan, 98–117 CE		
		Sasanid Empire supplants Parthia, 224 CE		
	Red Eyebrows uprising, 23 CE			
	Wang Mang usurps the Han throne, 9–23 CE		Yellow Turbans uprising, 184 CE	
	Eastern (Later) Han, 25–220 CE		Popular rebellions against Han rule, 184 CE	

almost solely on a huge population of free peasant farmers; this enormous labor pool, together with their remarkable bureaucracy, enabled the Han to achieve great political stability. The millions of peasant farmers who were the backbone of rural society in the Roman Empire were much more loosely integrated into the structure of the state. They never had the sense of belonging to a cohesive social whole, and they never unified to revolt against their government and overthrow it, as did the raging millenarian peasant movements of Later Han China.

By Chinese standards, the Roman Empire was relatively fragmented and underadministered. What is more, philosophy and religion never underpinned the Roman state in the way that Confucianism served the dynasties of China. But both empires were aided by the spread of a uniform language and imperial culture. This process was more comprehensive in China than in Rome, whose empire tended to divide into a two-language world—Latin was dominant in the western Mediterranean, Greek in the east. Both states fostered the development of a common imperial culture, at nonelite as well as elite levels of society, and once entrenched, these cultures and languages lasted well after the end of empire and formed deep-seated links between one imperial age and the next.

Their basic differences in human resources, languages, and ideas led the Roman and Han states to evolve in unique ways. In both places, however, the faiths of outsiders, Christians and Buddhists, eclipsed the secular classical ideals that grounded their respective states. And the transmission of the ideas of these new faiths was considerably assisted by the new communications networks fashioned to serve the empires' interests. These new religions added to the cultural mix that succeeded the Roman Empire and the Han dynasty. Yet despite their cultural and social significance, neither Christianity nor Buddhism ever challenged the political status quo, nor did they offer viable alternatives to the state systems that the Roman Empire and Han China had perfected.

At their height, Rome and Chang'an exercised uniform rule over vast expanses of land and large numbers of people for great lengths of time—a huge step beyond the scale of anything yet witnessed on the globe. Each state surpassed its forebears by translating unprecedented military power into the fullest form of state-based organization, as large, well-trained standing armies enforced its will. The complex organization of the state was supported by the systematic control, counting, and taxing of its population. In both cases, the general increase of the population, the growth of huge cities, and the success of long-distance trade contributed to the new scales of magnitude. The Han would not be superseded in East Asia as the model empire until the Tang dynasty in the seventh century. In western Afro-Eurasia, the Roman Empire would not be surpassed in scale or intensity of development until the rise of powerful European nation-states more than a millennium later.

STUDY QUESTIONS

 WWNORTON.COM/STUDYSPACE

1. Compare and contrast the labor systems in the Qin and Han dynasties of East Asia with that of the Roman Empire in the Mediterranean world. To what extent did each rely on systems of forced labor?

2. Analyze the impact of Xiongnu pastoralists on imperial policies of the Qin and Han dynasties of East Asia. How did each dynasty attempt to counter the threat of nomadic incursions into their territorial heartlands?

3. Compare and contrast the methods through which Han and Roman leaders enlisted the support of those they governed. What emphasis did each dynasty place on ideology, civil bureaucracy, and military organization?

4. Explain the influence of Confucian ideas on East Asia during the Han dynasty. How did Confucian ideas shape political and social hierarchies during their empire?

5. Explain the concepts of the *Pax Sinica* and *Pax Romana*. How did Han and Roman leaders promote long periods of peace and prosperity in Eastern and Western Afro-Eurasia, respectively?

6. Describe the process through which the Roman city-state created a vast empire in the Mediterranean world. How did Roman attitudes toward military service influence the growth of the empire?

7. Compare and contrast the concept of emperor in the Han dynasty with that in the Roman Empire. What role did each emperor play in the governing structure of his respective empire?

8. Explain the social and legal hierarchies that governed Roman urban life. To what extent did residents of towns and cities enjoy personal autonomy?

9. Describe the appeal of early Christianity in the Roman Empire. How did the *Pax Romana* promote the spread of Christian communities?

10. Compare and contrast Roman strategies for promoting peace and stability along its borders with those of the Han dynasty. How different were the threats that each empire faced from borderland peoples?

FURTHER READINGS

Bodde, Derk, *China's First Unifier: A Study of the Ch'in Dynasty as Seen in the Life of Li Ssu (280?–208 B.C.)* (1938). A classic account of the key Legalist adviser who formulated the Qin policy to enhance its autocratic power.

Bowman, Alan K., *Life and Letters on the Roman Frontier: Vindolanda and Its Peoples* (1994). An introduction to the exciting discovery of writing tablets at a Roman army base in northern Britain.

Bradley, Keith, *Slavery and Society at Rome* (1994). The best single overview of the major aspects of the slave system in the Roman empire.

Chevallier, Raymond, *Roman Roads*, trans. N. H. Field (1976). A guide to the fundamentals of the construction, maintenance, administration, and mapping of Roman roads.

Coarelli, Fillipo (ed.), *Pompeii*, trans. Patricia Cockram (2006). A lavishly illustrated large volume that allows the reader to sense some of the wondrous wealth of the buried city of Pompeii.

Colledge, Malcolm A. R., *The Parthians* (1967). A bit dated but still a fundamental introduction to the Parthians, the major power on the eastern frontier of the Roman empire.

Cornell, Tim, *The Beginnings of Rome: Italy and Rome from the Bronze Age to the Punic Wars, c. 2000 to 264 B.C.* (1995). The single best one-volume history of Rome through its early history to the first war with Carthage.

Cornell, Tim, and John Matthews, *Atlas of the Roman World* (1982). A history of the Roman world; much more than simply an atlas. It is provided not only with good maps and a gazetteer but also with marvelous color illustrations and a text that guides the reader through the basics of Roman history.

Csikszentmihalyi, Mark, *Readings in Han Chinese Thought* (2006). A volume presenting a representative selection of primary sources to illustrate the growth of ideas in early imperial times; a useful introduction to the key strains of thought during this crucial period.

Dixon, Suzanne, *The Roman Family* (1992). The best one-volume guide to the nature of the Roman family and family relations.

Garnsey, Peter, and Richard Saller, *The Roman Empire: Economy, Society, and Culture*, (1987). A perceptive and critical introduction to three basic aspects of social life in the empire.

Giardina, Andrea (ed.), *The Romans*, trans. Lydia Cochrane (1993). Individual studies of important typical figures in Roman society, from the peasant and the bandit to the merchant and the soldier.

Goldsworthy, Adrian, *The Roman Army at War: 100 B.C.– A.D. 200* (1996). A summary history and analysis of the Roman army in action during the late Republic and early Empire.

Goodman, Martin, *The Roman World: 44 B.C.– A.D. 180* (1997). A newer basic history text covering the high Roman Empire.

Harris, William, *Ancient Literacy* (1989). A basic survey of what is known about communication in the form of writing and books in the Roman Empire.

Hopkins, Keith, *Death and Renewal: Sociological Studies in Roman History*, vol. 2 (1983). Innovative studies on Roman history, including one of the best on gladiators and another on death and funerals.

———, *A World Full of Gods: Pagans, Jews and Christians in the Roman Empire* (1999). A somewhat unusual but interesting and provocative look at the world of religions in the Roman Empire.

Juliano, Annette L., and Judith A. Lerner (eds.), *Nomads, Traders and Holy Men Along China's Silk Road* (2003). A description of the travelers along the Silk Road in human terms, focusing on warfare, markets, and religion.

Kraus, Theodore, and Leonard von Matt, *Pompeii and Herculaneum: The Living Cities of the Dead*, trans. Robert E. Wolf (1975). A huge, lavishly illustrated compendium of all aspects of life in the buried cities of Pompeii and Herculaneum as preserved in the archaeological record.

Loewe, Michael, *The Government of the Qin and Han Empires: 221 BCE–220 CE* (2006). A useful overview of the government of the early empires of China. Topics include the structure of central government, provincial and local government, the armed forces, officials, government communications, the laws of the empire, and control of the people and the land.

Millar, Fergus, *The Crowd in the Late Republic* (1998). An innovative study of the democratic power of the citizens in the city of Rome itself.

———, *The Emperor in the Roman World, 31 B.C.–A.D. 337* (1992). Everything you might want to know about the Roman emperor, with special emphasis on his civil role as the administrator of an empire.

Potter, David, *Roman Empire at Bay: A.D. 180–395* (2004). A new basic text covering the later Roman Empire, including the critical transition to a Christian state.

Potter, David S., and David J. Mattingly (eds.), *Life, Death, and Entertainment in the Roman Empire* (1999). A good introduction to basic aspects of Roman life in the empire, including the family, feeding the cities, religion, and popular entertainment.

Qian, Sima, *Records of the Grand Historian: Qin Dynasty*, trans. Burton Watson, 3rd ed. (1995). The classic work of Chinese history in a readable translation. The Han dynasty's Grand Historian describes the slow rise and meteoric fall of the Qin dynasty from the point of view of the succeeding dynasty, which Sima Qian witnessed or heard of during his lifetime.

Southern, Pat, *The Roman Army: A Social and Institutional History* (2006). A fundamental guide to all aspects of the Roman army.

Todd, Malcolm, *The Early Germans*, rev. ed. (2004). A basic survey of the peoples in central and western Europe at the time of the Roman Empire.

Vainker, Shelagh, *Chinese Silk: A Cultural History* (2004). A work that traces the cultural history of silk in China from its early origins to the twentieth century and considers its relationship to the other decorative arts. The author draws on the most recent archaeological evidence to emphasize the role of silk in Chinese history, trade, religion, and literature.

Wells, Peter S., *The Barbarians Speak: How the Conquered Peoples Shaped Roman Europe* (1999). The cultures of the peoples of central and northern Europe at the time of the Roman Empire and their impact on Roman culture.

Wood, Francis, *The Silk Road: Two Thousand Years in the Heart of Asia* (2004). A work illustrated with drawings, manuscripts, paintings, and artifacts to trace the Silk Road to its origins as far back as Alexander the Great. The author stresses the importance of the Silk Road to cultural and religious movements.

Woolf, Greg (ed.), *The Cambridge Illustrated History of the Roman World* (2005). A good guide to various aspects of Roman history, culture, and provincial life.

8

THE RISE OF UNIVERSAL RELIGIONS, 300–600 CE

Around 180 CE, a group of relatively humble persons (three men and three women) stood trial before the provincial governor at Carthage. They claimed to be Christians, and their only crime was a refusal to worship the gods who protected the Roman Empire. The governor was unimpressed; his god was "the protecting spirit of our lord the emperor." To this, one Christian retorted that his god was also an emperor, but that he could not be seen, for he stood "above all kings and of all nations." There was an unbridgeable gap between the governor and the Christians. The governor had no choice but to read out a death sentence, ordering their immediate execution. "Thanks be to God!" cried the Christians, and straightaway they were beheaded.

As the centuries unfolded, the tables would turn dramatically. Old ideas of the supremacy of an emperor-lord gave way to those of the Lord God as emperor. This period witnessed the conjunction of religions with universal aspirations spreading across different geographic zones. It was the combination of a different kind of spiritual fervor with more numerous social and political contacts that gave religious beliefs their powerful significance. In

321

effect, religiosity became a powerful integrative force, while also setting in motion a long-term process of creating new world divides. This advent of religion as a global influence was anything but simple. It also built on the expansive reach of the Roman and Han empires and the closer commercial and intellectual connections that bound east and west together. But how did new religious movements shape political structures? Were those structures reinforced, or were they undercut? How did this process remap relations between world societies?

UNIVERSAL RELIGIONS AND COMMON CULTURES

> → *How did religion bring worlds together and drive them apart?*

In the three centuries from 300 to 600 CE, the whole of the Afro-Eurasian landmass experienced a surge of religious ferment. In the West, Christianity became the state faith of the Roman Empire. In India, Vedic religion (Brahmanism) evolved into a far more formal spiritual system that came to be called Hinduism, while in northern India, all across central Asia, and even in China, Buddhism, originally a code of ethics enunciated by an inspired individual, became a religion. Across much of the world, spiritual concerns became more and more important to everyday life, integrating dispersed communities into shared faiths.

Politics shaped religion, and religion shaped politics. Indeed, the new Afro-Eurasian spirituality took shape within imperial frameworks. Christianity arose in western Europe alongside a decaying Roman state. In the eastern Mediterranean it provided inspiration and strength for a revived eastern Roman *imperium,* Byzantium. In India, Hinduism and Buddhism vied for cultural preeminence; in central Asia and China, Buddhism flourished as the old polities foundered.

Elsewhere, in sub-Saharan Africa and the Americas, dynamic and mobile populations demonstrated that universalistic religions were not essential for creating empires of the mind. They, too, reached beyond local communities and wove them together into common spiritual worlds. In Africa a relatively small group of Bantu-speaking peoples, residing in the southeastern corner of present-day Nigeria, began to spread themselves and their way of life throughout the entire southern half of the landmass. Their latter-day ancestors became the dominant peoples in central, eastern, and southern Africa. Similarly, in the Americas, the Mayans established political and cultural institutions over a large portion of Mesoamerica.

A wide variety of societies around the world were caught up in various forms of spiritual ferment. By writing of "spiritual ferment" we do not mean that people became more excitable, more otherworldly, or more escapist. Rather, the phrase implies that religion touched more areas of society and culture than before and that it touched them in different, more demanding ways. People felt deeply about religion because it was through religious filters that they processed the meaning of what had always been important to them. Issues of truth, of loyalty, and of solidarity were discussed in religious terms, and framed by religious leaders who claimed to know the truth about an invisible other world.

Focus Questions THE RISE OF UNIVERSAL RELIGIONS

→ *How did religion bring worlds together and drive them apart?*

→ *How did empires such as the Roman and Sasanian help religions such as Christianity become universalizing?*

→ *How did the actions and activities of central Asians influence the geographic spread of universal religions and other cross-cultural developments during this time?*

→ *To what extent did South Asia develop a widespread common culture despite the region's political, religious, and social diversity?*

→ *To what extent did new influences from other parts of Afro-Eurasia transform Chinese culture and politics during this era?*

→ *How similar and different were spiritual developments in worlds apart from Afro-Eurasia during this time?*

WWNORTON.COM/STUDYSPACE

It helps to step back and consider how many questions in our own world are assumed to be answerable by science. In many respects, religion functioned in that age as science does in ours. It claimed to give clear answers about the nature of human beings, about why they lived in society, about why they married and had children, about whom they should obey, and about the degree of allegiance they owed to something unseen (God, the gods, or a supernaturally guaranteed code of conduct) rather than to any ruler. Even more, as the case of the Christian martyrs showed, it was religion that told them what they should die for.

Because religion claimed to enable its followers to distinguish sharply between right and wrong, it freed people from the past. The extreme age of local religious practices that might have existed since time immemorial did not make the old beliefs true. As this shift reverberated, and cultures shrugged off their older heritages bound to local customs and traditions, the new religious belief systems enabled people to bond together into new identities shaped by a shared faith, across much broader scales than hitherto imaginable. As we will see in this chapter, some religious systems, such as Buddhism and Christianity, would spread far and wide because they professed universal precepts; later, Islam would follow the same pattern (see Chapter 9).

The new spiritual ferment also freed individuals from the restraints imposed by preexisting social bonds. Knowing—and believing in—sharp distinctions between right and wrong drew new lines between peoples. In this way, religion provided a new wedge to drive worlds apart, as absolute conviction left little room for tolerance. Centuries of harmonious interaction offered few protections to neighbors now perceived to be "wrong" in their beliefs—and because of their errors, they could be ostracized, exiled, or killed. For wrong beliefs were held to be as dangerous as today's counterfeit medicines. Like noxious drugs, they had to be removed from circulation as quickly as possible. Conflict, even violence and religious persecution, went with this new sense of certainty.

Moreover, like science, religious beliefs were held to apply equally from one end of Afro-Eurasia to the other. Religious leaders, carrying written texts (books, scrolls, or tablets of wood or palm leaf), often traveled widely, and wherever they were, what they said and read was both true and relevant. Everywhere, universal religions were on the move. That Christians from Persia went to China demonstrates the fundamental error of associating Christianity exclusively with "Europe." Buddhism also migrated, journeying from South Asia to Afghanistan and the caravan routes of Central Asia, and to China. In 643, the Chinese Buddhist Xuanzang brought back to Chang'an (at the time, the world's largest city) an entire library of Buddhist scriptures—527 boxes of writings and 192 birch-bark tablets—that he had collected on a pilgrimage, begun in 630, to Buddhist holy sites in South Asia. He lodged them in the Great Wild Goose Pagoda, which still towers above the city, and immediately began to translate every line of them into Chinese. He had traveled 10,000 miles to bring these books to China. Here was the "truth" of Buddhism—propositions as true, in Xuanzang's opinion, as anything found in a modern science textbook, and as exciting and as healing when they reached distant China as when Buddhist thinkers had first elaborated them in northern India, more than 5,000 miles away.

Voyages, translations, long-distance pilgrimages, and sweeping conversion campaigns remapped the spiritual landscape of the world. New religious leaders were the brokers of more encompassing but also more intolerant worldviews, premised on a new relationship between gods and their subjects. Religions and their brokers profoundly integrated societies. But they also created new ways to drive them apart.

Xuanzang. This painting c. 900 CE, which survives in the caves of Dunhuang along the Silk Road, portrays the Chinese pilgrim Xuanzang accompanied by a tiger on his epic travels to South Asia to collect important Buddhist scriptures.

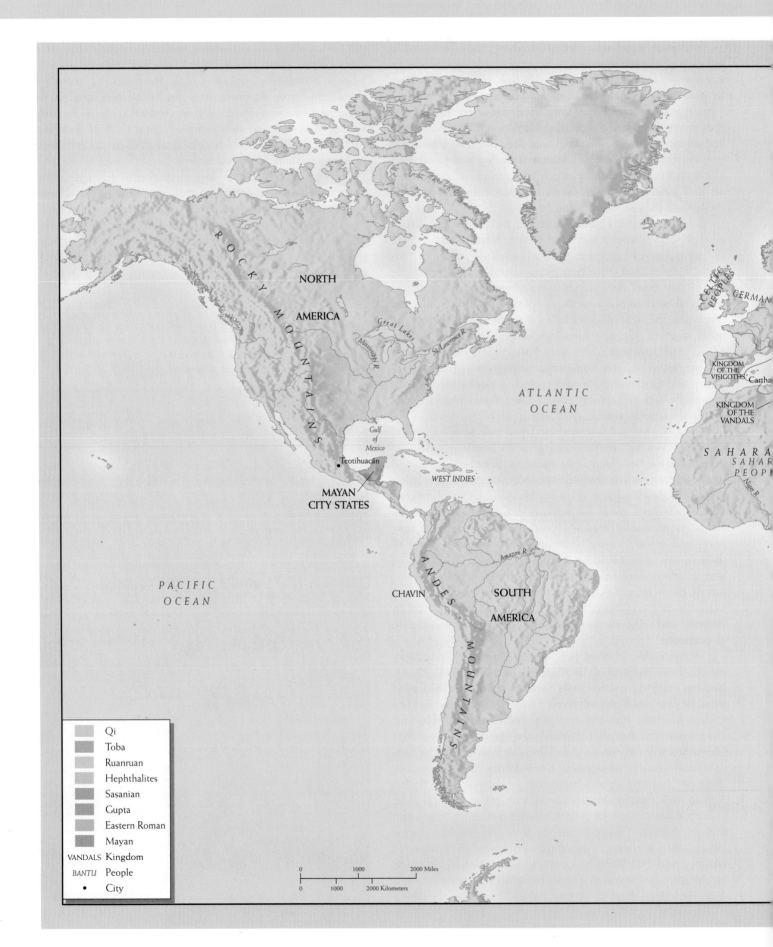

NORTH
AMERICA

Great Lakes

Mississippi R.

St. Lawrence R.

ATLANTIC
OCEAN

CELTIC
PEOPLES

GERMAN

KINGDOM
OF THE
VISIGOTHS   Cartha

KINGDOM
OF THE
VANDALS

S A H A R A

SAHAR
PEOP

Niger R.

Gulf
of
Mexico

• Teotihuacán

WEST INDIES

MAYAN
CITY STATES

Amazon R.

A
N
D
E
S

CHAVIN

SOUTH

AMERICA

M
O
U
N
T
A
I
N
S

PACIFIC
OCEAN

R
O
C
K
Y

M
O
U
N
T
A
I
N
S

	Qi
	Toba
	Ruanruan
	Hephthalites
	Sasanian
	Gupta
	Eastern Roman
	Mayan
VANDALS	Kingdom
BANTU	People
•	City

0   1000   2000 Miles

0   1000   2000 Kilometers

MAP 8-1 EMPIRES AND COMMON CULTURES FROM 300 TO 600 CE

The period between 300 and 600 CE was a time of great political change around the world. Which polities are new? Which polities have disappeared? Which have expanded or contracted? What fundamental historical factors are driving these changes in the political landscape?

MAP 8-2   THE SPREAD OF UNIVERSAL RELIGIONS IN AFRO-EURASIA, 300–600 CE

The spread of universal religions and the shifting political landscape of Afro-Eurasia in the first half of the first millennium were intimately connected. Using Map 8-1, identify the major polities in Afro-Eurasia during this era. How did these political configurations differ from those in the era covered in Chapter 7? Compare and contrast Map 8-1 with Map 8-2. Where did Hinduism, Buddhism, and Christianity emerge, and where did they spread? How did the rise and fall of empires affect the expansion of universal religions? To what extent did the polities identified in Map 8-1 use universal religions to establish their legitimacy?

EMPIRES AND RELIGIOUS CHANGE IN WESTERN AFRO-EURASIA

> → *How did empires such as the Roman and Sasanian help religions such as Christianity become universalizing?*

In the western region of Afro-Eurasia, the Roman Empire reigned supreme in 300 CE, but it was hardly the political and military juggernaut it had been 300 years earlier. Surrounded by peoples who coveted its great wealth while resisting its power, Rome was in the process of fragmenting. Rome's endurance proved a boon to new religious ferment, which took hold in its decaying structures. The populations of the western parts of the Roman Empire were eventually overrun by the barbarians on their peripheries, but in many ways they continued to feel "Roman." They looked to the new faith of Christianity to maintain order and continuity with the past, eventually founding a papacy in Rome to rule the remnants of empire.

This Christian empire split almost from the start. In Rome's east, on the other hand, a powerful successor state appeared in the form of the Byzantine Empire based at Constantinople. Its claim to be the political arm of Christianity seemed more viable than that of the western European Christian church based in Rome. But it faced a new foe still further east. The Sasanian Empire of Persia, like the papacy at Rome and the Byzantine state, was unlike the previous polities of the area. Indeed, these states represented something new in Afro-Eurasian polities. They claimed the blessing of new (or transformed) religions, and their rulers were concerned that their subjects should worship the correct gods in the correct manner. Those who did not were treated as outsiders, both in this life and in the next—where hell awaited them.

THE RISE OF CHRISTIANITY

It is one of the paradoxes of Western history that the most crucial change ever to happen to the Roman Empire had little to do with distant frontier wars. Instead, it grew from a religious war fought, from the bottom up, in the peaceful and tightly administered towns that were the nerve centers of the Roman Mediterranean.

The rise of Christianity coincided with the appearance of a new figure in matters of spiritual belief. Those who were executed by Roman authorities were called *martyrs* by the Christians, and many of them were indeed remarkable wit-

Saint Perpetua in Heaven. The Christian martyr Perpetua came to be represented as an upper-class Roman matron with carefully covered hair. Set in a circle of bright blue, in the golden dome of a church, she looks out from a distant, peaceful Heaven.

nesses to their faith. In 203, a well-to-do mother in her early twenties, Vibia Perpetua, faced a horrible punishment for her refusal to sacrifice to the gods. Denied even the benefit of a human executioner, she and her companions were condemned to be exposed to wild beasts in the amphitheater of Carthage. The amphitheater is still there, a little to the south of modern Tunis. It is a mean, small place—not a gigantic stadium. The condemned and the spectators would have had eye contact with each other throughout the fatal encounter.

Before her death, Perpetua dictated to her fellow Christians a prison diary that is unique in Roman literature. Here a woman speaks to us with a full religious message. She described her relief at being allowed to have her baby stay with her: "My prison had suddenly become a palace, so that I wanted to be there rather than anywhere else." More important, she recounted powerful visions of the next world, from which she and her companions derived strength and courage. Perpetua stepped every night into paradise, which appeared to her as a place of peace and abundance. "I saw an immense garden," she related, "and in it a gray-haired man sat in a

RELIGIOUS DEBATE AND CHRISTIAN UNIVERSALISM

The spread of religious ideas in the Roman Empire changed how people viewed their present existence. Believing implied that something bigger and more important loomed behind the world of physical matter. Feeling contact with this "other" world gave individual worshippers a sense of worth; it guided them, in this life, and they would eventually meet their guides and spiritual friends there. This was the power of Perpetua's visions. But it is important to note that the sharp taste for paradise had developed even beyond Christian circles. The fervor was potent enough that a little more than a century after Perpetua's execution, a Roman emperor, Constantine, considered that he had been led to military victory by a vision sent to him by Christ. From 312 onward, Constantine and his successors would place the huge authority of the Roman state behind a Christian church that up to then had been marginal and, often, persecuted.

Religion was no longer something that could be taken for granted—instead, it was supposed to engage the minds of those who practiced it. The reform of Judaism by the rabbis, which was also under way between 200 and 600 CE, took part in the same movement of ideas. As they struggled to rethink their religion after the loss of the Temple of Jerusalem (destroyed by the Romans in 70 CE), they recast time-honored oral traditions into the codified written volumes of the Talmud of Jerusalem, produced by the rabbis of Galilee around 400 CE. The efforts of the rabbis were intended to enable Jews to create, in their own homes and in their synagogues, "virtual temples" echoing the solemnity and purity of a temple that no longer existed. Even more influential was the Babylonian Talmud—the famous Bavli—produced by the rabbis of Mesopotamia sometime between 500 and 600 CE. Polytheists, Jews, and Christians alike unleashed their intellectual energies not, as had the ancient Greeks, in debates on how best to live in the polis but in fierce arguments about how to live in relation to God or the gods.

Religion was coming to take a form more familiar to modern Westerners. The gods were no longer local powers who had to be placated by dimly understood, archaic rituals associated with specific sacred places. Many gods became omnipresent figures to whom human beings might come close through loving attachment (similarly, as described below, the rise of *bhakti* piety among India's Hindus at this time brought individual gods closer to their worshippers). Humans might even hope to meet these divine beings again in another, happier world—and thus the sense that there must be an afterlife became stronger.

Above all, at this time, the gods expected to be obeyed, as one would obey a human lord. And it was on the issue of obedience to God rather than to a human ruler that the Christians entered with zest into a Mediterranean-wide debate on the nature of religion. Like the Jews, the Christians

Criminals and Martyrs. This detail from a mosaic found in a Roman circus in North Africa shows a criminal tied to a stake and being pushed on a little cart toward a lunging leopard. Christian martyrs were treated much the same as criminals: they were executed—exposed to animals without even the "privilege" of suffering at the hands of a human executioner.

shepherd's garb; tall he was, and milking sheep. And around him were many thousands of people clad in white garments. He raised his head, looked at me and said: 'I am glad you have come, my child.'"

Other religions, including Judaism and later Islam, honored martyrs who died for their faith. But because Christianity saw itself as being based directly on "the blood of martyrs," in the words of Tertullian (197 CE), martyrdom took on unusual significance in the Christian church in its early centuries. Moreover, the remembered heroism of women martyrs—as numerous as men—acted as a constant imaginative balance to the increasingly all-male leadership (the bishops and clergy) of the institutionalized Christian church.

claimed to possess divinely inspired scriptures in which their God had told them what to believe and what to do, even when those actions went against the laws of the empire. The little group of martyrs who appeared in Carthage carried into court a satchel containing "books and letters of a righteous man called Paul"—the Gospels and the letters of Saint Paul.

In their emphasis on texts, the Christians were moving with the times. After 200 CE, new forms of published writings, directed toward a wider audience, made their appearance in the Roman world. By 300 CE, a revolution in book production had taken place. The scroll that all ancient readers had used (and that still survives in the Torah scrolls of Jewish synagogues) was replaced by the codex: separate pages bound together to form what is the modern book. The English word "code" comes from the Latin *codex,* and even today it connotes a set of legally binding regulations ("the federal tax code") or of technical requirements ("a house built according to code"). Christians spoke of their scriptures as "a divine codex." Bound together in a compact volume (or, more usually, a set of volumes)—a form that, unlike the unwieldy

scrolls, made quick reference to precise pages quite easy—this was, in their view, the definitive Code of God's law.

THE CONVERSION OF CONSTANTINE

Born sometime after 280 CE in Naissus (Niš), in modern southern Serbia, near the Danubian frontiers of the empire, Constantine belonged to a class of professional soldiers whose careers took them a long way from the Mediterranean. He had been proclaimed emperor by his troops in the far north, in York, in 306 after the death of his father, the emperor Constantius. It was a time of political confusion, with two co-emperors and sub-emperors, and several claimants fought for power. In 312, Constantine's armies closed in on Rome in his first bid to rule the heartlands of the Mediterranean.

Like other Roman emperors before him, Constantine looked for signs from the gods and put great credence in them when they came. Before the decisive battle for the control of Rome, he claimed to have had a dream in which he was shown an emblem bearing the words "In this sign conquer."

Scroll and Codex. (*Left*) The Torah scroll still used in Jewish synagogues is the same as that used in the ancient world. Sheets of papyrus were carefully glued together to produce a continuous roll. (*Right*) The codex of the Christian Scriptures is written in simple letters. Each column of text is put on a separate page, and the pages are then bound together to form a book.

He was told to place this mysterious sign—later known as the *labarum*—on the shields of his soldiers. It took the form of an X (the Greek letter chi, representing a "ch" sound) placed over P (the Greek letter rho, or "r")—the opening letters of the name of Christ—and it soon became known all over the Roman world.

The recently persecuted Christian Church was the immediate beneficiary of Constantine's strange vision. In 313 CE, he issued a famous proclamation, exalting the work of Christian bishops and giving them tax exemptions for their services. But the significance of this edict was much broader. It was the first public evidence for what was soon labeled the "conversion" of Constantine, and it took a typically Roman approach to a powerful new god: it gave privileges to a favored religious group who were responsible for that god's worship. The order displayed no direct intention to make Christianity into a majority religion, still less to make it the exclusive religion of the empire. But, as is so often the case, an act's unintended effects were long-lasting; it would be through the institutions and across the byways of the Roman Empire that Christianity would spread.

Christians, taking Constantine's conversion as evidence of total victory for their faith, exploited their new privileges with fierce alacrity. Though still a minority within the empire (10 percent of the population, at most), they reacted to their earlier victimization by strenuously pushing their rights to the fore, even at the expense of others. Thus, as the century proceeded, the other religions of the Roman world felt the consequences of Constantine's conversion. Some resisted better than others. Notably, Judaism did not wither away. The archaeology of modern Israel and elsewhere has shown that Jewish communities remained proud and prosperous, despite the hostility of Christian emperors and Christian local violence, which was more frequent than any assaults by pagans against the Jews.

In 400, most inhabitants of the empire were still polytheist, but they were simply declared by Christians not to count. Christians in the Latin world gave them the pejorative name *pagani* (pagans), a word previously applied to those who were outside the privileged class of imperial officials (and who thus were second-class citizens). Being a *paganus* also meant to be a "local"—a person tied to his or her *pagus* (village), as in the modern French *paysan*, Spanish *paesano*, and English *peasant*. By using this name, Christians placed the entire world of ancient polytheism on a lower level than their own universal, urbane religion, which had taken shape from the preaching and reading of Christians in towns all over the Roman Empire.

The Conversion of Constantine. In this painting, the seventeenth-century artist Rubens uses "period" details for historical accuracy: the XP (the first letters of the name of Christ in Greek) in the sky; beneath them, the "dragon" standard of the Roman cavalry of the year 312 (the standard came from China and passed to Rome via the cavalry-nomads of Central Asia); beside the dragon, the eagle of the traditional Roman standard.

CHRISTIANITY IN THE CITIES

It took a long time for Christianity to become the majority religion of the Roman world. But Christianity soon established itself at the top of society, and it became a majority religion in the cities.

After 312 CE, the large churches built in every major city, many with the help of imperial funding, were a sign of Christianity's growing strength. They were gigantic meeting halls, often with room for more than a thousand worshippers. Called *basilicas*, from the Greek *basileus* (king), the solemn halls were indeed worthy of royalty. But unlike the ancient temples, which housed the gods inside (often in a small, dark sanctuary chamber) while the people milled around in the outdoors, they were open to all. Those entering a basilica found a vast enclosed space, shimmering with the light of oil lamps playing on shining marble and mosaics. Rich silk hangings, swaying between the rows of columns, increased the sense of mystery and directed the eye to the far end of the building—a semi-circular apse furnished with particular splendor. They had come into a different world. This was heaven on earth.

And it was a very orderly heaven. The bishop and priests sat at the very end of the building, under the dome of the apse, which represented the dome of heaven itself. The bishop had a special throne, called his *cathedra* (the Latin word regularly used both for a teacher's seat and for the throne of a governor). The space around the bishop and clergy was holy, marked off from the rest of the building by low marble screens and especially vivid floor mosaics. (The church at Verona even had under-floor heating in this area!) Ordinary members of the congregation would stand, as a gesture of respect, while the bishop sat and preached, usually from his space in the apse.

Such churches became the new urban public forums. They were ringed with spacious courtyards in which every city's poor would gather. In return for the tax exemptions that Constantine had given to the bishops of "his" church, the bishops were made responsible for the metropolitan poor, becoming in effect their governors. Christian poor relief helped the cities of the Mediterranean to weather financial crises in the fourth and fifth centuries.

Bishops also became judges. Constantine turned the process by which Christian bishops had acted as arbiters in disputes between fellow Christians into a more formal kind of small claims court. It was by such means—offering the poor shelter, quick justice, and moments of unearthly splendor in grand new basilicas on the holy days and festivals of the Christian year—that the bishops in the cities of the Roman world built up for themselves a position that would last (in many areas within and beyond Europe) until modern times. In many societies of Afro-Eurasia, as we will see, the weakening of grandiose imperial institutions often favored

Basilica Interior. The interior of a basilica was dominated by rows of ancient marble columns and was filled with light from upper windows, so that the eye was led directly to the apse of the church, where the bishop and clergy would sit under a dome, close to the altar.

the rise of local power blocs formed by religious groupings, who could hold the hearts and minds of smaller communities that discovered they were living in an increasingly dangerous world. In western Europe, those power blocs were headed by the Christian bishops. In their basilicas, "Rome" lived on for centuries after the empire had disappeared.

THE CHRISTIAN EMPIRE

Here was a universalizing religion and its practices. But how did it spread across parts of Southwest Asia, Africa, and Europe? Constantine and his successors were impressed by the Christian Church's unity and emphasis on expansion. Christianity was spreading into the hinterlands of Africa and Southwest Asia as part of a drive to reach out from the cities, where Greek or Latin predominated, to broader, more ethnically diverse populations. These efforts required the breaking of language barriers. After around 300 CE, the Christian clergy in Egypt replaced the hieroglyphs that were still being used to write the language—a system that only a few temple priests could read—with a more accessible, "modern" script, based on Greek letters: it is known today as Coptic (from the Greek word meaning "Egyptian," *Aigyptios*). With this innovation, the Christian clergy also brought the countryside and

Primary Source

EUSEBIUS

Eusebius declared that the Roman Empire had always owed its success to divine providence. He viewed the birth of Christ during the rule of the emperor Augustus as no coincidence: it showed God's choice to come to earth at a time when the preaching of his message could coincide with an almost uncanny era of peace and unity in the Roman world. Christianity had ridden to its favored position on the providential tide of a unified world empire.

Now formerly all the peoples of the earth were divided, and the whole human race cut up into provinces and tribal and local governments, states ruled by despots or by mobs. Because of this continuous battles and wars, with their attendant devastations and enslavements, gave them no respite in countryside or city. . . .

But now two great powers—the Roman Empire, which became a monarchy at that time, and the teaching of Christ—proceeding as if from a single starting point, at once tamed and reconciled all to friendship. Thus each blossomed at the same time and place as the other. For while the power of our Savior destroyed the multiple rule and polytheism of the demons [the old gods] and heralded the one kingdom of God to Greeks and barbarians and all men to the furthest end of the earth, the Roman Empire, now that the causes of manifold governments had been abolished, subdued the visible governments of, in order to merge the entire race into one unity and concord. . . .

Moreover, as One God and one knowledge of this God is heralded to all, one empire has waxed strong among men, and the entire race of mankind has been re-directed into peace and friendship as all acknowledged each other as brothers. . . . All at once, as if sons and daughters of one father, the One God, and children of one mother, true religion, they greeted and received each other peaceably, so that from that time the whole inhabited world differed in no way from a single well-ordered and related household. It became possible for anyone who pleased to make a journey and to leave home for wherever he might wish with all ease. Thus some from the East moved freely to the West, while others went from here [the East] back there, as easily as if traveling to their native lands.

→ *What do you think of this praise of Constantine as the first Christian emperor, which comes from a seventy-year-old bishop who had witnessed the "Great Persecution" of Christians (launched by the emperor Diocletian in 303 CE)?*

→ *What elements in the history of Christianity at this time would have led Eusebius to emphasize its role as a unifying force in the Roman world?*

→ *Was his belief in a relation between the expansion of a world religion and the expansion of an empire an assumption that was unique to Christians?*

SOURCE: Eusebius, *Tricennial Oration* 16.2–7 [Jubilee Oration on the Thirtieth Year of the Reign of Constantine, delivered on July 25, 336], translated by H. L. Drake in *In Praise of Constantine: A Historical Study and New Translation of Eusebius' Tricennial Orations* (Berkeley: University of California Press, 1976), pp. 119–21.

its local languages closer to the towns and the towns to the countryside. A similar pattern unfolded in Africa along the Nile, not just in Egypt but also in Nubia and Ethiopia, each of which developed its own scripts and language under Christian influence. And in the crucial corridor that joined Antioch to Mesopotamia, Syriac, an offshoot of the Semitic language Aramaic, became a major Christian language. Christianity also spread further east, to Georgia in the Caucasus and to Armenia, and Christian clergy, around 450 CE, created the written languages that are still used in those regions.

Constantine hoped to increase the unity of his empire by fostering the universal outreach of the Christian Church. In 325 CE, he celebrated his final conquest of the eastern provinces in Southwest Asia by summoning all the bishops to a gathering at Nicaea (modern Iznik in western Turkey), where he himself presided. Though their religion has since produced many denominations, all Christians still look back to the Council of Nicaea as the foundational moment when the Christian faith was first summed up in what is now known as a "creed"—from the Latin *credo,* "I believe." The belief that the essence of an entire religion could be captured in a written formula (rather than carried by memory, as was the case for oral societies and most "pagan" cults) typified the high hopes that the intellectual revolution of the third century had inspired. It was a statement of religious belief formulated in technical, philosophical terms. Jews and, later, Muslims expected believers to make formal statements that their God was the only God; Christians asked believers to balance three separate Gods in terms that required an expert to explain.

The effort did not succeed: Christians found themselves unable to come to universal agreement on such crucial questions as how Jesus could be both human and God in human form. More than a century later, the Council of Chalcedon (451 CE) fared no better. These were not issues that could be solved by a committee, even one backed by a Roman emperor; bishops did not always think alike. But, at Nicaea, they agreed on one crucial point: they agreed to hold Easter, the day on which Christians celebrated the resurrection of Christ from the tomb after his crucifixion, on exactly the same day in every church of the Christian world.

Constantine died in 337 CE. His legacy was monumental: he had converted to Christianity, but he had done so in such a way that Christianity itself was converted to the Roman Empire. Writing in the very last years of Constantine's reign, an elderly bishop of Caesarea in Palestine, Eusebius (c. 263–339?), presented a vision of the Roman Empire that would have surprised the martyrs of Carthage, who had died (less than a century and a half before) rather than recognize any "empire of this world."

From the time of Constantine onward, many Christians—especially in the Greek-speaking provinces of the empire, where Christianity was stronger and the empire was more secure—loudly trumpeted Eusebius's view of the history of Rome. Around the eastern Mediterranean, at least, Christians came to believe that Christianity, empire, and culture had flowed together.

But after the year 400 CE, Christians had to confront a new issue. What was the relative position of the "Christian" Mediterranean in a far wider sphere, where the world empire of Rome (which Christians such as Eusebius had come instinctively to identify with "civilization") was subject to increasing challenge from its own margins?

THE FALL OF ROME: A TAKEOVER FROM THE MARGINS

After 400 CE, the Roman world began to fall apart. The western European provinces went their own way, because there the frontiers had never been borders in the modern sense. They did not constitute a clear defensive line, separating the inhabitants of the empire from the tribal world outside it. Indeed, over the centuries, the presence of Roman armies and of Roman cities along the Rhine and Danube had blurred the boundary between the Roman and the non-Roman world. A common zone had emerged, as Roman skills and the impact of the Roman economy reached deep into Germany and as non-Roman customs reached deep into Roman territory—including the shocking "barbarian" custom of wearing trousers. The ancient Roman dress code, which insisted on the loosely folded toga for civilians, gave way, in the course of the fourth century, to a tight, brightly embroidered shirt and trousers covered by a great cloak, itself pinned to one shoulder by brooches that were now of exquisite barbarian workmanship. This became the fashion favored by top military personnel in the Roman armies. The men who wore such attire might be Romans, but they were proud to look like warriors drawn from the tribes across the frontier.

WHO WERE THE BARBARIANS?

Romans and non-Romans were drawn together along the Rhine and the Danube through an active market in military manpower. In the societies that bordered the empire, young men grew up knowing that their personal status (the precious freedom of a male warrior in Germanic societies) depended on their ability to fight. In the absence of a strong state, order was maintained by the blood feud. Hence fighting was a part of everyday life as well as military campaigns. Such societies produced surplus warriors almost as a modern country in the developing world produces cash crops with export value (for example, bananas or coffee). So, too, non-Roman soldiers were exports sold for Roman gold. In the course of the third and fourth centuries, every civil war within the Roman Empire had been accompanied by massive immigrations of manpower from across the frontier that supplemented the armies of the rival claimants to the position of emperor.

What is often referred to as the "barbarian invasions" of the late fourth and fifth centuries were simply a more violent and chaotic form of this steady immigration. Today we use *barbarian* to label someone uncultivated or savage, but the core meaning of the word is simply "foreigner" (with overtones of inferiority). The inhabitants of the western provinces had become used to non-Roman soldiers from across the frontiers, and for them *barbarian* was virtually synonymous with "soldier." Soldiers could be destructive, and Roman civil wars were murderous affairs. But nobody feared that the presence of barbarians fighting in armies on Roman territory would bring the end of Roman culture.

As arresting as the popular image of bloodthirsty barbarian hordes streaming into the Roman Empire might be, it bears little resemblance to reality. In fact, the barbarians

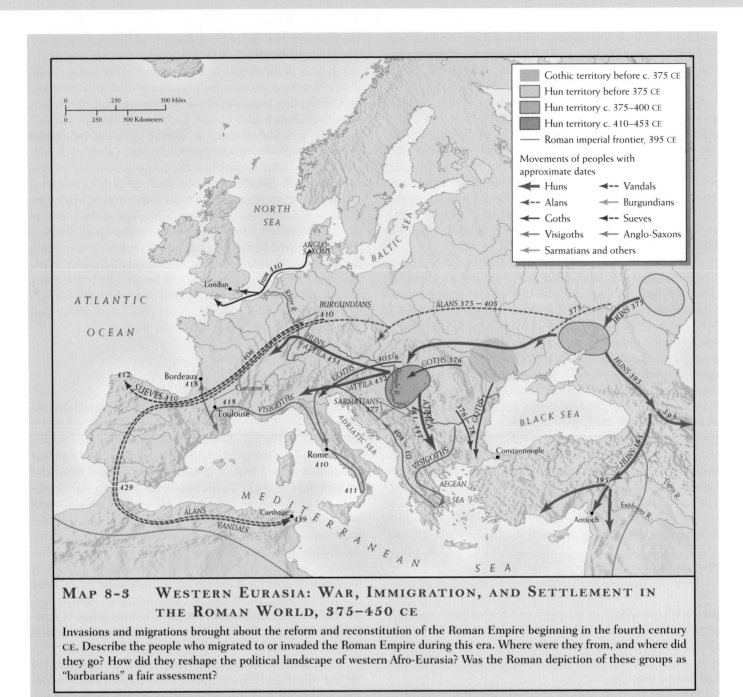

MAP 8-3 WESTERN EURASIA: WAR, IMMIGRATION, AND SETTLEMENT IN THE ROMAN WORLD, 375–450 CE

Invasions and migrations brought about the reform and reconstitution of the Roman Empire beginning in the fourth century CE. Describe the people who migrated to or invaded the Roman Empire during this era. Where were they from, and where did they go? How did they reshape the political landscape of western Afro-Eurasia? Was the Roman depiction of these groups as "barbarians" a fair assessment?

were sucked into the empire in ever greater numbers by the Roman need for soldiers. The process reached a crisis point when, in 376 CE, Visigothic tribes from across the Danube petitioned the emperor Valens (ruled 365–378 CE) to let them immigrate into the Roman Empire. In need of manpower, Valens encouraged their entrance. But the Roman authorities failed to feed their new guests. It was famine and anger at the breakdown of supplies from the Roman side—and not innate bloodlust—that turned the Visigoths against Valens. When Valens marched against them at the flat plains outside Adrianople (modern Edirne, in European Turkey) in the hot August of 378 CE, he was not seeking to halt a barbarian invasion. Rather, he had come to teach a lesson in obedience to his newly recruited military stoop laborers. But the Visigoths, driven to desperation by famine, had brought with them cavalry from the steppes north of the Danube, and the charge of this cavalry proved decisive. Valens and a large part of the Roman army of the East vanished in a cloud of red dust, trampled to death by the men they had hoped to hire.

Even the most notorious incidents of the so-called barbarian invasions follow a similar pattern, as most involved armies from across the frontier drawn into the empire by Roman civil wars. Intermittent and murderous civil wars had long been a feature of Roman society, but the Roman state could not survive this bout, constantly fed by non-Roman recruits. The "fall" of the Roman Empire in western Europe was not a sudden collapse; instead, it was the culmination of a long process—the result of what historians have called overextension. Rome could never be nearly as strong along its frontiers as it was around the Mediterranean, because those frontiers were simply too far away. Despite the deservedly famous Roman roads, travel time between the Rhine border and Rome was more than thirty days. Because the Romans did not have the vast network of canals that enabled the Chinese emperors to move goods and soldiers by water, Roman power could be felt in the north only at the cost of constant effort and high taxes. After 400 CE, neither men nor funds were available to exert that power.

It became plain that the western emperors could no longer raise the taxes required to maintain control of the provinces. While some loss of revenue was attributable to military defeat and the perpetual disruption brought about by civil wars, the primary cause may have been the rise of an aristocracy of great Roman landowners throughout the provinces of the West. Their imposing villas dominated the landscape outside the cities. Often fortified with strong towers on every corner, these buildings were harbingers of the castles that would rise in medieval Europe. Those who lived in them controlled their peasantry for miles around as completely as the later feudal lords would. They could manage, if need be, without an empire.

In 418 CE, the Visigoths finally settled in southwest Gaul, between present-day Bordeaux and Toulouse. Ruled by their own king, who kept his military following in order, they were welcomed by the local landowners. The Goths, as they were more generally known, became a form of local militia, capable of maintaining law and order. In particular, they were able to suppress the peasants' revolts that had begun occurring with alarming frequency along the margins of Gallic society. Though never as savage or as widespread as the uprisings that had brought about the end of the Han dynasty in China, they created a mood of emergency. The threat of chaos made the Roman landowners of Gaul and elsewhere anxious to ally themselves with new military leaders rather than face the worse disruption that would follow social revolution and the raids of even more dangerous armies. The Goths came as allies of the aristocracy, not as enemies of Rome.

> *The "fall" of the Roman Empire in western Europe was not a sudden collapse; instead, it was the culmination of a long process—the result of what historians have called overextension.*

CONTINUITY IN CHANGE

Such accommodation ensured that a "Roman" style of life survived around the western Mediterranean long after the empire that had claimed to protect it had vanished. Even today, the names of some of the most famous vineyards in the valley of the Garonne and Bordeaux in southwestern France, such as Loupiac and Paulliac (the villages of Lupus and Paulinus) outside Bordeaux, still bear the names of the Romans who owned them around the year 400. Across the Mediterranean, outside Carthage, the chance discovery of a cache of estate documents written in careful Latin in 497 (twenty years after the departure of the last Roman emperor of the West) show that little had changed on the ground. Large estates made up of olive plantations continued to produce stunning wealth for local landowners with Roman names. The olive trees were still being rented out, sold, and planted according to legal rulings that went back more than 350 years, to the age of the emperor Hadrian.

Romans, and the non-Romans with whom they had allied and fought, also drew together because both suddenly confronted a common enemy. As happened many times in the history of Afro-Eurasia, a nomad confederation—in this case, that of the Huns, from eastern Inner Asia—reached out along the steppe corridor north of the Black Sea (modern Ukraine) to bring a new style of warfare and a new political ideology to the very edge of western Europe. For twenty chilling years, from 433 to 453, a single king, Attila, imposed himself as sole ruler of all the Hunnish tribes. His euphemistic name—"little Daddy," in Gothic—did nothing to soften the reality: he was a harsh overlord who frightened the Germanic peoples even more than he frightened the Romans. The Romans had walls to hide behind—Hadrian's Wall, town walls, villa walls, city walls. In the open plains north of the Danube, however, the Hunnish cavalry found only scattered villages and open fields, whose harvests they would plunder on a regular basis, reducing the Germanic population to starvation.

Attila was so formidable because he intended to be a "real" emperor. Having seized (perhaps from the Chinese empire) the notion of a "mandate of heaven"—in his case, a divine right to rule the tribes of the north—he fashioned the first opposing empire that Rome ever had to face in northern Europe. Its traces clearly remain in the archaeology of Ukraine, of Hungary, and of central Europe. Spectacular jewelry of a Hunnish style, often bearing dragon motifs that had come all the way from China, showed that a true warrior-aristocracy could exist across the Rhine and the Danube. Rather than having to sell his people's services to Rome, Attila extracted thousands of pounds of gold coins from the Roman emperors in the form of tribute. With Roman gold, he could dominate the barbarian world. The result: the Roman empire in the West vanished only twenty years after the death of the great Hun. In 476, the last Roman emperor of the West, a young boy with the pretentious name of Romulus Augustulus —namesake of both Rome's heroic founder and, as "Mini-Augustus," its first emperor—resigned to make way for a so-called barbarian king in Italy.

Rule from Rome was over, but not its legacies. Future rulers had to make alliances with the landowning classes that had prospered during the days of the empire. The Roman landowners of southern Europe had survived, and among them, by the year 500, the Visigoths felt fully at home. Their king could call himself Alaric II, proudly underscoring his connection to the man who had sacked Rome in 410. At the same time, he could also now count on the warm support of the great Roman landowners, some of whom claimed to be descended from members of the ancient Roman Senate stretching back to the time before the empire was established. In 506, Alaric II even issued for them a simplified code of imperial law that owed nothing to the non-Roman world. This carefully chosen condensation of the essence of Roman law provided his Roman subjects with all that was necessary to maintain a Roman way of life in a world without empire.

Such an alliance was not unique. In China as well, the great landowning families survived the passing of the Han empire. From 200 to 550 CE, they stood for a way of life that was sufficiently well-rooted in the land to outlive the unwieldy political superstructure of a unified empire. In Europe, as in China, there was a price to pay: alliance with outsiders. Non-Romans had been stereotyped, for centuries, as "barbarians"—violent, foreign, lacking all culture. But the landowners in Roman territories, as in China, proved to be adaptable realists. Though they now lacked an empire, they remained confident of the superiority of their "Roman" way of life. Nevertheless, they lived in a poorer world: the huge cities and the extensive trade networks that had characterized the Roman Empire at its height were drastically curtailed. The population of Rome itself dropped vertiginously —from half a million in 350 CE to about 80,000 in 500. Smaller, weaker states that were ruled by a warrior upper class became the norm.

The sense of unity of the Roman Empire was replaced by a sense of the continued unity of the church. This process is dramatically exemplified by the well-known story of the "Apostle of Ireland"—Saint Patrick (died c. 470). A Roman-Briton, he was first brought to Ireland as a slave, but he later returned to the island as a missionary. He believed that in making the Irish people Christian, he also made them "Romans." Once baptized, he argued, they were no longer "barbarians." They were then entitled to the same respect as any other "Roman" Christian. The "Catholic" (literally, "universal") Church became the one institution to which all Chris-

tians in western Europe, Romans and non-Romans alike, felt that they belonged. As a result, the bishops of Rome eventually emerged as "popes"—as the symbolic head of the western Christian churches. Rome ceased to be an imperial capital. Instead, it became a spiritual capital. By 700 CE, the great Roman landowning families had vanished (unlike the more tenacious families of China). They were replaced in the power structure by religious leaders, who wielded vast moral authority—a clergy that was often descended from them and that continued to regard Latin culture as the only culture suited to an international Catholic Church.

BYZANTIUM, ROME IN THE EAST: THE RISE OF CONSTANTINOPLE

The collapse of empire in the fifth-century West was a development restricted to a small corner of Afro-Eurasia. Elsewhere, the Roman Empire was alive and well. From the borders of Greece to the borders of modern Iraq, and from the Danube River to the future location of the Aswan Dam in Egypt and the borders of Saudi Arabia (over a territory now occupied by ten separate modern states), the Roman Empire survived undamaged. Rich and self-confident, it saw itself as a new and more fortunate version of Old Rome.

The new Roman empire of the East already had its own Rome. In 324 CE, a year before he assembled the Christian bishops at Nicaea, Constantine decided to build a grandiose new city on the European side of the straits of the Bosporus, which separated Europe from Asia. He chose the site of the ancient Greek city of Byzantium; he first called it New Rome, but it soon took on his own name, "Constantine's City" (in Greek, *Kōnstantinou polis*).

In the next centuries, Constantinople grew explosively, becoming not just a new Rome but a bigger and better Rome. By 500 CE, when Rome itself had dwindled to fewer than 80,000 inhabitants, its population numbered more than half a million. It was one of the most spectacularly successful cities in Afro-Eurasia, boasting 4,000 new palaces. Every year, more than 20,000 tons of grain were shipped in from Egypt, to a dockside one and a half miles in length along the Bosporus and in the sheltered inlet of the Golden Horn. A gigantic hippodrome (a deliberate echo of Rome's Circus Maximus) straddled the central ridge of the city, flanking an imperial palace whose opulent, carefully enclosed spaces stretched down the hillside to the busy shore of the Bosporus. As in Rome, the emperor would sit in his imperial box, witnessing the chariot races as rival teams careened around the stadium. The Hippodrome was also the place where eastern imperial might was put on display. Ambassadors came to the Hippodrome, on bended knees, from as far away as central Asia, northern India, and Dongola in Nubia (modern Sudan).

Constantinople also had the resources of a world capital. In the early sixth century (long after their western colleagues had been declared bankrupt), the emperors of Constantinople had a yearly budget of 8,500,000 gold pieces. On his death in 518 CE, the emperor Anastasius left a surplus of 23 million gold pieces. No other state west of China had tax revenues so gigantic or regular. It is important to recall that by Roman standards, nowhere could be more "Roman" than Constantinople. Constantinople was a predominantly Greek city. But Greeks had accepted Roman rule for half a millennium. They were proud (and obliged) to be ruled by Roman law, a circumstance that made them "Romans"—*Rhomaioi*. This was the Constantinople to which the future emperor Justinian came, as a young man from an obscure village in the Balkans, to seek his fortune around 510 CE. He became emperor in 527 CE. He thought of himself as the successor of a long line of forceful Roman emperors—and he believed that he would outdo them.

First, Justinian reformed the Roman laws. Working at headlong speed, by 533 CE a commission of lawyers created the *Digest:* a solid volume of 800,000 words that condensed the contents of 1,528 Latin law books. It was accompanied by the *Institutes,* which was to serve as a teacher's manual in the schools of Roman law. The best ones had long been not in Rome but in Beirut, on the eastern Mediterranean coast of ancient Phoenicia. These works were the foundation of what all later ages came to know as "Roman law," as followed both in eastern and in western Europe.

Justinian was equally determined to reassert the authority of the Roman emperors in the western Mediterranean. Relying on formidable naval superiority and small regiments of his crack troops, which included units of Hunnish horse archers armed with the most advanced bows, he crushed the once-formidable Vandals in Africa. In 533 CE, Carthage became part of the "true" Roman empire once again. He then turned his attention to the heart of the old empire, wresting Rome itself from the Ostrogoths in 536 CE and reclaiming the former imperial capital of Ravenna in northern Italy, beside the Adriatic, in 540 CE.

Our only portraits of Justinian and his wife, Theodora, come from a mosaic that he set up in the church of San Vitale in Ravenna to celebrate his brisk reconquest of Italy. In brilliant colors, the emperor is shown, surrounded by his entourage, as he advances beside the bishop to offer his gifts at the altar. His remarkable wife—a former strip dancer in the Hippodrome turned high-class courtesan (so her enemies said)—stands on the other side, swathed in imperial finery, bringing a large chalice up to the silken veils of the sanctuary. The two portraits, carefully placed on either side of the holiest part of the basilica, are still there, a reminder that Justinian did not only fashion himself the successor of Augustus and the reformer of Roman law, but also as the direct heir of Constantine. Justinian's empire was victorious because it was a Christian empire.

The perfect example of the marriage of Christianity and empire was the building of the church of the Hagia Sophia at the far end of the Hippodrome. With characteristic boldness and energy, Justinian took advantage of the burning in 532 CE of the city's old basilica church, destroyed in the course of a riot that started in the Hippodrome and almost cost him

Justinian and Theodora. These portraits face each other on either side of the altar in the apse of the church of San Vitale at Ravenna. Both Justinian and Theodora are shown presenting lavish gifts. As emperor, Justinian heads the procession. On his left are the clergy; on his right are guards with Constantine's XP symbol on their shields and his lay advisers. Thus, both church and state line up behind their leader, the emperor. Theodora is more secluded. She is surrounded by ladies with veiled heads and by beardless eunuchs, who draw back the curtains for her to make her appearance.

The Hagia Sophia. After the conquest of Constantinople by the Muslim Ottomans in 1453, the Hagia Sophia was made into a mosque by having minarets (slender, high towers) added to each corner. Otherwise, it looks exactly as it did in the days of Justinian. In modern times, it became the model for the domed mosques that appear all over the Islamic world.

his throne. Finished within a few years, Hagia Sophia (literally, "Holy Wisdom") would have come as a complete surprise to those who first entered it. No church of this size had ever been seen in the world; few buildings so large had been constructed in Roman times. The nave was twice the span of the former basilica—230 feet wide—and the new church was more than twice as high as its predecessor. The largest church built by the emperor Constantine, the basilica of Saint Peter in Rome, would have reached only as high as its lower galleries. Above all, the solemn straight lines of the traditional Christian basilica were transformed. Great cliffs of stone, sheathed in multicolored marble and supported on gigantic columns of green and purple granite, rose to a dreamlike height. Audaciously curved semi-circular niches placed at every corner made the entire building seem to dance. Instead of a pitched or flat wooden roof, a spectacular dome, in which light was trapped in the refulgent depths of gold mosaics, floated almost 200 feet above it all.

In later centuries, Hagia Sophia was called, by the Greek and non-Greek Christians of the East, "the eye of the civilized world." It represented in stone the flowing together of Christianity and imperial culture that, for another thousand years, would be the distinctive feature of the eastern Roman empire of Constantinople.

SASANIAN PERSIA

Justinian had the misfortune of having to rule an empire at the western edge of Asia when Asia itself was changing dra-

matically. To begin with, the contacts between east and west intensified. The first, most unexpected, and most deadly reminder of the influence of the east was a sudden onslaught of the bubonic plague—the grim gift of the Indian Ocean, a region of latent plague. In 542 CE, the plague first appeared in the Egyptian port of Pelusium (near modern Port Said and the outlet of the modern Suez Canal), which linked the Mediterranean to the commercial route that reached down the Red Sea and across the Indian Ocean, to Kerala and Ceylon. We are not sure of the actual origin of the plague—whether it was South Asia or the Great Lakes region of Africa—but it quickly emptied the cities of the Mediterranean. A third of the population of Constantinople died of bubonic plague within a few weeks. Justinian himself survived and lived until 565 CE, but he was forced to rule an empire whose traditional heartland had been crippled.

The quick spread of epidemic diseases was one reminder of the growing interconnectedness of distant Afro-Eurasian worlds; another was border clashes between empires whose frontiers bumped up against each other. Rivalry for territorial control escalated. Justinian's empire was locked in conflict with a formidable eastern rival for the control of Southwest Asia. Beginning at the Euphrates River and stretching for eighty days of slow travel by land across the modern territories of Iraq, Iran, Afghanistan, and much of central Asia—a distance of more than 1,500 miles—a great landbased empire, the Sasanian empire of Persia, extended across the land routes of western Asia.

KING OF KINGS OF ERAN AND AN-IRAN

As we saw in Chapter 7, the Sasanians had replaced the less ambitious Parthians as the rulers both of the Iranian plateau and of the rich lands of Mesopotamia by the mid-220s CE. For the sake of convenience, westerners (Romans included) tended to call their domain the empire of Persia, but its precise title is more revealing. The Sasanian ruler was the King of Kings of Eran and An-Eran—of the Iranian and the non-Iranian lands. A royal dynasty and an aristocracy drawn from the heartlands of the Iranian plateau claimed to rule, by divine right, the non-Iranian territories of Mesopotamia. The ancient, carefully irrigated fields of what is modern Iraq were very different from the stark, dry plateau of Iran itself. They were the economic heart of the empire. The Sasanians placed their capital—Ctesiphon—where the Tigris and the Euphrates Rivers come close, only twenty miles south of modern Baghdad. The presence of the King of Kings at Ctesiphon was symbolized by a vast vaulted arch (more than 110 feet high, with a span exceeding 75 feet) framed by a high facade, decorated with rows of windowlike arches. Though it may have been built as early as 300 CE, the great arch was known throughout the Middle Ages as the Taq-e Kesra, the "arch of

Kesra/Kisra," from the name of Justinian's exact contemporary and rival, Khusro I Anoshirwan—Khusro of the Righteous Soul—who reigned from 530 to 579 CE.

In Southwest Asia during this period, Khusro Anoshirwan stood for the model ruler, and his name was identified with strong, just rule. Khusro's image in the east, as an ideal monarch and the personification of justice, was quite as glorious as that enjoyed by Justinian in the west, as the epitome of a Christian Roman emperor. For both Persians and Arab Muslims of later ages, the Arch of Khusro was as awe-inspiring and as seemingly indestructible as Justinian's Hagia Sophia appeared to be to Christians.

As Khusro's long reign unfolded, it became increasingly obvious that the vast Sasanian Empire was more than the equal of the Mediterranean empire of Rome, for it controlled the crossroads of Afro-Eurasia. Sasanian control of the western oases of central Asia ensured that the precious Silk Road passed through Iran before it reached the Romans at Antioch. But the control of trade was only part of the story. The flat lands around the Oxus River were the military laboratory of Afro-Eurasia, and developments there were studied keenly by Persians and Chinese alike. The Chinese emperors demanded "blood-sweating horses" from the plains of eastern central Asia for their own cavalry.

Christian forces met their match in the form of Iranian heavily armored cavalry, a fighting machine adapted from many years of Persian competition with the nomads of central Asia. On the plains of Syria, the Romans marched into a slaughterhouse. Covered from head to foot in flexible scale armor (small plates of iron sewn on to leather), these Persian horsemen were true harbingers of the medieval knight. More important still, the Sasanians had gleaned from northern India the art of making steel: their swords and armor were light and flexible. With such cavalry behind him, Khusro captured and sacked Antioch in 540 CE. The unexpected campaign proved to be no more than a smash-and-grab raid, and Khusro returned to Persia with vast plunder. But it was a warning, at the height of Justinian's glory in the west, that (as in the days of the Assyrians and then of the Achaemenids) Mesopotamia could reach out, once again, to conquer the shoreline of the eastern Mediterranean.

Under Khusro II, "the Victorious" (590–628 CE)—the grandson of Khusro I—the confrontation between Persia and Rome escalated into the greatest war that Southwest Asia had seen for centuries. Between 604 and 628 CE, Khusro II's armies conquered Egypt and Syria and even reached the threshold of Constantinople. Khusro II was finally defeated by the emperor Heraclius (ruled 610–641 CE) in a series of brilliant campaigns in northern Mesopotamia. Never had either empire reached so far into the heart of the other, and the effort exhausted both. For that reason, both fell easily to the Arab invasion that would occur only a few years later (see Chapter 9).

AN EMPIRE AT THE CROSSROADS

In their confrontations with Rome, Khusro I and Khusro II were helped by many factors. Culturally, Southwest Asia was already more united than its political boundaries implied. The political frontier between the two empires cut across an

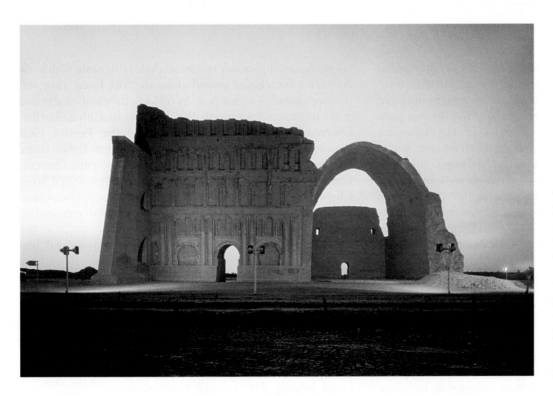

The Great Arch. For a Persian king-of-kings, the prime symbol of royal majesty was the great arch marking the entrance gate of his palace. Here, in a Middle Eastern tradition that reached back for millennia, the king would appear to his subjects to deliver judgment. This building was associated with Khusro I, who came to be remembered as an ideal ruler.

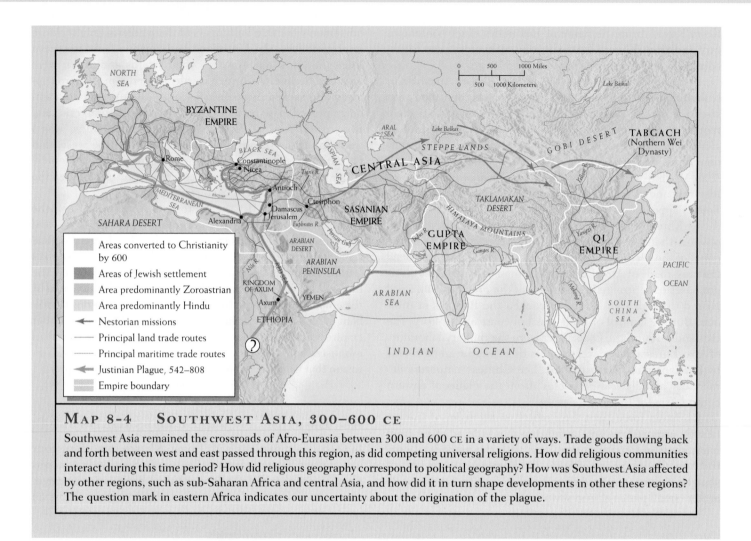

MAP 8-4   SOUTHWEST ASIA, 300–600 CE

Southwest Asia remained the crossroads of Afro-Eurasia between 300 and 600 CE in a variety of ways. Trade goods flowing back and forth between west and east passed through this region, as did competing universal religions. How did religious communities interact during this time period? How did religious geography correspond to political geography? How was Southwest Asia affected by other regions, such as sub-Saharan Africa and central Asia, and how did it in turn shape developments in other these regions? The question mark in eastern Africa indicates our uncertainty about the origination of the plague.

exuberant common zone, in which Syriac was spoken and into which Christianity had spread. Strong Christian communities were established, under Sasanian rule, in northern Mesopotamia; to the south, at the head of the Persian Gulf; and along the trade routes of central Asia. The Sasanians themselves remained loyal to the Zoroastrian religion, which they had inherited from the distant past, calling it "the Good Religion." But they were forbearing rulers. Jews and Christians enjoyed a tolerance in Mesopotamia that no Christian emperor had extended to any non-Christians within the territories of the autocratic Christian Roman Empire. Protected by the King of Kings, the rabbis of Mesopotamia compiled the monumental and definitive Babylonian Talmud at a time when their western peers, in Roman Palestine, were beginning to feel the cramping pressure of a Christian state.

Christians particularly throve in this empire. Named by their enemies "Nestorian" Christians (from Nestorius, a former bishop of Constantinople, deposed for heresy because he emphasized the human rather than the divine qualities of Jesus), these members of the "Church of the East," based in Ctesiphon, made full use of the horizons opened up by Sasan-

ian trade and diplomacy to spread their faith more widely. As Nestorian merchants passed along the Silk Road, they settled communities across Asia; by 635 CE, they had established monasteries and a church in Chang'an in China. Earlier, Christian merchants operating out of the Persian Gulf founded colonies on the west coast of southern India. Those colonists have survived up to today, known as "Saint Thomas's Christians" because they claimed to be descended from Christians converted by Thomas the Apostle, the companion of Jesus. In fact, they were the product of the wide economic outreach of the Persian Empire.

Tolerance paid off. When, in a burst of Christian zeal, Justinian finally forbade "pagans" to teach philosophy in Athens in 527 CE, the philosophers promptly went to Ctesiphon—and were made welcome by Khusro. At the same time, the Sasanian court embraced offerings from northern India, including the *Pancantantra* stories (moral tales played out in a legendary kingdom of the animals), polo, and the game of chess. Khusro's was truly an empire of Afro-Eurasia's crossroads, where the cultures of central Asia and India met the Greek culture of the eastern Mediterranean.

RELIGIOUS CONFLICT IN IMPERIAL BORDERLANDS

Through the Persian Gulf, the Sasanian Empire reached out to control the trade on the Indian Ocean. This effort brought Persians into conflict with Roman merchants, who had striven to reach India from the Red Sea. The entire region bounded by present-day Ethiopia, at the western end of the Red Sea; Yemen, in southern Arabia; and the Persian Gulf became a field of conflict between the Roman and Sasanian empires.

Their clash took religious as well as commercial and political form. Both Ethiopia (then known as Axum) and Himyar (modern-day Yemen) were rich lands. They were amply watered by the same rains from equatorial Africa that caused the annual rising of the Nile. Both regions had embraced monotheism, expressed in the worship of a Most High God, known as al-Rahmānān (the Merciful One). In Ethiopia, this monotheism was Christian. As in the empire of Constantine and his successors, Christ was seen as the protector of the kings of Ethiopia and the Cross of Christ was their talisman in battle. The leaders of Yemen and the southern coast of Arabia were Jewish, and they dismissed Jesus as a crucified sorcerer.

The kings of Axum occupied the African side of the southern end of the Red Sea, looking down on the sea from the foothills of the well-watered and populous mountains of Ethiopia. Their formidable warrior-kingdom stretched as far as the Nile to the northwest, south into equatorial Africa, and eastward across the Red Sea to southern Arabia and Yemen. Axum's rulers, who became Christian around 340 CE, celebrated their victories on gigantic granite obelisks; larger than any known in the Roman Empire, they were monuments to a God that was very much a god of battles.

Faced by the aggressive Christian kingdom of Axum, the Sasanians reached out to support the kings of Himyar, who since 380 CE had been Jewish. Thus two monotheisms faced each other across the narrow southern opening of the Red Sea. Each was associated with a rich and aggressive kingdom. Each was backed by a Great Power—Ethiopia by Christian Rome and Himyar by the Persians.

Between 522 and 530 CE, a Jewish king of Himyar popularly known as Dhu-Nuwas (the Man with the Forelock) drove the Ethiopian Christian garrisons out of southern Arabia. He turned churches into synagogues (just as, in the Christian empire far to the north, many synagogues had been turned into churches). In 523 CE, the Christians of the oasis city of Najran were ordered to become Jewish. After all, Dhu-Nuwas told them, it was not as if he was asking them to become "pagans." They simply had to worship the One God, whom Jews and Christians shared, and to agree that Jesus of Nazareth had been a mere man—for, he insisted somewhat disingenuously, "All countries understand that he was a man and not a God." Those who refused to become Jews, Dhu-Nuwas burned on pyres of brushwood piled into a deep trench.

Swept by these rivalries, the Arabian peninsula was no longer a world apart, seemingly shut off from "civilization" by its cruel deserts and by the nomadic lifestyle of its inhabitants. Far from it. Arabia had become a giant soundboard that amplified claims about the pros and cons of Judaism and Christianity, argued over in Arabic and among Arabs, with unusual intensity for an entire century. The "nonaligned" Arabs of the intermediate regions (between southern Arabia and Mesopotamia) still worshipped their ancestral tribal gods. But they had heard much, of late, about Jews and Christians, Romans and Persians. Arab tribes around Yathrib (modern Medina) adopted Judaism and remained in touch with the rabbis of Galilee along the caravan routes of northern Arabia. Here was a new kind of borderland between empires and between religions, stretching from the West Coast of Africa to the Red Sea. It would be from this borderland that a new religion and a new prophet would emerge. His name was Muhammad.

THE SILK ROAD

> → *How did the actions and activities of Central Asians influence the geographic spread of universal religions and other cross-cultural developments during this time?*

Crucial to the growing interconnectedness of the Afro-Eurasian landmass was the region of central Asia. Through its mountain passes and across its difficult terrains, merchants, scholars, and travelers joined the two ends of Afro-Eurasia. They helped transmit the commodities, technologies, and ideas that flowed with increasing rapidity between the Mediterranean worlds and China and across the Himalayas into northern India. Although the zone of Afro-Eurasia from the Mediterranean to Iran and from the Caucasus to Ethiopia was dominated by the rivalry of Rome and Persia, the widely distant regions of East Asia were connected to each other by trade, imperial ambitions, and the spread of world religions. In particular, the Sogdian peoples, residing in central Asia's commercial entrepôts, maintained the stability and accessibility of the Silk Road.

It was only through central Asia that the peoples of the Mediterranean world and China could learn about each other. This sharing of knowledge began in earnest during the period when Christianity and Buddhism were spreading, and when traditional Vedic religion (Brahmanism) was also developing a scholarly written tradition. Early evidence of a heightened eastern Roman interest in the area can be seen in the dispatch of ambassadors from Constantinople to the nomads of eastern central Asia. Attempting to circumvent the Sasanian Empire, in 568 CE these emissaries brought back firsthand reports of the great empire of China. Long known for the fabulous wealth of its silk, China struck them as a miraculously stable state.

Chinese observers were also impressed by the eastern and western Roman empires. They caught a distant echo of a strong and prosperous military empire, governed by rulers who (in the western empire, in the fifth century) came and went in rapid succession. According to the "History of the Later Han Dynasty," written by Fan Ye in the fifth century, "They have no permanent rulers, but when an extraordinary calamity visits the country, they elect a new king."

It was the political and economic dynamism of central Asia, as described in previous chapters, that enabled the empires at the opposite ends of Afro-Eurasia to be visible to one another. The trading links provided the routes through which universalistic religious movements could flow, and in so doing helped reinforce cross-cultural connections. This was a region of great oasis cities. The Sasanians controlled Merv in the west (in modern-day Turkmenistan), and the Sogdian

cities of Samarkand and Panjikent in the east (on the edge of the Tienshan Mountains, in today's Uzbekistan and Tajikistan) were absorbed into ambitious nomadic kingdoms. The first of these was the kingdom of the Hephthalites or "White Huns," who had crossed the Altai Mountains into Sogdiana around 400 CE. After 560 CE, the Hephthalites were replaced by an equally wide-ranging Turkish confederacy, which would eventually leave the name Turkistan—the region of the Turks—on the countries north of Afghanistan.

As the Kushan kingdom of central Asia had previously done (see Chapter 6), these confederacies joined western and eastern Afro-Eurasia by patrolling the Silk Road between Iran and China. Like the Kushans, they also joined north to south, as they passed through the mountains of Afghanistan into the plains of northern India. As a result, central Asia between 400 and 600 CE was the hub of a system of Afro-Eurasia-wide contacts. The religious and cultural aspects of these contacts are essential for understanding the spread and appeal of universalistic religious ideals in this period.

BETWEEN IRAN AND CHINA: THE SOGDIANS AS LORDS OF THE SILK ROAD

The nomadic confederacies of Central Asia made possible a remarkable contribution of borderlanders to world history. Sogdians in the large oasis cities of Samarkand and Panjikent served as human links between the two ends of Afro-Eurasia. Their religion was a syncretic blend of Zoroastrian and Mesopotamian beliefs, inflected with Brahmanic influences. Their language was the common tongue of the early Silk Road, and their shaggy camels bore the commodities that moved back and forth, east to west, through their oasis trading hubs. The splendid mansions of the Sogdians (recently excavated at Panjikent) show that they shared fully in the epic culture of the warrior-aristocracy of Iran. The palace walls are covered with gripping frescoes of armored riders, such as had revolutionized the art of cavalry warfare from Rome to China. But the Sogdians were known as far away as China as merchants. They were the first to organize the caravan trade

Simurgh, the legendary dog-headed bird of Persian mythology, as shown on this seventh-century silver plate from Sasanian Persia, was a favored motif on textiles, sculptures, paintings, and architecture from the Byzantine Empire to Tang China.

A LETTER FROM A SOGDIAN MERCHANT CHIEF

Perhaps the clearest demonstration of how the Sogdians brought the ends of Eurasia together is a vivid document discovered in western China. In the year 313 CE (that is, a year after Constantine's famous "conversion" outside distant Rome), a Sogdian merchant chief, Nanai-vandak, wrote a letter from a station in modern Gansu, China, to his partner in Samarkand, his homeland some 2,000 miles to the west. He describes a state of civil war made more violent by the involvement of barbarian armies, much as had happened in the Roman Empire in the fifth century. He also describes the "business as usual" attitude of traders. The letter never reached Samarkand, however. It was among several Sogdian letters in a mailbag found in one of the guard posts of the Great Wall of China, near Dunhuang.

And sirs, it is three years since a Sogdian came from "inside" [i.e., from China]. And now no one comes from there so that I might write to you about the Sogdians who went inside, how they fared and which countries they reached. And, sirs, the last emperor, so they say, fled from Luoyang because of the famine and fire was set to his palace and to the city, and the palace was burnt and the city [destroyed]. Luoyang is no more, Ye is no more! And sirs, we do not know whether the remaining Chinese were able to expel the Huns [from] Chany'an, from China, or whether they took the country beyond . . .

And from Dunhuang up to Jincheng . . . to sell, linen cloth is going [selling well?], and whoever has made cloth or woolen cloth . . .

And, sirs, as for us, whoever dwells in the region from Ji[ncheng] up to Dunhuang, we only survive so long as the . . . lives, and we are without family, old and on the point of death. . . .

. . . Moreover, four years ago, I sent another man named Artikhu-vandak. When the caravan left Guzang, Wakhushakk . . . was there, and when they reached Luoyang . . . the Indians and the Sogdians there had all died of starvation.

→ *What does the letter tell us about the nature of long-distance travel and trade along the Silk Road?*
→ *What does it tell us about the relationship between the Han Chinese and the "barbarian" Huns?*
→ *What does it tell us about the lives of the foreign traders in Han China?*

SOURCE: Annette L. Juliano and Judith A. Lerner (eds.), *Monks and Merchants: Silk Road Treasures from Northwest China Gansu and Ningxia, 4th–7th Century* (New York: Harry N. Abrams with the Asia Society, 2001), p. 49.

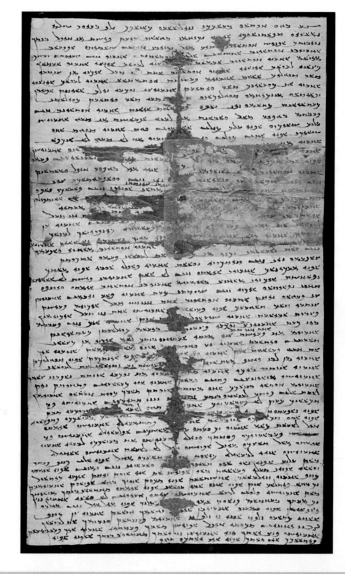

across the Taklamakan Desert to Chang'an, which served as the eastern terminus of the Silk Road in northwest China. To the Chinese, they were persons "with honey on their tongues and gum on their fingers"—to sweet-talk money out of others' pockets and to catch every stray coin.

Through the Sogdians, the products from West Asia and North Africa came into China. Goods decorated with Persian motifs—such as the legendary simurgh bird and prancing rams with the fluttering ribbons that, in Iran, were the symbol of good fortune and royalty—joined Roman glass, produced in the cities of the Mediterranean. Along with Sasanian silver coins and even gold pieces minted in Constantinople, these exotic products of the Western Lands traveled as far east as Japan, where some can still be seen in the treasury of the Shoso-in at Nara.

BUDDHISM ON THE SILK ROAD

Unstable political systems did not hinder the flow of ideas or commodities. On the contrary, the civil wars that marked the end of the Han Empire simply rendered China more open to the populations and the cultures of its far western regions. South of the Hindu Kush Mountains, in northern India, the conquests of the Hephthalite White Huns made the roads from India into central Asia safe to travel. It was over the mountainous corridor of Afghanistan that a new Buddhism came to spread, transforming the Chinese empire almost as dramatically as Christianity had transformed the world of Rome. That spread made Buddhism, for the first time, a

major world religion. Buddhism in this era involved monks bearing holy books, offering salvation to the average layperson (to use a Christian term), traveling widely, and establishing themselves more securely in their host communities than did armies, diplomats, or even merchants.

In Bamiyan, a valley of the Hindu Kush Mountains that stretches off the road from northern Afghanistan and central Asia to Kabul, two gigantic statues of the Buddha—one 121 feet and another 180 feet in height—were hewn from the stone face of the cliff during the fourth to the fifth centuries CE. Until their destruction in 2001, they looked out over a high, vividly green valley of intensive cultivation. Standing at one of the major entrances to South Asia, the colossal Buddhas beckoned travelers from far away to the Buddhist monasteries that lay at their feet.

Starting at Bamiyan, Buddhist cave monasteries accompanied the traveler all the way through the oases on the edges of the Taklamakan Desert to North China. For China, in those centuries, was also ruled by emperors of nomadic origin drawn from the steppes of the "lands of the West"—from Inner Asia—much as Germanic warriors had been sucked into the provinces of the western Roman empire. The emperors of the Northern Wei (c. 386–534 CE), successors to the Han dynasty, came from a nomadic group known as the Xianbei, who represented a federation of non-Han groups; of these groups, the Tuoba were the most important. They commissioned five huge Buddhas—carved from cliffs, like the Buddhas of Bamiyan—which were fashioned in Yungang during the late fifth century. Two have survived: one is about 55 feet high, the other about 45 feet. While those at Bamiyan

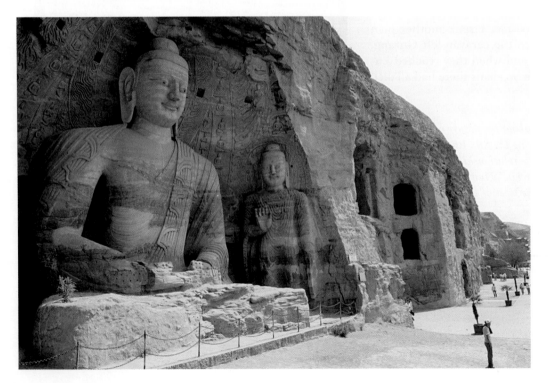

Yungang Buddha. This is one of the five giant statues of the Buddha in Yungang, created under the emperors of the Northern Wei, a dynasty built by nomads who invaded and occupied north China. Sitting at the foothills of the Great Wall, the Buddhas marked the eastern destination of the Central Asian Silk Road.

→ *How did Central Asians influence the geographic spread of cross-cultural developments?*

MAP 8-5   BUDDHIST LANDSCAPES, 300–600 CE

Buddhism spread from its heartland in northern India to central and East Asia during the first millennium CE. According to the map, what role did increasingly extensive trade routes play in pushing this movement? What was the relationship between Buddhist centers and rock-carved temples, trade routes, and the spread of this universal faith? How did the travels of Xuanzang symbolize growing connections between East and South Asia? To what extent did each region share a common culture?

had stood with royal majesty, the Buddhas of Yungang are shown seated, in meditation postures. Surrounding the Buddhas, more than fifty caves shelter more than 50,000 statues, representing both Buddhist deities and patrons who subsidized the construction. The Yungang Buddhas, seated

just inside of the Great Wall, welcomed travelers to the market in China. They marked the eastern end of the central Asian Silk Road.

These two groups of the Buddhas, placed more than 2,500 miles apart, are a reminder that at this time, in both the western and the eastern stretches of Afro-Eurasia, religious ideas had taken on a momentum of their own as they began to create world empires of the mind. Religions such as early Christianity and Buddhism saw themselves as not belonging to the kingdom of this world. They claimed to bring a universal message, contained in holy scriptures, and they were endowed with greater reach and greater cultural flexibility than the ponderous empires that *were* of this world—whether Roman, Hephthalite, or Chinese. Religion traveled light and traveled faster than did armies.

But as the conversion of the emperor Constantine showed, at the other end of Afro-Eurasia, "otherworldly" religions were not indifferent to the world. They were employed to validate ambitious new political structures. The sense of enjoying the blessing of Christ had encouraged Constantine to create nothing less than a New Rome on the Bosporus. Similarly, when the barbarian emperor Xiaowen moved the imperial capital of China from Pingcheng, at the foothills of the Great Wall, to Luoyang in the Yellow River valley in 494 CE, he formed a new religious center by having giant statues of the Buddha carved on the cliffs of Longmen, near the new capital. The nomadic rulers of the Northern Wei claimed that they were the incarnations of the Buddha, entitled by their identification with a new, divine world figure to rule their Chinese subjects in their own way. They could rule non-Chinese populations who were fellow Buddhists and could expect the Chinese to tolerate non-Chinese "barbarians" as fellow believers.

A Gold Coin of Chandragupta II. The Gupta dynasty, based in the middle and lower Ganges plain, was known for its promotion of indigenous Indian culture. Here, Chandragupta II, the most famous king of the dynasty, is shown riding a horse in the style of the invaders from the Central Asian steppes.

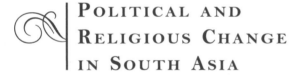

POLITICAL AND RELIGIOUS CHANGE IN SOUTH ASIA

> → *To what extent did South Asia develop a widespread common culture despite the region's political, religious, and social diversity?*

South Asia, especially the area that is now India, was also swept up in the religious enthusiasm of this period. Its major cultural system, Brahmanism (Vedic religion), did not claim to be a universal faith, with aspirations to reach outside India. But it did strive to meet all needs and to explain all theological problems, much as its rival, Buddhism, had done. Like Christianity in the Mediterranean and Southwest Asia, and Buddhism in China, religion in India helped unify diverse peoples. And here as in those regions, political opportunities aided the spread of spiritual forces.

Religious change in South Asia took a dramatic turn during the Gupta dynasty. The largest political entity in South Asia from the early fourth to the mid-sixth century—a sev-

enth century historian suggests there may have been as many as 70 states at this time—it provided the political stability that facilitated commercial and cultural exchange, much as the Roman Empire had done in its united territories. Chandra Gupta (ruled c. 320–335 CE)—who shared his name with Chandragupta, the founder of the Mauryan Empire 600 years earlier—titled himself "King of Kings, Great King." His son, Samudra Gupta (ruled c. 335–375 CE), expanded the Gupta territory to the entire northern Indian plain and even made a long expedition to southern India. Military achievements made the third king of the Gupta line, Chandra Gupta II (ruled c. 375–413 CE), the most famous, as did his generous patronage of many poets and singers in his court. Among them was Kalidasa, the poet and playwright whose works included *Sakuntala,* a famous play about a romantic encounter between a king and a daughter of an ascetic dwelling in a forest, and *Meghaduta (Cloud Messenger),* a lyric about a Yaksha, a man of a tribe outside of mainstream society, who sent a message through the monsoon cloud to his beloved wife in their faraway home while describing the cities and landscape—virtually all of India—on the cloud's route. Kalidasa and other poets of the time took episodes from the two great epics *Mahabharata* and *Ramayana*—finally set down in classical Sanskrit during this period—to write drama and narrative poems. The epics were no longer just lyrics for entertainment but a religious canon. All stories in the epics and derived works embodied *dharma,* or religious teachings. Hinduism was developing into a truly inclusive cultural complex.

THE TRANSFORMATION OF THE BUDDHA

In the centuries known as the Gupta period, the two main contemporary schools of Buddhism underwent fundamental changes as they increasingly took on universalistic features. From being regarded by his disciples as a contemplative atheist, the Buddha came to be worshipped as a god. The doctrines of both schools of this period—the Mahayana (Greater Vehicle) and the Hinayana (Lesser Vehicle)—had become quite different from what the Buddha had preached in the sixth to the fifth centuries BCE. As we saw in Chapter 5, the historical Buddha was a sage of the Shakya people who was believed to have entered *nirvana,* ending the pain of consciousness. In the earliest Buddhist doctrine, there was no god and no room for supernatural powers. But by 200 CE, as noted in Chapter 6, a crucial transformation had taken place in Buddhism: his followers had begun to view the Buddha as a god. Mahayana also extended worship to mediating demigods, the many bodhisattvas who bridged the gulf between the serene perfection of the Buddha and the world's sadly imperfect peoples. Some Buddhists, though, fully accepted Buddha as the god but could not accept the divinity of bodhisattvas; these adherents belonged to the school of Hinayana. It was especially in the wider, more inclusive form of Mahayana that Buddhism became a universal religion, whose adherents now worshipped divinities rather than simply acknowledging the worth of great men. Spreading along the Silk Road, this new religion, with claims to universality that rivaled Christianity's, would eventually appeal to peoples all over East Asia.

THE HINDU TRANSFORMATION

The ancient Vedic religion associated with the Brahmans responded to the new challenges of world religion with a revival and transformation of its own. Like Christianity, Buddhism and Jainism (another influential challenge to Brahmanic thinking, as described in Chapter 5) had become dominant in cities and in commercial communities. Ascetic and highly intellectual (and furnished with written scriptures), these two urban religions had pushed their rivals to one side, relegating the more conservative Brahmans and their religious practices to rural India.

Under this pressure, the Brahmanic (Vedic) religion changed profoundly, emerging to dominate Indian society as what we know today as Hinduism. Hinduism is a modern word coined from *Hindu,* the people who live in Hind, the Arabic word for India. People in India did not call themselves Hindus. In this new form of Brahmanical religion, the Brahmans became vegetarians, forsaking the animal sacrifices that had been so important to their earlier rituals. With this important change, totally abandoning the customs associated with pastoralists and nomads and absorbing in the process Buddhist and Jain practice, the Brahmans came to identify themselves with agricultural culture. Their new rituals were linked to self-sacrifice—denying themselves meat rather than offering up massive gifts of slaughtered animals to the gods, as they had in previous centuries. Three major deities, Brahma, Vishnu, and Siva, formed a trinity, representing both the three consecutive phases of the universe—birth, existence, and destruction, respectively—and the three expressions of the eternal self, known as the *atma.*

The Hindu trinity made it possible for believers to claim to be monotheists, since the three gods that they worshipped were thought to be embodiments of a single god, Atma. This belief also created a hierarchy around which to organize the numerous deities inherited from Vedic times. Vishnu, who embodied the present, was undoubtedly the most popular of the three. He came to the world in various avatars or incarnations, such as Krishna, the dark-skinned cowboy of Mathura who was the charioteer of the ancient hero Arjuna. Even the Buddha was adopted by Hindus as yet another avatar of Vishnu. The next most popular was Siva, who stood for the future. All three had female consorts—some beautiful goddesses, others fierce-looking.

The new Hindu pantheon was larger and more accessible than the Vedic one, enabling more believers to be incorporated into a single faith. Hindus did not wish to approach the gods only through sacrificial rituals, at which Brahmans alone could officiate. They sought to devote their passion and faith to an individual form of each one of the great gods. This religious practice of personal devotion to gods was called *bhakti.* *Bhakti* attracted Hindus of all social strata to the many deities, while a great body of mythological literature wove the deities into an intriguing heavenly order presided over by the trinity.

A CODE OF CONDUCT INSTEAD OF AN EMPIRE

Besides setting heaven in order, the Brahmans in this era also set about establishing a "correct" social order on earth. What emerged were new ways of thinking about governance and

Hindu Statue. This huge statue of a three-headed god in a cave on a small island near Mumbai (Bombay) represents the monotheistic theology of Hinduism. Brahma, the creator, Vishnu, the keeper, and Shiva the destroyer are all from one *atma,* or the single soul of the universe.

Primary Source

THE LAWS OF MANU

The Laws of Manu were compiled during the first or the second century CE, when the Kushan Empire ruled over much of South Asia. The compiler was a Brahman or a group of Brahmans. Among the many law codes that appeared in different periods of Indian history, that of Manu holds the most authority among the Hindus, as its coverage is the most comprehensive. It not only describes the origins of the four castes but also designates the occupations that provide members of each with their livelihood, as the following passage shows.

87. But in order to protect this universe He, the most resplendent one, assigned separate (duties and) occupations to those who sprang from his mouth, arms, thighs, and feet.

88. To Brâhmanas he assigned teaching and studying (the Veda), sacrificing for their own benefit and for others, giving and accepting (of alms).

89. The Kschatriya he commanded to protect the people, to bestow gifts, to offer sacrifices, to study (the Veda), and to abstain from attaching himself to sensual pleasures;

90. The Vaisya to tend cattle, to bestow gifts, to offer sacrifices, to study (the Veda), to trade, to lend money, and to cultivate land.

91. One occupation only the lord prescribed to the Sûdra, to serve meekly even these (other) three castes.

→ *The Brahmans, Kshatriyas, Vaishyas, and Shudras are the major four categories in the Hindu religious hierarchy. How are the differences in religious status reflected in the jobs that the people in different castes can take?*

SOURCE: *The Laws of Manu*, I.87–91; translated by G. Bühler, vol. 25 of *The Sacred Books of the East* (Oxford: Clarendon Press, 1886), p. 24.

---

the bonds between rulers and subjects. They were not enough to transcend the political fissures that crisscrossed the region. But they laid the foundation for an alternative ethic of statecraft, steeped in a universalizing faith, that would eventually bring legitimacy to an integrated polity. Unlike China and Rome, India did not have a centralized empire that this new ethic could revitalize. The empires that arose in central Asia, after the fall of the Mauryan Empire in the second century BCE left a vacuum in northern India, were governed by rulers who had no contact with the populations from whom they collected taxes and tariffs. Largely untouched by the empires' elaborate political structures, the local populations relied on religious and social institutions such as castes and guilds to maintain civic order during periods of frequent warfare and regime change (much as, in the west, Christian bishops had provided guidance and protection to Roman city dwellers and thereby spread their religion). To maintain order,

the Brahmans compiled many law codes, drawing their inspiration from Hindu moral precepts and customary law. Among them, the Laws of Manu, which were probably compiled in the first or the second century CE, stood out as the most comprehensive and widely valid. In Hindu mythology, Manu was the father of the human race (in Sanskrit, *manu* means "human"), and the Laws of Manu were considered applicable to all persons, irrespective of the states in which they lived. Kingdoms might come and go; but the "true" order of society, appropriate to "true" human beings and summed up in the Laws of Manu, remained the same.

Above all, the Laws of Manu offered clear guidance for living in a caste system, whose origins lay centuries earlier, in ways that embraced the entire complicated society. They ruled that every member of a certain caste could marry only within the caste and must follow the profession and dietary rules of that particular caste in order to perpetuate its status.

Thus tremendous social and religious pressure, but not government coercion, was exerted to keep all individuals within specific categories, obeying the social norms.

Though seemingly rigid, the Laws of Manu offered those who obeyed them a way to cope with a constantly changing Indian society, for the code's purview extended far beyond the frontiers of the major states of northern India. In providing the regulations and the mechanisms for absorbing new groups into the caste system, it helped Hinduism propagate into areas that the state could not control or even reach. Further, the *bhakti* form of religious devotion made Hinduism especially absorptive. Deities of folk religion joined the Hindu pantheon as new objects of worship were created. At the same time, the basic text or code reinforced what it meant to belong to a community of believers, especially as the faithful no longer lived close to one another. For with the universalizing of religious systems came the challenge of establishing norms and rules, principles set forth in writing and enforced by a priestly class. In this sense, the Laws of Manu functioned very much like the Jews' Torah, the Confucian Analects, the more recent "New Testament," and eventually the Muslim Quran, laying out basic precepts about religious life. These texts were also, it bears repeating, easily transported—they were certainly more mobile than armies or populations. Such holy scriptures could be conveyed great distances to those who were not yet members of the community of believers, potent weapons in the arsenal of religious conversion.

Behind these developments was a remarkable movement of internal colonization, as settlers from northern India pushed ever more southward, into lands that had formerly been outside the Brahmans' domain. In these territories south of the Deccan plateau, Brahmans met Buddhists as equals. Buddhist teachers were expected (like Brahmans) to speak refined Sanskrit, the "perfect" language, and they used the same vocabulary as the Brahmans while debating with them many topics, ranging from theology to theories of the structure of the universe to mathematics, logic, and botany. In essence, large Buddhist monasteries—such as Nalanda, with about 10,000 residential faculty and students in northeast India—became universities, responsible for both the spiritual and the intellectual growth of young men. Brahmans followed the models of Buddhist practice and established schools called *matha*. The meetings, often in open spaces sponsored by kings, were decisive historically, as the constant debates that they provoked helped to create a shared "Indic" culture. Most people spoke a dialect with imperfect grammar, but they could still understand the essentials of the debate in perfect Sanskrit. Although divided politically and religiously, the peoples living in what is now the country of India began between the fourth and sixth centuries to fashion a common culture organized around a shared vocabulary on crucial subjects such as concepts of the universe and the cyclical time scheme of life and death.

This widespread cultural unity physically covered no fewer than one million square miles (equaling the greatest extent of the Roman Empire) and affected a large and diverse population whose exact numbers are still not known. Although India was not under one polity (as was the case in China), or dominated by a single religious system (as would happen in the Christian Roman Empire and in medieval western Europe), it was becoming a region held together by a distinctive common culture—as outsiders clearly recognized. Xuanzang, a Chinese Buddhist pilgrim, began his account of a visit to India in the 630s and 640s CE by discussing the name *Indu*. For him and others, Indu, or what we today would refer to as India, began after a traveler crossed the valley of the Hindu Kush (modern Afghanistan). Geographically it was bounded by oceans on three sides (the east, south, and west) and by the snowy mountains of the Himalayas to the north. Politically, the region was split into more than seventy states. Yet it was culturally cohesive. Throughout this large land, Xuanzang observed, the Brahmans were the highest caste, and he thus suggested that it could also be called "the land of the Brahmans." In short, Xuanzang described India as an area of great diversity of regimes, climates, and local customs, but still a unity—possibly even a country.

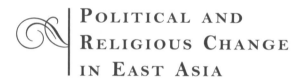

POLITICAL AND RELIGIOUS CHANGE IN EAST ASIA

> → *To what extent did new influences from other parts of Afro-Eurasia transform Chinese culture and politics during this era?*

In the first century CE, Han China had been the largest state in the world, with a population of approximately 60 million registered taxpayers (as great a population, that is, as the Roman Empire at its height). Its emperor ruled an area of 4 million square miles (more than twice the size of the Roman Empire) and regularly extracted an annual income of millions of pounds of rice and bolts of cloth and conscripted millions of regular and emergency corvée laborers. The end of the Han Empire (after 200 CE) was regarded, by later Chinese, as great a disaster as the end of the Roman Empire came to be viewed by western Europeans. Successive generations looked back to the centuries after the fall of the Han as a period marked by the barbarization of the Chinese world.

In reality (as was also true of the Roman Empire in the west), "barbarization" meant the opening up of a proud society to the cultures of the wider world that had grown up along its margins. In the case of post-Han China, the Silk Road, the military talents of the nomads, and the religious skills of proselytizing Buddhist monks from what the Chinese called the Western Regions provided new inspiration and new influences. In this invasion from the west, Buddhism took much the same role as Christianity played in Rome, adapting itself to the Chinese empire and gaining in strength and popularity as a result of imperial and elite patronage. Here Buddhism evolved into a Chinese religion with universalistic appeal—even extending its reach beyond China into Korea and Japan (as discussed in Chapter 9).

DOWNSIZING: NORTHERN AND SOUTHERN CHINA

After the fall of the Han in 220 CE, several kingdoms—initially three, though at times as many as sixteen—competed for total power. The Shu state in the southwest (Sichuan), the Wu kingdom in the south (the lower Yangzi region), and the Wei state in the northwest region all sought to restore the Han Empire and to monopolize political power to further their own interests. Civil wars raged between these three powerful states and their allies from 220 to 589 CE, a time often called the Six Dynasties period, when no single state was able to conquer more than half of China's territory. One of the major turning points of this era came in 311, when the Xiongnu confederacy from the northern steppes of Inner Eurasia, which had played a central role in forming the Silk Road and in bringing down the Han dynasty, sacked the former Han capital of Luoyang. Ultimately, the most successful regime was that of the Tuoba, a people originally from Inner Mongolia on the eastern edge of the steppe lands. Nearly seventy-five years after their first contact with the northern Chinese rulers, the Tuoba founded the Northern Wei dynasty in 386; it lasted one and half centuries, ending in 534 CE. As a result of the northern invasions, China was divided by polity, culture, and ethnicity for nearly three centuries. But the idea that it should be united still endured.

The northern and southern divide was the most pronounced. Many of the powerful families in the south were the descendants of aristocratic northerners and their supporters who had fled in disgust and fear at the thought of being ruled by barbarians from the steppes such as the Xiongnu and the Tuoba. The southerners thus regarded themselves as the true representatives of Chinese culture, and they scorned the allegedly barbarian rulers who had usurped power in the north. The flow of migrants from the north never stopped, but life in the southern reaches of

> *As a result of the northern invasions, China was divided by polity, culture, and ethnicity for nearly three centuries. But the idea that it should be united still endured.*

China over the next several centuries proved difficult. The hot and wet climate of the southern region of China was ideal for growing rice, but it also fostered diseases—especially malaria—that ravaged the population. The exiles tried to return, but their military expeditions to reconquer the north were like the efforts of the emperor Justinian to reconquer Italy and re-create the "true" Roman Empire: despite some initial successes, they ultimately failed.

Undeterred by the contempt of the Han peoples and scholars for their rough manners, the "barbarian" rulers in northern China—first the Xiongxu, then the Tuoba—maintained many of their preconquest forms of state and society. Because they had lived within the Chinese imperial orbit as tributary states before they conquered North China, they were "civilized" by imperial standards—yet still, in the minds of the Han, inferior. Nevertheless, they maintained many Chinese traditions of statecraft and court life; thus, they taxed land and labor on the basis of a census, conferred official ranks and titles, practiced court rituals, preserved historical archives, and promoted classical learning and the use of classical Chinese for record keeping and political discourse. Though they were nomadic warriors, they adapted their large standing armies to city-based military technology, which required large-scale public works such as dykes, fortifications, canals, and walls. Following the Qin-Han Chinese precedent, they drafted huge numbers of workers as corvée to complete such enormous projects as rebuilding a new capital city at Luoyang for the Northern Wei dynasty.

Rulers of the Northern Wei dynasty faced many challenges, including the need to consolidate authority over their own highly competitive nomadic people. One approach to bringing more control and order to their society, pursued strenuously but with little success over the course of nearly a century, was to make their own government more "Chinese." Emperor Xiaomen (ruled 471–499) encouraged Tuoba warriors to emulate Chinese society and customs. The royal family changed their name, adopting the Chinese family name of Yuan. All court officials were required to speak Chinese and wear Chinese clothing. The Tuoba families resisted these policies, continuing to speak in their native tongues and to wear native clothing. At the same time, the Wei rulers sought to cultivate stronger relationships with the great Han families of Luoyang that had not migrated to southern China, hoping that offers of more political power (greater opportunities to serve as officials in the Wei bureaucracy) and more land might persuade these families and their supporters to stay in the north.

A key figure in attempting to sinicize, or "make more Chinese," Tuoba rule and to win support of the Han Luoyang families was the Dowager Empress Fang (regent 476–490 CE), grandmother of Emperor Xiaomen. Her most substantial initiative on this front centered on a series of progressive land reforms. The need for the Han Chinese families to continue growing crops was urgent, both to feed the city dwellers and to maintain a strong tax base (the nomadic Tuoba were not required to pay land taxes). Under the land reform policies, young men who agreed to cultivate the land would receive two allotments of land, one at the age of eleven and one at fifteen, which they could pass on to their heirs. After age seventy, they would no longer be required to pay taxes on the land. But even this rather appealing plan, pursued over several decades, failed to bridge the cultural divides between the "civilized" Han of Luoyang and the "barbarian" Tuoba Wei because the latter showed no interest in farming. The boldest attempt to unify northern China would be made by Emperor Xiaomen, who rebuilt the old Han capital of Luoyang and made it the seat of his government in an effort to recapture the glory of the Han dynasty. His untimely death in 499 CE cut short his efforts to unify the north. Several decades of intense fighting among military rulers followed, leading ultimately to the downfall of the Northern Wei dynasty.

BUDDHISM IN CHINA

By the third and fourth centuries CE, when Chinese imperial power had reached a low point, Buddhist travelers arriving from central Asia had already become frequent visitors in the streets and temples of the competing Chinese capitals of the various warring states: Chang'an, Luoyang, and Nanjing. Great movements of peoples swept fascinating individuals into China. For example, in 383 CE, regional Chinese forces in the northwest seized Kucha (now Xinjiang), then under Tibetan rule. There they found Kumarajiva (344–413 CE), a renowned Buddhist scholar and missionary, whom they brought back to China proper. Beginning in 401 Kumarajiva resided at the court in Chang'an, where he both taught and practiced magic rituals and became known as a promoter of Buddhist holistic medicine.

Spreading the universalizing faith required brokers, endowed with texts or codes, to convey its message. Kumarajiva was the right man, in the right place, at the right time to spread Buddhism in China, where it already had toeholds but coexisted with many other faiths. He was, above all, a bearer of exotic holy books (not unlike the Christians of the Roman Empire), and his influence on Chinese Buddhist thought was critical. Not only did he translate previously unknown Buddhist texts into Chinese, including many of the most important titles in the Chinese Buddhist canon, but he also clarified Buddhist terminology and philosophical concepts for Chinese adepts. He and his disciples established a Mahayana branch known as Madhyamika (Middle Way) Buddhism in China, which used irony and paradox to show that reason was limited. They sought enlightenment through transcendental visions and spurned experiences in the material world of sights and sounds.

Kumarajiva represented just the beginning of a major cultural shift. After 300 CE Buddhism began to expand in northwestern China, taking advantage of imperial fragmentation and the decline of state-sponsored classical learning. The Buddhists stressed devotional acts and the saving power of the Buddha and the saintly bodhisattvas. They encouraged the Chinese to join the clergy. The idea that persons could be

Amitabha. This exquisite tapestry is an illustration for the *Amitabha Sutra,* the "Sutra of the Western Pureland." Since the text was translated into Chinese by Kumarajiva in the fourth century CE, Amitabha has been one of the most popular bodhisattvas in China. A devotee who invokes the name of Amitabha ten times before death would be saved to this Western Pure Land, where the Seven Treasures decorated the quiet landscape.

defined by faith rather than kinship was not entirely new in Chinese society, as the Han dynasty Daoist rebels showed (see Chapter 7), but it had special appeal in a time of unprecedented crisis. In the south, the immigrants from the north found that membership in the Buddhist clergy and monastic orders offered a way to restore their lost prestige.

Even more important, in the northern states—now part-Chinese, part-barbarian—Buddhism provided legitimacy. The presence of Buddhists at "Sino-barbarian" courts—taking prominent positions in government, medicine, and astronomy—enabled the ruling houses in northern states to espouse a philosophy and worldview that could provide them a defense against the Han Chinese who favored classical learning and despised "barbarians" for their lack of culture and education.

Despite its appeals to universalism, Buddhism, which did not have a central ecclesiastical authority, took on different forms in the different regions of South and East Asia as it adapted to realities on the ground. It did not have the hard edges that defined Christianity in the Roman Empire as a religion that was the same in all places and at all times. On the contrary, as the expression of a cosmic truth as timeless and as varied as the world itself, Buddhism easily took on new appearances in new places. It absorbed as its own the gods and the wisdom of every country into which it came. A particularly interesting variant emerged in South China, where Buddhism and Daoism borrowed many common practices from each other. In fact, there the two faiths became so amalgamated that quite often only scholars could elucidate the fine distinctions between them and explain the origins of various practices. In effect, Buddhism in South China had taken on a Chinese tinge through its borrowing from Daoist practices.

DAOISM, ALCHEMY, AND THE TRANSMUTATION OF THE SELF

Daoism had gained ground as a popular Chinese religion during the Han period. At that time, Daoist clergy challenged the Confucian state and its scholar-officials, first as leaders of rebellious local groups and, later, as leaders of massive armies. Beginning in the period of disunity, however, Daoism quickly lost its political edge and adapted to the society then in place. Two new traditions of Daoist thought flourished in this era of self-doubt in China. The first was community-oriented and involved heavenly masters guiding local religious groups or parishes. Followers sought salvation through virtue, confession, and liturgical ceremonies. Through ecstatic and orgiastic initiation rites, which were often achieved through an "external alchemy"—that is, using drugs and chemicals to cause transformations (in this context, in the self)— the Daoist clergy brought believers into contact with the divine.

A second Daoist tradition was more individualistic. In the Yangzi delta, personal expressions of religious faith emerged. Ge Hong (283–343 CE), a student of esoterica, sought to reconcile Confucian classical learning with Daoist religious beliefs in the occult and magical. He focused on "internal alchemy": that is, the use of trance and meditation alone to control human physiology. Through such mental and physical exertions, an adept accumulated enough religious merit to prolong his life. The quantification of merit and demerit in Daoist circles had important affinities with the Buddhist notion of karmic retribution (the cosmic assessment of the sum total of one's acts in this life that determines whether one will be reborn into a better or worse next life; see Chapter 5).

The Shaolin Monastery. This monastery on Mount Song, Henan province, is famous for its martial art, or "gongfu." But the martial art tradition was established quite a few hundred years after the monastery came into being in c. 495 CE, under the Northern Wei dynasty. In 527, an Indian priest, Bodhidharma, arrived there to initiate the Zen school of Buddhism in China. The more than 230 small pagodas contain relics of the head monks who managed the monastery in the last 1500 years.

THE ART OF RELIGIOUS FERVOR IN CHINA

Above all, the religious fervor of this period changed the visual environment of China. The decorations for pottery and metal objects from this time show strong central Asian and Sasanian influences, which were transmitted primarily through Buddhism. The impact on architecture was even more striking. In India, Buddhists had adapted a form of dome-shaped tombs called stupas into shrines used to house relics of the Buddha. Huge pagodas represented a Chinese attempt in wood to imitate stone and brick stupas in India. Regarded by Koreans and Japanese (and later by Westerners) as quintessentially Chinese, the pagoda was in fact a distant echo, on Chinese soil, of northern Indian Buddhism. Similarly, the complexes of cave temples at Longmen and Yungang were inspired by Indian and central Asian examples. In these ways, a universal religion created common artistic themes that stretched from central to East Asia.

One site that featured the work of central Asian artisans was the oasis city of Dunhuang. Located along the Silk Road, it contained a number of cave temples. Since 400 CE, they had been adorned with paintings and statues, and between the fifth and eighth centuries hundreds of cave chapels were decorated with wall paintings. Some illustrated Buddhist legends, and others depicted scenes of paradise. The caves were sealed in 1035 to save them from raiding Tibetans, and they have survived to this day. In 1900, the cave housing the great Buddhist library at Dunhuang was found unopened. The dry climate had preserved thousands of manuscripts, including Buddhist texts and works of popular literature.

→ *What do the architectural links from India to China, Japan, and Korea tell us about Buddhism?*
→ *Why are the Dunhuang caves so essential to our understanding of Chinese Buddhism in medieval times?*

Pagoda on Mount Song. This is probably the earliest pagoda in China. The solid stone structure shows the influence of pagodas in the contemporary eastern part of India, such as the one in Mahabodhi Monastery in Bodhgaya.

The Western Pure Land. This mural painting of the Western Pure Land is from Dunhuang, close to the eastern end of the Silk Road. The facial features of the celestial beings and the art style are more Chinese than Indian. Lazulite blue, a pigment made from lapis lazuli from Badakshan, Afghanistan, is the dominant color here, as it is on all the cave art along the central Asian Silk Road.

For the Daoists, however, eternal life—not the Buddhist ideal of release from the cycle of rebirth—was the ultimate goal. Older alchemical writings were reinterpreted in light of notions of Daoist breath control and the meditation techniques introduced by Buddhists. Both external and internal alchemy thus relied on natural processes for creating perfected substances to ingest or for creating a new self by practicing meditation. Each could confer eternal life.

By 400 CE China had more than 1,700 Buddhist monasteries and about 80,000 monks and nuns. By contrast, in 600 CE (after two centuries of monastic growth), Gaul and Italy—the two richest regions of western Europe—had, altogether, only 320 monasteries, many of them with fewer than thirty monks. In this emphasis on the cloister, the two ends of Afro-Eurasia resembled each other. Both in China and in large regions of Europe, the principal bearers of the new religion were monks, set apart from "worldly" affairs in their refuges, where they were piously supported by royal courts and by warriors whose lifestyle differed sharply from their own. Yet in China, the Buddhists were challenged as the major cultural force in the region, though their religion was one of the most dominant.

We will see in Chapter 9 that when the Chinese empire was reunified under the Sui (581–618) and Tang (618–907) dynasties, its officials brought Confucianism back into ascendancy. They spearheaded a renaissance based on the classical teachings that Buddhism and Daoism had overshadowed since the fall of the Han dynasty.

FAITH AND CULTURES IN THE WORLDS APART

> → *How similar and different were spiritual developments in worlds apart from Afro-Eurasia during this time?*

Sub-Saharan Africa was only loosely connected to the Eurasian and North African landmass, and the Americas were wholly separate. Where these worlds stood apart, ideas, institutions, peoples, and commodities did not circulate easily and quickly. Cultures that were based on world religions or principles held to apply everywhere in the world were therefore more difficult to create; as we have observed, however, Christianity spread up the Nile through the Nubian corridor into Ethiopia and the Sudan, two parts of sub-Saharan Africa that had always maintained close contacts with North Africa and many other parts of Eurasia. But elsewhere, we do not see the development of universalizing faiths. Rather, belief systems and their deities were localized. This is not to say that sub-Saharan Africa and the Americas lacked the elements for creating profound and integrated cultural systems

around communities of faith. Indeed, Africans and Americans alike had prophetic figures who were said to have communicated with the deities and brought to humankind divinely prescribed rules of behavior. Moreover, peoples in both regions had canonical beliefs and rules that, though not preserved in texts, were passed down orally from generation to generation. They, too, were intended to guide behavior and to establish social mores. The calendar of rituals across these regions was closely governed by relationships with deities in whose hands Africans and Americans believed their fortunes to lie.

BANTUS OF SUB-SAHARAN AFRICA

Almost all of Africa south of the Equator is inhabited today by peoples speaking some variant of more than 400 Bantu languages, no more distinct from each other than are the Germanic languages of northern Europe. Early Bantu history is shrouded in mystery. At present, scholars using oral traditions and linguistic evidence can trace the narrative of these peoples no further back than 1000 CE. The first Bantu speakers apparently lived in the southeastern part of modern Nigeria, where they began to shift from a hunting, gathering, and fishing economy to practicing settled agriculture. The areas into which they spread as they began to move about 4,000 or 5,000 years ago demanded an immense amount of work. To ready a new acre of land in the tropical rain forest for cultivation required the removal of some 600 tons of moist vegetation, and the early migrant groups brought to this task only simple tools (mainly machetes and billhooks). In fact, their most effective technique for the initial clearing was controlled bush burning, but it left a great deal of burned vegetation to be removed. Moreover, the African equatorial forests, the primary zones of Bantu habitation, were almost totally devoid of indigenous food plants. Yams were native to Africa, but new varieties were later introduced from Southeast Asia, as were bananas; and maize, manioc, and sweet potatoes arrived only after the Europeans had reached the Americas. As a consequence, these peoples had to make do with woodland plants such as yams and mushrooms, as well as palm oils and kernels.

Bantu migrants traveled out of West Africa along river beds and elephant trails, in two great population waves. One group moved eastward across the Congo forest region to East Africa, aided early in their migration by their knowledge of iron smelting, which enabled them to use iron tools in their agricultural activities. Because the habitats into which they moved permitted them to maintain a mixed economy of animal husbandry and sedentary agriculture, they became relatively prosperous. The second branch moved southward through the rain forests in present-day Congo, eventually reaching the Kalahari Desert, but they were not so fortunate. Their tsetse fly–infested environment did not permit them to rear livestock, and thus they were limited to subsistence farming. They learned to use iron later than those who had moved to the east.

Precisely when these Bantu migrations began cannot yet be known with certainty, but once under way, the travelers moved with extraordinary rapidity. Genetic and linguistic evidence demonstrates that they swept all else before them, absorbing most of the hunting-and-gathering populations who had originally inhabited these areas. A few remnants of the earlier residents do survive, however, most notably the pygmy hunters and cultivators in the Ituri forest of central Africa and the Khoisan hunters of the Kalahari Desert in southern Africa.

What enabled the Bantus to prevail and then to prosper was their skill as settled agriculturalists. They knew how to cultivate the soil, and they were able to adapt their farming to widely different environments. They thrived equally well in the tropical rain forests of the Congo River basin, the high grasslands around Lake Nyanza, and the highlands of Kenya,

MAP 8-6 BANTU MIGRATIONS

The migration of Bantu speakers throughout much of sub-Saharan Africa in the first millennium CE dramatically altered the cultural landscape of the region. According to the map, where were the Bantu speakers' migrations? What skills did they possess that enabled them to populate the lands they migrated to and dominate the peoples who were already living there? Did the Bantu migrations create a common culture below the Sahara Desert during this time?

even though they had to grow different crops in each of these locations.

For the Bantu of the equatorial rain forests of central Africa, known as the Western Bantu, the introduction of the banana plant was decisive. Linguistic evidence suggests that it first arrived in the Upper Nile region, and from there it was carried into the rest of Africa by small groups migrating from one favorable location to another; the earliest proof of its presence is a record from the East African coast dated to 525 CE. Eventually it spread into the equatorial rain forests, where its adaptability to local conditions was unmatched. Not only did it provide more nutrients than the yam crop, which it ultimately replaced, but it better withstood heavy rainfalls. In addition, banana plantings required farmers to clear fewer trees from the land than did yam cultivation and created an environment that was free of the anopheles mosquito, the

carrier of malaria. Taking full advantage of the benefits of banana cultivation, the Western Bantu filled up the equatorial rain forest areas of central Africa—perhaps as early as 500 CE, certainly by 1000 CE.

But did these peoples create a Bantu culture, as some scholars claim? Clearly, they could not establish the same political, social, and cultural institutions in widely different ecological zones. The Great Lakes in eastern Africa presented them with savanna lands, which allowed for relatively easy communications. Here, they eventually created centralized polities whose kings ruled by divine right. Mostly, however, they moved into heavily forested areas—tropical rain forests similar to those they had left in southeastern Nigeria. These locations supported a distinctive way of life that remained fundamentally unaltered for perhaps a millennium and a half (400 to 1900), withstanding the impact of the Atlantic slave

Primary Source

INSTRUCTIONS TO A YOUNG MAN IN WEST AFRICA

The words that were traditionally spoken to a young man coming of age in the Cameroons in West Africa reflect the importance that families attached to being a strong and enterprising individual.

The grandfather gave an ivory bracelet and said:

"This elephant which I put on your arm, become a
   man of crowds,
a hero in war, a man with women
rich in children, and in many objects of wealth
prosper within the family, and be famous
   throughout the villages."

The grandmother gave a charm of success as a belt and said:

"Father, you who are becoming a man
Let toughness and fame be with you as this sap of the
Baillonella toxisperma tree is glued to this thread.

Become dominant, *a great man,*
a hero in war, who surpasses strangers and visitors;
prosper, Have us named!"

→ *Why were gifts in these coming-of-age ceremonies typically charms?*
→ *Why did the sub-Saharan peoples organize themselves around "big men" rather than kings or other sorts of rulers?*

SOURCE: Jan Vansina, *Paths in the Rainforests: Toward a History of Political Tradition in Equatorial Africa* (Madison: University of Wisconsin Press, 1990), pp. 73–74.

---

trade and withering only under European colonialism in the twentieth century. The western Bantu-speaking communities of the lower Congo rain forests formed small-scale societies that relied on family and clan connections. They organized themselves socially and politically into age groups, the most important of which were the ruling elders. Within these age-based networks, individuals of demonstrated talent in warfare, commerce, and politics regularly came to the fore and provided decisive leadership.

Lacking chiefs and kings, the highly fluid and loosely organized Bantu societies rallied around these so-called big men, whose talents inspired others and attracted followers, thereby promoting territorial expansion. In the rain forest, land was relatively abundant but labor was in short supply. Hence, individuals able to attract a large community of followers and to marry many women and sire many children could lead their bands into new locations and establish dominant communities.

Although dispersed, these rain forest communities embraced a common view of the world. They believed that the natural world was inhabited by spirits, many of whom were their own heroic ancestors. These spiritual beings intervened in people's lives and required constant attention and appeasement. Diviners helped men and women understand the ways of the spirits, and charms warded off the misfortune that aggrieved spirits might wish to inflict. Both diviners and charms were also important in protecting people from the injuries that living beings—witches and sorcerers—could inflict on them. Much of the misfortune that occurred in the world was thought to be the work of these malevolent forces, especially as wielded by witches and sorcerers. Indeed, the big men were often thought to control such forces and to use them to punish opponents and reward friends. These beliefs, like the rest of the Bantu worldview, would survive unchallenged for well over a millennium.

The Bantu migrations filled up an immense part of Africa, not less than half of its landmass. The diverse population groups that moved out from their original location in southeastern present-day Nigeria introduced settled agriculture into all corners of the southern part of the landmass. They brought with them a political and social order based on family and clan structures that at the same time allowed considerable leeway for individual achievement—and maintained an intense relationship to the world of nature that they believed, for good or ill, was shot through with supernatural forces.

MESOAMERICANS

As in sub-Saharan Africa, the process of settlement and expansion in Mesoamerica differed from that in the large empires of Afro-Eurasia. In the case of Teotihuacán, the first major community to emerge since the Olmecs, we see the growth of a city-state that ruled over a large, mountainous valley in present-day Mexico. While it did not evolve into a territorial state, it traded as well as warred with neighboring peoples, and created a smaller-scale common culture. In the case of the more famous Mayans, we witness the emergence of a "big" common culture, one that also ruled over large stretches of Mesoamerica; it was composed of a series of kingdoms, each built around ritual centers rather than cities. The Mayan people aggressively engaged neighboring peoples in warfare and trade, expanding their borders through tributary relationships. The extraordinary feature of Mayan society was that its people were defined not by a great ruler, or great capital city, but by their shared religious beliefs, worldview, and sense of purpose. But there is a mystery at the heart of Mesoamerican societies. For as great as were the early so-

cieties of the Olmecs, the people of Teotihuacán, and the Mayans, there was less carryover from one society to the next. Cultural development was much less cumulative here than in Afro-Eurasia, where new regimes built on the old—in part because frequently they absorbed their predecessors. In the Americas, decline often set in before newcomers could take advantage of the learning and breakthroughs of those who had preceded them. As a result, in Mesoamerica empires and common cultures did not emerge on the same scale as in Afro-Eurasia before 1000 CE.

The factors responsible for the repeated interruptions in development remain a mystery. Some argue that the lack of domesticated beasts of burden limited humans' ability to control nature and amass resources. Others point out that what was so essential to Afro-Eurasian developments—the constant contact with neighbors and strangers that fostered learning from others—here vanished once the land bridge across the Bering Straits sank. Inhabitants of the Americas were thereafter on their own, truly in a world apart.

TEOTIHUACÁN Around 300 BCE, the people of the central plateau and the southeastern districts of Mesoamerica, where the dispersed villages of an Olmec culture had risen and fallen, began to gather in larger concentric settlements and to create state systems. The growing scale of political and social integration led to city-states, the largest of which was Teotihuacán, in the heart of the fertile valley of central

Teotihuacán. The ruins of Teotihuacán convey the importance of monumental architecture to Aztec culture. In the foreground is the Plaza of the Moon, leading to the Street of the Dead, with the Pyramid of the Sun to the left. These massive structures were meant to confirm the importance of spiritual affairs in urban life.

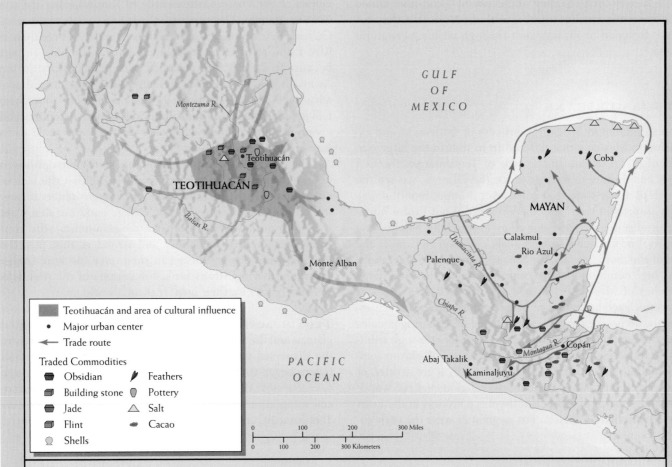

MAP 8-7 MESOAMERICAN WORLDS, 200–700 CE

In the first millennium, two cultural groups dominated Mesoamerica: one was centered at the city of Teotihuacán in the center, and the other, the Mayans, was in the south. According to the map, how did each group create a common culture in surrounding regions? Do common trade goods suggest common cultural outlooks? To what extent do you believe the people of the Teotihuacán and Mayan worlds influenced each other?

Mexico; indeed, it became by far the largest center of the Americas before the Aztecs almost a half-millennium later. Its influence was felt across Mesoamerica, from the deserts in the north to the jungles of the south, and from the Gulf Coast to the Pacific.

The fertility of Teotihuacán's land and the ample supply of water from the marshes and lakes of the valley fostered high agricultural productivity, though the methods of cultivation were still technologically primitive. At the city's zenith, the local food supply sustained a metropolis of probably 100,000 people (as many as 200,000, by some estimates), living in more than 2,000 apartment compounds lined up and down the city's streets. At one corner were the massive pyramids of the sun and the moon, the focus of spiritual life for the city dwellers. The city's center was given over to the huge royal compound, or Ciudadela; it contained its own stepped stone pyramid, the Temple of the Feathered Serpent, whose

grandeur and refinement were famed throughout Mesoamerica at the time and probably influenced Mayan pyramid builders. The awesome promenade, known as "the Street of the Dead," culminated in the hulking Pyramid of the Moon, where, as archaeologists have discovered, foreign warriors and dignitaries were mutilated, sacrificed, and often buried alive to consecrate the holy structure, an edifice designed to raise believers closer to their deities.

Teotihuacán was a powerful city-state that did not mutate into an empire. Though it did not conquer vassal states or create a centralized bureaucracy, its military muscle was imposing. Its rivals were soon either overwhelmed or annexed; by 300 CE, Teotihuacán controlled the entire basin of the Valley of Mexico. It dominated its neighbors and demanded gifts, tribute, and humans for ritual sacrifice. Its massive public architecture was adorned with art commemorating decisive battles, defeated neighbors, and captured

→ *How similar and different were spiritual developments in worlds apart from Afro-Eurasia during this time?*

Quetzalcoatl. The artisans of Teotihuacán decorated the sides of their monumental buildings with sculptures. Here, feathered serpents, denoting the god Quetzalcoatl, burst from the sides of a wall to stare menacingly at passers-by.

fighters. Warfare was instrumental for the city's command of distant hinterlands, even if the vanquished were not made into formal provinces of Teotihuacán.

But the city's political influence beyond the basin was limited. Far more important was its cultural and economic diffusion. Teotihuacán's merchants traded throughout Mesoamerica, outside its formal sphere of control. Ceramics, ornaments of marine shells, and all sorts of decorative and valued objects (especially of highly prized green obsidian) made by Teotihuacano artisans were shipped out on the backs of porters and exchanged far and wide. For instance, a modest Mayan community near the coast of present-day Belize used Teotihuacán green obsidian objects, such as elegant figurines that resembled the Temple of the Feathered Serpent, in burial offerings. At the same time, Teotihuacán imported pottery, feathers, and other goods from distant lowlands.

This kind of expansion therefore left much of the political and cultural sovereignty of neighbors intact, with only the threat of force keeping them in check. But as that threat began to wane, Teotihuacán ran into trouble. Reasons for the demise of the city remain unclear. It likely fell at the hands of invaders near the end of the fifth century, probably after a generations-long decline that left it vulnerable to attack. Whatever the precise circumstances, invaders attacked the city, burned it, and smashed the carved figurines of the central temples and palaces, targeting their destructive energies at its institutional and spiritual core; Teotihuacán's gods, helpless or resigned, watched the assailants' rampage.

THE MAYANS Teotihuacán's power eventually spread as far as the Caribbean region of the Yucatán and its interior hinterlands. These became the areas occupied by the Mayan people, who expanded gradually from about 250 CE to reach their zenith in the eighth century. The Mayans have been a never-ending mystery to historians and archaeologists. They lived in an inhospitable region—hot, with infertile soils, lacking large navigable river systems, and vulnerable to periodic hurricanes. Still, they managed to develop large concentrations of peoples, trade over long distances, and make stunning scientific and mathematical innovations. They were also great artists and builders, and it is largely from the remains of their prodigious constructions that we know much about them. Like the Olmecs before them, the Mayans accomplished magnificent things, only to collapse, leaving their ancient centers deserted for centuries and entire provinces utterly depopulated.

In contrast to those who dwelled in Teotihuacán (or in Baghdad or Constantinople, for that matter), the Mayans achieved greatness without founding a single great metropolis. Instead, they settled across present-day southern Mexico to western El Salvador. In this region divided by many ecological zones, hundreds, possibly thousands, of agrarian villages sprang up; their people shared the same Mayan language and were connected by trade. Villages were also linked together through tribute payments, chiefly from lesser settlements to central, mainly sacred, towns, in honor of deities and family rulers. Because the population growth rates were high and sustained for many centuries, at their peak the Mayans may have numbered as many as 10 million—a figure that certainly qualifies them as a "big" culture. Bigness in a cultural system without big cities made them unique.

The Mayans were divided into a variety of kingdoms that revolved around major hubs and their hinterlands. Palenque,

Palenque. Deep in the Lacandon jungle lies the ruin of the Mayan city of Palenque. Its pyramid, on the left, overlooks the site; on the right, the Tower of the Palace shadows a magnificent courtyard where religious figures and nobles gathered. There is no mistaking how a city like Palenque could command its hinterland with religious authority.

Copán, and Piedras Negras, for instance, were closer to the model of a city-state with hinterlands, similar in some respects to the Mesopotamian city-states surrounded by the transhumant societies; they were politically sovereign but culturally and economically interconnected. Some larger polities, such as Tikal and Kalak'mul, became substantial, sprawling cities with dependent provinces. The ambitions of rulers in these larger states frequently and repeatedly embroiled them in hostilities.

Thus a single culture was internally divided into about a dozen kingdoms, with shifting borders, that shared many features. Each was highly stratified, displaying an elaborate class structure. At the center was a shamanistic king who legitimated his position by extolling his lineage, which reached back to a founding father and ultimately the gods, and who promoted public ceremonies to honor him as well as his ancestors. Kings sponsored elaborate rituals to reinforce their divine lineages, including ornate processions down the main boulevards of their cities to pay homage to gods and their descendants, the rulers. Lords and their wives performed ritual blood sacrifice to feed their ancestors. Though a priestly ruling caste has sometimes been credited with great powers, the pillars of these societies were their scribes, legal experts, military advisers, and skilled artisans. Indeed, many artists and scribes rose to high political positions because they bestowed an aura of greatness on rulers whose grasp on power was often insecure.

Most of the Mayan people remained tied to the land, which was capable of sustaining a high population but not in concentrated settlements. In much of the region, the soil was poor and quickly exhausted. Limited water was also an impediment to large-scale agriculture, as major rivers or irrigation systems were lacking. Mayans therefore employed a combination of agrarian systems adapted to the ecology. Where possible, they created terraces and drained fields—thereby allowing more intensive cultivation. But in much of the region they relied on swidden (slash and burn) agriculture, which pushed the arable frontier further into the dense jungle of Mesoamerica. Either way, farmers could not become too specialized. The result was largely a subsistence economy of diversified agrarian production. Villagers cultivated maize, beans, and squash, rotating them to prevent soil nutrients from being depleted. Where possible, some farmers supplemented these staples—and their diets—with root crops such as sweet potato and manioc. Cotton was the basic fibrous staple used for robes, dresses, and blouses; it was frequently grown amid rows of other crops as part of a diversified mix.

Commerce connected the dispersed Mayan worlds, as did a shared culture: a common set of beliefs, codes, and values that rulers supported. Villagers spoke dialects of roughly the same language. Writing developed very early, though only very recently have epigraphers been able to make sense of the Mayan script—and that new knowledge has revolutionized modern understanding of the Mayan world. The advent of

Wood Tablet. This detail of a wood-carved tablet from a temple in the city of Tikal (c. 741 CE) is a fine example of the ornate form of scribal activity, which combined images and portraits with glyphs that tell a narrative.

writing created an important caste of scribes, who were vital to the integration of Mayan society. Rulers handsomely rewarded scribes with great titles and honors, as well as material comforts, for their ability to write grand epics telling the story of dynasties and their founders, great battles, marriages, deaths, and sacrifices. Such writings taught generations of Mayan subjects that they shared common histories, beliefs, and gods, and that these were associated with the narratives of ruling families.

The Mayans also were skilled in mathematics, which they used in devising a calendar and pursuing the study of astronomy. Keen readers of the stars, they charted regular celestial movements with amazing accuracy. They clearly had developed a method for marking the passage of time by precise lunar as well as solar cycles. By counting and watching the stars, the Mayans could map heavenly motions onto their sacred calendars and rigorously observe their rituals at the proper times.

Here was a world riven by political divisions and often crippling warfare, but with common religious and cultural features. A common faith provided a powerful human resource that rulers could exploit. Cities, and even their rem-

POP	UO	ZIP	ZOTZ	TZEC
XUL	YAXKIN	MOL	CHEN	YAX
ZAC	CEH	MAC	KANKIN	MUAN
PAX	KAYAB	CUMHU	uayeb	

Mayan Pictograms. The Mayans were famous for keeping records of time with an elaborate calendar. Pictograms, each with a separate image, represented the months of the year. All literate Mayans would have recognized this index.

nants after intense periods of warfare, reflected a ruler's ability to summon his subjects to work and contribute to the greatness of the kingdom. Mayan cities lacked street grids. Instead, plazas, ball courts, terraces, and palaces were simply added on to existing neighborhoods, in an early form of urban sprawl. The hubs of activity revolved around royal palaces, whose sophistication was intended to manifest a ruler's grandeur, and massive ball courts, where teams of players met before enthusiastic audiences in a contest that was more religious ritual than game. Moreover, great rulers exhorted their people to build not just outward but upward. The Mayans excelled at the building of skyscrapers—especially as tombs. In Tikal, for instance, surviving buildings include six steep funerary pyramids, whose massive superstructures are made of thick masonry walls and contain grand corbel-vaulted ceilings and chambers; the tallest temple soars above the treetops, more than 220 feet high. The outsides are embellished with giant carvings and paintings, and deep within are the crypts that held the bodies of royal family members.

The elites were obsessed with blood: spilling it was a way to honor dynastic lineages while paying homage to gods. This rite led to chronic warfare, especially among the high-ranked members of rival dynasties, to capture victims whose blood could be shed. Rulers also would frequently shed their own blood at intervals set by the calendar. Royal wives drew blood from their tongues; men underwent a more delicate ritual, as it involved using a stingray spine or sharpened bone to perforate the ruler's penis. Such bloodletting was undertaken only by those of noble descent, with the aid of instruments that were adorned and sanctified; beautiful scenes carved and painted on stelae portrayed blood cascading from the mutilated bodies of great rulers.

Warfare could cut two ways. It enabled rulers to consolidate control over subjects. It brought tribute, sacrificial victims, and honor to commanders. It also led to the grandeur of some of the sovereign polities and their hinterlands. But constant seesawing across the Mayan region among the substates also brought constant territorial flux. The frontiers of each kingdom expanded and contracted in the jostling with neighbors. Such shifts help explain why the Mayan era lasted for so long—in fact, kingdoms rose and fell during this time. Neighbors eclipsed each other in sequence across seven centuries even though we now treat them all as part of "Mayan" culture. Some lesser states became dependencies of greater ones and were expected to bestow honor on their patrons with royal visits, gifts, eligible marital partners, and subjects for sacrifice.

The spiral of warfare doomed the Mayans, especially after the ravages of devastating wars between Tikal and Kalak'mul between the fourth and seventh centuries. With each outbreak of more encompassing war, rulers drafted larger armies and insisted on sacrificing greater numbers of captives, and their resolve only fueled the carnage. Crops were ruined. People fled. Food supplies began to dwindle. After centuries of spreading misery, it began to seem as if the gods themselves were abandoning the Mayan people and their rulers. This appears to have been the cycle that contributed to their ultimate demise.

Warfare therefore engulfed the fractured Mayan polities. With the collapse of ruling households, entire states fell. The cycle of violence destroyed the cultural underpinnings of elite rule that were so important for keeping the Mayan world together. There was no single catastrophic event, no great defeat by a rival power. Spiritual centers of Mayan cultures were abandoned; cities became ghost towns. As populations declined, jungles overtook temples. Eventually, the hallmark of Mayan unity—the ability to read a shared script—was lost.

CONCLUSION

The breakdown of two ancient imperial systems—Rome around the Mediterranean and Han China in East Asia—provided the opening to an era in which religion and shared common culture rather than political structure and institutions became the social and cultural glue holding together large areas of Afro-Eurasia. The demise of these empires yielded to new efforts to bring peoples together, relying more on faith and culture than on military conquest and incorporation. Between 300 and 600 CE, the unity of the Roman Empire gave way to a religious unity, first represented by Christian dissenters and then co-opted by the emperor Constantine. This sense of a unity not limited by the frontiers of any empire formed the basis of a universal church in western Europe, which called itself "Catholic" and believed that it was the true religion that should be spread to all peoples. In the eastern Mediterranean, where the Roman Empire had survived, Christianity and empire coalesced to reinforce the feeling that true religion, high culture, and empire went hand in hand. This Christianity called itself "Orthodox," convinced that beliefs about God and Jesus were given their most correct and most splendid expression within the eastern Roman empire and in its capital, Constantinople. At this time, it showed little interest in evangelizing.

Similarly, in East Asia, the weakening of the mighty Han dynasty enabled Buddhism to become a dominant force in Chinese culture. Without a unified state in China, Confucian officials languished in obscurity, while Buddhist priests and monks gained wide patronage from regional rulers, local warriors, and commoners seeking solace and legitimation in an age of decentralized political and social units. In India, too, a political vacuum helped make possible the unfolding of a new culture. The Brahman elites were also aided by the movement of populations into new territories beyond the reach of the old power structures as they set the agenda for the ritual organization of daily life on every level of society.

By the same token, differences in belief could also create new divides. Not all regions of the world felt the spread of universalizing religions. In sub-Saharan Africa and the Americas, where long-distance transportation was harder, where language systems had not yielded texts that could be shared with and easily conveyed to neighboring cultures of nonbelievers, belief systems were much more localized. But spiritual life was no less profound an influence governing daily existence. What is more, in both Bantu regions of sub-Saharan Africa and in Mesoamerica, religion could integrate peoples far more effectively than political or military influences—which often tended to fracture states rather than centralize them. In these two more distant regions, it was the strong sense of a shared worldview, a shared sense of purpose, and a shared sense of faith that enabled common cultures to develop. Indeed, the Bantus and Mayans would become large-scale common cultures, but ones that were ruled at the local level. This bottom-up approach in sub-Saharan Africa and Mesoamerica created the longer-term means to integrate both regions under similar cultural and religious frames.

Chronology

	1 CE	100 CE	200 CE	300 CE	400 CE
THE MEDITERRANEAN AND NORTH AFRICA		Emperor Constantine legalizes Christianity in Roman Empire, 313 CE ∎ Christianity becomes dominant in Roman cities after 312 CE ∎ ∎ Nicaean Creed developed, 325 C "Barbarian" invasions of Roman Empire, late 4th and 5th centur ∎ Christianity spreads among peoples of the Roman Empire			
SOUTHWEST ASIA	Sasanians create empire in Iran, Mesopotamia, 220s ∎ Constantine establishes new Roman capital at Constantinople, 324 CE ∎ Jewish Talmud produced in the Levant, 400 CE ∎ ∎ Buddhism spreads through Central Asia				
CENTRAL ASIA		Hephthalites rule much of Central Asia, 400–560 CE ∎ Sogdian merchant communities dominant trade routes through Central Asia ∎ ∎ Buddhism spreads through Central Asia			
SOUTH ASIA	∎ Transformation of Brahmanism to Hinduism begins, 1st or 2nd centuries CE Gupta dynasty rules much of northern India, 320–550 CE ∎				
EAST ASIA		∎ Han Empire collapses, c. 220 CE ∎ Six Dynasties Period, 220–589 CE Daoism reforms and revives in popularity ∎ Buddhism spreads among Chinese society, 300–600 CE ∎			
SUB-SAHARAN AFRICA					
MESOAMERICA	Early Classic Mayan Period begins in Yucatan Peninsula, 250 CE ∎ City of Teotihuacán dominates valley of Mexico, 300 CE to late 5th century ∎				

Hence, the three centuries from 300 to 600 CE were marked by the emergence of three great cultural units in Afro-Eurasia, each defined in religious terms: Christianity in the Mediterranean and Southwest Asia, Brahmanism in South Asia, and Buddhism in East Asia. They gave the world a new set of markers and signposts that would illustrate the ways in which peoples were converging under larger and larger religious tents, while at the same time becoming more clearly distinguished from each other. Although these religions did not always replace imperial institutions, they provided transitional alternatives in each region from one form of empire to the next. Universal religions, whether Christian or Buddhist, and universal codes of behavior, such as the Brahmanic Laws of Manu, offered people a way to define themselves, their families, and their loyalties. But this pattern would soon change, when empire returned to East Asia in the form of the mighty Tang and when the inhabitants of a zone stretching from Morocco to central Asia found themselves suddenly united in a gigantic imperial system, created by the unexpected conquests of the Arab followers of the Prophet Muhammad.

STUDY QUESTIONS

 WWNORTON.COM/STUDYSPACE

1. Describe the spread of universal religions in Afro-Eurasian societies between 300 and 600 CE. How did this process reshape, remap, and realign cultural configurations between and among a variety of societies?

2. Describe the connections between the growth and power of Christianity and the political reconfiguration of the Roman Empire between 300 and 600 CE. How did the popularity of Christianity reshape identities among societies in western Asia?

3. Analyze the role of the Sasanian Empire in the spread of universal religions and the development of common cultures in Afro-Eurasia between 300 and 600 CE. How did the geographic context of the empire heighten its role in cross-cultural dissemination?

4. Explain the role of Sogdians and other central Asian peoples in the geographic dispersion of universal religions between 300 and 600 CE. How and through what means did they influence East Asian societies in particular?

500 CE	600 CE	700 CE	800 CE	900 CE	1000 CE

▌ *Collapse of Roman authority in western empire, 5th century* CE

▌ *Byzantine Empire flourishes in the eastern part of former Roman Empire by 500* CE

    ▌ *Emperor Justinian revises Roman law, attempts to revive Roman Empire, 533–540* CE

    ▌ *Justinian commissions construction of Hagia Sophia in Constantinople, 532* CE

    ▌ *Bubonic plague ravishes Southwest Asia starting in 542* CE

    ▌ *Sasanian/Byzantine Wars*

▌ *Rock temple at Bamiyan constructed, 507 and 554* CE

    ▌ *Turkish Confederacy rules much of Central Asia beginning 560* CE

Nestorian Christianity spreads along the Silk Road, 5th–7th centuries CE

    ▌ *Xuanzang, Chinese Buddhist pilgrim, visits South Asia, 630s, 640s*

    ▌ *Sui dynasty revival of Confucianism begins, 581* CE

▌ *Tuoba Wei dynasty rules northern China to 534* CE

    Bantu migrations from West Africa into Central and Southern Africa occur over centuries, 3000 BCE–1000 CE ▌

▌ *Mayan culture reaches its zenith, 8th century*

5. Describe how South Asian Brahmanism (Vedic religion) evolved into Hinduism during this era. What factors contributed to this development?

6. Identify key changes in Buddhist thought and practice in South Asia during this era. How did these refinements aid the spread of this religious outlook outside Buddhism's South Asian homeland?

7. Explain the role of written texts such as the Laws of Manu, the Talmud, the Analects, and the New Testament in universalizing religion in this era. How did these texts reshape social attitudes toward spiritual behavior and identity?

8. Analyze how political decentralization affected the growing popularity of Buddhist and other religious ideas in East Asia between 300 and 600 CE. To what extent did they challenge Confucian ideas on social and political organization?

9. Analyze the impact of the Bantu migration on the social and cultural geography of sub-Saharan Africa. Did a common set of beliefs unite societies in this region of the world during this time?

10. Compare and contrast Mayan society with that of Teotihuacán in Mesoamerica. To what extent did each represent a common religious and cultural outlook in this region at different times?

11. Analyze the extent to which universalizing religions and the enlargement of common cultures fostered common artistic themes among a variety of societies during this era. How, in particular, did a common artistic theme accompany the geographic spread of Buddhism in this period?

12. Analyze the extent to which universal religions brought worlds together and pushed worlds apart. To what extent did religion create new cultural boundaries and rivalries in Afro-Eurasia during this era?

FURTHER READINGS

Bowersock, Glen W., Peter Brown, and Oleg Grabar, *Late Antiquity: A Guide to the Postclassical World* (1999). Essays and items for the entire period 150–750 CE. The volume covers the Roman, East Roman, Sasanian, and early Islamic worlds.

Brown, Peter, *The Rise of Western Christendom: Triumph and Diversity, A.D. 200–1000*, 2nd ed. (2003). The rise and spread of Christianity in Europe and Asia, with up-to-date bibliographies on all topics, maps, and time charts.

———, *The World of Late Antiquity: From Marcus Aurelius to Muhammad, AD 150–750* (1989). A social, religious, and cultural history of the late Roman and Sasanian empires, with illustrations and a time chart.

Bühler, G. (trans.), *The Laws of Manu* (1886). The classic translation of one of India's most important historical, legal, and religious texts.

Coe, Michael D., *The Maya*, 6th ed. (1999). A work by the world's most famous Mayanologist, with up-to-date evidence, analyses, and illustrations.

Cowgill, George L., "The Central Mexican Highlands and the Rise of Teotihuacan to the Decline of Tula," in Richard Adams and Murdo Macleod (eds.), *The Cambridge History of the Native Peoples of the Americas*, vol. 2, *Mesoamerica, Part 1* (2000). The most recent and thorough review of findings about urban states in central Mexico.

Fash, William L., *Scribes, Warriors and Kings: The City of Copan and the Ancient Maya* (2001). A fascinating and comprehensive study of one of the most elaborate of the Mayan city-kingdoms.

Fowden, Elizabeth Key, *The Barbarian Plain: Saint Sergius between Rome and Iran* (1999). The study of a major Christian shrine and its relations to Romans, Persians, and Arabs.

Fowden, Garth, *Empire to Commonwealth: The Consequences of Monotheism in Late Antiquity* (1993). A study of the relation between empire and world religions in western Asia.

Gombrich, Richard F., and Sheldon Pollack (eds.), *Clay Sanskrit Library* (2005–2006). All major works from the Gupta and post-Gupta periods, in both Sanskrit and English versions. During the Gupta period, classical Sanskrit literature reached its apex, with abundant drama, poetry, and folk stories.

Gordon, Charles, *The Age of Attila* (1960). The last century of the Roman Empire in western Europe, vividly illustrated from contemporary sources.

Harper, Prudence, *The Royal Hunter: The Art of the Sasanian Empire* (1978). The ideology of the Sasanian Empire as shown through excavated hoards of precious silverware.

Heather, Peter, *The Fall of the Roman Empire: A New History of Rome and the Barbarians* (2006). A military and political narrative based on up-to-date archaeological material.

Herrmann, Georgina, *Iranian Revival* (1977). The structure and horizons of the Sasanian Empire as revealed in its monuments.

Hillgarth, Jocelyn (ed.), *Christianity and Paganism, 350–750: The Conversion of Western Europe*, rev. ed. (1986). A collection of contemporary sources.

Holcombe, Charles, *In the Shadow of the Han: Literati Thought and Society at the Beginning of the Southern Dynasties* (1994). A clear and concise account of the evolution of thought in China after the fall of the Han dynasty in 220 CE. The book presents the rise of Buddhism and Daoism as popular religions as well as elite interests in classical learning in a time of political division and barbarian conquest in North and South China.

La Vaissière, Étienne de, *Sogdian Traders: A History*, trans. James Ward (2005). A summary of historical facts about the most important trading community and their commercial networks on the Silk Road, from the early centuries CE to their demise in the ninth century CE.

Liu, Xinru, and Lynda Norene Shaffer, *Connections across Eurasia: Transportation, Communication, and Cultural Exchanges on the Silk Roads* (2007). A survey of trade and religious activities on the Silk Road.

Maas, Michael, *Readings in Late Antiquity: A Source Book* (1999). Well-chosen extracts that illustrate the interrelation of Romans and non-Romans, and of Christians, Jews, and pagans.

Maas, Michael (ed.), *The Cambridge Companion to the Age of Justinian* (2005). A survey of all aspects of the eastern Roman empire in the sixth century.

Moffett, Samuel, *A History of Christianity in Asia*, vol. 1 (1993). Particularly valuable on Christians in China and India.

Munro-Hay, Stuart, *Aksum: An African Civilization of Late Antiquity* (1991). The origins of the Christian kingdom of Ethiopia.

Murdock, George P., *Africa: Its Peoples and Their History* (1959). A vital introduction to the peoples of Africa and their history.

Oliver, Roland, *The African Experience: From Olduvai Gorge to the Twenty-First Century* (1999). An important overview, written by one of the pioneering scholars of African history and one of the leading authorities on the Bantu migrations.

Pregadio, Fabrizio, *Great Clarity: Daoism and Alchemy in Early Medieval China* (2006). An examination of the religious aspects of Daoism. The book focuses on the relation of alchemy to the Daoist traditions of the third to sixth centuries CE and shows how alchemy was integrated into the elaborate body of doctrines and practices of Daoists at that time.

Tempels, Placide, *Bantu Philosophy* (1959). A highly influential effort to argue for the underlying cultural unity of all the Bantu peoples.

Vansina, Jan, *Paths in the Rainforests: Toward a History of Political Tradition in Equatorial Africa* (1990). The best work on Bantu history.

Walker, Joel, *The Legend of Mar Kardagh: Narrative and Christian Heroism in Late Antique Iraq* (2006). Christians and Zoroastrians in northern Iraq and in Iran.

Wells, Peter, *The Barbarians Speak: How the Conquered Peoples Shaped the Roman Empire* (1999). A view, based on archaeology, of the Roman Empire from the non-Roman side of the frontier.

Yarshater, Ehsan, *Encyclopedia Iranica* (1982–). A guide to all aspects of the Sasanian Empire and to religion and culture in the regions between Mesopotamia and central Asia.

Zürcher, E., *The Buddhist Conquest of China: The Spread and Adaptation of Buddhism in Early Medieval China*, 3rd ed. (2007). A reissue of the classic account of the assimilation of Buddhism in China during the medieval period, with particular focus on the religious and philosophical success of Buddhism among Chinese elites in South China.

9

NEW EMPIRES AND COMMON CULTURES, 600–1000 CE

*I*n 754 CE, when the Muslim caliph al-Mansur (ruled 754–775 CE) began his search for a new capital city, Islam was already more than a century old and into its second dynasty, the Abbasids. Al-Mansur wanted to relocate his primary city from Damascus, the capital of Islam's first dynasty, in order to shift the center of imperial power toward the Iranian plateau, the Abbasids' home region. Traveling the length and breadth of the Tigris and Euphrates rivers, the caliph eventually decided to build near a small, unimposing village called Baghdad, located along the west bank of the Tigris.

He had good reasons for his selection. The site lay between Mesopotamia's two great rivers, where they were only twenty-five miles apart and were linked by canals. As one contemporary observer noted, the area was "surrounded by palm trees and near water so that if one district suffers from drought or fails to yield its harvest in due season, there will be relief from another" (Hodges, *Mohammed*, p. 126). Al-Mansur also knew that his metropolis would arise close to the illustrious ancient capital of the Sasanian Empire, Ctesiphon, where the old Arch of Khusro was still standing. This was also the site of earlier Sumerian and

367

Babylonian imperial power. Rulers decided to build at Baghdad with the intention of reaffirming Mesopo- tamia's centrality in the Afro-Eurasian world, and in so doing exalting the universalizing ambitions of Islam. Al-Mansur proceeded with the vigor that characterized the new Abbasid regime. He laid the first brick in 762 CE; within five years, a set of towering inner city walls surrounded what soon became known as the "round city."

Al-Mansur's choice was inspired. As the new capital of Islam, Baghdad also became a crossroads for Africa and Eurasian commerce; as the nexus of a universalizing faith, it also became an economic point of world convergences. Overnight, this city turned into a bustling world emporium. Chinese merchants supplied it with silk, paper, and porcelain. Indian traders shipped it pepper, and East Africa was its source for gold, ivory, and slaves. While Chinese goods arrived by land and sea, commodities originating in Inner Eurasia came via the well-traveled Silk Road from Khurasan. Large camel caravans wound across Baghdad's western desert, linking the capital with Syria, Egypt, North Africa, and even southern Spain. In effect, the unity that the Abbasids imposed with their impressive capital at Baghdad redoubled the movement of peoples, ideas, innovations, and commodities. Baghdad's reputation quickly spread. Seen as the "navel of the earth," Baghdad attracted people "from all countries far and near, and people from every side have preferred Baghdad to their own homelands." To its inhabitants and visitors, Iraq was "the most elegant country," from which goods "can be procured so readily and so certainly that it is as if all the good things of the world were sent there, all the treasures of the earth assembled there, and all the blessings of creation reflected there" (Yaqubi and Muqaddasi, in Lewis, p. 70).

These were the words of the ninth-century Arab Muslim intellectuals Yaqubi and Muqaddasi. For them, Baghdad's eminence and prosperity needed no explanation. After all, the city was the center of the Islamic world, which in turn was

God's gift to his believers. The transformation was remarkable. Here was a tribal people from a distant and remote part of the Arabian Peninsula, founders of a religion that by 762 CE had sliced through the territory of the once dominant Christian Byzantine Empire and totally absorbed the Zoroastrian Sasanian Empire. Here was an empire that replaced the eastern and southern regions of the old Roman Empire and that represented a polity as powerful as the Tang empire in China. The rise of Islam is yet another example of how religion and empire entwined to create the foundations of the world's modern social geography.

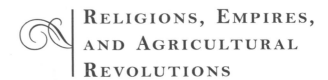

RELIGIONS, EMPIRES, AND AGRICULTURAL REVOLUTIONS

> → *How did the growth of Islamic empires lead to a revolution in agriculture across Afro-Eurasia?*

But Islam's origins illustrate how the entwinings of religion and empire were not all the same. Islam alters the pattern displayed by the ascent of Christianity and Buddhism. As we saw in Chapter 8, empire served as the main vehicle for the growth of those two universalizing religions. Moreover, they played significant political and spiritual roles in societies weakened by the breakdown of the Roman, Mauryan, and Han empires. In the case of Islam, in contrast, it was religion that led to the creation of empires. Having swept aside their predecessors in Southwest Asia, Muslim leaders had to form their own imperial system. Although they borrowed liberally from the Byzantines and Persians, their underlying reason for

Focus Questions NEW EMPIRES AND COMMON CULTURES

→ *How did the growth of Islamic empires lead to a revolution in agriculture across Afro-Eurasia?*

→ *What factors created a common cultural outlook among Muslim communities in Afro-Eurasia during this era?*

→ *How did the Tang state balance its desire to restore Confucian principles to China with the growth of new universal religions in East Asia?*

→ *To what extent did Japanese and Korean states and societies emulate Tang China during this era?*

→ *How did two Christianities come to exist in western Eurasia?*

 WWNORTON.COM/STUDYSPACE

establishing an imperial system was new: to secure, defend, and spread their religion. Christianity and Zoroastrianism converted empires to their own views; Islam created its empire from scratch.

When we consider how religions had pervaded the lives of the Afro-Eurasian populations in the previous three centuries, we should not be surprised that a charismatic and prophetic figure would arise among the Arabs, proclaiming new religious precepts. By this time, religions had become the currency of life. Christianity and Buddhism were now laying claim to universal truths, and groups seeking to compete with them in making a mark on the Afro-Eurasian landmass at the end of the sixth century had to speak their language of universal religion. The Tang dynasty in China alone withstood the universalizing claims of religion that swept across the region in this period, as Confucianism and Daoism responded to the upsurge of Chinese Buddhism—proving again that China would follow a somewhat different path from the other Afro-Eurasian empires by maintaining its commitments to its past traditions and customs.

At the same time that Islam was spreading, the Muslim world was experiencing significant developments in agriculture. Islam may well have been a crucial factor in this transformation. As a syncretic culture, it assimilated the ideas, institutions, and beliefs of many different peoples and geographical zones—a feature that was as fully apparent in the agricultural realm as in other areas of culture. Farmers in the early Muslim empire became agricultural innovators, introducing a host of new crops and employing new agrarian techniques that made possible rapid population growth, rising standards of living, and urbanization.

By the dawn of the Common Era, India had replaced Mesopotamia as the source of a wide range of new crops. In fact, most of the new cultigens in Afro-Eurasia in the first millennium CE had their origins in Southeast Asia, made their way only gradually to India, and dispersed from there throughout the Muslim world. Southeast Asia provided Indian cultivators with rice, taro, sour oranges, lemons, limes, and most likely coconut palm trees, sugarcane, bananas, plantains, and mangoes. Sorghum and quite possibly cotton and watermelons arrived from Africa. Only the eggplant was indigenous to India. Although many of these crops spread quickly and easily to East Asia, where they became staples in the Chinese diet, their movement westward was not so rapid. A few crops made their way into Sasanian Persia and the Arabian Peninsula, but it was not until the Muslim conquest of Sindh in the lower Indus region of northern India in 711 CE that the territories to the west were fully opened up to the crop innovations pioneered in South Asia.

Most of the new cultigens had their origins in Southeast Asia, made their way only gradually to India, and dispersed from there throughout the Muslim world.

Writing in the fourteenth century, the Arab historian Ibn Khaldun once observed about his peoples that "all of their customary activities lead to travel and movement" (Ibn Khaldun, *Prologomena*). India fascinated them, and their travelers, merchants, scholars, and landed gentry exploited the new agriculture of India to the hilt. Between 700 and 1000 CE nothing less than a revolution in cultigens and diet swept through the Muslim world. Sorghum supplanted millet and the other grains of antiquity because it was hardier, had higher yields, and required a shorter growing season. Citrus trees added flavor to the diet and provided refreshing drinks during the heat of the summer, and the spread of cotton cultivation led to increased demand for textiles.

During the first three and half centuries after the appearance of Islam, farmers from northwest India in the east to Spain, Morocco, and West Africa in the west used these new cultigens to expand the area under cultivation; they increased agricultural output, became a more productive workforce, slashed fallow periods, and grew two and sometimes even three crops on lands that had previously yielded only one. (See Map 9-1.) The results were impressive. Farmers could feed larger urban communities and offer consumers more diversified and healthier diets. We lack population figures for this period, but the evidence from Arab travelers and geographers is incontrovertible. Cities grew, and the countryside became more densely populated and more productive. According to one writer, the Fayyum region of Egypt had no fewer than 360 villages, each of which, by his account, was so productive that its cultivators could provision the whole of Egypt for a day. Once Islam began to consolidate its command over much of the region spanning North Africa to the edges of India, it acted as a massive conveyor belt of these agrarian breakthroughs, with dramatic repercussions for the peripheries of Eurasia and Africa. In the long run, the Afro-Eurasian world was set on a path of population increase and ever-larger cities; its growth accelerated after 1000 CE and was not interrupted until the fourteenth century, when the Black Death produced dying and suffering on a scale that few had seen before.

The transformation also swept through East Asia. China, too, experienced an agricultural surge between 600 and 1000 CE, receiving—often directly from Southeast Asia rather than through India—the same crops that Islamic cultivators were carrying westward. Rice was critical. New varieties entered China from the south; as populations migrated down from the north, fleeing the political turmoil that followed the collapse of the Han empire, they eagerly took up the new crops. By the eleventh century, Chinese farmers had become the world's most intensive wet-field rice cultivators. Early- and

MAP 9-1(A & B)   THE SPREAD OF ISLAM AND AGRICULTURAL DIFFUSION IN THE FIRST MILLENNIUM

The second half of the first millennium saw a revolution in agriculture throughout Afro-Eurasia. As the map on page 371 demonstrates, agriculturalists across the landmass increasingly cultivated similar crops. How does the map suggest these cultigens diffused across a wider geographic area? What role did the spread of Islam and the growth of Islamic empires play in this process? How did the spread of this new religion act as a massive conveyor belt for crop diffusion? How did this process shape the history of Afro-Eurasia?

late-ripening seeds made it possible to harvest two or three plantings during a single year. Champa rice, introduced from central Vietnam, was the most widely used. It was drought resistant, had low gluten content, and ripened faster than the older strains.

The introduction of new grains and new technologies opened vast new arable lands in China's south to feed an expanding populace. In 742 CE, 60 percent of China's 80 million people lived in the wheat- and millet-producing areas of the Yellow and Wei rivers in the north and northwest. By 980, only 38 percent of China's 100 million people still lived in the north. This shift was made possible by improvements in irrigation techniques and the expansion of the road and water transportation system. Rice needs ample supplies of water, and Chinese hydraulic engineers designed water-lifting devices while peasant farmers built more canals linking lakes and rivers and drained swamps, alleviating the malaria that had long troubled the region. These developments created a booming and constantly moving rice frontier. (See Map 9-2.)

Europe was the exception to these agricultural breakthroughs. Most of the new crops were tropical and semitropical cultigens, suited only to the Mediterranean basin. Moreover, cultivators in northern Europe were still in the early stages of clearing the primeval forest. The critical ingredients for agricultural growth in Europe were the axe, the steel plow, and the harnessed horse; in China they were new seeds, dams, sluice gates, and sophisticated hydraulic devices. In Europe, agrarian innovation lagged and took longer to flourish, but it, too, would soon come, as the next chapter will illustrate.

So it was that a vibrant new universalizing faith erupted onto the Afro-Eurasian stage just as an agrarian transformation was about to spread across the middle latitudes of the landmass. The two movements—the diffusion of a rural revolution and a spiritual riptide—reinforced each other and heightened the potential of each to change the cultural, political, and economic geography of the world. They did so in league with new imperial formations in the heartlands, integrating the dispersed peoples of the middle of Southwest Asia and North and East Africa into an increasingly common cultural system. The long-term effect was to strengthen the linkages across even longer distances, from China to Africa. These linkages were the interlocking effects of three significant changes: an agrarian revolution (which fostered more commerce and denser populations), the resurgence of empires in the wake of Roman and Han collapses (which created institutional structures with greater unity to facilitate some stability within polities), and the appearance of a new, vibrant universalizing faith in the region straddling western and eastern Afro-Eurasia. It was the ascent of Islam out of Arabia, its unifying effects on the territories between the two other spreading universal faiths—Christianity and Buddhism—and its provision of the spiritual foundations for a new empire in Southwest Asia and Africa that brought the world together in historically unprecedented ways. It also laid the basis for a new set of divisions that would drive worlds apart, as a politicized Islam created internal and external sources of conflict across these regions.

THE ORIGINS AND SPREAD OF ISLAM

> → *What factors created a common cultural outlook among Muslim communities in Afro-Eurasia during this era?*

Any explanation of Islam's emergence as a universalizing religion that sowed the seeds for a widespread common culture must begin where Islam's story began: inside Arabia. Despite its remoteness and sparse population, by the sixth century CE Arabia was feeling the influence of outside currents of long-distance trade, religious disputation, and imperial politics. Toward the end of the sixth century, as we learned in Chapter 8, Byzantine and Sasanian imperial pressures had intruded deeply into Arabia. Commodities from Egypt, Syria,

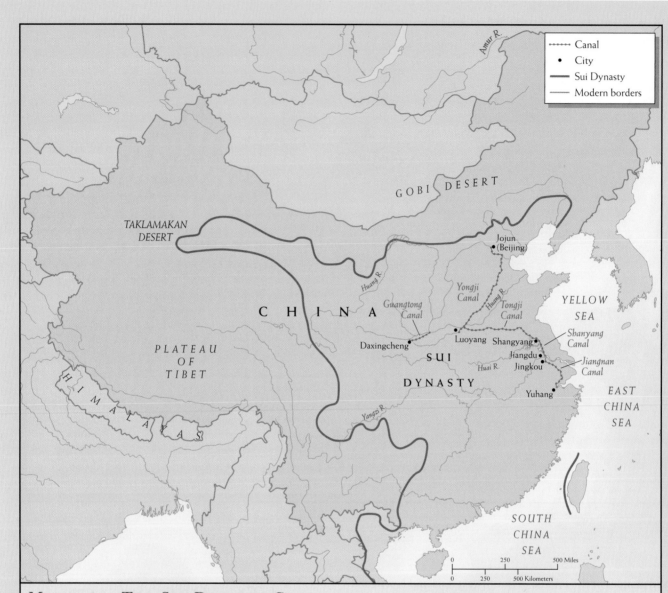

MAP 9-2 THE SUI DYNASTY CANALS

China, like the Islamic world, experienced an explosion in population during this period (see the discussion on page 370). What role did the building of the Sui dynasty canals play in this growth? What role might the canals have played in fostering massive internal migrations in China? What other advantages might the presence of these canals provide to the Chinese state and its peoples?

and Iraq circulated in local markets, and learned men debated the doctrinal tenets of Christianity and Judaism. The Hijaz, the western region of Arabia bordering the Red Sea, was connected to the outside world by trading routes that led all the way up the coast to the Mediterranean. Yet without the actions of a deeply inspired and powerful religious leader, the Prophet Muhammad, it is doubtful that the peoples of Arabia would have entered the mainstream of world history so forcefully.

Mecca, in the Hijaz, was not an imposing place. A pre-Islamic poet wrote of it that "winter and summer are equally intolerable. No waters flow . . . [and there is] not a blade of grass on which to rest the eye; no, nor hunting. [Here there are] only merchants, the most despicable of professions" (Peters, p. 23). Hardly more than a village, Mecca was composed of simple mud huts whose inhabitants sustained themselves less as traders than as caretakers of a revered sanctuary, the kaaba, an otherwise unprepossessing collection of unmortared rocks piled one on top of the other that local peoples regarded as the dwelling place of deities. But it was here that a great prophet was born.

A VISION, A TEXT

Born in Mecca around 570 CE into a well-respected tribal family, Muhammad enjoyed only moderate success in his career as a trader. Little in his early life suggested the momentous events that were in the offing. Then came a revelation, one that would convert this broker of commodities into a proselytizer of a new faith. In the year 610 CE, while he was on a monthlong spiritual retreat in a cave on Mount Hira (near Mecca), God himself, or possibly the angel Gabriel, came to him in a vision and commanded him to recite the following words, which eventually became Sura 96 of the Quran:

> Recite in the Name of the Lord who createth,
> Createth man from a clot
> Recite: And thy Lord is the most Bounteous who
>   teacheth by the pen
> Teacheth man that which he knew not.

Further revelations followed. The early ones were like the first: short, powerful, and full of instructions for his fellow Meccans. Note in particular the injunction to teach, to carry the message to nonbelievers. They were eminently memorable, an important feature in an oral culture where no art form was more highly prized than poetry recitation. Muhammad's early preaching had a sharp and clear message. He enjoined his followers to act righteously, to set aside false

deities, to submit themselves to the one and only true God, and to care for the less fortunate, for the Day of Judgment was imminent. Muhammad's most insistent message was the oneness of God, a belief that has remained at the core of the faith ever since.

When finally compiled into a single authoritative version sometime around 650 CE, more than a decade after the Prophet's death, the Quran consisted of 114 chapters, known as suras, which were arranged in descending order of length; the longest ran to 300 verses and the shortest, a mere three. According to Arab historians, the verses were at first written down on "bits of parchment, thin white stones, leafless palm branches, and the bosoms of men" (Arberry, p. viii). Accepted as the very word of God, they were transmitted without flaw through God's perfect instrument, thee Prophet Muhammad.

Like basic works described in earlier chapters, such as the Jewish Torah, the Christian Bible, and other foundational texts, this was one meant to inscribe the tenets of a faith to unite a people and to convey a set of stable messages to other cultures, to expand the frontiers of the new faith. Here was one God, one set of lessons, one text, and a providential purpose to spread the word.

Muhammad saw himself as the last of the long line of prophets—or, as he said, the seal of the prophets. He believed that he was in the tradition of Moses, other Hebrew prophets, and Jesus and that he communicated with the same God that they did. As we have seen, Christian and Jewish religious ideas and communities existed in the Arabian peninsula at the time of Muhammad. A substantial Jewish community resided in the city of Yathrib (later called Medina). Just how deeply Muhammad understood the tenets of Judaism and Christianity is difficult to determine, but his professed

Mecca. At the great mosque at Mecca, which many consider the most sacred site in Islam, hundreds of thousands of worshippers gather for Friday prayers. Many are performing their religious duty to go on a pilgrimage to the holy places in the Arabian Peninsula.

THE QURAN

These two suras from the Quran are relatively short ones, but they provide some of the essence of Muhammad's message and the faith of Islam. The Quran opens with a sura known as the fatiha, *which in its powerful prayerlike quality lends itself to frequent recitation. Sura 87, "The Most High," provides a deeper insight into the nature of humanity's relationship with God.*

THE EXORDIUM

IN THE NAME OF GOD THE COMPASSIONATE THE MERCIFUL

Praise be to God, Lord of the Universe,
The Compassionate, the Merciful,
Sovereign of the Day of Judgement!
You alone we worship, and to You alone we turn for help.
Guide us to the straight path,
The path of those whom You have favoured,
Not of those who have incurred Your wrath,
Nor of those who have gone astray   (1.1–1.7)

THE MOST HIGH

IN THE NAME OF GOD, THE COMPASSIONATE, THE MERCIFUL

Praise the Name of your Lord, the Most High, who has created all things and proportioned them; who has ordained their destinies and guided them; who brings

forth the green pasture, then turns it to withered grass.

'We shall make you recite Our revelations, so that you shall forget none of them except as God pleases. He has knowledge of all that is manifest, and all that is hidden.

We shall guide you to the smoothest path. Therefore give warning, if warning will avail. He that fears God will heed it, but the wicked sinner will flout it. He shall burn in the gigantic Fire, where he shall neither die nor live. Happy shall be the man who purifies himself, who remembers the name of his Lord and prays.

Yet you prefer this life, although the life to come is better and more lasting.

All this is written in earlier scriptures; the scriptures of Abraham and Moses.   (87.1–87.19)

→ *What themes can you glean from these passages about humanity's relationship to God?*
→ *Do you find any similarities to the tenets of Judaism and Christianity as you have encountered them in this volume?*

SOURCE: *The Koran,* trans. with notes by N. J. Dawood (London: Penguin, 1993), pp. 9, 424.

---

indebtedness to and affiliation with their tradition is a part of Islamic belief.

THE MOVE TO MEDINA, 622 CE

Muslims date the beginning of the Muslim era from the year 622 CE, when Muhammad and a small group of followers, persecuted by the leaders of Mecca, escaped to Yathrib (later renamed Medina)—an event known as the Hegira (in Arabic *Hijra,* "breaking off of relations" or "departure"). The perilous 200-mile journey accomplished more than a flight. It yielded an entirely new form of communal unity: the *umma*

(band of the faithful), which supplanted traditional family, clan, and tribal affiliations with loyalty to Muhammad as the one and true Prophet of God. Medina became the birthplace of a new faith, called Islam, which means "submission" (to the will of God), and a new collectivity, called Muslims (literally, "those who submit"). Its believers accepted the prophecy of Muhammad. From Medina Muhammad's adherents broadcast their new faith and their new mission, first to the recalcitrants of Mecca and then, after Mecca had been converted, to all inhabitants of Arabia and even beyond—to the larger world of Asia, Africa, and Europe. In this way, Islam joined Christianity in seeking to bring the whole known world under its authority—asserting a logic of world integration,

The Battle of Badr. This image depicts the battle of Badr, which took place in 624 and marked the beginning of Muhammad's reconquest of Mecca from his new base in the city of Medina.

but also laying out a fundamental new division between the worlds of believers and nonbelievers.

CONQUESTS, 632–661 CE

In 632, in his early sixties, the Prophet passed away. Islam could easily have withered. What kept the new religious movement moving forward were the inspiration of the founder himself and the energy of the early leaders—especially the first four successors to Muhammad, referred to in later Muslim accounts as the "rightly guided caliphs." The word caliph, or *khalīfa*, means "successor" in Arabic, and in this context it referred to the successors to Muhammad as political rulers over the Muslim peoples and the expanding state.

The expansive spiritual force of Islam galvanized its imperial political authority. Muhammad's successors decided to implement the Prophet's plans to send Arab-Muslim armies into Syria and Iraq. Spurred on by religious fervor and a desire to enrich their growing empire with the wealth of conquered territories, Muslim soldiers embarked on military conquests; this expansion of the Islamic state was one aspect of the struggle that they referred to as *jihad* (another aspect focuses on the daily personal struggle for faith). Within a decade and a half they had control over Syria, Egypt, and Iraq. These centerpieces of the Byzantine and Sasanian empires then became the pillars of an even larger new Islamic empire. Mastery of desert warfare and inspired military leadership help explain these astonishing exploits, but equally important was the exhaustion of the Byzantine and Sasanian empires after generations of continuous warfare. The Byzantines saved the core of their empire by pulling most of their troops back to highlands of Anatolia, where they had more defensible frontiers, and conceding the more distant and discontented parts of their territories. In contrast, Sasanian rulers gambled all on a final effort: they hurled their remaining military resources against the armies of the Muslim believers, only to be crushed and then to collapse. Having lost Iraq and unable to defend the Iranian plateau, the Sasanian Empire passed out of existence, its remnants absorbed into a new imperial regime.

AN EMPIRE OF ARABS, 661–750 CE

When the last of the first four caliphs, Ali, was assassinated in 661 CE, new men took over. A political vacuum had opened, and a branch of one of the Meccan clans, the Umayyads, seized the opportunity to lay claim to Ali's legacy. As the governors of the province of Syria under Ali, this first dynasty moved the core of Islam out of Arabia and introduced the principle of a hereditary monarchy to resolve leadership disputes. Cosmopolitan traders who were adaptable in their outlook, they ruled from the city of Damascus until they were overthrown by the Abbasids in 750 CE.

By then, the core practices and beliefs of every Muslim had already crystallized and were known early on as the five "pillars" of Islam. These tenets built on long-standing practices. In addition to a declaration of a belief in one God and in the role of Muhammad as Messenger, ritual prayer, fasting, pilgrimage, and alms were prescribed in the text of the Quran, and were similar to either familiar Jewish practices or old Arabian customs. They became solid parts of Islamic practice in the first decades of Muhammad's career as a prophet.

In its early days, converting to Islam was a simple affair. The religion was also open to blending with older belief systems, an openness that enhanced its ability to spread by adaptation. Rather than insisting that followers abandon all of their former ways of life, the new faith called on them to add adherence to its key beliefs, which involved allegiance to Muslim authorities and payment of alms. Another major incentive to convert was a reduction in the *jizra,* or "toleration tax." The simplicity of these core doctrines, especially the first and essential pillar affirming a belief in one God and the prophecy of Muhammad, may have attracted early converts, but Islam in fact made many demands on its faithful, particularly after the full elaboration of its legal system, the sharia, a century after Muhammad's death.

There was, however, a political limit to Islam's ability to integrate others. Although tolerant of conquered populations, the ruling groups during the Umayyad dynasty did not permit non-Arabic-speaking converts to rise to high political offices. The overthrow of Umayyad rule ended the "Arabs only" empire, paving the way for the incorporation of non-Arab populations into the Islamic core. This changed the nature of the incipient empire. For as the political center of Islam moved out of Arabia to Syria, and then with the Abbasids to Mesopotamia, it sacrificed ethnic purity for geographic expansion. So while this universalizing religion spread the word to create a more common spiritual world, it became more and more diverse within the Islamic world. To be sure, obstacles to converts' acceptance still existed, and the pace of conversion was often slow—fastest in Persia, sluggish in Egypt. By the middle of the eighth century, probably less than 20 percent of the peoples residing in the Islamic empire were Muslims.

THE ABBASID REVOLUTION

As the Umayyad dynasty spread Islam beyond Arabia to integrate more people and provinces, it created resistance to its authority. The province of Khurasan in central Asia contained many who had accepted the Islamic faith and resented discrimination at the hands of the Arab peoples. Here, religious reformers and political dissidents stressed doctrines of religious purity and depicted the Umayyads as irreligious and politically repressive. A coalition emerged led by the Abbasi family, which claimed descent from the Prophet's family. Disgruntled provincial authorities and their military allies joined the Abbasid movement, which also found strong support among the non-Arab converts to Islam—individuals known as *Mawali,* or freedmen, who had made themselves clients to Muslim Arabs, embraced Islam, and learned Arabic, only to discover that they were still regarded as second-class citizens. This coalition amassed a sizable military force and trounced the Umayyad ruler in 750 CE. The Abbasid triumph in turn shifted the center of the caliphate to Iraq, signifying the eastward sprawl of the faith and of its empire. It also represented a success for non-Arab ethnic groups within Islam without entirely eliminating Arab influence at the center of the new dynasty, as indicated by the Abbasids' decision to make Baghdad in Arabic-speaking Iraq the capital of their empire.

MAP 9-3   THE SPREAD OF ISLAM DURING THE FIRST MILLENNIUM

Islam emerged in the Arabian Peninsula in the seventh century. Within 150 years, leaders of this religious community had conquered a vast amount of territory. Identify the areas that came under Islamic armies' control by the eighth century. How were Arab armies able to defeat their Byzantine and Sasanian counterparts? To what extent did Islamic conquests lead to widespread conversion to the religion among those they conquered during this era? How did Islam expand beyond these areas of conquest?

But conversion to Islam rested on the zeal of evangelizers and the appeal of the new faith to converts. Some turned to it for practical reasons, seeking a reduction in their taxes or aspiring to exercise power. Others were impressed with the message of Islam. They regarded the new way of life as offering superior answers to a range of secular and spiritual questions. Not only did the Abbasids move aggressively to open Islam to Persian peoples, they also encouraged the Islamic world to embrace Greek and Hellenistic learning, Indian science, and Chinese innovations. No doubt the origins of the Abbasid dynasty broadened their worldview, as peoples along the Silk Road in central Asia were exposed to elements from all major cultures. The result was to make Islam in the Abbasid period truly cosmopolitan. It successfully merged the contributions of peoples from vastly different geographical expanses and widely different intellectual backgrounds into a rich yet unified culture.

> *Not only did the Abbasids move aggressively to open Islam to Persian peoples, they also encouraged the Islamic world to embrace Greek and Hellenistic learning, Indian science, and Chinese innovations.*

RALLYING POINTS: THE CALIPHATE One of the first questions that the Abbasid rulers had to answer was how traditional or "Arab" they could be and still rule over so vast an empire. They chose to retain the bedrock political institution of the early Islamic state—the caliphate, a political and spiritual head of the Islamic community—which the early Islamic community had recognized as the successor to the incandescent leadership of Muhammad. Although from the outset the caliphs exercised temporal and spiritual authority over the Muslim community, Muhammad's successors did not inherit his prophetic powers. Nor were they expected to exercise authority in the realm of religious doctrines: that power was reserved to specialist religious scholars, called *ulama* (the Arabic plural of *alim*, meaning "scholar"). But the Abbasid caliphs differed from their predecessors, the Umayyads and the first four Meccan caliphs, in leadership style. The new approach revealed how syncretic imperial Islam had become. Exposure to Byzantine and Persian political influences significantly altered what the community of believers expected of their rulers and how they were chosen. The Persians stressed the leader's absolute authority, such as that wielded by the rulers of the Achaemenid Empire. And like Byzantine rulers, Abbasid caliphs lived in secluded palaces, cut off from their subjects and protected by eunuchs and professional bodyguards.

The rulers of imperial Islam mingled practices of absolute authority with decentralized exercise of power through their envoys in the provinces. It was a delicate and ultimately unsustainable balancing act. As the empire grew it became increasingly decentralized, making it possible for regional governors and even counter-caliphates in Spain and Egypt to

take hold. The political result was an Islamic world characterized by multiple nodes of power, nominally led by a weakened Abbasid caliphate. But as its political center shifted in the coming centuries, the spiritual center of the faith always remained fixed in Mecca.

RALLYING POINTS: THE ARMY The Abbasids, like all rulers, relied on force to integrate their empire; and for imperial Islam, as was true of the Romans, the exercise of military power necessitated the involvements of warriors and soldiers from different ethnic backgrounds from across Afro-Eurasia. How "Arab" should the Muslim armies be? In the early stages of conquest, leaders had conscripted their military forces from local Arab populations, creating, in effect, citizen armies. But as Arab populations settled down in new garrison cities, the rulers turned to professional soldiers. The Abbasids looked to the peripheries of the empire for their military forces, recruiting from the Turkish-speaking communities in central Asia and from Berbers and black Africans in the West. Their reliance on these foreign (non-Arab) groups as the core of their military, much like that of the second- and third-century Romans on the Germanic peoples and Goths, represented a major historical shift in the Islamic world. Not only did the change bring new populations into the empire, but by the ninth and tenth centuries these groups had begun to wield decisive political authority, just as the "barbarians" had done in the last centuries of the Roman Empire. Having begun as an Arab state and then incorporated strong Persian influence, the Islamic empire now embraced Turkish elements from the pastoral belts of Inner and central Asia. So, as the universalizing religion spread, it became increasingly multicultural while uniting diverse peoples into a single community of believers. Like other universalizing religions, this faith brought people together in more integrated political and religious structures, and in doing so created polities that were more ethnically and culturally diverse. The presence of the nomadic Turkish warriors in particular reminds us of the important role that pastoral peoples continued to play throughout the history of the early world. Ultimately, the Ottoman Turks would become the successor state to the Umayyad dynasty and rule over stretches of southern Europe and Southeast Asia for more than eight centuries.

RALLYING POINTS: ISLAMIC LAW (THE SHARIA) AND THEOLOGY In the Abbasid period, not just the caliphate but also a crucial foundation of Islam—Islamic law, known as the *sharia*—took shape. Sharia law covers all aspects of practical as well as spiritual life, providing legal principles for marriage contracts, trade regulations, and religious prescriptions such as prayer, pilgrimage rites, and ritual fasting. It was the work of generations of religious scholars, rather than of men of the sword, courtiers, and bureaucrats—and its life has continued until today all over the Muslim world, independent of empires.

The early Muslim communities prepared the ground for the sharia, endeavoring (guided by the Quran) to handle legal matters in ways that they thought Muhammad would have wanted. But because the Quran dealt mainly with family concerns, religious beliefs, and social relations—not legal questions—local judges exercised their own judgment where the Quran was silent. The most influential of these early legal scholars was an eighth-century Iraqi, al-Shafi'i, who was determined to make the laws of the empire entirely Islamic. He insisted that the laws that Muhammad had laid out in the Quran, with the addition of the Prophet's sayings and actions that were written down in later reports known as *hadith,* provided all the legal guidance that Islamic judges needed.

The triumph of scholars such as Shafi'i marked an important development in the Muslim world. It placed the ulama, the Muslim scholars, at the heart of Islam. Ulama, not princes and kings, became the lawmakers, insisting that the caliphs could not define or make religious law. Only the scholarly class had the right to interpret the Quran and determine which hadith were authentic. The emergence of the ulama opened a sharp division within Islam between the secular realm, where the caliphs and their representatives exercised power, and the religious sphere, where a wide range of religious officials and scholars—judges (*qudah,* or qadis), experts on Islamic jurisprudence or *fiqh,* teachers, and holy men (*a'immah,* or imams)—held forth.

RALLYING POINTS: GENDER IN EARLY ISLAM An area in which early Islam adapted new rules to older arrangements was its handling of the relations between men and women. Pre-Islamic Arabia was one of the last regions in Southwest Asia where patriarchy had not triumphed. Instead, men still married into women's families and moved to their wives' locations, as was common in tribal communities. Some women were known to engage in a variety of occupations and even, if they became wealthy, to marry more than one husband. But here, too, the status of women was changing, as the communities of Arabia became more settled and entered into closer contact with the rest of Southwest Asia.

Muhammad's own personal biography and his evolving relations with women reflected the changes that were occurring around him. As a young man, he married a woman fifteen years his senior—Khadija, an independent trader—and took no other wives before she died. During some of the crucial battles between Mecca and Medina, he allowed women to fight at his side. Later in life, however, he took younger wives and insisted on their veiling. He married his favorite wife, Aisha, when she was only nine or ten.

Hence, by the time that Islam spread through Southwest Asia and North Africa, where strict gender rules existed and where women had already become deeply subordinated to men, the new faith had already begun to accommodate itself to the already-established patriarchal way of life. Muslim men could divorce freely; women could not. A man could take four wives and numerous concubines, while a woman could have only a single husband. Well-to-do women were veiled and lived secluded from male society. Still, the Quran did offer women some protections. Men were required to treat each wife with respect if they took more than one. Women could inherit property, although only a half of what a man received. Infanticide was prohibited. Marriage dowries were paid directly to the bride rather than to the bride's guardian, indicating that women had independent legal standing; and while a woman's adultery was harshly punished, its proof required eyewitness testimony. The result was a legal system that helped reinforce the dominance of men over women but gave to magistrates superior powers to oversee the definition of male honor and proper behavior.

THE BLOSSOMING OF ABBASID CULTURE

The arts flourished during the Abbasid period, a blossoming that left its imprint throughout society. Within a century, Arabic had superseded Greek as the world's most widely used language in poetry, literature, medicine, science, and philosophy. Like Greek, it spread beyond its native speakers to become the language of the educated classes. Arabic scholarship made many important contributions to the world of learning, including the preservation and extension of Greek and Roman thought and the transmission of Greek and Latin treatises to Europe. Scholars at Baghdad translated the principal works of Aristotle; essays by Plato's followers; many works by Hippocrates, Ptolemy, and Archimedes; and above all the medical treatises of Galen, the second-century CE court physician. This extensive borrowing exemplified the most substantial effort by one culture to assimilate the learning of other peoples since the Roman conquest of Greece. To house these and other scholarly manuscripts, the patrons of the arts and sciences, including the caliphs themselves, opened massive—and magnificent—libraries.

The acts of borrowing, translating, storing, and diffusing written works helped bring worlds together. The Muslim world in this period absorbed the scientific breakthroughs of China and other areas and circulated them throughout thee Islamic world and beyond, incorporating into its societies the use of paper from China, siege warfare from China and Byzantium, and knowledge of plants from the old Greek texts. From Indian sources, scholars borrowed a numbering system based on the concept of zero and units of ten—what we today call Arabic numerals. Arab mathematicians were pioneers in

PREMODERN LIBRARIES: FROM ROYAL ARCHIVES TO REPOSITORIES OF UNIVERSAL KNOWLEDGE

Libraries invariably accompanied urbanization, centralized governments, and writing. Not surprisingly, in the ninth and tenth centuries the biggest, most carefully organized, and most actively used were found in the Islamic and Chinese empires. These were the great centers of learning and government; their cultures extolled the written word. Respect for books and libraries was especially plentiful in the Islamic world, for in the Quran Muhammad had brought the very words of God to his followers. Later generations added to Islam's religious traditions by collecting sayings attributed to the Prophet and the Prophet's companions and the early caliphs (hadith), writing treatises on religious law (the sharia), and assimilating the knowledge of the Greeks, Persians, Indians, and Chinese when they overran their territories or came into contact with their merchants, travelers, and scholars. Moreover, since Egypt and Southwest Asia had seen the world's earliest writing, these areas—the heartland of Islam—already had strong literary and library traditions in place.

The world's very first libraries arose, predictably, in Mesopotamia, where writing itself first appeared. These libraries were quite different from modern repositories of learning. They did house literary masterpieces, like the Sumerian *Epic of Gilgamesh,* but their principal function was to serve as government archives, holding the important records of the kings and the state to which future rulers and government bureaucrats might need to refer. The library often considered to be the first storehouse of written materials was that created by King Ashurbanipal II of Assyria, who ruled over the Assyrian Empire from his capital city at Nineveh in the seventh century BCE. Like other monarchs aspiring to universal sway, he set about to collect all significant literary works. His library, which numbered perhaps as many as 25,000 tablets, contained omens, incantations, and hymns; it also held the literatures of the many Mesopotamian languages, including Assyrian, Sumerian, Ugaritic, and Aramaic.

Because the "books" of King Ashurbanipal II's library were clay tablets etched in cuneiform, hardened through baking in kilns, they were safe from the destroyer of many later libraries—fire. Those in its famous successor in Alexandria were not so fortunate. That magnificent library was established by Ptolemy I and Ptolemy II (ruled 323–285, 285–246 BCE), two enlightened kings who believed that the arts, sciences, and literature of the Greeks were unmatched in the world and had to be preserved for future generations. They set their administrators the task of collecting anything written in Greek. Though the size of Alexandria's holdings (housed in several buildings) is unknown, it was by all estimates almost unimaginably large for this period, whether as little as 40,000 scrolls or, at the other extreme, half a million separate works. But beginning in the first century BCE, these collections were repeatedly subject to burning and looting. By the fourth century CE, an immense body of literature had been almost wiped out, and the peoples of this region in Afro-Eurasia were forced to start over again.

The Muslims led the way, as impressive and large libraries arose in the heartland of Islam. They appeared first in the early mosques, including those in Cairo, Damascus, and Baghdad. But book and manuscript collecting spread rapidly to the outskirts of the Islamic world, where libraries

arithmetic, geometry, and algebra, and they expanded the frontiers of plane and spherical trigonometry.

ISLAM IN A WIDER WORLD

As Islam spread and became more decentralized, it gave rise to a series of dazzling and often competitive dynasties in Spain, North Africa, and points further east in central Asia. Each of these dynastic states put on display the Muslim talent for achieving high levels of artistry in locations far from the political and cultural heartland. Spreading the message brought more and more peoples under the roof provided by the Quran, its priests, and its scholarly interpreters. Such expansion invigorated a world of Islamic learning and science. But the growing diversity of peoples gave rise to a problem: the political structures Islam invented could not hold its widely dispersed believers under a single regime. Many legal elements were shared, especially those controlled by Islamic texts and its enforcers. But when it came to secular power, Islam was deeply divided—and remains so to this day. (See Map 9-4.)

in Timbuktu in West Africa, Samarkand in central Asia, and Jakarta in Southeast Asia earned deservedly high reputations for their extraordinary collections of religious and scientific treatises.

Compared with those in Christian Europe, the Muslim libraries were immense. The library at Cordova in Muslim Spain at the end of the tenth century was reported to hold 600,000 books, or more than two books for every household in the city. Ibn Sina, the great Muslim scholar of the eleventh century, marveled at the library holdings at the Saminid court in Persia. There he found Greek books that he had not seen anywhere else and that most of the best Muslim scholars barely knew of. Probably the largest collection of them all was Cairo's vast library, known as the House of Learning, assembled over time by the Fatimid caliphs. At its height at the beginning of the eleventh century, when the caliph al-Hakim merged his collection with that of one of his predecessors, the caliph al-Aziz, the collection was said to number 1.5 million books. By contrast, Germany's Reichenau, one of the largest monastic libraries in Christian Europe, the West, had only 450 volumes in parchment—almost one-third of them prayer books. It did, however, have a catalog and a system of interlibrary loans that served monasteries spread across Germany, northern Italy, and France.

As befit another empire that had a strong literary tradition and relied on written records for administrative purposes, China was very much the equal of the Islamic world in its wealth of libraries. Indeed, the Chinese had many advantages over the western neighbors with whom they shared the Afro-Eurasian landmass. They had invented paper during the Western Han Dynasty and printing during the Tang era. As a result, scholarship, book production, and libraries became vital ingredients of the cultural fabric of China. Accompanying the highbrow classical works printed for literati during the Tang and Song dynasties were lowbrow works of popular literature and primers that circulated more widely among a commoner audience.

The Chinese infatuation with the printed word and book collecting led to the emergence of a small, elite class of bibliophiles. These individuals located source materials and created the reference works necessary to found coherent scholarly disciplines. Although Chinese libraries housed printed books, unpublished manuscripts formed a more substantial portion of many collections.

During the Han, private libraries did not exceed 10,000 "rolls" (each holding about a chapter) of books or manuscripts. But in the Tang era, many Buddhist monasteries accumulated thousands of books and religious sutras. Some 30,000 rolls, for example, survived in the precious Buddhist grottoes of Dunhuang along the Silk Road, which were made public in 1907. The largest collection was gathered at the emperor's command to form the imperial library in the capital. Bibliophiles played an important role in creating the Tang imperial library, which was staffed by tens of scholars who as collators and editors recompiled the Confucian classics and dynastic histories for the examination system and for posterity. The Tang imperial catalog indicates that by the early eighth century, the imperial library contained some 54,000 unique titles and, including duplicates, about 200,000 rolls. Then as now, libraries were crucial repositories of knowledge and culture.

SPAIN One such Muslim state that vied with the others arose in Spain under that region's most dynamic ruler, Abd al-Rahman III, al-Nasir (the Victorious), who reigned from 912 until 961 CE. The Muslim kingdom in Iberia had been founded at the time of the Abbasid revolution of 750 CE, when a member of the defeated Umayyad family fled Damascus and established an independent kingdom in Spain. Abd al-Rahman brought peace and stability to a frontier region whose commerce and intellectual exchanges had been disrupted by civil conflict and much violence. His evenhanded approach to governance facilitated amicable relations among the Muslims, Christians, and Jews, and his extensive diplomatic relations with Christian potentates as far away as France, Germany, and Scandinavia promoted prosperity among all of the communities of western Europe and North Africa. He expanded and beautified the capital city of Cordova, and his successor, al-Hakim II, made the Great Mosque of Cordova one of Spain's most stunning sites. With room for 20,000 worshippers, it could have comfortably held the total population of Paris in the mid–tenth century!

As in the Mediterranean lands and Southwest Asia after Alexander the Great, competition between rival rulers spurred

MAP 9-4   POLITICAL FRAGMENTATION IN THE ISLAMIC WORLD, 750–1000

By 1000, the Islamic world was politically fractured and decentralized. The Abbasid caliphs still reigned in Baghdad, but they wielded very limited political authority. Why were Abbasid caliphs unable to create and sustain political unity in the Islamic world? In what regions, according to the map, did other Islamic powers emerge? How did the Sunni-Shiite schism among the Islamic faithful contribute to political decentralization?

creativity in the arts. By the tenth century, the Islamic world resembled a series of dazzling lanterns, each vying to exceed the brightness of the others as each powerful center strove to outdo the others in glory. Abd al-Rahman built an extravagant city, Madinat al-Zahra, next to Cordova; it was intended to overshadow the splendor of Islam's most fabled cities, including Baghdad and al-Qayrawān, the great North African city in northeast Tunisia. He surrounded the main administrative offices and mosque of its city center with gardens, pools, fountains, and aqueducts. Madinat al-Zahra was meant to be paradise on earth.

A CENTRAL ASIAN GALAXY OF TALENT At the other end of the Islamic empire, 8,000 miles east of Spain, the region beyond the Oxus River in central Asia experienced an equally spectacular cultural flowering in the eighth and ninth

centuries. In a territory where Greek culture had once sparkled and where Sogdians had emerged as the leading intellectuals, Islam now became the dominant faith and the source of intellectual ferment. The Abbasid rulers in Baghdad delighted in surrounding themselves with learned men from this region in whose accomplishments they took great pride. The famous Barmaki family, who for several generations held high administrative offices during the Abbasid caliphate, came from the central Asian city of Balkh. They had been Buddhists living close to the great carved Buddhas of Bamiyan (see Chapter 8). The Barmakis prospered under Islam and enjoyed remarkable influence in Baghdad. According to the tenth-century Arab historian Ali al-Mas'udi, the Barmaki family was responsible for building the Abbasid bureaucratic system and opening the Islamic world to many inventions from Central Asia, including papermaking. Loyal

> → *What factors created a common cultural outlook among Muslim communities in Afro-Eurasia during this era?*

The Great Mosque of Cordova. The great mosque of Cordova was built in the tenth century by the caliph al-Hakim II, who succeeded Abd al-Rahman III, considered by many historians to have been the most powerful and effective of the Spanish Umayyad caliphs.

servants of the caliph, they ensured that all the wealth and talent from the crossroads of Asia made their way to Baghdad, as they themselves had done.

In turn, the Barmakis aided their native region as patrons of the arts. They collected and had Arabic translations made of Persian, Greek, and Sanskrit manuscripts, and they encouraged scholars from central Asia to enhance their learning by moving to Baghdad. One of their protégés, the highly regarded Islamic cleric al-Bukhari (d. 870 CE), from Bukhara, was Islam's most dedicated collector of hadith, which provided vital knowledge about the Prophet's life.

Others from the area made notable contributions to science and mathematics. Al-Khwarizmi (c. 780–850 CE) modified the Indian digits into Arabic numerals, wrote the first book on algebra, and through the Latinized version of his name is the source of the word *algorithm*. He became one of the most valued members of Baghdad's famous translation center, the House of Knowledge, using his deep familiarity with the geography of the regions described by the Alexandrian polymath Ptolemy (fl. 127–148 CE) to correct many of Ptolemy's mistakes. The renowned Abbasid philosopher al-Farabi (d. 950 CE), from a Turkish military family, also made his way to Baghdad, where he studied Hellenistic Christian teachings. Although he regarded himself as a Muslim, he thought formal religions were for the common people, not

Materia Medica. A page from an Arabic translation of the classical text of Dioscorides, *Materia Medica*. The translated text is dated to 1224 and comes from Iraq, which was one of the centers for the translation of classical Greek and Roman works into Arabic.

the intellectual elite. In his view, good societies would naturally embrace the idea of a single God, but they would succeed only if their rulers implemented the political tenets espoused in Plato's *Republic*. He championed a virtuous "first chief" to rule over an Islamic commonwealth in much the same way that Plato had favored a philosopher-king.

As the power of the Abbasid caliphate began to decline in the eleventh century because of the same problems that had faced the Roman Empire—overextension and the influx of outsider groups—scholars from central Asia no longer made the trek to the caliph's court at Baghdad. Yet the intellectual vitality of central Asia did not suffer, for young men of learning began to find patrons among local rulers. Consider Ibn Sina, known in the West as Avicenna (980–1037 ce). He never made it to Baghdad; he grew to adulthood in Bukhara, practiced medicine in the courts of various Islamic rulers, and spent the last fifteen years of his life in Isfahan, in central Persia. Schooled in the Quran, the Arabic secular literature known as *adab*, philosophy, geometry, and Indian and Euclidean mathematics, Ibn Sina had mastery over many disciplines. His *Canon of Medicine* was the standard medical text in both Southwest Asia and Europe for centuries.

ISLAM IN SUB-SAHARAN AFRICA Islam also crossed the Sahara and entered Africa, carried by traders and scholars rather than by soldiers. (See Map 9-5.) Its movement depended largely on camels, which were domesticated well before the Common Era but were not used for crossing the Sahara Desert until the third century CE; these animals, able to carry heavy loads and to go weeks without water, enabled long-distance traders to traverse the deserts with almost as much ease as they traveled through settled areas and across seas. By the seventh and eighth centuries, large numbers of Islamic adventurers were arriving in sub-Saharan West Africa, where in exchange for weapons and textiles they received gold, salt, and slaves. The lively trading networks included the old city of Jenne in modern-day Mali, whose archaeological remains can be dated to around 400 BCE. Four centuries later, it had become a bustling entrepôt, with residences and town buildings taking up about 100 acres and surrounded by a large protective wall.

Trade did more than join West Africa to North Africa. It also generated wealth, which in turn facilitated the creation of centralized political kingdoms in West Africa. The most celebrated of these kingdoms was Ghana, located north and east of the modern country of that name, in the eastern region of modern Mauritania. It lay at the terminus of North Africa's major trading routes.

Of Ghana, we know little. The first to mention it was the Baghdadi scholar al-Fazari, who in the eighth century described Ghana as "the land of gold." A century later, the Arab traveler and geographer al-Yaqubi wrote of "the kingdom of Ghana, the king of which is very powerful. In his country there are gold mines. Under his authority are other kingdoms

Ibn Sina. Ibn Sina was a versatile scholar, most famous for his *Canon of Medicine,* which was for centuries the standard medical text in Southwest Asia and Europe.

. . . and gold is found in all of these regions" (Fage, p. 15). Although Muslim traders frequented the state, its rulers were not Muslims. Still, the pomp and power of the state impressed visitors; in 1067–1068, the Andalusian geographer al-Bakri wrote of a powerful and resplendent king who heard "grievances against officials in a domed pavilion around which stand ten horses covered with gold-embroidered materials.

→ *What factors created a common cultural outlook among Muslim communities in Afro-Eurasia during this era?*

Direction of trade
Trade route
Extent of the Ghana Empire, c. 1050 CE
Swahili settlement in the 14th century

Commodities
△ Salt
⬭ Gold
⬤⬤⬤ Slaves
✕ Weapons
◣ Textiles

▨ Gold source
▲ Major salt source

MAP 9-5 ISLAM AND TRADE IN SUB-SAHARAN AFRICA, 700–1000

Islamic merchants and scholars, not Islamic armies, carried Islam into sub-Saharan Africa soon after their religion emerged. According to the map, what kinds of goods were Islamic merchants seeking below the Sahara? How did increased trade with the broader Afro-Eurasian world affect societies below the Sahara? How did trade and commerce lead to the further geographic expansion of the Islamic faith?

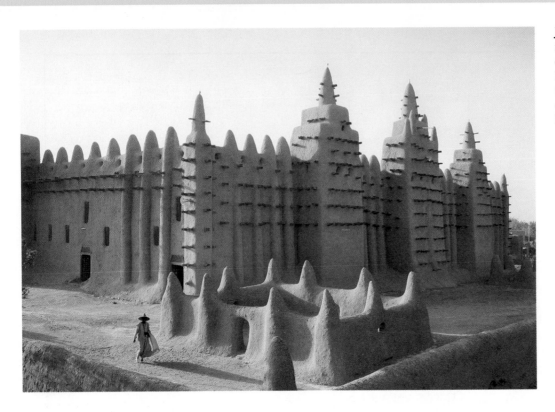

Jenne Mosque. This fabulous mosque arose in the kingdom of Mali when it was at the height of its power. It speaks to the depth and importance of Islam's roots in the Malian kingdom.

Behind the king stand ten pages holding shields and swords decorated with gold and on his right are the sons of the (vassal) kings of his country wearing splendid garments and their hair plaited with gold" (Levtzion and Spaulding, p. 16).

Seafaring Muslim traders carried Islam into East Africa as Islam became a dominant mercantile force in the Indian Ocean. A small Islamic trading community had come into being in the eighth century at Lamu, along the northern coast of present-day Kenya. By the middle of the ninth century, other East African coastal trading communities had sprung up. On the island of Pate, off the coast of Kenya, the inhabitants of Shanga constructed the region's first mosque, a simple structure replaced 200 years later by a mosque capable of holding all of the adult members of the community when they gathered for their Friday prayers. These communities, an amalgam of African and Arab populations, exported ivory and possibly slaves. Already by the tenth century, the East African coast featured a mixed African-Arab culture. The evolving Bantu language of the region took in Arabic loanwords—at first a few and later, especially after the fifteenth century, many more—and before long was given a new name, Swahili (derived from the Arabic plural of the word meaning "coast").

OPPOSITION WITHIN ISLAM, SHIISM, AND THE RISE OF THE FATIMIDS

Islam's whirlwind rise generated internal tensions from the start. Such a powerful religious movement fostered a shared reverence for a basic text and a single God. But there was not much else that was shared. The divisions were apparent from the time of Muhammad's proselytizing campaigns, and only grew deeper as Islam spread into new corners of Eurasia and Africa. Once the charismatic Prophet died, in 632 CE, the latent fissures came to the surface as believers disagreed over who should take his place and how to preserve some authority. Strains associated with the selection of the first four caliphs after Muhammad's death left a legacy of protest; to this day, they represent the greatest challenge facing Islam in its efforts to create a unified culture.

Early and spirited opposition originated during the seventh century among a group calling itself the Kharijites, who came together in Arabia during the dispute over the succession to Muhammad. Spurning all of the conservatives' choices for caliphs, the Kharijites believed that the rulers of Islam should only be individuals of impeccable religious credentials—individuals who most resembled Muhammad himself. The doctrine found support especially among those peoples who felt deprived of power, appealing to the highlander Berber peoples of North Africa and the inhabitants of lower Iraq, who complained that the leaders of the faith discriminated against them, despite the teaching that all Muslims belonged equally to the community of believers.

The Kharijite movement died out. It was too individualistic to challenge the authority of established political elites. But another, more powerful, movement of opposition arose in many of the same areas where Kharijism had been influential. In North Africa, lower Iraq, and the Iranian plateau, the mat-

Primary Source

GHANA AS SEEN BY A MUSLIM OBSERVER IN THE ELEVENTH CENTURY

The following excerpt is taken from a manuscript written in the eleventh century by a Muslim serving under the Umayyad regime in Spain. Its author, Abdullah Abu Ubayd al-Bakri, produced a massive general geography and history of the known world, as did many of the most accomplished Muslim scholars of this period. This manuscript has special value because it provides information about West Africa, a region in which the Spanish rulers had a great interest and into which Islam had been spreading for several centuries.

Ghana is the title of the king of the people. The name of the country is Aoukar. The ruler who governs the people at the present time—the year 460 AH (after the Hijra and 1067–68 CE)—is called Tenkamein. He came to the throne in 455 AH. His predecessor, who was named Beci, began his reign at the age of 85. He was a prince worthy of great praise as much for his personal conduct as for his zeal in the pursuit of justice and his friendship to Muslims. . . .

Ghana is composed of two towns situated in a plain. The one inhabited by Muslims is large and contains twelve mosques, in which the congregants celebrate the Friday prayer. All of these mosques have their imams, their muezzins, and their salaried readers. The city possesses judges and men of great erudition. . . . The city where the king resides is six miles away and carries the name el-Ghaba, meaning "the forest." The territory separating these two locations is covered with dwellings, constructed out of rocks and the wood of the acacia tree. The dwelling of the king consists of a chateau and several surrounding huts, all of which are enclosed by a wall-like structure. In the ruler's town, close to the royal tribunal, is a mosque where Muslims come when they have business with the ruler in order to carry out their prayers. . . . The royal interpreters are chosen from the Muslim population, as was the state treasurer and the majority of the state ministers. . . .

The opening of a royal meeting is announced by the noise of a drum, which they call a *deba*, and which is formed from a long piece of dug-out wood. Upon hearing the drumming, the inhabitants assemble. When the king's coreligionists appear before him, they genuflect and throw dust on their heads. Such is the way in which they salute their sovereign. The Muslims show their respect for the king by clapping their hands. The religion of the Negroes is paganism and fetishism. . . . The land of Ghana is not healthy and has few people. Travelers who pass through the area during the height of the agricultural season are rarely able to avoid becoming sick. When the grains are at their fullest and are ready for harvesting is the time when mortality affects visitors.

The best gold in the land comes from Ghiarou, a town located eighteen days journey from the capital. All of the gold found in the mines of the empire belongs to the sovereign, but the sovereign allows the people to take gold dust. Without this precaution, the gold would become so abundant that it would lose much of its value. . . . It is claimed that the king owns a piece of gold as large as an enormous rock.

→ *From this excerpt, how much can you learn about the kingdom of Ghana?*
→ *What influence did Islam have in the empire?*
→ *What elements of Ghana most interested the author, al-Bakri?*

SOURCE: Abou-Obeïd-el-Bekri, *Description de l'Afrique septentrionale*, revised and corrected edition, translated by [William] Mac Guckin de Slane (Paris: A. Maisonneuve, 1965), pp. 327–31; translated from the French by Robert Tignor.

ter of who should succeed the Prophet and how the succession should take place was a source of fundamental disagreement from the outset. Some repudiated the Umayyad and Abbasid rulers and the claims to succession defended by those who came to be known as Sunnis (from the Arabic word meaning "tradition"). Among the earliest dissidents were the Shiites (literally, members of the party of Ali), who believed that the proper successors to the Prophet should have been Ali, who had married the Prophet's daughter Fatima, and his descendants. Shiites also believed that Ali's descendants, whom they called imams, had religious and prophetic power as well as political authority and should enjoy spiritual primacy even over

Muslim scholars with more extensive religious training. Like Kharijism, Shiism appealed to groups whom the Umayyads and Abbasids had excluded from power; it became Islam's most potent dissident force and created a permanent divide within Islam. Shiism was well established in the first century of Islam's existence.

But not until the tenth century, after nearly 300 years of struggling, did the Shiites finally seize power. Repressed in Iraq and Iran, Shiite activists made their way to North Africa, where they joined with dissident Berber groups to bring down several rulers. In 909 CE, a Shiite religious and military leader, Abu Abdallah, overthrew the Sunni ruler in North Africa. Thus began the Fatimid regime; after conquering Egypt in 969 CE, it set itself against the Abbasid caliphs of Baghdad, refusing to acknowledge their legitimacy and claiming authority to speak for the whole of the Islamic world. The Fatimid rulers established their capital in a new city that arose alongside al-Fustat, the old Umayyad capital. They called this place al-Qahira (or Cairo), "the Victorious." Although intended simply as a royal refuge, Cairo soon overshadowed al-Fustat, and the Fatimid rulers promoted its beauty. One of their first acts was the founding of a place of worship and learning, the Azhar mosque, which attracted scholars from all over Afro-Eurasia and spread Islamic learning outward from Egypt; they also built other elegant mosques and centers of learning. The Fatimid regime remained in power until the end of the twelfth century, though its rulers made little headway in persuading the Egyptian population to embrace their Shiite beliefs.

By 1000 CE Islam had become the dominant political and cultural force in the middle regions of the Afro-Eurasian landmass. At Afro-Eurasia's peripheries, its armies, merchants, and scholars had finally run out of energy, leaving much of western Europe and China outside the Islamic domain. Moreover, by the beginning of the new millennium Muslims were ceasing to be a minority within their own lands. A rapidly increasing rate of conversions reduced the Christian, Jewish, and other non-Muslim populations living in polities ruled by Muslim kings and princes. Yet the political unification of the whole Muslim world had not followed. Although the Abbasid caliphate made claims to universal political power, breakaway regimes disputed these claims. Powerful separatist Muslim states emerged in Spain and North Africa.

THE TANG STATE

> → *How did the Tang state balance its desire to restore Confucian principles to China with the growth of new universal religions in East Asia?*

The rise of the Sui (581–618 CE) and Tang (618–907 CE) empires in China and their pervasive impact on Korea and Japan paralleled Islam's explosion out of Arabia in the seventh cen-

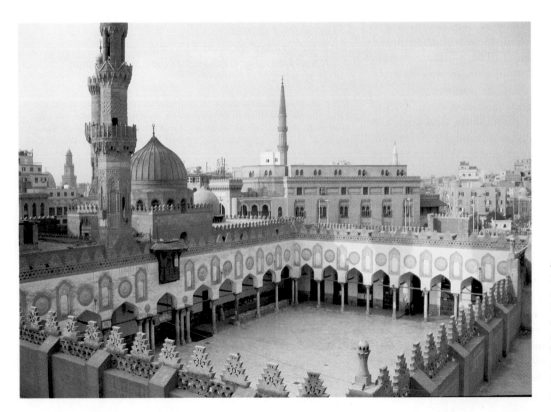

Al-Azhar Mosque. The mosque of al-Azhar is Cairo's most important ancient mosque. Built in the tenth century by the Fatimid conquerors and rulers of Egypt, it quickly became a leading center for worship and learning, frequented by Muslim clerics and admired in Europe.

tury and its rise to prominence throughout Afro-Eurasia in the eighth, ninth, and tenth centuries. Once again, the Afro-Eurasian landmass had two centers of power. Islam, stretching to Africa and Iberia, replaced the Roman Empire in providing a counterbalance to the power and wealth of China.

But in one fundamental way, this bipolar world differed from that of the Roman and Han empires: in the centuries since their waning, Eurasian and African worlds had been brought much closer together by trade, conversion, and more regular political contacts. The two most powerful political and cultural systems of Afro-Eurasia now had common borders. They converged and then competed for dominance in central Asia, were influenced by one another and even shared populations, admired features of the other, and encouraged travelers and traders to share information about the other society. The world had, indeed, become smaller. Peoples, ideas (especially technological innovations), and commodities moved rapidly across political boundaries.

Yet in China, religion did not play the role in shaping the formation of states and empires seen in the rest of Afro-Eurasia. Instead, its religious and political histories ran on separate but not parallel rails. China's political fortunes did not rest nearly as much on sacred foundations as did the smaller dynasties of India or Europe, or the powerhouse of the caliphate and Islam. Underneath a single dynastic and imperial culture in China lay a plurality of religions and sects—an amalgamation of belief systems rather than a single integrated culture functioning as the polity's bulwark. In this regard, China exemplifies the many ways in which Eurasian and African worlds balanced the forces of integration and diversity as they neared the end of the first millennium.

China was both at the receiving end of foreign influences and a source of influences on its neighbors. Indeed, it was becoming the hub of East Asian integration. Like the Umayyads and the Abbasids, the Tang promoted a cosmopolitan culture that absorbed and digested many new cultural elements arising at a great distance. Buddhism, medicine, and mathematics from India via central Asia gave China's chief cities an international flavor. Buddhist monks from Bactria; Greeks, Armenians, and Jews from Constantinople; Muslim envoys from Samarkand and Persia; Vietnamese tributary missions from Annam; chieftains of nomadic tribes from the Siberian plains; officials and students from Korea; and monkish visitors from Japan rubbed elbows in the streets of the dual Tang capitals at Chang'an and Luoyang, previously the Qin and Han capitals. Ideas floated to the east as well—notably in the middle of the first millennium CE, when the early societies and states in Korea and Japan emerged in the shadow of China. Even when China was disunited politically after the fall of the Han, the impact of Chinese religions, particularly Daoism and Buddhism, in Korea and then Japan was marked. Similarly, Chinese statecraft—as enunciated principally through the Confucian classics—seemed to the early Korean and Japanese scholars and courtiers to provide the best and most universally applicable model for their own state building.

Yet conversely, even during the Tang dynasty (608–907 CE), when the Chinese empire revived as never before, China's impact on Korea and Japan was limited. The latter never became "little Chinas." Each culture adapted and appropriated Chinese institutions, values, and religions in ways that suited its own political and social conditions. To be sure, for the sake of trade relations each paid lip service to the Middle Kingdom's efforts to define them as subordinate states that had to pay tribute in their economic and diplomatic exchanges with China. But each maintained cultural autonomy and often turned Chinese learning and cultural and political concepts to its own purposes, sometimes with unexpected consequences.

Throughout its history, China was the "Middle Kingdom" (*Zhongguo*), but this name mainly differentiated between those who considered themselves Chinese and those who were seen as outsiders. During the Warring States era (see Chapter 5), the key states were referred to in aggregate as "Zhongguo," that is, the "middle states." Under the Tang, the name differentiated the "Middle Kingdom" of China proper from her non-Chinese provinces. During the Song and thereafter, the term demarcated the Middle Kingdom (and its Han civilization) from the steppe barbarians (and their allegedly uncivilized ways). The Mongol and Manchu conquests of China made this last distinction moot, as they both equated their dynasties with the Middle Kingdom.

CHINESE TERRITORIAL EXPANSION UNDER THE SUI AND TANG DYNASTIES

After the fall of the Han in 220 CE, China faced a long period of political instability (see Chapter 8). But it was only a matter of time before a new set of the rulers (the Sui and Tang) took advantage of military weaknesses and political fragmentation to restore Han models of empire building. Their claims that a big imperial system could outperform small states found a receptive audience in a populace fatigued by internal chaos. Both dynasties expanded the boundaries of the Chinese state and reestablished China's dominance in East and central Asia.

Leading the way back to empire was Yang Jian, who had served as an official of the militarily strong Northern Zhou dynasty (557–580 CE). His struggles for unification ended in the Sui dynasty, which heralded the revival of Han imperial ideals. The Sui reunification continued reforms begun at the Northern Zhou court that were aimed at enhancing the state's power over the aristocracy. The two emperors of Sui, Wendi (ruled 581–604 CE) and Yangdi (ruled 605–616 CE), father and son, championed the notion that bigger is better as they channeled the state's domestic energy into territorial expansion into Korea, Vietnam, Manchuria, Tibet, and central Asia. Yet those efforts, particularly the costly and disastrous military campaigns undertaken against Silla Korea in the early seventh century, fatally weakened the dynasty. In addition, as so often occurred throughout Chinese history (e.g., see Chapter 7), a precipitous change in the course of the Yellow River, causing extensive flooding on the North China plain, led to popular revolts; they set the stage for Li Yuan, a Sui general, to march on Chang'an and take the throne for himself. Li Yuan promptly established the new Tang dynasty in 618 CE and began building a powerful central government. He increased the number of prefectures and counties and expanded the bureaucracy. By doubling the number of government offices, the emperor tightened his control over individual governors. By 624 CE the initial steps needed to found the new Tang dynasty had been completed. (See Map 9-6.)

THE ARMY AND IMPERIAL CAMPAIGNING

An expanding Tang state required a large and professionally trained army, capable of defending far-flung frontiers and squelching recalcitrant populations. The military organization created by the Tang emperors consisted of aristocratic cavalry and peasant soldiers. The aristocrats were used primarily on the northern steppes in Inner Eurasia to deal with nomadic peoples, who similarly fought mounted; at its height the Tang military had some 700,000 horses. At the same time, between 1 and 2 million peasant soldiers garrisoned the south and were also used for public work projects.

MAP 9-6   THE TANG STATE IN EAST ASIA

The Tang dynasty, at its territorial peak in 750, was the most powerful, most advanced, and best administered empire in the world. It controlled a state that extended from central Asia to the East China Sea. How did Tang rulers promote order and stability in such a diverse realm? In particular, how did they foster and try to control the growth and spread of religious communities? According to the map, how did Tang policies promote an economic revolution in China? To what extent did the empire influence other peoples in Afro-Eurasia not ruled directly ruled by the Tang state?

Much like the Islamic forces, the Tang's frontier armies, especially those that operated beyond the Great Wall—newly repaired now that China was reunified—became increasingly reliant on pastoral nomadic soldiers from the Inner Eurasian steppe. Notable among them were the Uighurs, Turkish-speaking steppe peoples who had moved into the Tarim basin in western China and who by 750 CE had become the most potent military force in the empire. The Tang military also enabled the westward expansion of the state, which brought the first Chinese penetration of parts of Tibet, then emerging as a powerful centralized kingdom in the southwest and along the Silk Road. The Red River valley in northern Vietnam and Manchuria in the north came under Chinese suzerainty as well. Briefly, Tang authority stretched from Tibet and central Asia to Korea.

Though it rested on earlier imperial foundations, the Tang's spread into East and central Asia was no less dramatic than the expansion of Islam. By 650 CE, as Islamic armies were moving toward central Asia, the Tang were already the new colossus of the region, claiming to have surpassed even the Han in scope and scale. At this empire's height, Tang armies controlled more than 4 million square miles of territory—an area that was as large as and was much more centrally administered than the whole of the Islamic world in the ninth and tenth centuries. The Tang population of more than 80 million surpassed the Han peak of 60 million and was far greater than the populations under Islamic rulers in the eighth and ninth centuries. Once the Tang administrators had brought the rich farmlands of South China under cultivation—draining swamps, building an intricate network of canals and channels to complement those in the north, and connecting lakes and rivers to the rice lands—the state was able to collect taxes from no fewer than 10 million families in agricultural labor, representing 57 million individuals.

In spite of the Abbasid Empire's precocious spread, China in 750 CE was the most powerful, most advanced, and best administered empire in the world. Korea and Japan, its neighbors in East Asia, recognized its superiority in every material aspect of life. Muslims were among the people who arrived from the four corners of the world to pay homage. Persians, Armenians, and Turks brought tribute and merchandise via the busy Silk Road or by sea, and other travelers and traders came from Southeast Asia and Japan.

This was the peak of Chinese power—at the very moment that the Abbasids were expanding into the Tang portions of central Asia. The map of Afro-Eurasia was now connected by bordering empires on the east and west, filling in the political landscape with powerful states, some of them bursting with religious energy. The rivalry for Afro-Eurasian supremacy brought the worlds together, but not peaceably. Muslim forces drove the Tang from Turkistan in 751 CE at the battle of Talas, and their success emboldened new groups such as the Sogdians and Tibetans to challenge the Tang in the west. As a result, the Tang were forced to retreat from central Asia

and mainland Southeast Asia into the old heartlands of China along the Yellow and Yangzi rivers. Even in the Wei River valley, Chinese rulers saw their capital in Chang'an fall to invading Tibetans and Sogdians in the middle of the eighth century. Misrule, court intrigues, economic exploitation, and popular rebellions weakened the empire, but the dynasty held on for over a century more until northern invaders brought an end to it in 907 CE. The next half century saw the fragmentation of China into five northern dynasties and ten southern kingdoms, a brief repeat of the era of disunity after the fall of the Han dynasty in 220 CE. Wars and rebellions devastated the population.

ORGANIZING AN EMPIRE

The Tang empire was a worthy successor to the Han and deservedly ranks as one of China's great dynastic polities. In its nearly 300-year tenure, it was exceeded only by the Han (202 BCE–220 CE) and it surpassed the Ming (1368–1644) and Qing (1644–1912) dynasties, China's other long-lasting empires. Although Tang rulers emulated the Han in many ways, including the compilation of their own legal code (which drew heavily on that of the Han) in 624 CE, they also introduced new institutions, the most significant and enduring of which was the imperial examination system. Moreover, as an empire in an age of universalistic and proselytizing religions, the Tang had to deal with the arrival of global religions inside their borders and accommodate these new religious institutions and agents within their imperial framework. Its methods for achieving and maintaining power often differed from those employed by the Abbasid Empire, Afro-Eurasia's other superpower at this time.

CONFUCIAN ADMINISTRATORS Even though the Tang ultimately relied on military force, their day-to-day control of

China Trade. In this seventh-century silk painting, we see envoys from the busy Silk Road bearing tribute to gain access to the lucrative China trade.

the empire depended on an efficient and loyal civil service. Unlike the multilingual, multiethnic, and even multireligious Islamic empire, which was held together by a shared spiritual commitment to Islam, the Tang had to devise other formulas for integrating their remote territories and diverse ethnicities and linguistic groups. Instead of a single universalizing faith, the Tang provided the political framework for a spiritual mosaic of Buddhism, Confucianism, and Daoism. In some areas, local deities continued to flourish. Rather than relying on a world religion to anchor their empire, to maintain order the Tang created a formidable and unifying political culture based on Confucian teachings composed in the classical written language that was mastered by Mandarin-speaking officials and China's educated elites.

Chinese integration began at the top. To enter the ruling group required knowing the ideas of Confucius and all of the subsequent commentaries on the classics that he had transmitted to his disciples. It also entailed handling the intricacies of the classical Chinese language, in which all such literature was written. These skills were as powerful in forging cultural and political solidarity as Islam was for the Abbasid state or Christianity for Europe and the Byzantine Empire. Thus a common written language (classical Chinese) and a common philosophy (Confucianism) served as a surrogate for the universalistic religions that created common cultures elsewhere in Eurasia and Africa. Confucian thought, learned and embraced by a privileged group of individuals from elite families, provided a set of common characteristics for the rulers and administrators of Tang society. Indeed, we have seen that the adoption of a common language—Latin, Greek, Arabic—at least among elites, can be a powerful element unifying an empire.

Of the highest importance in exalting the powers of the Tang state was the world's first written civil service examination system. Examinations now became the mechanism for making knowledge of a specific language and the Confucian classics the only route to power and the means of uniting the Chinese state, and no innovation was more significant for promoting the obedience and loyalty of state appointees. Candidates for office, whom local elites recommended, gathered in the capital to take qualifying examinations that required them to know the classics and display highly developed literary skills. Those who were successful underwent further trials to evaluate their character and determine the level of their appointments. New officials were selected from the pool of examination graduates on the basis of deportment, eloquence, skill in calligraphy and mathematics, and legal knowledge. When Emperor Li Shimin (ruled 627–649 CE) first observed the new officials obediently parading out of the examination hall, he slyly noted, "The heroes of the empire are all in my pocket!" (Miyazaki, *China's Examination Hell*, 13).

Having assumed the mandate of heaven (see Chapter 4), the Tang rulers and their supporters were intent on estab-

Tang Official. Tang officials were selected through competitive civil examinations in order to limit the power of Buddhist and Daoist clerics. This painted clay figure of a Tang official c. 717 was excavated in 1972.

lishing a common code of moral values for the whole empire. Building on Han models, they expanded the state school in the capital into an empire-wide hierarchy of select state schools that prepared those who had already mastered the required Confucian texts for the civil examinations. But Tang rulers and officials also favored the continued use of the Daoist classics as texts for the examinations, because the rulers and many elites still regarded the early Daoists as an important stream of ancient wisdom. What the Tang managed to do was to amalgamate this range of texts, codes, and

Primary Source

INTEGRATING EMPIRE BY EXAMINATION

The young and old competed equally in the Tang examination market, bringing different experiences into the examination halls. The rituals of success looked alluring to youths, while the tortures of failure were common among their older competitors still seeking an elusive degree. For all, however, the emotional tensions they felt when the list of successful candidates was posted—following years of preparation for young boys, and even more years of defeat for old men—were the private, human response to success or failure. The few that passed would look back on that day with relief and pride.

In the Southern Court they posted the list. (The Southern Court was where the Board of Rites ran the administration and accepted documents. All prescribed forms together with the stipulations for each [degree] category were usually publicized here.) The wall for hanging the list was by the eastern wall of the Southern Court. In a separate building a screen was erected which stood over ten feet tall, and it was surrounded with a fence. Before dawn they took the list from the Northern Court to the Southern Court where it was hung for display.

In the sixth year of Yuanhe [AD 811] a student at the University, Guo Dongli, broke through the thorn hedge. (The thorn hedge was below the fence. There was another

outside the main gate of the Southern Court.) He then ripped up the ornamental list [*wenbang*]. It was because of this that afterwards they often came out of the gateway of the Department [of State Affairs] with a mock list. The real list was displayed a little later.

→ *Why were the stakes so high in the civil examinations?*
→ *Was the Tang civil examination system an open system that tested talent—that is, a meritocracy?*
→ *What happened to those that failed?*

SOURCE: Wang Dingbao (870–940), quoted in Oliver J. Moore, *Rituals of Recruitment in Tang China* (Leiden: Brill, 2004), p. 175.

---

tests into a common intellectual and cultural credo for the governing classes.

CHINA'S FIRST FEMALE EMPEROR Not all Tang power brokers were men. Women also played influential roles in the court, usually behind the scenes—but sometimes publicly. Consider the example of Empress Wu, who dominated the Tang court in the late seventh and early eighth centuries. She deftly used the examination system to check the power of aristocratic families and helped consolidate courtly authority by creating cadres of loyal bureaucrats, who in turn preserved loyalty to the dynasty at the local level.

Born into a rich and noble family, Wu Zhao (626–706 CE) played music and mastered the Chinese classics as a young girl. By thirteen, because she was witty, intelligent, and beautiful, Wu was recruited to Li Shimin's court, where she soon became his favorite concubine. She also became enamored of

his son. When Li Shimin died, his son assumed power and became the Emperor Gaozong (ruled 649–683 CE). Wu quickly became the new emperor's favorite concubine as well and gave birth to the sons he required to succeed him. As the mother of the future emperor, Wu's prestige in court was heightened, and her political power grew. Subsequently, she took the place of Gaozong's Empress Wang by accusing her—falsely—of killing Wu's newborn daughter. Gaozong believed Wu and married her.

When Emperor Gaozong suffered a stroke in 660 CE, Wu Zhao became administrator of the court, a position equal to the emperor's. She created a secret police force to spy on her opposition, and she jailed or killed those who stood in her way, including the unfortunate Empress Wang. Upon the emperor's death, Wu outmaneuvered her eldest sons and placed her youngest son in power; she named herself as his regent. Shortly afterward she seized power in her own right as Empress Wu (ruled 684–705 CE), becoming the first and only female ruler in Chinese history, though initially reigning in the name of her son. She expanded the military and recruited her administrators from the civil examination candidates to oppose her enemies at court.

Challenging Confucian beliefs that subordinated women, Wu elevated their position. She ordered scholars to write biographies of famous women, and she empowered her mother's clan by giving her relatives by marriage high political posts. Later, she moved her court away from the seat of traditional power in Chang'an to Luoyang, where she tried to establish a new "Zhou dynasty" in imitation of the time of Confucius.

Despite the ruthlessness of her climb to power, her rule proved to be benign and competent. During her reign, Empress Wu elevated Buddhism over Daoism as the favored state religion. She invited the most gifted Buddhist religious scholars to her capital at Luoyang, built Buddhist temples, and subsidized the building of spectacular cave sculptures, particularly in northwest China. Chinese Buddhism achieved its highest officially sponsored development in this period.

As she grew older, Empress Wu lessened the power of her secret police, but she became superstitious and fearful. Sorcerers and corrupt court favorites flattered her. Finally, in 705 CE, she gave up the throne in favor of her third son. Later that year, she died in retirement at age eighty.

Although official careers were in theory open to anyone of talent, in practice members of many groups were excluded. Despite Empress Wu's prominence, women were not permitted to serve, nor were sons of merchants and those who could not afford a classical education. The Tang restored the Han dynasty state school in the capital, but because there were still no public schools, initially many candidates—as in Zhou and Han times—still came from aristocratic families. Tang civil examinations over time forced aristocrats to compete with rising southern families, commoners whose economic wealth and new educational resources made them the equals of the old elites. Under the banner of a classical meritocracy that Empress Wu enforced, a new aristocracy of academic ability emerged in the upper echelons of the Tang government. Through examinations, this new elite of southern commoners eventually outdistanced the sons of the landed northern aristocracy in the Tang government.

The system also indirectly benefited the poor by impressing on them the value of an education as the primary avenue for entering the ruling elite. Even poor families sought the best classical education they could for their sons. Although few from the ranks of the less well-off succeeded in the civil service examinations, many boys and even some girls learned the fundamentals of reading and writing. The Buddhists played a crucial role in extending education across society, for their temple schools introduced many children to primers based on classical texts as part of their charitable empire-wide mission. Relatively few of these students became fully literate in classical Chinese, but in a society containing nearly 16 million families and 80 million people in 750 CE, many were at least functionally literate.

EUNUCHS Abbasid and Tang rulers alike defended themselves and their most valued possessions, including their womenfolk, from opponents and enemies by surrounding themselves with loyal and well-compensated men. The caliphs in Baghdad chose young male slaves, frequently Turks, as their personal guards, although males known as eunuchs, who were surgically castrated as youths to perform a specific social function, also protected the harem. Similarly, Tang emperors in Chang'an and Luoyang relied on castrated males from the lower classes to guard the harem and protect the royal family because they were rendered sexually impotent. By the late eighth century, however, eunuchs in China were fully integrated into the empire's institutions, wielding a great deal more court power than those of the male slaves in Baghdad.

The numbers provide a sense of their growing power: in 820 CE the Tang government included 4,618 eunuchs, and 1,696 of them served at the highest administrative grade. The Chief Eunuch controlled the military, and through him the military power of court eunuchs extended to every province

Empress Wu. When she seized power in her own right as Empress Wu, Wu Zetian became the first and only female ruler in Chinese history. Although ruthless toward her court enemies, she expanded the military and recruited administrators from the civil examination candidates. She also challenged Confucian beliefs that subordinated women.

Eunuchs. Castrated males, known as eunuchs, guarded the harem and protected the royal family of Tang emperors. By the late eighth century, eunuchs were fully integrated into the government and wielded a great deal of military and political power.

Tang Court Women. This tenth-century painting of elegant ladies of the Tang imperial court enjoying a feast and music tells us a great deal about the aesthetic tastes of elite women in this era. It also shows the secluded "inner quarters," where court ladies passed their daily lives far from the hurly-burly of imperial politics.

and garrison station in the empire, forming an all-encompassing network. In effect, the eunuch bureaucracy mediated between the emperor and provincial governments.

Under Emperor Xianzong (ruled 806–820 CE), eunuchs acted as a third pillar of the government, working alongside the official bureaucracy and the imperial court. By establishing clear career patterns for eunuchs that paralleled those in the civil service, Xianzong empowered them and sparked a striking rise in their levels of literacy and their cultural attainments. More eunuchs acquired enough classical training to handle imperial documents and official reports. Yet by 838 CE, the delicate balance of power that had existed between the throne, eunuchs, and civil officials had evaporated. Eunuchs became an unruly political force in late Tang politics, and their machinations equaled those of the slaves guarding the Abbasid caliph and his harem.

AN ECONOMIC REVOLUTION

In the Abbasid caliphate and in Tang China, political stability fueled remarkable economic achievements. Rising agricultural production based on an egalitarian land allotment system for peasant farmers, an increasingly fine handicrafts industry, a diverse commodity market, and dynamic urban life highlighted China's dramatic successes. The Sui had started this

economic progress by building canals—especially the Grand Canal linking North and South China—throughout the country (see Map 9-2). The Tang continued the canal-building endeavor, centering their efforts on the Grand Canal and the Yangzi River, which flows from west to east. These new waterways aided communication and transport to all parts of the empire and helped raise living standards. Granaries built along the canals enabled the Tang to transport rice from the south to the north. The south grew richer, largely through the hard work of northern immigrants. Fertile land along the Yangzi became China's new granary, and areas south of the Yangzi became the demographic center of the Chinese empire.

Chinese merchants took full advantage of the Silk Road to trade with India and the Islamic world; but when mid-eighth-century rebellions in northwest China and the rise of Islam in central Asia jeopardized the land route, the "silk road by sea" blossomed. From all over Asia and Africa, merchant ships arrived in South China ports bearing cargos of spices, medicines, and jewelry; they left carrying Chinese silks and porcelain. The capital, Chang'an, became the richest and arguably the most populous city in the world. Its million or so residents included minorities from many countries. Fortified with a wall and moat, the city was divided into government and residential quarters; in its two main markets full of shops and stores, more than 200 types of businesses sold a wide variety of domestic and international goods.

Tang Tripod Jar. Tricolor glazed stoneware was all the rage in the early and middle Tang court and among elites in Chang'an, Loyang, and the provinces. This glazed jar from the eighth century imitated ancient Zhou bronzes (see Chapter 4). Such stoneware was displaced in the late Tang by the exquisite jadelike porcelains made in high-fired kilns.

In the larger cities of the Yangzi delta—debatably the world's first industrial heartland—workshops proliferated; they were admired far and wide for the elegance of their wares, which included brocades, fine paper, printed woodblocks, iron casts, and high-fired porcelains. Chinese industrialists used locally grown cotton to produce clothing of the highest quality. The textile industry prospered as painting and dyeing technology improved, and superb silk products were a major source of tax revenue. Asian art collectors valued what became known as Tang "tricolor porcelain," decorated with brilliant hues of yellow, green, white, brown, and blue. Many of these pieces moved through the river and lake systems of the middle Yangzi region to major urban centers and then on to Chang'an and Luoyang in the northwest. Conspicuous consumption of manufactured fineries stimulated Tang producers of high-value textiles and porcelain. Chinese luxuries dominated the domestic and international trading networks that reached Southwest Asia, Europe, and Africa via the Silk Road and Arab ships from the Indian Ocean.

DEALING WITH WORLD RELIGIONS

The Confucian ideology at heart was secular. Although it posited a heaven from which the ruling dynasty claimed the authority to govern, it did not hold out the promise of an afterlife or threaten unbelievers with eternal damnation. Not surprisingly, therefore, the early Tang emperors tolerated a remarkable amount of religious diversity. Nestorian Christianity (originally based in the old Persian capital of Ctesiphon), Zoroastrianism, and Manichaeanism (a radical Christian sect) had entered China through central Asia from Persia at the time of the Sasanian Empire. Islam came later. These—together with Buddhism and the indigenous teachings of Daoism and Confucianism—spread throughout the empire and were not at first viewed as conflicting with state power.

THE GROWTH OF BUDDHISM Buddhism, in particular, thrived under Tang rule. Many foreign students from Korea and Japan journeyed to China in the early years of the dynasty to study it.

Emperor Li Shimin distrusted Buddhist monks because they avoided serving the government and paying taxes. Yet once Buddhism was accepted as one of the "three ways" of learning—joining Daoism and Confucianism—Li endowed monasteries, sent emissaries to India to collect texts and relics, and commissioned Buddhist paintings and statuary. To provide devotional sites where the people could practice Buddhism through good works and prayer, huge monasteries were built with imperial patronage. Giant carvings of the Buddha in northwestern temple sanctuaries dotted the trading routes to central Asia, and less monumental temples filled with ornate statuary provided sites for religious refuge throughout South China. Such temples provided shelter, and gave some measure of autonomy to commoners and women burdened by the rigid Tang social hierarchy. Chinese pilgrims braved the Silk Road and the heights of the Pamirs to travel to India, where they learned Sanskrit; when they returned, they brought back Buddhist texts. One of these pilgrims was Xuanzang, whose story was told in Chapter 8. On returning, Xuanzang won many followers in Japan as well as in China. His life inspired the widely read novel *Journey to the West* (c. 1590), a classic of the Ming dynasty.

ANTI-BUDDHIST CAMPAIGNS By the middle of the ninth century, the Tang empire contained nearly 50,000 monasteries and hundreds of thousands of Buddhist monks and nuns. By comparison, the Carolingian Empire under Charlemagne in France had only 700 major monasteries (see the following section). Such success by a foreign religion, in conjunction with the beginning of the decline of the Tang dynasty in the mid–eighth century, threatened the Confucian and Daoist leaders. They therefore attacked Buddhism, arguing that its values were at variance with Confucian and Daoist traditions.

One example of a Confucian response comes from the scholar-official Han Yu (768–824 CE). Han Yu represented the rising literati from the south, who championed ancient writing forms based on Confucian classics. Han Yu's Memorial of 819 protested the emperor's plan to bring a relic of the Buddha to the capital for exhibition. Striking a xenophobic note that would have been inconceivable during the cosmopolitanism of the early Tang, Han Yu attacked Buddhism as a foreign doctrine of barbarian peoples who were different in language, culture, and knowledge. For raising these objections, Han was exiled to the southern province of Guangdong. Yet, two decades later, the state began suppressing Buddhist monasteries and confiscating their wealth.

Secular rulers grew more and more concerned that religious loyalties would undermine political ones. Increasingly intolerant Confucian scholar-administrators argued that the Buddhist monastic establishment threatened the imperial order. They accused Buddhists of undercutting kinship values and undermining the cardinal family relations of father and son, husband and wife, and so on. They claimed that the clergy were conspiring to destroy the state, the family, and the body—a conspiracy that they labeled the "Three Destructions" of Buddhism.

Piecemeal measures against the monastic orders gave way in the 840s CE to open persecution. Emperor Wuzong (ruled 841–847 CE) closed more than 4,600 monasteries and destroyed 40,000 temples and shrines. More than 260,000 Buddhist monks and nuns were forced to return to secular life, and the state parceled out monastery lands to taxpaying landlords and peasant farmers. Two important points can be made about the persecution of Buddhism in this period. First, in China the Tang government brought the Buddhist monastic communities under its control; in Latin Europe, in contrast, the Christian church dominated feudal states. Second, because the Chinese bureaucracy was steeped in the traditions of Confucianism and Daoism, its traditions had a power base that Buddhism lacked. China's most prominent universalizing religion was thus vulnerable once Emperor Wuzong began to persecute it.

To expunge the cultural impact of Buddhism, classically trained literati emphasized the revival of ancient prose styles and the teachings of Confucius and his followers. Linking classical scholarship, ancient literature, and Confucian morality, they constructed a cultural fortress that reversed the early Buddhist successes in China. Scholars such as Liu Zongyuan (773–819 CE) claimed that skill in writing ancient prose verse forms was still the best measure of talent and should remain the core of the civil examinations. The Tang poets Li Bai (701–761 CE), Du Fu (c. 712–c. 770 CE), and Bo Juyi (772–846 CE) extolled verse, always popular with the literate population, as the most effective genre for expressing moral concerns and personal emotions, thereby obviating the need to turn to the Buddhist religion for solace.

Among the many remarkable feats of the Tang era was the triumph of the homegrown ideologies of Confucianism and Daoism over the universalistic ethos of Buddhism. The result was persistent religious pluralism within China. Tang China stands out in this age of world religions as the one cultural zone that remained committed to a secular common culture and that resisted the pressures to embrace universalistic religions.

THE FALL OF TANG CHINA

China's deteriorating economic conditions in the ninth century resulted in peasant uprisings, some led by failed examination candidates. These revolts, which began in 859 CE, ultimately brought down the dynasty. In the tenth century, China fragmented into as many as ten regional states. The result was a new era of decentralization, which even the Song dynasty that emerged in 960 CE could not overcome. Only the Mongols, invading steppe peoples, were later able to restore the glory of the Han and Tang empires.

EARLY KOREA AND JAPAN

> → *To what extent did Japanese and Korean states and societies emulate Tang China during this era?*

At the same time that China was opening up to the cultures of its western regions, such as Chinese Turkestan, versions of its culture colored by Buddhism (and thereby rendered more flexible and less distinctly Chinese) reached out to the east—to Korea and, eventually, to Japan. (See Map 9-7.) To comprehend Korean and Japanese history of this era, we need to gain some understanding of the developments that predated the Koryo kingdom and the Japanese experience of the ninth and tenth centuries.

EARLY KOREA

Chinese cultural influences in Korea can be documented as early as the third century BCE, when Chinese immigrants from the northeast helped locals set up a small state called Lelang (also called Lolang) at the present-day site of Pyongyang. By the fourth century CE, three independent states had emerged on the peninsula that jutted into the Yellow Sea: Koguryo in the north, Paekche in the southwest, and Silla in the southeast. Koguryo subsequently expanded its influence northward into Manchuria. By contrast, because of its location on the southwest coast facing the Yellow Sea and Shandong province in China, Paekche had close ties with North China. This division into what was known as the "Three Kingdoms" of Korea lasted until 668 CE, when the southeastern kingdom of Silla gained control over the entire peninsula and unified it for the first time. During this period, Japan also maintained a small enclave on Korea's southern coast at Kaya (also called Mimana).

Extent of Silla power, 670–935 CE
Extent of Nara state by 600 CE
⊙ Capital
• City
⌂ Buddhist temple
⊗ Shinto shrine
▲ Holy mountain
Bohai

Amur R.

BOHAI

SEA OF
JAPAN

*HOKKAIDO
AINU*

HONSHU

Pyongyang
Wonsan
SAKCHU
HANCHU

MYONGJU

KOREA

SANGJU

UNGJU
SILLA ⊙ Kumsong (Kyongju)
CHONJU YANGJU
KANGU
MUJU ▲

YELLOW
SEA

JAPAN

Heian-kyo
Ise
Osaka
Heijo-kyo
Nara

SHIKOKU

PACIFIC
OCEAN

KYUSHU

EAST
CHINA
SEA

0   50   100 Miles
0   50   100 Kilometers

MAP 9-7   BORDERLANDS: KOREA AND JAPAN, 600–1000

The Tang dynasty held great sway and power over emerging Korean and Japanese states in East Asia, although it never directly ruled either region. Study the map above. How did state formation evolve in Korea and Japan between 600 and 900? What connections existed between these states and the Tang empire during this era? To what extent did Korean and Japanese states adapt Tang traditions and customs during this time?

Silla's unification of Korea after 670 CE enabled the Koreans to establish a unified government modeled on the Tang Chinese imperial state. Silla dispatched annual embassies to the Chinese capital at Chang'an, as well as regularly sending students and monks to China. Like Latin among diverse populations in Europe, literary Chinese became the written language of Korean elites. Koreans later devised a phonetic system for writing their own language that simplified Chinese characters, but most official writing remained in Chinese. Early Korean society, like China's, was based on a hereditary aristocracy who monopolized official posts. But like Japan, Korea initially resisted the classical meritocracy that would be introduced into Tang China through the civil service examinations.

Silla's own fortunes were entwined with those of the Tang. In the wake of the Tang decline, the state of Silla also began to fragment. In 936 CE, Wang Kon, a rebel leader, absorbed Silla into the northern-based Koryo kingdom (918–1392 CE), an act that tenuously reunified the country. The Koryo dynasty, from which the country's modern name derives, began to construct a new cultural identity for itself by enacting an unprecedented bureaucratic system aimed at replacing the archaic tribal system that had continued under the Silla. Unlike in Japan, Tang dynasty–style civil service examinations to select the most capable officials to govern at court and in the provinces were successfully put in place in Korea. Wang Kon's heirs consolidated control over the peninsula and strengthened its political and economic foundations by more closely following the bureaucratic and land allotment systems of Tang China.

Yet during this period, Korea, like Tang China itself, was harassed continuously by northern tribes such as the Khitan people. As we will see in Chapter 10, the Khitan also took advantage of the fall of the Tang dynasty to control northern Chinese lands after 907 CE, establishing the rival Liao dynasty (907–1126 CE) in northeast China. During this troubled period, Korean artisans anxiously carved wooden printing blocks for 81,258 scriptures from the Buddhist canon as an offering to the Buddha to protect them from invading enemies—but in vain. After being overwhelmed by the Khitan in 1010, the Koryo dynasty revived, only to be invaded by the Mongols in 1231 (see Chapter 10). Despite these temporary invasions, the dynasty managed to last until 1392.

EARLY JAPAN

Beginning in the Ice Age, tribal groups known as the Jomon (from 10,000 years ago to 400 BCE; see Chapter 2) and succeeding Yayoi peoples (400 BCE–250 CE) dominated prehistoric Japan. Subsequently, in the middle of the third century, a warlike group from northeast Asia arrived by sea from Korea and aggressively imposed their military and social power on southern Japan. These conquerors, known today as the "Tomb Culture" because of their elevated necropolises near present-day Osaka, unified Japan by extolling their imperial ancestors and maintaining the social hierarchy that they had brought with them from Korea and Manchuria. They also brought with them a belief in the power of female shamans, who married into the imperial clans; like Himiko, discussed below, these women became de facto rulers of early Japanese kinship groups, combining religious and political power.

Chinese dynastic records describe the early Japanese, with whom imperial China had contact in this period, as a "dwarf" people who maintained a rice and fishing economy. The Japanese farmers had also mastered Chinese-style sericulture. According to the Chinese, the Japanese were united under a shaman-queen, Himiko, who sent an envoy in 239 CE to the state of Wei—one of the Three Kingdoms in China after the fall of the Han. The complex aristocratic society that developed under the leaders of the Tomb Culture became the basis of an emerging Yamato Japanese state, which in successive waves incorporated many natives and Korean migrants. The rise of the Japanese state coincided with the Three Kingdoms era in Korea; they were linked for a long time and at least until 688 CE, when Silla, with Tang military help, occupied the Japanese enclave of Kaya on the Korean peninsula. Many Koreans, along with Japanese who had fought on the side of Paekche, crossed the straits and settled in the island kingdom.

THE YAMATO EMPEROR AND THE ORIGINS OF JAPANESE SACRED IDENTITY Ancestor worship, though influenced by China, was native to Japan and lay at the heart of a belief system that emerged after the fourth century. Ancestral rites that predated the influx of Buddhism and Confucianism from Paekche in the sixth century underwent significant transformation in the hands of the early Japanese aristocratic clans. For the early Japanese, a person's *tamashii*, his or her soul or spirit, became a *kami* or local deity when it was fully nourished and purified through the proper rituals and festivals after death. Before the imperial Yamato clan

Tomb Culture. Daisenryo Kofun, in Osaka, is allegedly the tomb of Emperor Nintoku, dating from the fifth century.

Creation Myth. Tsukioka Yoshitoshi (1839–1892) depicted Japan's creation myth in "Amaterasu Appearing from the Cave." To entice Amaterasu, the goddess of the sun, out so that light would be returned to the world, the other gods performed a ribald dance.

became dominant, each clan had its own pantheon of ancestral deities; but after 500 CE, the ancestors of the Yamato clan were increasingly worshipped by all Japanese. Other regional ancestral deities were later subordinated to the Yamato deities, who claimed direct lineage from Amaterasu, the Sun Goddess and creator of the sacred islands of Japan.

After 587 CE, the Soga kinship group—originally from Korea—became Japan's leading family and controlled the Japanese court. The Soga were particularly sympathetic to the Buddhist religion of the southwestern kingdom of Paekche, which also faced China, and sympathy flowed the other way as well. From the polity's inception, aristocratic birth and kinship, tied to descent lines from the *kami*, were the overriding qualification for social status and advancement within the Yamato imperial clan. The imperial line justified it-

self by embracing a tradition that used both Buddhism and Shinto to sacralize the Japanese state and Japanese society.

The political developments in Japan differed strikingly from those in China or Korea, where a more secular state took hold: the Yamato scribes wove together a unique historical blend that presented their emperor as the living embodiment of Japan and its peoples. They created a sacred past in which the divine and human realms coalesced in the imperial state to form the "way of the deities" (Shinto). Its divine characteristics placed the Yamato aristocratic families at the top of the Japanese state and its aristocratic society.

PRINCE SHOTOKU AND THE TAIKA POLITICAL REFORMS By 600 CE, just as the new Sui dynasty (581–618 CE) was bringing together North and South China under a single ruler for the first time in 300 years, the Japanese had gained a sense of themselves as a distinct and unified people. Looking back on this era a century later, and eager to believe that they owed little or nothing to outside influences, the Soga kinship group attributed everything that was innovative in the culture of the early Japanese Yamato state to their own creative young Prince Shotoku (574–622 CE). Contemporary Japanese scribes claimed that Prince Shotoku rather than Korean immigrants had introduced Buddhism to Japan and that his illustrious reign had touched off Japan's rise as an exceptional and powerful island kingdom in East Asia. Indeed, the Japanese Buddhists saw in Prince Shotoku what the Christians of the Roman Empire saw in Constantine: the founding religious figure and chief political icon. But Shotoku's actual historical role remains, at the very least, overstated.

When the Sui dynasty took power, Prince Shotoku allegedly sent envoys to China to inquire about their strengths, and Chinese artists, craftsmen, and clerks were brought to help Japan reshape its institutions. In addition, Shotoku was given credit for preparing a seventeen-article treatise in 1604 that promoted governmental reforms along the Chinese lines; then, the model was the Sui dynasty. At the end of Prince Shotoku's regency, Japan's neighbor underwent a momentous change, as the Sui dynasty quickly gave way to the Tang. For Korea and Japan, such success transformed the Tang empire into a model for up-to-date statecraft, culture, religion, the arts, and society in East Asia.

As in China, Japanese rulers tolerated, and even promoted, a mosaic of religions. Increasing political integration was cover for growing religious pluralism. Shotoku promoted Buddhism and Confucianism; though the groundwork for their growth had been laid by Korean immigrants the century before, he was given credit for introducing them into a native religious culture, Shintoism, which had been wholly Japanese. The prince's prestige has also been associated with several Buddhist temples modeled on Tang pagodas and massive halls; one of these, built in Nara (near present-day Kyoto and Osaka), was the Horyuji Temple; it is still extant, the oldest surviving wooden structure in the world. Its frescoes include figures derived directly from the art of Iran and central Asia. They are a reminder that within two centuries, Buddhism had dispersed its visual culture along the full length of the Silk Road, from Afghanistan to China, and then on to Korea and the island kingdom of Japan in the Pacific Ocean. In Japan, it contributed to the variety of religions.

Political integration was not necessarily the same as political stability. In 645 CE, another leading kinship group known as the Nakatomi came to power via a violent coup d'état that eliminated the Soga and their allies. The leader of the coup, Nakatomi no Kamatari (614–669 CE), and his family used their power over the throne to enact the Taika Reform edicts, which were based on Confucian principles of government allegedly first enunciated by Prince Shotoku in

Taishi. Prince Shotoku Taishi was instrumental in the establishment of Buddhism in Japan, although his actual historical role was overstated. In this hanging scroll painting from the early fourteenth century, he is idealized as a sixteen-year-old son, holding an incense censer and praying for the recovery of his sick father, the Emperor Yomei (r. 585–87).

604 CE. These reforms were sponsored by Nakatomi courtiers in the Yamato court who advanced a new Japanese imperial ideology. According to these edicts, the ruler was no longer simply an ancestral kinship group leader. Instead he became an exalted "emperor" (*tenno*) who ruled by the mandate of heaven, as in China, and exercised absolute authority.

By adapting the Chinese notion of the mandate of heaven, the Yamato court elevated the religious prestige of the Japanese emperor. But not all aspects of Chinese culture were welcomed. Even when Tang institutions of governance were introduced during the Taika reforms of 645, the Japanese court refused to institute the Chinese civil service examination system for fear that doing so would destabilize the aristocrats in power. In the early eighth century, the imperial court at the first Japanese capital of Nara prepared a political narrative about themselves, written in classical Chinese. They linked religious reverence for earlier imperial Yamato ancestors with legitimate political power in Japan.

MAHAYANA BUDDHISM AND THE SANCTITY OF THE JAPANESE STATE Religious influences continued to flow into Japan, contributing to spiritual pluralism while bolstering its rulers. Although Prince Shotoku and later Japanese emperors turned to Confucian models for government, they also dabbled in the occult arts and in Daoist purification rituals. In addition, the Taika edicts under the Nakatomi promoted Buddhism as the state religion of Japan, following Shotoku's lead. Though the imperial family did not cease to support native Shinto traditions, association with Buddhism gave the Japanese state extra status by affiliating it with a universal religion whose appeal stretched to Korea, China, and India.

State-sponsored spiritual diversity led native religions to formalize credos of their own. The introduction of Confucianism and Buddhism to Japan motivated the adherents of native Shinto cults to organize what had been an amorphous body of religious practices into something comparable to these two well-organized belief systems—much as Buddhism had spurred a transformation of Vedic religion in distant India a few centuries earlier. Shinto priests now collected ancient liturgies, and Shinto rituals were incorporated into the official Department of Religion.

The Japanese did not fully accept the traditional Buddhist view of the state as purely a vehicle to protect and propagate moral and social justice for both the ruler and his subjects. The Japanese emperor was the object of more explicit worship as the sacred ruler, one in a line of luminous Shinto gods. He was not simply the temporal ruler who turned the wheel of the law (*dharmaraja*) and patronized the Buddhist monasteries from afar. Unlike rulers in Korea and China, the Japanese emperor was a supreme *kami*—a divine force in his own right. Buddhism as a universal religion imported from China and Paekche was adapted and spread in Japan to also serve the interests of the state, much as Christianity would be used by

European monarchs and Islam by the various Islamic dynasties. But in one respect Japan fundamentally differed from Christianity and Islam. Whereas a single faith—splintered and fractious, to be sure—integrated the latter, Shinto and Buddhism became symbiotically intertwined in the political and religious life of the Japanese. Moreover, unlike in China, emperors in Japan rarely wielded direct power themselves. We will see in Chapter 10 that other individuals, whether next of kin or warrior elites, usually invoked the religious aura of the emperor to legitimate their own political protection of the imperial line.

THE CHRISTIAN WEST, 600–1000 CE

> → *How did two Christianities come to exist in western Eurasia?*

Seen from the Mediterranean and the Islamic world, post-Roman Europe during the period from 600 to 1000 CE seemed little more than a warrior-dominated world. In the fifth century, the mighty Roman military machine gave way to a multitude of warrior leaders whose principal allegiances were local affiliations. Indeed, ever since the days of the ancient Celts, small societies of farmers and herders (living in scattered homesteads or in villages with populations rarely larger than 300) had been dominated by warlords. Yet, here, too, major innovations were under way. The leading force was Christianity, and the leading agents of the Christianization of the European peoples were missionaries and monks. The political ideal of the Roman Empire cast a vast shadow over the western Europeans, but the inheritor of the mantle of Rome was increasingly a spiritual institution—the Roman Catholic Church—whose powerful head, the pope, was based in Rome.

CHARLEMAGNE'S FLEDGLING EMPIRE

In 802 CE, Harun al-Rashid, the ruler of Baghdad, sent the gift of an elephant to Charlemagne, the king of the Franks, in northern Europe. The elephant, named Abuldabaz—after Abu Abbas, Harun's ancestor and the founder of the Abbasid dynasty—caused a sensation among the Franks, who saw the gift as an acknowledgment of Charlemagne's power. In fact, Harun, like the Sasanian King of Kings centuries before him, often sent rare beasts to distant rulers as a gracious reminder of his own formidable power. In his eyes, Charlemagne's "empire" was a minor principality. Indeed, the region would have struck those accompanying the elephant from Baghdad as

profoundly underdeveloped. Northern Europe contained few cities—the largest, Paris, had only 20,000 inhabitants—and they were smaller than the long-deserted Roman settlements now in ruins.

This was an empire that Charlemagne ruled with tireless energy from 768 to 814 CE, often traveling 2,000 miles a year on campaigns of plunder and conquest. By 802 CE, he controlled much of western Europe, lands reaching across the Pyrenees Mountains as far south as Catalonia in modern-day Spain, as far east as across the Alps, and as far south as Naples in modern-day Italy. Yet, compared with the rulers of the Islamic world, he was a political lightweight. His empire had a population of less than 15 million; he rarely commanded armies larger than 5,000; and he had only the most rudimentary tax system. At a time when the palace quarters of the caliph at Baghdad covered nearly 250 acres, Charlemagne's newly built palace at Aachen was merely 330 by 655 feet. (Baghdad itself was almost 40 square miles in area, whereas there was virtually no "town" outside the palace at Aachen.) Constructed in 796 CE (only a generation after the foundation of Baghdad), it was little more than a large country house set in the middle of open countryside, close to the

Charlemagne's Throne. From this raised throne, Charlemagne presided over services performed by the clergy. Constructed of slabs of marble transported all the way from Rome to Aachen, the throne showed that Charlemagne was the "new" emperor of the West and heir of the emperors of Rome.

Charlemagne's Palace and Chapel. Though not large by Byzantine or Islamic standards, Charlemagne's palace and chapel were heavy with symbolic meaning. A royal hall for banqueting in Frankish, "barbarian" style was linked by a covered walkway to the imperial domed chapel, which was meant to look like a miniature version of the Hagia Sophia of Constantinople. Outside the chapel was a courtyard, like that outside the shrine of Saint Peter at Rome.

woods of the Ardennes where Charlemagne and his Franks loved to hunt wild boar on horseback.

He and his men were representatives of the warrior class that had come to dominate post-Roman western Europe. Set against the broader history of northern and western Europe, there was nothing unusual about the Franks. Roman rule, which inaugurated a period when large towns were privileged over the countryside and educated civilians valued over warriors, had briefly imposed an alien way of life. That Mediterranean empire had withdrawn, and from 500 CE onward, war became, once again, the duty and the joy of the aristocrat: buoyed up by their chieftains' mead—a heavy beer made with honey, "yellow, sweet and ensnaring"—young men were expected to follow their lords into battle, "among the war horses and the blood-stained armor" (Aneirin, *Y Gododin*, ll. 102, 840).

And though the Franks vigorously engaged in trade, that trade was based on war: Europe's principal export at this time was Europeans. The Frankish empire was financed by the massive sale of prisoners of war. From Venice, which grew rich from its role as middleman in human trafficking, the captives were sent across the sea to Alexandria, Tunis, and southern Spain. The main victims of this trade were Slavic-speaking peoples, tribal communities of hunters and cultivators whose populations had slowly grown in eastern Europe. Their long oppression is preserved in the English language,

for the medieval Latin *sclavus* (which originally meant "Slavic") replaced the classical Latin *servus* to denote "slave"; *servus*, by contrast, was applied to those who stayed at home and became the English word "serf"—a peasant tied for life to the estates of the aristocracy.

Yet in this seemingly uncivilized and inhospitable zone, a religion with universalistic aspirations—Christianity—began to sink down roots. Although its worldwide expansion did not occur for centuries, its spiritual conquest of the European peoples established institutions and fired enthusiasms that would later drive believers to carry its message to faraway lands.

A CHRISTIANITY FOR THE NORTH

Charlemagne's empire was unquestionably primitive when compared with the Islamic empire or the Tang empire of China. But what mattered most about it was *where*, not what, it was. Far removed from the old centers of high culture, it had left the Roman Mediterranean behind. Charlemagne's empire was a polity of the borderlands. It was also based on an expansionist and proselytizing Christianity that drew energy from its rough frontier mentality. (See Map 9-8.)

As the fuzzy frontier lines between the Roman Empire and the territories to its north vanished forever, Christianity was pulled into a new world profoundly different from the Mediterranean cities in which it had taken form.

Through its evangelizing efforts, the Christianity of the West bridged the ancient gulf between the Mediterranean world and the non-Roman world of the north. As a result, Christians felt that theirs was the only truly universal religion. It could bring hitherto opposed groups into a single "catholic" church that, as we have seen, had begun to replace a political unity lost in western Europe when the Roman Empire fell.

As far back as 410 CE, reacting to the Visigothic sack of Rome, the great Christian bishop Augustine of Hippo (a seaport in modern Algeria) had laid down the outlines of this belief. Of Augustine's many books, the most important for future centuries was his *City of God*. He wrote it to persuade contemporary Christians that the barbarian takeover already happening around them was not the end of the world. The "city of God" was represented on earth by the Catholic Church, and the Catholic Church was not for Romans only—it was for all times and for all peoples, "in a wide world which has always been inhabited by many differing peoples, that have so many different customs and languages, so many different forms of organization and so many languages, and who have had so many different religions" (Augustine, *The City of God*, 14.1). Nonetheless, only one organization would bring them all to paradise: the Catholic Church.

Such confidence may appear paradoxical. After all, around 800 CE barely 25 percent of the Christians in the

MAP 9-8   CHRISTENDOM, 600–1000

The end of the first millennium saw much of Europe divided between two versions of Christianity, each with different traditions and histories. Identify the regions where each version of Christianity held sway. Why do you think the Catholic Church based in Rome was successful in expanding its influence in the west, but not the east? Why did the Orthodox version of Christianity based in Constantinople expand into eastern Europe, but not the west? How influential was Charlemagne's empire in promoting this division?

world were found in western Europe. Most lived in the richer and more populous Byzantine Empire—the eastern Roman empire of Constantinople—or in the large and sophisticated Christian communities that were thriving under a relatively tolerant Muslim rule. Independent Christian kingdoms still flourished in Africa, in Nubia on the Upper Nile and in the highlands of Ethiopia. Beyond the Islamic lands, to the east, Nestorian Christianity was a major presence on the Silk Road. Yet none of these offshoots of Christianity felt quite the certainty of being truly, and exclusively, the one universal

Primary Source

CHRISTENDOM ON THE EDGE: A VIEW OF EMPIRE IN IRELAND

A young Christian Briton of Roman citizenship who lived near Hadrian's Wall experienced the pull of Christianity around 400. In his teens, Patricius was captured by Irish slave raiders and spent six years herding pigs on the Atlantic coast of Mayo. He escaped and years later decided to return in order to convert his former captors to Christianity. He believed that in making the fierce Irish Christians, he also made them "Romans." He thus brought Christianity to the Atlantic edge of the known world. Patricius, who died around 460, is remembered today as Saint Patrick.

16 But after I reached Ireland, well, I pastured the flocks every day. . . . I would even stay in the forests and on the mountain and would wake to pray before dawn in all weathers, snow, frost, rain. . . .

17 And it was in fact there that one night while asleep I heard a voice saying to me: 'You do well to fast, since you will soon be going to your home country;' and again, very shortly after, I heard this prophecy: 'See, your ship is ready.' And it was not near at hand but was perhaps two hundred miles away, and I had never been there and did not know a living soul there. And then I soon ran away and abandoned the man with whom I had been for six years. . . . till I reached the ship.

23 And again a few years later I was in Britain with my kinsfolk. . . . And it was there that I saw one night in a vision a man coming as it were from Ireland . . .

with countless letters, and he gave me one of them, and I read the heading of the letter, 'The Voice of the Irish,' and as I read these opening words aloud, I imagined at that very instant that I heard the voice of those who were beside the forest of Foclut which is near the western sea; and thus they cried, as though with one voice: 'We beg you, holy boy, to come and walk again among us.'

→ *What does this passage tell us about life in the Celtic worlds?*

→ *What does this passage reveal to us about how St. Patrick's spiritual experiences compare to those of priests in the older Christian communities in the Mediterranean worlds of Rome and Constantinople?*

SOURCE: *St. Patrick: His Writings and Muirchu's Life,* edited and translated by A. B. E. Hood (London: Phillimore, 1978), pp. 41, 44–46, 50.

church that was enjoyed by the Catholic Church of Europe in the age of Charlemagne.

Several developments helped give rise to this attitude. First, the arrival of Christianity in northern Europe had provoked a cultural revolution. Preliterate societies made contact, for the first time, with a sacred text in a language that seemed utterly strange to them. Latin became a sacred language, and books themselves became charged vehicles of the holy. As we saw in Chapter 8, Roman Christians had already moved from the clumsy scroll to the bound codex, but it was still a messy object. Written on papyrus, the codex had none of the features that Europeans today associate with a modern book—no divisions between the words, no punctuation, no

paragraphs, and no chapter headings. The reader was assumed to know Latin well enough (as a spoken language) that no further aids to understanding were needed. The same assumption could not be made of an Irishman, a Saxon, or a Frank who had never spoken Latin but wished to read and understand the Bible. Hence the care lavished in the new Christian north on the Latin scriptures. The few parchment texts that circulated in northern Europe were carefully prepared, with the words in them separated, the sentences correctly punctuated and introduced by uppercase letters, and chapter headings provided: they were far more like the book you are reading now than anything available to Romans at the height of the empire.

Monasticism rapidly took hold because it appealed to a deep sense that precisely the men and women who had least in common with those whose lives were "normal" were best able to mediate between the believer and God. Just as in Buddhism, in the monastic Christianity of western Europe the relation between the members of religious orders and the laity was grounded in religious "merit," or spiritual credit. Lay persons gave gifts to the monasteries and offered their protection. In return for these righteous acts, they gained the prayers of the monks and nuns and the very real reassurance that although they themselves were warriors and men of blood, the monks' and nuns' intercessions would keep them from going to hell.

With the spread of monasticism, the Christianity of the north took a decisive turn. In Muslim (as in Jewish) societies, religious leaders tended to emphasize their commonalities with those around them: many of the greatest scholars, theologians, and mystics of Islam were married men, including merchants and courtiers. In the Christian West, the opposite was true: preliterate warrior societies honored small groups of men and women who were utterly unlike themselves—unmarried, unfit for warfare, and intensely literate in an incomprehensible tongue. Even their hair looked different. Unlike warriors, these men were close-shaven; by contrast, the Orthodox clergy of the eastern Roman empire sported long, silvery beards (signifying wisdom and maturity and not, as in the West, the warrior's masculine strength). The heads of Catholic monks and priests were shaved as well, in a rite known as "tonsure." Such deliberate differentiation shows that the Catholic Church of northern Europe owed its ambitious horizons, as a missionary religion, to the same principles that explained the spread of Buddhism in central and Inner Asia (and later in Japan): it was a religion of monks, whose communities represented an otherworldly alternative to the warrior societies in which they found themselves. By the year 800 CE, few regions of northern Europe were without great monasteries, many of which held more than 300 monks or nuns (they were larger, that is, than the local villages). Supported by thousands of serfs donated to them by kings and local warlords, these were powerhouses of prayer, which kept the regions safe.

Northern Christianity also gained new ties to an old imaginative center. As the cleric leading the gigantic former capital of the empire, the Christian bishop of Rome had always enjoyed much prestige around the Mediterranean. But he was only one bishop among many. He was often overshadowed and contradicted by his peers in Carthage, Alexandria, Antioch, and Constantinople. Though he was spoken of with respect as *papa*, as "the grand old man," many others shared that title.

By the year 800 CE, this picture had dramatically changed. As believers looked down into the Mediterranean from the distant north, they saw only one *papa* left in western Europe: Rome's pope. The papacy as we know it rose because of the

Celtic Bible. Unlike the simple codex of early Christian times, the Bible came to be presented in Ireland and elsewhere in the northern world as a magical book. Its pages were filled with mysterious, intricate patterns, which imitated on parchment the jewelry and treasure for which early medieval warlords yearned.

Second, those who produced the new Bibles were starkly different from ordinary men and women. They were monks and nuns. Monasticism, which had been a feature of Mediterranean Christianity since 300 CE, had originated in Egypt, and its technical terms underscore its eastern source. The root of "monastic" (and of "monk") is the Greek *monos*, "alone": a man or a woman who chose to live alone, without the support of marriage or family. And "hermit" derives from the Greek *herēmos*, "man of the desert," for zealous Christians had retired to the desert to find solitude.

Monasticism had been immensely popular in Egypt, Syria, and elsewhere, but it also suited the missionary tendencies of Christianity in northern Europe particularly well. It placed small, well-organized groups of men and women in the middle of societies with which they had nothing in common.

St. Gallen Monastery. The great monasteries of the age of Charlemagne were like Roman legionary settlements. Placed on the frontiers of Germany, they were vast, stone buildings, around which entire towns would gather. Their libraries, the largest in Europe, were filled with parchment volumes, carefully written out and often lavishly decorated in a "northern," Celtic style. Though dwarfed by the Islamic libraries of the same time, they were the places where Latin literature was preserved. All Latin "classical" texts known to us survive because they were copied by monks in such monasteries at this time.

fervor with which the Catholic Church of western Europe united to support a single and exclusive symbolic center, represented by the popes at Rome. This movement had begun at the time of the collapse of the Roman Empire in the west, and sometime after 750 CE it achieved its goal. The popes owed their position in the Christian West to two developments: the Arab conquests, which had removed Rome's competition by abruptly slicing the Mediterranean in two, and the increased need of new Christians who had grown up in the northern borderlands to create a more vibrant, more exclusively religious focus for their hopes.

Charlemagne recognized this need very well. In 800 CE, he went out of his way to celebrate Christmas Day by visiting the shrine of Saint Peter at Rome. There, Pope Leo III acclaimed him as the new "emperor" of the West. The hurried ceremony added nothing to his power, but it ratified the aspirations of an age. A "modern" Rome—inhabited by popes, famous for the shrines of the martyrs, and protected by a "modern" Christian monarch from the north—and not the "ancient" Rome of pagan emperors was what his subjects wanted.

Stone Beehive Huts. Monasticism was also about the lonely search for God at the very end of the world, which took place in these Irish monasteries on the Atlantic coast. The cells, made of loose stones piled in round domes, are called "beehives." Beyond, in the ocean, is the rock of Saint Michael (Skellig Michál), a place of total isolation for monks known as "hermits"—men of the deep desert. Having no deserts, the Irish turned to offshore rocks and islands to find a place to be alone with God.

THE AGE OF THE VIKINGS, 800–1000 CE

Harun's elephant died in 813—one year before Charlemagne himself. Abuldabaz's death was recorded because the Franks viewed it as an omen of coming disasters. The great beast keeled over when he was marched out to confront the army

The Coronation of Charlemagne. This is how the coronation of Charlemagne at Rome in 800 was remembered in medieval western Europe. This painting stresses the fact that it was the pope who placed the crown on Charlemagne's head, thereby claiming him as a ruler set up by the Catholic Church for the Catholic Church. But in 800 contemporaries saw the pope as recognizing the fact that Charlemagne had already deserved to be emperor. The rise of the papacy to greater prominence and power in later medieval Europe caused this significant "re-remembering" of the event.

of a Viking king from Denmark. In the next half century, the Vikings from Scandinavia exposed the weakness of Charlemagne's self-confident regime. His once powerful empire of borderland peoples met its match on the widest border of all: that between the European landmass and the mighty Atlantic. (See Map 9-9.)

The motives of the Vikings were simple and announced in their name, which is derived from the Old Norse *vik*, "to be on the warpath." The Vikings sought to loot the now wealthy Franks and replace them as the dominant warrior class of northern Europe. It was their turn to extract plunder and to

Oseberg Ship. The Viking ship was a triumph of design. It could be rowed up the great rivers of Europe, and, at the same time, its sail could take it across the Atlantic.

sell droves of slaves across the water. They succeeded because of a deadly technological advantage: ships of unparalleled sophistication, developed by Scandinavian sailors in the Baltic Sea and the long fjords of Norway. Light and agile, with a shallow draft, they could be rowed up the rivers of northern Europe and even carried overland from one river system to another. Under sail, the same boats could tackle open water and cross the hitherto unexplored wastes of the North Atlantic.

In the ninth century, the Vikings set their ships on both courses. They emptied northern Europe of its treasure, sacking the great monasteries that had sprung up in precisely those places most vulnerable to attack from the sea—along the Atlantic and North Sea coasts of Ireland and Britain and on the banks of the Rhine and the Seine, great, slow rivers that led into the very heart of Charlemagne's Frankish empire. At the same time, Norwegian adventurers colonized first the hitherto uninhabited island of Iceland, and then Greenland. By 982 CE, they had even reached the New World and established a substantial settlement at L'Anse aux Meadows on the coast of Labrador. Viking goods have been found as far west as the Inuit settlements of Baffin Island to the north of Hudson Bay, carried there along intricate trading routes by Native Americans.

The consequences of this spectacular reach across the ocean to the coast of America were short-lived, but the penetration of eastern Europe by Viking ships had lasting effects. Ruthless and supremely well equipped to penetrate long river systems, the Vikings sailed east along the Baltic and then turned south, edging up the rivers that flowed into the Baltic to cross the watershed of central Russia, where the Dnieper, the Don, and the Volga begin to flow south into the Black Sea and the Caspian. By opening this link between the Baltic and what is now Kiev in modern Ukraine, they created an av-

MAP 9-9   THE AGE OF VIKINGS AND THE SLAVE TRADE, 800–1000

Vikings from Scandinavia dramatically altered the history of Christendom in the late first millennium. What impact did Viking raiders have on western Christendom during this era? Was their influence on the communities of eastern Europe similar or different? What influence did Vikings have on people beyond the Afro-Eurasian world? What role did the Vikings and the Holy Roman emperors play in expanding the slave trade during this period?

enue of commerce that, for the first time, linked Scandinavia and the Baltic directly to Constantinople and Baghdad. What they added was yet more slaves; Muslim geographers bluntly called this newly opened route "The Highway of the Slaves." The fortified trading posts of the Scandinavians would eventually form the spine of medieval Russia.

THE SURVIVAL OF THE CHRISTIAN EMPIRE OF THE EAST

On reaching the Black Sea, the Vikings made straight for Constantinople. In 860 CE, more than 200 of their long ships gathered ominously in the straits of the Bosporus, beneath the walls of the city. What they found was not Charlemagne's rustic Aachen but a proud city with a population exceeding 100,000, surrounded by well-engineered late Roman walls.

The Vikings had come up against a state hardened by battle. For two centuries on end, the empire of East Rome, centered on Constantinople, had held Islamic armies at bay. Once Southwest Asia as a whole had fallen to the Islamic empire of Baghdad, the East Romans fought across Anatolia and the eastern Mediterranean for their own survival. From 640 to 840 CE they faced almost yearly campaigns launched by an empire that grew to be ten times greater in extent than their own, with a budget fifteen times greater. For years on end, Muslim armies and navies came within striking distance of Constantinople. Each time they failed, outmaneuvered by highly professional generals and unable to prevail against a skillfully constructed line of fortresses that controlled the roads across Anatolia. Muslim writers took the Christian empire of East Rome—Rûm—seriously, as they never took the Franks. The Christian empire of East Rome fought the caliphs of Baghdad to a draw.

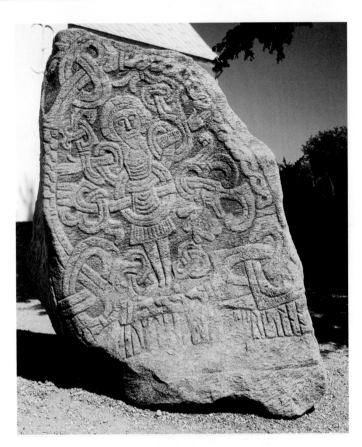

Jelling Stone. Carved on the side of this great stone, Christ appears to be almost swallowed up in an intricate pattern of lines. For the Vikings, complicated interweaving like serpents or twisted gold jewelry was a sign of majesty: hence, in this, the first Christian monument in Denmark, Christ is part of an ancient pattern of carving, which brought good luck and victory to the king.

Moreover, this empire had its own technological advantage, one used to deadly effect in naval warfare: Greek fire, a combination of petroleum and potassium that, when sprayed from siphons, would explode in a great sheet of flame on the water. In 717 CE, the emperor Leo III used it for the first time to destroy the Muslim fleet as it lay at anchor within sight of the imperial palace of Constantinople. A century and a half later, the experience and weaponry of East Rome were too much for the Vikings, and their raid was a spectacular failure.

In the long run, the sense of having outlasted an endless series of military emergencies bolstered the morale of East Roman Christianity and led to its unexpected flowering in distant lands. Not just Constantinople but Justinian's glorious church, the Hagia Sophia, its heart, had survived. That great building and the solemn Greek liturgy that was performed in it might not impress Catholic Franks. But Scandinavian adventurers from the new slave markets of Kiev and the Volga—like their medieval Russian successors—were prepared to be immensely impressed. Here was the central church of a Christian empire that for half a millennium had represented all that was most dignified and venerable in the Christian tradition. In the tenth century, as Charlemagne's empire collapsed in western Europe, large areas of eastern Europe became Greek Orthodox, not Catholic. As a result, Greek Christianity gained a spiritual empire that eventually offset the losses of the eastern Roman empire in Southwest Asia.

The conversion of Russian peoples and the Balkan Slavs to Orthodox Christianity was a complex process. But it was based on an admiration for Constantinople, on the part of Russians, Bulgarians, and other Slav princes, as intense as that of any Western Catholic for the Roman popes. This admiration amounted to awe, as shown by the famous story, preserved in a Russian chronicle, of the conversion to Greek Christianity in 987 CE of the rulers of Kiev (descendants of Viking adventurers from the Baltic):

> The envoys reported[,] . . . "We went among the Germans [the Catholic Franks] and we saw them performing many ceremonies in their churches; but we beheld no glory there. Then we went to Greece [in fact, to Constantinople and Hagia Sophia], and the Greeks led us to the edifices where they worship their God, and we knew not whether we were in heaven or on earth. For on earth there is no such splendor or such beauty, and we are at a loss to describe it. We only know that God dwells there among men, and their service is fairer than the ceremonies of other nations. For we can not forget that beauty. (Cross and Sherbowitz-Westor, *The Russian Primary Chronicle*, 111)

By 1000, two Christianities existed: one was the new and confident "borderland" Catholicism of western Europe, and the other was an ancient Greek Orthodoxy, protected against constant threat of extinction by the iron framework of a "Roman" state inherited directly from Constantine and Justinian. Western Catholics believed that their church was destined to expand everywhere. East Romans were less euphoric but more tenacious. They believed that their Christian empire would, somehow, forever survive the regular ravages of invasion. It was a significant difference in attitudes, and neither side liked the other. East Romans considered the Franks barbarous and grasping: "no one deserves to have a Frank as their neighbor" was an East Roman proverb of the age of Charlemagne. For their part, Western Catholics contemptuously called the East Romans "Greeks" and condemned them for "Byzantine" cunning—failing to recognize that the generals and diplomats of Constantinople managed for centuries to fend off Baghdad's aggression largely by living by their wits. And locked in this confrontation, both Catholics and Orthodox tended to forget the sizable Christian communities to the east and south of them, from Ethiopia to Armenia, who continued under Muslim rule or on the frontiers of the Islamic empire, largely unaffected by what happened in either Europe or Byzantium.

Thus, like Islam, the Christian world was divided, though in this case the main division was into just two distinct entities—Western and eastern Christianity. Their differences

Viking Longhouse. A simple turf bunker was built by the Vikings on the coast of Canada. Low-lying for protection against wind and snow, it was built as a permanent settlement and trading post with the Eskimos. Viking trade goods appear far to the north in Baffin Island.

at that time were not doctrinal, like those of Shia and Sunni Islam. They were differences in heritage, customs, and levels of civilization. At that time, the orthodox world was considerably more ancient and more cultured than that of the Catholic west. Both encountered the expansionist ambitions of Muslim warriors, but they dealt with Islam differently. At Constantinople, capital of eastern Christianity and heir to the eastern part of the Roman Empire, Christianity held off Muslim forces that constantly threatened the integrity of the great city and its Christian hinterlands. In the west, on the other hand, Muslim expansionism ran its course confined to the Iberian Peninsula, behind the Pyrenees Mountains. Western Christendom, led by the Roman papacy, did not feel the same degree of political and cultural intimidation from Islam. It set about the task of spreading Christianity to the pagan tribes to the north, and as the period drew to a close it began to contemplate retaking lands from the Muslims.

Also like Islam, western Christianity expanded its geographic reach into new frontiers by harnessing faith to empire. (Byzantine Christianity tended to keep within its own frontiers and used the religion only for matters of interstate diplomacy.) In this fashion, universalizing religions reinforced the claims to power of aspiring rulers; but they also relied on rulers' armies to subdue or incorporate nonbelievers into the expanding circle of common spirituality. But much more than in Islam, where conquering armies more effectively centered the faith in Baghdad, Christendom was cleaved between east and west, and within the west it was splintered among rivalrous warrior provinces with only nominal allegiance to popes and other central authorities. Religion adapted itself to the localized political structures. And in contrast to China, where new rulers rebuilt integrated empires using traditional means

of rulership while accommodating and even promoting growing religious pluralism, in Christendom, especially in the west, we see increasing religious homogeneity and common faith, but no recovery of the bygone power of Rome—to which ambitious pretenders continued to aspire.

 # CONCLUSION

The four centuries from 600 to 1000 CE were marked both by extraordinary fluidities and by striking rigidities. Eurasian and North African societies witnessed a radical reordering of their political and cultural maps that encouraged movement across cultural boundaries and over long distances while at the same time insisting on the distinctiveness and often the superiority of individual political and cultural systems. Commodities, technological innovations, ideas, travelers, merchants, adventurers, and scholars moved with unusual rapidity from one end of Afro-Eurasia to the other, and up and down coastal Africa. This mercantile activity was accompanied by missionizing into new frontiers. The proximity and relatively porous boundaries of the two great political and cultural units of this period—Abbasid Islam and Tang China—abetted the movement of people and commodities; in this regard, the two empires stood in glaring contrast to their two powerful predecessors, Han China and Rome, which had occupied the far corners of the Afro-Eurasian landmass and were separated by great distances. The Silk Road was now even more widely traveled than in the previous centuries. And the agrarian revolution that swept much of middle Afro-Eurasia only fueled the bounty and population growth.

Yet in spite of the circulation of peoples and ideas throughout Eurasia and Africa, a new set of political and cultural boundaries were developing that would split this landmass in ways that it had not known before. The most important of these dividing forces was the new universalistic religion, Islam, which emerged in the first half of the seventh century and immediately challenged and slowed the spread of an equally determined universalistic religion, Christianity. As a consequence, Afro-Eurasia's highly differentiated major cultural zones now began to compete with one another in their universalistic religious and cultural doctrines. The Abbasid empire pushed back the borders of the Tang empire. But the intensity of interimperial conflict grew particularly high be-

tween the Islamic and Christian worlds, where the clash involved faith as well as frontiers.

The Sui and Tang empires revived Confucianism, insisting on its primacy within the Chinese political and moral system as the foundation of a new imperial order; and they embraced the classical written language as another unifying element in a new common culture. They thereby successfully counteracted the powerful global forces that brought foreign religions, notably Buddhism but also Islam, into the Chinese state. The same adaptive strategies, promoting religious amalgamation of new and old belief systems while elevating the powers of centralizing dynasties, also influenced the creation of new systems on the Korean Peninsula and in Japan.

Chronology

	MAJOR TRENDS	200 CE	300 CE	400 CE	500 CE
THE ISLAMIC WORLD	Afro-Eurasian agricultural revolution begins				
EAST ASIA		Three Kingdoms dominate Korea from the 3rd century		Yamato clan becomes dominant in Japan, 500	
EUROPE					

There were, therefore, many ways to cope with the emergence and spread of universalizing religions across Eurasia and Africa, but all were linked to empire. In some circumstances, faith followed empire and relied on rulers' support or tolerance, as well as some measure of political stability, to spread the word. This was the case especially in East Asia. At the opposite extreme, empire followed faith, as in the case of Islam, whose believers imagined an empire out of new cloth. To be sure, emerging dynasts exploited older symbolic resources, like the allure of a "restored" Mesopotamian centrality. But for the most part, the Islamic empire—and its successors—represented a new force on the world stage: expanding political power backed by one God whose instruc-

tions to believers was to spread his message. In the worlds of Christianity, a common faith yielded to elements of a common culture (shared books, a language for learned classes), but in the west only in name did rulers overcome the intense allegiance to local sources of political authority.

While this was an age in which universalizing religions expanded and common cultures grew, especially among literati and learned groups who aligned themselves with state power, there was also enormous debate and dissent within each religion over basic principles. In spite of the diffusion of basic texts inscribed in "official" languages, many variations of Christianity, Islam, and Buddhism existed, proliferating even more as each of these belief systems spread into new

600 CE	700 CE	800 CE	900 CE	1000 CE

▌ *Muhammad born in Mecca, 570*

    ▌ *Muhammad and small group of followers flee Mecca for Medina, 622*

    ▌ *Death of Muhammad, 632*

        ▌ *Arab armies conquer Southwest Asia, North Africa, Spain, Central Asia, and parts of South Asia, 650–750*

        ▌ *Ummayad caliphate rules from Damascus, 661–750*

        ▌ *Shiism emerges as major dissident force within Islam, late 7th century*

        ▌ *Abbasid caliphate rules from Baghdad, 750–1258*

        ▌ *Al-Khwarizmi (c. 780–850) writes first book on algebra*

        Fatimid Shiite regime forms, based in Egypt, 969 ▌

        Ibn Sina (980–1037) produces Canon of Medicine ▌

▌ *Prince Shotoku (574–622) initiates Taika political reforms*

▌ *Sui state unites much of China, 581–618*

    ▌ *Tang state emerges in China, 618*

    ▌ *Tang dynasty establishes strong influence on Central Asia by 650*

    ▌ *Silla state unifies Korea, 668*

    ▌ *Empress Wu reigns over Tang state, 690–705*

        ▌ *Tang army loses battle of Talas in 751 to Islamic forces, beginning Tang retreat from Central Asia*

        ▌ *Tang state embarks on anti-Buddhist campaigns*

        ▌ *Peasant uprising begins, 859*

        ▌ *Tang dynasty disintegrates, 906*

    Koryo kingdom assumes control of Korea, 918 ▌

        ▌ *Khitan invasion*

    ▌ *Arab armies conquer much of Byzantine Empire's lands in Southwest Asia, but the empire survives, 632–661*

        ▌ *Missionaries and monastic orders begin converting much of northern Europe into Christian communities loyal to the popes in Rome (had been converted by 800)*

        ▌ *Catholic Church based in Rome dominates Christian West*

        ▌ *Charlemagne (768–814) unites much of western Europe into a short-lived kingdom*

        ▌ *Vikings plunder northern Europe, 9th century*

        ▌ *Vikings establish strong commercial links across eastern Europe to Constantinople*

        Vikings reach North America, 982 ▌

        Russian leaders convert to Orthodox Christianity, 987 ▌

regions. As the first millennium drew to a close, religion, reinforced by prosperity and imperial resources, was a means to bring peoples together in unprecedented ways. But it was also, as the next chapter will illustrate, a new means to drive them apart in bloodcurdling confrontations.

STUDY QUESTIONS

WWNORTON.COM/STUDYSPACE

1. Analyze the impact of the spread of Islam on the various societies of Afro-Eurasia. How did the emergence of a large Islamic empire shape the movement of peoples, ideas, innovations, and commodities across the vast landmass?

2. Describe the process through which the spread of Islam fostered an agricultural revolution in Afro-Eurasia. What crops and cultivation techniques were involved in this process?

3. Compare and contrast the spread of Islam, Christianity, and Buddhism between 600 and 1000. What was the geographic range of each religious community? Through which methods did each religion gain new converts?

4. Explain the origins and basic concepts of Islam. How similar to and different from other religions that began in Southwest Asia, such as Judaism, Christianity, and Zoroastrianism, was this new religious outlook?

5. Analyze the successes and failures of Islamic leaders in creating one large empire to govern Islamic communities. What opponents emerged to challenge this goal?

6. Describe the Tang dynasty's attempts to restore political unity to East Asia. How did Tang leaders react to the growth of universal religions within their realm?

7. Explain the significance of the year 751 in world history. How did the battle of Talas shape the history of Afro-Eurasia?

8. Describe the state structure that emerged in Korea and Japan during this era. How were these new states shaped by other developments in Afro-Eurasia, such as the growth of universal religions?

9. Compare and contrast Christian communities in western Europe to those in eastern Europe and the Byzantine Empire. What factors contributed to each region's distinctiveness?

10. Analyze the impact of Viking communities on world history during this era. How did Vikings shape developments in the Christian world especially?

FURTHER READINGS

Ahmed, Leila, *Women and Gender in Islam* (1992). A superb overview of the relations between men and women throughout the history of Islam.

Aneirin, *Y Gododdin: Britain's Oldest Heroic Poem*, ed. and trans. A. O. H. Jarman (1988). A sixth-century Welsh text that describes the battle of the last Britons against the invading Anglo-Saxons.

Arberry, Arthur J., introduction to *The Koran Interpreted: A Translation*, trans. Arthur J. Arberry (1986). One of the most eloquent appreciations of this classical work of religion.

Augustine, *The City of God*, trans. H. Bettenson (1976). An excellent translation of Augustine's monumental work of history, philosophy, and religion.

Berkey, Jonathan P., *The Formation of Islam: Religion and Society in the Near East, 600–1800* (2005). A recent overview of the history of Islam before the modern era. It is particularly sensitive to the influence of external elements on the history of the Muslim peoples.

Bol, Peter, *This Culture of Ours: Intellectual Transitions in T'ang and Sung China* (1994). A study tracing the transformation of the shared culture of the Chinese learned elite from the seventh to the twelfth centuries.

Brown, Peter, *The Rise of Western Christendom: Triumph and Diversity, AD 200–1000*, 2nd ed. (2003). A description of the changes in Christianity in northern Europe and the emergence of the new cultures and political structures that coincided with this development.

Bulliet, Richard W., *Conversion to Islam in the Medieval Period: An Essay in Quantitative History* (1979). A determined and largely successful effort to measure the rate at which the populations overrun by Arab conquerors in the seventh century CE embraced the religion of their rulers.

Cook, Michael, *The Koran: A Very Short Introduction* (2000). A useful overview of Islam's holy book.

———, *Muhammad* (1983). A brief but careful life of the Prophet that takes full account of the prolific and often controversial preexisting scholarship.

Cross, S. H., and O. P. Sherbowitz-Westor, trans., *The Russian Primary Chronicle* (1953).

Donner, Fred M., *The Early Islamic Conquests* (1981). The best account of the Arab conquests in the Persian and Byzantine empires in the seventh century.

Fage, J. D., *Ghaua: A Historical Introduction* (1966). A brief but authoritative history of Ghaua from earliest times to the present.

Fisher, Humphrey J., *Slavery in the History of Muslim Black Africa* (2001). A general history of the relations between North Africa and black Africa, focusing on one of the most important aspects of contact—the slave trade.

Graham-Campbell, James, *Cultural Atlas of the Viking World* (1994). A positioning of the Vikings against their wider background in both western and eastern Europe.

Hawting, G. R., *The First Dynasty of Islam: The Umayyad Caliphate, A.D. 661–750* (2000). The essential scholarly treatment of Islam's first dynasty.

Herrmann, Georgina, *Iranian Revival* (1977). The structure and horizons of the Sasanian Empire as revealed in its monuments.

Hillgarth, J. N. (ed.), *Christianity and Paganism, 350–750: The Conversion of Western Europe*, rev. ed. (1986). A collection of contemporary sources.

Hodges, Richard and David Whitehouse, *Mohammed, Charlemagne, and the Origins of Europe* (1983). A spirited comparison of Islam and the rise of Europe.

Hodgson, Marshall G. S., *The Venture of Islam: Conscience and History in a World Civilization* (1977), 3 vols. A magnificent history of the Islamic peoples. Its first volume, *The Classical Age of Islam*, is basic reading for anyone interested in the history of the Muslim world.

Holdsworth, May, *Women of the Tang Dynasty* (1999). An account of women's lives during the Tang dynasty.

Hourani, Albert, *History of the Arab Peoples* (2002). The best overview of Arab history.

Jones, Gwynn, *The Norse Atlantic Saga* (1986). The Viking discovery of America.

Kennedy, Hugh, *The Prophet and the Age of the Caliphate: The Islamic Near East from the Sixth to the Eleventh Century* (2004). A very good recent synthesis.

Lee, Peter, et al. (eds.), *Sources of Korean Tradition*, vol. 1 (1996). A unique view of Korean history through the eyes and words of the participants or witnesses themselves, as provided in translations of official documents, letters, and policies.

Levtzion, Nehemia, *Ancient Ghana and Mali* (1980). The best introduction to the kingdoms of West Africa.

Levtzion, Nehemia, and Jay Spaulding, *Medieval West Africa: Views from Arab Scholars and Merchants* (2003). An indispensable source book on early West African history.

Lewis, Bernard, *The Middle East: Two Thousand Years of History from the Rise of Christianity to the Present Day* (1995). A stimulating introduction to an area that has seen the emergence of three of the great world religions.

——— (trans.), *Islam from the Prophet Muhammad to the Caphre of Constantinople* (1974). Vol. 2: Religion and Society. A fine collection of original sources that portray various aspects of classical Islamic society.

Middleton, John, *The Swahili: The Social Landscape of a Mercantile Community* (2000). An exciting synthesis of the Swahili culture of East Africa.

Miyazaki, Ichisada, *China's Examination Hell* (1981).

Nurse, Derek, and Thomas Spear, *The Swahili: Reconstructing the History and Language of an African Society, 800–1500* (1984). A work laying out what we know at present about the history of the Muslim peoples who lived along the coast of East Africa.

Peters, F. E., *Muhammad and the Origins of Islam* (1994). A work that explores the early history of Islam and highlights the critical role that Muhammad played in promoting a new religion and a powerful Arab identity.

Schirokauer, Conrad, et al., *A Brief History of Japanese Civilization*, 2nd ed. (2005). A balanced account; chapters focus on developments in art, religion, literature, and thought as well as on Japan's economic, political, and social history in medieval times.

Smith, Julia, *Europe after Rome: A New Cultural History, 500–1000* (2005). A vivid analysis of society and culture in so-called Dark Age Europe.

Twitchett, Denis, *The Birth of the Chinese Meritocracy: Bureaucrats and Examinations in Tang China* (1976). A description of the role of the written civil examinations that began during the Tang dynasty.

———, *Financial Administration under the Tang Dynasty* (1970). A pioneering account—based on rare Dunhuang documents that survived from medieval times in Buddhist grottoes in central Asia—of the political and economic system undergirding the Chinese imperial state.

Whittow, Mark, *The Making of Byzantium, 600–1025* (1996). A study on the survival and revival of the eastern Roman empire as a major power in eastern Europe and Southwest Asia.

Wood, Ian, *The Missionary Life: Saints and the Evangelization of Europe, 400–1050* (2001). The horizons of Christians on the frontiers of Europe.

10

BECOMING "THE WORLD," 1000–1300 CE

In the late 1270s, two Christian monks, Bar Sāwmā and Markōs, voyaged into the heart of Islam. They were not Europeans. They were Uighurs, a Turkish people of central Asia, among whom the Nestorian Christians had established churches in the seventh century CE. Sent by the mighty Mongol ruler Kubilai Khan on the eve of his becoming the first emperor of China's Yuan dynasty (1280–1368), the monks were supposed to worship at the temple in Jerusalem. But the Great Khan also had political ambitions—he had his eyes on conquering Jerusalem, held by the Muslims. Accordingly, he dispatched the monks to help make alliances with Christian kings of western Afro-Eurasia and to gather intelligence on his potential enemy's readiness in Palestine.

By 1280, conflict and conquest had transformed many parts of the world. But friction was simply one manifestation of cultures around the world brushing up against each other. Another had become more important: trade. Indeed, Bar Sāwmā and Markōs were delayed at the magnificent trading hub of Kashgar in what is now far western China, where caravan routes of Afro-Eurasia converged in a market for jade, exotic spices, and precious

417

silks. They were following the pathways of traders and migrants who were bringing Afro-Eurasian worlds into greater contact with each other. The monks detoured to Baghdad, and from there they parted ways. Bar Sāwmā himself visited Constantinople (where the king gave him gold and silver), Rome (where he met with the pope at the shrine of Saint Peter), and Paris (where he saw that city's university, teeming with students), before deciding to return to China, where the Christians of the East awaited his reports. In the end, neither monk ever returned. Yet their voyages exemplified the crisscrossing of people, money, and goods along the trade routes and sea-lanes that connected the world's parts. For just as religious conflict was a hallmark of this age, so too was a surge in trade, migration, and global exchange.

During the period from 1000 to 1300, people from distant regions often borrowed ideas, tools, and norms from other cultures. It was an era of great population growth, rising wealth, and social transformation, which propelled the world's cultures into heightened cross-cultural contact—a far cry from the common view that the world moved in slow motion before 1500 and the advent of modern institutions and technologies. But it was equally an age of conflict, carnage, and colonization, in which warfare fractured old states and created militarized new ones. Economic splendor, social change, and political upheaval entwined in the first three centuries of the second millennium in the Common Era. Commerce, conflict, and conquest did not make the world's people at the beginning of the second millennium more alike, however. To the contrary: contact and exchange reinforced

the sense of difference across cultures and created a feeling of apartness, of living within bounded cultural worlds that would soon come to be called "Europe," or "China," or "India." Even the minimal contact with other cultures experienced by the more separate areas of the world, such as sub-Saharan Africa, Japan, and the Americas, strengthened their identities. The paradoxical result was that the world was becoming more interconnected, while its regions became more clearly differentiated. The more geographical boundaries were crossed, the more they were reinforced by distinct cultural identities—which began to map out the world's regions as we recognize them today.

COMMERCIAL CONNECTIONS

> → *What factors led to the explosion of global trading activity between 1000 and 1300?*

The pace of economic change started to gather speed during this period. The effects of the agrarian and commercial breakthroughs of earlier periods began to make themselves felt in hitherto remote regions of Afro-Eurasia, drawing them closer together and making them more and more interdependent. The Americas, a region truly apart from the structures of

Focus Questions BECOMING "THE WORLD"

- → *What factors led to the explosion of global trading activity between 1000 and 1300?*
- → *How did trade and migration affect sub-Saharan Africa between 1000 and 1300?*
- → *How did trade and migration affect the Islamic world between 1000 and 1300?*
- → *In what ways did India remain a cultural mosaic?*
- → *What transformations in communication, education, and commerce contributed to the emergence of a distinct Chinese identity during this era?*
- → *How were Southeast Asia, Japan, and Korea influenced by sustained contact with other regions in this era?*
- → *How did Christianity produce a distinct identity among the diverse peoples of Europe?*
- → *Where did societies in the Americas demonstrate strong commercial expansionist impulses?*
- → *How did Mongol conquests affect cross-cultural contacts and regional development in Afro-Eurasia?*

 WWNORTON.COM/STUDYSPACE

long-distance trade and migration, also saw greater regional trade, urbanization, and population growth. The most visible sign of these prosperous times was the global explosion of trading activity.

REVOLUTIONS AT SEA

In the centuries after 1000 CE, traders took to the seas. By the tenth century, sea routes were eclipsing old land-based trading networks for long-distance trade. The combination of improved navigational aids, refinements in shipbuilding, better mapmaking, and breakthroughs in commercial laws and accounting practices made shipping easier and slashed the costs of seaborne long-distance trading. The numbers testify to the power of the maritime revolution: while a porter could carry about 10 pounds of commodities over long distances, and animal-drawn wagons could move 100 pounds of goods, the large Arab dhows that plied the Indian Ocean were capable of transporting as many as 5 tons of cargo. The result was that some small coastal ports, like Mogadishu in present-day Somalia, on the east coast of Africa, became in the eleventh century vast transshipment centers for a thriving trade across the Indian Ocean.

A new instrument made available to navigators was crucial in this boom: the needle compass. This Chinese invention was initially intended to find auspicious locations and orientations for houses and tombs, but it was also employed by sailors from Canton in the eleventh century to help guide them on the high seas. Use of the device spread rapidly from there. By the early thirteenth century, the compass was a vital tool on all vessels plying the sea-lanes between Southeast Asian and Indian trading hubs. Not only did it make sailing under cloudy skies possible—thus opening up the Mediterranean, which in Roman times had been too dangerous to travel from November to March, to year-round travel—but it made mapmaking less arduous and more accurate. And, of course, it made all the oceans, including the Atlantic, easier to navigate.

Shipping became less dangerous. Navigators relied on their trusty vessels—lateen-rigged dhows between the Indian Ocean and the Red Sea, heavy junks in the South China seas. They could also rely on the protection of political authorities, such as the Song dynasts in China, in guiding the trading fleets in and out of harbors. The Fatimid caliphate (909–1171 CE) in Egypt, for instance, profited from the maritime trade and therefore agreed to defend merchant fleets from pirates. Armed convoys of five or three ships escorted commercial fleets, a system called *karim* that regularized the traffic on the Indian Ocean and Red Sea. Because of its success, the system soon spread west to North Africa and southern Spain. *Karimi* firms were often family-based, and they sent young men of the family, sometimes servants or even slaves, to work in India. Housewives in Cairo could expect gifts from their husbands to arrive with the *karim* fleet.

Dhow. This modern dhow in the harbor of Zanzibar displays the characteristic triangle sail. The triangle sail can make good use of the trade monsoon and thus has guided dhows on the Arabian Sea since ancient times.

Antique Chinese Compass. Chinese sailors from Canton started to use needle compasses in the eleventh century. By the thirteenth century, needle compasses were widely used on ships in the Indian Ocean and were starting to appear in the Mediterranean.

The needle compass and changes in navigation ushered in the slow demise of the overland routes. Just as the merchants of the Silk Road had adapted by moving to southern routes in earlier centuries, so they eventually pulled up their stakes from the camel trains, fragrant caravansaries, and oasis hubs as they abandoned the road for the sea-lanes. It took centuries for the shift to be completed, but overland routes and camels were no commercial match for multiple-masted cargo ships laden with tons of silks, spices, and even more basic tradable staples. As the end of the first millennium drew near, a new interregional and increasingly global set of connections emerged on the high seas, bringing the parts of the world together, and thereby also creating new divisions.

COMMERCIAL CONTACTS

The opening of the sea-lanes sparked a commercial transformation. It also tapped into changes occurring in world agriculture. Agricultural development in Afro-Eurasia, and especially in western Europe, altered the nature of trade and transportation. (See Map 10-1.)

For a long time it was thought that agriculture remained primitive, not much more advanced than in Neolithic times, until the introduction of modern husbandry and the application of science. This view, we now know, misses the gradual and fundamental shifts occurring by 1000. The centuries of great irrigation works began to yield their enormous returns.

MAP 10-1 AFRO-EURASIAN TRADE, 1000–1300

During the early second millennium, Afro-Eurasian merchants increasingly turned to the Indian Ocean to transport their goods. Larger commercial flows profoundly shaped the history of the region. What revolutions in maritime travel facilitated this development? Why were ocean-based commercial routes more lucrative than land-based routes? Identify Quilon, Alexandria, Cairo, and Guangzhou. What role did they play in connecting the peoples of Afro-Eurasia?

Farmers learned how to rotate their crops to preserve soil fertility. The development of new strains of cereals, especially of barleys, ryes, and oats, and in the Americas the refinement of maize, enabled the cultivation of grains in vast areas that had formerly been too cold and arid to sustain them. Clover, alfalfa, and newly domesticated grasses of other sorts became fodder for grazing healthier, stronger, and fatter animals. Agriculture pushed into new regions, buoying population growth and yielding surpluses in many provinces—surpluses that now could be shipped great distances.

The Silk Road had conveyed luxuries, such as gemstones, fragrances and spices, silk textiles, woolen rugs, and tapestries. Their value was high, and they were light and easily carried. But now rice and other agrarian staples joined manufactured goods such as porcelains and silks in the long-distance trading systems. Ships made it feasible and lucrative to transport bulky and lower-value commodities—goods whose shipment was impossible or impractical when technologies of distribution were less developed: tea, rice, palm oil, woolen linen, and cotton textiles. Some goods, like the popular celadon porcelain ware, were not only heavy but fragile; they often shattered when carried on the backs of camels. Ships were a better means of conveying such delicate commodities to distant markets. In addition, the weight of porcelain added ballast necessary for long-distance sailing vessels.

GLOBAL COMMERCIAL HUBS

Long-distance trade spawned a new kind of metropolis: the commercial city. These hubs, the meeting points between distant cultures that we call entrepôts, became cosmopolitan nerve centers of an increasingly integrated world. Beginning in the late tenth century, three places emerged as the major anchorages of the maritime trade linking the landmasses of Afro-Eurasia, including the islands of Southeast Asia and Africa. In the west, the city of Cairo-Fustat (old Cairo) was a commanding headquarters for commerce between the Mediterranean and the Indian Ocean through the Red Sea. In the east, Quanzhou was the major port handling China's international trade. And Quilon, a port near the tip of Indian peninsula, which pushed deeply into the Indian Ocean's shipping lanes, functioned as the way station for voyages between the South China Sea and the Red Sea. All of these great trading centers thrived, in part because the free-for-all of trade and market life flourished under the political stability provided by big, powerful dynasts who recognized that the wealth created by trade would benefit their regimes.

THE EGYPTIAN ANCHORAGE The Egyptian cities of Cairo and Alexandria were Europe's main maritime commercial centers with ties to the Indian Ocean and beyond. Cairo, some 100 miles up the Nile, was home to numerous Muslim and Jewish trading firms, and Alexandria was their lookout

Persian Book. Books, such as this hand-copied one written in Kufic style, were traded in the Afro-Eurasian market starting in the tenth century.

post on the Mediterranean. These trading firms were kin-based, made up of family members, servants, and even slaves; they therefore took form within a single religion and conducted business according to rules set by their respective religious authority. Yet Jews, Muslims, and Christians were close partners in trade. On the Indian Ocean, Muslim firms owned most of the ships ferrying cargoes of Jewish traders to India.

Silk yarn and textiles were the most commonly traded commodities. It was through Alexandria that Europeans acquired silks from China, especially the coveted *zaytuni* (satin) fabric from Quanzhou. Spanish silks also passed through Alexandria on their way to eastern Mediterranean markets. But the entrepôts handled much more. Traditional goods from the Mediterranean included olive oil, glassware, flax, corals, and various metals. Gemstones and aromatic perfumes made from plants and animals poured in from India. Long-distance traders also shipped many staples such as minerals and chemicals for dying textiles or tanning skins, and raw materials such as timber and bamboo. The real novelties were paper and books. Hand-copied Bibles, Talmuds, works of legal and moral instruction, grammars in various languages, and Arabic books became the first best sellers of the Mediterranean.

Cairo and Alexandria prospered because Islamic leaders created sophisticated commercial institutions. Success began with the states that took seriously their obligation to protect merchants from predators. As noted above, the powerful Fatimid caliphate began regularly dispatching armed convoys to escort commercial fleets in the Mediterranean and the Red Sea, enabling the *karimi* firms and their family members to send goods and information on schedule. So regular were these fleets that they soon became the basis of an effective postal system. Thus, when an Egyptian trader who had traveled to Quilon around 1100 was delayed on his journey home, he could send a consoling message to his wife in Cairo. He could also send tokens of his love. In his letter he apologized for his absence from home but promised several gifts, including pearl bracelets, garments of red silk, a bronze basin, a ewer, and a six-year-old slave girl: "I shall send them, if God wills it, with somebody who is traveling home in the *Karim*" (Goitein, "New Light," 179).

The Islamic legal system also was involved in creating an environment favorable to conducting business. Those efforts are perhaps best exemplified in the techniques that specialists in law employed to get around the rule that would probably have brought commerce to a halt—the injunction in the sharia against usury, which prohibited earning any interest on loans. With the blessing of the clerics, Muslim traders formed partnerships, called *commenda* in medieval Europe, between those who had capital to lend and those who needed money to expand their businesses. These partnerships enabled owners of capital or merchandise to entrust their money or commodities to agents who, after their work was done, returned the initial investment and a share of the profits to the owners, keeping the rest as their reward. The English word "risk" derives from the Arabic *rizq*, the extra allowance paid to merchants in lieu of interest.

> *The English word "risk" derives from the Arabic* rizq, *the extra allowance paid to merchants in lieu of interest.*

THE ANCHORAGE OF QUANZHOU At the other end of Afro-Eurasia, in China, Quanzhou was as busy as the cities of Cairo and Alexandria, although trade there was not a free-for-all. The Song government set up offices of Seafaring Affairs in its three major ports: Canton, Quanzhou, and an area near present-day Shanghai in the Yangzi delta. In return for taking a portion of the taxes, these offices registered and examined cargoes, sailors, and traders, while archers employed as guards kept a keen eye on the traffic.

All foreign traders were guests of the governor, who doubled as the Chief of Seafaring Affairs. Part of his mandate was to host an annual ritual intended to summon favorable winds for ships. Unlike in the Arabian Sea, where monsoons make the wind direction predictable, winds in the Taiwan Strait do not fall into regular seasonal patterns. Every year, the governor took his place on a high perch facing the harbor, in front of a rock cliff filled with inscriptions that recorded the wind-calling rituals. Traders of every origin witnessed the rite, then joined the governor and local dignitaries for a large banquet. Quanzhou sailors, foreigners as well as Chinese, also frequently sought protection at the shrine of the goddess Mazu. According to the local legend, before assuming godhood Mazu had lived from 960 to 987 and had performed many miracles. Her temple became prominent after 1123, when the governor of Quanzhou survived a bad storm at sea while returning home from Korea. Ever since then, sailors as well as their wives and mothers regularly burned incense for the goddess and prayed for her aid in keeping them safe at sea.

Ships departing from Quanzhou and other Chinese ports were junks—large flat-bottomed ships with internal sealed bulkheads and stern-mounted rudders. Those from Quanzhou headed for Srivijaya, or Java, in the Malay Archipelago, navigating through the Strait of Melaka, a choke point between the South China Sea and the Indian Ocean. The final destination was Quilon, on the Malabar Coast of southwest India. Traders wishing to go further west unloaded their cargo and boarded small Arabian dhows, to make passage in Arab-dominated seas. Conversely, traders from Islamic countries arriving at Quilon in dhows and wishing to travel further east had to change to big Chinese ships.

Chinese traders had the best ships in the world. Multiple watertight compartments increased their stability and seaworthiness, and the larger ships contained as many as four decks, six masts, and a dozen sails and could carry 500 men. Navigators used up-to-date charts and compasses to reach foreign ports.

The traders who arrived at Chinese ports on junks were not all Chinese. Arabs, Persians, Jews, and Indians traded at Quanzhou, and quite a few stayed on to manage their businesses. Perhaps as many as 100,000 Muslims lived in Quanzhou's trading communities during the Song dynasty. Foreign traders could become power brokers in their own right. Consider the Pu family, which owned several hundred ships that plied the routes between India and Islamic countries. To promote good relationships in the community, it made large donations over several generations for public projects such as bridges, and the contributions even garnered official positions for some male family members. After the Mongols conquered the Southern Song in the late thirteenth century, Pu Shougeng, the patriarch of the family, turned over all the ships and the city of Quanzhou. The new emperor, Kubilai, was pleased with his services—and granted him the position of administrating the port's overseas trade.

Foreign merchants did not stay in isolated neighborhoods, apart from the rest of the city. Indeed, their residences and graves were scattered throughout Quanzhou. However, they had their own buildings for religious worship and indicated their faith on their gravestones. A well-built mosque from this period is still standing on a busy street. Hindu traders who lived in Quanzhou worshipped in a Buddhist shrine, Kaiyuan Si, where statues of the Hindu deities Hanuman and Krishna stand beside Buddhist gods. Like so many of the new global entrepôts, Quanzhou was simultaneously a power base in its own state and a home for world traders and travelers.

THE TIP OF INDIA In the tenth century, the Chola dynasty in modern Tamil Nadu rose as a major power in south India. It supplied the political support and protection for a new commercial nerve center for maritime trade between

China and the Red Sea and the Mediterranean. As the Chola dynasts profited from their commercial ventures, they expanded their reach. Following their conquest of Sri Lanka, they moved on to extend their influence over key ports on the southern Malay Peninsula, Sumatra, and eventually to the all-important Strait of Malacca, the seagoing gateway to Southeast and East Asia (see more on the islands of Southeast Asia below).

A commercial revolution swept the Indian Ocean as networks of Chola traders fanned out to establish entrepôts around the sea's rim. Indian merchant ships benefited from the Chola patronage to sail to Chinese ports. However, the Chola golden age lasted only about two generations. Indian Ocean trade continued to flourish after the Chola hegemony. Beginning in the mid–eleventh century, Islamic traders, both Arabs and Iranians, made adjustments to their trading arrangements. Many Muslim traders settled in Malabar, on the southwest coast of the Indian peninsula, and Quilon became a major hub. Dhows arrived, laden with goods from the Red Sea and Africa, and unloaded their cargoes. Passengers, traders, sojourners, and fugitives also disembarked and made Quilon into a cosmopolitan city. Big Chinese junks entered the port to unload their wares of silks and porcelain, and to pick up passengers and commodities for East Asian markets. Sailors and traders strictly observed the customs of this entrepôt; as they knew well, it was good business to respect others' norms and values while engaging in commerce with them.

Muslims constituted the largest foreign community, living in their own neighborhoods. They shipped horses from Arab countries to India and southeast islands. Kings of the tropical countries viewed horses as symbols of royalty, and because the animals could not survive long in those climates the demand was constant. Elephants and cattle from tropical countries were also sold in Quilon, though the bulk of the goods traded were spices, perfumes, and textiles. Traders who frequented Quilon knew each other well, and personal relationships were key in their transactions. When trying to strike a deal with a local merchant, a Chinese trader would mention his Indian neighbor in Quanzhou and the residence of that family in Quilon. Global commercial hubs relied on friendship and family to keep their businesses humming across religious and regional divides.

SUB-SAHARAN AFRICA COMES TOGETHER

> → *How did trade and migration affect sub-Saharan Africa between 1000 and 1300?*

The dawn of the new millennium produced dramatic transformations in sub-Saharan Africa's relationship to the rest of the world, while heightening North Africa's integration into an emerging global economy. Before 1000 CE, sub- Saharan Africa had never been a world truly apart, but after this date its integration became firmer. Africans and outsiders now became more determined to overcome the sea, river, and desert barriers that had blocked the peoples who lived below the Sahara Desert from participating in long- distance trade and intellectual exchanges. (See Map 10-2.) During this period, hardly a region within Africa escaped the effects of the outside world, though many inhabitants who lived far away from the new routes bearing trade and culture were unaware of how events outside of Africa were now altering their lives.

WEST AFRICA AND THE MANDE-SPEAKING PEOPLES

Ever since the camel had bridged the great Sahara Desert (see Chapter 9), trade, commodities, and ideas linked Africa south of the Sahara to the Muslim world of North Africa and Southwest Asia. As the savanna region of West Africa became increasingly connected to Afro-Eurasian developments, the mobile Mande-speaking peoples emerged as the primary agents for integration within and beyond West Africa, using their expertise in commerce and political organization to edge out other groups living in the area. The Mande languages are a branch of the large Niger-Congo family, which contains most of the African languages below the Sahara (including those in the Bantu branch). But Mande was more than a linguistic category. It was also associated with a way of life, as its speakers shared a common culture.

The home to the Mande or Mandinka peoples was, and continues to be, the vast area between the bend in the Senegal River to the west and the bend of the Niger River to the east (1,000 miles wide), a territory stretching from the Senegal River in the north to the Bandama River in the south (a distance of more than 2,000 miles). This was the locale in which the kingdom of Ghana had come into being around the eighth century and where Ghana's successor state—the Mandinka state of Mali, discussed below—emerged around 1100 CE.

The Mande-speaking peoples were constantly on the go, and they were marvelously adaptable. By the eleventh century they were spreading their cultural, commercial, and political hegemony from the high grasslands of the West African savanna southward into the woodlands and the tropical rainforests that stretched to the Atlantic Ocean. Those who lived in the rain forests of West Africa organized themselves into small-scale societies led by local councils, while those who occupied the savanna lands of the interior of West Africa became adept at centralized forms of government. It was in these high grasslands that the Mande and other groups developed an institution that marked the centralized polities of West Africa: sacred kingships. The inhabitants of these polities believed that their kings had descended from the gods

MAP 10-2 SUB-SAHARAN AFRICA, 1300

Increased commercial contacts continued to influence the religious and political geography of sub-Saharan Africa between 1000 and 1300. Compare this map to Map 9-5 (p. 385). Where had strong Islamic communities emerged by 1300 and what factors facilitated their growth? How did Mande speakers heighten the cultural integration of sub-Saharan societies? To what extent had sub-Saharan Africa "come together"?

and that they enjoyed the blessing of the gods. As the Mande broadened their territory from the interior of West Africa all the way to the Atlantic coast, they gained access to the tradable items much sought after in the interior, notably kola nuts and malaguetta peppers, for which they exchanged iron products and textile manufactures. By 1300, the Mandinka merchants had followed the Senegal River to its outlet on the northern coast of present-day Senegal, and then pushed their commercial frontiers further inland and down the coast. Thus, even before the arrival of European explorers and traders in the middle of the fifteenth century, West African peoples had created dynamic trading networks that linked the African hinterlands with coastal trading hubs.

In the period from the eleventh century to the end of the fifteenth century, the most vigorous and profitable businesses were those that stretched across the Sahara Desert. The Mande-speaking peoples, with their far-flung commercial networks and highly dispersed populations, dominated this trade as well. Here one of the most prized items of trade was salt, mined in the northern Sahel, around the city of Taghaza; it was in demand on both sides of the Sahara. Another highly valued commodity was gold, mined within the Mande homeland itself and borne by camel caravans to the northern societies on the far side of the Sahara, where it was exchanged for a variety of manufactures. Equally important in West African commerce were slaves, who were shipped to the settled Muslim communities of North Africa and Egypt.

THE EMPIRE OF MALI

Booming trade spawned new political organizations. The empire of Mali was the Mande successor state to the kingdom of Ghana. Founded during the first half of the twelfth century, it exercised political sway over a vast area up until the fifteenth century, when it gave way to yet another sprawling Muslim state, Songhai, whose center was based further to the east. The Mali Empire represented the triumph of horse warriors, and its origins have long been enshrined in an epic involving the dynasty's founder, the legendary Sundiata. According to *The Epic of Sundiata,* a powerful but deformed youngster eventually overcame unjust and irreligious rulers to install a righteous Islamic state in the new capital city of Niamey. Many historians believe that an individual named Sundiata actually existed, noting that the famed Arab historian Ibn Khaldun referred to him by name a full century later and reported that he was "their [Mali's] greatest king. He overcame the Susu, conquered their country, and seized the power from their hands" (Levtzion, p. 64). He—or if not he, then someone very much like him—lived in the early part of the thirteenth century, and his triumph, as narrated in *The Epic,* marked the victory of the new cavalry forces over traditional foot soldiers. Henceforth, horses—which had always existed in some parts of Africa—became prestige objects of the savanna peoples, the essential symbols of state power.

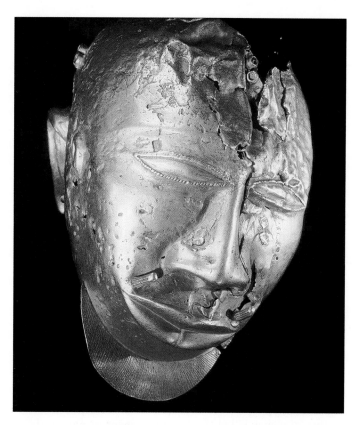

Asanti Gold. Although this gold head from the kingdom of Asante was made in the eighteenth century, it nicely shows the artistic abilities of the West African peoples. The head probably belonged to the Asante ruler, known as the Asantehene, and symbolized his power and wealth.

The Mali Empire was a thriving polity, and its commerce was in full swing in the fourteenth century. Because Mande trade routes ran through the rain forests to the Atlantic Ocean and crossed the Sahara Desert, West Africa was no longer a distant, isolated periphery of the central Muslim lands. The noted Arab traveler Ibn Battuta, who visited Mali in the early thirteenth century, praised the Muslims of the area for their punctuality in carrying out the five daily prayers required of the faithful. Mali's most famous sovereign, Mansa Musa, who ruled from 1312 until 1332, made a celebrated hajj, the pilgrimage to Mecca, in 1325–1326, traveling through Cairo and impressing crowds of merchants and clerics with the size of his retinue and with his displays of wealth, which usually featured items made from gold.

The Mali Empire boasted two of West Africa's largest cities. Jenne, an ancient northern commercial entrepôt, was a vital assembly point for caravans of salt, gold, and slaves about to set out on their long journeys west to the Atlantic Ocean coastal area and north over the Sahara. An urban settlement first appeared here around 200 BCE, and from that time on it became an important gathering place for traders. The town itself arose as the area became more arid and was no longer subject to annual Niger River flooding. The first

Primary Source

AN AFRICAN EPIC

The traditional story of the founding of the kingdom of Mali is long and complex; it was passed down orally from generation to generation by griots, counselors, and other official historians to the royal family. Only in 1960 was it finally written down in French. Because the narrative involves many complicated stories as it recounts the life of Sundiata, the heroic founder of the Mali state, no single excerpt can fully capture its flavor. The following short passage provides some insight into the role of the narrator (the griot) in the Malian kingdom and identifies the qualities of good and bad rulers.

We are now coming to the great moments in the life of Sundiata. The exile will end and another sun will arise. It is the sun of Sundiata. Griots know the history of kings and kingdoms and that is why they are the best counsellors of kings. Every king wants to have a singer to perpetuate his memory, for it is the griot who rescues the memories of kings from oblivion, as men have short memories.

Kings have prescribed destinies just like men, and seers who probe the future know it. They have knowledge of the future, whereas we griots are depositories of the knowledge of the past. But whoever knows the history of a country can read its future.

Other peoples use writing to record the past, but this invention has killed the faculty of memory among them. They do not feel the past any more, for writing lacks the warmth of the human voice. With them everybody thinks he knows, whereas learning should be a secret. The prophets did not write and their words have been all the more vivid as a result. What paltry learning is that which is congealed in dumb books!

I, Djeli Mamoudou Kouyaté, am the result of a long tradition. For generations we have passed on the history of kings from father to son. The narrative was passed on to me without alteration and I deliver it without alteration, for I received it free from all untruth.

Listen now to the story of Sundiata, the Na'Kamma, the man who had a mission to accomplish.

At the time when Sundiata was preparing to assert his claim over the kingdom of his fathers, Soumaoro was the king of kings, the most powerful king in all the lands of the setting sun. The fortified town of Sosso was the bulwark of fetishism against the word of Allah. For a long time Soumaoro defied the whole world. Since his accession to the throne of Sosso he had defeated nine kings whose heads served him as fetishes in his macabre chamber. Their skins served as seats and he cut his footwear from human skin. Soumaoro was not like other men, for the jinn had revealed themselves to him and his power was beyond measure. So his countless sofas [soldiers] were very brave since they believed their king to be invincible. But Soumaoro was an evil demon and his reign had produced nothing but bloodshed. Nothing was taboo for him. His greatest pleasure was publicly to flog venerable old men. He had defiled every family and everywhere in his vast empire there were villages populated by girls whom he had forcibly abducted from their families without marrying them.

→ Are you able to understand the function of the griot after reading this passage?
→ How reliable do you think this kind of oral history is?
→ Soumaoro was the adversary of Sundiata and exemplified the characteristics of a bad ruler. Sundiata, in contrast, prevailed because he embodied good kingly qualities. What were they?
→ Comment on the role of religion in the founding of this empire.

SOURCE: *Sundiata: An Epic of Old Mali*, translated by D. T. Niane (Harlow: Longman Group, 1965), pp. 40–41.

houses were made of mud, but most of these had been replaced by 1000 CE with more substantial brick structures. Around the city, running for more than a mile, was an impressive wall more than eleven feet thick at its base. Even more spectacular than Jenne was the city of Timbuktu; founded around 1100 as a seasonal camp for nomads, it grew in size and importance under the patronage of different Malian kings. By the fourteenth century the city was a thriving commercial and religious center, famed for its two large mosques, which are still standing. In addition to being a

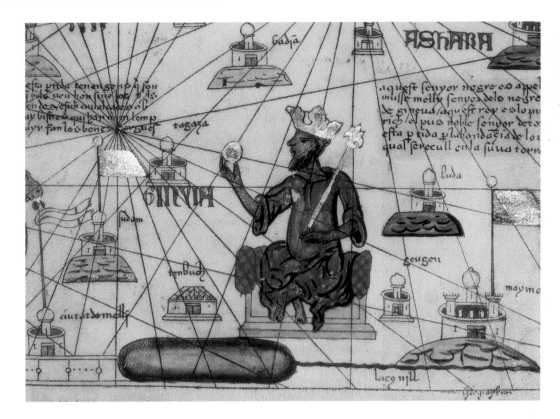

King of Mali. This 1375 picture shows the king of Mali on his throne, surrounded by images of gold. The Europeans considered the interior of West Africa to be an important source of gold.

booming commercial center, it was also renowned for its intellectual vitality. Here, West African Muslim scholars congregated to debate the tenets of Islam and to ensure that Islam even when distant from the Muslim heartland was rigorously practiced, with no taint of pagan observances. These clerics acquired learned treatises on Islam from all over the world for their personal libraries, remnants of which remain to this day.

East Africa and the Indian Ocean

Eastern and southern African regions were also integrated into long-distance trading systems. The monsoon winds, blowing from the southwest in January and the northeast in July, had made East Africa a logical end point for much of the Indian Ocean trade; Swahili peoples living along that coast became active brokers intermediating between the peoples of the Arabian Peninsula, the Persian Gulf territories, and the west coast of India. The city of Kilwa soon caught up with the booming port of Mogadishu as a great entrepôt. Merchants in Kilwa, along the coast of present-day Tanzania, brought ivory, slaves, gold, and other items from the African interior and shipped them to destinations around the Indian Ocean.

The most valued commodity for Swahili traders was gold. It was the key to the commercial revolution along the East African coast—and fueled the extravagant success of the In-

dian Ocean trading system. Located in the highlands between the Limpopo and Zambezi rivers, gold was mined by Shona-speaking peoples, who had established their dominance in the region around 500 CE. By the beginning of the new millennium, the Shona had already founded as many as fifty small centers of religious and political significance; each was dominated by stone structures that displayed its political and religious power and was surrounded by many small peasant villages. Around 1100 one of these centers, Great Zimbabwe, emerged as supreme among the Shona peoples. It was built on the fortunes made from gold, and its most impressive landmark was a massive elliptical building—32 feet high, 17 feet thick in parts, and stretching for more than 800 feet—made of stone so expertly that its fittings needed no grouting. The buildings of Great Zimbabwe were probably intended to house the king, known as *monomotapas,* whose religious and political powers were greatly extolled and feared. They probably also contained the smelters for melting down the gold that had been mined or panned nearby.

The commercial integration of the Swahili and Shona peoples enabled gold and other products to flow from the interior of eastern and southern Africa across the Indian Ocean. Before Europeans accidentally happened upon the Americas, Africa was the world's largest source of precious metals.

One of the great meeting grounds of the Indian Ocean trading system was the island of Madagascar—the fourth-largest island of the world, lying just 150 miles off the coast of East Africa. Indeed, during this period so intense was the

Great Zimbabwe. These walls surrounded the city of Great Zimbabwe, which was a center of the gold trade between the East African coastal peoples and traders plying the Indian Ocean. Great Zimbabwe flourished during the thirteenth, fourteenth, and fifteenth centuries.

interchange of peoples, plants, and animals from mainland Africa and around the rest of the Indian Ocean that Madagascar became one of the most intermixed and multicultural places in the world. The minority population came from Bantu-speaking peoples, who by then dominated the southern part of the African landmass (see Chapter 8); the majority were of Malay-Indonesian origin. Early seafarers from Indonesia, plying large, seaworthy outrigger canoes, hugged the shores of the Indian Ocean as they sailed from their homes past Sri Lanka and South Asia, and were carried by the monsoon winds to the African coast. Then they sailed south, perhaps picking up Bantu-speaking peoples along the way, and finally arrived at the island of Madagascar. The first evidence of human settlement does not occur until the eighth century CE. Thereafter, the island became a regular stopover

point, as well as an import-export market, for traders crossing the Indian Ocean.

THE TRANS-SAHARAN AND INDIAN OCEAN SLAVE TRADE

African slaves were as valuable as African gold in shipments to the Mediterranean and Indian Ocean markets. Unlike gold, slave populations left a permanent imprint, since they eventually merged into the North African and Indian Ocean communities. There had been a busy trade in African slaves, mainly from Nubia, into pharaonic Egypt well before the Common Era. After Islam spread into Africa and sailing techniques improved, the slave trade across the Sahara and Indian Ocean boomed. As noted above, slaves were an important component of West African commerce.

This slave system was unlike the chattel slavery found much later in the Americas (the form of slavery most familiar to us today). The Prophet Muhammad had found slavery to be a well-established institution in the Arabian Peninsula when he was promulgating his message in the seventh century. The Quran attempted to mitigate its severity, requiring Muslim slave owners to treat their slaves with kindness and generosity and praising the manumission of slaves as an act of piety. Nonetheless, the African slave trade flourished under Islam, and slaves filled a great variety of roles in the slave-importing societies.

African slaves were obtained in this period much as they were later on: some were taken in wars; others were judged to be criminals and sold into slavery as punishment. Their duties in slave-importing societies were quite varied. Some slaves were pressed into military duties, rising in a few instances to positions of high authority. Others were valued for their seafaring skills and were used as crewmen on dhows or dockworkers servicing dhows in the Indian Ocean's port cities. Still others, mainly women, were domestic servants, and not a few African slave women became concubines of powerful Muslim political figures and businessmen. African slaves were also used on plantations, the most notorious and oppressive being the agricultural estates of lower Iraq—very early forerunners of the plantations of the antebellum South in the United States; there slaves worked under fearsome discipline and carried out a revolt in the ninth century. Yet in this era, such labor was more the exception than the rule. Slaves were more prized as adjuncts to family labor or as status symbols for their owners. Although the precise numbers are not known, the Arab Muslim slave traders transported many millions of Africans across the Sahara or the Indian Ocean from the beginning of the seventh century until the end of the nineteenth century. Slavery was therefore widespread. But in the words of the American historian Ira Berlin, these were societies with many slaves rather than slave societies—that is, societies whose basic economic fortunes and social structures rested on the widespread ownership of human beings as a source of labor.

وَكَأَنَّ اَحَدَ اِنَّهُ سَيَنْظُرُ شَرَرًا اِلَى وَغُلَى السِّمَةِ عَلَى اَحَلَّ ...

Slave Market. Slaves were a common commodity in the marketplaces of the Islamic world. Turkish conquests during the years from 1000 to 1300 put many prisoners into the slave market.

ISLAM IN A TIME OF POLITICAL FRAGMENTATION

> → *How did trade and migration affect the Islamic world between 1000 and 1300?*

Islam underwent the same burst of expansion, prosperity, and cultural diversification that swept through the rest of the Afro-Eurasian world in the three centuries after 1000. (See Map 10-3.) However, in contrast to many other regions, where prosperity fostered greater integration, the peoples of Islam remained politically fractured despite sharing a common faith and culture. The Islamic empire's population at the turn of the millennium (excluding India and Africa below the Sahara) was well below that of China and India at this time—a mere 34 million, just slightly less than that of Europe (including European Russia). This was a paradoxical age, in

which the dream of a unified Islam became precisely that: a dream nurtured in a bountiful present by the sense of a glorious past. As in China, efforts to unite under a common rulership failed, giving way to defeats by marauding outsiders. The attempt to uphold centralized rule ended cataclysmically in 1258 with the Mongol sacking of Baghdad and the execution of the last Abbasid caliph.

Islam responded to its political fragmentation not by turning inward but by undergoing major changes, many prompted by contacts (and conflicts) with neighbors. Commercial networks, sustained by active Muslim merchants, carried the word of the Quran far and wide. As Islam spread, it attracted more converts. But new converts often carried on many traditions that the ulama and other Islamic leaders condemned as incompatible with the religion. This conflict between orthodox Muslims and newer converts threatened to divide the wider Islamic community. At the same time (as discussed below), many Sufi orders emerged that blended orthodox and unorthodox practices in a fashion that held broad appeal and linked diverse communities. Also, as the commercial revolution driven by the dramatic expansion of Afro-Eurasian trade within the old Islamic heartlands brought urban and peasant masses into trading relations, it introduced them to a faith that previously had been shared mainly by political, commercial, and scholarly elites. In these three centuries, Islam became an even more open and accommodating religious system, embracing Persian literature, Turkish ruling skills, and Arabic language contributions in the fields of law, religion, literature, and science. In this way the world acquired another "core" region centered in what we now call the Middle East—the lands between the "Far East" of China and Japan and the "Near East," or the countries of the eastern Mediterranean—united by a shared faith and pulsating with frenetic commercial energies.

But by the thirteenth century, India and China, rather than the Islamic world, were the most technologically advanced and prosperous agrarian societies. Cultivation in Islamic societies began to stagnate and, in some places, even decline. Trade became the main source of prosperity when the agrarian innovations that Islam had so dynamically spread across Afro-Eurasia stalled. Muslim merchants became the world's premier traders in this era; the old Islamic heartland became the crossroads for Afro-Eurasian commercial networks.

AFRO-EURASIAN MERCHANTS

The peoples most responsible for integrating the sprawling Islamic worlds were long-distance merchants. They also were the main cultural brokers mediating between Islamic peoples and the rest of the world. Afro-Eurasia's expanding populations and rising material prosperity offered unprecedented opportunities for the merchants of Islam to enrich themselves; Southwest Asia was poised at the center of the Afro-Eurasian landmass, its merchants settled in key nodal points.

These merchants were as diverse as their businesses. Islam's lack of violent turmoil, the spread of the Arabic

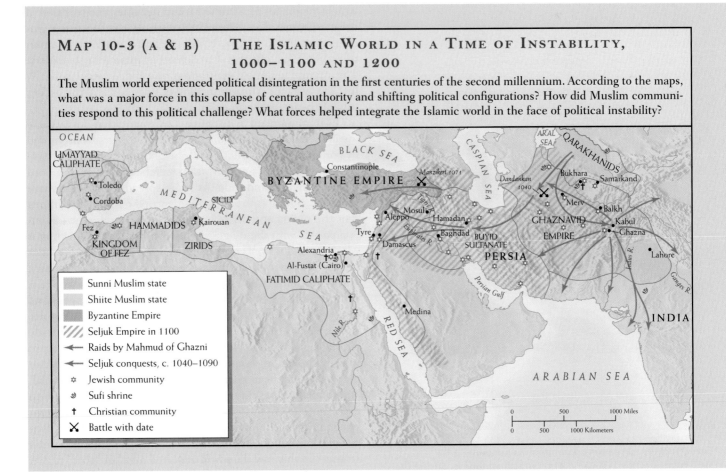

MAP 10-3 (A & B)   THE ISLAMIC WORLD IN A TIME OF INSTABILITY, 1000–1100 AND 1200

The Muslim world experienced political disintegration in the first centuries of the second millennium. According to the maps, what was a major force in this collapse of central authority and shifting political configurations? How did Muslim communities respond to this political challenge? What forces helped integrate the Islamic world in the face of political instability?

language, and Islamic law enabled entrepreneurs of many different ethnic and religious backgrounds to flourish. While Muslims played a major part in the brisk long-distance trading of this period, Armenian, Indian, and Jewish traders who were based in Islam's major cities and connected with families in North Africa and Central Asia also expanded their commercial networks. Documents discovered in a Jewish synagogue in Cairo that date back to this era reveal how voluminous and far-reaching this trade was. Jewish merchants, residing in major cities from Morocco to India, oversaw a booming trade from intermediate points such as Aden.

Long-distance trade surged because it was supported by a highly sophisticated legal framework. Traders drew up elaborate contracts; and when the contracts were breached, merchants took their cases to the courts. Although disputes involving Jewish, Armenian, or Christian coreligionists were often resolved by local religious tribunals, many merchants appeared before Islamic *qadis* (judges), who presided over the Islamic courts and whose expertise in commercial matters was greatly admired. Yet, in truth, merchants rarely needed to seek legal recourse. The mercantile community was self-policing; its members severely punished those who violated trust, sometimes ending their careers. Relying on partner-

ships, using letters of credit, and possessing knowledge of local trading customs and currencies, traders and their customers were confident that agreements made in India would be honored in Southeast Asia, Egypt, and North Africa.

DIVERSITY AND UNIFORMITY IN ISLAM

Not until the ninth and tenth centuries did Muslims become a majority within their own recently ascendant Abbasid Empire. From the outset, Muslim rulers and clerics had to deal with large non-Muslim populations, even as these populations were gradually converting to Islam. Borrowing freely from subject peoples and regarding those with their own scriptures as fellow "peoples of the book," Muslim rulers accorded non-Muslims religious toleration as long as they accepted Islam's political dominion. Jewish, Christian, and Zoroastrian communities were permitted to choose their own religious leaders and to settle internal disputes in their own religious courts. They were, however, obligated to pay a special tax, called the *jizya,* and to be properly deferential to their rulers. Especially in times of heightened religious tension, such deference could entail wearing special clothing and dis-

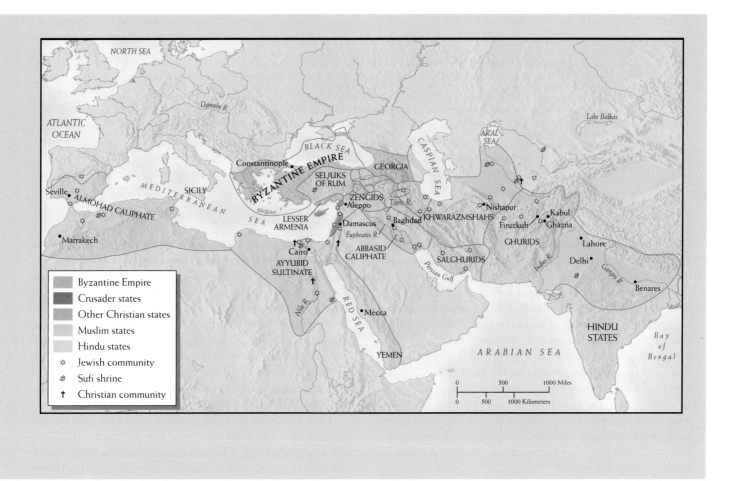

mounting from horses when they passed important Muslim personages.

These regulations, which shaped what was known as the *dhimma* system, granted protections to religious minorities. They therefore spared the Islamic world some of the religious conflict that afflicted other areas. Non-Muslims were free to worship in their traditional ways and were encouraged to make significant contributions to the economic and political well-being of Islamic lands. Such tolerance helped make Islamic cities hospitable environments for traders from around the world.

Still, Islam was an expansionist faith. Some intense proselytizing carried the sacred word to new frontiers, and in the process reinforced the spread of Islamic institutions that supported more commercial exchanges. There were also moments of intense religious passion within Islam's frontiers, especially when Muslim rulers feared that Christian minorities would make common cause with the Europeans who were pressing on their borders. Ugly incidents erupted, and some churches were burned. Pressures to convert to Islam were unremitting at this time; after a surge of conversions to Islam from the ninth century onward, the Christian Copts of Egypt shrank to a small community and never recovered their numbers.

Islam was hardly uniform. One strong element was the mystical movement known as Sufism, a name derived from the wool garments (*suf* in Arabic) that many of its adherents wore. By performing such ecstatic rituals as repeating over and over again the name of God, dancing, and most notably whirling, they sought to liberate the soul from the body and even to come face to face with God. It was inside the Sufi brotherhoods (*turuq* in Arabic) that Islam truly became a religion for the people. Indeed, Sufi orders brought about mass conversions from Christianity to Islam.

The formalizing of Sufi brotherhoods did little to lessen mystics' desire to experience the love of God. Some expressed that desire in poetry, and several of Islam's most highly regarded mystical love poets belonged to Sufi orders. The most admired of all, Jalal al-Din Rumi (1207–1273), was the spiritual founder of the Mevlevi Sufi order, famed for the ceremonial dancing of its whirling dervishes. Rumi, who wrote in Persian, celebrated all forms of love, spiritual and sexual, and preached a universalistic religious message:

What is to be done of Muslims? For I do not recognize myself,
I am neither Christian, nor Jew, nor Gabr [Zoroastrian], nor Muslim.

Primary Source

THE MERCHANTS OF EGYPT

The most comprehensive collection of eleventh- and twelfth-century commercial materials from the Islamic world comes from a repository originally connected to the Jewish synagogue in Cairo. It was the custom of the Jewish community to preserve all texts that mention God in a special store-room called a geniza. A huge collection of such documents came to light just before 1890 when the Cairo Geniza became known to the outside world. Most of these papers, which are a rich source of information about the Jewish community in Egypt at that time, were purchased for the University Library of Cambridge University. The documents touch on all manner of activities: cultural, religious, judicial, political, and commercial. The following letter is addressed to Joseph ibn 'Awkal, one of Egypt's leading merchants in the eleventh century.

Dear and beloved elder and leader, may God prolong your life, never take away your rank, and increase his favors and benefactions to you.

I inform you, my elder, that I have arrived safely. I have written you a letter before, but have seen no answer. Happy preoccupations—I hope. In that letter I provided you with all the necessary information.

I loaded nine pieces of antimony (kohl), five in baskets and four in complete pieces, on the boat of Ibn Jubār—may God keep it; these are for you personally, sent by Mūsā Ibn al-Majjānī. On this boat, I have in partnership with you—may God keep you—a load of cast copper, a basket with (copper) fragments, and two pieces of antimony. I hope God will grant their safe arrival. Kindly take delivery of everything, my lord.

I have also sent with Banāna a camel load for you from Ibn al-Majjānī and a camel load for me in partnership with you—may God keep you. He also carries another partnership of mine, namely, with 'Ammār Ibn Yijū, four small jugs (of oil).

With Abū Zayd I have a shipload of tin in partnership with Salāma al-Mahdawī. Your share in this partnership with him is fifty pounds. I also have seventeen small jugs of s[oap]. I hope they arrive safely. They belong to a man [called . . .]r b. Salmūn, who entrusted them to me at his own risk. Also a bundle of hammered copper, belonging to [a Muslim] man from the Maghreb, called Abū Bakr Ibn Rizq Allah. Two other bundles, on one is written Abraham, on the other M[. . .]. I agreed with the shipowner that he would transport the goods to their destination. I wish my brother Abū Nasr—may God preserve him—to take care of all the goods and carry them to his place until I shall arrive, if God wills.

Please sell the tin for me at whatever price God may grant and leave its "purse" (the money received for it) until my arrival. I am ready to travel, but must stay until I can unload the tar and oil from the ships.

I have no doubt that you have sent me a letter containing all the quotations.

I have learned that the government has seized the oil and that Ibn al-Naffāt has taken the payment upon himself. I hope that this is indeed the case. Please take care of this matter and take from him the price of five skins (filled with oil). The account is with Salāma.

Al-Sabbāgh of Tripoli has bribed Bu 'l-'Alā the agent, and I shall unload my goods soon.

Kindest regards to your noble self and to my master [. . . and] Abu 'l-Fadl, may God keep them.

→ *What can you learn from the letter about the commodities traded?*

→ *What does the letter tell us about the ties among merchants, and about how they conducted their business?*

SOURCE: *Letters of Medieval Jewish Traders*, translated with introductions and notes by S. D. Goitein (Princeton, NJ: Princeton University Press, 1973), pp. 85–87.

Another Sufi mystic and advocate of the universality of religions, the Spanish Muslim poet Ibn Arabi (1165–1240), wrote in Arabic:

My heart has been of every form; it is a pasture for
  gazelles and a convent for Christian monks.
And a temple for idols and the pilgrim's kaaba, and the
  tables of the Torah and the book of the Quran.

Dervishes. Today, the whirling dance of dervishes is almost a tourist attraction, as shown in this picture from the Jerash Cultural Festival in Jordan. Though Sufis in the early second millennium CE were not this neatly dressed, the whirling dance was an important means of reaching union with God.

POLITICAL INTEGRATION AND DISINTEGRATION, 1050–1300

Just as the Islamic faith was increasing its global reach from Africa to India and ultimately into Southeast Asia, its political bulwarks collapsed. Islam's religious and cultural influences transcended its political powers. For a century, from 950 to 1050, it appeared that Shiism would be the vehicle for uniting the whole of the Islamic world. While the Fatimid Shiites established their authority over Egypt and much of North Africa (see Chapter 9), the Abbasid state in Baghdad fell under the sway of the Shiite Buyid family. Each created universities—in Cairo and Baghdad, respectively—thereby ensuring that Islam's two leading centers of higher learning in the eleventh century were Shiite. But the divisions also sapped Shiism; Sunni Muslims began to challenge Shiite power and to establish their own strongholds. The last of the Shiite Fatimid rulers gave way to a new Sunni regime in Egypt. In Baghdad, the Shiite Buyid family surrendered to an unrelated group of Sunni strongmen.

Those strongmen were mainly Turks, who had been migrating into the Islamic central core from the steppe lands of Asia since the eighth century, bringing with them superior military skills and an intense devotion to Sunni Islam. Ensconced in Baghdad, they established outposts in Syria and Palestine, and then moved into Anatolia after defeating Byzantine forces at the battle of Manzikert in 1071. But this Turkish state also crumbled, as Turkish-speaking tribesmen quarreled with one another for preeminence. Thus, by the thirteenth century the Islamic core area, stretching from Morocco in the west to the Oxus River in the east, was fractured into three distinctive regions. In the east (central Asia, Iran,

and eastern Iraq), the remnants of the old Abbasid state persevered. Here, caliphs succeeded one another, still claiming to speak for all of Islam yet lacking the ability to enforce their directives. They deferred without fail to their Turkish military commanders. Even in the central core of the Islamic world (Egypt, Syria, and the Arabian Peninsula), where Arabic was the primary tongue, military men of non-Arab origin held the reins of power. Further west, in the Maghreb, Arab rulers prevailed—but there the influence of Berbers, some from the northern Saharan region, was extensive. Islam was a vibrant faith, but its polities were splintered.

WHAT WAS ISLAM?

Buoyed by Arab dhows on the high seas and carried on the backs of camels, following commercial networks, Islam evolved from Muhammad's original goal of creating a religion for Arab peoples. By 1300, its influence was spreading across Eurasia and Africa. It lacked only an American toehold. It attracted urbanites and rural peasants alike, as well as its original audience, desert nomads. Its extraordinary appeal to such diverse populations generated an intense Islamic cultural flowering at the turn of the millennium in 1000 CE.

Some worried about the preservation of Islam's true nature. The Arabic language ceased to be the idiom of Islamic believers. True, the devout read and recited the Quran in its original tongue, as the religion mandated. But Persian was now often employed in Muslim philosophy and art, and Turkish in law and administration. Moreover, Jerusalem and Baghdad no longer stood alone as Islamic cultural capitals. There were now many important cities, and consequently many universities and centers of learning, boasting alternative, vernacular versions of Islam. In fact, some of the most dynamic thought came from Islam's fringes. To confront the question of Islam's identity meant dealing with its great—and ever growing—heterogeneity.

At the same time, heterogeneity fostered cultural efflorescence, as was apparent in all fields of high learning. Arabic remained a preeminent language of science, literature, and religion in 1300. Indicative of Islam's and Arabic's prominence in thought was the culture's most influential and versatile thinker—the legendary Ibn Rushd (1126–1198). Known as Averroës in the Western world, where scholars pored over his writings, he wrestled with the same theological issues that troubled Western scholars. Steeped in the writings of Aristotle, Ibn Rushd became Islam's most thoroughgoing rationalist. His knowledge of Aristotle was so great that it influenced the thinking of the Christian world's leading philosopher and theologian, Thomas of Aquino (Thomas Aquinas, 1225–1274). Above all, Ibn Rushd believed that faith and reason could be compatible. He also argued for a new kind of social hierarchy, in which learned men would command influence akin to Confucian scholars in China or Greek philosophers in Athens. Ibn Rushd believed that the proper forms of reasoning had to be entrusted to the educated class—in the case of Islam, the ulama—who would serve the common folk.

Equally powerful works were produced in Persian, which by the eleventh century was seen as a language capable of expressing the most sophisticated ideas of culture and religion. The intellectual who best represented the new Persian ethnic pride was Abu al-Qasim Firdawsi (920–1020), a devout Muslim who also believed in the importance of pre-Islamic Sasanian traditions. In the long epic poem *Shah Namah,* or *Book of Kings,* he celebrated the origins of Persian culture and narrated the history of the peoples of the Iranian highlands from the dawn of time to the Muslim conquest. As part of his effort to extol a pure Persian culture, Firdawsi attempted to compose the whole of his poem in Persian unblemished by other languages, avoiding Arabic loanwords.

By the fourteenth century, Islam had achieved what early converts would have considered unthinkable. No longer a religion of a minority of peoples living amid larger Christian, Zoroastrian, and Jewish communities, it had become the people's faith. The agents of conversion were mainly Sufi saints and Sufi brotherhoods and not the ulama, whose exhortations and knowledge of legal and philosophic texts had little impact on common people. The Sufis had carried their faith to the Berbers of North Africa, to villagers living on the plateaus of Anatolia, and to West African animists. Indeed, Ibn Rushd worried about the growing influence and appeal of what he considered an "irrational" piety. But his message failed, because he did not appreciate that Islam's expansionist powers rested on its appeal to common folk. While the sharia was the core of Islam for the educated and scholarly

classes, Sufism spoke to the religious beliefs and experiences of ordinary men and women.

INDIA UP FOR GRABS

> ⇥ *In what ways did India remain a cultural mosaic?*

Trade and migration affected India, just as it did the rest of Asia and Africa. As in the case of Islam, however, prosperity led to growing social and cultural interconnections; but there was little political continuity or integration. Under the large canopy of Hinduism, India remained a cultural mosaic; in fact, in this period the Islamic faith joined with others in South Asia to make the region even more of a cultural mosaic. (See Map 10-4.) India, in this sense, was a crossroads of various parts of Eurasia and Africa; it illustrates how integration into long-distance, cross-cultural networks can just as easily preserve diversity as promote internal unity.

Turks spilled into India as they had the Islamic heartlands, carrying with them their newfound Islamic beliefs. But in India, these newcomers, like all previous invaders, encountered an existing ethnic and religious mix to which they would add something new without greatly upsetting the balance. India became an intersection for the trade, migration, and culture of Afro-Eurasian peoples—a vital nerve center of the world. Moreover, with 80 million inhabitants in 1000,

Hindu Temple. When Buddhism started to decline in India, Hinduism was on the rise. Numerous Hindu temples were built, many of them adorned with ornate carvings like this small tenth-century temple in Bhubaneshwar, east India.

MAP 10-4   SOUTH ASIA IN 1300

As the fourteenth century began, India was a blend of many cultures. Politically, Muslim Turks dominated the region. To what extent did the rulers of the Delhi Sultanate integrate India into the broader Islamic world during this era? What factors accounted for Hinduism's continued appeal despite the political power of Muslim leaders? How did Muslim communities integrate themselves into the larger cultural mosaic in South Asia?

India had the second-largest population in Afro-Eurasia at the time, not far behind China's 100 million but well ahead of Islamic Southwest Asia and North Africa (34 million) as well as Christian Europe (36 million).

India was rich, but it remained splintered into the rivalrous chiefs called *rajas*. By the end of the tenth century, their constant struggles had left them all exhausted. So, when northern invaders began encroaching on their frontiers, both the will and the resources to put up a fight were scarce. Before large-scale invasions by the Turks, central Asian invaders to India did not seek to conquer all the rajas; instead they accommodated and reinforced local rajas' power bases. Claiming *kshatriya* (warrior) status, the invaders cemented an alliance with the local rajas through marriages. Meanwhile, rajas old and new solicited support from high-caste Brahmans by making land concessions to them. Much of the land was not under cultivation. Brahmans took the leadership in reclaiming the wastelands. First they built temples, and then they converted the indigenous hunter-gatherer peoples to the Hindu faith. Then they showed the new converts how to cultivate the land. The Brahmans simultaneously spread their faith and greatly expanded the agrarian tax base for themselves and the rajas. Brahmans reciprocated for their good fortunes by compiling elaborate genealogies for the rajas, endowing them with a lengthy (and therefore legitimizing) ancestry. For their part, the rajas demonstrated that they were well-versed in Sanskrit culture, including equestrian skills and courtly etiquette, and they became the patrons of artists and poets. Ultimately, many of the warriors and their heirs became Indian rajas. However, Turkish invaders were armed with Islam, so the conquerors remained sultans instead of becoming rajas.

INVASIONS AND CONSOLIDATIONS

Turkish warlords entered India in a series of waves that began in the tenth century, introducing their customs into the fertile lands between the Indus and Ganges basins, while also accepting many of the existing political structures. Concerned to uphold their image as promoters of Islamic culture, they constructed grandiose mosques and built impressive libraries where scholars could toil and share their wisdom with the court. The first wave of invaders did not intend to stay in India. Mahmud of Ghazna (971–1030), who launched many expeditions from the Afghan heartland into the wealthy northern provinces of India, was one such conqueror, seeking to make his capital, Ghazni, a great center of Islamic learning in order to win status within Islam. The booty of his invasions—especially the jewels and precious goods plundered from the Hindu temples—also helped boost his status. Worse than Mahmud, Muhammad Ghuri in the 1180s led another wave of Islamic Turkish invasions from Afghanistan and dispersed across the Delhi region in north India. Wars over the control of the plains between the Indus and Ganges rivers raged until one by one, all the way to the lower Ganges valley, the fractured kingdoms toppled.

The now land-bound Turkish Muslim regime of northern India was known as the Delhi Sultanate (1206–1526), and its rulers strengthened the cultural diversity and tolerance that had already become a hallmark of the Indian social order. Although the Delhi sultans knew how to exploit a rich agricultural society, they had little knowledge of or interest in the flourishing commercial life that had sprung up along the Indian coast. They therefore permitted these areas to develop on their own. Persian Zoroastrian traders settled on the Konkan coast in the northwest, around modern-day Mumbai (Bombay). The Malabar Coast to the south became the preserve of Arab traders, who further developed the trade that their ancestors had started. The Delhi Sultanate was a rich and powerful regime that brought political integration but did not enforce cultural homogeneity.

WHAT WAS INDIA?

The entry of Islam into India made the region more of a cultural mosaic, not less. The local Hindu population treated the arrival of the Turks in India as they had done earlier invaders from central Asia: they expected to assimilate their conquerors. The Turks cooperated, but only up to a point. They became Indians but retained their Islamic beliefs and their steppe ways. They behaved as they had in their highland redoubts, wearing their distinctive trousers and robes and riding their horses. The Turks also did not eliminate all the rajas. Some rajas continued to rule certain areas under the sultans.

Although the sultans spoke Turkish languages, they regarded Persian literature as a high cultural achievement and made Persian the sultanate's courtly and administrative language. Meanwhile, most of their Hindu subjects continued to speak local languages that had evolved out of Sanskrit and to

Lodi Gardens. The Lodi Dynasty was the last Delhi sultan dynasty. Lodi Gardens, the cemetery of Lodi sultans, places Central Asian Islamic architecture in the Indian landscape, thereby creating a scene of "heaven on the earth."

follow their caste regulations in daily life. Moreover, they adhered to their local adaptations of the Hindu faith. The sultans did not meddle with the beliefs and cultures of the conquered but merely collected the special *jizya* tax that they paid.

Despite the reluctance of most people in India to embrace Islam, the faith flourished. Islam did not have to be a conquering religion to prosper. As rulers, sultans granted lands to Islamic scholars, the ulama, and Sufi saints, much as Hindu rajas had earlier granted lands to Brahmans. Prestigious scholars and saints in turn attracted followers to their large estates and forests to enjoy the benefits of membership in this community of believers.

The Delhi sultans built strongholds to defend their conquests. Every new sultanate built a fortress in the Delhi region, employing both local workers and foreign artisans from central Asia and Iran. The curves of domes and arches on mosques, tombs, and palaces, formed in the shape of the lotus flower, were uniquely South Asian in flavor. As expenditures at court attracted traders and artisans of all sorts, the palaces and fortresses quickly evolved into prosperous cities.

Although newcomers and locals lived in separate worlds, their customs began to merge. Delhi sultans maintained their steppe lifestyle and equestrian culture, and they were delighted when conquered peoples adopted nomadic customs and artifacts. They realized, however, that they had to learn the local language to rule the country effectively. Court scholars and Sufi holymen started to use local dialects to write and teach. Hindustani, an Indian language full of Persian and Arabic words, was taking shape and became the ancestral language of both Hindi and Urdu. Foreign artisans who arrived with their rulers produced the silk textiles, rugs, and appliances to irrigate gardens that the leading families of Delhi so cherished. Their talents spread beyond the palaces and influenced the manufacturing techniques of the local population. Before long, Indians had learned from the Muslim workers how to extract long filaments from silk cocoons and were themselves weaving fine silk textiles. The merging of cultures became even more apparent when the common people began to wear Turkish–style trousers and robes and when the Persian wheel, a water-lifting device, became widely used by farmers.

By this period, Buddhism in India had already been in decline for centuries. When Vedic Brahmanism evolved into Hinduism (see Chapter 8), it absorbed many doctrines and practices from Buddhism, such as the doctrine of *ahimsa* (non-killling) and the practice of vegetarianism. The two religions became so similar that Hindus simply considered the Buddha to be one of their deities—specifically, an incarnation of the great god Vishnu. Many Buddhist moral teachings were mixed and became Hindu stories. Artistic motifs were similarly adopted and adapted. Following the onslaught of the Turkish invaders, who destroyed many monasteries in the thirteenth century, several leading Buddhist scholars re-

Vishnu. With Buddhism disappearing from India, Buddha was absorbed by the cult of Vishnu and became one of the incarnations of the Hindu god. This late-twelfth-century Angkor Wat style sculpture from Cambodia shows Vishnu asleep; from his nostril sprouts the lotus that will give birth to Buddha.

treated to Tibet, where they helped lead a flowering of Buddhism on the plateau. Bereft of local spiritual leaders and lacking dynastic support, Buddhists in India were assimilated into the Hindu population or converted to Islam.

SONG CHINA, 960–1279

→ *What transformations in communication, education, and commerce contributed to the emergence of a distinct Chinese identity during this era?*

The preeminent world power in 1000 CE was still China, despite its recent experience of turmoil. That turbulence would give rise to a long era of stability and splendor—a combination that made China one of the main regional engines of Afro-Eurasian prosperity. After the end of the Tang dynasty (907 CE), China entered the Five Dynasties period. For two centuries the Tang dynasty's power had waned until North and South China broke into a series of regional kingdoms, usually led by military generals. But one of those generals, Zhao Kuangyin, put a stop to the fragmentation in 960 CE. Overthrowing the boy emperor of his own kingdom, Zhao moved quickly to reunify China by conquering three more of the seven major regional kingdoms between 963 and 975 CE. He was succeeded after his death in 976 CE by his younger brother, who finished the reunification effort by annexing the last three kingdoms. Thus, the Song dynasty took over the mandate of heaven.

The three centuries of Song rule in China would witness many economic and political successes, but powerful nomadic tribes in the far northern stretches of China kept the Song from completely securing their reign. (See Map 10-5.) Their efforts to fight off or pay off these warriors from the north would ultimately prove unsuccessful, and in 1127, the Song finally would lose control of northern China to the nomadic Jurchen, the ancestors of the Manchu. After reconsti-

tuting their dynasty in southern China, the most populous and economically robust region of their empire, they would enjoy another century and a half of rule before falling to the Mongols in 1276.

A CHINESE COMMERCIAL REVOLUTION

China's commercial revolution during this period had agrarian roots. Without vast fields of rice, the population would never have reached 120 million in the twelfth century—doubling its size from the previous millennium. Agriculture

MAP 10-5 (A & B)   EAST ASIA, 1000–1300

Several states emerged in East Asia between 1000 and 1300, but none as strong as the Song dynasty in China. What geographic and political factors contributed to the Song state's economic dynamism? What factors contributed to the Song state's loss of territory to the Jurchen Jin dynasty? How did the Jin state demonstrate the continued impact of pastoral groups on East Asian history in this era?

→ *What transformations contributed to the emergence of a distinct Chinese identity during this era?*

benefited from breakthroughs in metalworking. China's farmers were able to employ new and stronger iron ploughs, which they harnessed to sturdy water buffalo, to break the tough soil in the south, and to extend the farming frontier. In 1078, for example, total Song iron production peaked somewhere between 75,000 and 150,000 tons, roughly the equivalent of European iron production at the start of the eighteenth century. The Chinese piston bellows were a marvel of the age, of a size unsurpassed anywhere in the world until the nineteenth century.

Manufacturing flourished. In the early years of the tenth century, Chinese alchemists were mixing saltpeter with sulfur and charcoal to produce a product that would burn and

could be deployed on the battlefield. By 1040, the first gunpowder recipes were being written down. Over the next 200 years, Song entrepreneurs invented a remarkable array of incendiary devices that flowed from their mastery of techniques for controlling explosions. Song Chinese also devised an "eruptor," a weapon that functioned like a cannon, and it was quickly emulated by their enemies. This was not the only manufacturing breakthrough to astonish the world. Building on their predecessors' techniques, Song artisans produced lighter, more durable, and stunningly more beautiful porcelains. Before long, Song porcelain (now called "china") had become the envy of all Afro-Eurasia. China's artisans also produced vast amounts of clothing and handicrafts from the hemp, mulberry, and cotton that its farmers were growing in great abundance. In effect, the Song Chinese brought about the world's first manufacturing revolution, producing finished goods on a large scale for consumption far and wide.

The growth of commerce transformed the role of money and its worldwide circulation. By the middle of the eleventh century, the Song government was annually minting nearly two million strings of currency—each string containing 1,000 copper coins—far in excess of the Tang maximum of about 300,000 strings. Indeed, the inability of the supply of metal currency to keep pace with demand fueled East Asia's thirst for East African gold in this era. At the same time, merchants began to tinker with printed paper certificates; their guilds in northwestern Shanxi developed the first letters of exchange, which were called "flying cash." These letters linked northern traders with their colleagues in the south. The paper habit spread, and by the thirteenth century printed money had eclipsed coins. Even the government became heavily dependent on paper currency, as it found itself now able to collect more than half of its tax revenues in cash rather than in grain and cloth. The government also turned to its own printing presses to issue more and more notes to pay its bills—a practice that ultimately contributed to the world's first case of runaway inflation, which destabilized the Song and later the Yuan regimes.

NEW ELITES

The commercial revolutions enabled the early Song emperors to champion civilian rule over military values and to usher in a period of social and cultural vitality. The Song undercut the powers of the hereditary aristocratic elites, establishing instead a society governed by a central bureaucracy of scholar-officials chosen through competitive civil service examinations whose scope exceeded that of the Tang. The shift of loyalties from aristocratic clans to the ruling house solidified during the reign of Zhao Kuangyin, also known as Emperor Taizu (ruled 960–976 CE), who in 973 himself administered the final test for all those who had passed the highest-level palace examination. In subsequent dynasties, the emperor became the nation's premier examiner, symbolically demanding oaths of allegiance from successful candidates for public office. Civil officials were now drawn almost exclusively from the ranks of learned men, and by 1100 they had accumulated sufficient power to become China's new ruling elite.

NEGOTIATING WITH NEIGHBORS

As the Song flourished, nomads on the outskirts eyed Chinese successes closely. At the dynasty's northern borders, Khitan, Tungusic, Tangut, and Jurchen nomadic societies formed their own dynasties and adapted Chinese techniques to their

Song Civil Service. Song emperors championed civilian rule to undercut the remaining Tang aristocratic elites. A civil service composed of scholar-officials selected through competitive examinations in both the provinces and the capital took hold. Here we see a painting of an examination being administered during Emperor Renzong's reign (1023–1031).

own advantage. Located within the boundaries of the "greater China" established by the Han and Tang dynasties, these non-Chinese polities watched with envy as China's core amassed extraordinary wealth and prestige. It was only a matter of time before nomadic armies such as those of the Khitan and Jurchen saw China proper as an object of conquest.

In one important way the Song dynasts were weak: they had limited military power, despite their sophisticated weapons. Steel tips increased the effectiveness of Song arrows used with crossbows, and Song armies also boasted flame-throwers and "crouching tiger catapults" for lobbing incendiary bombs at their enemies. But none of these breakthroughs was secret. Warrior neighbors on the steppe, such as the Khitan tribal confederation and Jurchen, mastered the new arts of war more fully than did the Song dynasts themselves.

China's strength as a manufacturing powerhouse made economic diplomacy an option. To keep borderlanders at bay, the Song relied on "gifts" and generous trade agreements with the peoples on the fringes. Defeated militarily by the Liao dy-

Trebuchet. Derived from the sling, the trebuchet served as a siege engine to smash masonry walls or throw flaming projectiles over them. Trebuchets were invented in China in about the fourth century BCE and came to Europe in the sixth century CE. All trebuchets were made of wood and could fling a three hundred–pound (140 kg) projectile at high speed. The illustration here shows a Song Dynasty naval river ship c. 1044 equipped with a traction trebuchet catapult.

nasty in 1004, the Song agreed to make annual payments of 100,000 ounces of silver and 200,000 bolts of silk. The treaty enabled the Song to live in relative peace for more than a century. Another Inner Asian tribal confederation, the Tangut, pressed on the Song's northwestern border. The Tangut state also received an annual subsidy from the Song when an agreement was reached in 1044. Securing peace meant emptying the state coffers—and thus the state turned to its printing presses to make more paper money. The resulting runaway inflation added economic instability to military weakness, making the Song an easy target when the Jurchen invaders made their final assault.

WHAT WAS CHINA?

Paradoxically, the increasing contact and exchange between outsiders and insiders within China hardened the lines that divided them. This was a pattern displayed centuries earlier, in the entanglements of the nomadic Northern Wei rulers with the Han people in China proper (see Chapter 8). The exchanges that did take place, and there were many, wound up nurturing a "Chinese" identity for those who considered themselves true insiders and referred to themselves as Han.

Thus, transformations in communications and education intensified the sense among the Han Chinese that they were authentically Chinese, and that outsiders were radically different. Driven from their ancient homeland in the north beginning in the eleventh century, the Han Chinese grew increasingly suspicious and resentful toward the outsiders living in their midst. They once again called them "barbarians" and treated them accordingly, drawing a dividing line between the nomadic warrior cultures of the Eurasian steppe and their own society based on the large-scale cultivation of grain and rice. Yet these identities were not completely fixed: Han Chinese and non-Han barbarians, insiders and outsiders, were in fact mutually dependent. For long periods, the two groups had easily coexisted, particularly in northwestern and northern China, with much interchange of cultures and technologies. But despite the nomadic borrowing of Chinese ways, and the assimilation of warrior elites to Han Chinese ways, the differences between civilized "China" and the barbarian "other" became a durable stereotype. To be authentically Chinese, even if ruled by outsiders, meant valuing civilian mores, especially for those educated Chinese who were steeped in the civil examination system. It meant being literate—able to read, write, and live by codes inscribed in foundational texts.

Of all the Afro-Eurasian societies in 1300, the Chinese had created the most advanced print culture. The Song government published a wide variety of works, using its plentiful supply of paper to print books, especially medical texts, and to distribute calendars. The private publishing industry also expanded, and printing houses sprang up throughout the country. They produced the Confucian classics, works on

Chinese and Barbarian. After losing the north, the Han Chinese grew resentful of outsiders. They drew a dividing line between their own agrarian society and the nomadic warriors, calling them "barbarians." Such identities were not fixed, however. Chinese and so-called barbarians were mutually dependent.

history, philosophical treatises, and literature, all of which were employed in the civil examinations, which were administered not just centrally but in provincial capitals throughout the country. In Fujian province alone, some 17,000 to 18,000 candidates gathered in the coastal capital city triennially to take the provincial examination. Buddhist publications were also available everywhere. Song printing directly influenced the precocious Koryo dynasty (918–1392) in Korea, which also made great headway in printing by developing movable metal type in 1234, about two centuries before its independent invention in Europe.

CHINA'S NEIGHBORS, 1000–1300

→ *How were Southeast Asia, Japan, and Korea influenced by sustained contact with other regions in this era?*

Under its Song rulers, China became the most populous and wealthiest of the world's regions. Its population of more than 120 million in 1100 projected the influence of Chinese culture, through trade and migration, across all of Afro-Eurasia, especially into Korea, Japan, and Southeast Asia. Chinese commodities found ready markets in neighboring cultures, as local elites had a growing appetite for manufactured textiles, porcelains, and other luxuries. In return, they shipped staples to Chinese cities along the coast, both foodstuffs and industrial inputs. The Koryo rulers in Korea, for example, actively imitated Song culture, religions, and technology, which they passed on to Japan. Their capital, Kaesong, was one of the world's most impressive cities. Koryo rulers ordered the construction of hundreds of Buddhist temples in the Tang-Song style, as well as the creation of countless religious artworks.

THE RISE OF WARRIORS IN JAPAN

As China became an economic and political powerhouse, the cultures around its rim were forced to adapt. They could not help but feel the gravitational pull of China. Often these neighbors responded by consolidating internal political authority to resist being swallowed up, while increasing their participation in commercial transactions. In Japan, rulers had to resolve some endemic problems to create a stable regime out of feuding warrior factions. Their solution was to amalgamate the Heian court's imperial authority with the military power of the more rusticated provincial warriors in the east.

The pattern of regents ruling in the name of the sacred emperor was repeated many times in Japanese history, but it began in the Heian period (794–1185). First court nobles—an entrenched aristocracy—in the new capital of Heian (today's Kyoto) dominated Japan, and later rough-and-ready warriors followed their model in literally winning possession of the throne to "protect" its sanctity as an object of popular veneration. They captured it to gain the symbolic power of the emperor, which was transferred to his protectors.

By intermarrying with and ruling through the Heian imperial family for two centuries, the influential Fujiwara family added considerably to the power of their ancestors, the powerful Nakatomi kinship group in Nara (described in Chapter 9). The Fujiwara nobles presided over a refined Heian culture of flower and tea ceremonies. They also exchanged poetry written in classical Chinese and their native language and dressed in the elegant costumes that have influenced Japanese public life and private taste up to this day.

Political marriages enabled the Fujiwara to control the throne, but the rise of large private estates (called *shōen*) outside the capital shifted the balance of power from the court to the regional elites in the provinces. A hierarchy of land tenures emerged in the countryside: peasant cultivators were at the bottom, managers and estate officials in the middle, and absentee patrons at the top. By 1100 more than half of Japan's rice land was controlled by these large estates, and the revenue and power of the state fell considerably. In the midst of such privatization, Heian became for aristocrats a theater state—politically weak but culturally influential—while the hinterlands provided their economic wealth.

Heian aristocrats ruled through political stealth and artistic style and disdained the military. In 792—even before Heian became the capital—the conscription system to raise imperial armies was abolished. In the provinces, however, trained warriors affiliated with specific kinship groups gathered strength. The rural elites were expert horsemen who fought in armor, and they defended their private estates by relying on their skill with the bow and sword. As incipient samurai, they formed local warrior organizations in the outlying regions, particularly on Kantō Plain (where today's Kamakura and Tokyo are located), well to the east of the capital.

Japan became the home to multiple sources of power: an aristocracy, an imperial family, and local warriors (known as samurai). It was a combustible mix, a recipe for intrigue and double-dealing. Although the sanctity of the Japanese emperor and the Heian aristocracy remained intact, outside warrior groups such as the Minamoto and Taira families provided a new bridge between the elites of the capital and the nouveaux riches in the provinces. Using native Japanese script developed in the Heian era, Lady Murasaki Shikibu (c. 976–c. 1031) described the elegant lives and sordid affairs of the courtiers and their women in *The Tale of Genji*, Japan's—and possibly the world's—first novel. Neither nobles nor warriors refrained from political intrigue, as they grasped at any and all possible alliances that would propel them into power. First, beginning in 1168, the Taira kinship group ruled as

Heiji Rebellion. This illustration from the Kamakura period depicts a battle during the Heiji Rebellion, which was fought between rival subjects of the cloistered emperor Go-Shirakawa in 1159. Riding in full armor on horseback, the fighters on both sides are armed with devastating long bows.

samurai elites in the name of the emperor. Next General Yoritomo (1147–1199) led his Minamoto kin (also called the Genji) to a dramatic victory over the Taira at the sea battle of Dan no Ura off the southern island of Shikoku in 1185. Ultimately, it was the alliance of local potentates and military commanders under the Kamakura shoguns (1192–1333)—generalissimos who served as military "protectors" of the ruler in Heian—that brought more stable rule to Japan. The Kamakura age thus provided the fierce warriors who successfully fended off the Mongol naval invasions of 1274 and 1281. Moreover, the shogunate form of military government remained intact under the theoretical sovereignty of the Japanese emperor in Heian until 1868.

THE CULTURAL MOSAIC OF SOUTHEAST ASIA

Southeast Asia, like India, became a crossroads of Afro-Eurasian influences. (See Map 10-6.) Its population was still relatively low (probably not more than 10 million in 1000), especially when compared with that of its nearest neighbors, China and India. Certainly, the dominance of island life and island culture, particularly as developed on the lands that were to become Indonesia in modern times, set the peoples of this unique geographical area off from others. But the Southeast Asian communities were not immune to the influences of the peoples that flocked into this region. Like India,

the archipelago became a cultural mosaic, its sea-lanes (and peoples) connecting China with Asia and Africa. The elongated Malay Peninsula became the home to many trading ports and stopovers for traders shuttling between India and China, and thus connected the Bay of Bengal and the Indian Ocean with the South China Sea.

Indian influence had been prominent both on the Asian mainland and in island portions of Southeast Asia since 800 CE. Islamic expansion into the islands that comprised maritime Southeast Asia after 1200 gradually superseded these cultural influences. Only Bali and a few other outlying islands located far to the east of the Malayan crossroads, for example, were able to preserve their Vedic religious origins relatively intact. Elsewhere in Java and Sumatra, Islam irrevocably became the universalistic religion of the islands. In Vietnam and northern portions of mainland Southeast Asia, Chinese cultural influences and northern schools of Mahayana Buddhism were especially prominent.

The prosperity and cultural vitality of the heavily populated regions of China and India spilled over into the maritime and Asian mainland worlds of Southeast Asia, especially benefiting the Thai, Vietnamese, and Burmese peoples who gradually emerged as the largest population groups on the mainland. Island residents of the Malay Archipelago—especially of Java and Sumatra—controlled much of the region's maritime activity. Each population group adjusted as Chinese and Indian influences rose and fell, selecting those aspects of "Indo-Chinese" civilization that they found compatible with local

THE TALE OF GENJI

Lacking a written language of their own, Heian aristocrats adopted classical Chinese as the official written language while continuing to speak Japanese. Men at the court took great pains to master the Chinese literary forms imported from the Tang dynasty via the Heian tributary missions periodically sent to Chang'an. Japanese court ladies, however, were not expected to master Chinese writing. For example, Lady Murasaki, the author of The Tale of Genji, *went to great pains to hide her knowledge of Chinese, fearing that she would be criticized for being unladylike. In the meantime, the Japanese developed a syllabary for their own language by simplifying Chinese written graphs and tying them directly to native sounds. Using this syllabary, Lady Murasaki began a diary in Japanese that she kept up for two years. In it she gave vivid accounts of Heian court life, whose frivolity she herself disliked. Lady Murasaki noted that some might also view writing fiction as frivolous, but she made clear that fiction could be as truthful as a work of history in capturing human life and its historical significance.*

So saying she pushed away from her the book which she had been copying. Genji continued: "So you see as a matter of fact I think far better of this art than I have led you to suppose. Even its practical value is immense. Without it what should we know of how people lived in the past, from the Age of the Gods down to the present day? For history-books such as the *Chronicles of Japan* show us only one small corner of life; whereas these diaries and romances which I see piled around you contain, I am sure, the most minute information about all sorts of people's private affairs. . . ." He smiled, and went on: "But I have a theory of my own about what this art of the novel is, and how it came into being. To begin with, it does not simply consist in the author's telling a story about the adventures of some other person. On the contrary, it happens because the storyteller's own experience of men and things, whether for good or ill—not only what he has passed through himself, but even events which he has only witnessed or been told of—has moved him to an emotion so passionate that he can no longer keep it shut up in his heart. Again and again something in his own life or in that around him will seem to the writer so important that he cannot bear to let it pass into oblivion. There must never come a time, he feels, when men do not know about it. That is my view of how this art arose.

"Clearly then, it is no part of the storyteller's craft to describe only what is good or beautiful. Sometimes, of course, virtue will be his theme, and he may then make such play with it as he will. But he is just as likely to have been struck by numerous examples of vice and folly in the world around him, and about them he has exactly the same feelings as about the pre-eminently good deeds which he encounters: they are more important and must all be garnered in. Thus anything whatsoever may become the subject of a novel, provided only that it happens in this mundane life and not in some fairyland beyond our human ken.

"The outward forms of this art will not of course be everywhere the same. At the court of China and in other foreign lands both the genius of the writers and their actual methods of composition are necessarily very different from ours; and even here in Japan the art of storytelling has in course of time undergone great changes. There will, too, always be a distinction between the lighter and the more serious forms of fiction. . . . Well, I have said enough to show that when at the beginning of our conversation I spoke of romances as though they were mere frivolous fabrications, I was only teasing you. Some people have taken exception on moral grounds to an art in which the perfect and imperfect are set side by side. But even in the discourses which Buddha in his bounty allowed to be recorded, certain passages contain what the learned call *Upāya* or 'Adapted Truth'—a fact that has led some superficial persons to doubt whether a doctrine so inconsistent with itself could possibly command our credence. Even in the scriptures of the Greater Vehicle there are, I confess, many such instances. We may indeed go so far as to say there is an actual mixture of Truth and Error. But the purpose of these holy writings, namely the compassing of our Salvation, remains always the same. So too, I think, may it be said that the art of fiction must not lose our allegiance because, in the pursuit of the main purpose to which I have alluded above, it sets virtue by the side of vice, or mingles wisdom with folly. Viewed in this light the novel is seen to be not, as is usually supposed, a mixture of useful truth with idle invention, but something which at every stage and in every part has a definite and serious purpose."

→ *What does this account tell us about the relation between historical fact and fictional romance?*

→ *How are "truth and error" displayed in religious writings, which, like novels, use stories in pursuit of their didactic purpose?*

Source: *Sources of Japanese Tradition*, compiled by Ryūsaku Tsunoda, Wm. Theodore de Bary, and Donald Keene (New York: Columbia University Press, 1964), vol. 1, pp. 177–79.

→ *How were Southeast Asia, Japan, and Korea influenced by sustained contact with other regions in this era?*

MAP 10-6   SOUTHEAST ASIA, 1000–1300

Cross-cultural influences strongly shaped the development of Southeast Asian societies between 1000 and 1300. According to the map, how did East and South Asian societies influence various communities in Southeast Asia? What aspects of Chinese and Indian culture did Southeast Asian societies import? In this chapter, the term "cultural mosaic" is used to describe both South and Southeast Asia. How did the mosaic in Southeast Asia differ from that in India during this era?

state formation and cultural activities. Chinese and Indian peoples also became part of the new trading milieu.

Cambodian, Burmese, and Thai peoples founded powerful mixed polities along the Mekong, Salween, Chaophraya, and Irriwaddy river basins of the Asian mainland. The important Vedic and Buddhist kingdoms of the Khmer (today's Cambodia), Pagan (today's Burma), and Siam (today's Thailand) emerged as political buffers between the strong states in China and India. These Southeast Asian kingdoms were

soon robust enough to consolidate their hold on these borderlands, thereby bringing stability and furthering the commercial prosperity of the region.

Consider the great kingdom that ruled Angkor in present-day Cambodia. With their capital in Angkor, the Khmers (889–1431) created the most powerful and wealthy empire in Southeast Asia between the tenth and thirteenth centuries. Countless water reservoirs enabled the Khmers to flourish on the great plain to the west of the Mekong River. Public works

Aerial View of Angkor Wat. Mistaken by later European explorers as a remnant of Alexander the Great's conquests, the enormous temple complexes built by the Khmer people in Angkor borrowed their intricate layout and stupa architecture from the Brahmanist Indian temples of the time. As the capital, Angkor was a microcosm of the world for the Khmer, who aspired to represent the macrocosm of the universe in the magnificence of Angkor's buildings and their geometric-astronomic layout.

and magnificent temples dedicated to the glory of the revived Vedic gods from India went hand in hand with the earlier influence of Indian Buddhism in mainland Southeast Asia. Eventually the Khmer kings gathered enough military strength to unite adjacent kingdoms and extend Khmer influence to the Thai and Burmese states along the Chaophraya and Irriwaddy rivers.

One of the greatest temple complexes in Angkor exemplified the heavy borrowing by the Khmer peoples from Indian temples and architecture. By this time, the Brahmanist revival of Vedic religion in India circa 1000 CE had eclipsed Buddhism there, except on the island of Ceylon. Angkor aspired to represent the universe in the magnificence of its buildings. As signs of the ruler's power, the pagodas, pyramids, and terra-cotta friezes presented the life of the gods on earth. The royal palace alone extended 1,970 feet east to west and 820 feet north to south; it was crowned by the magnificent Vaishnavite temple of Angkor Wat, measuring about a mile square and probably the largest religious structure ever built. The buildings and statues represented the revival of the Hindu pantheon of gods in the Khmer royal state, such as Shiva and Vishnu, in great detail and with great artistry, but far less Buddhist influence is visible.

Because of its strategic location and proximity to Malayan tropical produce, Melaka became perhaps the most international city in the world. Indian, Javanese, and Chinese merchants and sailors spent months at a time in such ports selling their goods, purchasing a return cargo, and waiting for the winds to change so that they might reach their next destination. Seasonal shifts in the monsoon winds across the Bay of Bengal, the South China Sea, and the Java Sea allowed Chinese and Japanese ships to arrive from January to March and then return home in August. Ships from India came from May to early October and sailed back west in winter. During peak season, Southeast Asian ports were filled with foreign sailors and traders from all over Asia who accompanied their own merchandise. They gathered in large numbers at crossroads where agriculture sustained the local population and maritime trade routes converged.

CHRISTIAN EUROPE

> → *How did Christianity produce a distinct identity among the diverse peoples of Europe?*

In the far western corner of the Afro-Eurasian landmass, a people were building a culture revealingly different. (See Map 10-7.) Although their numbers were still relatively small compared with the rest of Afro-Eurasia in 1000 (36 million in Europe, compared to 80 million in India and 100 million in China), their population was rapidly rising and would soar to 80 million before the arrival of the Black Death at the beginning of the fourteenth century.

This was a region of contrasts. On the one hand, the first three centuries of the second millennium witnessed an intense localization of politics. There was no successor to the Roman or Carolingian empires (see Chapter 9). On the other hand, the territory was ever more united by a progressively

→ *How did Christianity produce a distinct identity among the diverse peoples of Europe?*

MAP 10-7 LATIN CHRISTENDOM IN 1300

Catholic Europe expanded geographically and integrated culturally during this era. According to this map, into what areas did Western Christendom successfully expand? What factors contributed to the growth of a widespread common culture and shared ideas? How did long-distance trade shape the history of the region during this time?

greater shared sense of its place in the world. Indeed, in these years some even began for the first time to believe in the existence of something called "Europe," whose inhabitants were increasingly referring to themselves as "Europeans."

A WORLD OF KNIGHTS

The collapse of the Carolingian empire (768–814 CE) had exposed much of northern Europe to invasion, principally from the Vikings, and left the region's peasantry with no central authority to protect them from the power of local warlords. These warlords collected taxes and imposed forced labor. Armed with new and more deadly weapons, the warrior class came to stand out as the unchallenged rulers of society. In this growth of a warrior aristocracy, northern France led the way. The Franks (who gradually came to be called "Frenchmen" in this period) were the self-proclaimed trendsetters of eleventh- and twelfth-century western Europe.

The most important change was the subjugation of the peasantry to the knightly class. Previously, well-to-do peasants

The Bayeux Tapestry. This tapestry was prepared by a queen and her ladies to celebrate the victories of William the Conqueror. It shows the fascination of the entire "feudal" class, even women, with the sinews of war on which they depended—great horses, tightly meshed chain mail, long shields, and the stirrups that made such cavalry warfare possible.

had carried arms, and doing so had marked themselves as "free" men. The moment the farmers lost their right to carry arms, they were no longer free. They slipped back to being mere agricultural laborers. Each peasant was under the authority of a lord, who controlled every detail of his or her life. This was the basis of a system known as feudalism.

Assured of control of the peasantry, feudal lords watched over an agrarian breakthrough—which formed the basis of a commercial transformation that would link Europe to the rest of the global trading networks. This breakthrough was largely due to massive deforestation, which, in turn, implied more advanced use of metal tools (axes and ploughs) and heavier livestock to pull the ploughs that turned the heavy, root-infested sods of northern Europe. Above this stood the castle—a threatening presence that ensured that (unlike many other regions of the world) the peasantry did not simply vanish into the woods that they had cleared. They stayed within range of the collector of rents and services for the lords and of tithes for the Church. In this blunt way, "feudalism" harnessed agrarian energy to its own needs. The population of western Europe as a whole leaped forward, most spectacularly in the north. By 1300, northern Europe contained almost half of Europe's inhabitants. As a result, northern Europe (from England to Poland) finally ceased to be an underdeveloped barbarian appendage of the Mediterranean.

EASTERN EUROPE

Nowhere did pioneering peasants develop more land than in the wide-open spaces of eastern Europe, the region's land of opportunity. Between 1100 and 1200, some 200,000 farmers emigrated from Flanders (modern Belgium), Holland, and northern Germany into eastern frontiers. Well-watered landscapes, covered with vast forests, in what are now Poland,

the Czech Republic, Hungary, and the Baltic states filled up. "Little Europes," whose castles, churches, and towns echoed the landscape of France, sprang up to replace economies that had been based on gathering honey, hunting, and the slave trade. In Silesia (western Poland), for instance, 1,200 villages were founded within a century. For a thousand miles along the Baltic Sea, from the city of Lübeck in Germany to Riga in present-day Latvia, forest clearings dotted with new farmsteads and small towns edged inward from the coast up the river systems.

The social structure in eastern Europe was a marriage of convenience between migrating peasants and local elites. Western European peasants sought to enjoy, in a different land, some of the freedoms that had been lost to their feudal overlords. Eastern Europe offered the promise of freedom from arbitrary justice and from the imposition of forced labor.

Olavinilinna Castle. This castle in Finland was the easternmost extension of a "western," feudal style of rule through great castles. It was built at the very end of the Baltic, to keep away the Russians of Novgorod.

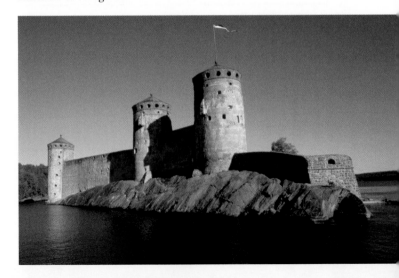

Even the harsh landscape of the eastern Baltic (where the sea froze every year and vast forests blocked the way of settlers from the coast) was preferable to life in the feudal west. For their part, the elites of eastern Europe—the nobility of Poland, Bohemia, and Hungary and the princes of the Baltic—wished to live well, in the "French" style. But they could do so only if they attracted manpower to their vast lands by offering peasants and townspeople a liberty that they had no hope of enjoying in the west.

THE RUSSIAN LANDS

In Russian lands, western settlers and knights met an eastern brand of Christian devotion. This was a world that had chosen to look toward Byzantium. Russia was a giant borderland between the interior steppe lands of Afro-Eurasia and the booming feudalisms of Europe, bridging east and west. Its cities lay at the crossroads of overland trade and migration, and Kiev became one of the greatest cities of Europe. Standing on a bluff above the Dnieper River, it straddled newly opened trade routes. With a population of well over 20,000, partly made up of merchants drawn from all over eastern Europe, western Europe, and the Middle East, Kiev was larger than Paris—larger even than the much-diminished city of Rome.

Kiev looked south to the Black Sea and to Byzantium. Under Iaroslav the Wise (1016–1054), it was carefully re- built so as to become a small-scale Constantinople on the Dnieper. A stone church called St. Sophia was placed (as in Constantinople) beside the imperial palace. Indeed, with its distinctive "Byzantine" domes, it was a miniature Hagia Sophia. Almost a hundred feet high from the floor to the top of the dome, it was at its completion the largest structure ever built in Europe east of the Elbe. Splendid mosaics covered the walls with images of Byzantine saints, which faithfully echoed the religious art of Constantinople. But the message was political as well as religious, for the ruler of Kiev similarly was cast in the mold of the emperor of Constantinople. He was now called *tsar* from the ancient Roman name given to the emperor, Caesar. From this time onward, *tsar* was the title of rulers in Russia.

The Russian form of Christianity embraced the Byzantine style of churches and replicated them up the great rivers leading to the largely independent trading cities of the north and northeast. These were not centers of growing agrarian settlement and dense populations but entrepôts, the hubs of expanding long-distance trade across Afro-Eurasia. Each city became a small-scale Kiev, and thus became a smaller-scale echo of the Great City—Constantinople. The Orthodox religion associated with Byzantium's Hagia Sophia, and not the Catholic religion associated with the popes in Rome, was their form of Christianity. Russian Christianity remained the Christianity of a borderland—a series of vivid oases of high culture, set against the backdrop of vast forests and widely

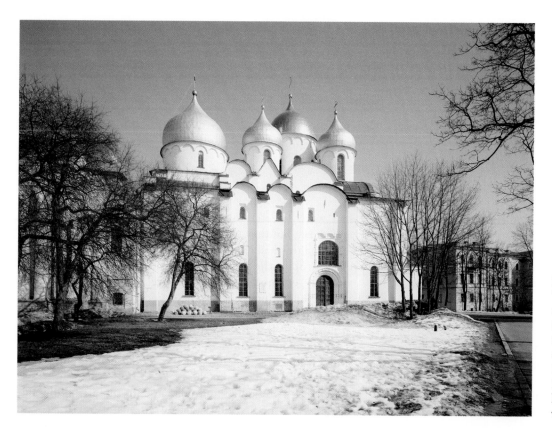

Hagia Sophia, Novgorod. The cathedral of Novgorod (as that of Kiev) was called Hagia Sophia. It was a deliberate imitation of the Hagia Sophia of Constantinople, showing Russia's roots in a glorious Roman/Byzantine past that had nothing to do with western Europe.

Primary Source

VOICES FROM THE PAST: THE BIRCH BARK LETTERS OF NOVGOROD

From 1951 onward, the excavations of Russian archaeologists in Novgorod have revealed almost a thousand letters and accounts scratched on birch bark. Written on wood, they were preserved in the sodden, frequently frozen ground. Reading them we realize what a remarkable place Novgorod must have been in the twelfth and thirteenth centuries.

First, we meet the merchants. Many letters are notes by creditors of the debts owed to them by trading partners. The sums are often expressed in precious animal furs. They contain advice to relatives or to partners in other cities:

> Giorgii sends his respects to his father and mother: Sell the house and come here to Smolensk or to Kiev: for the bread is cheap there.

Then we meet neighborhood disputes:

> From Anna to Klemiata: Help me, my lord brother, in my matter with Konstantin. . . . [For I asked him,] "Why have you been so angry with my sister and her daughter. You called her a cow and her daughter a whore. And now Fedor has thrown them both out of the house."

There are even glimpses of real love. A secret marriage is planned:

> Mikiti to Ulianitza: Come to me. I love you, and you me. Ignato will act as witness.

And a poignant note from a woman was discovered in 1993:

> I have written to you three times. What is it that you hold against me, that you did not come to see me this Sunday? I regarded you as I would my own brother. Did I really offend you by that which I sent to you? If you had been pleased you would have torn yourself away from company and come to me. Write to me. If in my clumsiness I have offended you and you should spurn me, then let God be my judge. I love you.

> → *What does the range of people writing on birch bark tell us about these people?*
> → *What does the final note tell us about the expression of love among the peoples from the northern stretches of Afro-Eurasia?*

SOURCE: A. V. Artsikhovskii and V. I. Borkovski, *Novgorodskie Gramoty na Bereste*, 11 vols. (Moscow: Izd-vo Akademii nauk SSSR, 1951–2004), document nos. 424, 531, 377, and 752.

---

scattered settlements. As the settlement frontier pushed outward, it merged with the shamanistic cultures of the Arctic and Siberia, and, in the south, with the nomad corridor that linked Europe to central Asia along the coast of the Black Sea.

WHAT WAS CHRISTIAN EUROPE?

In this era, Catholicism became a mass faith, a transformation that shaped the emergence of the region then coming to be known by some as "Europe." The Christianity of post-Roman Europe had been a religion of monks, and its most dynamic centers were great monasteries. Members of the laity were expected to revere and support their monks, nuns, and clergy, but they were not encouraged to imitate them. By 1200, all this had changed. The internal colonization of western Europe—the clearing of woods and the founding of villages—ensured that parish churches arose in all but the wildest landscapes. Their spires could be seen and their bells could be heard from one valley to the next. The graveyards around the churches were the only places where a good Christian could be buried; criminals and outlaws were piled into "heathen" graves outside the cemetery walls. Even the bones of the believers helped make Europe Christian.

The clergy reached more deeply into the private lives of the laity. For the first time in Christian history, marriage and

Amiens Cathedral. The cathedrals of northern France and elsewhere in Europe were built largely by local townsmen with the wealth that came to them through trade and industry. Each town strove to build its own cathedral ever higher and higher. No building was as high in Roman times. Even the Hagia Sophia was dwarfed by these light and lofty marvels of engineering.

divorce (which had been treated, by aristocrats and peasants alike, as family matters over which the clergy had no jurisdiction) became a full-time preoccupation of the church. Sin, for instance, was no longer dealt with as an offense that just happened to the laity. It was a matter that the laity could do something about, preferably on a day-to-day basis. After 1215, for the first time ever, regular confession to a priest was made obligatory for all Catholic, western Christians. The followers of Francis of Assisi (1182–1226)—a man from a merchant background, whose father traded wool in northern France—emerged as an order of preachers who brought to the towns a message of repentance. They did not tell their audiences to enter the monastery (as would have been the case in the early Middle Ages). Instead, the listeners were to weep, to confess their sins to their local priests, and to try to be better Christians. Franciscans instilled in the hearts of all believers a new, Europe-wide Catholicism, based on daily remorse and on the daily contemplation of the sufferings of Christ and his mother, Mary. From Ireland to Riga and Budapest, Catholic Christians shared a common piety.

UNIVERSITIES AND INTELLECTUALS During this era, Europe acquired its first class of intellectuals. Since the end of the twelfth century, scholars had tended to come together in Paris. There they formed a *universitas*—a term borrowed from the merchant communities, where it denoted the equivalent of the modern "union." Those who belonged to the *universitas* were protected by their fellows and were allowed to continue their trade. Similarly protected by their union, the scholars of Paris set about wrestling with the new learning from Arab lands. And when in 1212 the bishop of Paris forbade this undertaking, they simply moved to the Left Bank of the Seine, so as to place the river between themselves and the officials of the bishop, who lived around the cathedral of Notre Dame.

The ability of the scholars to organize themselves gave them an advantage not enjoyed by their Arab contemporaries, despite the latter's immense cultural resources. For all his genius, Ibn Rushd had to spend his life courting the favor of

Medieval Lecture. Crowded lecture halls, open to a wide audience, were a creation of the medieval university. Previously, learning had taken place in small groups over long periods of time.

individual monarchs to protect him from conservative fellow Muslims. Frequently his books were burned. Ironically, European scholars congregating in the Schools of Paris could quietly absorb the most persuasive elements of Arabic thought, like Ibn Rushd's. Yet, at the same time, they endeavored to show that everything gradually converged to prove that Christianity was the only religion that fully met the aspirations of all rational human beings. Such was the message of the great teacher and intellectual Thomas Aquinas, born in southern Italy, whose *Summa contra Gentiles* (*Summary of Christian Belief against Non-Christians*) was written in 1264.

The Europe of 1300 was more culturally unified than it had been in previous centuries. It was more fully permeated by a version of its dominant Catholicism, made more accessible than ever before to the laity of the new towns through preachers such as Saint Francis and through stunning monuments such as the new Gothic cathedrals of northern France. Its leading intellectuals extolled the virtues of Christian learning and thought. Such a confident region was not, however, a happy place for heretics, Jews, or Muslims.

TRADERS Western Europeans were expanding frontiers around the Mediterranean and pushing beyond it. Great trading hubs emerged, most famously Venice and Genoa, as the nodes of commerce and finance linking Europe, Africa, and Asia. Powerful families commanded trading fleets and used their deep pockets to influence dealings far and wide. They also possessed the means to meddle in political affairs. Indeed, both Venice and Genoa set their sights on the waning power of Constantinople and on its eastern trade, vying for access to Asia Minor, the Black Sea, and the thriving commercial hinterlands of Afro-Eurasia. The Genoese showed, on a worldwide stage, what urban magnates could do when they combined sea power with a zest for organization. By 1300, Genoese ships had linked the Mediterranean to the coast of Flanders through regular sailings along the Atlantic coast of Spain, Portugal, and France. In 1291, some ventured as far as the Azores in the Atlantic, only to be lost as they pushed further southwest. Genoese maps displayed the entire coast of West Africa—including the kingdom of Mali, ruled by Mansa Musa (see above), which was the source of the gold dust that was now carried across the Sahara to the coast of North Africa.

CRUSADERS By the tenth and eleventh centuries, Europe had gained a strong enough sense of its separate identity that its elites and even many of its common folk regarded the area as a distinct region. Western Christianity was on the move. It spread into Scandinavia, southern Italy, the Baltic, and eastern Europe. Its ambitions to reconquer Spain and Portugal, which had been under Islamic control since the eighth century, demonstrated one of the effects of the flourishing of feudal power: the self-confidence of lords, their belief in their

military capability, and their pious sense of manifest destiny were all inflated. Besides, the wealth of the east, fueled by the prosperity of trading cities, was irresistible to those whose piety was entwined with an appetite for plunder. Nor were feudal lords alone in mixing opportunism and a passion for sacred causes. The leaders of the eastern and western churches were keen to recover or gain strength. Rome and Byzantium both sought to gain the upper hand in the scramble for religious command in Europe; each considered a blow to the "infidel" a cunning ploy to out-do the other. Yet the two Christendoms formed an uneasy alliance to roll back the expanding frontiers of Islam.

Crusader. Kneeling, this Crusader promises to serve God (as he would serve a feudal lord) by going to fight on a crusade (as he would fight for any lord to whom he had sworn loyalty). The two kinds of loyalty—to God and to one's lord—were deliberately confused in Crusader ideology. Both were about war. But fighting for God was unambiguously good, while fighting for a lord was not always so clearcut.

In 1095, at the Council of Clermont, Pope Urban II called for the First Crusade in the following words:

> Oh, race of Franks, race from across the mountains, race chosen and beloved by God, as shines forth in very many of your works, set apart from all nations by the situation of your country, as well as by your Catholic faith and the honor of the Holy Church! To you our discourse is addressed, and for you our exhortation is intended. We wish you to know what a grievous cause has led us to your country, what peril, threatening you and all the faithful, has brought us.

The "grievous cause" was the occupation of the Holy City of Jerusalem by the Islamic empire. Formed within the complex relationship between the Byzantine Empire and the western Christian papacy and kingdoms of Europe, the religious motivation behind the Crusades became the subject of many literary renditions of the tumultuous events. It also generated emotionally stirring and polemical writing, depicting either a Muslim or Christian enemy (depending on the work's author).

Polemics are often passionate, harsh, and emotional. They are also often meant to inspire and reinforce the conviction of fellow believers, with little concern for the accuracy of their portrayals. Thus authors of polemic in the time of the Crusades were usually too biased, too distant from the events or people they described, or simply too misinformed to present accurate portraits of the enemies against whom they were pitting themselves. But occasionally, firsthand accounts in the form of chronicles and histories offer us unique glimpses into Christian-Muslim relations in the age of the Crusades.

Consider Usāmah ibn Munqidh (1095–1188), the deeply learned ruler of the city of Shaizar on the Orontes River in western Syria. Skirmishes, truces, and the ransoming of prisoners were part of his daily life, and Usāmah socialized with his Frankish neighbors quite as much as he fought with them. He offers a dismissive opinion of his enemies. Basically, they struck him as "animals possessing the virtues of courage and fighting, but nothing else." In particular, their medical practice appalled him. More strange yet, the Franks allowed their wives to walk about freely and to talk to strangers unaccompanied by male guardians. How could men be at once so brave and yet so lacking in a proper, Arab sense of honor, which would lead a man to protect his women? In fact, sexual laxity seemed to be one of the aspects of Frankish life that most appalled Usāmah, who claimed that the Franks were "void of all zeal and jealousy," meaning that they were unconcerned with relatively loose sexual mores. Unlike other Muslim authors of his time, however, Usāmah does not refer to the Franks in derogatory terms such as "infidels" or "devils." In fact, he occasionally refers to some of them as his companions, and writes in one case of a Frank who used to call him "my brother" (*An Arab-Syrian Gentleman and Warrior in the Time of the Crusades,* 16).

Christian authors had similar interests in documenting the habits and customs of their enemies in battle. Jean de Joinville (1224/1225–1317) was a chronicler of medieval France. He also composed a biography of King Louis II, at the request of Jeanne of Navarre, the queen. In 1309 Joinville completed his work on the *Histoire de Saint Louis,* which documents how he himself had been in the service of the king. During the crusade launched from 1248 to 1254, Joinville, one of the king's confidants, had occasion to note the social behavior of the Muslims:

> Whenever the Sultan was in the camp, the men of the personal Guard were quartered all round his lodging, and appointed to guard his person. At the door of the Sultan's lodging there was a little tent for the Sultan's door-keepers, and for his musicians, who had Arabian horns and drums and kettledrums; and they used to make such a din at daybreak and at nightfall that people near them could not hear one another speak, and that they could be heard plainly all through the camp. The musicians never dared sound their instruments in the daytime unless by the order of the Chief of the Guard. Thus it was, that whenever the Sultan had a proclamation to make he used to send for the Chief of the Guard, and give him the order; and then the Chief would cause all the Sultan's instruments to be sounded; and thereupon all the host would come to hear the Sultan's commands.

Although we should regard literary renditions of the events described with a certain degree of caution, they are useful for gleaning personal details that may be left out of other types of works. The colorful accounts by authors such as Usāmah ibn Munqidh and Joinville have proven invaluable as resources for the social and cultural history of the Crusader era.

The result was that Europeans took war outside their own borders on a mass scale. In the late eleventh century, western Europeans launched the wave of attacks that we now know as the Crusades. The First Crusade began in 1095, when Pope Urban II appealed to the warrior nobility of France to put their violence to good use. They should combine their role as pilgrims to Jerusalem with that of soldiers and free Jerusalem from Muslim rule. What the pope and clergy proposed, in effect, was a novel kind of war. Previously, the clergy had regarded war as a dirty business and a source of sin (not unlike sex). Now the clergy told the knights that good and just wars were possible. Such wars could cancel out the sins of those who waged them.

Starting in 1097, an armed host of around 60,000 men—a force larger than any "barbarian" wave at the end of the Roman Empire—moved all the way from northwestern Europe to Jerusalem. In all, there would be four "crusades," over the course of two centuries. They cannot be described as successful. Only a small proportion of Crusaders stayed behind to guard the territories they had won. No more than 1,200 knights remained to defend the Kingdom of Jerusalem after the First Crusade. Most knights returned home, their epic pilgrimage completed. The fragile network of small Crusader lordships could only occasionally pose a threat to the true heartlands of the Islamic world. On July 4, 1187, the Frankish heavy cavalry was lured on to the dry plateau above the Sea of Galilee, where they were slaughtered in the blazing heat by Saladin (Salah ad-Din, "Righteous in Faith"), the Kurdish commander who had made himself ruler over Egypt. Subsequent forays were equally disastrous. Stretched thin, with feeble supply lines, the dwindling forces of Christian occupiers (or "liberators," depending on one's perspective) were too easy to pick off, surround and besiege, or simply overrun. Against such odds, western Christian forces took out their frustrations against other Christians and allies. In one infamous "crusade" Frankish armies went on a rampage in the Byzantine capital and sacked Constantinople in 1204. According to one Byzantine monk, "nothing worse than this has happened nor will happen." When news reached the far-off Scandinavian world, Christian I, king of Norway and Denmark, saw it as a signal of the forthcoming apocalypse, when the beast would rise from the waters, as described in the New Testament.

Muslim leaders did not see the Frankish knights as much of a threat to their heartland. From the point of view of the Muslim Middle East, the Crusades were largely irrelevant. As far as the average Muslim of the region was concerned, the Crusaders had blundered into a no-man's-land of little importance. The principal long-term effect of these assaults was to harden Muslim feelings against the *Ferangi* (Franks) of the West and to bring about a worsening of the condition of many millions of non-Western Christians who had previously lived peacefully in Egypt and Syria.

Other Crusade-like campaigns of Christian expansion undertaken around this time were considerably more successful. Rather than being overseas ventures, these were launched from a secure home base. In this period, the Spanish Reconquista got under way. Beginning with the capture of Toledo in 1061, the Christian kings of northern Spain (who could count on support from their immediate Christian neighbors across the Pyrenees) slowly but surely pushed back the Muslims. Eventually, they reached the rich heart of Andalusia and in 1248 they conquered Seville, a victory that permanently added more than 100,000 square miles of territory to Christian Europe. Another force from northern France crossed Italy to conquer Muslim-held Sicily in 1091, thereby ensuring that a rich island only seventy-five miles away from the coast of Africa and in a position to control the middle of the Mediterranean was subject to Christian rule. These two conquests accomplished in less than a century, and not the fragile foothold of the Crusaders on the edge of the Middle East, were the events that truly turned the tide in the relations between Christian and Muslim power in the Mediterranean.

THE AMERICAS

> → *Where did societies in the Americas demonstrate strong commercial expansionist impulses?*

Alone in the world, untouched by the increasing connections across the Afro-Eurasian regions, were the Americas. Simply put, the revolution in communications did not enable Asian, African, or European navigators to cross the large oceans that separated the Americas from other lands. However, isolation did not mean that the Americas were stagnant. Many of the commercial and expansionist impulses that swept the rest of the world occurred independently in the Western Hemisphere and similarly brought the peoples of the Americas into closer contact with each other.

ANDEAN STATES

Growth and prosperity in the Andean region led to the formation of South America's first empire. Known as the Chimú Empire, it developed during the first century of the second millennium in the fertile Moche Valley, bordering the Pacific Ocean. (See Map 10-8.) At its height, the Moche people had expanded their influence across a number of valleys—and thus incorporated a wide number of ecological zones, from pastoral highlands to rich valley floodplains to the fecund fishing grounds of the Pacific Coast. As their geographical reach grew, so did their wealth. The Chimú regime lasted until Incan armies invaded the coastal strongholds in the 1460s and incorporated the Pacific state into its own immense empire.

The Chimú economy was successful because it was highly commercialized. Agriculture was its base, and complex irrigation systems turned the arid coast into a string of fertile oases capable of feeding an expanding and far dispersed population. Cotton became a lucrative export to distant markets along the Andes. Parades of llamas and porters lugged these commodities up and down the steep mountain chains that are the spine of South America. As in China, a large, well-trained bureaucracy was responsible for constructing and maintaining canals, with a hierarchy of provincial administrators to watch over commercial hinterlands.

Between 850 and 900 CE, the Moche peoples founded their biggest city, Chan Chan, with a core population of 30,000 inhabitants. A sprawling metropolis surrounded by twenty-six-foot-high walls, covering nearly ten square miles with extensive roads circulating through adobe neighborhoods, it had ten huge palaces at its center. These were residence halls, protected by thick walls thirty feet high, whose prestige and opulence demonstrated the rulers' power over other Moche subjects. Within the compound, emperors erected mortuary monuments, which became stores for their accumulated riches. In them archaeologists have found

MAP 10-8   ANDEAN STATES

Although the Andes region of South America was isolated from Afro-Eurasian developments before 1500, it was not a stagnant region. Indeed, political and cultural integration brought the peoples of this region closer together. What kind of empire was the Chimú? What kinds of ecological niches did it govern? How did each polity encourage greater cultural and economic integration?

Chan Chan. This is what is left of Chan Chan. The city covered fifteen square miles and was divided into distinct neighborhoods for nobles, artisans, and commoners, with the elites living closest to the hub of governmental and spiritual power. Adobe was the basic construction material; it held up well in the arid conditions of the Peruvian coast.

Tihuanaco Buildings. The buildings of Tihuanaco were made of giant, hand-hewn stones assembled without mortar. Engineers had not discovered the principle of curved arches and keystones and instead relied on massive slabs atop gateways. Gateways were important symbolic features, for they were places where people acknowledged the importance of sun and moon gods. In this building, a giant monolith stood in the gateway that looked out over the Andean horizon.

treasures of fine cloth, gold and silver objects, splendid *Spondylus* shells, and piles of other high-status goods. Around the emperors' compound were neighborhoods for nobles and artisans; in the further reaches of the city stood small rows of houses for Moche commoners.

The Andes also saw its first highland empires during this period. On the shores of the high plateau lake Titicaca, the people of Tiahuanaco forged a high-altitude state. Though neither as large nor as wealthy as the Chimú Empire, it was complex, and it converted the seemingly inhospitable highlands into an environment where farmers and herders thrived. There is, moreover, extensive evidence of long-distance trade between the highland peoples and neighbors in semitropical valleys, and even signs of highlanders migrating down to the lowlands to set up agrarian colonies to produce staples for their kin in the mountains. Dried fish and cotton came from the coast; fruits and vegetables came from lowland valleys. Trade was active enough to sustain an enormous urban population of up to 115,000 people. Looming over the skyline of

Lake Titicaca. This is the setting for the first great Andean polity of Tihuanaco (Tiwanaku). Surrounded by the glacial peaks of the Andes, Tihuanaco grew up near the shores of Lake Titicaca, a source of water, fish, and legends about the birth of gods. To cultivate the steep mountainsides, farmers developed complex terrace systems. Most settlements were nestled, like these ruins, on valley floors or by the shores of the lake.

Tiahuanaco was an imposing pyramid of massive sandstone blocks; its advanced engineering system conveyed water to the summit, from which the liquid flowed in an imitation of rainfall down the carefully carved sides—an awesome spectacle of engineering prowess in such an arid region.

NORTH AMERICAN CONNECTIONS

By 1000 CE, Mesoamerica had seen the rise and fall of several complex societies. Caravans of porters worked the intricate roads that connected the coast of the Gulf of Mexico and the Pacific, and the southern lowlands of Central America to the arid regions of modern Texas. (See Map 10-9.) Its heartland was the rich valley of central Mexico. The Toltecs rose to power with great rapidity because they were able to fill the political vacuum left by the decline of the great city of Teotihuacán (see Chapter 8) and tap into the commercial network that radiated from the valley.

The Toltecs themselves were hybrids—a combination of migrant groups, refugees from the south, and farmers from the north—who settled northwest of Teotihuacán as the city waned. Their capital was Tula, growing in the shadow of the Mesoamerican metropolis. The Toltecs relied on a maize-based economy, supplemented by beans, squash, and dog, deer, and rabbit meat, as local agrarian production covered the population's needs. Rulers, however, relied on the enterprise of merchants to provide them with status goods such as ornamental pottery, rare shells and stones, and precious skins and feathers.

Tula was a commercial hub. But it was also a political capital and a ceremonial center. While the city's layout differed from Teotihuacán's, many features revealed borrowings from other Mesoamerican peoples. Temples were made of giant pyramids topped by colossal stone soldiers, and the ball courts where subjects and conquered peoples alike played their ritual sport were ubiquitous. The architecture and monumental art bespoke the mixed and migratory origins of the Toltecs: a combination of Mayan and Teotihuanacu influences decorated the city's great public works. At its height, the Toltec capital was home to around 60,000 people—a huge metropolis by contemporary European standards.

Cities at the hubs of trading networks could be found all across North America. North of Tula, the largest was Cahokia, by the shores of the Mississippi River (near modern-day East St. Louis), a city of about 15,000 (which would make it about the size of London at the time). Farmers and hunters settled in the region around 600 CE, attracted by the combination of good soil, availability of woodlands for fuel and game, and access to the trading artery of the mighty Mississippi. Eventually, fields planted with rows of maize (their main staple) and other crops fanned out into the horizon. The hoe replaced the trusty digging stick, increasing yields, and smaller satellite towns put up granaries to hold foodstuffs.

Cahokia became a commercial center for regional and long-distance trade. The hinterlands produced staples for urban consumers. In return, Cahokia's crafts were exported, carried inland on the backs of porters and to distant North American markets in canoes. The city's woven fabrics and ceramics were desired by faraway consumers. In exchange, traders brought to the rich city mica from the Appalachian Mountains, seashells and sharks' teeth from the Gulf of Mexico, and copper from the upper Great Lakes. Indeed, Cahokia became more than an importer and exporter: it was the

Toltec Temple. Tula, the capital of the Toltec Empire, carried on the Mesoamerican tradition of locating ceremonial architecture at the center of the city. The Pyramid of the Morning Star cast its shadow over all other buildings. And above them stood columns of the Atlantes, carved Toltec god-warriors, the figurative pillars of the empire itself. The walls of this pyramid were likely embellished with images of snakes and skulls. The north face of the pyramid has the image of a snake devouring a human.

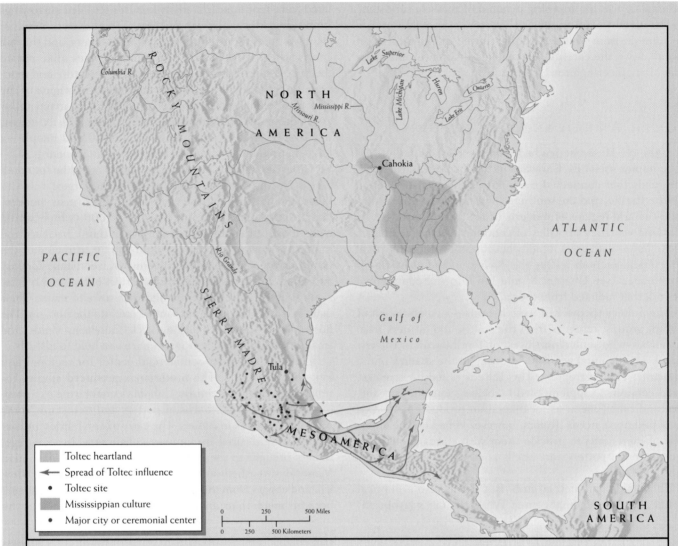

MAP 10-9   **COMMERCIAL HUBS IN MESOAMERICA AND NORTH AMERICA, 1000**

Both Cahokia and Tula, shown on the map above, represented commercial hubs of vibrant regional trade networks between 1000 and 1300. What kinds of goods do your readings suggest circulated through these cities? How much political influence on the surrounding region do you think each city maintained? Do you think that the trade networks anchored by each city ever interacted with each other during this time?

entrepôt for an entire regional commercial network, containing many trading nodes where salt, tools, pottery, woven stuffs, jewelry, and ceremonial goods could be procured from traders from other places.

Cahokia's urban landscape was dominated by mounds, really big mounds (which is one reason Cahokians are often known as "mound people"). These earth monuments were delicately maintained: Cahokians enveloped their shells with layers of sand and clay to prevent their foundations from drying and then cracking. It was from these great artificial hills that Cahokians paid homage to spiritual forces. Of course, building this kind of infrastructure without draft animals, hy-

draulic tools, or even wheels was labor-intensive. To solve this problem, Cahokians recruited other North Americans to serve in working brigades. Around the city was an endless palisade made from neighboring forests, to protect the metropolis from marauders and enemies.

In the end, the city outgrew its environment. The woodlands were cleared and arable soil began to lose nutrients. Timber and food became scarce. Because the city lacked a means of transportation to ship bulky items over long distances, Cahokia's success bred its downfall. When the creeks that fed its water system could not keep up with demand, engineers changed their course, to no avail. By 1350, the city

Cahokia Mounds. This is all that is left of what was once a large city organized around temple mounds in what today is Illinois. The largest of the temples, known as Monks' Mound, was likely a burial site, with four separate terraces for crowds to gather. Centuries of neglect and erosion have taken their toll on what was once the largest human-made earthen mound in North America.

was practically empty. Nevertheless, Cahokia represented the growing networks of trade and migration across North America, and it demonstrated the ability of North Americans to organize vibrant commercial societies and powerful states.

THE MONGOL TRANSFORMATION OF AFRO-EURASIA

> → *How did Mongol conquests affect cross-cultural contacts and regional development in Afro-Eurasia?*

The world's sea-lanes grew crowded with ships; ports buzzed with activity. Commercial networks were clearly one way to integrate the world. But just as long-distance trade connected people, so could conquerors—as we have seen throughout the history of the early world. In this instance, these transformative conquerors came from the inner Eurasian steppe lands, the same place where horse-riding warriors such as the Xiongnu originated centuries earlier (see Chapters 6 and 7). Like the Xiongnu and the Kushans before them, the Mongols would both conquer peoples and intensify trade and cultural exchange. By setting up a latticework of states across northern and central Asia, the Mongols created a new empire that straddled the east and west. (See Map 10-10.) It was unstable, and not as durable as other dynasties. It did

not even have a shared faith; the mother of the conquering emperors, Hulagu and Kubilai Khan, was a devout Christian, reflecting the success of Nestorian missionaries who had been laboring for centuries to bring about conversions among the animistic nomads. Many Europeans hoped and prayed that the entire empire would convert. But it did not; the Mongols were a religious patchwork of Afro-Eurasian belief systems. Yet the Mongols succeeded in bringing parts of the world together.

Who were these conquerors of territories so much larger than their own? The Mongols were a combination of forest and prairie peoples. Residing in circular, felt-covered tents, which they shared with some of their animals, the Mongols lived by a combination of hunting and livestock herding. A mobile society, they changed campgrounds with the seasons, hunting game and herding livestock south in winter and north in summer. Life on the steppes was a constant struggle, which meant that only the strong survived. Their food, consisting primarily of animal products from their herds or from game they hunted, provided high levels of protein, which built up their muscle mass and added to their strength. Always on the march, the Mongols created a society that resembled a perpetual standing army. Their bands were organized into strictly disciplined military units led by commanders chosen for their skill. Mongol archers, using a heavy compound bow, made of sinew, wood, and horns, could fire an arrow more than 200 yards at full gallop with accuracy. Mongol horses were stocky, and capable of withstanding extreme cold. Their saddles had high supports in front and back, enabling the warriors to ride and maneuver at high speeds. Iron stirrups permitted the riders to rise in their saddles to shoot their arrows without stopping. The Mongols were expert horsemen, who could remain in the saddle all day and night, even sleeping while their horses continued on the move. Each warrior kept many horses, enabling Mongol armies to travel as many as sixty or seventy miles per day. Between military campaigns, soldiers kept sharp by engaging in winter hunting.

Mongol tribes were imperialists in a special way: while they conquered they also adjoined their conquests by extending kinship networks. In this fashion, the empire was made of a confederation of familial tribes. The tents (households) were interrelated mostly by marriage; that is, they were alliances sealed by exchange of daughters. Conquest involved marrying conquering men to the women of the conquered, and selecting conquered men to marry the conqueror's women. Chinggis Khan is said to have had more than 500 wives, most of them daughters of tribes that he conquered or that sought alliance with him. As a result a great proportion of steppe chiefs were kin. Patrimony was king, but empire was achieved through the exchange of women.

Women in Mongol society were responsible for child-rearing as well as shearing and milking livestock and processing their pelts for clothing. But women also took part in

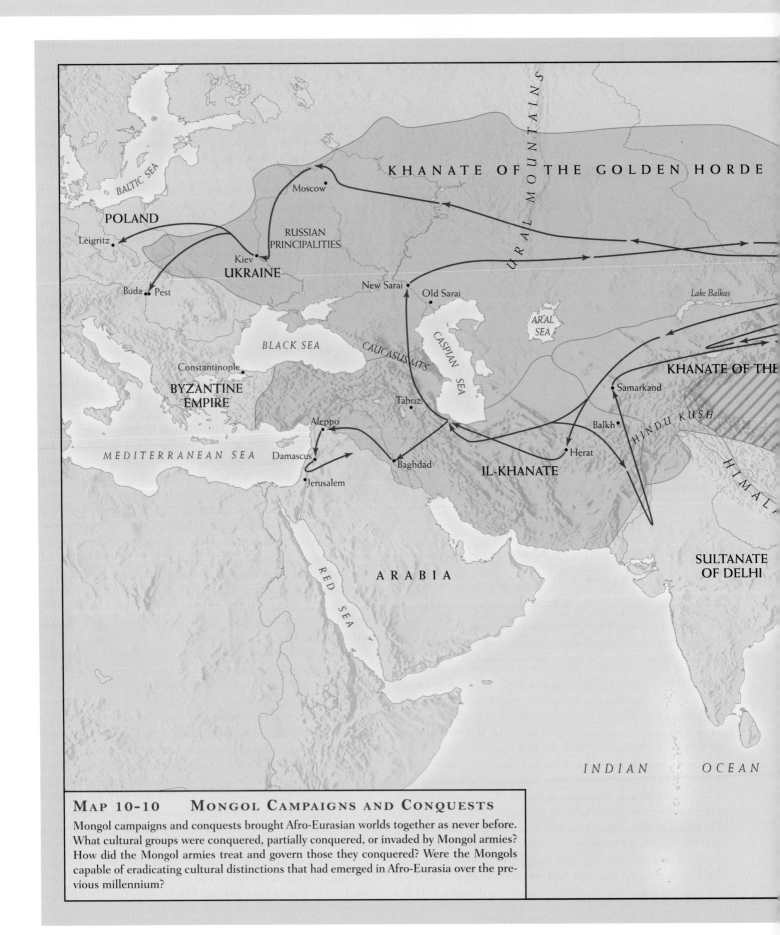

MAP 10-10 MONGOL CAMPAIGNS AND CONQUESTS

Mongol campaigns and conquests brought Afro-Eurasian worlds together as never before. What cultural groups were conquered, partially conquered, or invaded by Mongol armies? How did the Mongol armies treat and govern those they conquered? Were the Mongols capable of eradicating cultural distinctions that had emerged in Afro-Eurasia over the previous millennium?

→ *How did Mongol conquests affect cross-cultural contacts and regional development in Afro-Eurasia?*

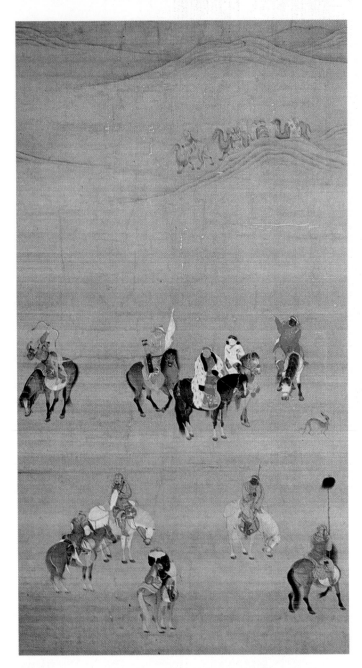

Mongols on Horseback. Even after the Mongols became the rulers of China, the emperors remembered their steppe origin and maintained the skills of horse-riding nomads. This detail from a thirteenth/fourteenth-century silk painting shows Kubilai Khan at hunting.

that each son acquired a different second language that would aid in administrating conquered lands. She gathered Confucian scholars to prepare Kubilai Khan to rule China. Chabi, Kubilai's senior wife, followed a similar pattern, offering patronage to Tibetan monks who set about converting the Mongol elite in China to Tibetan Buddhism.

At least initially, the nomads' desire for conquests may have been fueled by their need for grazing lands. Then, as the Mongols moved into new lands, they were able to increase their wealth enormously by extracting taxes through their tributary system. Trade disputes were also a powerful spur to their expeditions. The Mongols were dependent on trade with settled peoples, seeking especially grain but also manufactured goods (including iron for tools, wagons, weapons, bridles, and stirrups), and their first expansionist forays followed caravan routes. Here were opportunities to raid instead of trade.

The nomads' expansionist thrust began in 1206, when a cluster of tribes joined into a united force. A large gathering of clan heads acclaimed one of those present as Chinggis (Genghis) Khan, or Supreme Ruler. Chinggis (c. 1155–1227) subsequently launched a series of conquests southward across the Great Wall of China, and westward through central Asia to Afghanistan and Persia. The Mongols also launched a massive invasion of Korea in 1231. Although the Korean armies fiercely resisted, the Koryo state was no match for the well-organized horsemen from the northern steppe. The armies of Chinggis's son and first successor reached both the Pacific Ocean and the Adriatic Sea. His grandsons founded dynasties in China, Persia, and on the southern Eurasian steppes east of Europe. One of them, Kubilai Khan, enlisted thousands of Koryo men and ships for ill-fated invasions of Japan in 1274 and 1281. Thus, a realm took shape that was more than 6,000 miles wide and touched all four of Afro-Eurasia's main worlds.

Mongol raiders built a permanent empire by incorporating conquered peoples and by absorbing some of their ways. By stretching their power across the northern arch of Afro-Eurasia, horsemen bypassed the Pamir watershed, which divides central Asia into eastern and western portions. This unification was far more surprising and sudden than the ties developed incrementally by traders and travelers on ships. Now, Afro-Eurasian regions were connected by land and by sea, in historically unparalleled ways.

MONGOLS IN CHINA

In 1200, the north of China was still under the control of the Jin dynasty (1115–1234), which was led by Jurchen, who had driven the Song into the south. The Song court and its Chinese followers had regrouped in the south and called themselves the "Southern Song." As the political and military upheaval continued in the north, much of the economic ac-

battles. Kubilai Khan's niece Khutulun became famous for besting men in wrestling matches and claiming their horses as spoils. Although women were often bought and sold, Mongol wives had the right to own property and even to divorce. Elite Mongol women played important political roles. Sorghaghtani Beki, Kubilai Khan's birth mother, helped to engineer the rule of her sons. Illiterate herself, she made sure

Mongolian Warriors. This miniature painting is one of the illustrations for *History* by Rashid al Din, the most outstanding scholar under the Mongol regimes. Note the relatively small horses and strong bows used by the Mongol soldiers.

tivity of trade and finance moved southward and focused on their new capital, Hangzhou. This former provincial seaport became the political center of the Chinese people in their ongoing struggles with northern steppe nomads. It also became one of China's gateways to the rest of the world via the South China Sea. Agrarian staples and precious manufactures poured out of southern China to feed and clothe people in distant markets, as Chinese precious goods were coveted by elites far and wide.

The Jin fell fairly quickly in 1234 because of the Mongols' superiority in cavalry on the North China Plain. But below the Yangzi River, the climate and weather changed, no longer favoring the Mongol horsemen against Southern Song forces. They grew ill from diseases such as malaria, and their horses perished from the heat. To conquer the semitropical south, the Mongols increasingly took to boats and fought along rivers and canals, as Chinese had done since the Three Kingdoms period and during the Sui and Tang reunifications. Kubilai, Chinggis's grandson, completed the conquest of the grandest prize of all—southern China—after 1260. His generals marched their cavalries through the higher plateaus of Sichuan and Yunnan in southwest China, and then attacked South China's economic heartland from the west. The Southern Song army, composed of hired mercenaries, proved unable to withstand the onslaught of warriors who were armed with the latest gunpowder-based weapons (developed from a technology originally invented by the Chinese themselves).

Still, Mongol armies pressed south until they reached the outskirts of Hangzhou; this last Song capital succumbed to the invaders in 1276. Rather than see the invaders pillage the city and the tombs of the emperors, they bowed to the inevitable. The Song court was in disarray: the young emperor had died suddenly in 1274, and all his heirs were minors. The new regents for the successor and the Empress Dowager were unable to handle the internal chaos and the advancing army. Meanwhile, Kubilai Khan's most trusted and able commander, Bayan, led his crack Mongol forces as they seized town after town, ever closer to the capital. The Empress Dowager tried to buy off the invaders, as the Chinese had often done in the past, proposing regular and substantial tribute payments—250,000 taels of silver and 250,000 bolts of silk—but Bayan had his eye on the prize: Hangzhou.

On the eve of the city's fall in 1276, the Empress Dowager presented Bayan with the Song dynasty's seal, the sign that she had given up. Later the Song emperor appeared in person and submitted to the new masters of the city. Bayan was magnanimous in his victory. He ordered his men to conduct a census of Hangzhou and register its granaries and treasury. He also prohibited his men from plundering the suburban tombs of the Southern Song emperors—in contrast to the Jin conquerors, who in 1127 had pillaged the Northern Song tombs outside Kaifeng. Bayan also escorted the Song emperor and the Empress Dowager to Beijing, where Kubilai treated them with honor. Pockets of resistance persisted after 1276, but within three years Song China's defeat was complete. Having extended their military sway over all of South China, the Mongols established the Yuan dynasty (1280–1368) with a new capital at Dadu ("Great Capital," present-day Beijing).

THE TRAVELS OF MARCO POLO AND IBN BATTUTA

Although no traveler crossed the Atlantic or Pacific oceans, an increasing number ventured through the lands of Africa, Europe, and Asia. The most famous of these thirteenth- and fourteenth-century travelers, Marco Polo and Ibn Battuta, encountered a world tied together by trade routes that crossed the Afro-Eurasian landmass and the Indian Ocean that often had as their ultimate destination the imperial court of the Great Khan in China. These two men and similar, though less-celebrated travelers, observed worlds that were both highly localized and yet had culturally unifying features.

In 1271, Marco Polo (1254–1324), the son of an enterprising Venetian merchant, set out with his father and uncle on a journey to East Asia. Making their way along the fabled silk route across central Asia, the Polos arrived in Xanadu, the summer capital of the Mongol empire, after a three-and-a-half year journey. There they remained for more than two decades. When they returned to their home in Venice in 1295, fellow townsmen greeted them with astonishment, so sure were they that the Polos had perished years before. So, too, Marco Polo's published account of his travels generated an incredulous reaction. Some of his European readers considered his tales of Eastern wonders to be mere fantasy, yet others found their appetites for Asian splendor whetted by Polo's descriptions.

A half-century after Polo commenced his travels, the Moroccan-born scholar Muhammad ibn Abdullah ibn Battuta (1304–1369) embarked on a journey of his own. Then just twenty-one, Ibn Battuta vowed to visit the whole of the Islamic world without traveling the same road twice. It was an ambitious assignment, for Islam's domain extended from one end of the Eurasian landmass to the other and far into Africa as well. On his journey, Ibn Battuta eventually covered some 75,000 miles and traveled through West and East Africa, across the interior of Asia, and beyond the realm of Islam to China. Along his way, he claimed to have met at least sixty rulers, and in his book he recorded the names of more than 2,000 persons whom he knew personally.

Marco Polo and Ibn Battuta provide a wealth of information on the well-traversed lands of Africa, Europe, and Asia. What they and other travelers observed was the extreme diversity that characterized the peoples living in Afro-Eurasia, where numerous ethnicities, many political formations, and varied religious faiths and practices prevailed. In addition, they observed that the vast majority of people lived deeply localized lives, the primary goal of which was to obtain the basic necessities of everyday living. Yet, they were also aware that these very same societies, however local their orientations, welcomed and even encouraged contact, trade, and cultural exchange over long distances and between regions. In fact, they wrote most eloquently about the way in which each of the four major cultural systems of the Afro-Eurasian landmass—Christian, Muslim, Indian, and Chinese—struggled to articulate definitions of themselves. Interestingly, if Ibn Battuta and Marco Polo had been able to travel in the "unknown" worlds—the African hinterlands, the Americas, and Oceania—they would have witnessed to varying degrees similar phenomena and challenges.

The exploits of Marco Polo and Ibn Battuta suggest that a few men and women, mainly merchants and scholars, routinely traversed immense distances. These travelers used and strengthened existing trade routes between regions and fostered contacts across cultural boundaries. Their journeys revealed a Eurasian world linked from the Mediterranean in the west to China in the east. Along the trade routes, merchants, travelers, commodities, and ideas circulated freely through great port cities such as Surat and Calicut along the Malabar coast in India; Zanzibar and Kilwa in East Africa; and Genoa, Venice, and Alexandria along the northern and southern shores of the Mediterranean Sea.

Although it fell in 1276, Hangzhou survived the Mongol conquest reasonably intact. However, the tombs of the Song royal family were ransacked for valuables in 1285 to raise funds for the construction and renovation of Buddhist monasteries and temples. It was still, when the Venetian traveler Marco Polo visited it in the 1280s and the Muslim traveler Ibn Battuta in the 1340s, one of the greatest cities in the world. They both agreed that neither Europe nor the Islamic world had anything like it.

After defeating the Jin in northern China in 1234 and the Southern Song by 1280, the Mongol conquest changed the political and social landscape. The population in the north, especially in Kaifeng, already had begun to drop precipitously under the Jin. When the demand for iron ores and coal dried up, steel production declined; it came to almost a total halt after the Yellow River shifted south in 1194, severing Kaifeng, as the key industrial city in the north, from its iron mines and smelters. By 1330, now under the Mongols, the once magnificent Kaifeng, with a population once exceeding a million, had become a ramshackle town of fewer than 90,000 inhabitants.

Mongol rule did not involve the imposition of rough ways of the steppe lands on "civilized" urbanite Chinese (though such was the view of Han ideologues). True, China acquired a new ruling hierarchy. Chinese Confucian insiders were relegated to a subordinate station—and withdrew to exercise power, to the extent they were permitted, at the local level. Outsiders, non-Chinese known as the *semu* (categorized peoples), took over political control. They themselves were a heterogeneous group of Afro-Eurasian peoples—Mongols, Tanguts, Khitan, Jurchen, Muslims, Tibetans, Persians, Turks, Nestorians, Jews, Armenians—a new conquering elite that ruled over a vast Han majority. The result was a segmented ruling system, in which incumbent Chinese elites governed locally while newcomers who came from around Afro-Eurasia handled the levers of the central dynastic polity and collected taxes for the Mongols.

MONGOL REVERBERATIONS IN SOUTHEAST ASIA

Southeast Asia was also whiplashed by the Mongol conquests. Circling Song defenses along the rivers and lakes in South China, the Mongols marched into the southwest and conquered the states of Dali and Pyu in Yunnan and Burma. From there, in the 1270s, the armies turned back to China, heading directly east into the soft underbelly of the Song state. In this sweep, portions of mainland Southeast Asia became part of the Mongol empire and thus were annexed to China for the first time. As the kingdom of Dali and other polities became prefectures of Mongol-ruled China, the autonomy that the southwest had enjoyed since the Han and Tang dynasties came to an end. Even the distant Khmer regime felt the consequences of the Mongol conquest of the Song dynasty when the Mongol fleet passed by on the way to attack and take Java—unsuccessfully, as it turned out—in 1293.

THE FALL OF BAGHDAD

As in China, in Islamic lands the brunt of foreign invasions was borne by the empire's core. By this time Baghdad had become a mere shadow of its former glorious self, though caliphs continued to sit on the throne, proclaiming their dominion over all the Islamic world. From their earlier attacks on the Islamic borderlands of central Asia, Mongol raiding parties learned of the weaknesses and divisions of Islamic rulers in the heartlands.

In the thirteenth century, Mongol tribesmen streamed west out of the eastern steppes, crossing the whole of Asia and entering into the eastern parts of Europe. Mongke Khan, a grandson of the great Mongol unifier and war leader Chinggis, made clear the Mongol aspiration for world domination, appointing his brother Kubilai to rule over China, Tibet, and the northern parts of India and commanding another brother, Hulagu, to add the western territories of Iran, Syria, Egypt, Byzantium, and Armenia to the Mongol imperium.

When Hulagu reached Baghdad in 1258, he encountered a feeble foe: merely 10,000 horsemen faced his army of 200,000 soldiers, who were eager to acquire the booty of a wealthy city at the crossroads of Afro-Eurasian commerce. Even before the battle had taken place, Baghdadis knew the fate that awaited them. Poets were composing elegies for the dead and mourning the defeat of Islam.

The slaughter was vast, and few were spared. Hulagu himself boasted to one of the European kings that he had taken the lives of at least 200,000 people. The Mongols gave no quarter, pursuing their adversaries everywhere. They hunted them in wells, latrines, and sewers and followed them into the upper floors of buildings, killing them on rooftops until, as the Iraqi Arab historian Ibn Kathir observed, "blood poured from the gutters into the streets. . . . The same happened in the mosques and . . . Baghdad, which had been the most civilized of all cities, became a ruin with only a few inhabitants" (Lewis, pp. 82–83). In a few weeks of sheer terror, the venerable Abbasid caliphate was demolished. Hulagu's forces showed no mercy to the caliph himself, who was rolled up in a carpet and trampled to death by horses, his blood soaked up by the rug so it would leave no mark on the ground. With Baghdad crushed, the Mongol armies pushed on to Syria, slaughtering Muslims along the way. A succession crisis in the Mongol heartland pulled Hulagu away from the front, however.

In the end, the Egyptian Mamluks, an Islamic regime built by slave-soldiers, stemmed the advance of the Mongol armies in 1261, thereby preventing Egypt from falling into Mongol hands. The Mongol empire had reached its outer limits. Better at conquering than controlling, defeating rather than governing, the Mongols struggled to rule their vast possessions in makeshift states. But bit by bit, and with gathering speed, they ceded control to local administrators and dynasties who promised to govern as their surrogates. There was also chronic feuding among the Mongol dynasts, especially between jealous sons. In China and in Persia, Mongol rule collapsed in the fourteenth century.

Mongol conquest reshaped the social landscape of Afro-Eurasia. Islam was decisively transformed: never again would it have a unifying authority like the caliphate or a powerful center like Baghdad. Though not sundered in quite the way Islam's heartland was, China was divided and changed in other ways. The Mongols introduced many Persian, Islamic, and Byzantine influences on China's architecture, art, science, and medicine. The Yuan policy of benign tolerance for foreign creeds and consistent contacts with western Asia also brought elements from Christianity, Judaism, Zoroastrianism, and Islam into the Chinese mix. The Mongol thrust into China thus led to a flowering and great opening, as fine goods, traders, and technology would flow unstintingly from China to the rest of the world in the ensuing centuries. Finally, the Mongol state, after its bloody conquests, settled down and promoted an Afro-Eurasian interconnectedness that this huge territorial landmass had not known before and would not experience again for many centuries. Out of conquest and translandmass warfare would come centuries of trade, migration, and increasing contacts among Africa, Europe, and Asia.

Chronology

	700 CE	800 CE	900 CE	1000 CE
SUB-SAHARAN AFRICA				
THE AMERICAS		Moche people found Chan Chan, c. 900 ▮ Toltec Empire in Mexico Valley, c. 900–1100 ▮	Cahokia flourishes as a commercial hub in Mississippi River valley, c. 1000 ▮ Chimú Empire, 1000–1460 ▮	
THE ISLAMIC WORLD			Muslims become a majority in Abassid caliphate ▮	
SOUTH ASIA			Turkish invasions from Central Asia begin ▮	
EAST ASIA		▮ Heian period in Japan, 794–1185 Koryo dynasty rules, 918–1392 ▮ Lady Shikibu (c. 976–c. 1031) writes The Tale of Genji ▮	Song dynasty founded, 960 ▮ Gunpowder invented ▮	
SOUTHEAST ASIA		Khmer kingdom, 899–1431 ▮		
CHRISTIAN EUROPE			Iaroslav the Wise (1016–1054) rebuild Kiev as a small scale Constantinop	

CONCLUSION

Between 1000 and 1300, the world of Afro-Eurasia was being divided into large cultural spheres. At the same time, as people traded and migrated across longer distances, the regions of Afro-Eurasia prospered and became more integrated. In the center of Afro-Eurasia, Islam was firmly ensconced, its merchants, scholars, and travelers taking full advantage of their location to serve as commercial and cultural intermediaries joining the entire landmass together. As Indian Ocean seaborne trade expanded, India, too, became a commercial crossroads. Merchants set up businesses in the Indian port cities and welcomed traders who arrived from the Arab lands

to the west, from China, and from Southeast Asia. China also boomed, pouring its manufactures into trading networks that encompassed all of Afro-Eurasia and reached into African frontiers.

Trade helped delineate the parts of the world. The prosperity it brought also helped create new classes of peoples—thinkers, writers, and naturalists—who more clearly defined what it meant to belong to the regions of Afro-Eurasia. By 1300, learned priests and writers had begun to reimagine each of the world's regions as more than just territories: they were ideas that were now maturing into cultures with definable—and defensible—geographic boundaries. More and more these intellectuals sought to deliver their messages to commoners as well as to rulers.

1100 CE	1200 CE	1300 CE	1400 CE

- Kingdom of Mali emerges
- Great Zimbabwe
- Swahili emerges as a distinct language linking the coast of East Africa
- Mandinka merchants establish vast commercial networks linking West Africa
- King Mansa Musa of Mali (ruled 1312–1332) completes the hajj, 1325–1326

- Turkish forces defeat Byzantine armies at Manzikert, 1071
- Ibn Rushd (1126–1198) refines rationalist philosophy
- Jalal al-Din Rumi (1207–1273) spreads Sufi ideas
- Mongol forces sack Baghdad, end Abassid caliphate, 1258

- Turkish warriors found Delhi Sultanate in northern India, 1206–1526
- Buddhism loses almost all influence in India

- Japan fends off Mongol invasions, 1274–1281
- Song iron production peaks, 1078
- Mongols conquer Southern Song dynasty, 1279
- Song dynasty loses North China to Jurchen Jin dynasty, 1127
- Mongol invasions of Korea
- Kamakura shogunate, 1192–1333
- Yuan dynasty, 1280–1368

- Islamic influence increases in city-states
- Mongols invade southwestern China and Burma
- Mongol fleet attacks Java, 1293

- Francis of Assisi (1182–1226) preaches message of repentance
- Genoese ships link northern and southern Europe by sea
- Spanish Reconquista, 1061–1492
- Half of Europe's population lives in its west
- Crusades, 1095–1272
- Roman Catholic farmers migrate from the western to central and eastern European frontier zones

While Afro-Eurasia was increasingly carved up into large cultural blocs with more rigid identities and boundaries, neither the Americas nor sub-Saharan Africa saw quite the same degree of integration. But trade and migration in these areas of the world did have profound effects. Great African cultures flourished as they came into contact with the commercial energy of trade on the Indian Ocean. Indeed, Africans' trade with one another grew, bringing together coastal and interior regions into an ever-more integrated world. American peoples also built great cities that dominated large cultural areas and thrived through long-distance and regional trade. American cultures shared significant common features—reliance on trade, maize, and the exchange of similar status goods, such as shells and precious feathers. And larger and larger areas honored the same spiritual centers.

By 1300, trade, migration, and conflict were making the Afro-Eurasian regional worlds interconnected in unprecedented ways. When Mongol armies swept into China, into Southeast Asia, and into the heart of Islam, they applied a veneer of political integration to these dispersed parts and built on strong commercial links that already existed. But it is worth reminding ourselves that most people lived local lives, governed by the perennial need for subsistence and by the micro-level powers of spiritual and governmental agents who acted at the behest of distant and very remote authorities. Still, locals could see and hear the evidence of cross-cultural exchanges everywhere—in the clothing styles of provincial elites, such as Chinese silks in Paris or Quetzal plumes in northern Mexico; in enticements to move (and forced removals) to new frontiers; in the news of faraway conquests or advancing armies. In these ways, worlds were coming together within themselves and across their territorial boundaries, while remaining apart as they sought to maintain their own identity and traditions. In Afro-Eurasia especially, as the movement and goods and peoples shifted from ancient land routes to sea-lanes, these long-distance contacts were more frequent and far-reaching. Never before had the world seen so much activity that connected its parts. Nor within those parts had it ever seen so much shared cultural affinity—linguistic, religious, legal, and military. Indeed, by the time of the rise of the Mongol empire, the regions that composed the globe were those that we now recognize as the cultural spheres of today's world.

STUDY QUESTIONS

 WWNORTON.COM/STUDYSPACE

1. List the major cultural regions that existed in the thirteenth century that are explored in this chapter and explain where they were. Which of these regions were "together" and which were "apart"? How were regions connected?

2. List the four major cultural regions in Afro-Eurasia and briefly explain the defining characteristics of each. What did the various people and groups in these geographic areas all have in common that distinguished them from others?

3. Explain the role of global commercial hubs in India, China, and Egypt in fostering global commercial contacts across Afro-Eurasia. How did they reflect revolutions in maritime transportation?

4. Explain which areas of sub-Saharan Africa were parts of the larger Afro-Eurasian world by 1300. How did contact with other regions shape political and cultural developments in sub-Saharan Africa?

5. Describe the cultural diversity within the Islamic world during this era. How were these diverse communities integrated into a uniform regional identity?

6. Analyze the impact of Muslim Turkish invaders on India between 1000 and 1300. To what extent did India remain distinct from the Islamic world in this era?

7. Describe how the Song dynasty reacted to the military strength of its pastoral neighbors. How did these relationships foster a separate and distinct Chinese identity during this era?

8. Compare and contrast cultural and political developments in Korea, Japan, and Southeast Asia during this era. How were these societies influenced by other regional cultures?

9. Describe how Christianity expanded its geographic reach during this era. How did this expansion affect Latin Christianity in western Europe and Orthodox Christianity in eastern Europe?

10. Analyze the extent to which peoples in the Americas established closer contact with each other during this era. How extensive were these contacts compared with those in the Afro-Eurasian world?

11. Describe the empire created by the Mongols in the thirteenth century. How did Mongol policies bring the various regions of Afro-Eurasia into greater contact with each other?

FURTHER READINGS

Allsen, Thomas, *Commodity and Exchange in the Mongol Empire: A Cultural History of Islamic Textiles* (1997). A study that uses golden brocade, the textile most treasured by Mongol rulers, as a lens through which to analyze the vast commercial networks facilitated by the Mongol conquests and control.

———, *Culture and Conquest in Mongol Eurasia* (2001). A work that emphasizes the cultural and scientific exchanges that took place across Afro-Eurasia as a result of the Mongol conquest.

Bartlett, Robert, *The Making of Europe: Conquest, Colonization and Cultural Change, 950–1350* (1993). The modes of cultural, political, and demographic expansion of feudal Europe along its frontiers, especially in eastern Europe.

Bay, Edna G., *Wives of the Leopards: Gender, Politics, and Culture in the Kingdom of Dahomey* (1998). A work that stresses the role of women in an important West African society and dips into the early history of this area.

Beach, D. N., *Shona and Zimbabwe, 900–1850: An Outline of Shona History* (1980). A good place to start for exploring the history of Great Zimbabwe.

Brooks, George E., *Landlords and Strangers: Ecology, Society, and Trade in Western Africa, 1000–1630* (1993). A survey assembled from primary sources of early West African history that stresses transregional connections.

Buzurg ibn Shahriyar of Ramhormuz, *The Book of the Wonders of India: Mainland, Sea and Islands,* ed. and trans. G. S. P. Freeman-Greenville (1981). A collection of stories told by sailors, both true and fantastic; they help us imagine the lives of sailors of the era.

Chappell, Sally A. Kitt, *Cahokia: Mirror of the Cosmos* (2002). A thorough and vivid account of the "mound people"; it explores not just what we know of Cahokia but how we know it.

Christian, David, *A Short History of Russia, Central Asia, and Mongolia,* vol. 1, *Inner Eurasia from Prehistory to the Mongol Empire* (1998). Essential reading for students interested in interconnections across the Afro-Eurasian landmass.

Curtin, Philip, *Cross-Cultural Trade in World History* (1984). A groundbreaking book on intercultural trade with a primary focus on Africa, especially the cross-Saharan trade and Swahili coastal trade.

Dawson, Christopher, *Mission to Asia* (1980). Accounts of China and the Mongol Empire brought back by Catholic missionaries and diplomats after 1240 CE.

Foltz, Richard C., *Religions of the Silk Road: Overland Trade and Cultural Exchange from Antiquity to the Fifteenth Century* (1999). A study of the populations and the cities of the Silk Road as transmitters of culture across long distances.

Franklin, Simon, and Jonathan Shepherd, *The Emergence of Rus: 750–1200* (1996). The formation of medieval Russia between the Baltic and the Black Sea.

Gibb, Hamilton A. R., *Saladin: Studies in Islamic History,* ed. Yusuf Ibish (1974). A sympathetic portrait of one of Islam's leading political and military figures.

Goitein, S. D., *Letters of Medieval Jewish Traders* (1973). The classic study of medieval Jewish trading communities based on the commercial papers deposited in the Cairo Geniza (a synagogue storeroom) during the tenth and eleventh centuries; it explores not only commercial activities but also the personal lives of the traders around the Indian Ocean basin.

———, *A Mediterranean Society: An Abridgment in One Volume,* rev. and ed. Jacob Lassner (1999). A portrait of the Jewish merchant community with ties across the Afro-Eurasian landmass, based largely on the documents from the Cairo Geniza (of which Goitein was the primary researcher and interpreter).

———, "New Light on the Beginnings of the Karim Merchant," *The Journal of Social and Economic History of the Orient* 1 (1958). Goiten's description of Egyptian trade.

Harris, Joseph E., *The African Presence in Asia: Consequences of the East African Slave Trade* (1971). One of the few books that looks broadly at the impact of Africans and African slavery on the societies of Asia.

Hartwell, Robert, "Demographic, Political, and Social Transformations of China, 750–1550," *Harvard Journal of Asiatic Studies* 42 (1982): 365–442. A pioneering study of the demographic changes that overtook China during the Tang and Song dynasties, which are described in light of political reform movements and social changes in this seminal era.

Historical Relations across the Indian Ocean: Report and Papers of the Meeting of Experts Organized by UNESCO at Port Louis, Mauritius, from 15 to 19 July, 1974 (1980). Excellent essays on the connections of Africa with Asia across the Indian Ocean.

Hitti, Philip, *An Arab-Syrian Gentleman and Warrior in the Period of the Crusades: Memoirs of Usāmah ibn-Munqidh* (1929). The Crusaders seen through Muslim eyes.

Holt, P. M., *The Age of the Crusades: The Near East from the Eleventh Century to 1517* (1984). The Crusades period as seen from the eastern Mediterranean and through the lens of a leading British scholar of the area.

Hymes, Robert, and Conrad Schirokauer (eds.), *Ordering the World: Approaches to State and Society in Sung Dynasty China* (1993). A collection of essays that traces the intellectual, social, and political movements that shaped the Song state and its elites.

Ibn Battuta, *The Travels of Ibn Battuta,* trans. H.A.R. Gibb (2002). A readable translation of the classic book, originally published in 1929.

Ibn Fadlan, Ahmad, *Ibn Fadlan's Journey to Russia: A Tenth Century Traveler from Baghdad to the Volga River,* trans. with commentary by Richard Frye (2005). A coherent summary of the first-hand observations by an envoy who traveled from Baghdad to Russia.

Irwin, Robert, *The Middle East in the Middle Ages: The Early Mamluk Sultanate, 1250–1582* (1986). Egypt under Mamluk rule.

Lancaster, Lewis, Kikun Suh, and Chai-shin Yu (eds.), *Buddhism in Koryo: A Royal Religion* (1996). A description of Buddhism at its height in the Koryo period, when the religion made significant contributions to the development of Korean culture and monasteries of great beauty were constructed.

Levtzion, Nehemia, and Randall L. Pouwels (eds.), *The History of Islam in Africa* (2000). A useful general survey of the place of Islam in African history.

Lewis, Bernard (trans.), *Islam from the Prophet Muhammad to the Caphre of Constantinople* (1974). Vol. 2: Religion and Society. A fine collection of original sources that portray various aspects of classical Islamic society.

Lopez, Robert S., *The Commercial Revolution of the Middle Ages, 950–1350* (1976). An account focusing on the development around the Mediterranean of commercial practices such as the use of currency, accounting, and credit.

Maalouf, Amin, *The Crusades through Muslim Eyes,* trans. Jon Rothschild (1984). The European Crusaders as seen by the Muslim world.

Marcus, Harold G., *A History of Ethiopia* (2002). An authoritative overview of the history of this great culture.

Mass, Jeffrey, *Yoritomo and the Founding of the First Bakufu: The Origins of Dual Government in Japan* (1999). A revisionist account of how the Kamakura military leader Minamoto Yoritomo established the "dual polity" of court and warrior government in Japan.

McDermott, Joseph, *A Social History of the Chinese Book: Books and Literati Culture in Late Imperial China* (2006). The history of the book in China traced since the Song dynasty, with comparisons to the role of books in other civilizations, particularly the European.

McIntosh, Roderik, *The Peoples of the Middle Niger: The Island of Gold* (1988). A historical survey of an area often omitted from other textbooks.

Moore, Jerry D., *Cultural Landscapes in the Ancient Andes: Archaeologies of Place* (2005). The most recent and up-to-date analysis of findings based on recent archaeological evidence, emphasizing the importance of local cultures and diversity in the Andes.

Niane, D. T. (ed.), *Africa from the Twelfth to the Sixteenth Century,* vol. 4 of *General History of Africa* (1984). The general UNESCO history of Africa's volume on four centuries of African history. This work features the scholarship of Africans.

Oliver, Roland (ed.), *From c. 1050 to c. 1600,* vol. 3 of *The Cambridge History of Africa,* ed. J. D. Fage and Roland Oliver (1977). Another general survey of African history. This volume draws heavily on the work of British scholars.

Parry, J. H., *The Age of Reconnaissance: Discovery, Exploration and Settlement, 1450–1650* (1981). This book connects intellectual and technological developments of the Renaissance to the explorations of the new world.

Peters, Edward, *The First Crusade* (1971). The Crusaders as seen through their own eyes.

Petry, Carl F. (ed.), *Islamic Egypt, 640–1517,* vol. 1 of *The Cambridge History of Egypt,* ed. M. W. Daly (1998). A solid overview of the history of Islamic Egypt up to the Ottoman conquest.

Polo, Marco, *The Travels of Marco Polo,* ed. Manuel Komroff (1926). A solid translation of Marco Polo's famous account.

Popovic, Alexandre, *The Revolt of African Slaves in Iraq in the 3rd/9th Century,* trans. Leon King (1999). The account of a massive revolt against their slave masters by African slaves taken to labor in Iraq's mines and fields.

Scott, Robert, *Gothic Enterprise: A Guide to Understanding the Medieval Cathedral* (2003). The meaning and social function of religious building in medieval cities in northern Europe.

Shaffer, Lynda Norene, *Maritime Southeast Asia to 1500* (1996). A history of the peoples of the southeast fringe of the Eastern Hemisphere, up to the time that they became connected to the global commercial networks of the world.

Shimada, Izumi, "Evolution of Andean Diversity: Regional Formations (500 BCE–CE 600)," in Frank Salomon and Stuart Schwartz (eds.), *South America,* vol. 3 of *The Cambridge History of the Native Peoples of the Americas* (1999), part 1, pp. 350–517. A splendid overview that contrasts the varieties of lowland and highland cultures.

Steinberg, David Joel, et al., *In Search of Southeast Asia: A Modern History* (1987). An account of the emergence of the modern Southeast Asian polities of Cambodia, Burma, Thailand, and Indonesia.

Tyerman, Christopher, *God's War: A New History of the Crusades* (2006). The balance of religious and nonreligious motivations in the Crusades.

Waley, Daniel, *The Italian City-Republics,* 3rd ed. (1988). The structures and culture of the new cities of medieval Italy.

Watson, Andrew, *Agricultural Innovation in the Early Islamic World: The Diffusion of Crops and Farming Techniques, 700–1100* (1983). An impressive study of the spread of new crops throughout the Muslim world.

Abd al-Rahman III Islamic ruler in Spain who held a countercaliphate and reigned from 912 to 961 CE.

Agones Athletic contests in ancient Greece.

Ahmosis An Egyptian ruler in the southern part of the country who ruled from 1550 to 1525 BCE; Ahmosis used Hyksos weaponry—horse chariots in particular—to defeat the Hyksos themselves.

Ahura Mazda The Supreme God of the Persians believed to have created the world and all that is good and to have appointed earthly kings.

Alaric II Visigothic king who issued a simplified code of innovative imperial law.

Alexander the Great Alexander came from the frontier state of Macedonia, to the north of Greece. He was a path-breaking conqueror who transformed the Mediterranean world. In the fourth decade of the fourth century BCE, Alexander brought under the rule of his Greek-speaking forces all the lands that had comprised the Persian Empire that extended from Egypt and the shores of the Mediterranean to the interior of what is now Afghanistan and as far as the Indus River valley.

Alexandria A port city in Egypt named after Alexander the Great. Alexandria was a model city in the Hellenistic world. It was built up by a multiethnic population from around the Mediterranean world.

Al-Khwarizmi A scientist and mathematician who lived from 780 to 850 CE and is known for having modified Indian digits into Arabic numerals.

Allomothering A system by which mothers relied on other women, including their own mothers, daughters, sisters, and friends, to help in the nurturing and protecting of children.

Amorites A name that Mesopotamian urbanites called the transhumant herders from the Arabian desert. Around 2300 BCE, the Amorites, along with the Elamites, were at the center of newly formed dynasties in southern Mesopotamia.

Amun A once insignificant Egyptian god elevated to higher status by Amenemhet (1991–1962 BCE). Amun means "hidden" in Ancient Egyptian; the name was meant to convey the god's omnipresence.

Analects Texts that included the teachings and cultural ideals of Confucius.

Anatolia Now mainly the area known as modern Turkey; in the sixth millennium BCE, people from Anatolia, Greece, and the Levant took to boats and populated the Aegean. Their small villages endured almost unchanged for two millennia.

Angkor Wat A magnificent Khmer Vaishnavite temple that crowned the royal palace in Angkor. It had statues representing the Hindu pantheon of gods.

Animal domestication A gradual process that occurred simultaneously with or just before the domestication of plants, depending on the region.

Annals Historical records. Notable annals are the cuneiform inscriptions that record successful Assyrian military campaigns.

Aramaic A dialect of a Semitic language spoken in Southwest Asia; it became the lingua franca of the Persian Empire.

Aristotle Philosopher who lived from 384 to 322 BCE; he was a pupil of Plato's but came to different conclusions about nature and politics. Aristotle believed in collecting observations about nature and discerning patterns to ascertain how things worked.

Aryans Nomadic charioteers who spoke Indo-European languages and entered South Asia in 1500 BCE. The early Aryan settlers were herders.

Ashur One of two cities on the upper reaches of the Tigris River that were the heart of Assyria proper (the other was Nineveh).

Aśoka Emperor of the Mauryan dynasty from 268 to 231 BCE, he was a great conqueror and unifier of India. He is said to have embraced Buddhism toward the end of his life.

Aśvaghosa The first known Sanskrit writer. He may have lived from 80 to 150 CE and may have composed a biography of the Buddha.

Atma Vedic term signifying the eternal self, represented by the trinity of deities.

Atman In the Upanishads, an eternal being who exists everywhere. The atman never perishes but is reborn or transmigrates into another life.

Attila From 433 to 453, Attila was the sole ruler of all Hunnish tribes. Harsh and much feared, he formed the first empire to oppose Rome in northern Europe.

Augustus In 27 BCE, Octavian (63–14 BCE) assumed the title Augustus, "Revered One." This was one of many titles he assumed; others included *imperator*, *princeps*, and *Caesar*.

Australopithecus africanus A hominid species that appeared 3 million years ago. It had a brain capacity of approximately one pint, or a little less than one-third of the brain size of a modern human and about the same size as modern-day African apes. These beings were different from other animals because they walked on two legs.

Avesta A compilation of holy works transmitted orally by priests for millennia and eventually recorded in the sixth century BCE.

A1

Bactrian camel Domesticated in Central Asia around 2500 BCE, the two-humped camel was heartier than the one-humped dromedary and became the animal of choice for the harsh and varied climates typical of Silk Road trade.

Baghdad Founded in 762 CE, Baghdad (in modern-day Iraq) was the capital of the Islamic Empire under the Abbasid dynasty. In the medieval period, it was a center of administration, scholarship, and cultural growth for what came to be known as the Golden Age of Islamic science.

Bamboo Annals Shang stories and foundation myths that were written on bamboo strips and later collected.

Banana plant For the Bantu of the equatorial rain forests of central Africa, known as the Western Bantu, the introduction of the banana plant around 525 CE was a major development.

Bantu Language first spoken by people who lived in the southeastern area of modern Nigeria around 1000 CE.

Barbarian A derogatory term used to describe pastoral nomads, painting them as enemies of civilization; the term "barbarian" used to have a more neutral meaning than it does today.

Barbarian invasions A violent migration of people in the late fourth and fifth centuries into Roman territory. These migrants had long been used as non-Roman soldiers.

Basilicas Early church buildings, based on old royal audience halls.

Beghards (1500s) Eccentric European group whose members claimed to be in a state of grace that allowed them to do as they pleased—from adultery, free love, and nudity to murder; also called Brethren of Free Speech.

Bell beaker An artifact from Europe, this ancient drinking vessel was so named because its shape resembles an inverted bell.

Berenice of Egypt An Egyptian "queen," she helped rule over the Kingdom of the Nile from 320 to 280 BCE.

Beringia A prehistoric thousand-mile-long land bridge that linked Siberia and North America (which had not been populated by hominids). About 18,000 years ago, *Homo sapiens* edged into this landmass.

Bhakti A religious practice that grew out of Hinduism and emphasizes personal devotion to gods.

Bipedalism Walking on two legs, thereby freeing hands and arms to carry objects such as weapons and tools; one of several traits that distinguished hominids.

Black Death Great epidemic of the bubonic plague that ravaged Europe, East Asia, and North Africa in the fourteenth century, killing large numbers, including perhaps as many as one-third of the European population.

Bodhisattvas In Mahayan Buddhism, enlightened demigods who were ready to reach *nirvana* but delayed so that they might help others attain it.

Book of the Dead An Ancient Egyptian funerary text that contains drawings and paintings as well as spells describing how to prepare the jewelry and amulets that were buried with a person in preparation for the afterlife.

Brahma One of three major deities that form a trinity in Vedic religion. Brahma signifies birth. *See also* Vishnu *and* Siva.

Brahmans Vedic priests who performed rituals and communicated with the gods. Brahmans provided guidance on how to live in balance with the forces of nature as represented by the various deities. The codification of Vedic principles into codes of law took place at the hands of the Brahmans. They memorized Vedic works and compiled commentaries on them. They also developed their own set of rules and rituals, which developed into a full-scale theology. Originally memorized and passed on orally, these may have been written down sometime after the beginning of the Common Era. Brahmanism was reborn as Hinduism sometime during the first half of the first millennium CE.

Bronze An alloy of copper and tin brought into Europe from Anatolia; used to make hard-edged weapons.

Bubonic plague Acute infectious disease caused by a bacterium that is transmitted to humans by fleas from infected rats. It ravaged Europe and parts of Asia in the fourteenth century. Sometimes referred to as the "black death."

Cahokia A commercial center for regional and long-distance trade in North America. Its hinterlands produced staples for urban consumers. In return, its crafts were exported inland by porters and to North American markets in canoes.

Caliphs The spiritual and political leaders of the Islamic community.

Caravan cities A set of networks at long-distance trade locations where groups of merchants could assemble during their journeys. Several of these developed into full-fledged cities, especially in the deserts of Arabia.

Carthage A city in what is modern-day Tunisia; emblematic of the trading aspirations and activities of merchants in the Mediterranean. Pottery and other archaeological remains demonstrate that trading contacts with Carthage were as far-flung as Italy, Greece, France, Iberia, and West Africa.

Çatal Hüyük A site in Anatolia discovered in 1958. It was a dense honeycomb of settlements filled with rooms whose walls were covered with paintings of wild bulls, hunters, and pregnant women. Çatal Hüyük symbolizes an early transition into urban dwelling and dates to the eighth millennium BCE.

Cathedra A bishop's seat, or throne, in a church.

Cato the Elder Often seen as emblematic of the transition from a Greek to a Roman world, Cato the Elder wrote a manual for the new economy of slave plantation agriculture, invested in shipping and trading, learned Greek rhetoric, and added the genre of history to Latin literature. He lived from 234 to 149 BCE.

Cave drawings Images on cave walls. The subjects are most often large game, although a few are images of humans. Other elements are impressions made by hands dipped in paint and pressed on a wall or abstract symbols and shapes.

Chan Chan Between 850 and 900, the Moche people founded the city of Chan Chan in what is now modern-day Peru, with a core population of 30,000 inhabitants.

Chandra Gupta II In South Asia, this king, who reigned from 320 to 335 CE, shared his name with Chandragupta, the founder of the Mauryan Empire.

Chandravamsha One of two main lineages (the lunar one) of Vedic society, each wth its own creation myth, ancestors, language, and rituals. Each lineage included many clans. *See* Suryavamsha.

Chariots Horse-driven carriages brought by the pastoral nomadic warriors from the steppes that became the favored mode of transportation for an urban aristocratic warrior class and for other men of power in agriculture-based societies. Control of chariot forces was the foundation of the new balance of power across Afro-Eurasia during the second millennium BCE.

Charlemagne Emperor of the West and heir to Rome from 764 to 814 CE.

Chattel slavery Form of slavery that sold people as property, the rise of which coincided with the expansion of city-states. Chattel slavery was eschewed by the Spartans, who also rejected the innovation of coin money.

Chavín A people who lived in what is now northern Peru in the period from 1400 to 200 BCE. They were united more by culture and faith than by a unified political system.

Chimu Empire South America's first empire, it developed during the first century of the second millennium in the Moche Valley on the Pacific Ocean.

China's Sorrow Name for the Yellow River, which, when it changed course or flooded, could cause mass death and waves of migration.

City-states Small self-governing polities across the Mediterranean; they integrated an otherwise geographically dispersed region. The Greek city-states produced generations of thinkers and philosophers who influenced Western politics and philosophy.

Civil service examination system The world's first written civil service examination system instituted by the Tang. These exams helped to unite the Chinese state by making knowledge of a specific language and Confucian classics the only route to power.

Clovis people Early humans in America who used basic chipped blades and pointed spears in pursuing prey. They extended the hunting traditions they had learned in Afro-Eurasia, such as establishing campsites and moving with their herds. They were known as "Clovis people" because the arrowhead point that they used was first found by archaeologists at a site near Clovis, New Mexico.

Codex An early form of book, with separate pages bound together; it replaced the scroll as the main medium for written texts. The codex emerged around 300 CE.

Coins This form of money replaced goods, which previously had been bartered for services and other products. Originally used mainly to hire mercenary soldiers, coins became the commonplace method of payment linking buyers and producers throughout the Mediterranean.

Colosseum A huge amphitheater completed by Titus and dedicated in 80 CE. Originally begun by Flavian, the structure is named after a colossal statue of Nero that formerly stood beside it.

Confucian ideals By 50 BCE, the Han dynasty had made the Confucian ideals of honoring tradition, emphasizing the responsibility of the emperor, and respect for the lessons of history the official doctrine of the empire.

Confucius Influential teacher, thinker, and leader in China from 551 to 479 BCE.

Cong tubes A ritual object crafted by the Liangzhu. A cong tube was made of jade and was used in divination practices.

Constantine Roman emperor who converted to Christianity in 312 CE. In 313, he issued a proclamation that gave Christians new freedoms in the empire. He also founded Constantinople (at first called "New Rome").

Constantinople Capital city, formerly known as Byzantium, which was founded as the New Rome by Constantine the Great.

Coptic A form of Christianity practiced in Egypt. It was doctrinally different from Christianity elsewhere, and Coptic Christians had their own views of Christology, or the nature of Christ.

Council of Nicaea A church council convened in 325 CE by Constantine and presided over by him as well. At this council, a Christian creed was articulated and made into a formula that expressed the philosophical and technical elements of Christian belief.

Creed A formal statement of faith or expression of a belief system. A Christian "creed" or "credo" was formulated by the Council of Nicaea in 325 CE.

Crossbow Innovative weapon used at the end of the Warring States period that allowed archers to shoot their enemies with accuracy, even from a distance.

Crusades In the late eleventh century, western Europeans launched the wave of attacks called the Crusades. The First Crusade began in 1095, when Pope Urban II appealed to the warrior nobility of France to free Jerusalem from Muslim rule. Four subsequent Crusades were fought over the next two centuries.

Cultigen An organism that has diverged from its ancestors through domestication or cultivation.

Cuneiform As people combined rebus symbols with other visual marks that contained meaning, they became able to record and transmit messages over long distances by using abstract symbols or signs to denote concepts; such signs later came to represent syllables, which could be joined into words. By impressing these signs into wet clay with the cut end of a reed, scribes engaged in a form of wedge-shaped writing that we call *cuneiform*.

Cyrus the Great Founder of the Persian Empire, this sixth-century ruler (559–529 BCE), conquered the Medes and unified the Iranian kingdoms.

Daoism A school of thought contemporary with others at the end of the Warring States period, but with a great emphasis on the Dao, or the natural way of the cosmos. It did not have the same emphasis on ritual as Confucianism.

Darius I After Cyrus's death, Darius I (521–486 BCE) put the emerging unified Persian Empire onto solid footing.

Dear Boy The nickname of an early human remain discovered in 1931 by a team of archaeologists named the Leakeys. They discovered an almost totally intact skull. Other objects discovered with Dear Boy demonstrated that by the time of Dear Boy, early humans had begun to fashion tools and to use them for butchering animals and also, possibly, for hunting and killing smaller animals.

Delhi sultanate The Turkish regime of northern India, which lasted from 1206 to 1526.

Democritus Thinker in ancient Greece who lived from 470 to 360 BCE; he deduced the existence of the atom and postulated that there was such a thing as an indivisible particle.

Demotic writing The second of two basic forms of ancient Egyptian writing. Demotic was a cursive script written with ink on papyrus, on pottery, or on other absorbent objects. It was the most common and practical form of writing in Egypt and was used for administrative record keeping and in private or pseudo-private forms like letters and works of literature. *See also* Hieroglyphs.

Devshirme System of taking non-Muslim children in place of taxes in order to educate them in Ottoman Muslim ways and prepare them for service in the sultan's bureaucracy.

Dhamma A moral code espoused by Aśoka in the Kalinga edict, which was meant to apply to all—Buddhists, Brahmans, and Greeks alike.

Dhows Ships used by Arab seafarers; the dhow's large sails were rigged to maximize the capture of wind.

Diogenes A Greek philosopher who lived from 412 to 323 BCE and who espoused a doctrine of self-sufficiency and freedom from social laws and customs. He rejected cultural norms as out of tune with nature and therefore false.

Djoser This ancient Egyptian king reigned from 2630 to 2611 BCE. He was the second king of the Third Dynasty and celebrated the Sed festival in his tomb complex at Saqqara.

Dong Zhongshu Emperor Wu's chief minister, who advocated a more powerful view of Confucius by promoting texts that focused on Confucius as a man who possessed aspects of divinity.

Double-outrigger canoes Vessels used by early Austronesians to cross the Taiwan Straits and colonize islands in the Pacific. These sturdy canoes could cover over 120 miles per day.

Egyptian Middle Kingdom Lasting from about 2040 to1640 BCE, this period of Egyptian history was characterized by a consolidation of power and building activity in Upper Egypt.

Ekklesia A church or an early gathering committed to leaders chosen by God and fellow believers.

Elamites A people with their capital in the upland valley of modern Fars who became a cohesive polity that incorporated transhumant people of the Zagros Mountains. A group of Elamites who migrated south and west into Mesopotamia helped conquer the Third Dynasty of Ur in 2400 BCE.

Entrepôts Trading stations at the borders between communities, which made change possible among many different partners. Long-distance traders could also replenish their supplies at these stations.

Epicurus A Greek philosopher who espoused emphasis on the self. He lived from 341 to 279 BCE and founded a school in Athens called The Garden. He stressed the importance of sensation, teaching that pleasurable sensations were good and painful sensations bad. Members of his school sought to find peace and relaxation by avoiding unpleasantness or suffering.

Etruscans Until the fourth century BCE, the Etruscan states were dominant on the Italian peninsula. They were part of the foundation of the Roman Empire.

Eunuchs Both Abbasid and Tang rulers relied for protection on a cadre of loyal and well-paid men who were surgically castrated as youths and remained in service to the caliph or emperor.

Examination system Examinations that were open to most males and used to recruit officials and bureaucrats in imperial China.

Fatimids The Shiite dynasty that ruled parts of the Islamic Empire beginning in the tenth century CE. They were based in Egypt and founded the city of Cairo.

Ferangi An Arabic word meaning "Frank" that was used to describe Crusaders.

Fertile Crescent The site of the world's first agricultural revolution, this area is in Southwest Asia, bounded by the Mediterranean Sea in the west and the Zagros Mountains in the east.

Feudalism A system instituted in medieval Europe after the collapse of the Carolingian Empire (814 CE) whereby each peasant was under the authority of a lord.

Five Pillars of Islam The five tenets, or main aspects, of Islamic practice are the testification or bearing witness that there is no God other than God (Allah, in Arabic) and that Muhammad is the messenger of God; praying five times a day; fasting from sunup to sundown every day during Ramadan (a month on the Islamic calendar); giving alms; and making a pilgrimage to Mecca.

Flagellants European social group that came into existence during the bubonic plague in the fourteenth century; they believed that the plague was the wrath of God.

Floating population Poor migrant workers in China who supplied labor under Emperor Wu.

Flying cash Letters of exchange—early predecessors of paper cash instead of coins—first developed by guilds in the northwestern Shanxi. By the thirteenth century, paper money had eclipsed coins.

Fondûqs Complexes in caravan cities that included hostels, storage houses, offices, and temples.

Forbidden City The palace city of the Ming and Qing dynasties.

Gendered relations A relatively recent development, these imply roles that emerged only with the appearance of modern humans and perhaps Neanderthals. When humans began to think imaginatively and in complex symbolic ways and give voice to their insights, perhaps around 150,000 years ago, gender categories began to crystallize.

Genoa In 1300 CE, Genoa and Venice were two nodes of commerce linking Europe, Africa, and Asia. Genoese ships linked the Mediterranean to the coast of Flanders through consistent routes along the Atlantic coasts of Spain, Portugal, and France.

Ghana The most celebrated medieval political kingdom in West Africa.

Gilgamesh A heroic narrative written in the Babylonian dialect of Semitic Akkadian. This story and others like it were meant to circulate and unify the kingdom.

Goths One of the groups of "barbarian" migrants into Roman territory in the fourth century.

Government schools Schools founded by the Han dynasty to provide an adequate number of officials to fill positions in the administrative bureaucracy. The Imperial University had 30,000 members by the second century BCE.

Gracchus brothers In 133 and 123–21 BCE, two Tribunes, the brothers Tiberius and Gaius Gracchus, attempted to institute land reforms that would guarantee all Rome's poor citizens a basic amount of land that would qualify them for army service. Both men were assassinated.

Grand Canal Created in 486 BCE, this was a thousand-mile-long connector between the Yellow and Yangzi rivers, linking the north and south, respectively.

Grand unity A guiding political idea embraced by Qin rulers and ministers, with an eye toward joining the states of the Central Plain into one empire and centralizing administration.

Great Flood The Sumerian King List refers to an event known as the Great Flood, one of many traditional Mesopotamian stories that were transmitted orally from one generation to another before being recorded. The Great Flood, a crucial event in Sumerian memory and identity, assigned responsibility for Uruk's demise to the gods.

Griot Counselors and other officials to the royal family in African kingships. They were also responsible for the preservation and transmission of oral histories and repositories of knowledge.

Gunpowder By 1040, the first gunpowder recipes were being written down. Over the next 200 years, Song entrepreneurs invented several incendiary devices and techniques for controlling explosions.

Hagia Sophia An enormous and impressive church sponsored by Justinian and built starting in 532 CE. At the time, it was the largest church in the world.

Hammurapi and his code Hammurapi, the most famous of the Mesopotamian rulers, reigned from 1792 to 1750 BCE. He sought to create social order by centralizing state authority and creating a new legal code, a grand legal structure that embodied paternal justice. The code was quite stratified, dividing society into three classes: free men, dependent men, and slaves, each with distinct rights and responsibilities.

Han agrarian ideal A guiding principle for the free peasantry that made up the base of Han society, this was a system in which peasants were honored for their labors, while merchants were subjected to a range of controls, including regulations on luxury consumption, and were belittled for not engaging in physical labor.

Han Chinese Inhabitants of China proper who considered others to be outsiders. They felt that they were the only authentic Chinese.

Han Fei A Chinese state minister who lived from 280 to 223 BCE; he was a proponent and follower of Xunzi.

Han military Like its Roman counterpart, the Han military was a ruthless military machine that expanded the empire and created stable conditions that permitted the safe transit of goods by caravans. Emperor Wu heavily influenced the transformation of the military forces and reinstituted a policy that made military service compulsory.

Hangzhou This city and former provincial seaport became the political center of the Chinese people in their ongoing struggles with northern steppe nomads. It was also one of China's gateways to the rest of the world by way of the South China Sea.

Hannibal A great Roman general from Carthage whose campaigns in the third century BCE swept from Spain toward the Italian peninsula. He crossed the Pyrenees and the Alps mountain ranges with war elephants. He was unable, however, to defeat the Romans in 217 BCE.

Harappa One of two cities that, by 2500 BCE, began to take the place of villages throughout the Indus River valley. The other was Mohenjo Daro. Each covered an area of about 250 acres and probably housed 35,000 residents.

Harem Secluded women's quarters in Muslim households.

Harnesses Tools made from wood, bone, bronze, and iron for steering and controlling chariot horses. Harnesses discovered by archaeologists reveal the evolution of headgear from simple mouth bits to full bridles with headpiece, mouthpiece, and reins.

Hatshepsut Known as Ancient Egypt's most powerful woman ruler, Hatshepsut served as regent for her young son, Thutmosis III, whose reign began in 1479 BCE. She remained co-regent until her death.

Hegira The "emigration" of Muhammad and his followers out of a hostile Mecca to Yathrib, a city that was later called Medina. The year in which this journey took place, 622 CE, is also year 1 of the Islamic calendar.

Heian period The period from 794 to 1185, during which began the pattern of regents ruling Japan in the name of the sacred emperor.

Hellenism The process by which the individuality of the cultures of the earlier Greek city-states gave way to a uniform culture that stressed the common identity of all who embraced Greek ways. This culture emphasized the common denominators of language, style, and politics to which anyone, anywhere in the Afro-Eurasian world, could have access.

Hieroglyphs One of two basic forms of Egyptian writing that were used in conjunction throughout antiquity. Hieroglyphs are pictorial symbols; the term derives from a Greek word meaning "sacred carving"—they were employed exclusively in temple, royal, and divine contexts. *See also* Demotic writing.

Hinayana Buddhism A form of Buddhism that accepted the divinity of Buddha himself but not of demigods, or bodhisattvas.

Hittites One of the five great territorial states. The Hittites campaigned throughout Anatolia, then went east to northern Syria, though they eventually faced weaknesses in their own homeland. Their heyday was marked by the reign of the king Supiliulimua (1380 to 1345 BCE), who preserved the Hittites' influence on the balance of power in the region between Mesopotamia and the Nile.

Hominids Humanlike beings who walked erect and preceded modern humans.

Homo A word used by scientists to differentiate between pre-human and "true human" species.

Homo erectus A species that emerged about 1.5 million years ago and had a large brain and walked truly upright. *Homo erectus* means "Standing man."

Homo habilis The scientific term for "Skillful man." Toolmaking ability truly made *Homo habilis* the forerunners, though very distant, of modern humans.

Homo sapiens The first humans; they emerged in a small region of Africa about 200,000 years ago and migrated out of Africa about 100,000 years ago.

Homogeneity Uniformity of the languages, customs, and religion of a particular people or place. It can also be demonstrated by a consistent calendar, set of laws, administrative practices, and rituals.

Horses By the second millennium BCE, full-scale nomadic communities dominated the steppe lands in western Afro-Eurasia. Horse-riding nomads moved their large herds across immense tracts of land within zones defined by rivers, mountains, and other natural geographical features. In the arid zones of central Eurasia, the nomadic economies made horses a crucial component of survival.

Hyksos A western Semitic-speaking people whose name means "Rulers of Foreign Lands"; they overthrew the unstable Thirteenth Dynasty in Egypt around 1640 BCE. The Hyksos had mastered the art of horse chariots, and with those chariots and their superior bronze axes and composite bows (made of wood, horn, and sinew), they were able to defeat the pharaoh's foot soldiers.

Ibn Sina Philosopher and physican who lived from 980 to 1037 CE. He was also schooled in the Quran, geometry, literature, and Indian and Euclidian mathematics.

Iliad An epic Greek poem about the Trojan War, composed several centuries after the events it describes. It was based on oral tales passed down for generations.

Il-khanate Mongol-founded dynasty in thirteenth-century Persia.

Imperium A Latin word used to express Romans' power and command over their subjects. It is the basis of the English words "empire" and "imperialism."

Indo-Greek The fusion of Indian and Greek culture in the area under the control of the Bactrians, in the northwestern region of India, around 200 BCE.

Indu What we would today call India. Called "Indu" by Xuanzang, a Chinese Buddhist pilgrim who visited the area in the 630s and 640s CE.

Internal and external alchemy In Daoist ritual, this refers to the use of trance and meditation or chemicals and drugs, respectively, to cause transformations in the self.

Iron A cheap and highly durable metal, harder than tin or copper; iron went into the creation of tools and weapons that were instruments of major change in the first millennium BCE. The advent and use of iron affected warfare and agrarian culture across cultures.

Irrigation Technological advance whereby water delivery systems and water sluices in floodplains or riverine areas were channeled or redirected and used to nourish soil.

Jacquerie (1358) French peasant revolt in defiance of feudal restrictions.

Jade The most important precious substance in East Asia. Jade was associated with goodness, purity, luck, and virtue, and was carved into such items as ceremonial knives, blade handles, religious objects, and elaborate jewelry.

Jainism Along with Buddhism, one of the two systems of thought developed in the seventh century BCE that set themselves up against Brahmanism.

Janissaries Corps of infantry soldiers recruited as children from the Christian provinces of the Ottoman Empire and brought up with intense loyalty to the Ottoman state and its sultan. The Ottoman sultan used these forces to clip local autonomy and to serve as his personal bodyguards.

Jatis Subcaste of laborers who were outside the Vedic line but joined the agricultural economy of ancient South Asia.

Jihad Literally, "striving or struggle," this word also connotes military efforts or "striving in the way of God." It also came to mean spiritual struggles against temptation or inner demons, especially in Sufi, or mystical, usage.

Jong Large ocean-going vessels, built by Southeast Asians, which plied the regional trade routes from the fifteenth century to the early sixteenth century.

Judah The southern kingdom of David, which had been an Assyrian vassal until 612 BCE, when it became a vassal of Assyria's successor, Babylon, against whom the people of Judah rebelled, resulting in the destruction of Jerusalem in the sixth century BCE.

Julius Caesar A formidable Roman general who lived from 100 to 44 BCE. He was also a man of letters, a great orator, and a ruthless military man who boasted that his campaigns had led to the deaths of over a million people.

Junks Trusty seafaring vessels used in the South China Seas after 1000 CE. These helped make shipping by sea less dangerous.

Justinian Roman or Byzantine emperor who ascended to the throne in 527 CE. In addition to his many building projects and military expeditions, he issued a new law code.

Karma Literally "fate" or "action," in Confucian thought; this is a universal principle of cause and effect.

Kassite Nomads who entered Mesopotamia from the eastern Zagros Mountains and the Iranian plateau as early as 2000 BCE. They gradually integrated into Babylonian society by officiating at temples. By 1745 BCE, they had asserted order over the region, and they controlled southern Mesopotamia for the next 350 years, creating one of the territorial states.

Kharijites A radical sect from the early days of Islam, the Kharijites seceded from the "party of Ali" (who themselves came to be known as the Shiites) because of disagreements over succession to the role of the caliph. They were known for their strict militant piety.

Khmers In what is modern-day Cambodia, the Khmers created the most powerful empire in Southwest Asia between the tenth and thirteenth centuries.

Khufu This pyramid, among those put up in the Fourth Dynasty in ancient Egypt (2575–2465 BCE), is the largest stone structure in the world. It is in an area called Giza, just outside of modern-day Cairo.

Khusro I Anoshirwan Sasanian emperor who reigned from 530 to 579 CE. He was a model ruler and was seen as the personification of justice.

Kiev After the eleventh century, Kiev became one of the greatest cities of Europe. It was built to be a small-scale Constantinople on the Dnieper.

Kingdom of Jerusalem What Crusaders set out to liberate when they launched their attack.

Knossos Area in Crete where, during the second millennium BCE, a primary palace town existed.

Koine Greek A common form of Greek that became the international spoken and written language in the Hellenistic world. This was a simpler everyday form of the Ancient Greek language.

Koryo dynasty Leading dynasty of the northern-based Koryo kingdom in Korea. It is from this dynasty that the name "Korea" derives.

Kshatriyas Originally the warrior caste in Vedic society, they were dominant clan members and a ruling caste who controlled the land.

Kumarajiva A renowned Buddhist scholar and missionary who lived from 344 to 413 CE. He was brought to China by Chinese regional forces from Kucha, modern-day Xinjiang.

Kushans A northern nomadic group that migrated into South Asia in 50 CE. They unified the tribes of the region and set up the Kushan dynasty. The Kushans' empire embraced a large and diverse territory and played a critical role in the formation of the Silk Road.

"Land under the Yoke of Ashur" Lands not in Assyria proper, but under its authority; they had to pay the Assyrian Empire exorbitant amounts of tribute.

Language A system of communication reflecting cognitive abilities. Natural language is generally defined as words arranged in particular sequences to convey meaning and is unique to modern humans.

Language families Related tongues with a common ancestral origin; language families contain languages that diverged from one another but share grammatical features and root vocabularies. More than a hundred language families exist.

Laozi Also known as Master Lao; perhaps a contemporary of Confucius and the person after whom Daoism is named. His thought was elaborated upon by generations of thinkers.

Latifundia Broad estates that produced goods for big urban markets, including wheat, grapes, olives, cattle, and sheep.

Law Book of Manu Part of the handiwork of Brahman priests, this was a representative code of law that incorporated social sanctions and practices.

Legalism Also called Statism, a system of thought about how to live an ordered life. It was developed by Master Xun, or Xunzi (310–237 BCE). It is based on the principle that people, being inherently inclined toward evil, require authoritarian control to regulate their behavior.

Liangzh Spanning centuries from the fourth to the third millennium BCE, the Liangzhu represented the last new Stone Age culture in the Yangzi River delta. The culture, one of the Ten Thousand States, was highly stratified and is known for its jade objects.

Linear A and B On the island of Crete and on the mainland areas of Greece, documents of the palace-centered societies were written on clay tablets in two scripts that were linear. These were first discovered on Crete in 1900. Linear A script, apparently written in Minoan, has not yet been deciphered. Linear B was first deciphered in the early 1950s.

"Little Europes" Between 1100 and 1200 CE, these were urban landscapes comprised of castles, churches, and towns in what are today Poland, the Czech Republic, Hungary, and the Baltic States.

Liu Bang Reigned from 206 to 195 BCE; after declaring himself the prince of his home area of Han, in 202 BCE, Liu declared himself the first Han emperor.

Llamas Similar in utility and function to camels in Afro-Eurasia, llamas could carry heavy loads for long distances.

Longshan peoples The Longshan peoples lived in small agricultural and riverine villages in East Asia at the end of the third millennium BCE. They set the stage for the Shang in terms of a centralized state, urban life, and a cohesive culture.

Lucy In 1974, an archaeological team working at a site in present-day Hadar, Ethiopia, unearthed a relatively intact skeleton of a young adult female australopithecine in the valley of the Awash River. The researchers nicknamed the skeleton Lucy. She stood just over three feet tall and walked upright at least some of the time. Her skull contained a brain within the ape size range. Also, her jaw and teeth were humanlike. Lucy's skeleton was relatively complete and was the oldest hominid skeleton ever discovered.

Ma'at In ancient Egypt, this term referred to stability or order, the achievement of which was the primary task of Egypt's ruling kings, the Pharaos.

Maccabees Leaders of a riot in Jerusalem in 166 BCE; the riot was a response to a Roman edict outlawing the practice of Judaism.

Mahayana Buddhism A school of Buddhist theology that believed that the Buddha was a deity, unlike previous groups that had considered him a wise human being.

Maize Grains, the crops that the settled agrarian communities across the Americas cultivated, along with legumes (beans) and tubers (potatoes).

Mandate of heaven Ideology established by Zhou dynasts to communicate the moral transfer of power. Originally a pact between the Zhou people and their supreme god, it evolved in the first century BCE into Chinese political doctrine.

Mande The Mande or Mandinka people lived in the area between the bend in the Senegal River and the bend in the Niger River east to west and from the Senegal River and Bandama River north to south. Their civilization emerged around 1100 CE.

Martyrs People executed by the Roman authorities for persisting in their Christian beliefs and refusing to submit to pagan ritual or belief.

Mastaba This word means "bench" in Arabic; it refers to a huge flat structure identical to earlier royal tombs of ancient Egypt.

Mauryan Empire From 321 to 184 BCE, from the Indus Valley to the northwest areas of south Asia, in a region previously controlled by Persia, the Mauryans extended their dynasty. It was the first large-scale empire in South Asia and was to become the model for future Indian empires.

Mawali Non-Arab "clients" to Arab tribes in the early Islamic Empire. Because tribal patronage was so much a part of the Arabian cultural system, non-Arabs who converted to Islam affiliated themselves with a tribe and became clients of that tribe.

Mayans The civilization that ruled over large stretches of Mesoamerica; it was composed of a series of kingdoms, each built around ritual centers rather than cities. The Mayans engaged neighboring peoples in warfare and trade and expanded borders through tributary relationships. They were not defined by a great ruler or one capital city, but by their shared religious beliefs.

Mecca Arabian city in which Muhammad was born. Mecca was a trading center and pilgrimage destination in the pre-Islamic and Islamic period. Exiled in 622 CE because of resistance to his message, Muhammad returned to Mecca in 630 CE and claimed the city for Islam.

Medes Rivals of the Assyrians and the Persians, the Medes inhabited the area from the Zagros Mountains to the modern city of Tehran; known as expert horsemen and archers, they were eventually defeated by the Persians.

Megaliths Literally, "great stone"; the word *megalith* is used when describing structures such as Stonehenge. These massive structures are the result of cooperative planning and work.

Megarons Large buildings found in Troy (level II) that are the predecessors of the classic Greek temple.

Mencius A disciple of Confucius who lived from 372 to 289 BCE.

Meroe Ancient kingdom in what is today Sudan. It flourished for nearly a thousand years, from the fifth century BCE to the fifth century CE.

Minoans Around 2000 BCE, a large number of independent palace centers began to emerge on Crete, at Knossos, and elsewhere. The people who built these elaborate centers are called the Minoans, after the legendary King Minos, said to have ruled Crete at the time. They sailed throughout the Mediterranean and by 1600 BCE had planted colonies on many Aegean islands, which in turn became trading and mining centers.

Mitochondrial DNA A form of DNA found outside the nucleus of cells, where it serves as cells' microscopic power packs. Examining mitochondrial DNA enables researchers to measure the genetic variation among living objects, including human beings.

Moche At the height of the Chimu Empire, the Moche people extended their power over several valleys in what is now modern-day Peru, and their wealth grew as well.

Mohism A school of thought in ancient China, named after Mo Di, or Mozi, who lived from 479 to 438 BCE. It emphasized one's obligation to society as a whole, not just to one's immediate family or social circle.

Monasticism A Christian way of life that originated in Egypt and was practiced as early as 300 CE in the Mediterranean. The word itself contains the meaning of a person "living alone" without marriage or family.

"Mound people" A name for the people of Cahokia, since its landscape was dominated by earthen monuments in the shapes of mounds. The mounds were carefully maintained and were the loci from which Cahokians paid respect to spiritual forces.

Mu Chinese ruler (956–918 BCE) who put forth a formal bureaucratic system of governance, appointing officials, supervisors and military captains to whom he was not related. He also instituted a formal legal code.

Muhammad Born in 570 CE in Mecca in Saudi Arabia, Muhammad was the prophet and founder of the Islamic faith. Orphaned when young, Muhammad lived under the protection of his uncle. His career as a prophet began around 610 CE, with his first experience of scriptural revelation.

Mycenaeans The mainland competitors of the Minoans; they took over Crete around 1400 BCE. Migrating to Greece from central Europe, they brought their Indo-European language, horse chariots, and metalworking skills, which they used to dominate until 1200 BCE.

Neanderthals Members of an early wave of hominids from Africa who settled in western Afro-Eurasia, in an area reaching from present-day Uzbekistan and Iraq to Spain, approximately 150,000 years ago.

Needle compass A crucial instrument made available to navigators after 1000 CE that helped guide sailors on the high seas. It was a Chinese invention.

Negritos Hunter-gatherer inhabitants of the East Asian coastal islands who migrated there around 28,000 BCE but by 2000 BCE had been replaced by new migrants.

Nehemiah A Jewish eunuch of the Persian court who was given permission to rebuild the fortification walls around the city of Jerusalem from 440 to 437 BCE.

Neo-Assyrian empire In around 950 BCE, the Neo-Assyrians came to dominate. They were Afro-Eurasia's empire, extending their control over resources and people beyond their own borders. The empire lasted for three centuries.

Nestorian Christians A denomination of Christians whose beliefs about Christ differed from those of the official Byzantine church. Named after Nestorius, former bishop of Constantinople, they emphasized the human aspects of Jesus.

Nirvana Literally, nonexistence; nirvana is the state of complete liberation from the concerns of worldly life, as in Buddhist thought.

Noble Eightfold Path Buddhist concept of a way of life by which people may rid themselves of individual desire to achieve Nirvana. The path consists of wisdom, ethical behavior, and mental discipline.

Nok culture Spectacular culture that arose in what is today Nigeria, in the sixth century BCE. Iron smelting occurred there around 600 BCE. Thus the Nok people made the transition from stone to iron materials.

Nomads People who move across vast distances without settling permanently in a particular place. Often pastoralists, nomads and transhumant herders introduced new forms of chariot-based warfare that transformed the Afro-Eurasian world.

Odyssey Composed in the eighth century BCE, this is the epic tale of the journey of Odysseus, who traveled the Mediterranean back to his home in Ithaca after the siege of Troy.

Oikos The word for "small family unit" in ancient Greece, similar to the *familia* in Rome. Its structure, with men as heads of household over women and children, embodied the fundamental power structure in Greek city-states.

Olmecs Emerging around 1500 BCE, the Olmecs lived in Mesoamerica. The name means those who "lived in the land of the rubber." Olmec society was comprised of decentralized villages. Its members spoke the same language and worshipped the same gods.

Oracle bones Shang diviners applied intense heat to the shoulder bones of cattle or to turtle shells, which caused them to crack. Diviners would then interpret the cracks as signs from the ancestors regarding royal plans and actions.

Orrorin tugenensis A predecessor to hominids that first appeared 6 million years ago.

Pagani A pejorative word used by Christians to designate pagans.

Palace The palace, both as an institution and as a set of buildings, appeared around 2500 BCE, about a millennium later than the Mesopotamian temple. The palace quickly joined the temple as a defining landmark of city life. Eventually, it became a source of power rivaling the temple, and palace and temple life often blurred, as did the boundary between the sacred and the secular.

Palmyra A Roman trading depot in modern-day Syria; part of a network of trading cities that connected various regions of Afro-Eurasia.

Papacy The institution of the pope; the Catholic spiritual leader in Rome.

Parthians A horse-riding people who pushed southward around the middle of the second century BCE and wiped out the Greek kingdoms in Iran. They then extended their power all the way to the Mediterranean, where they ran up against the Roman Empire in Anatolia and Mesopotamia.

Pastoral nomadic communities Around 3500 BCE, western Afro-Eurasia witnessed the growth and spread of pastoral nomadic communities that herded domesticated animals with demanding grazing requirements.

Pastoralism The herding and breeding of sheep and goats or other animals as a primary means of subsistence.

Paterfamilias The father of the family, which itself was the foundation of the Roman social order.

Patrons In the Roman system of patronage, men and women of wealth and high social status acted as "patrons," protecting dependents or "clients" of a lower class.

Pax Romana Latin for "Roman Peace," this term refers to the period between 27 BCE and 180 CE during which conditions in the Roman Empire were settled and peaceful.

Pax Sinica A period of peace (the first century BCE) during which agriculture, commerce, and industry flourished in East Asia under the rule of the Han.

Peloponnesian War A war fought between 431 and 404 BCE between two of Greece's most powerful city-states, Athens and Sparta.

Periplus A book that reflected sailing knowledge; in such books captains would record landing spots and ports. The word *periplus* literally means "sailing around."

Persepolis Darius I's capital city in the highlands of Fars; a ceremonial center and expression of imperial identity as well as an important administrative hub.

Petra City in modern-day Jordan that was the Nabataean capital. It profited greatly by supplying provisions and water to travelers and traders. Many of its houses and shrines were cut into the rocky mountains. Petra means "rock."

Phalanx The military formation used by Philip II of Macedonia, whereby heavily armored infantry were closely arrayed in battle formation.

Philip II of Macedonia The father of Alexander the Great, under the rule of whom Macedonia developed into a large ethnic and territorial state. After unifying Macedonia, Philip went on to conquer neighboring states.

Philosophia Literally "love of wisdom"; this system of thought originally included speculation on the nature of the cosmos, the environment, and human existence. It eventually came to include thought about the nature of humans and life in society.

Phoenicians Known as the Canaanites in the Bible, they were an ethnic group in the Levant under Assyrian rule in the seventh century BCE; they provided ships and sailors for battles in the Mediterranean. The word *Phoenician* refers to the purple dye they manufactured and widely traded, along with other commercial goods and services, throughout the Mediterranean. While part of wider Mesopotamian culture, their major contribution was the alphabet, first introduced in the second millennium BCE, which made far-reaching communication possible.

Phonemes Primary and distinctive sounds that are characteristic of human language.

Plant domestication Plant domestication occurred as far back as 5000 BCE, when plants began to naturally retain their seeds. With the domesticated plant, seeds could be harvested. Most were used for food, but some were saved for planting in subsequent growing cycles, resulting in a steady food supply. This process happened first in the southern Levant and spread from there into the rest of Southwest Asia.

Plato A disciple of the great philosopher Socrates, Plato lived from 427 to 347 BCE; his works are the only record we have of Socrates' teaching. He was also the author of formative philosophical works on ethics and politics.

Plebs In Rome, this term referred to the "common people." Their interests were protected by officials called Tribunes.

Potassium-argon dating A major dating technique based on the changing chemical structure of objects over time, since over time potassium decays into argon. This method makes possible the dating of objects up to a million years old.

Potter's wheel An advance made at the city of Uruk, where potters made significant technical breakthroughs using a fast wheel that enabled them to mass-produce vessels in many different shapes.

Pottery Vessels made of mud and later clay that were used for storing and transporting food. The development of pottery was a major breakthrough.

Proto-Indo-European The parent of all the languages in the Indo-European family, which includes, among many others, English, German, Norwegian, Portuguese, French, Russian, Persian, Hindi, and Bengali.

Qanats Underground water channels, vital for irrigation, which were used in Persia. Little evaporation occurred when water was being moved through qanats.

Questions of King Milanda (Milindapunha) The name of a second-century BCE text espousing the teachings of Buddhism as set forth by Menander, a Yavana king. It featured a discussion between the king and a sophisticated Buddhist sage named Nagasena.

Quran The scripture of the Islamic faith. Originally a verbal recitation, the Quran was eventually compiled into a book in the order in which we have it today. According to traditional Islamic interpretation, the Quran was revealed to Muhammad by the angel Gabriel over a period of twenty-three years.

Radiocarbon isotope C^{14} All living things contain the radiocarbon isotope C^{14}, which plants acquire directly from the atmosphere and animals acquire indirectly when they consume plants or other animals. When living things die, the C^{14} isotope they contain begins to decay into a stable nonradioactive element, C^{12}. The rate of decay is regular and measurable, making it possible to ascertain the date of fossils that leave organic remains for ages of up to 40,000 years.

Raja "King" in the Kshatriya period in South Asia; could also refer to the head of a family, but indicated the person who had control of land and resources in South Asian city-states.

Rajanya Meaning "group of brilliant ones," a senior clan of a Vedic lineage.

Rebus Probably originating in Uruk, a rebus is a representation that transfers meaning from the name of a thing to the sound of that name. For example, a picture of a bee can represent the sound "b." Such pictures opened the door to writing: a technology of symbols that uses marks to represent specific discrete sounds.

Reconquista The Spanish reconquest of territories lost to the Islamic Empire, beginning with Toledo in 1061.

Red Turbans Diverse religious movement in China during the fourteenth century that spread the belief that the world was drawing to an end as Mongol rule was collapsing.

Renaissance Term meaning "rebirth" that historians use to characterize the expanded cultural production of European nations between 1430 and 1550. Emphasized a break from the church-centered medieval world and a new concept of humankind as the center of the world.

Res publica Literally "public thing"; this referred to the Roman republic, in which policy and rules of behavior were determined by the Senate and by popular assemblies of the citizens.

Rift Valley An area of northeastern Africa where some of the most important early human archaeological discoveries of fossils were found, especially one of an intact skull that is 1.8 million years old.

Riverine Denoting an area whose inhabitants depended on irrigation for their well-being and whose populations are settled near great rivers. Egypt was, in a sense, the most riverine of all these cultures, in that it had no hinterland of plains as did Mesopotamia and the Indus valley. Away from the banks of the Nile, there is only largely uninhabitable desert.

Roman army The Romans devised a military draft that could draw manpower from a huge population. In their encounter with Hannibal, they lost up to 80,000 men in three separate encounters and still won the war.

Roman law Under the Roman legal system, disputes were brought to the public courts, and decisions were made by judges and sometimes by large juries. Rome's legal system featured written law and institutions for settling legal disputes.

Royal Road A 1,600-mile road from Sardis in Anatolia to Susa in Iran; used by messengers, traders, the army, and those taking tribute to the king.

Sack of Constantinople In 1204 Frankish armies went on a rampage and sacked the capital city of Constantinople.

Sacred kingships Institution that marked the centralized politics of West Africa. The inhabitants of these kingships believed that their kings were descendants of the gods.

Sahel region Area of sub-Saharan Africa with wetter and more temperate locations, especially in the upland massifs and their foothills, villages, and towns.

Saint Patrick A former slave brought to Ireland from Briton who later became a missionary, or the "Apostle of Ireland." He died in 470 CE.

Sargon the Great Reigning from 2334 to 2279 BCE, Sargon was the king of Akkad, a city-state near modern Baghdad; he helped bring the competitive era of city-states to an end and sponsored monumental works of architecture, art, and literature.

Sasanians An empire that succeeded the Parthians in the mid 220s CE in Inner Eurasia.

Satrap The governor of a province in the Persian Empire. Each *satrap* was a relative or intimate associate of the king.

Scythian ethos In part the result of the constant struggle between settlers, hunter-gatherers, and nomads on the northern frontier of Europe, this was a warrior ethos that embodied the extremes of aggressive mounted-horse culture, c. 1000 BCE.

Sea Peoples Migrants from north of the Mediterranean who invaded the cities of Egypt and the Levant in the second millennium BCE. Once settled along the coast of the Levant, they became known as the Philistines and considerably disrupted the settlements of the Canaanites.

Second-generation cultures Societies that expanded old ideas and methods by incorporating new aspects of culture and grafting them onto, or using them in combination with, established norms.

Seleucus Nikator A successor of Alexander the Great who lived from 358 to 281 BCE. He controlled Mesopotamia, Syria, Persia, and parts of the Punjab.

Semu This term referred to "outsiders" or non-Chinese people—Mongols, Tanguts, Khitan, Jurchen, Muslims, Tibetans, Persians, Turks, Nestorians, Jews, and Armenians—who became a new ruling elite over a Han majority population in the late thirteenth century.

Shah Traditional title of Persian rulers.

Shandingdong Man A *Homo sapiens* whose fossil remains and relics can be dated to about 18,000 years ago. His physical characteristics were closer to those of modern humans, and he had a similar brain size.

Shang State Dynasty in northeastern China that ruled from 1600 to 1045 BCE. Though not as well defined by borders as the territorial states in the southwest of Asia, it did have a ruling lineage. Four fundamental elements of the Shang state were a metal industry based on copper, pottery making, standardized architectural forms and walled towns, and divination using animal bones.

Sharecropping A system of farming in which tenant farmers rented land and gave over a share of their crops to the land's owners. Sometimes seen as a cheap way for the state to conduct agricultural affairs, sharecropping often resulted in the impoverishment and marginalization of the underclass.

Sharia Literally, "the way"; now used to indicate the philosophy and rulings of Islamic law.

Shiism One of the two main branches of Islam. Shiites recognize Ali, the fourth caliph, and his descendants as rightful rulers of the Islamic world; practiced in the Safavid empire.

Shiites The group of supporters of Ali, Muhammad's cousin and son-in-law, who wanted him to be the first caliph and believed that members of the Prophet's family deserved to rule. Although always a minority sect in the Islamic world, Shiism itself contains several subsects, each of which has slightly different interpretations of theology and politics. The leaders of the Shiite community are known as "Imam," which means "leaders."

Shoguns From 1192 to 1333, the Kamakura shoguns were generalissimos who served as military "protectors" of the ruler in the city of Heian.

Shotoku Prince in the early Japanese Yamoto state (574–622 BCE) who is credited with having introduced Buddhism to Japan.

Shudras Literally "small ones," these people were workers and slaves from outside the Vedic lineage.

Siddhartha Gautama Another name for the Buddha; the most prominent opponent of the Brahman way of life; he lived from 563 to 483 BCE.

Silk A luxury textile that became a vastly popular export from China (via the Silk Road) to the cities of the Roman world.

Silk Road Trade route linking China with Central Asia and the Mediterranean; it extended over 5,000 miles, land and sea included, and was so named because of the quantities of silk that were traded along it. The Silk Road was a major factor in the development of civilizations in China, Egypt, Persia, India, and even Europe.

Silla One of three independent Korean states that may have emerged as early as the third century BCE. These states lasted until 668 CE, when Silla took control over the entire peninsula.

Siva The third of three Vedic deities, signifying destruction. *See also* Brahma *and* Vishnu.

Slave plantations A system whereby labor was used for the cultivation of crops wholly for the sake of producing surplus that was then used for profit; slave plantations were a crucial part of the growth of the Mediterranean economy.

Small seal script A unified script that was used to the exclusion of other scripts under the Qin, with the aim of centralizing administration; its use led to a less complicated style of clerical writing than had been in use under the Han.

Sogdians A people who lived in central Asia's commercial centers and maintained the stability and accessibility of the Silk Road. They were crucial to the interconnectedness of the Afro-Eurasian landmass.

Song dynasty This dynasty took over the mandate of heaven for three centuries starting in 976 CE. It was an era of many economic and political successes, but they eventually lost northern China to nomadic tribes.

Song porcelain A type of porcelain perfected during the Song period that was light, durable, and quite beautiful.

Speciation The formation of different species.

Spiritual ferment After 300 CE religion touched more areas of society and culture than before and touched them in different, more demanding ways.

Spring and Autumn period Period between the eighth and fifth centuries BCE, during which China was ruled by the feudal system. Considered an anarchic and turbulent time, there were 148 different tributary states in this period.

Stoicism A widespread philosophical movement initiated by Zeno (334–262 BCE). Zeno and his followers sought to understand the role of people in relation to the cosmos. For the Stoics, everything was grounded in nature. Being in love with nature and living a good life required being in control of one's passions and thus indifferent to pleasure or pain.

Strait of Malacca The seagoing gateway to Southeast and East Asia.

Sufi brotherhoods Mystics within Islam who were responsible for the expansion of Islam into many regions of the world.

Sultan An Islamic political leader. In the Ottoman Empire, the sultan combined a warrior ethos with an unwavering devotion to Islam.

Sumerian King List The Sumerian King List is among the texts that recount the making of political dynasties and depict great periodic floods. Recorded around 2000 BCE, it organizes the reigns of kings by dynasty, one city at a time.

Sumerian pantheon The Sumerian gods, each of whom had a home in a particular floodplain city. In the Sumerian belief system, both gods and the natural forces they controlled had to be revered.

Sumerian temples Temples were thought of as homes of the gods and symbols of Sumerian imperial identity. They also represented the ability of the gods to hoard wealth at sites where people exchanged goods and services. In addition, temples distinguished the urban from the rural world.

Sunni Orthodox Islam, as opposed to the Shiite Islam.

Sunnis The majority sect of Muslims, who originally supported the succession of Abu Bakr over Ali, and supported the rule of consensus rather than family lineage for the succession to the Islamic caliphate.

Superior man In the Confucian view, a person of perfected moral character, fit to be a leader.

Suryavamsha The second lineage of two (the solar) in Vedic society. *See* Chandravamsha.

Tale of Genji Written by Lady Murasaki, a Japanese work that gives vivid accounts of Heian court life; Japan's first novel (early eleventh century).

Talmud Huge volumes of oral commentary on Jewish law eventually compiled in two versions, the Palestinian and the Babylonian, in the fifth and sixth centuries BCE.

Talmud of Jerusalem The codified written volumes of the traditions of Judaism; produced by the rabbis of Galilee around 400 CE.

Teotihuacán A city-state in a large, mountainous valley in present-day Mexico; the first major community to emerge after the Olmecs.

Territorial state A political form that emerged in the riverine cities of Mesopotamia, which was overwhelmed by the displacement of nomadic peoples. These states were kingdoms organized around charismatic rulers who headed large households; each had a defined physical border.

Tiglath Pileser III Ruling the Assyrians from 745 to 728 BCE, this leader instituted reforms that changed the administrative and social structure of the empire to make it more efficient and also introduced a standing army.

Tiwanaku Another name for Tihuanaco, the first great Andean polity, on the shores of Lake Titicaca.

Toltecs By 1000, the Toltecs had filled the political vacuum created by the decline of the city of Teotihuacán.

Tomb culture In the middle of the third century CE, a warlike group from northeast Asia arrived by sea and imposed their military and social power on southern Japan. These conquerors are known today as the "Tomb culture" because of their elevated necropolises near present-day Osaka.

Topkapi Palace Political headquarters of the Ottoman Empire, it was located in Istanbul.

Transhumant migrants Nomads who entered settled territories in the second millennium BCE and moved their herds seasonally when resources became scarce.

Trickle trade Also called "down the line trade," this is a method by which a good is passed from one village to another, as in the case of obsidian among farming villages; the practice began around 7000 BCE.

Troy Founded around 3000 BCE, Troy was an important third millennium BCE site in Anatolia, to the far west. Troy is legendary as the site of the war that was launched by the Greeks (the Achaeans) and that was recounted by Homer in the *Iliad*.

Tsar/czar Russian word derived from the Latin "Caesar" to refer to the Russian ruler of Kiev, and eventually to all rulers in Russia.

Tula The Toltec capital city; a commercial hub and political and ceremonial center.

Ulama An Arabic word that means "learned ones" or "scholars"; used for those who devoted themselves to knowledge of Islamic sciences.

Umayyads A family who founded the first dynasty in Islam. They established family rule and dynastic succession to the role of caliph. The first Umayyad caliph established Damascus as his capital and was named Mu'awiya ibn Abi Sufyan.

Umma The Arabic word for "community"; used to refer to the "Islamic politu" or "Islamic community."

Universitas Beginning at the end of the twelfth century, this term denoted scholars who came together, first in Paris. They formed a *universitas*, a term borrowed from the merchant communities, where it denoted the equivalent of the modern "union."

Untouchables Caste in the Indian system whose jobs, usually in the more unsanitary aspects of urban life, rendered them "ritually and spiritually" impure.

Upanishads Collected in the first half of the first millennium BCE, this Vedic wisdom literature took the form of dialogues between disciples and a sage.

Urban-rural divide One of history's most durable worldwide distinctions, the division between those living in cities and those living in rural areas eventually encompassed the globe. In areas where cities arose, communities adopted lifestyles based on the mass production of goods and on specialized labor. Those living in the countryside remained close to nature, cultivating the land or tending livestock. They diversified their labor and exchanged their grains and animal products for necessities available in urban centers.

Vaishya Householders or lesser clan members in Vedic society who worked the land and tended livestock.

Vardhamana Mahavira Advocate of Jainism who lived from 540 to 468 BCE; he emphasized interpretation of the Upanishads to govern and guide daily life.

Vedas Rhymes, hymns, and explanatory texts composed by Aryan priests; the Vedas became their most holy scripture and part of their religious rituals. They were initially passed down orally, in Sanskrit. Brahmans, priests of Vedic culture, incorporated the texts into ritual and society. The Vedas are considered the final authority of Hinduism.

Vedic people People who came from the steppes of Inner Asia around 1500 BCE and entered the fertile lowlands of the Indus River basin, gradually moving as far south as the Deccan plateau. They called themselves Aryan, which means "respected ones," and spoke Sanskrit, an Indo-European language.

Veiling Introduced by Assyrian authorities in the thirteenth century BCE, this practice of modest dress was required of respectable women in the empire.

Venus figures Representations of the goddess of fertility drawn on the Chauvet Cave in southeastern France. Discovered in 1994, they are probably about 35,000 years old.

Vikings A people from Scandinavia who were literally "on the warpath." They wanted to replace the Franks as the dominant warrior class in northern Europe and set about doing so in the ninth century.

Vishnu The second of three Vedic deities, signifying existence. *See also* Brahma *and* Siva.

Viziers Bureaucrats of the Ottoman Empire.

Wang Mang Han minister who usurped the throne in 9 CE because he believed that the Han had lost the mandate of heaven. He ruled until 23 CE.

Warring States period This period extended from the fifth century BCE to 221 BCE, when the regional warring states were unified by the Qin dynasty.

White and Blue Niles Rising out of central Africa and Ethiopia, the two main branches of the Nile are called the *White and Blue Niles*. They come together at the present-day capital city of Sudan, Khartoum.

Witnessing Dying for one's faith, or becoming a martyr.

Wu or Wudi Known as the "Martial Emperor" because of his many military campaigns during the Han dynasty. He reigned from 141 to 87 BCE.

Wu Zhao Chinese empress who lived from 626 to 706 CE. She began as a concubine in the court of Li Shimin and became the mother of his son's child. She eventually gained more and more power, equal to that of the emperor, and named herself regent when she finagled a place for one of her own sons after their father's death.

Xiongnu The most powerful and intrusive of the nomadic peoples; originally pastoralists from the eastern part of the Asian steppe in what is modern-day Mongolia. They appeared along the frontier with China in the late Zhou dynasty and by the third century BCE had become the most powerful of all the pastoral communities in that area.

Xunzi A Confucian moralist whose ideas were influential to Qin rulers. He lived from 310 to 237 BCE and believed that rational statecraft was more reliable than fickle human nature and that strict laws and severe punishments could create stability in society.

Yavana kings In Sanskrit culture, Greek rulers were known as Yavan kings, a name which derives from the Greek name for the area of western Asia Minor called Ionia, a term that then extended to anyone who spoke Greek or came from the Mediterranean.

Yellow Turbans One of several local Chinese religious movements that emerged across the empire, especially under Wang Mang's officials, who considered him a usurper. The Yellow Turbans, so-called because of the yellow scarves they wore around their heads, were Daoist millenarians.

Yin City that became the capital of the Shang in 1350 BCE, ushering in a golden age.

Yuan dynasty After the defeat of the Song, the Mongols established this dynasty, which was strong from 1280 to 1386 CE; its capital was at Dadu, or modern-day Beijing.

Yuan Mongols Mongol rulers of China who were overthrown by the Ming dynasty in 1368.

Yuezhi A Turkic nomadic people who roamed on pastoral lands to the west of the Xiongnu territory of central Mongolia. They had friendly relationships with the farming societies in China, but the Yuezhi detested the Xiongnu and had frequent armed clashes with them.

Zheng King during the Qin era who defeated what was left of the Warring States between 230 and 221 BCE. He assumed the mandate of heaven from the Zhou and declared himself First August Emperor, to distinguish himself from other kings.

Zhong Shang The administrative central complex of the Shang.

Ziggurat By the end of the third millennium BCE, the elevated platform base of a Sumerian temple had transformed into a stepped platform called a *ziggurat*.

Zoroaster Sometimes known as Zarathustra, he was thought to have been a teacher around 1000 BCE in eastern Iran and is credited with having solidified the region's religious beliefs into a unified system that moved away from animistic nomadic beliefs. The main source for his teachings is a compilation called the Avesta.

World political map and world satellite map appear in the book courtesy of the National Geographic Society.

PRIMARY SOURCE DOCUMENTS

ROBERTUS AVESBURY: "Flagellants in England" from "The Black Death," *Manchester Medieval Sources*, Rosemary Horrox, trans./ed., pp. 153–54. Reprinted with permission of Manchester University Press.

SSU-MA CH'IEN: "Sima Qian on the Ruler's Mandate" from *The Grand Scribe's Records*, ed. William H. Nienhauser Jr. Copyright © 2002 by William H. Nienhauser Jr. Reprinted by permission of Indiana University Press.

STEPHANIE DALLEY: "The Epic of Gilgamesh" from *Myths from Mesopotamia: Creation, the Flood, Gilgamesh, and Others*, pp. 100–101, ed. Stephanie Dalley (1989). Reprinted with permission of Oxford University Press.

N. J. DAWOOD: Excerpt from *The Koran*, translated and with an introduction by N. J. Dawood. Copyright © N. J. Dawood, 1956, 1959, 1966, 1968, 1974, 1990, 1993, 1997, 1999, 2003. Reproduced by permission of Penguin Books Ltd.

DE BARY AND BLOOM: "A Qin Legal Document: Memorial on the Burning of the Books" from *Sources of Chinese Tradition*, Volume 1, eds. William Theodore de Bary and Irene Bloom, © 1999 Columbia University Press. Reprinted with the permission of the publisher.

PATRICIA BUCKLEY EBREY: "Proclamations of the HongWu Emperor" and "Qui Jin: An Address to Two Hundred Million Fellow Countrywomen." Reprinted with the permission of The Free Press, a division of Simon & Schuster Adult Publishing Group, from *Chinese Civilization: A Sourcebook*, Second Edition, Revised and Expanded by Patricia Buckley Ebrey. Copyright © 1993 by Patricia Buckley Ebrey. All rights reserved.

ROBERT FAGLES: "The Truce Erupts in War" from *The Iliad* by Homer, translated by Robert Fagles, copyright © 1990 by Robert Fagles. Used by permission of Viking Penguin, a division of Penguin Group (USA), Inc.

J. GONZALEZ: "The Lex Irnitanta: A New Copy of the Flavian Municipal Law," from *Journal of Roman Studies*, Vol. 76 (1986). Reprinted with permission of the Society for the Promotion of Roman Studies.

SARAH BLAFFER HRDY: From *Mother Nature* by Sarah Blaffer Hrdy, copyright © 1999 by Sarah Blaffer Hrdy. Published by Chatto & Windus. Used by permission of Pantheon Books, a division of Random House, Inc., and The Random House Group Ltd.

AHMET KARAMUSTAFA: "Dervish Groups in the Ottoman Empire, 1450–1550" from *God's Unruly Friends: Dervish Groups in the Islamic Later Middle Period*, pp. 6–7. Oneworld Publications, Oxford, 2006. Reprinted with the permission of Oneworld Publications.

RICHARD B. LEE AND IRVEN DEVORE: "Problems in the Study of Hunters and Gatherers" from *Man the Hunter*, pp. 3 and 5. Copyright © 1968 Transaction Publishers. Reprinted with permission.

NANAK: "Nanak's Teachings in India" from *Sources of Indian Tradition*, ed. William Theodore de Bary, © 1958 Columbia University Press. Reprinted with the permission of the publisher.

JAMES PRITCHARD: "The Admonitions of Ipuwer" from *Ancient Near Eastern Texts Relating to the Old Testament*, Third Edition with Supplement. Copyright © 1950, 1955, 1969, renewed 1978 by Princeton University Press. Reprinted by permission of Princeton University Press.

SHEREEN RATNAGAR: "The Mystery of Harrapan Writing" from *Understanding Harappan Civilization in the Greater Indus Valley*, 2001, Tulika Publishers.

ADRIAN RECINOS: *Popol Vuh: The Sacred Book of the Ancient Quiché Maya*, trans. Delia Goetz and Sylvanus G. Morley, pp. 165–67. Reprinted with permission of University of Oklahoma Press.

JIA YI: "Faults of the Qin" from *Sources of Chinese Tradition*, Volume 1, eds. William Theodore de Bary and Irene Bloom, © 1999 Columbia University Press. Reprinted with the permission of the publisher.

DONG ZHONGSHU: "Responsibilities of Han Rulership" from *Sources of Chinese Tradition*, Volume 1, eds. William Theodore de Bary and Irene Bloom, © 1999 Columbia University Press. Reprinted with the permission of the publisher.

ART AND PHOTOS

CHAPTER 1: pp. 2–3: Erich Lessing/Art Resource; p. 5: Granger Collection; p. 7: Robert Preston/Alamy; p. 11: Kenneth Garrett/National Geographic Image Collection; p. 12: (top): Des Bartlett/Photo Researchers; (bottom): John Reader/Photo Researchers; p. 13: Staffan Widstrand/Corbis; p. 14: JTB Photo Communications, Inc./Alamy; p. 15: Pascal Goetgheluck/Photo Researchers; p. 16: Lionel Bret/Photo Researchers; p. 17: John Reader/Photo Researchers; p. 20: Images of Africa Photobank/Alamy; p. 22: Archivo Iconografico, S.A./Corbis; p. 23 (both): French Ministry of Culture and Communication, Regional Direction for Cultural Affairs–Rhône-Alpes Region–Regional Department of Archaeology; p. 24: Archivo Iconografico, S.A./Corbis; p. 25: Ancient Art & Architecture/Danita Delimont; p. 34 (top): Copyright © Christie's Images Ltd. All rights reserved; (bottom): Lowell Georgia/Corbis; p. 36: Image courtesy of Professor Jeremy B. Rutter, Department of Classics, Dartmouth College; p. 37: Bruce Smith, *The Emergence of Agriculture* (New York: Diane Publishing Company, 1998), p. 104; p. 38: Boltin Picture Library/Bridgeman Art Library; p. 40: Interfoto/Pressebildagentur/Alamy; p. 42: Erich Lessing/Art Resource; p. 43: Catalhoyuk Research Project, Institute of Archaeology, University College London.

CHAPTER 2: pp. 50–51: © The Trustees of the British Museum/Bridgeman Art Library; p. 53: *Illustrated London News*; p. 59: Granger Collection; p. 60: Peter Bull Art Studio; p. 61: Dean Conger/Corbis; p. 62: © The Trustees of the British Museum; p. 63 (from left to right): HIP/Art Resource; Granger Collection; University of Pennsylvania Museum of Archaeology and Anthropology, B16693; p. 65: University of Pennsylvania Museum of Archaeology and Anthropology; p. 66: image copyright © The Metropolitan Museum of Art/Art Resource; p. 68: Scala/Art Resource; p. 71: Diego Lezama Orezzoli/Corbis; p. 72 (top): Réunion des Musées Nationaux/Art Resource; (bottom): Borromeo/Art Resource; p. 73: Roger Wood/Corbis; p. 76: Kenneth Garrett/National Geographic Image Collection; p. 77: © The Trustees of the British Museum; p. 78 (clockwise from top left): Gianni Dagli Orti/Corbis; Christine Osborne/Corbis; The Art Archive/Corbis; p. 79 (left): Scala/Art Resource; (right): Sandro Vannini/Corbis; p. 83: Asian Art & Archaeology, Inc./Corbis; p. 85: HIP/Art Resource; p. 86: The Museum of East Asian Art/Heritage Images/The Image Works; p. 89: Werner Foreman/Topham/The Image Works; p. 90: Adam Woolfitt/Corbis; p. 91: Ashmolean Museum, University of Oxford.

CHAPTER 3: pp. 96–97: JTB Photo Communications/Alamy; p. 102: Department of Archaeology and Museums, Karachi. A. H. Dani, "Recent Archaeological Discoveries in Pakistan," The Center for East Asian Cultural Studies. UNESCO Japan: 1988. p. 103 (clockwise from top left): Scala/Art Resource; JTB Photo Communications/Alamy; Art Resource; p. 107: Roger Wood/Corbis; p. 109: Sandro Vannini/Corbis; p. 111: Berlin Museum; p. 114: Erich Lessing/Art Resource; p. 115: Vanni/Art Resource; p. 116: National Museum of India, New Delhi; p. 117: A. H. Dani, "Recent Archaeological Discoveries in Pakistan," The Center for East Asian Cultural Studies. UNESCO Japan: 1988; p. 123 (left): Yale University Art Gallery/Art Resource; (right): HIP/Art Resource; p. 124: Louis Mazzatenta/National Geographic Image Collection; p. 125: Zhenyu Ji Luo, *Yin xu shu qi jing hua*. China: Shangyu Luo shi, Minguo 3: 1914; p. 128 (top): Albrecht G. Schaefer/Corbis; (bottom): Bob Krist/Corbis; p. 130 (clockwise from top left): Institute of Nautical Archaeology, Bodrum, Turkey (2); Gianni Dagli Orti/Corbis; p. 131 (left): Peter Clayton; (right): University of Cincinnati; p. 132: Erich Lessing/Art Resource; p. 133: The Art Archive/National Archaeological Museum, Athens/Dagli Orti.

CHAPTER 4: pp. 140–41: Dagli Orti/Louvre/Bridgeman Art Library; p. 146 (left): © A. Paul Jenkin/Animals Animals; (right): S. Muller/Peter Arnold, Inc.; p. 148: © The Trustees of the British Museum; p. 149 (left): Erich Lessing/Art Resource; (right): HIP/Art Resource; p. 151: British Museum/Bridgeman Art Library; p. 154 (top): SEF/Art Resource; (bottom): Alinari/Art Resource; p. 156 (top): Bibliotheque Nationale, Paris, France,

Bridgeman Art Library; (bottom): Dagli Orti/Louvre/Bridgeman Art Library; p. 157 (top): EmmePi Iran/Alamy; (bottom): Lloyd Cluff/Corbis; p. 158: The Art Archive/Dagli Orti; p. 159: Erich Lessing/Art Resource; p. 160: Scala/Art Resource; p. 162: akg-images/Peter Connolly; p. 164: Dagli Orti/Art Archive; p. 165: Art Archive; p. 166: Louvre/Lauros/Giraudon/Bridgeman Art Library; p. 173: Giraudon/Art Resource; p. 175 (left): Asia Society, New York: Mr. and Mrs. John D. Rockefeller 3rd Collection 1979, 100a, b. Photograph by Lynton Gardiner; (right): HIP/Art Resource; p. 176: Louvre/Lauros/Giraudon/Bridgeman Art Library; p. 177: Victoria & Albert Museum, London/Art Resource.

CHAPTER 5: pp. 182–83: (from left to right): National Library of China; Scala/Art Resource; Erich Lessing/Art Resource; p. 191 (top): Asian Art & Archaeology, Inc./Corbis; (bottom): Erich Lessing/Art Resource; p. 192: Smithsonian Freer Gallery of Art and Arthur M. Sackler Gallery; p. 193 (left): British Library; (right): The Art Archive/Private Collection, London; p. 197: Borromeo/Art Resource; p. 198 (top): Paul Almasy/Corbis; (bottom): Corbis; p. 199: courtesy joelcoins.com; p. 201: Erich Lessing/Art Resource; p. 206 (both): Gillett Griffin; p. 208: JTB Photo Communications, Inc./Alamy; pp. 209–10: Princeton University Art Museum; p. 211: The Art Archive/Xalapa Museum, Veracruz, Mexico/Gianni Dagli Orti; p. 212: Maunus; p. 214: Vanni/Art Resource; p. 215 (left): Erich Lessing/Art Resource; (right): Michael Freeman/Corbis; p. 218: Erich Lessing/Art Resource; p. 219 (top): Peter Willi/Bridgeman Art Library; (bottom): Erich Lessing/Art Resource; p. 220: Bridgeman Art Library; p. 221 (left): Erich Lessing/Art Resource; (right): HIP/Art Resource; p. 222: Ashmolean Museum, University of Oxford, UK/Bridgeman Art Library; p. 223 (left): Scala/Art Resource; (right): Erich Lessing/Art Resource.

CHAPTER 6: pp. 230–31: © The Cleveland Museum of Art; p. 236 (top): Erich Lessing/Art Resource; (bottom): Brian A. Vikander/Corbis; p. 238: Lauros/Giraudon/Bridgeman Art Library; p. 241: Vanni/Art Resource; p. 242: akg-images/Peter Connolly; p. 244: Erich Lessing/Art Resource; p. 245 (top): Illustration by Jean-Claude Golvin from *L'Afrique Antique* (Paris: Tallandier, 2001); (bottom): Bildarchiv Preussischer Kulturbesitz/Art Resource; p. 246: Landesmuseum, Mainz, Germany; p. 247: Stapleton Collection/Corbis; p. 249 (left): Bridgeman Art Library; (right): Brian A. Vikander/Corbis; p. 250: Réunion des Musées Nationaux/Art Resource; p. 254 (all): Courtesy of Bill Welch, "What I Like About Ancient Coins"; p. 256: © The Cleveland Museum of Art; p. 257 (top): David Gurr/Eye Ubiquitous/Corbis; (bottom): Lindsay Hebberd/Corbis; p. 258: The Metropolitan Museum of Art. Gift of Muneichi Nitta, 2003 (2003.593.1). Image © The Metropolitan Museum of Art; p. 259: Image copyright © The Metropolitan Museum of Art/Art Resource; p. 263: Bruno Morandi/Robert Harding World Imagery/Corbis; pp. 265–66: The Art Archive/Palmyra Museum, Syria/Dagli Orti; p. 267: NASA/JPL; p. 268: Alfred Ko/Corbis; p. 270: wikipedia.com.

CHAPTER 7: pp. 274–75: Viktor Korotayev/Reuters/Corbis; p. 278 (left): Viktor Korotayev/Reuters/Corbis; (right): Asian Art & Archaeology, Inc./Corbis; p. 280 (left): HIP/Art Resource; (right): National Library of China; p. 282: Louis Mazzatenta/National Geographic Image Collection; p. 284: Bridgeman Art Library; p. 286: Lauros/Giraudon/Bridgeman Art Library; p. 288: Princeton University Art Museum; p. 290 (top): British Museum/Art Resource; (bottom): British Museum/Art Resource; p. 291: Model of House, Chinese, 1st century CE, Eastern Han Dynasty (25–220 CE). Earthenware with unfired coloring, 52 ⊠ 33 1/2 ⊠ 27 inches (132.1 ⊠ 85.1 ⊠ 68.6 cm). The Nelson-Atkins Museum of Art, Kansas City, Missouri. Purchase: Nelson Trust, 33-521. Photograph by Jamison Miller; p. 292 (top): Princeton University Art Museum; (bottom left): Asian Art & Archaeology, Inc./Corbis; (bottom right): Royal Ontario Museum/Corbis; p. 293 (both): Asian Art & Archaeology, Inc./Corbis; p. 294: Liu Dunzhen et al., *Zhongguo gudai jianzhu shi*. Peking: Zhongguo jianzhu gongye chuban-she, 1980; p. 295 (top): Erich Lessing/Art Resource; (bottom): dk/Alamy; p. 296: AM Corporation/Alamy; p. 297: The Art Archive/Genius of China Exhibition; p. 301: Araldo de Luca/Corbis; p. 303: Robert Harding Picture

Index

Page numbers in *italics* refer to illustrations, maps, and timelines.